THE Enduring Strategic Brand

How brand-led organisations over-perform sustainably

THE Enduring Strategic Brand
How brand-led organisations over-perform sustainably

Luc Bardin
with Clara and Elsa Bardin

URBANE
Publications

urbanepublications.com

First published in Great Britain in 2016
by Urbane Publications Ltd
Suite 3, Brown Europe House, 33/34 Gleaming Wood Drive,
Chatham, Kent ME5 8RZ
Copyright © Luc Bardin, Clara Bardin, Elsa Bardin, 2017

A CIP catalogue record for this book is available
from the British Library.

ISBN 978-1-911-583-49-3

Design and Typeset by Michelle Morgan

Cover by Rouge Absolu

ROUGE ABSOLU

Printed and bound by CPI Group (UK) Ltd, Croydon, CR0 4YY

urbanepublications.com

FSC
www.fsc.org
MIX
Paper from
responsible sources
FSC® C013604

WHAT THEY ARE SAYING...

"Luc Bardin's book is opening the door to strategic value creation. He captures the magic of the brand and translates the alchemy of an intangible asset base into 13 elements, which allow every reader to understand the fascinating art of enduring brand building."

Professor Klaus Schwab, Founder and Executive Chairman of the World Economic Forum

"I valued Luc Bardin's counsel when we worked together. There is good reason why he is a globally renowned marketer and I would encourage other leaders to take insights and courage from his suggested framework on how to build and grow an enduring strategic brand."

Lord John Browne, former Group CEO BP

"Those CEOs who already grasp the strategic value of their brand will find this book welcome, research-based validation. Those still doubtful will find it highly enlightening. And those who ignore it may continue to struggle to make strategic sense of their companies. I hope it's hugely influential."

Sir Martin Sorrell, Founder and CEO WPP

"Luc's work highlights the connection between the creation of enduring and increasingly valuable brands and successful strategies, implemented and adjusted as markets and circumstances warrant."

John Rice, Vice Chairman General Electric

CONTENTS

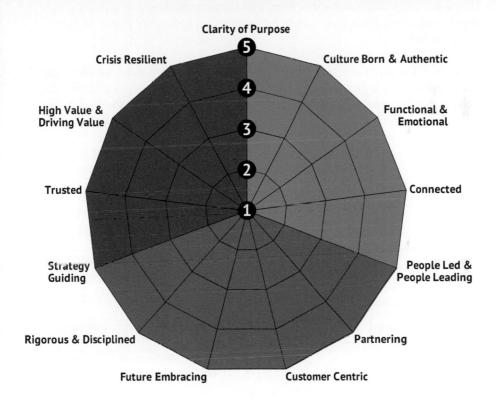

"The defining factor that has kept us in business and growing for more than 40 years has been the strength and reputation of the brand. The way a company brands itself is everything - it will ultimately decide whether or not a business survives"

Richard Branson, Founder at Virgin Group

On 20th April 2010, the BP-commissioned Deepwater Horizon oil rig exploded and sank. Eleven people tragically died, and for 87 days oil flowed into the Gulf of Mexico in what was the largest accidental marine oil spill in history. Each second of each day that the oil continued to spill caused concern and damage for local communities and their surroundings. For the thousands of BP employees directly involved, like me, it was the most challenging and difficult time of our professional lives.

'THE Enduring Strategic Brand' is not a book solely concerned with lessons learned from my decades in senior leadership growing branded businesses - nor is it a book about crisis management. However, the months spent in the eye of the storm during The Deepwater Horizon crisis clarified many valuable lessons about the essence, power and limitations of brands and how they relate to an organisation's ability to form a sustainable future.

And there have been numerous other moments during my professional life, including a groundbreaking global partnership between BMW and Castrol that resulted in a co-branded 'filler' cap inside the BMW's engine, that have fed this interest for what makes an Enduring Strategic Brand.

What is it precisely that makes one brand more likely to stand out and overperform than others? How do we build and grow an Enduring Strategic Brand fit for our ever-changing world? How do we ensure our brands fulfil their potential?

ILLUSTRATION I.1	BP BRAND ALTERATIONS DURING THE DEEPWATER HORIZON CRISIS

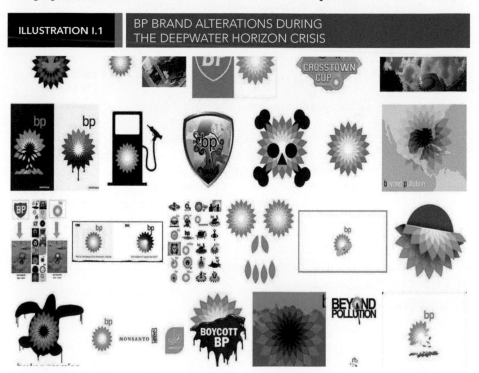

ILLUSTRATION I.2   THE BMW – CASTROL OIL FILLER CAP

I have come to realise as a practitioner and through many conversations with other C-suite brand champions that the secret lays in 13 vital imperatives – all of which are required to create THE Enduring Strategic Brand. This thinking is built on practical experience and the understanding of what would have made me a better, more effective CMO during my time on the frontline of strategic marketing.

I have subsequently underpinned this with some 'science', that is a framework all brands can use to build insights and assess their own strategic strengths and weaknesses. To support the 13-imperatives thesis, I have chosen 20 exemplary brands that are all sources of great learning and on a journey of transformation - and drawn on the expertise of a panel of business and marketing leaders to analyse their successful formula.

But does it work? The results are striking. We compared the brand performances of our Exemplary Strategic Brands against the performance of the S&P 500 over a period of nine years from 2006-2015. The Exemplary Strategic Brands grew earnings 3.5 times faster than the S&P 500 average and revenues by 8 per cent CAGR versus 3 per cent - more on this later.

WHY WRITE 'THE ENDURING STRATEGIC BRAND'?

I had this book on my chest, as the convergence of three drivers:

First driver - This book is set against the backdrop of tension for society and brands – on the one hand, the surreal pace of change in the digital revolution and on the other, a number of fundamental truths that remain the same as ever.

On change, and as represented in Illustration I.3, just look at what happens in an Internet minute; or how the communication landscape is changing radically, with Facebook and Google alone capturing 72% of the world's online advertising (aside China).

"It is fashionable to talk about changing man. A communicator must be concerned with unchanging man, with its obsessive drive to survive, to be admired, to succeed, to love, to take care of his own."

| ILLUSTRATION I.3 | CONSIDERABLE DIGITAL – LED CHANGES |

- 763,888 people use Facebook
- 69,444 hours watched on Netflix
- 150 million emails
- 1,389 rides on Uber
- 51,000 app downloads
- $203,596 in sales on Amazon
- 65,900 videos and photos posted
- 38,052 hours of listening on Spotify
- 972,222 swipes on tinder

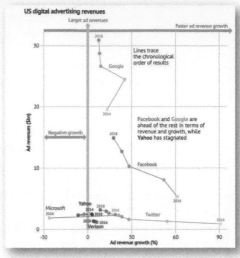

Credit – Nicola Mendelsohn, Marketing Society Conference & Presentation November 2016

Source – FT, 30 – 31 July 2016

And, despite all these huge changes, we must remember advertising guru, Bill Bernbach's wisdom who said: *"It is fashionable to talk about changing man. A communicator must be concerned with unchanging man, with its obsessive drive to survive, to be admired, to succeed, to love, to take care of his own."*

I have seen first-hand how organisations and leaders wrestle with these two apparently opposed realities; let alone are they able to grab their inherent strategic opportunity. It is these different forces which have cemented my intention to write *'THE Enduring Strategic Brand'* – to avoid getting lost in the noise of the latest digital flash and focus on what is strategic, so our brands achieve what Don Fabrizio Corbera, the Prince of Salina, said in The Leopard: *"Everything needs to change, so everything can stay the same."*

Second driver - The Deepwater Horizon disaster put me in front of a hard truth: hardly any brand is fit for the extremes.

This crisis was the ultimate test for a brand, a $60 billion one. It exposed that ours was not sufficiently ready, because it was not at the highest level of group strategy before the events. This is true in the vast majority of enterprises, meaning that we are all foregoing a massive opportunity, both defensive when the storm hits or to overperform in peace times.

Long time Group Vice-President, Business CEO and Group Chief Sales & Marketing Officer, I have lived the BP – Beyond Petroleum brand at the forefront, from inception to shift, crisis to recovery. I will tell the revealing story of the textbook but unfinished BP brand from the inside and in three key stages, as an incentive to bring up the importance of brands.

Third driver - Over the last 30 years or more of my business life I have lived and breathed brands.

From organising our family and friend gatherings for the Super Bowl so I can cook and serve during the game, and stand riveted to the screen when the ads appear.

To taking my children as toddlers on weekend mystery shopper expeditions to the supermarkets to make sure our category plan had been implemented on the motor oil shelves, much to my colleagues dismay on Monday mornings.

And of course, leading branded businesses over my entire business life, building their brands to sustain faster business growth and higher returns.

"Brands mean the world to me."

Building Enduring Strategic Brands

The brand is our North Star. We need to push aside the latest gadget, the latest marketing agency's 'killer invention', or digital disruptor and look at what's inherently important. That's not to say that we should disregard progress, trends or new tools, but rather master them and put them in perspective - because it is the major trends we are really interested in.

There's nothing more powerful than a Strategic Brand, it acts as a compass to the entire business and creates long-term value - so why are so many brands unable to reach their full potential?

How many enterprises manage to 'own' their brand's space? Which organisations have maintained their brand purpose and mission for decades, creating an unparalleled stakeholder preference? How many brands have such a clear positioning that businesses, shareholders and customers see it in the same way?

The purpose of *'THE Enduring Strategic Brand'* is to reflect on the transformational journey from being a brand to becoming an Enduring Strategic Brand. What does it takes in practice to achieve this shift in the times of the Fourth Industrial Revolution?

What is an Enduring Strategic Brand?

Many of us believe that brands have never been and will never be as important as they are now.

So what is a Strategic Brand? There are two shorthand ways of looking at how it manifests: a brand that is 'too good to miss'; or an enterprise which has become a 'brand led organisation' rather than runs a 'business led brand'.

"A brand that is 'too good to miss'; or an enterprise which has become a 'brand led organisation' rather than runs a 'business led brand'."

For me, brands are first and foremost relationships. Strategic Brands are extraordinary relationships, developed at scale day after day over a long period of time, imbuing authority and permission to drive action and behaviour from stakeholders. These relationships are transformational and perform some kind of alchemy, changing products into joyful experiences.

Perhaps because relationships are the essence of a brand, I have always compared brands to people. A person's substance is like the functional attributes of a brand, while a person's charisma is the brand's emotional side, its authentic values and character.

ILLUSTRATION I.4	A BRAND AS A PERSON

What we do and the value we bring to society

▶ **Role** – what we do in life, our main function in society

▶ **Purpose** – why we exist and what we want to achieve within our role

▶ **Differentiator** – what we do that is distinctive, to achieve our purpose

Who we are

▶ **Personality** – how we show up; how others see and describe us

▶ **Values** – what we believe and helps us make decisions

▶ **Behaviours** – daily actions by all staff that represent/ signal our personality and values

Back to the Future

'THE Enduring Strategic Brand' was born from and is grounded in leadership practice - and projects practical knowledge through the examples of the many brands in the book. If I had been given the opportunity to step back and write this while in post, I would probably have been a better business CEO and CSMO, with greater clarity, more confidence and a stronger practice – and consequently more radically transformational. I would therefore exhort you to step back and get deeper into the strategy of brand, as it will transform what you do.

'THE ENDURING STRATEGIC BRAND' SYSTEM: 13 VITAL IMPERATIVES

Learning from concrete best practice cases, *'THE Enduring Strategic Brand'* identifies 13 dimensions, which are considered vital to being a Strategic Brand. We call these the 'Strategic Brand Imperatives'. All 13 elements are needed to create a Strategic Brand.

A first cluster of imperatives – such as 'Culture born' or 'Radically authentic' – is about the raison d'être, the identity and character of a Strategic Brand [WHY & WHO the brand is]; a second cluster relates to the modus operandi of Strategic Brands, such as the role of people or partnerships [HOW the Brand operates]; and finally, a third cluster relates to the impact of the Strategic Brand, such as creating value or being trusted [the WHAT/Performance of the Brand].

"Learning from concrete best practice cases, 'THE Enduring Strategic Brand' identifies 13 dimensions, which are considered vital to being a Strategic Brand. We call these the 'Strategic Brand Imperatives."

The 13 Enduring Strategic Brand Imperatives are a nod to the traditional marketing funnel, loved by our marketing fathers and a simple tool that I continue to find relevant. The logical steps of these two systems are similar: you start with building and understanding who you are; you then take stock and determine how you operate and finally achieve your performance.

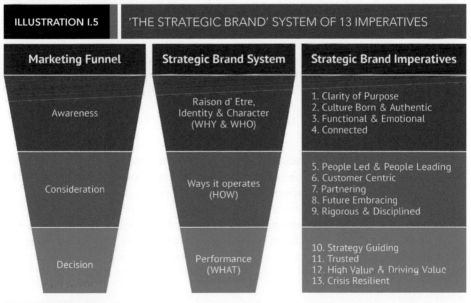

ILLUSTRATION I.5	'THE STRATEGIC BRAND' SYSTEM OF 13 IMPERATIVES	
Marketing Funnel	**Strategic Brand System**	**Strategic Brand Imperatives**
Awareness	Raison d' Etre, Identity & Character (WHY & WHO)	1. Clarity of Purpose 2. Culture Born & Authentic 3. Functional & Emotional 4. Connected
Consideration	Ways it operates (HOW)	5. People Led & People Leading 6. Customer Centric 7. Partnering 8. Future Embracing 9. Rigorous & Disciplined
Decision	Performance (WHAT)	10. Strategy Guiding 11. Trusted 12. High Value & Driving Value 13. Crisis Resilient

© THE Enduring Strategic Brand

Let's take a helicopter view of the 13 Strategic Brand Imperatives, with brief perspectives of some of the brand champions we talked to:

1. Clarity of Purpose

In simple terms, an organisation's purpose is the reason why it exists and has been given the right by society to participate: *"All business in a democratic society begins with public permission and exists by public approval,"* said Arthur W. Page. It is the response to the question by each associate: *"Why am I here"*

This purpose goes beyond making money: at a basic level, it might be how an organisation improves the life of its stakeholders. The best brand purposes stretch beyond this to reflect the organisation's commitment to make society and the world better. Purpose is crucial to longevity: only the simplest, clearest brand purposes will endure and have impact in a changing society.

The value power of a strong brand purpose is compelling. Jim Stengel's research concludes on about three times faster growth for 'ideals-led' brands than for their competitors.

Lord John Browne, former Group CEO BP, comments: *"The brand is the glue that keeps the company together and expresses the forward paths, the direction, which is communicable to everybody. The enterprise brand actually has little to do with how you signify what you sell. Of course it is important but it is not the same thing. While the brand is the glue, purpose is the litmus test of sustainability in business. Without brand or purpose, no company."*

2. Culture Born and Authentic

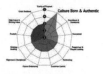

Culture is the central definer of what an organisation and a brand are. I will argue that everything, including purpose, should emanate from a deep understanding of the enterprise underlying culture.

I will contend that a culture can't be changed, except by changing people, but rather evolve. We will review some culture 'science', so a more rigorous approach is taken on this 'make or break' pillar of an enterprise and its brand. And highlight how a brand built on culture mobilises its employees and benefits from their spontaneous support.

In a world where stakeholders are empowered by the digital revolution, organisations must show an unprecedented level of transparency and cultural genuineness. Takeshi Uchiyamada, Chairman of Toyota Motor Company, talks about the importance of culture born authenticity: *"I have been with Toyota for forty years. The way Toyota thinks is entirely influenced by how it was founded. Toyota began with the invention of Sakichi Toyoda. His son, Kiichiro Toyoda, wanted to establish an automobile industry in Japan. The overwhelming culture within Toyota today is a continuation of Kiichiro's legacy: to be challenged to create something entirely new and to support those who take on this challenge."*

3. Functional and Emotional

A Strategic Brand starts with the foundation of a relevant, tangible, valued, purpose-led functional benefit, which it continuously improves.

But in a competitive world where supply often exceeds demand, and there is limited differentiation in terms of manufacturing or distribution, a Strategic Brand must also imbue strong emotional benefits to satisfy customers.

The big question is on how to build this winning combination and we will observe the way the BMW brand provides best-in-class functional benefits and deep emotional fulfilment.

Former American Express CMO, John Hayes, explains the importance of 'Functional and Emotional' in his experience: *"There is a gravity in business, particularly in the US, towards left-brain thinking and rational understanding of everything. But as we have learned with recent polls and elections, those things don't necessarily reflect the true understanding of the marketplace.*

"Emotional issues are fundamental but difficult to deal with because they are uncomfortable. I would often say to people: 'Let's talk for a moment about your spouse. Let's talk about how you decided to make this commitment of a lifetime. I'd like to go through the research studies that were done...' 'What research studies?' they would ask. And I'd say: 'You didn't research? It is such an important decision!' We'd agree that they made their decision based on emotion, solely. And I'd say: 'That was a very risky thing to do.' By having this conversation, people begin to understand that in other parts of their life, they operate differently than in business. It is so important because that is the level at which you need to operate to truly create a brand."

4. Connected

The Strategic Brand is deeply connected. It develops an extensive knowledge of its audience to anticipate expectations and learn from stakeholders. It develops a relationship model through which people can feel valued and are ready to give discretionary contributions to the brand, including loyalty and advocacy.

Connected Strategic Brands change the code from targets to audiences, from communicating to being in dialogue, from transaction to trust. In local markets, Strategic Brands adopt the cultural symbols, practices and expectations of the national culture.

As Nicola Mendelsohn, VP for EMEA at Facebook, points out: *"Brands are increasingly important because they provide people with a shorthand; they help them cut through all the choices that are available today. They provide an emotional connection that you have with a product based on a shared understanding of what it means."*

5. People Led and People Leading

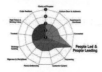

The Strategic Brand leads people and acts as their guide: the brand is their ultimate frame of reference to make decisions, as well as determining their behaviours.

Symmetrically, every employee is a brand ambassador and impactful Strategic Brands are transparently and authentically 'Inside – Out'.

Organisationally, the CEO and the CMO play a very special role in tandem – enabling the Strategic Brand to start and finish with people. As their context is changing dramatically, we will discuss how the CEO needs to be ever more the 'brand champion' and the CMO, the 'chief value officer'.

Greg Welch, senior partner, Spencer Stuart, believes that *"the heartbeat of the brand in most companies, needs to sit with the CMO. This needs to be a loud, consistent, colourful voice. I also use the words 'disciple' or 'orchestra leader' to illustrate the idea that someone needs to be the architect, the owner and the keeper, the shepherd of that brand. And I think the CMO is the best person to do that."*

6. Partnering

Why would we want to do it all alone? Can we be best at everything? Do we possess infinite resources?

The Strategic Brand collaborates with its stakeholders. It creates deep partnerships and rich ecosystems to innovate and deliver its services. It understands the power of advocacy. It achieves much higher returns because partners and stakeholders magnify its activities.

But partnering is a 'hit and miss' process that fails far more times that it succeeds. We will examine the art and the science of partnerships to tap into their transformational potential for the brand.

Kevin Bishop, former VP IBM Brand System and Workforce Enablement explains: *"Ideally, partnering is part of your DNA, as it is for IBM. Publicly we make it an explicit part of our culture - expectations are clear with everybody that it is important. Partnering needs to be imbued with empathy and always be a win-win union."*

7. Customer Centric

Customer centricity is an over-used notion. While every organisation claims to be customer centric, in reality very few truly succeed. A Strategic Brand places the customer at the heart of the organisation's intent, with zero compromise. Says the O2 brand: *"If it is good for you, it's good for us"*

The Strategic Brand must be clear about who their ultimate customers are. This understanding defines the organisation's focus on providing an experience or a lifestyle platform which will inspire their target customers.

Amazon epotimises customer centricity. Says Jeff Bezos, CEO Amazon: *"Our focus is on customer obsession rather than competitor obsession, eagerness to invent and pioneer, willingness to fail, the patience to think long-term and the taking of professional pride in operational excellence".*

8. Future Embracing

Today, organisations are faced with change at a faster pace than ever before – whether that's 'uberisation', platformisation or any other type of transformation. The Strategic Brand develops two magic powers to deal with this – see, shape and create the future; and be future proof, to enable the enterprise's transition into the future.

Deep into the Fourth Industrial Revolution, we will review some of the ongoing societal and cross – category shifts that are forming the future and are essential to sustainable brand development.

Says Haier Group Corporation: *"The Internet Age brings with it segmentation of marketing. The production-inventory-sales model of traditional businesses can no longer meet the personalised demands of users, and a firm has to transform from self-centred product selling to a user-centric sale of services, i.e. a user-driven 'on-demand manufacturing and delivery' mode. The Internet has also given rise to the integration of global economies… and therefore Haier has consolidated global resources in R&D, manufacturing and marketing to create a global brand."*

9. Rigorous and Disciplined

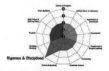

Rigour, discipline and consistency of execution are considered pre-requisites today, which means they are hardly talked about. But thoroughness in execution is not only essential to building a Strategic Brand, it will remain a major point of differentiation in the future because it is so hard to achieve.

Are we enchanted with the consistency of execution of our banks, airlines or utility companies? 'Implementation is strategy' and we will review principles and practices of those brands high on the scale of disciplined execution.

Lisa Baird, CMO of the US Olympic Committee considers how the Olympic Brand guides discipline: *"The Olympic brand is powerful: it has such well-understood clarity of meaning and purpose; it has one of the most powerful logos in the world, which uniquely brings us together; it continues to be itself and remind people what it stands for; it shapes the Games through storylines and relationships which portray the event in a positive manner; it has the right broadcasters around the world, whose interest it is to invest in making the brand as strong as possible. These are the things which make it an extraordinary brand."*

10. Strategy Guiding

The Strategic Brand leads the organisation's strategy, making the business 'brand led' rather than the brand an outcome of changing business strategies.

The Strategic Brand is the organisation's compass, driving its participation strategy, activities, people and relationships, and practices. The Strategic Brand acts as an enduring guide, simplifying decision and action, and empowering people to operate accordingly.

Keith Weed, Chief Marketing and Communications Officer, Unilever, explains: *"Unilever's brand purpose is intrinsic to the business model. We have always been clear that this (The Sustainable Living Plan) was not something we were doing because it was a moral obligation or a nice thing to do. This was an economic strategy, and it is now paying off. The corporate purpose remains constant, though the expression may change."*

11. Trusted

A brand is 'owned' by its stakeholders. Its value is defined by how these stakeholders appreciate and respect the whole organisation. Trust is the most coveted outcome of everything an organisation does. Across sectors and geographies, trust translates into reputation, which leads to better outcomes. But trust has to be earned.

"Trust has been the essential pillar for the way in which the Tata Group has been viewed by stakeholders over generations," says Dr Mukund Rajan, Chief Ethics Officer and Chair of the Global Sustainability Council, Tata Group. *'The feedback we get is that Tata is a trusted brand, a corporate group that you do business with, whose products and services are truly intended to deliver value for customers and who will never renege on a commitment.*

"Our social commitment extends to concern and care for the natural environment in the communities in which we work. That social commitment creates an affinity, which enhances the brand in the eyes of the stakeholders".

"So there is a strong sense that Tata is a group that not only has a commitment to doing good business, but is also in the business of doing good."

12. High Value and Driving Value

Perhaps I should have started the book with this chapter because ultimately, a brand is all about value – financial but by far not only. Indeed, brand and value make the perfect marriage – but achieving this union is challenging. How do we demonstrate the brand's power to create value in such ways that the financial market, CEOs and CFOs rally behind it? And how do we capture and measure the value of a brand?

What does Apple teach us, with net margins from products over forty per cent? The business model has to link clearly brand to value generation. Consequently, investing in the brand will not be sporadic, but a business imperative to protect and drive value creation and growth.

What does Apple tell us, with its brand alone valued over $100 billions? A true Strategic Brand independently measured intrinsic value is high and continuously growing – put simply, the brand is a high value asset by itself.

Nina Bibby, Chief Marketing Officer at O2, explains *"At O2 the brand is so central to value creation that we are not a business that runs a brand, we are a brand that runs a business. The brand is the backbone, it's at the heart of where the business is seeking to create value and how the business delivers its products or services."*

"In our world, a large part of profitability is determined by how much it costs to acquire versus retain a customer; the cost differential hits our bottom line immediately. We can quantify all of this and say precisely to our CFO: this is what we're investing because this is the pay back.

13. Crisis Resilient

Only few brand builders talk about this vital pillar of a Strategic Brand. Crisis is the ultimate test of whether a brand is Strategic. Indeed, the true Strategic Brand will have been developed in the context of a potential major crisis.

The Strategic Brand must have a strong reservoir of goodwill so that it can survive any crisis – not only to recover from it but also to surpass pre-crisis status. Says Kathy Leech, Executive Director of Corporate Brand and Advertising for Comcast NBCUniversal *"A Strategic Brand acts. It shows. It doesn't tell."*

We will follow the BP Brand facing the Deepwater Horizon crisis in 2010 onwards. Says Tony Hayward, BP's Group CEO at the time: *"The tougher it became, the more tightly bound the BP family became. So the greater the adversity, the greater the feeling of BP against the world… Everyone was supporting each other and battling this thing. It was a unique moment in terms of a united company.*

Everyone could see that we were trying to do the right thing. We weren't hiding behind words but trying our upmost to be fully accountable and responsible in the crisis. BP was a rallying cry."

Assembling and using '*THE* Enduring Strategic Brand' System

As you will see throughout the book, I like data and measures. Not because they hold the truth but because they help build insights. So how do we use the 13 Strategic Brand Imperatives?

As a board member or CEO, you can use the framework to assess your organisation or to ask yourself and your team a few deep questions; you can use it if you are the CMO, the communication guru, the branded business lead, and want to self assess or guide team work; and if you are a stakeholder, shareholder or a customer, you can use it as a simple tool to assess your partner, investment or supplier.

On writing '*THE Enduring Strategic Brand*', we created a small panel of business and marketing leaders to assess ca. 20 different, handpicked brands against the 13 imperatives. You might find it useful to benchmark your own business with these as they appear throughout the book.

By way of illustration, diagram I.6 represents '*THE Enduring Strategic Brand*' system in action with Apple, the world's most valuable brand over the last five years. And as brilliant as we all know the Apple brand to be, our 13-imperatives system suggests some grounds of potential improvements in the areas of 'Partnering', 'Future embracing' and 'Crisis resilience' - more on this later.

Enduring Strategic Brands

Based on the 13 imperatives and through selected real-life case stories and best-in-class experiences, '*THE Enduring Strategic Brand*' discusses concrete approaches to creating and developing extraordinary and transformational Strategic Brands. Each imperative is presented using some of the best (and sometimes worst) practice cases as examples. To this extent, the book acts as a repository of modern best practice for Strategic Brand management.

ILLUSTRATION I.6   THE ENDURING STRATEGIC BRAND IMPERATIVES - APPLE

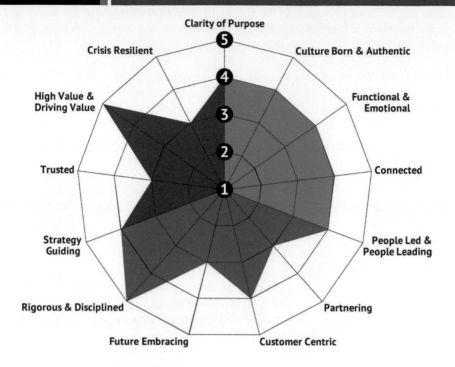

Exemplary Strategic Brands

Each 'Imperative' chapter presents an 'Exemplary Brand' – or occasionally more than one. We chose the word 'exemplary' with care. In the Oxford English Dictionary it is defined as: *'serving as a desirable model; very good and characteristic of its kind or illustrating a general rule'*.

Each Exemplary Brand is arguably already an Enduring Strategic Brand but it also provides a world-class example of best practice for that particular imperative whether it's Airbnb for 'Connected' or Toyota for 'Culture born and authentic'.

In reading each Exemplary Brand story, you might find that I spend extensive time on other imperatives than their top one. The striking observation is that other imperatives feed coherently into their world-class one – as a system. A bit like these best pupils at school who have a major but are good at everything.

During our multiple interviews and discussions, there was one common thread across all Exemplary Brands: none are satisfied with the status quo and most are undertaking considerable transformation from their strong base. A lot also continuously happens to great brands and some have faced interesting times as we were writing these lines – the

Kraft Heinz's $143 billion offer for Unilever; the eventful succession at Tata Sons and more. We did not attempt to capture all aspects of these developments and events but are considering publishing an updated version of 'THE Enduring Strategic Brand' in the future to reflect on their continuing journeys.

'THE Enduring Strategic Brand' System

So here is 'THE Enduring Strategic Brand' system, with this book's selection of Exemplary Brands. As you can see on Illustration I.7, each brand gets a top mark of five for the imperative they stand against e.g. Apple and Disney for 'High value & driving value' or Tata for 'Trusted'.

ILLUSTRATION I.7 — THE EXEMPLARY STRATEGIC BRANDS

In a few cases, the high-mark does not mean that this brand is necessarily best in class, but rather that the journey they have gone through or are undertaking, is one that we can all learn from - whether it's VW on 'Crisis resilient' or RBS on 'People led & People leading'.

Choosing Exemplary Brands was a challenge. To help the selection process we also tried to span sectors and geographies, although my personal and business fascination with the automotive sector and its inherent complexity is also reflected in the final selection. Illustration I.8 represents the sector – country mix matrix.

ILLUSTRATION I.8	SECTOR AND REGION OF ORIGIN OF EXEMPLARY STRATEGIC BRANDS							
	USA	China	Japan	India	Europe	Germany	UK	Swiss
Energy							bp	
Banking & Financial Ser.	American Express						Royal Bank of Scotland	
Pharma	Johnson & Johnson							
Retailing						ALDI		
Automotive			TOYOTA			BMW VW		
Service	airbnb Hertz							
Telecom							O₂	
Conglomerate	GE			TATA				
Consumer Goods	Apple Walt Disney	Haier			Unilever		DIAGEO	
Technology	facebook							
B2B	IBM							
NFP							Olympic Rings	

Is it useful to be an Enduring Strategic Brand?

And there's no question that this approach to strategic branding works. Brand performances are often compared to the S&P 500 (Ref. Chapter 12), so we measured them from 2006 to 2015. The results are striking: the Exemplary Strategic Brands have grown their revenues by 8 per cent CAGR versus 3 per cent for the S&P 500 average.

ILLUSTRATION I.9	PERFORMANCE OF THE EXEMPLARY STRATEGIC BRANDS VS. S&P 500

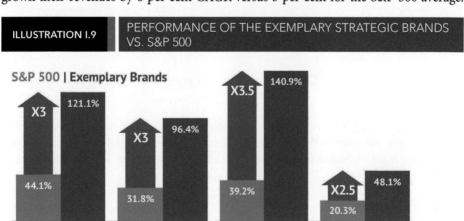

S&P 500 | Exemplary Brands

	Market Cap	Sales	Earnings	Employees
S&P 500	44.1%	31.8%	39.2%	20.3%
Exemplary Brands	121.1% (X3)	96.4% (X3)	140.9% (X3.5)	48.1% (X2.5)

Their market caps have grown almost 3 times more, and their earnings 3.5 times faster than the S&P 500. They have created far more jobs by increasing their workforce by close to 50 per cent, compared to 20 per cent for the S&P 500.

WPP's Group CEO Martin Sorrell says: *"Investing in brands works. In the last 10 years, a measurement of the strongest brands from the BrandZ Top 100 as a stock portfolio shows their share price has risen over three times more than the MSCI World Index, a weighted index of global stocks, and substantially outperformed the S&P 500 too"*

ILLUSTRATION I.10	STRONG BRANDS LARGELY OUTPERFORM THE MARKET

Credit – BrandZ Top 100

WHAT TO EXPECT FROM READING 'THE ENDURING STRATEGIC BRAND'

This is not an academic book. Nor is it an exhaustive study with strict lessons to be followed to the letter. Instead, it is a collection of insights and experiences, questions and tensions, which many Boards, CEOs and CMOs have wrestled with over brand.

"This is a strategy book, not an overview of tactics; a book about foundations, not final decoration; about drawing a map, not the driving details. It aims to prevent people losing the strategic angle or the ability to separate what's important from what's not in such destabilizing times, so they can build their ultimate 'weapon', THE brand."

We want to show the way things are, rather than tell the theory of how they should be. And then, turn these real life examples gathered from C-suite practitioners into a well-understood and well-practised Strategic Brand system.

This is a strategy book, not an overview of tactics; a book about foundations, not final decoration; about drawing a map, not the driving details. It aims to prevent people losing the strategic angle or the ability to separate what's important from what's not in such destabilizing times, so they can build their ultimate 'weapon', THE brand. As Dr Ian Robertson, Member of the BMW AG Board of Management, responsible for global sales and marketing, says: "*A Strategic Brand drives the company, rather than anything else. You have to have the flexibility in your brand to be able to evolve but the consistency to have it anchored*"

Having seen the importance and impact – but also the limitations – of brand management and development, and how so many brands fail to fulfill their potential, this book is a rallying cry to build Enduring Strategic Brands.

It is the voice of Exemplary Strategic Brands through the eyes of a practitioner with over thirty years of experience. During my time at the 'coalface' of executive leadership, I have lived in the eye of the storm through BP's Gulf of Mexico crisis, led year-on-year double-digit growth of branded customer-facing businesses, gone through extreme business cycles and transformations. I have been immensely privileged to see the inside workings of many major companies with whom I was developing extraordinary partnerships. I have worked with CEOs who were not brand or marketing savvy and with others who were the other extreme. I have developed friendships at the highest level of strategy, business leadership and strategic marketing around the world.

THE Enduring Strategic Brand practitioners

First and foremost, this book is a collection of real-life evidence, experiences and journeys of great brands and great leaders, whom I want to thank wholeheartedly for their amazing contribution to the book. Their voices and words make up close to half of the text because it is their experiences and practical wisdom, which provide the richest learning opportunities.

"THE Enduring Strategic Brand' is a passionate cry to provide an opportunity to step back, transform the approach to brand and focus on what is strategic."

Among these forty voices or so, current or previous Chairmen, Board Members or CEOs of BMW, BP, Castrol, GE, Glencore, Hertz, Johnson Matthew, Toyota Motor Company; Group Executives or CMOs of Airbnb, AmEx, Diageo, Facebook, Ford Motor Company, IBM, Lloyds Banking Group, O2, RBS, Tata, Unilever, the International Olympic Committee; and world leading personalities such as Lord John Browne, Professor Klaus

Schwab - WEF, Sir Martin Sorrell - WPP or agency principals, like John Seifert - Ogilvy, Greg Welch - Spencer Stuart and others.

'THE Enduring Strategic Brand' is a passionate cry to provide an opportunity to step back, transform the approach to brand and focus on what is strategic. From BMW's transcendental brand ethos which imbues every element of the organisation, to Paul Polman's courage as Unilever's CEO to change the way business success is valued, following the Pole Star of a Strategic Brand is transformational.

And hopefully, *'THE Enduring Strategic Brand'* will be fun to read, share and discuss.

Next, we will delve into the detail of our first strategic imperative – 'Clarity of Purpose'. And we will describe how purpose can transform your brand through the story of BP and Beyond Petroleum.

CHAPTER 1
CLARITY OF PURPOSE

Clarity of Purpose

Crisis Resilient · Culture Born & Authentic · High Value & Driving Value · Functional & Emotional · Trusted · Connected · Strategy Guiding · People Led & People Leading · Rigorous & Disciplined · Partnering · Future Embracing · Customer Centric

"Simple, clear purpose and principles give rise to complex, intelligent behaviour. Complex rules and regulations give rise to simple, stupid behaviour"

Dee Hock, Founder of Visa

THE INSIDE STORY

Imagine this. It is 19th March 2001 and a global oil company invites you, as a member of its leadership team, to a seminar at Cambridge University. From the honey-coloured cloistered walls of your building overlooking Downing College, where Monty Python's John Cleese dabbled in comedy and theoretical physicist John Pendry began work that would lead to the development of the first invisibility cloak, a small team of suited scientists, engineers, finance and marketing executives step out of their normal lives to look at the world differently. For three days they think long and hard about the world. How could they make resources available sustainably and allocate them fairly?

An Alaskan biodiversity expert talks about the lifecycle of whales – how the gray whale commutes over 400,000 miles in its lifetime, the equivalent of a trip to the moon and back, how the heart of a blue whale is as large as a car. They discover there is circularity in energy. That whale oil was replaced by petroleum as an energy source in 1859…

They play role model games according to world group representation, simulating the "global village": so if two out of 10 people are Chinese, two around a table become Chinese; if one out of 10 in the world suffers from deep hunger, one person around the table must hold this position fiercely and fight for food.

I was one of them, and we argued and debated, we learned new ways of considering the world and its fragility. What would we do at the end of these three days? Would we wipe the experience from our mind and pretend it never happened? Would we drill the earth and provide the world with oil without wider considerations? Or would we try to think bigger and consider alternatives? This seminar was life-changing and is seared into my memory.

The reason I'm telling this story is because this is just one of many examples over its 100-year history of how BP tried to redefine what it means to be an energy company.

Why would an oil company choose to expose its workers to forces contradictory to its traditional business model? Because it was bold. BP used these experiences to embed its brand purpose of 'Beyond Petroleum'. They exposed us to different ideas and encouraged us to think for ourselves about the enterprise's role in wider society. In this way, we could 'own' BP's North Star and help drive it to success.

CLARITY OF PURPOSE

In simple terms, an organisation's purpose is the reason WHY it exists: *"All business in a democratic society begins with public permission and exists by public approval,"* said Arthur W. Page, the 'father of corporate public relations' and VP, AT&T from 1927 to 1946.

The purpose responds to both the simple and complex question: why do we exist, why are we here? And it is more than making money: at a basic level, it might be how an organisation improves the life of its stakeholders. The best brand purposes go beyond this and reflect the organisation's commitment to make the world better.

While it is generally accepted that the need for purpose is indispensible, the distinctive characteristic of a Strategic Brand is to achieve the highest level of clarity and simplicity of purpose. This purpose has to be understood, remembered, and followed through; stakeholders must rally behind its idea.

As Comcast NBCUniversal Kathy Leech explains: *"A true Strategic Brand is one where the purpose is at the heart of the organisation, and is relevant and real because the CEO is effective at communicating it in an engaging way. Then it's not just the CEO who believes in it but also the employees, the board, the suppliers and partners. Business decisions are made based on purpose: when it comes down to the inevitable decision: 'do we go along with what is consistent with our purpose or not?', it should always be to go with what is consistent."*

Purpose is crucial to longevity: only the simplest, clearest brand purposes will endure and have true sustainable impact in a changing society.

Exemplary Brands have a compelling purpose

Throughout this book, we have included the experience of brands we consider to be 'exemplary'. All of these brands have a simple and powerful purpose:

IBM's *'Using technology to make the world work better'* has guided the company through its successive reinventions and reframed its position in a fast-moving technological and societal context.

The Olympics' *'Building a better world through sport'* represents Olympism as a philosophy of life, which places sport at the service of humankind. This purpose informs the actions of the wider global Olympic movement.

Walmart's *'We save people money so they can live better'* returns the retailer to the founder Sam Walton's original intent with the purpose of lower prices to help people provide better lives for their families.

Tata's *'Committed to improving the quality of life of the community we serve'* was first guided by the group's founder Jamsetji Tata and still gives Tata's employees a sense of higher purpose about the work they do, while imbuing trust with the group's stakeholders.

Unilever's *'To make sustainable living commonplace'* creates a unique connection between business and society. In order to make the purpose intrinsic to every part of the company, each brand in the portfolio is required to develop an offer with a mutually reinforcing economic and social mission.

Facebook's *'To make the world more open and connected'* was described memorably by CEO Mark Zuckerberg in 2012, and restated in February 2017. This purpose guided the company's groundbreaking transformation into mobile phones and now to infrastructure that informs us.

Ford's *'Make people's lives better through automotive and mobility leadership'* originates from Henry Ford's determination to build a car the average American could afford. This has shaped today's world and given Ford an enduringly distinctive sense of mission.

Airbnb's *'To make people around the world feel like they could belong anywhere'* drives the company's relentless effort to create a world of more belonging. Airbnb's purpose is to extend their idea of belonging from homes into 'everything' in the future.

Nike's *"To bring inspiration and innovation to every athlete in the world"* drives the company's systematic approach to improve every aspect of people's exercise, shifting from products to experiences and lifestyle.

Johnson & Johnson adorable *"Caring for the world, one person at a time"* exudes personal warmth while involving people in the bigger picture.

BP's *'Beyond Petroleum'* expresses the enterprise's commitment to play its part in making the required energy resources available, while acknowledging that they are not perfect and therefore being determined to improve their societal performance.

'Doing well' and 'doing good' are the same

There are plenty of other brands with a clear and guiding purpose, whether they're legacy or emerging brands, product or digital led, Western or Asian. What they all have in common is their clarity and simplicity – and success.

"This realisation created the ultimate test for a Strategic Brand's 'clarity of purpose': is the business model, the way it creates value, synonymous with or embedded in its purpose?"

I have come to observe that the enduring good fortune of these brands results from the fact that 'doing well' and 'doing good' are the same, and are mutually reinforcing. This realisation created the ultimate test for a Strategic Brand's 'Clarity of purpose': is the business model, the way it creates value, synonymous with or embedded in its purpose?

Is Unilever's Sustainable Living Plan helping the company's performance? The enterprise is very clear that it does, and states: *"Unilever has a simple but clear purpose – to make sustainable living commonplace. We believe this is the best long-term way for our business to grow."*

Facebook's Mark Zuckerberg is equally passionate that *"it is by focusing on our mission that we will create the most value for our shareholders and partners over the long term."*

Are other enterprise brand purposes as robustly intertwined with the company's business model? Was BP's purpose equally grounded into and associated with how it made money? If your brand and its purpose are not symbiotic with your organisation's economic model, I would advise you to consider evolving its purpose, transforming its business model or changing both as soon as possible to avert disappointment.

A wide spread acceptance for deep purpose

Most CEOs, C-Suites, CMOs and professionals adhere to the idea that it's critically important for an organisation to have purpose. Multiple researches validate the compelling business value of strong brand purpose and here are a few evidences:

Jim Stengel's 10-year growth study with Millward Brown of 50,000 brands revealed that the top 50 businesses in his research - "The Stengel 50" could all be characterized as 'ideals-led' businesses, grew three times faster than their competitors and would have been 400 percent more profitable than an investment in the S&P 500 (Note 1)

For the last two years, Unilever has been reporting that its 'Sustainable Living Brands' have grown twice as fast as other brands in their portfolio (Note 2).

A Havas Group research on 1500 global brands has shown that 'meaningful brands' increase share of wallet by up to nine times, capture a 12 per cent pricing premium and an additional five per cent repurchase compared to average (Note 3).

This chapter is therefore not an advocation of the idea – because the 'WHY a purpose' is clear to many. Rather, I will focus on the WHAT and HOW: what does it mean to be deeply purposed? How do you develop a simple and compelling guiding purpose for your organisation?

Years of experience and practice have shown me the challenges of building a purposed brand and business – and raised the following questions: where does an enterprise purpose come from? How does strong and visionary leadership define it? How do you build and embed brand purpose as a fundamental driver for the enterprise? I have seen how purpose manifests and plays out; how it can be pervasive – and how it can get lost.

BP's Beyond Petroleum provides a textbook example of a brand purpose, so I will mainly focus on this story and its real life aspects – why the need for a BP purpose in 2000; what was the process to develop, embed and communicate it; how did it happen and work out?

You will find more examples throughout the book of how a deep brand purpose is sine qua non for Strategic Brands and makes such a difference to their enterprise - with most chapters showing how other enduring Strategic Brands have embedded their purpose and made it a guide for everything.

Why a 'New BP' Brand?

Many people have heard of BP, but may not know – or fully appreciate – the true BP and the story of its brand. This is another reason why I would like to tell the story, starting with a short introduction of the company.

BP's journey from the Anglo Persian Oil Company

Today, BP remains one of the world's largest companies with over 79,800 employees, operating in 70 countries, producing over 3.3 million barrels of oil equivalent per day.

BP was born in 1909 as the Anglo Persian Oil Company with a handful of employees and one asset: a promising concession, which eventually led to the discovery and production of oil in what is now Iran. In 1969, when John Browne graduated from Cambridge University and joined the oil company, BP struck oil in Alaska.

ILLUSTRATION 1.1	THE CHANGING FACES OF BP THROUGH THE AGES

Throughout BP's history – from Iran in 1909 to Alaska in the 1960s, the North Sea in the 1970s, and Angola, the Gulf of Mexico and the Caspian Sea today – the company has always worked at the frontiers of the energy sector, building relationships, applying its technology and know-how in ways that often push forward boundaries.

BP has always been at the cutting edge of **innovation**, for example in building the Trans-Alaska pipeline between 1974–77, a 1200km long system and the largest civil engineering project ever attempted in North America at the time; of **technology**, using imaging, remote sensing and other pioneering science to advance its position as one of the best oil and gas explorers in the world; of **major projects**, operating the world's largest supercomputer for commercial research in Houston as a worldwide hub for processing huge amounts of geophysical data. BP has continuously stood at the frontiers of **strategy**, continually reinventing itself, from the nationalisation by Colonel Gaddafi of its Libyan assets in 1971, to being over many years the biggest foreign investor in China through its stake in PetroChina and in Russia through TNK-BP.

Throughout its long history, BP has committed to its enduring purpose to deliver energy in a responsible manner to the world. Over the past two decades, the company has played a material role among other leading energy companies to power an unprecedented era of economic growth and global development. In this period, global GDP doubled (source: Worldeconomics) and energy consumption grew by nearly 50 per cent (source: BP energy outlook).

BP leads the industry global transformation

The 1990s was a momentous time for BP and the oil industry as a whole. Oil prices were at a record low, so industry economics were challenging and the outlook for some of the world's biggest, most successful energy companies was uncertain.

John Browne was not naïve to these challenges. He knew that hope for better days was not a strategy. He and his team recognised that BP would not thrive in a depressed market without true global scale and a more robust portfolio of energy assets to sustain future growth when industry economics recover.

When the oil price was at rock bottom at the end of the 1990s and assets were cheaper, he went on an acquisition spree, one of the boldest in business history, buying Amoco (a beloved US retail brand), Arco (a leading West Coast brand), Aral (a leading German retail brand) and Burmah Castrol, one of the world's largest lubricants businesses - where I was CEO for the Europe region.

| ILLUSTRATION 1.2 | BP'S ACQUISITION SPREE IN THE LATE 1990'S |

BP transformed itself into a leading global player. With the global stage came internal pressures – how did these acquisitions make a whole? What kind of brand would we become?

The genesis of the 'New BP' Strategic Brand

I joined BP in 2000 when it acquired Burmah Castrol, at the very time that this new and transformed company had some soul-searching to do. BP needed to answer some existential questions; it needed a purpose and a brand. Lord John Browne explains why he took such a strong leadership position on developing a clear brand purpose: *"A good Strategic Brand needs to be associated with a big idea. We were in the business of not just producing shareholder value, but about projecting the future. This was the big idea. That was the clarity of purpose."*

The metamorphosis of BP

Here are some of the questions BP was asking itself in 2000 in the midst of its metamorphosis: what happens when an audacious M&A-driven increase in scale means the sun will never set on BP's companies, now spread all over the world? What does it mean when a very British organisation becomes a world leader and guides the transformation of an entire industry? What are the forces on a company's culture when it nearly triples its number of people in just one year?

What is the result when a quantum leap in confidence sees BP accept responsibility for the world at large, setting a template for future generations of corporates to lead difficult environmental discussions? What does it mean when a company is transformed, a sector is challenged and political and business leaders are inspired or threatened to change? It's because of these questions – and many others – that I am putting BP's brand under the microscope.

I was privileged to work at BP for the following 14 years and lived through John's groundbreaking vision to redefine what an energy company might become. I worked with many of my colleagues to make it a reality, and experienced all the subsequent challenges that implementation at scale of big, bold ideas can bring.

Lots of people have written about the BP brand story, but what was it like on the inside during the evolution of British Petroleum to Beyond Petroleum? What was it like at these passionate internal meetings, when we faced resistance from the exploration & production (upstream) team about the brand? How did we cope with a change of era when we lost our iconic leader John Browne? Was life purpose-driven on the West Lake campus in Houston, USA, when we worked with the most committed people to contain and then repair the devastation of the Deepwater Horizon crisis?

The 'big' brand

Like all the best stories, BP's brand story is the tale of a journey with highs and lows, jeopardy and conflict. The early 2000s began with good fortune as the oil company led the sector's consolidation with a bold acquisition spree to assemble an unparalleled group of quality brands. This was followed by a radical resetting of the industry in 2007-8, the consequences of which I explain in Chapter 10. Bad fortune followed with the Deepwater Horizon crisis and then there was a subsequent period of gradual recovery. I analyse how we handled this disaster alongside the role the BP brand played in crisis management in Chapter 13.

"While the brand is the glue, purpose is the litmus test of sustainability in business. Without brand, no company."

All along the journey, the brand purpose was being built – and challenged. Recently John described to me what the brand meant to him: *"The brand is the glue that keeps the company together and expresses the forward paths, the direction, which is communicable to everybody. The enterprise brand has actually little to do with how you signify what you sell. Of course it is important, but it is not the same thing. While the brand is the glue, purpose is the litmus test of sustainability in business. Without brand, no company."*

In his book 'Connect', John also writes: *"The very greatest companies place human progress at the heart of their purpose. They do so based on a firm understanding of their place in the world."*

"The very greatest companies place human progress at the heart of their purpose. They do so based on a firm understanding of their place in the world."

The Sun King

A lot has been said and written about Lord John Browne. The Financial Times called him the Sun King. When talking about him around the Sunday dinner table I would describe him as the most intelligent man I have ever met, with a distinctive ability to enquire, gather data, structure thinking, develop vision and strategies, and represent them to others.

John taught me how to best combine fairness and toughness, to look high and far, and that *"the best is yet to come"*. He taught me that business is about choices and finding confidence in those choices. I remember a trip to Monaco for the F1 Grand Prix: over the course of two days, he wanted to know everything about 'customers'. That weekend saw the birth of the BP Strategic Accounts business, which I led for over ten years.

There is no doubt that over the last 15 years, the BP brand has aspired to define itself and become an Enduring Strategic Brand. Alongside commentary from John Browne and John Seifert, worldwide Chairman and CEO of Ogilvy & Mather and the WPP Group leader for the BP brand since its inception, I will reflect on the successes and weaknesses of our attempt.

Defining the 'New BP' Brand Purpose

With his visionary approach, John asked a refreshingly simple, but provocative question: "What does 'BP inside' mean?"

To answer this question, a small global brand team was formed in 2000, which included senior business leaders from all parts of BP, beyond the usual marketing boundaries. The agencies Ogilvy & Mather and Landor & Associates were appointed to support the work – less a formal process than a relationship based on John and BP's trust in Shelly Lazarus, now Chairman Emeritus of O&M, and John Seifert. I was not a full-time member of this team, as I had been newly 'acquired' by BP with Burmah Castrol – but kept close and was invited to provide thoughts and feedback, all of which would prepare me for later.

This team embarked on a fascinating and daunting journey to define a Strategic Brand for the new energy mammoth. In short, their mission was to create a 'New BP' brand for a new age in the energy business. They needed to consider how society's needs and our brand purpose might meet enduringly.

Beginning with the long gasoline lines and shortages of the 1970s and compounded by the economic and geopolitical roller coaster of oil markets in the 1980s and 1990s, the emotional connection between consumers and energy company brands was lower than just about every business sector one could look at, as can be seen in Illustration 3. When asked, 'How strongly has the leading brand in each category and sector bonded with consumers?', just 9 per cent stated motor fuel, compared with 60 per cent packaged goods and 41 per cent services. Even infrequently purchased brands (at 53 per cent) scored higher than our industry. There was much work to be done!

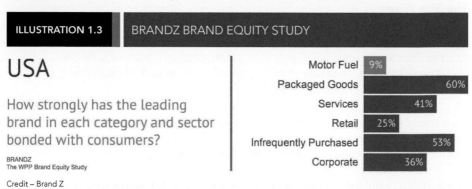

ILLUSTRATION 1.3   BRANDZ BRAND EQUITY STUDY

USA

How strongly has the leading brand in each category and sector bonded with consumers?

BRANDZ
The WPP Brand Equity Study

Motor Fuel	9%
Packaged Goods	60%
Services	41%
Retail	25%
Infrequently Purchased	53%
Corporate	36%

Credit – Brand Z

The energy paradox

And yet, oil is the basic energy source for much of today's economic prosperity and wealth. Without it we would still be drawing water from a well or riding to market in a horse and cart. Indeed, no business sector is more essential to the fundamental needs for society's quality of life: light, heat, mobility and economic growth.

It was equally true that the world was increasingly challenged by the consequences of an expanding industrial era and the societal problems resulting from that growth – from air and water quality issues to waste disposal, from traffic congestion to global urbanisation. Remember those times in the late 90s: we were very close to the tipping point, when 50 per cent of people in the world would live in cities – over the last ten years, the number of megacities in the world has doubled. Meanwhile, the science around man-made global warming was becoming more robust and convincing.

To the brand team, a "co-dependency" existed between producer and consumer. Societies everywhere needed energy companies for their livelihoods and better living standards. Would people be accepting when they turned on their lights in the morning to no effect? Would they tolerate mobility restrictions because of unavailability of fuel? Would it be OK to be cold in winter or without work if power was not available?

Yet, the consequences of our collective economic growth and improving lifestyle contributed to ever more negative consequences, resulting in frustration towards the producers of our most indispensible energy. And don't forget the simple correlation between energy consumption and development, which meant that the developing world would need a lot more energy. (Incidentally, the team was not thinking only about oil and gas but rather about the fast overall increase of energy demand, which was matched by coal to a significant extent.)

More energy and less environmental consequences

We called this the "energy paradox". It was the seemingly irreconcilable challenge facing the whole industry – but we concluded that no energy brand could thrive going forward without confronting this paradox head on. This plan of action was a natural continuation of years of John and BP's pioneering engagement in reconciling more energy with less environmental impact.

A unifying and purposed brand

So, BP set out to do just that. The BP brand team helped develop an enterprise agenda to unify a diverse new portfolio of companies (BP, Amoco, Arco, Burmah Castrol, etc.), each with their own distinctive heritage and brand point of view. At the same time, the brand would address the challenge of the "energy paradox".

John Browne recalls this as the moment when the 'New BP' began redefining its future, its purpose and its place in the world: *"The element of the future is critical. Otherwise, we could have stuck with the brand that we had, which was the BP shield. And therein lies the important piece of the visual identity, because the visual identity connoted a brand that was actually stuck in the past, and we wanted to do something different, which we felt was important.*

"The way we talked about our company had to change. If only because of the acquisitions, the old BP became the minority of the company, both in financial and human terms. Having all these new people, new places, new things, we were different and had to think deeply about this new reality. We stood for the same things, but they had to be further reinforced with the huge diversity of the company and our different future."

Similarly, John Seifert recalls: *"There was an extraordinary moment when, because of the external environment and the opportunity in the oil and gas and energy business, John had the vision and ambition to scale BP to a whole new level. This led to the acquisitions of Amoco, Burmah Castrol and ultimately ARCO, as parts of a grand design of a new enterprise. It was a big grand challenge moment: BP had a defining history but then, all of a sudden, the whole company becomes something different because of the scale and diversity of these acquisitions.*

"In my mind, that was an inflection point, the time when any large enterprise which has gone through that type of large-scale transformation has to ask itself: 'OK, are we going to be a conglomerate of pieces or are we going to try and invoke something distinctive and enduring, an idea that becomes the glue, the bonding agent for this new scaled entity?'"

For me, what is also fascinating to note is that at different points both leaders described the enterprise brand in the same language: as the 'glue'.

Addressing climate change

The vision we had for BP in 2000, the genesis of this new brand, was bold and brave. As John Seifert said: *"I can't think of another category where a single company brand was prepared to colour so far outside the lines of what was expected within the category."*

The first seeds of the idea were sown in the outside world in May 1997. Just three weeks after Tony Blair became Prime Minister of the UK, John delivered a now-famous speech to Stanford Business School which addressed climate change. He dramatically moved the conversation from collective denial to a more progressive dialogue on the connection between hydrocarbons and global climate change.

In this speech John talked about BP in terms of shared responsibility, and as a citizen. His words remain relevant twenty years later:

"We are all citizens of one world, and we must take shared responsibility for its future and sustainable development. We must do that in all our various roles: as business people with capital to invest, as legislators with the power to make law, as individual citizens with the right to vote, and as consumers with the power of choice.

"We've now come to an important moment in our consideration of the environment: the moment when we need to go beyond analysis to seek solutions and to take action. It is a moment for change and for a rethinking of corporate responsibility.

"But sustainability is about more than profits. Real sustainability is about simultaneously being profitable and responding to the reality and the concerns of the world in which you operate. We're not separate from the world. It's our world as well. To be sustainable, companies need a sustainable world. That means a world where the environmental equilibrium is maintained but also a world whose population can enjoy the heat, light and mobility which we take for granted and which the oil industry helps to provide. I don't believe those are incompatible goals.

"All the actions we're taking and will take at BP are directed to ensuring that these goals are not incompatible. There are no easy answers. No silver bullets. Just steps on a journey, which we should take together because we all have a vital interest in finding the answers. The cultures of politics and of science and of enterprise must work together if we are to match and master the challenges we all face."

The reaction to John's speech was immediate and incredible. He sent shockwaves around the world by breaking ranks with the rest of the oil industry in endorsing the science of climate change and publicly acknowledging the relationship between fossil fuels and climate shifts.

Stephen H. Schneider, a climate researcher and Stanford professor who wrote the first popular book on global warming, said then: *"Browne's speech was a welcome change of direction for an industry that has, until now, denied that global warming is a problem. They're out of climate denial."*

And James M. Strock, the founding Secretary of the California Environmental Protection Agency said: *"This bold move will set the world stage for other companies to emulate."*

THE CREATION OF THE BP - BEYOND PETROLEUM BRAND

As I mentioned earlier, three years after this speech, BP was an energy world leader in scale and had the opportunity to integrate its beliefs while it was defining its new entity. Internally, BP people were excited. We knew this was the beginning of something extraordinary. John Seifert recalls: *"We had spent almost a year talking internally in the company about the purpose, the promise. It was a long time. People were euphoric and this was pretty powerful. But the majority of employees probably didn't know at the time exactly what it would mean in terms of their own individual contribution and the consequences on their roles. Rather, everyone was basking in the glow of the promise."*

In Chapter 10, I analyse how we implemented this new enterprise brand in practice, connecting it to strategy. But with the benefit of hindsight, there is one question that strikes me (and a number of others at BP) now: did BP's Strategic Brand play a bigger role for others than it did for itself, in that it was ahead of its time? The 'energy paradox' idea pushed all the boundaries of what a brand might be and say – *"colouring outside the lines"*, to borrow John Seifert's language.

Could today's progressive companies like Unilever, which links its business growth to decoupling its environmental footprint, and Adidas – which is ranked the third most sustainable company in the world by Corporate Knights – have achieved as much without BP's inspirational role nearly twenty years before?

I had a fascinating conversation with Unilever's CEO Paul Polman on the night of the 6 November 2013, when he was appointed chairman of the World Business Council for Sustainable Development (WBCSD). Paul was extremely thoughtful about the importance of pathfinders in helping to create a vision and proof of concept to show that good business and sustainability could become one and the same and generous towards BP's own contribution.

BP was clearly an agent of change and John Seifert agrees: *"Did you believe in BP's efforts to go 'Beyond Petroleum' and raise the level of accountability for a major industrial company to deliver value in a more societally responsible context for the extraction and use and long-term consequences of energy. I absolutely have to believe that you would say it was positive.*

"It was a model of responsibility that otherwise would not have happened. I would also argue that a whole bunch of other companies, both within and beyond the sector, became sensitive to this opportunity and need because of BP."

Beyond Petroleum

This was the thinking behind the new BP brand in 2000. As you can perhaps sense, it was wide and deep, about history and the future. It was not about product or fuel station's branding, but about the long-term role and accountability of a global corporation in a highly sensitive sector. In short, it was about the deep purpose of the 'New BP', a purpose that would guide the daily actions of the hundreds of thousands of people in its extended workforce.

"In short, it was about the deep purpose of the 'New BP', a purpose that would guide the daily actions of the hundreds of thousands of people in its extended workforce."

John Browne comments: *"We embedded the brand with our future, what we stood for, wanted to do, how we dealt with people, how we thought about our position in the world."*

So how did the brand development work? The team had to boil down a highly strategic point of view into language, symbols and rites. There were many exercises, as you would expect in a structured and strategically-minded organisation - but there was also a lot of harmony in the decision-making process because the effort was grounded in facts and a vision of the future. What's more, the culture of the old BP was strong.

Culture and values

John Browne was well aware of the vital importance of culture – intimating that nothing is as important to a brand as the culture and values of the people who own and represent it.

Throughout its history, BP has experienced both tragedy and triumph and persevered through it all. This is testament to the character and culture of BP's people. At BP's core - cutting through the mechanics of strictly codified 'Values & Behaviours' exercises - I believe (though others might disagree) that the common beliefs shared by those in BP, its collective character, could be described as first and foremost:

- *'Doing the right thing'*
- *'Performance at the frontier'*
- In *'open dialogue with others'*

It made the company inspirational and inimitable – I examine this idea in more detail in Chapter 13, when talking about how BP's Strategic Brand played a pivotal role during crisis management.

From this rich and anchored heritage and with close to two-thirds of non 'natives' having just joined, all with their own strong cultures, the challenge ahead was to define the common and desired traits that would represent the 'New BP' shared culture.

Debates were rich and animated: what was the importance of heritage to BP's culture? Should we be more anchored in what exists or what we aspire to? What were the trade offs, for example between short-term 'performance' and 'being green'?

Ultimately, BP committed itself to a set of four core values, as represented in Illustration 1.4: Progressive, Green, Performance and Innovative.

ILLUSTRATION 1.4	BP'S VALUES

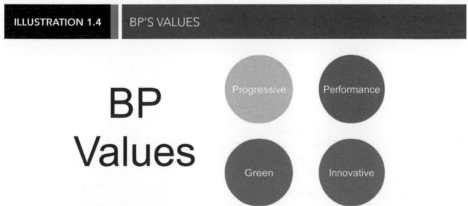

Credit: BP – Source: BP Corporate Site

It was clear that these values were essentially aspirational, that they underpinned the ongoing attempt to form a common culture behind an emotionally compelling vision of change and industry leadership.

Essence & Purpose

To magnify the new enterprise brand point of view, an identity system was created around the brand essence – 'Beyond Petroleum'.

The message implicit in Beyond Petroleum was, *"We make this resource and know it's imperfect, and you consume it. Let's work together to do better. To go beyond."*

And in practice, Beyond Petroleum would stand for the three journeys of:

- Meeting the growing demand for fossil fuels in better ways
- Manufacturing and delivering more advanced products and services
- Enabling the transition to a lower carbon economy

These three complementary journeys had been considered in depth and were core to the brand development. They had been created for their perfect ability to imbue purpose to every part of the 'New BP', while in turn, each would be playing a major role in delivering the enterprise's purpose.

Exploration & Production – Upstream would provide more of the energy required today, but in continuously improved ways.

Refining & Marketing – Downstream would reduce its products' environmental footprint, both in the way they are manufactured and consumed.

And a third business would be developed, Renewable Energy – solar, wind and bio fuels, to start the transition. Each and all of the three businesses would 'do their job' while contributing to the journey towards a lower carbon economy in their own way.

ILLUSTRATION 1.5	BP GROUP BRAND BRIDGE

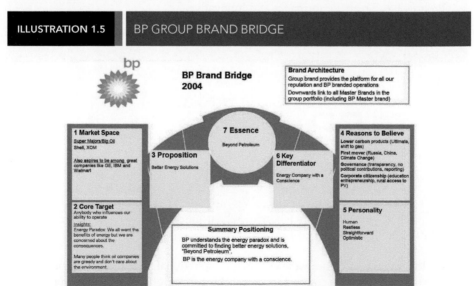

Credit – BP plc.

It was a strong purpose. In hindsight, we didn't embed it enough, both inside and outside of the organisation. Over time, too many people in the outside world focused only on our third journey and renewable energy – and too many people within BP only focused on the first journey. More on this later, but Beyond Petroleum was a deep purpose!

Brand architecture

Using the strictest Strategic Brand design methodology, the team, along with other BP leaders, developed a unifying brand platform illustrated by the BP, 'Beyond Petroleum' brand bridge (Ref. Illustration 1.5). I like this tool, which is similar to 'Brand Key' used by Unilever and other alike methods, as it forces a brand's core positioning to unite with its expression. The BP brand bridge was going to exert a leading influence in the energy sector, and of course within BP, for a number of years to come.

Symbols and descriptors

The enterprise, its purpose and mission were embodied by the new BP mark, the Helios. Making reference to the sun and nature, it was generally well received as appealing, evocative, fresh, hopeful and reassuring. Transformational and ambitious brand guidelines were also issued, notably *'no accidents, no harm to people, no damage to the environment'*.

ILLUSTRATION 1.6	BP'S HELIOS AND BEYOND PETROLEUM

beyond petroleum®

Credit – BP Corporate Site

There are a lot of myths and stories behind the choice of the Helios mark, in particular about it being up against another strong logo option, the 'V Formation'. John Browne was convinced of the importance of visual identity and determined it would represent 'the BP' he so passionately envisioned and was building. Those who were at the meeting to make the final decision on the logo report that John's mother played an important role in the final judgment.

It's a start

Now the 'New BP' Strategic Brand had been defined, it was time to express and communicate it.

Brand content and activation

The new brand proposition was activated through an innovative mix of '*on the street*' initiatives, which were designed to foster more relevant and emotionally engaging connections with thought leaders and, of course, everyday consumers. This communication format came to life with a large number of interviews held '*on the street*', where members of the public would be canvased for their opinions about energy issues and the energy paradox. The resulting video clips were then shown on TV, to invite and encourage participation in this important conversation.

While Beyond Petroleum was a sticky and provocative brand theme, "*It's a start*" was the true heart of our new brand proposition. We needed to make sure that Beyond Petroleum did not mislead stakeholders. We didn't want people to believe that BP was leaving the oil and gas business, or indeed that BP had a perfect set of energy solutions just now.

ILLUSTRATION 1.7	'IT'S A START' BEYOND PETROLEUM CAMPAIGN

Credit – Ogilvy & Mather

Rather, communication needed to reflect how Beyond Petroleum was intended as a commitment to engage the world differently – to confront the seemingly irreconcilable 'energy paradox' as a shared responsibility.

'*It's a start*' was a way to signal that we were clear it would be a long journey to a sustainable economy – but that we were determined to give it a good start and go through each step. '*It's a start*' was also an invitation to others to join and play their part, however big or small. It was a humble message, it did not overpromise and it was connected.

Being bold
While most advertising 'tag lines' are conceived to perfectly sum up the workings of an enterprise, BP's corporate reputation campaign was designed to be bold, a true signal of brand difference in a category that had been long regarded as out of touch. It certainly accomplished that.

Technically, the campaign made strides, including a Gold Effie Award from the American Marketing Association in 2007, which stated: *"The BP corporate campaign is a landmark platform for a company trying to change the way the world uses, and thinks about, the fuels that are vital to human progress."*

The brand purpose influences strategy and actions
The new brand agenda sparked a wave of internal innovation at BP, from new age solar-powered service stations to introducing cleaner fuels across 40 major cities.

BP operations in Upstream and Downstream refining or chemical plants reduced their environmental footprint significantly, by 30 to 50 per cent in many areas.

ILLUSTRATION 1.8	SERIES OF INITIATIVES AND INNOVATIONS

Credit – WBCSD, BP, Landor

BP engaged in lower carbon-driven partnerships with automotive OEMs to reduce emissions through the better technological combination of our products and their engines. We also joined up with major progressive users of energy – for example freight companies like Fedex, mining companies like BHP Billiton and retailers like Walmart – to jointly optimise energy at the consumption points. I ran these co-operations through a 'Strategic Partnerships' business, supported by a strategy group called 'Sustainable Mobility'.

BP pledged $8bn to the low financial return renewable energy businesses of wind, solar and bio fuels, a move that attracted bitter push back from some investors but still represents the biggest such commitment in the sector. We embarked on the journey of 'conserving' energy with green shoots like BP Target Neutral, an emission offset mechanism or campaigns to reduce consumers' fuel consumption through improving their driving cycles, and so on.

BP entered a flurry of conversations and partnerships with universities, such as Princeton in the US and Tsinghua in China, global business institutions like the WBCSD, and multiple NGOs around the world.

We even committed to a better retail experience – who wouldn't get emotional about a better gas station bathroom?

ILLUSTRATION 1.9	BP RETAIL 'A LITTLE BETTER' CAMPAIGN

Credit – Ogilvy & Mather

We measured and reported progress in our yearly Sustainability Reports, a common practice nowadays but something that BP originally pioneered and remained best in kind over many years.

These activities reflected how the brand purpose translated into actions, as well as how "*it's a start*" invited others to join and build stronger 'Beyond Petroleum' solutions together.

BP - A Purposed Strategic Brand

In the early 2000s, BP was undoubtedly a Strategic Brand – as shown on Illustration 10. Its 'Purpose', combined with strong leadership – 'People led', an unrivalled 'Future embracing' approach in the sector and its on-going actions – 'Strategy guiding', all resulted in strong performance – 'High value' – and unparalleled levels of 'Trust'. In just a short time, the brand had gone a long way.

Many of those working in BP embraced the brand's purpose and beliefs. We were able to recruit the best people, as they were inspired by the company. This is also what made me stay there and develop such affection and respect for BP.

As far as culture goes, from the moment you began employment, you read the BP code of conduct saying that: *"It is your personal commitment to do the right thing"*. We measured the way our brand values and behaviours were held by people in their performance scorecards. One of the best illustrations of how these values ran through people at BP like blood through their veins is the following sentence from former BP CEO Tony Hayward as he resigned in 2010: *"I was turned into a villain for doing the right thing."*

ILLUSTRATION 1.10	THE ENDURING STRATEGIC BRAND IMPERATIVES - BP IN 2003

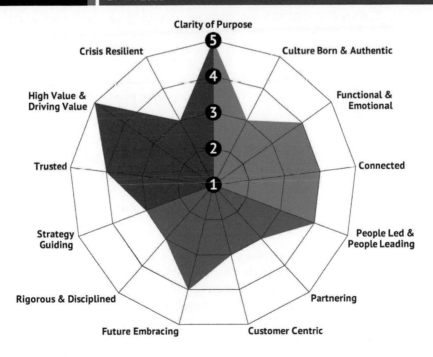

As for the purpose, what is more inspiring than to feel empowered to pave the way to a better future, while belonging to a successful enterprise!

A changing world

The world changed for everybody on 11 September 2001. Price spikes upstream and at the pump, coupled with geopolitical tensions in the Middle East post 9/11, along with the accelerated economic growth of China, India and other fast developing economies, led to some 'hard truths' and new challenges for the energy sector. Over time, this would intensify the debate on three critical societal demands, and how society would balance their respective importance: affordable access to energy, security of supply, and a lower carbon future.

ILLUSTRATION 1.11	THE THREE SOCIETAL DEMANDS FOR ENERGY

Affordable access

Security of supply

Lower carbon

While the world was changing, BP was also evolving. From 2003 onwards, I remember strong debates both inside and outside the company about how we were living the brand and the Beyond Petroleum purpose in reality. Six years had passed since John's groundbreaking rallying cry setting BP up as a corporate pioneer in the battle against climate change.

Over that period, society had started to shift from a time of aspiration to an era of realisation and implementation at scale. There were big questions to address: weren't we still a major oil producer and therefore indirectly a major polluter? What was the actual scale and weight of the bridge we were creating between fossil fuels and alternative energy?

A number of very demanding NGOs were starting to publicly question BP's real intent. This was based largely on a misunderstanding of the three journeys of Beyond Petroleum and what they really meant.

Internally, next to all the other challenges of who we were, what we did, how we performed, many teams wanted to simplify the way forward and return to focusing on what they had to do as a core job. All these debates raised critical questions about what this meant for the brand. It was the biggest test we'd had since 2000: could BP be not only a Strategic Brand but an Enduring Strategic Brand?

TWELVE STEPS TO BUILDING A STRATEGIC BRAND WITH PURPOSE

It is a challenge to reflect properly on the page the strong leadership, great work and practice that it took to redefine a 100-year-old enterprise as a powerful, aspiring and purposed Strategic Brand. But I believe a similar approach would serve well any organisation with a desire to develop or restate its brand purpose and pave the way to build itself into an Enduring Strategic Brand.

Here are the 12 most important things I have learned from my experience and journey in building a purposed 'New BP' and observing other exemplary brands:

1. **Purpose must be determined by and intertwined with the enterprise culture –** Can employees answer the question, *"Why are we here?"* and be satisfied with the response? The answer needs to fit with the employee's aspirations, what they value, the life they want to live and create for others – in short, with their culture and the organisation's culture. Inherently, I believe that Beyond Petroleum was attuned to BP's deep culture.

2. **Purpose must be reflective of the business model –** If the brand purpose is at odds with the main focus and performance objectives of the organisation, it will not permeate and survive, neither internally – business will do what it thinks is good for business – nor externally – shareholders and other stakeholders will push back hard. Unilever makes unparalleled efforts to drive unique value from its Sustainable Living Plan. Walmart would never accept a sustainability initiative that would raise costs. At BP we had many evidences of value – as example, I remember winning an exploration licence in Canada on the back of our purpose; or our OEM partnerships led to high mutual value creation. But it should have been more systematically spread across the enterprise, truly placing Beyond Petroleum at the heart of all core pillars of our business model.

3. **Purpose should be clear –** There should be no second interpretation to the brand purpose. At BP, the phrase 'Beyond Petroleum' could be read as exiting petroleum for alternatives. John Browne comments: *"I think there was a lot of mischief at play. Some people tried to push the world to take Beyond Petroleum literally – and make it happen now. We should have moderated it more by saying that we are not getting rid of today but building into a different future."*

4. **Purpose should be simple** – A brand and a fortiori a brand purpose will only anchor with people, inside or outside the company, if it is simple to understand, to remember and to appreciate and value. An example of the great success of such simplicity is when the brand name becomes the action verb, e.g. *"let's Airbnb there"*.

5. **Again, again and again** – The old rule of communication and advertising applies nowhere better than to purpose. Every aspect of living the brand should be consistently in tune with the purpose over a long period of time so that it will anchor. BMW's Ian Robertson explains, *"People develop the feeling because it is a consistent message. Words are easy to say, but you have to keep nurturing it."*

6. **In its time... into the future** – Audiences will only embrace a brand purpose if it also solves a problem and improves their situation now. Facebook's Nicola Mendelsohn says: *"Understand where the consumer is, where they are spending their time, how they are talking about your brand, and how they want to be communicated with - and bring those learnings upfront."* While John Browne tells us: *"The BP brand, its purpose and positioning were very much about reflecting the future."*

7. **Strong leadership – but not a single leader** – To drive game-changing purpose through all the peaks and troughs of business life takes immense leadership. Steve Jobs, Bill Gates, Paul Polman, Richard Branson, Jeff Bezos, John Browne and a number of other exceptional leaders have defined, lived and epitomised their organisation's purpose. Losing these figureheads often leaves the brand and purpose like orphans – this is certainly what we saw when John Browne and then Ian Conn left BP. Shelly Lazarus describes the worst (but frequent) risk which arises if the brand purpose is not co-owned: *"A new CEO comes in and, for example, says: 'Make me a new brand. What we have is not hip, it is boring, it is of the last generation.' This is just naïve and foolish, because you have to start where you are, and in most cases, the DNA and the purpose of the brand are pretty solid and permanent."*

8. **Only communicate when purpose has been translated into hard-tested strategic plans** – Behind Unilever's corporate purpose stands a robust plan, the 'Sustainable Living Plan', which in turn is backed up by the individual consumer brands' own 'Sustainable Living Plans'. In BP, we had some good plans and drove remarkable initiatives and innovations – but this was not systematic enough or fully robust - and driving purpose throughout became a challenge over time, particularly as the world context caused businesses to fight for survival and revert to basics.

9. **Execute like crazy** – Facts will speak louder than words. Never more than in our modern customer-led, digital-enabled society has every aspect of connection with a brand, what is called the full experience, been the continuing and compelling proof of living the purpose. Your purpose guides what you do; what you do reveals your purpose. *"The biggest impact comes from solving the biggest problems. And when you're faced with the choice between strategy and execution, choose execution,"* says Nicola Mendelsohn.

10. **Under promise, over deliver** – Manage expectations. Some brand purposes are simply amazing on their meaning and impact - and it is easy to get carried away and pushed by vested stakeholders to do more and faster than what is possible. The drivers are good but if you can't hold to your promise, disappointment and mistakes will happen. John Seifert remembers this about BP: *"Brand communications internally and externally delivered very strongly on the promise, as it was so genuinely appealing. In the end, the challenge became the ability to fully live up to it through enough actions in the short term."*

11. **Performance managed** – Even purpose should be performance managed. Firstly, for itself: how it is embedded [e.g. people surveys]; how it is lived [e.g. individual employee 'performance contracts']; how it is understood and valued [e.g. brand metrics, social media listening]. Then it should be measured for its outcomes – for example, Unilever measures and publicises metrics and milestones on the economic and social impact of its purpose-driven plans.

12. **Be prepared for a generation-long journey** – The ultimate measure of how embedded a purpose is and of its transforming impact is when it evolves culture, and becomes integral to it. A new business can be built entirely on its purpose. Established businesses need a generation to build and truly embed a restated purpose, the time it would have taken Beyond Petroleum if drama hadn't interceded. Erez Vigodman once said to me: *"A start up can begin the journey from the ultimate belief and end game. A large organisation does not have that luxury. It needs to portray the future and then execute on a step-by-step evolutionary basis."*

As we wish all brands success in this endeavour, let's follow the advice of Benjamin Disraeli: *"The secret to success is constancy of purpose."*

CHAPTER 2
CULTURE BORN AND AUTHENTIC

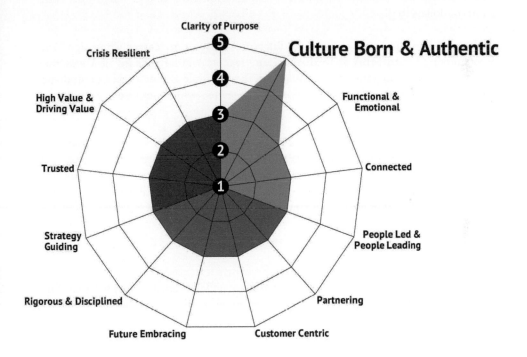

Clarity of Purpose

Culture Born & Authentic

Crisis Resilient

High Value &
Driving Value

Functional &
Emotional

Trusted

Connected

Strategy
Guiding

People Led &
People Leading

Rigorous & Disciplined

Partnering

Future Embracing

Customer Centric

"Culture is what people do when no one is looking"
Herb Kelleher, Chairman, Southern Airlines

Culture is where everything starts and finishes. Cultural differences can play out in myriad ways, sometimes bringing us down to earth with a bump.

The most striking evidence I ever had of the absolute dominance of culture was when BP faced the Deepwater Horizon crisis in 2010 in the Gulf of Mexico. As I describe in detail in Chapter 13, whatever crisis management processes there were in place, BP's people reverted to culture and acted accordingly. Tony Hayward jumped on the first plane to Houston and took charge immediately; BP people fought *'to do the right thing'*.

Later, in the heart of the legal battle, the main public and jurisdictional concerns centred on culture. The critical question of whether BP was grossly negligent mushroomed into a public debate on: *"did BP cut corners; was the culture of the company reckless?"* The response to this question on culture would determine the civil penalty to BP, with billions of dollars in play.

I took a watershed learning on cultural differences early in my career when, aged 24, I was studying for an MBA at INSEAD. Many readers will have heard of Markstrat, the strategic marketing enterprise simulation. The principle is that a team of students represents a company and plays against other teams, which represent competitor companies.

Our Markstrat team included Donna, an American lawyer, Takao, a Japanese 'observer', Francois, a Swiss engineer, John, an English IT specialist, Lourenco, a Portuguese aristocrat, and me, the French beginner. With all of us lacking any meaningful cultural awareness, this was a recipe for disaster – which culminated in Lourenco the Portuguese, who was 5.5 feet tall, physically attacking the unusually tall 6.2-foot Japanese Takao.

KEY LEARNINGS ON CULTURE

The notion of culture is such a broad church that we will address it in three ways in this chapter: by sharing some learning from the corporate world on its various forms; by investigating the science of national culture; and finally by examining a 'Culture born & authentic' Strategic Brand, Toyota.

But first, let me put my cards on the table and express a few convictions, which I will investigate in the rest of the chapter:

1. **Culture is the compelling definer** of what an organisation and a brand are, with its visible expressions and invisible drivers, as represented on Illustration 1. Everything should flow and emanate from a deep understanding of underlying culture, including the brand purpose, as noted in the previous chapter.

2. **Culture can't be changed rapidly.** Progressive evolutions are possible but I still hear many organisations and leaders claim that they will *"change culture... and do it fast"*.

This is simply as unreal as claiming that mankind will dominate nature - as changing culture means changing everything somebody is, the strongest force behind a person or an organisation. To change an organisation's culture, change the people! Or be ready for a one-generation-long (or more) evolution towards the destination culture.

3. **The associated imperative to living one's culture is authenticity.** An organisation aligned with its culture liberates its people because they can operate as they are. This gives the power of 'Inside-Out'. On the reverse, pretention or constraining an organisation and its people in a box that is not who they are will lead to disaster - and such an organisation will be caught out in our world of transparency.

4. **There is not enough depth and truth about culture.** Any Strategic Brand journey needs to start with a fully honest, unbiased cultural assessment. As described in Chapter 1, the emerging BP brand did some of this but chose to reference its brand and strategy in the context of an aspired culture rather than the established. I have seen good practice of brands starting their journey with soul-searching ethnological research.

| ILLUSTRATION 2.1 | VISIBLE AND INVISIBLE DIMENSIONS OF CULTURE |

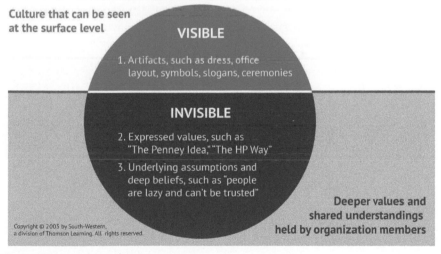

Levels of Corporate Culture

Culture that can be seen at the surface level

VISIBLE

1. Artifacts, such as dress, office layout, symbols, slogans, ceremonies

INVISIBLE

2. Expressed values, such as "The Penney Idea," "The HP Way"

3. Underlying assumptions and deep beliefs, such as "people are lazy and can't be trusted"

Deeper values and shared understandings held by organization members

Credit – South-Western, a division of Thomson Learning

Begin with the authenticity imperative

Culture and authenticity are intrinsically linked: without living its culture, an organisation stands no chance of being authentic. In our modern world there is no alternative to authenticity - you will be found out. It is impossible to pretend to be somebody you are not. And so it is with brands.

Authenticity can empower an organisation to be direct, energetic and spontaneous. And as long as what you do matches your target group's aspirations, authenticity will enhance your success because consumers will like and trust you. It's the same with friends. If you pretend to be somebody you are not, your friendships are less likely to be long lasting.

Some of the most challenging questions the BP Brand faced were often about its authenticity - how could BP champion energy efficiency when this meant reduced oil and gas consumption? How could BP promote alternative energy while all of its profit was made from hydro-carbons? Was our support of the Olympic and Paralympic Games just a means of looking good by association with them? From the inside, I know that our actions were authentic – but we needed to understand and respect how it might have looked different from the outside.

Considerable knowledge and experience has been developed on the authentic organisation, the "authentic enterprise" (Note 1). Illustration 2.2 lists key principles which lie behind it. This should be the mantra of any leadership when thinking about, setting up or evolving the company's culture and values - and building or managing multiple stakeholder relationships. And when it comes to communication, these principles can enable the enterprise to gain new media skills and tools.

ILLUSTRATION 2.2	THE AUTHENTIC ENTERPRISE PRINCIPLES

The Authentic Enterprise
The Page Principles

- Tell the truth.
- Prove it with action.
- Listen to the customer.
- Manage for tomorrow.
- Realize a company's true character is expressed by its people.

- Conduct public relations as if the whole company depends on it.
- Remain calm, patient and good-humored.

Credit – Arthur W. Page Society

Being authentic means living and projecting your true culture

So authenticity is about being yourself in the way you think and act. There are plenty of definitions for authenticity in an organisation and here is my own: *Authenticity is the straightforward expression of the organisation's culture in all that it is and does.*

Culture must be at the epicentre of a brand's purpose, mission and strategic plan: a brand cannot in any way be at odds with the culture of an organisation. When a brand is built on culture, it is able to mobilise its employees naturally and benefit from their support and energy.

IBM There are lots of stories of what Strategic Brands are able to do by turning to their core culture during times of crisis – for example, Lou Gerstner took the reins of an ageing, complacent IBM and, by bringing it back to its core, completely revitalised it.

Today three key contemporary changes – the digital revolution, globalisation and the empowerment of stakeholders – have driven organisations to show an unprecedented level of transparency with democratised access to information. Radical authenticity is now even more crucial to establish a distinctive brand and build long-term success. For customers, investors and employees alike, a brand must have a grounded sense of its culture: what defines it, why it exists, what it stands for and what differentiates it from others.

What is culture?

In an article for the *Harvard Business Review*, entitled "*What is Organisational Culture and Why Should We Care?*", Michael D Watkins explored the different definitions of culture (Note 2). Here I summarise those which I consider the most important ones for building a Strategic Brand:

"Culture is how organisations do things" – Robbie Katanga
"Culture is consistent, observable patterns of behaviour in organisations. Aristotle said, 'We are what we repeatedly do.' This elevates repeated behaviour or habits as the core of culture and deemphasises what people feel, think and believe. It focuses our attention on the forces that shape behaviour in organisations."

"Organisational culture is the sum of values and rituals, which serve as 'glue' to integrate the members of the organisation" – Richard Perrin
"Culture is a carrier of meaning. Cultures provide not only a shared view of 'what is' but also the 'why is'. In this view, culture is about the 'story' in which people in the organisation are embedded, and the values and rituals that reinforce that narrative. It also focuses attention on the importance of symbols and the need to understand them – including the idiosyncratic languages used in organisations – in order to understand culture."

"Organisational culture is civilisation in the work place" – Alan Adler
"Culture is a social control system. Here the focus is the role of culture in promoting and reinforcing 'right' thinking and behaving, and sanctioning 'wrong' thinking and behaving. Key in this definition of culture is the idea of behavioural 'norms' that must

be held, and associated social sanctions that are imposed on those who don't stay within the lines. This view also focuses attention on how the evolution of the organisation shaped the culture. That is, how have the existing norms promoted the survival of the organisation in the past? Note: implicit in the evolutionary view is the idea that established cultures can become impediments to survival when there are substantial environmental changes."

"Organisational culture is shaped by the main culture of the society we live in, albeit with greater emphasis on particular parts of it" – Elizabeth Skringar
"Organisational culture is shaped by and overlaps with other cultures – especially the broader culture of the societies in which it operates. This observation highlights the challenges that global organisations face in establishing and maintaining a unified culture when operating in the context of multiple national, regional and local cultures."

And it is this final definition on the influence of national culture by Elizabeth Skringar that we are especially interested in, because it is an area that many people and business leaders have opinions on, but very few are experts. This is something I'm currently investigating in a scientific study on culture and partnerships with UCL and how co-operations between companies are deeply influenced by their respective national culture.

Culture is brand, brand is culture

"Culture eats strategy for breakfast," said Peter Drucker. The picture on Illustration 2.3 shows how, while core strategies may aim in one direction, they will meet significant resistance if that direction is counter-cultural.

ILLUSTRATION 2.3	THE PREVAILING IMPACT OF CULTURE

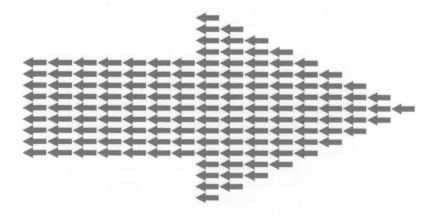

Culture eats strategy for breakfast

Therefore, it is vital to assess a company's organisational culture and character before beginning the brand journey. The brand must emanate from culture: it must be "culture born".

The brand must emanate from culture: it must be "culture born".

This is no easy feat – and it's something I have wrestled with at BP, not only in terms of the company's image but also when building partnerships with other organisations. As noted above, culture can actually hinder strategically important relationships. I remember a meeting in GE's Rockefeller Center in the very early days of the GE – BP partnership. Both teams were equally proud, confident, driven by their own belief – and instinctively hostile to one another. It was extraordinary to see how, by working on these cultural barriers, we were later able to build a strong partnership.

So, if culture is both the beginning and end of a Strategic Brand, how much do we actually understand it?

The fact is, we rationalize too little. Spencer Stuart describes this well in its PoV2015, 'Leading with Culture'. Vision, mission and strategy are explicitly articulated by leaders in order to guide an organisation's activities – but defining a culture is difficult because the underlying drivers are usually hidden, built upon unconscious sets of shared assumptions that have developed over time. Culture is pervasive and invisible, it works silently in the background, directing how people throughout an organisation think, make decisions and behave.

This elusive nature is both a challenge and an opportunity for business. It is hard to know if culture is helping or hurting when you can't see or describe it. Yet the right culture can capture the imagination and ignite a workforce's potential. In his book *Good to Great*, Jim Collins argues that companies with strong, well-aligned cultures are six times more successful than their competitors, generate twice the return on investment and deliver significantly better sales growth and return on assets than those with weaker or misaligned cultures (Note 3).

But culture is a double-edged sword. Once established, it is extremely hard to change. For example, if it is generally accepted that the way to be successful in a company is to avoid risks and stay under the radar, a new strategy that prioritises risk-taking and innovation will face irresistible resistance.

The start of our thesis is that leaders do not devote enough time, energy and consideration to culture. This is because, as Spencer Stuart says (Note 4): *"for many leaders, culture feels 'soft' and ambiguous… They don't know where to start and often define culture by the outcome they hope to achieve – a customer-oriented culture or a results-oriented culture, for example. But culture is not outcomes. Rather culture is the mindsets, assumptions and behaviours that produce those outcomes."* We contend that an enterprise needs to consider its culture or accept that it is not a Strategic Brand.

Where does culture come from?

Culture originates and develops under three main influences: the founder, the organisation's dominant vocation and the society we live in.

ILLUSTRATION 2.4	WHERE ORGANISATIONS' CULTURE COMES FROM

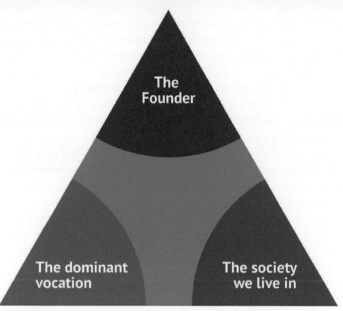

© THE Enduring Strategic Brand

The founder

During its early years, a company's culture is tied to the personality, background and values of its founder. There are many examples of founders in the modern world whose beliefs and behaviours define the culture of their organisations – for example Steve Jobs – Apple; Elon Musk – Tesla Motors, Space X; Jeff Bezos – Amazon; Mark Zuckerberg – Facebook; Brian Chesky, Joe Gebbia and Nathan Blecharczyk – Airbnb; Richard Branson – Virgin.

This is not a new experience - the cultures of Toyota, IBM, Ford, IKEA, Ogilvy and Eggon Zehnder just to name a few can all be traced back to their founders and often are eponym brands. Microsoft's rather aggressive nature is often attributed to Bill Gates's personal competitiveness.

Walmart ✳ Walmart founder Sam Walton's mission statement – *'Saving people money so they can live better'* – lives in every way in the organisation, from their modest offices in Bentonville, Arkansas, to their moderate salaries and famous 7:00 to 9:30 Saturday morning meetings.

IKEA® Similarly, Ingvar Kamprad, IKEA's frugal founder, was known to encourage managers to sleep in their Volvos to reduce expensive hotel bills – because IKEA's mission statement was all about looking after customers with 'thin wallets'.

The following list shows how the founder's shaping and guiding influence can be practised, maintained and strengthened, as explained by Dr. Talya Bauer and Dr. Berrin Erdogan in 'An introduction to Organisational Behaviour' (Note 5):

- Define it – notably in developing a clear mission statement, rules and policies
- Live it – through people attraction, selection and attrition; leadership style and priorities; visual elements such as physical layout; rituals and stories (Ref. Illustration 2.5)
- Teach it – through employee onboarding; toolboxes
- Measure it –through internal people surveys; balance score cards
- Reward it – through embedding cultural dimensions in the reward systems

ILLUSTRATION 2.5	VISUAL ELEMENTS OF CULTURE

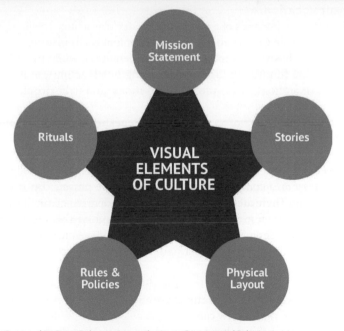

Credit – Dr. Talya Bauer and Dr. Berrin Erdogan - An Introduction to Organisational Behaviour

Let's hear John Seifert on new age founder brands: *"Companies like IBM, GE, American Express or Ford often start with the founders – for example, C. Watson with IBM and Henry Ford with the Ford Motor Company – so there is a strong association with the company name and everything that the business as a whole represents: the legacy and mythology that's been built and maintained over a period of history.*

"The golden thread that runs through all these brands is they are strategically important in defining the role, responsibility, point of view, actions, behaviours and performance of the company.

"Airbnb and Uber have completely reinvented the model: using their brands to change the way the world thinks and acts. This is the new reality of the digital economy and globalisation. This is different from a 100-year-old company with a founder, a philosophy, a set of values and a point of view, which has been building a Strategic Brand over time through the way they do business, the value they create and the nature in which they serve customers. This leads to a fundamental question: what's brand building going to look like in the future?

"There are important lessons to be learned from these older, respected brands – in particular, lessons about building trust. Because a new age founder brand like Airbnb could easily be replicated and replaced by another which is more trusted. The CEO of American Express and others are apparently inundated with questions from new age companies - they all want to understand how to build a trusted and enduring brand."

The dominant vocation

The characteristics and demands of a sector or industry play a huge role in the culture of their organisations (Note 6). To generalise, many companies in insurance and banking might have a culture based on stability and rule orientation, while those in high-tech industry might value innovation, agility and taking quick actions, and have a lower concern for rules or authority. Non-profit organisations tend to be people oriented.

As explained above, the culture of an organisation stems from its founders and leaders – and, more often than not, these people come from a dominant vocation.

bp

In BP, leaders are often mechanical or chemical engineers. Generally speaking, they are predisposed to a culture of orderliness, conservatism, well-defined processes, hierarchical structures and, in the extreme, can have an almost mechanistic view of the organisation. At the other end of the spectrum, software development start-ups will have a very different cultural view – for example, preferring a flatter structure.

This culture is reinforced by selection, training, development, assessments and rewards, which are all mostly geared to the dominant vocation within the organisation.

This doesn't necessarily mean that other vocations are unimportant: they can have an influence on the culture of an organisation. But we mustn't overstate this influence: when push comes to shove, the culture of the dominant vocation will take precedence over any other (this does raise the issue of diversity, but that's another story).

The society we live in

In my view – and to my continuing surprise – the society we live in (in other words, the national culture we come from) remains the source of culture which is both the most deeply influential and the least well understood, considered or managed.

Most of us working in global organisations have shared multiple cultural experiences similar to the one I described at INSEAD at the beginning of this chapter. Here is another memory.

Castrol When I was given the reins of Castrol Europe in the mid-90s, my leadership team was composed of Freddie the Dane, Bob the Englishman, Rob the Canadian, Torsten the German, Cesare the Italian, Gustav the Austrian and me, the Frenchman. These guys were strong personalities and superb business people, and we were the so-called "dream team" in the company. But without applying deep cultural understanding to our leadership practice, the reality was a risky situation. We all know the Heaven and Hell story - in Heaven, the cooks are French, the policemen are English, the mechanics are German, the lovers are Italian and the bankers are Swiss. In Hell, the cooks are English, the policemen are German, the mechanics are French, the lovers are Swiss and the bankers are Italian. In Castrol Europe, we didn't get it all perfect, and some of the deepest scars of my whole career stem from that time.

Culture is a major driver of an organisation, its brand and its marketing. Operating all my business life around the globe, I sometimes thought that I got it. But the more time passed, the more I felt the need for better science, understanding and rigour of application in this area.

THE PARAMOUNT IMPACT OF NATIONAL CULTURE

We will be investigating some scientific research around culture in the following section, which has been written with the help of Tom Fadrhonc and Huib Wursten of Itim International, to whom my deep thanks. (Note 7)

Globalisation does not mean reduction of culture differences

Since the early 1960s, participants in the discussion about the effects of globalisation have assumed that economic development would lead to standardization driven by converging needs and tastes of consumers. Harvard professor Ted Levitt's (1983) article "The globalisation of markets" is often quoted: *"The world's needs and desires have irrevocably homogenised…"*

In 2015 the Stanford School of Business conducted research on Cultural vs. Personal Knowledge or Values when making consumer judgments. General cultural knowledge is the values we learn from the most important people in our early years – parents and teachers. They become our default values.

But we may also gain personal and more general knowledge that conflicts with these accepted cultural values. For example, a girl growing up in China may accept the importance of keeping in harmony with family members. But being exposed to pictures of American cultural icons may lead her to wear clothes her parents don't like. When pressured to form a quick judgment, she may tend to rely on her cultural norms as a 'default', but when deliberating, waver aspects of her own culture – alike organisations who revert to deep culture in crisis times.

A recent INSEAD business study by André Laurent across 20 countries asked managers *"how important it is that leaders can answer subordinates' questions?"*. The differences across countries are remarkable, as shown on Illustration 2.6, with 78% of the Japanese saying important compared to 9% in Sweden.

ILLUSTRATION 2.6	IMPACT OF NATIONAL CULTURE IS EVEN MORE IMPORTANT IN MULTI-NATIONAL COMPANIES

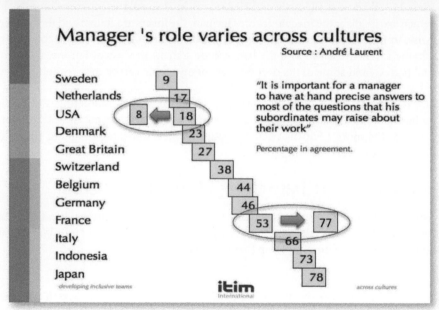

Credit – itim International

Very revealing is when the same question was asked of people working for international companies day to day with international colleagues - the differences increased. For example, the US percentage went from 18 per cent to 8 per cent, while the French percentage increased from 53 per cent to 77 per cent.

Impact of national culture – an example

Bottled water is a costly product compared to tap water, so one would presume that wealthier countries consume more. Yet, we see it is not at all correlated to income, with Belgium or Germany consuming ca. eight times more than the UK or Sweden.

The answer lies in culture. And the determining factor is the Uncertainty Avoidance Index (UAI), an indicator of how comfortable a culture is in coping with uncertainty. The higher the score, the more certainty that culture requires. It's not surprising then that Belgium and Germany, with their very high UAI, would want the certainty of bottled water. At the other end of the spectrum, UK consumers would be more inclined to take the "risk" of tap water.

ILLUSTRATION 2.7	CULTURE DRIVES CONSUMPTION OF BOTTLED WATER

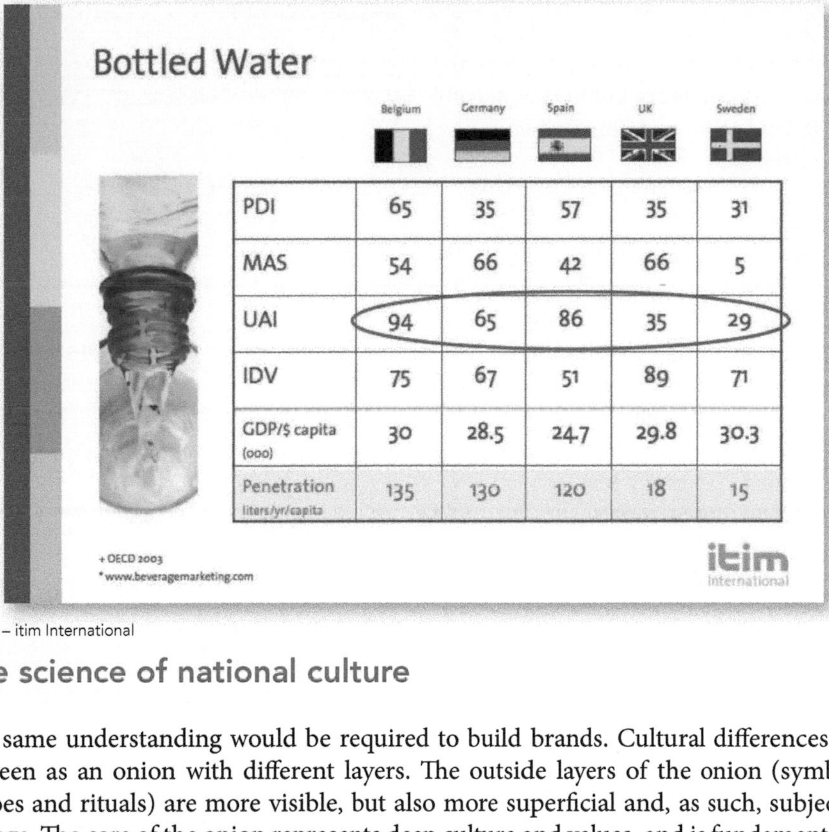

Bottled Water

	Belgium	Germany	Spain	UK	Sweden
PDI	65	35	57	35	31
MAS	54	66	42	66	5
UAI	94	65	86	35	29
IDV	75	67	51	89	71
GDP/$ capita (000)	30	28.5	24.7	29.8	30.3
Penetration liters/yr/capita	135	130	120	18	15

+ OECD 2003
* www.beveragemarketing.com

itim
International

Credit – itim International

The science of national culture

The same understanding would be required to build brands. Cultural differences can be seen as an onion with different layers. The outside layers of the onion (symbols, heroes and rituals) are more visible, but also more superficial and, as such, subject to change. The core of the onion represents deep culture and values, and is fundamental in understanding worldwide diversity.

Extensive research projects on cultural values were led by Geert Hofstede, one of the 20 most influential global business thinkers, according to *The Wall Street Journal*. Hofstede distinguishes the dimensions of national culture measured on a scale from 0 to 100. Original quantitative data were based on an extensive IBM study of 116,000 questionnaires in 72 countries and 20 languages. The results were re-validated through over 40 subsequent studies from a variety of disciplines. The scores for each country explain variations in behaviour of people and organisations.

Let's examine Hofstede's five cultural dimensions (5-D) and their consequences on brands, marketing and advertising.

Uncertainty avoidance (UAI).
This is the extent to which people feel threatened by uncertainty and ambiguity and try to avoid these situations. In cultures of high uncertainty avoidance, there is a need for rules to structure life. Competence is a strong value with deep belief in experts. In weak uncertainty-avoidance cultures people tend to be more innovative and entrepreneurial.

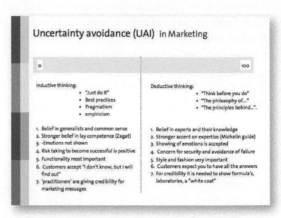

In **masculine cultures (MAS)** the dominant values are achievement, performance and success. Status shows success. Those in feminine cultures are caring for others and quality of life. Their people orientation makes small be beautiful and status not so important. In masculine cultures, roles are very different between males and females, whereas in feminine cultures, the role differentiation is much smaller.

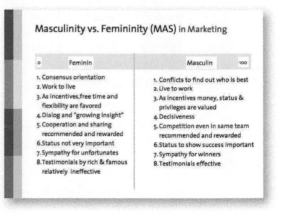

Power distance (PDI) is the extent to which less powerful members of a society accept that power is distributed unequally. In large power-distance cultures everybody has his/her rightful place in society, there is respect for old age, and status is important to show power. In small power-distance cultures people try to look younger and powerful people try to look less powerful.

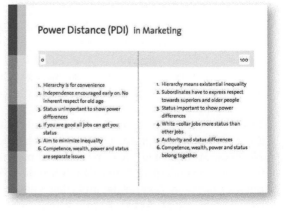

In **Individualistic** cultures **(IDV)** people look after themselves and their immediate family; in **Collectivist** cultures people belong to in-groups who look after them in exchange for loyalty. In collectivist cultures a person's identity is based on the social network to which they belong. In individualist cultures, communication is more explicit. In collectivist cultures, communication is implicit.

The Long-Term Orientation (LTO) index is the extent to which a society has a pragmatic future-oriented perspective rather than a near-term point of view. Low scoring countries are usually under the influence of monotheistic religions, e.g. Christianity, Islam or Judaism, and people in these countries believe there is an absolute truth, i.e. black or white answers. In high scoring countries, e.g. cultures practising Buddhism, Shintoism or Hinduism, truth depends on time and context. i.e. truth is shades of grey.

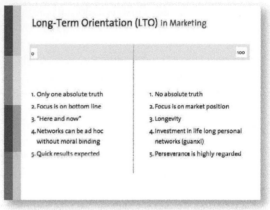

How applying culture science impacts brand and business

What does all this mean for aspiring global brands? What are the do's and don'ts for building a Strategic Brand efficiently and effectively across borders?

The desired outcome is that the brand means the same in China and Germany, in the US and Argentina. Some brands including Nike and Coca-Cola are cited as best practice for their consistency.

BMW's Ian Robertson elaborates on how the car company manages the delicate balancing act between consistency and cultural differences: *"We don't change things. The consistency of what the company stands for is exactly the same in Germany or America or Brazil. The only thing we change is how to express things. So in China, we looked to where the brand came from, because in China, longevity is a strong value. So a brand that's been around for a hundred years stands a good chance of being more successful."*

With this objective in mind and in the face of cultural differences, we cannot afford 100+ executions, one for each culture. We need economies of scale while still achieving cultural relevance.

Building a Global Brand efficiently – The Culture Clusters

Hence markets have been segmented into six Culture Clusters© across the globe, with Japan as a seventh. Rather than leaving companies with 210 country cultures and all their sub-variations, clusters help corporations organise their brand and business to achieve both cost effectiveness and maximum impact across and within cultures.

A culture cluster is a group of countries which share specific cultural characteristics based on Hofstede's 5-D Model. Culture clusters are fundamental social structures, in that they transcend demographics and industries, social and government institutions. The Six Culture Clusters© have an impact on issues such as negotiations, decision-making, customer behaviour, entrepreneurship, motivation, teamwork; and of course, brand, marketing and business development.

As represented on Illustration 2.8, three of the clusters are 'hierarchical' (PDI+), three others are 'egalitarian' (PDI -). Japan scores exactly in the middle on hierarchy and is discussed as a seventh cluster.

ILLUSTRATION 2.8	THREE LOW PDI AND THREE HIGH PDI CLUSTERS

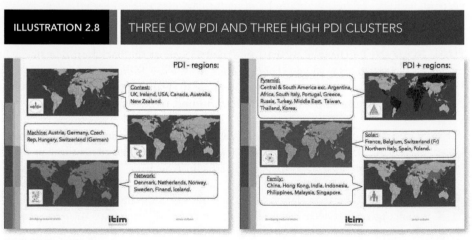

PDI - regions:

Contest: UK, Ireland, USA, Canada, Australia, New Zealand.

Machine: Austria, Germany, Czech Rep, Hungary, Switzerland (German)

Network: Denmark, Netherlands, Norway, Sweden, Finland, Iceland.

PDI + regions:

Pyramid: Central & South America exc. Argentina, Africa, South Italy, Portugal, Greece, Russia, Turkey, Middle East, Taiwan, Thailand, Korea.

Solar: France, Belgium, Switzerland (Fr) Northern Italy, Spain, Poland.

Family: China, Hong Kong, India, Indonesia, Philippines, Malaysia, Singapore.

Credit – itim International

Let's briefly explore each of the six Clusters and the brand consequences in each.

[The acronyms for the cultural dimensions are: PDI: Power Distance Index; UAI: Uncertainty Avoidance Index; MAS: masculinity score; IDV: individuality score ; LTO: long-term orientation]

Cluster 1 – The Contest Cluster

This includes the Anglo-Saxon countries, notably the US and UK. Here, the key is well-understood self-interest. The cultures involved all share a low score for PDI, high IDV, high MAS, low UAI and low LTO.

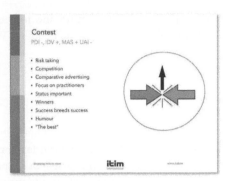

Brand and Marketing implications for the CONTEST Cluster:

1. Competition and showing winners are both seen as positive. It is motivational to show testimonials by successful people. Success breeds success. It is not seen as 'bragging' to say: *"I'm the best."*

2. Showing people taking risks to be successful is positive. Entrepreneurial behaviour is highly appreciated. Status symbols are seen as motivational.

3. Statements by practitioners are more appreciated than statements by experts. The thinking is 'inductive'. Analysing practical examples gets to conclude what is 'best practice'. Experts are less credible as they are perceived too 'academic' – for example, the Zagat approach is more popular than Michelin's.

HEINEKEN An example of culturally aware brand expression in the CONTEST cluster is Heineken's 'The Speech' ad by Guy Ritchie, starring Jose Mourinho. It portrays the Manchester United football manager as a god-like creature striding around a New York rooftop against the backdrop of a storm-lit night-time sky. *"Tonight, you don't play as lions, for you are Titans,"* says Mourinho. *"For tonight is match night!"* As he prepares a speech for his team Mourinho is the epitome of masculinity and leadership – this is all about winning. (Note 8)

NIKE Similarly, Nike's 'If You Let Me Play Sport' turns the concept of masculine competition on its head with a powerful social message on the benefits of sport for young girls, especially around self-esteem (Note 9).

Cluster 2 – The Network Cluster

This includes the Netherlands and Scandinavia. The combination they share is: low PDI, High IDV, Low MAS, low to middle UAI and low LTO

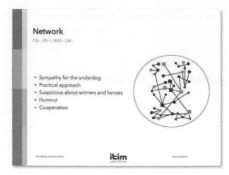

Brand and Marketing Implications for the NETWORK Cluster:
1. Sympathy for the underdog – people are suspicious of 'winners'. It is quickly seen as bragging. It is preferable to show humorous situations about 'underdogs'.
2. Cooperation is preferred – competitive behaviour makes people uneasy. This cluster prefers seeing successful people behaving 'normally' and being modest in their statements.
3. Practical evidence is more credible than expert testimonials – testimonials by people that are like 'you and me' are more appreciated than academic "evidence".
4. Status symbols are disliked: in reality there is a tendency to make people with too obvious status symbols the bait of cynical jokes.

An example of culturally aware brand expression in the NETWORK cluster is Volkswagen's ad where a teenage boy goes with his father to buy his first car, a second-hand Volkswagen Golf. The seller is an innocent-looking old lady who smiles benignly as the father checks the car. He thinks they are on to a good thing – the old lady must have driven it with restraint and caution. But nostalgic memories in the form of flashbacks reveal what the old lady really did in her car – handbrake turns, racing off the traffic lights and stunt driving over bridges. The father and son drive off happily in their new car, still ignorant of its wild past, while the old lady looks on very pleased. The strapline reads: *'Not every old lady is reliable. Luckily a Golf is.'* The reliability and longevity of a Golf are evoked through droll satire in an advert reminiscent of a comedy sketch and understated humour (Note 10).

Cluster 3 – The Well-Oiled Machine Cluster

This includes Germany and Austria. Here, the most important feature is the combination of a low PDI and a high UAI. This leads to an internalised need for structure.

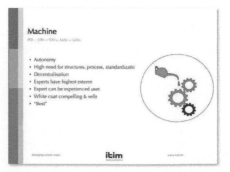

Brand and Marketing Implications for the WELL-OILED MACHINE Cluster:
There is an emphasis on expertise and experts. Reliability is very important, which calls for structure and accuracy. The approach towards the customer should be precise, factual and structured. The key in these cultures is to build up credibility, which requires the product or service to be supported by people who have the knowledge. Quality defects should be dealt with in an immediate, structured, professional and assured way.

1. Expert approach – people think deductively and the highest esteem is given to experts. People with academic titles are more credible than laymen or practitioners. The white coat as a symbol of scientific evidence is appreciated. An experienced 'user' of a certain product can also be a credible source.
2. People highly appreciate systematic approaches. An internalised need for structure is what defines this cluster.
3. Status is important to show success - symbols like expensive watches, clothing and fast cars are appreciated.

An example of culturally aware brand expression in the WELL-OILED MACHINE cluster is Audi's 'Vorsprung durch Technik' advert. The scene takes place in a futuristic, minimalist looking laboratory, where Audi designs its cars. An older-looking man, with an engineering and design 'expert' feel to him, is seen looking at Audi's engineering history through different high-tech 3-D media. With him acting as the magician, the viewer is taken through various firsts in Audi design, which occasionally have an almost 'magical' feel. At the end of the ad, the viewer moves out of the laboratory to look at contemporary Audi cars. The "*'Vorsprung durch Technik'* slogan is more than just words", says the voiceover, "*Drive an Audi and you are driving over 100 years of endeavour to find the answers before the question is asked.*" The whole ad is a grounded and passionate commitment to stay ahead through best engineering (Note 11).

Cluster 4 – The Pyramid cluster

This includes Turkey, Mexico, Portugal, Russia and the continent of Africa among others. The 'shared values' are high power distance, low IDV, and high UAI. MAS and LTO vary.

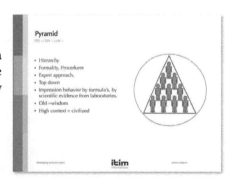

Brand and Marketing implications in the PYRAMID Cluster:
1. Hierarchy is important. Messages from important people carry high impact.
2. Style is appreciated. In high UAI countries, people are in general impressed by standards of behaviour. As a result formality and stylish behaviour is seen as positive.

3. Expert approach – as in the well-oiled machine cluster, people think deductively and high esteem is given to experts. People with academic titles and scientific evidence are appreciated.
4. Older people are more credible than younger people – age is equal to wisdom.
5. Indirect messages are appreciated and seen as more civilised – making sure people don't lose face is a real issue.

An example of culturally aware brand expression in the PYRAMID cluster is the Russian TV ad for Pedigree. A bully and his faithful gang of followers intimidate small children in the park. At some point, the bully spots a little boy holding something and demands to see what it is. The little boy opens his arms to reveal a sweet puppy. This is too much even for the bully – he melts at the sight of it, stroking and petting it. His gang dutifully follow suit. Back at home, the little boy feeds the puppy a bowl of Pedigree and the voiceover says *"Dogs make us better. And we try to do our best for them. Pedigree: for those who make us better."* This advert is typical of the Pyramid cluster: a gentle example of 'love' winning over 'hate', the sweetness of the puppy getting the better of the top of the 'hierarchy' bullies (Note 12).

Cluster 5 – The Family Cluster

This includes China and India and is in many respects similar to the Pyramid cluster – though the big difference is the low score on uncertainty avoidance (UAI).

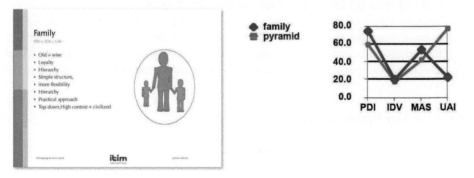

Brand and Marketing Implications in the FAMILY Cluster:
1. The low UAI means that change is faster and more flexible in the Family cluster than in the Pyramid one. There is less structure and fewer rules. This makes this cluster an easy culture to implement change in.
2. Older people are more credible than younger people – age equals wisdom.
3. As in the Pyramid cluster, indirect messages are appreciated and seen more civilized. Not losing face is critical.
4. Hierarchy is important. Messages from important people are obeyed and have status.

An example of culturally aware brand expression in the FAMILY cluster is the David Beckham TV commercial for Jaguar in China. Directed by Matthew Vaughn, it begins in black and white in the past with David Beckham preparing to race an old-fashioned Jaguar. Beckham is then seen driving different Jaguars across different, dramatic terrains as the advert slowly moves into colour. He finishes in London, at the head of a fleet of Jaguars, driving across the Thames over Westminster Bridge. His voiceover ends the advert with *'Never stop achieving.'* In China Beckham is an icon and his presence in the Jaguar advert brings prestige to the brand. He represents the key FAMILY cluster values of loyalty, benevolence, paternalism, performance and prestige – all which Jaguar wanted to convey through him (Note 13)

Cluster 6 – The Solar Cluster

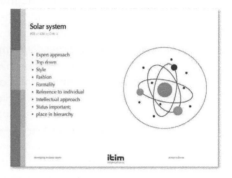

This includes France and Belgium. The big difference in this cluster compared to the Pyramid and Family clusters is the high score for Individualism, IDV. This creates tension: people obey when the 'Patron' is present, but prefer to follow their own path when the boss is away.

Brand and Marketing implications in the SOLAR Cluster:
1. Style is highly appreciated – in high UAI countries people are impressed by standards of behaviour. As a result formality and stylish behaviour are valued.
2. Expert approach – people think deductively and high esteem is given to experts. Evidence from people with academic titles is more credible and the white coat as a symbol of scientific evidence is valued.
3. Intellectual approach is appreciated. The thinking process is deductive, 'Cartesian'. People like intellectual role models.

An example of culturally aware brand expression in the SOLAR cluster is an Italian Alfa Romeo commercial. A successful businessman is driving his Alfa Romeo to St Petersburg airport to catch a private jet for a very important meeting in Berlin. However, the weather is bad, the snow is thick, and the pilot tells him they can't fly. The businessman looks at the private jet crew and then turns on his sat nav. *'Are you sure?'* he asks, as he sets off on his journey to Berlin by car. The trappings of success and prestige – the private jet, the attention of a beautiful woman, not to mention the Alfa Romeo itself, surround him. The advert imbues style, following one's own path, masculinity and status, with the businessman having the power to achieve things that others wouldn't. (Note 14)

In summary, deep attention to the science of culture and rigorous practice of clustering and segmenting give companies the means to deliver their brand objectives while using resources effectively and efficiently.

Cluster 7 - Japan

Japan is considered as the seventh cluster because of its unique characteristics. Let's look in greater detail, as understanding Japanese culture in some depth provides a useful background to the Toyota brand story to follow.

THE JAPANESE CULTURE

Mid-PDI and mid-IDV

Japan has a combination of mid-PDI (power-distance index) and mid-IDV (individuality score).

Mid-PDI means that management is both top-down and bottom-up. Decisions are made at every level, with middle managers having power and influence. Taking initiative is encouraged, although the implementation is up to the supervisor's approval.

Mid-IDV makes Japan the most individualistic country relative to other Asian countries. But it is a highly collectivist country compared to Western or Anglo-Saxon countries. Relationship and trust are important elements for success and harmony should never be disrupted (Ref. Illustration 2.9).

ILLUSTRATION 2.9	JAPAN CULTURAL PROFILE VERSUS CHINA AND THE USA

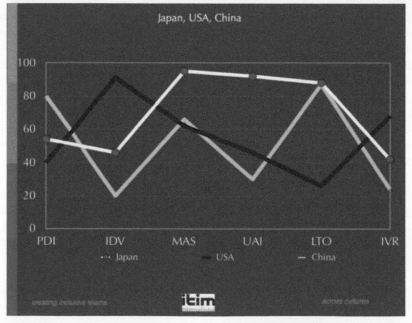

Credit – Itim International

Consequences of the combined mid-PDI and mid-IDV are reflected in culture-led practices, notably *Ho-ren-so* and *Nemawashi*:

- **Ho-ren-so: report, contact, consult.** A back-and-forth way of working which characterises how Japanese supervisors and subordinates interact. *Ho-ren-so* is based on the idea that work is a collaboration of supervisor and subordinate as a team. While the subordinate takes the lead, the supervisor provides guidance in the form of suggestions for revision and improvement.
- **Nemawashi: consensus building.** A consensus is built using one-on-one discussion with each member of a decision-making group. It is usually conducted before a formal meeting. In Japan, high-ranking people expect to be able to make suggestions and have input in new proposals before an official meeting. If they find out about something for the first time during the meeting, they will feel that they have been ignored, and they may reject it for that reason alone.

High-MAS and UAI

Japan also has high MAS (masculinity score) and UAI (uncertainty avoidance index). The Japanese live to work and the company comes before family. Competition in groups and being the best is important (*ichiban*/number one). Failure is not tolerated. The Japanese strive for perfection using tried and tested methods.

Consequences of high MAS and UAI are reflected in many culture-led practices, including the following:

- **Omotenashi** – This is more than hospitality – it's a completely selfless approach to receiving guests. This approach was demonstrated in the bid for the 2020 Olympic Games.
- **Monozukuri** – Skilled craftsman pouring their heart and soul into work, striving for perfection regardless of time or cost. 'Mono' is the object that is produced and 'Zukuri' means the act of making. But *Monozukuri* implies more than simply making things. It can be best compared to the word 'craftsmanship' in English.
- **Kaizen** – Relentless pursuit of improvement. The *kaizen* system of incremental improvement owes much to traditional craftsmen. It has become globally famous as a powerful approach to strive for perfection
- **Bushido** (code of the Samurai) – Inazo Nitobe describes *Bushido* as *"the code of moral principles and law written on the tablets of the heart."* Central to the code is honour, discipline, civility (politeness or courtesy) and responsibility.

Encompassing mid-PDI, mid-IDV, high-UAI and high-MAS, the *Ringi* system is the way consensus-building multi-layer decisions are made, in which each person has to sign-off on a certain decision using their *hanko* or personal seal. This is a formal, highly ritualised system which stems from Japan's high UAI score.

Japan's unique culture has considerable impact on society and brands. Broadly – and at the risk of over-simplification – Japanese culture values harmony, cooperation and the endless pursuit of perfection. Illustration 2.10 on the next page reflects this trilogy.

ILLUSTRATION 2.10 | JAPANESE CULTURE OF HARMONY, COOPERATION AND PERFECTION

Credit – Itim International

Japanese history

The unique culture of Japan stems from its fascinating history. Far from me to run through it here, except for one particularly revealing aspect: in 1600 and after a long period of near-anarchy, the shogun Tokugawa Ieyasu moved to reunify the country and successfully established the Tokugawa Shogunate. The *sakoku* policy, or 'locked country', enacted in 1633 by the Tokugawa Shogunate prevented foreigners from entering Japan on penalty of death. The same policy also prevented the Japanese from leaving Japan. This isolation continued for more than two hundred years, until 1852.

Japan's military rule, social order, interdependency, long self-imposed isolation, fear of threats, etc. explain to a large extent the unique attributes of Japanese culture.

Brand and Marketing consequences for Japan

Japan's unique strength is the ability to perfect. The Japanese desire to improve towards excellence over a long period of time is indicative of its high UAI and LTO. A good illustrative anecdote is how the rate of delayed trains in Japan is about 7 seconds per year, the result of immaculate revision and improvement.

It follows then that Japan is not one of the most innovative countries (Ref. The global innovation index). High MAS, IDV and low UAI in the Anglo Saxon world explain the drive and readiness to innovate fast and let precision follow. This is contrary to Japan's culture, seen in its mid PDI, mid IDV, high MAS and high UAI scores.

Innovations such as the camera, copier, telephone and automobile have mainly been taken to mass market in the US. Silicon Valley and other similar places are viewed as centres of global innovation. Yet shifts have taken place: American companies such as

Xerox and Kodak and, to a lesser extent, the big three US automobile companies, have faced challenging times from Japanese competitors, as the Japanese have perfected their inventions and succeeded in bringing high quality, desirable products to market.

Japanese brands, as well as other brands based in Japan, must be 'culture born', meaning that they must reflect, imbue and project the essence of Japanese culture.

An example of a culturally aware brand expression from a non-Japanese brand in Japan is this ad. by Nike. To the sound of Japanese schoolchildren chanting a morning mantra of Japanese values – which include 'don't push or disrupt', 'do not stray off your path', 'don't attempt to do things you cannot do' – young people are seen expressing themselves in different sporting ways: dancing, football, yoga, basketball, running, etc. Each of these expressions celebrates individuality and pushing yourself to the limit. As the scenes continue and move to a frenetic finish, the chanting reaches a climax with the repetition of 'know your place'. This culminates in the advert's message, '*Minohodoshirazu* (don't know your place); just do it' – which is a direct contradiction of the repeated chant. With his advert, Nike Japan on the one hand subverts a particular traditional Japanese value ('know your place') and on the other, connects to and acknowledges Japanese deep culture. In essence, Nike encourages individuals to express themselves, while also respecting the culture they come from (Note 15).

THE TOYOTA STRATEGIC BRAND

This background to Japanese culture is a helpful foundation when considering TOYOTA the success of the Toyota brand. And it is Toyota that we have selected as our Exemplary Strategic Brand in relation to 'Culture and Authenticity'.

| ILLUSTRATION 2.11 | THE CO-BRANDED TOYOTA WRC WINNING CAR |

Credit – Toyota and WRC

A long-term relationship and friendship

My relationship with Toyota began 25 years ago when I was CEO of Castrol France. We wanted to partner with high-quality OEMs – and Toyota was top of the list. So began a longstanding, co-operative relationship with Henri Combe and Jean-Paul Verret, the then leaders of Toyota France. As I became CEO of Castrol Europe, I led the group relationship with Toyota. We became partners in many ways – most visibly at the World Rally Championship (WRC) where we won joint crown together a few times, with a special title for me in 1994 when Didier Auriol took the coveted world champion title.

Two years after BP acquired Castrol in 2000, John Browne and my then entrepreneurial boss John Manzoni supported me in founding the BP Strategic Accounts division. A partnership with Toyota was a key aim – but this would be a challenge: BP had no branded presence in Japan and no meaningful previous connections to Toyota. Instead Toyota had enjoyed a long-lasting relationship with Exxon Mobil, since they had helped them to rebuild after the war.

But BP had two distinctive assets: Beyond Petroleum and Strategic Accounts.

Beyond Petroleum - Well aligned with Toyota's vision of sustainable mobility, BP's brand led both companies to engage in a number of initiatives for a lower carbon economy. One of these was the World Business Council for Sustainable Development (WBCSD). Together and over years, we literally shepherded a cross-sector effort to develop an industry pathway for sustainable mobility. The so-called SMP1 report on 'Mobility 2030' was concluded and ratified in 2003 by most global mobility and energy companies. For 10 years, I represented BP in the WBCSD Council and worked continuously with colleagues in Toyota on the joint and inter-related future of our industries.

I enjoyed unparalleled relationships there with Dr. Saito, Dr. Schichiro Toyoda and Mr. Cho. A great pride remains co-chairing another WBCSD watershed project with Dr. Toyoda, on city mobility entitled 'Mobility for Development' which was issued in 2009.

ILLUSTRATION 2.12	INTRODUCING DR. TOYODA TO PRINCESS ANNE AT LONDON 2012

Credit – Teruyuki Nakagawa

These years built deep friendships with many Toyota colleagues – including with Dr. Hiroyuki Watanabe, who sadly passed away in February 2016 and whom I want to pay tribute to in this book.

Strategic Partnership – The objective of BP's 'Strategic Accounts' Division was to build strategic relationships and bring about transformational mutual value over the long-term. Following early dealings with Toyota from London, a remarkable Partnership Manager, Teruyuki Nakagawa, was appointed to lead on the relationship. It was a marathon, which we started from a position of weakness as *'ichiguen'* , in Japanese, 'the not so-welcome one-time visitor'. But BP had a vision – Beyond Petroleum – it had a strategic point of view on global energy, it had technology capability in fuels and lubricants, and it had a good industrial and market footprint. By approaching the relationship from the angles of integrated mobility strategy and joint technology, we developed our partnership gradually over years until it became one of the deepest and most trusting I have ever experienced.

Over the years, I worked regularly and developed a deep respect for Toyota's leadership and notably Dr. Saito, Takimoto-san, Okamoto-san, Okuda-san, Uchiyamada-san (the father of the Prius and current TMC Chairman) and many others of their colleagues.

To cut a long story short, I was given the opportunity to experience Toyota, see their leaders in action and discover their vision and character over a long period of time – and to some extent from within. My belief in the company is fostered by the two ways in which Toyota contributes to society: by providing best-in-class cars and mobility solutions; and by striving to be a formidable force for good.

Toyota: the ultimate culture-born authenticity

This is about Toyota's ultimate authenticity. They are who they are: what you see is what you get. As explained earlier, their authenticity comes from the company's deep-rooted culture – and makes Toyota an Exemplary Brand.

Toyota's authenticity and coherence as a brand is shown by its maximum scores in six Strategic Brand Imperatives: 'Culture Born', 'Clarity of Purpose', 'People Led and People Leading', 'Partnering', 'Strategy Guiding' and 'Trusted' (Ref Illustration 2.13). I have observed first hand how these dimensions reinforce each other in echo to Toyota's deep culture.

Culture born and Authentic – I have never known an organisation so grounded in its roots as Toyota. Its relationship to Japan is strong and continues to evoke the principles of Sakichi Toyoda. You need only visit the Toyota museum in Toyota-City to observe this. Let's hear from Takeshi Uchiyamada, Chairman of Toyota Motor Company: *"I have been with Toyota for forty years. The way Toyota thinks is entirely influenced by how it*

ILLUSTRATION 2.13	THE ENDURING STRATEGIC BRAND IMPERATIVES - TOYOTA

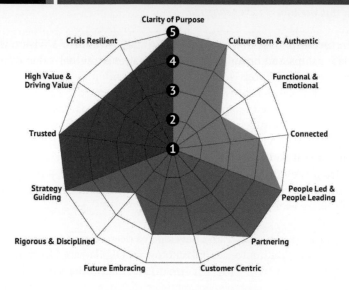

was founded. Toyota began with the invention of Sakichi Toyoda, who founded the Toyota Automatic Loom Company – today this is Toyota Industries. His son, Kiichiro Toyoda, wanted to establish an automobile industry in Japan: to develop not only a vehicle but also an entire industry. The overwhelming culture within Toyota today is a continuation of Kiichiro's legacy: to be challenged to create something entirely new and to support those who take on this challenge."

Didier Leroy, Executive Vice President of Toyota Motor Corporation and Member of the Board of Directors, also emphasises the importance of Toyota's deep cultural heritage: *"It is important to remember our past, our values and the behaviour that is consistent with them. We live in a digitalised world. Connectivity and speed are very important. For Toyota it is about how to live in this world, how to anticipate these factors, how to operate in societies in these circumstances and how to apply consistent thought and analysis, because the future is uncertain. We work within an environment that is changing dramatically and need to stick to a number of fundamental values which have been company strengths in the past. That's the difference between a company that always searches for the latest trend and forgets the past, and a company that is based on solid foundations, is inspired by the past but remains agile, flexible and completely adaptable.*

"Toyota retains a deep sense of what it owes Japanese society. During many years, the growth of Toyota was strongly supported by the Japanese customers. So the concept of giving back, of making a contribution to Japanese society and the life of the country, is extremely strong in everything we do and all that we are. There is an emotional side to this: a lot of people within Toyota ask me, how can we strengthen the image of Japanese society in the eyes of the world? Toyota's role at the Olympic and Paralympic Games in Tokyo 2020 will help to do this.

"Our culture stems from the fact that we always want to move forward together. You can never stop and say that you are the best: there is always progress to be made, and ultimately we are a company that is never satisfied."

ILLUSTRATION 2.14	TOYOTA GLOBAL VISION TREE OF 'ROOTS AND FRUITS'

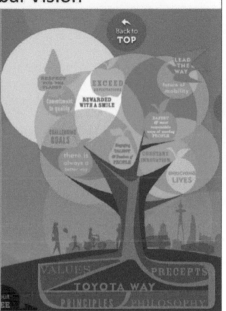

Toyota Global Vision

Toyota will lead the way to the future of mobility, enriching lives around the world with the safest and most responsible ways of moving people.

Through our commitment to quality, constant innovation and respect for the planet, we aim to exceed expectations and be rewarded with a smile.

We will meet our challenging goals by engaging the talent and passion of people, who believe there is always a better way.

Credit – Toyota Motor Corporation

Let's hear from Jack Hollis, Group Vice President and General Manager of the Toyota Division at Toyota Motor North America, on how this culture manifests itself: *"I love working for this company which doesn't ever stop. We never say: 'We've arrived and it's done.' This is more than just 'Kaizen', the Toyota business philosophy of continuous improvement. It is the idea that the things we want are just out of reach, so we need to keep making progress.*

"The downside is that often we're waiting for industry innovations. We will always strive to be number one with quality. But there is a saying: 'measuring twice and cutting once.' Sometimes our company measures five or six times before we cut. And because of that, we can sometimes be slow to move.

"Modern society is more accepting of mistakes – but Toyota's deep culture, especially in Japan, does not accept even one. This throws up questions about how certain cultural aspects might restrict some of the best innovation or risk-taking in the future. This is our opportunity to once again expedite our growth. We should honour the errors which are part and parcel of that risk-taking journey. That is a part of Japanese culture that still needs

to change and Akio (Toyoda) is doing just that. He is advocating for taking risks and this is one of the most encouraging truths that I have experienced in my 25 years with Toyota."

Toyota's societal vision and purpose emanate directly from its culture. Let me declare a personal bias up front: it is this purpose which I have seen repeatedly in action, and which is owned, projected and epitomised by its leadership, that makes me a committed friend to the brand [**Clarity of purpose**]

Didier Leroy: *"Toyota is emotionally attached to its desire to improve and change people's lives – in terms of mobility and in many other ways.*

"This desire translates into understanding the issues of today's world. Toyota wants to allow everyone to keep moving, give them ease of transport, provide mobility for the elderly, help them afford home care, improve air quality and reduce road accidents.

"Toyota strives to provide solutions that will improve the lives of future generations. We want to contribute to an ever better world. We may not provide yet the ultimate solution but perhaps we are ahead of the rest of the world in understanding how to address the issues. People ask me 'How do you want to do this?' The answer is in interacting with global society and learning from each other."

This view is fully shared by Jack Hollis: *"In the US, my legacy is to increase understanding about what the company stands for and why we exist. What I hear from Mr. Toyoda and Didier Leroy, I also believe in my own heart: that we exist to make individual people's lives better for the long term.*

"We have different brand taglines around the world but they are all centred on enriching people's lives, person by person, making an ever better society and an ever better Toyota."

People Led and People Leading – One of the most interesting aspects of Toyota, which I only realised after a number of years, is that it is one of the few companies that communicates its values very little. Instead, Toyota replaces theory and words by actions and expected behaviours, giving its associates a way of discovering and owning the values for themselves (ref. Robbie Katanga above - *"culture is how organisations do things"*). In other words, Toyota doesn't give out a theoretical view of their values but aims for everyone in the company to live out these values instead. Hence the Toyota Way is not simply about principles but about ways of being and doing things. These powerful action and behaviour guidelines are shown on Illustration 2.15.

These principles provide practical and useful guidance for everybody in Toyota – and beyond. They underpin Toyota's performance, clarity of purpose – and ultimately its authenticity.

Let's hear from Didier Leroy: *"There is a strong correlation between values and behaviour. Toyota is not a company that absorbs ideas in terms of theory: people cannot understand or grasp the abstract. They have to physically live out these ideas instead. This is part of the Japanese way of thinking. Look at the Japanese in terms of software: we are not good at working in total abstraction. If you ask us to write five lines of software, we become less effective because it's too theoretical. However, we are more than competent when it comes to making the best integrated circuits in the world: we make electronic components with great accuracy, quality and rigour which are not matched anywhere else. But the average Japanese person is not trained to understand complex concepts.*

ILLUSTRATION 2.15	THE TOYOTA WAY 14 PRINCIPLES
1	Long-term philosophy, even at the expense of short-term financial goals.
2	A continuous process flow to bring problems to the surface – Kaisen.
3	Use "pull" systems to avoid overproduction.
4	Level out the workload – Heijunka: work like the tortoise, not the hare. Hence, minimizing waste – Kuda not overburdening people or the equipment – Muri, and not creating uneven production levels – Mura.
5	Stop to fix problems, to get quality right the first time. Quality takes precedence – Jidoka.
6	Standardized tasks and processes are the foundation for continuous improvement and employee empowerment – Kaizen.
7	Use visual control so no problems are hidden – The 5S Program.
8	Use only reliable, thoroughly tested technology that serves your people and processes.
9	Grow leaders who thoroughly understand the work, live the philosophy, and teach it to others.
10	Develop exceptional people and teams who follow your company's philosophy.
11	Respect your extended network of partners and suppliers by challenging them and helping them improve.
12	Go and see for yourself to thoroughly understand the situation – Genchi Genbutsu.
13	Make decisions slowly by consensus, thoroughly considering all options; implement decisions rapidly – Nemawashi.
14	Become a learning organization through relentless reflection – Hansei and continuous improvement – Kaisen.

Credit – Restated from The Toyota Way by Dr. Jeffrey Liker, McGraw-Hill Publishing, 2004

"This means that the vast majority of the population will not be able to understand any value if it does not have an impact on a person's behaviour. So a company's values must be reflected in the behaviour of its employees. The Toyota Way comes from the company's extraordinary origins: the original ideas of being around people, partnering with them, understanding their problem and getting involved in the solution. This is not just a tool, it is a methodology: it is a way of thinking and an absolutely phenomenal way of life."

It is also about exceptional leadership. One example can be found in Toyota Chairman Takeshi Uchiyamada's story of his challenging journey to develop the Prius:

"In the Toyota Way, you will find very important keywords, such as 'teamwork' and 'respect' and, my favourite word, 'challenge'.

"My experience as chief engineer developing Prius taught me that trust in relationships is the most important element for success. It can be scary to try to make an advance even though you don't know the outcome, like we did with the Prius. In these circumstances, trusting relationships are crucial. I am an engineer and I sometimes had arguments with

my colleagues when I thought somebody's idea was wrong. I was always frank about my opinion, so discussions could be heated. However, if I was not able to convince others of my idea, I always tried to be open-minded and accept other people's opinions.

"In a risky project like developing the Prius, we usually come up with back-up plans in order to support the mainstream plan. However, in this particular case, we minimised back-up plans altogether. This meant that if an engineer came up with a good strategy, then I would adopt it completely and could say to him 'your plan is very good, so we are going to use it'. I would always do this face-to-face – as I think it is significantly more motivating when a chief engineer has directly told you something like that."

Didier Leroy builds on this idea and expresses what I have also always felt: *"Management is about creating a climate of trust in the teams, so that they will want to work with you, for you, for the company, with a common goal – because somewhere you are able to make them want to, even if it is a standard or uninteresting or repetitive or tiring job. Your goal is to give meaning to people and to what they do. One of Toyota's values is to give everyone challenges – whatever their level, a challenge which corresponds to their skills. The two pillars of Toyota are continuous improvement and respect. But this is a very different understanding of respect: it means respecting an individual by giving him or her challenges corresponding to his or her skill level. I think this is something [Western] society has lost and needs to recover."*

Partnering – It comes as no surprise then that Toyota considers partnering to be in line with its authentic, clearly purposed, people-led approach. I experienced Toyota's respect, commitment and ingenuity for more than ten years as the leader of BP's strategic partnerships. Here are Uchiyamada–san's views: *"When we form alliances with companies, we always think about whether we are able to establish trusting mid- and long-term relationships with those organisations. We don't just look at the short-term economic advantages. Perhaps financial investors would prefer it if Toyota were more interested in the short-term benefit. But we don't see things that way. We think it is more important to establish respect and a trusting relationship with such organisations: this enables us to share strategies and disclose data with each other in an open manner. If we didn't aim for a long relationship, we couldn't be as open. Frankly, if an aggressive and hurried company comes to Toyota with an attractive proposal, however appealing, I don't think we would get to it."*

Strategy guiding – Given everything we have discussed above, we now need to look at how these characteristics form and guide strategy – and how these strategies are fulfilled, notably in the company's global growth.

Toyota's generic strategy is a combination of cost leadership – first-time quality, minimal waste, inventory, response time, and so on; differentiation in all market segments; and geographic and market penetration – increasing share in new markets or selling to new market segments. But Toyota's purposeful long-term approach sees beyond all of this, into mobility of the future and a low-carbon society. As Toyota's website states: *"Through improvements of conventional technology, as well as pioneering efforts in the application of* new technologies, Toyota is taking great steps to develop eco-cars which will help us become a low-carbon society."

One of the most impressive strategic acts I have ever seen came from Akio Toyoda. Akio-san took the helm of the group in 2009, in the midst of the global economic downturn, shortly after Toyota reported its first annual loss in many years. He rapidly faced the 'unintended acceleration' crisis and recalls in the US in 2009 and 2010, the tsunamis in Japan and Thailand, and earthquakes bringing production lines to a halt. In the second half of 2013, with these turbulent times behind, it was time for him to share how Toyota was going on the offensive again. Here are few lines from his November 11th 2013 interview to *Automotive News*:

"Toyota has come close to 10 million units a year. No carmaker worldwide has exceeded the 10 million unit sales mark. But at today's Toyota, we are not pursuing volume. Going on the offensive means making ever-better cars and changing the way in which we produce cars. Our expansion in volume outpaced our development of human resources. We are trying to nurture people who can think about and understand what it really means to have competitiveness and sustainable growth. Volume will be the result. It's not our ultimate goal. I don't really agree with the idea that being number one means having the biggest volume... Unless you are successful in making cars one by one for each customer, you can't be successful on an aggregate level... What I am saying is: 'Let's make ever better cars, let's pursue sustainable growth, let's become a stronger company so we can make a contribution to society at large.' ... It is like kaizen: you never reach a final stage. The key is to make tomorrow better than today. After the kaizen is before the kaizen: when one improvement is finished, it is the beginning of the next."

This strong leadership from Akio Toyoda brought a united and unifying mobilisation, from every corner of the organisation, with a common goal to make 'ever-better cars'. Is this culture driving strategy? Absolutely!

Trusted – Trust is a key outcome of Toyota's culture-born authenticity: trust in what the company stands for and its ability to verify its actions; trust in the products; trust among employees; trust between Toyota and its dealers; mutual trust with partners, etc. There is much evidence of this – one among many is provided by the CR Consumer 2017 car brand reliability report in the US shown on illustration 2.16. Also, three out of ten best vehicle picks are from the Toyota Group.

Toyota: a natural 'Strategic Brand' character

So Toyota has a perfect scorecard when it comes to being 'Culture Born' and 'Authentic'. It gets top marks for its 'Clarity of Purpose', 'People Led and People Leading', 'Partnering', 'Strategy Guiding' and 'Being Trusted'. But Toyota does well in other imperatives too, albeit in its own way. Let's comment briefly on each one and link them to Toyota's culture:

Functional and Emotional

On 'Functional', Toyota is perceived as a solid, trustworthy brand that is perhaps best known for its high-quality products. As Jack Hollis explains: *"Our excellent products are at the core of what we do. We are 'a vehicle company that's unparalleled'. The functional aspect is strong and the products stand for themselves. People around the world pick Toyota because it's the best choice, it's the best value, it's the best product, the best quality, and has the best safety."*

ILLUSTRATION 2.16	THE TOYOTA BRANDS TOP THE 2017 RANKING FOR CAR RELIABILITY			
2017 Rank	**Change From 2016**	**Brand**	**No. of Models**	**Average Reliability Score**
More Reliable				
1	-	Lexus	9	86
2	-	Toyota	12	78
3	↑ 4	Buick	4	75
4	↓ 1	Audi	7	71
5	↑ 1	Kia	4	69
6	↓ 2	Mazda	5	68
7	↑ 2	Hyundai	7	66
8	↑ 16	Infiniti	4	62

Credit: CR Consumer Reports, October 24, 2016

Jack's take on the emotional side of Toyota (Ref. Illustration 2.17 on design/style, where Toyota does not appear in the leading 10 car manufacturers): *"My personal goal is for Toyota to be number one in the heart. If as a brand you can change people's lives forever, then people will live with the brand and allow it to be a part of their lives. It will become emotional: they will speak of the brand with joy and praise.*

To a certain extent, we are missing the love of our brand and what we stand for. Let's look at heart and head: head – we are number one in the world with the best practical products; heart – we are together with all kinds of companies.

I don't want Toyota to ever be compared to other automotive companies. That thinking is too narrow. When you think of our brand, it should be in the same emotional context that you might think of other brands which elicit an emotional response from the customer."

Didier Leroy brings this back to culture, explaining what he sees as the challenge and the opportunity: *"The emotional side of things is not a natural part of Japanese society. It is natural for people like Akio-san, who has great international vision, understanding and openness to the world. But for many people who run the daily operations, emotional means you must smile – so they smile. That is not our expectation.*

"Our long-term partnership with the Olympics and Paralympics will hopefully give the brand a more emotional image than we have today – and by brand I mean Toyota, Lexus and all our brands. We have an opportunity to strengthen the emotional side through sport and the impact that sport can have on society."

Connected and Customer Centric

There is an extraordinary dimension to the Toyota Brand which many people don't realise - it is indeed very connected though by different means to the traditional disciplined, centralised approach of brand management and communication.

Didier Leroy explains: *"Toyota's global marketing has not existed for long, less than five years. Before global marketing, everyone managed and developed the brand values in their area as they saw fit. We still believe it is important to have strong, marked local characteristics. We take a group approach to avoid duplications, and to look for coherency and synergies. But at the same time, we want to give space to each region and country to connect with the local culture. Regions remain at the centre and retain total authority."*

Jack Hollis agrees: *"The name Toyota does not necessarily mean the same thing in Japan, the US, Europe or around the world. We have a global name but not necessarily a global brand. That said, the Toyota Way is the baseline of what and how we do our work: respect for people and continuous improvement - kaizen, being our two primary values.*

"Our brand is built differently from most. An important part of our 'connectedness' and customer centricity is based on our relationship with retailers and dealers in the local community. I believe this is better than any other automotive company. In the US, Toyota is the most connected with the car owners and their communities. This owes a lot to our dealership investment and the mutual trusting relationship we have with retailers and distributors."

Rigorous and Disciplined

Given the way Toyota works, it is easy to conclude that it does not excel at managing its brand consistently and therefore with rigour and discipline. From a global perspective of the best-run brands with a strong centrally led approach, this is probably fair. Jack Hollis admits: *"Right now, one could argue Toyota is a conglomeration of regional brands, without an overarching brand as other companies would see it. We don't have global campaigns from a marketing standpoint, or even materials that everybody uses. Add to this 340,000 associates in the company, and you might get 10 to 15 different answers throughout the world about what the Toyota brand is. The main thing is that everyone is close on why they work for Toyota and what Toyota stands for."*

Future Embracing

I have worked with Toyota's R&D division for many years – and it is no wonder they develop some of the best cars across segments and customer needs. Their long-term perspective means they research and develop them day after day in a uniquely systematic manner. But culture is also an important factor - let's remember our earlier observations about Japanese culture: Japan is strong when it comes to getting something right first time, at perfecting something, but weaker when it comes to innovation and thinking outside the box. Arguably, this is to some extent the same with Toyota.

ILLUSTRATION 2.17	POTENTIAL AREAS OF IMPROVEMENT FOR THE TOYOTA BRAND

2013 Technology/Innovation

	Factor Score	Total Unaided Awareness	
	%	Count	%
Tesla	33.9	116	7.5
Mercedes-Benz	19.7	404	26.3
Toyota	19.5	920	59.8
Ford	19.5	1,202	78.1
BMW	18.2	411	26.7
Cadillac	18.1	372	24.2
Audi	16.5	241	15.7
Lexus	16.5	269	17.5
Chevrolet	11.3	1,039	67.6
Acura	11.3	197	12.8

2013 Design/Style

	Factor Score	Total Unaided Awareness	
	%	Count	%
BMW	20.4	411	26.7
Cadillac	20.4	372	24.2
Audi	20.2	241	15.7
Mercedes-Benz	19.6	404	26.3
Chevrolet	17.6	1,039	67.6
Ford	17.1	1,202	78.1
Lexus	17.0	269	17.5
Ferrari	16.0	134	8.7
Tesla	15.0	116	7.5
Dodge	13.3	589	38.3

Base: Household owns car

Credit – Consumer Reports National Research Center – January 2014

This reality is reflected in the survey on illustration 2.17, where Toyota appears at parity with Ford but behind Tesla and Mercedes-Benz on technology and innovation. (Of course there are always exceptions – and the invention of hybrid cars and the Toyota Prius is a huge one.)

Do these rankings in innovation and design matter? Perhaps not, as long as Toyota's leadership recognises these areas of relative weakness and acts accordingly, as it did recently by making a considerable investment in artificial intelligence in the Silicon Valley. This 'counter cultural' decision was explained in a June 2016 report from the *Financial Times*:

"The world's largest carmaker wrestles with the need to strengthen its software and data capability to survive the race to build intelligent cars that can act on their own to prevent accidents… Six months ago, Toyota launched an artificial intelligence and robotics research lab in the Silicon Valley… Gill Pratt, a former head of robotics at the US Defense department's research arm, joined Toyota and was given authority to do what Toyota is little known for: making quick decisions. Six months since the launch of the first lab, 70

employees have been hired, including James Kuffner, Google's former head of robotics. A third research facility has also been opened in Ann Harbor, Michigan, by tapping into a $1bn initial investment from Toyota."

The FT report comments on the cultural dimension of the move: *"It would have been unthinkable in the past for Toyota to act so quickly to poach a senior external executive and make a $1bn investment. It is out of character – and when companies do things that are out of character, we'll have to see how it plays out."*

High Value and Driving Value

The Toyota brand is the highest valued brand in the industry: in 2016 its brand was worth $43bn, a compelling 23% increase versus 2015.

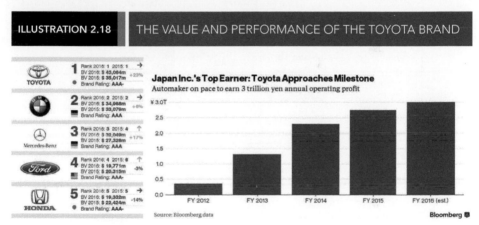

| ILLUSTRATION 2.18 | THE VALUE AND PERFORMANCE OF THE TOYOTA BRAND |

Credit – Brand Finance, Bloomberg

So it follows that the Toyota Brand also drives considerable value. In the fiscal year 2015-16, it earned a record 3 trillion Yen, the equivalent of $26 billion. This was more than the combined earnings of all other automotive companies in Japan, and made Toyota the first ever-Japanese company to reach this level of profit.

Crisis Resilient

As we mentioned earlier, Toyota has faced considerable challenges over recent years. The crisis most closely related to brand was in 2009 to 2011 in the US, when Toyota was forced to recall vehicles after drivers experienced unintended acceleration. I remember this well, and believe the response was absolutely true to Toyota's culture and brand - as well as deeply authentic, which brought its lots of highs and lows.

Response was 'Authentic and People Led' – the immediate response was somewhat out of touch and slow, grounded in Japanese culture and resulted in President Akio Toyota presenting his apologies to the American people and bowing in front of Congress.

But very quickly Toyota's employees became the personal, engaging, authentic voice of the company. Illustration 2.19 shows the successive steps of crisis communication and how the voices of Toyota's employees humanised the issue and its resolution. This serves as a textbook best-in-class practice of crisis communication...by a Strategic Brand.

ILLUSTRATION 2.19	TOYOTA CRISIS COMMUNICATION

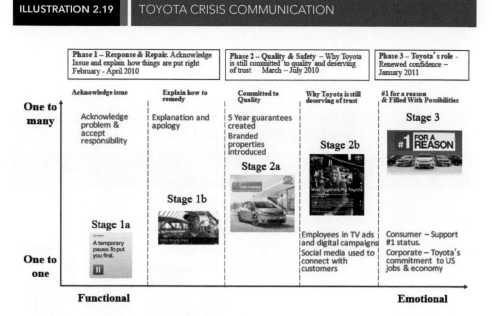

Credit – THE Enduring Strategic Brand, based on Ogily data.

Response was 'Purposed, Connected and Customer Centric' – No effort was spared to establish the cause of the problem and develop a systemic solution going forward. The recall of 4.2 million cars was structured with high levels of personal care and attention to consumers.

Response was 'Rigorous and Disciplined', as well as 'Partnering' – Together, Toyota and their dealers mobilised considerable resources to operate the recall as immaculately as possible.

Response was 'Future Embracing and Strategy Building' – Toyota undertook an extensive review of the events. One of the consequences taken was a revision of the organisational practice towards much greater devolution of authority to the regions and their leaders.

Ultimately, 'Trust' in Toyota was quickly restored, and the crisis had very little impact, if any at all, on sales, performance and brand perception.

CONCLUSION

As someone who has spent his entire career working with different cultures in global companies and tried to better understand how culture and authenticity influence brands, I know how hard it can be to be truly culturally attuned. For this reason, I have spent much time reflecting and leaning on the research and science of how culture influences brand's impact.

There is little question to me that Toyota is an Exemplary Strategic Brand which has found great success from its deeply engrained culture - and will continue to strive based on the strength of its anchoring. The reason is simple - Toyota's culture is grounded into what the world is looking more of, including deep purpose, authenticity and trustworthiness.

No culture is perfect and the world is changing – so as noted earlier, Toyota 's leadership is interrogating how to evolve culture by nurturing initiative and giving more deployed autonomy. In a circular manner, this explicit consideration talks to how vitally important Toyota's management sees culture - culture depth breeds culture excellence. And we should not be surprised that the enterprise's long-term commitment to the Olympics & Paralympics on the way to the Tokyo 2020 Games and beyond acts as a prime support to culture evolution over time.

It is finally my hope that Toyota's example and other evidence from this chapter encourage many more of us to put culture explicitly and systematically at the heart and genesis of our pursuit to build our brand into an Enduring Strategic Brand.

CHAPTER 3
FUNCTIONAL AND EMOTIONAL

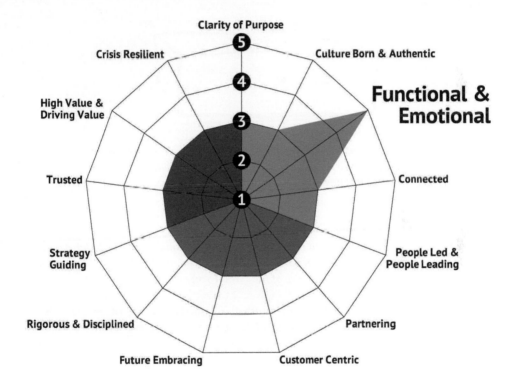

"I have learned that people will forget what you said, people will forget what you did, but people will never forget how you made them feel"
Maya Angelou, author

You might have read the story of the 'Little Prince' by Antoine de Saint-Exupéry and perhaps the chapter when the narrator meets the little hero. It goes like this:

"Draw me a sheep, said the Little Prince… Where I live, everything is very small. What I need is a sheep. Draw me a sheep."
So then I made a drawing. He looked at it carefully, then he said: "No. This sheep is already very sickly. Make me another." So I made another drawing. My friend smiled gently and indulgently. "You see yourself," he said, "that this is not a sheep. This is a ram. It has horns." So then I did my drawing over once more. But it was rejected too, just like the others. "This one is too old. I want a sheep that will live a long time."
By this time my patience was exhausted, because I was in a hurry to start taking my engine apart. So I tossed off this drawing.

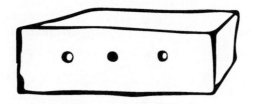

And I threw out an explanation with it. "This is only his box. The sheep you asked for is inside." I was very surprised to see a light break over the face of my young judge: "That is exactly the way I wanted it! Do you think that this sheep will have to have a great deal of grass?"
"Why?"
"Because where I live everything is very small…"
"There will surely be enough grass for him," I said. "It is a very small sheep that I have given you." He bent his head over the drawing. "Not so small that – Look! He has gone to sleep…"
And that is how I made the acquaintance of the Little Prince.

I have always liked this book from my youth. Not purely because of nostalgia but because it has the gift for imparting so many adult lessons. And here, the functionality – i.e. the way the sheep are drawn – is never good enough. It is only the imagination, the projection and the association – in one word, the emotion that – fulfils the Little Prince's needs. Reflecting on this idea in the business world of services and products, winning on functionalities alone is very hard – nay impossible – because perfection does not exist. Except when great functionalities are combined with strong emotional benefits.

DEVELOPING FUNCTIONAL AND EMOTIONAL BRANDS

I remember the day I received my first Montblanc pen. It was a present for my 18th birthday, a time of transition for me, from secondary education to university.

I had a strong, positive inward reaction to this present. How many times before had I tried to borrow a Montblanc pen from various family members and been rebuffed? Suddenly it felt like I had become somebody of standing.

The Montblanc brand promise, "*the art of writing*", embodies the combination of function – writing, and emotion – the art.

There are thousands of similar examples where an object or a service fulfils a functional role but where the emotion associated with it is at least as important.

Another memory serves as introduction to the exemplary brand that we will explore later in this chapter: BMW. In 1997 BMW and Castrol were in deep discussions to form a strategic partnership, which stretched well beyond purchase and supply into joint technology developments, supply chain co-operations, joint service offers to dealers and customers, motorsport and, ultimately, brand association - we will explore this in Chapter 6, Partnering.

My main contact was Karl-Heinz Kalbfell, then head of BMW's 'M Performance' motorsport division. Karl-Heinz had been passionate about motorbikes all his life – and I'd like to honour his memory here: he sadly lost his life in August 2013 at Brands Hatch enjoying his passion for classic motorcycle racing. One evening, years before, after a long day of meetings between the BMW and Castrol teams, we were having a drink at the Munich Airport Hilton. In the flow, Karl-Heinz shared his memories of his first bikes and the oil he used for them. He was always full of emotion about how this product, the Castrol R oil, had a very particular smell, which he, and many with him, loved so much. He explained how this feeling had guided his deep intuitive preference for building a functional partnership – with functional products like oils – with Castrol the emotionally charged brand of his youth.

Visiting the LEGO secret vault (LEGO's Memory Lane) at their HQ in Billund, Danish Jutland almost invariably engenders a similar flood of nostalgia in me… and this is another example of an emotionally driven brand preference. I compared notes with other visitors there, and the experience consistently touched them all in a way they didn't expect. This wasn't simply amazement but rather something else: a ticket back to the past, to days apparently long forgotten. The nostalgia hits you in the stomach, triggering all sorts of emotional images in your head, of Christmas, mother and father, birthdays, the smell of the plastic bricks. And what do you think I gave my children as presents so often?

Connected through functionalities, convinced by emotions

In my BP years as Group Chief Sales and Marketing Officer, I remained convinced that the BP brand needed to touch hearts at least as much as it tried to impress minds - and that it absolutely could. But it was not an easy battle with all our engineers!

Like many believers in brands, I am convinced that a Strategic Brand has to start by providing a relevant, tangible, valued, purpose-led, functional benefit to its customers and stakeholders. Indeed, Strategic Brands need to excel at what they are here to do, and they have to continuously improve and renew the quality of this service and offer. This is not easy, of course as it requires consistent flawless conception, execution and delivery.

But in a world where supply often exceeds demand, where manufacturing or distribution capacity is widely available and competition means brands strive to raise the quality of their offers, a Strategic Brand should be associated with strong emotions. A Strategic Brand needs to have benefits which satisfy a customer's emotional needs, either personal – lifestyle, or societal – 'me and the world'. When successful, these emotions result in a positive relationship between a customer and the brand. If functional is combined with love, affection, wellbeing or fulfilment, the customer will commit to a long-term relationship.

Cognitive Neuroscience informs brand building

The long-running debate on whether to build and communicate a brand with a rational OR emotional approach seems to have been largely resolved by science – establishing that logic and feeling are intertwined. The author of '*Unconscious Branding: How Neuroscience can Empower (and Inspire) Marketing*', Douglas Van Praet uses the following extreme case to justify this: *"the stronger the emotion, the stronger the belief, and the greater the tendency is to seek out supporting evidence. We are not rational, we are rationalizers"* (Note 1).

Enterprises and marketers are increasingly fascinated by the deeper mechanisms by which their stakeholders' brains make decisions. Extensive neuroscience knowledge is now available and establishes that entire brain regions are dedicated to perceiving and processing emotions. In '*The Science of Emotion in Marketing: How our Brains Decide What to Share and Whom to Trust*"(Note 2), Courtney Seiter summarizes numerous studies about: how joy and happiness live in our left pre-frontal cortex; how sadness lives in the same brain region but, by generating cortisol and oxytocin hormones, it can activate greater connection…and, for example, lead to giving more money to charity; how fear is controlled by the brain structure called the amygdala and increases the tendency to bond with people; how our brain hypothalamus is responsible for anger and engenders real and lasting effects to negativity and most specifically anger, such as making us more stubborn.

"Scientists have also established that people feel first and think second. 'The emotional brain processes sensory information in one fifth of the time our cognitive brain takes to assimilate the same input'."

Scientists have also established that people feel first and think second. *"The emotional brain processes sensory information in one fifth of the time our cognitive brain takes to assimilate the same input"* says Courtney Seiter. And Google's Abigail Posner insists that we can't underestimate the importance of understanding the science of emotion in marketing.

Neuromarketing gives rise to 'Functional and Emotional' brands

What does this mean for brands? Which is the right approach to 'Functional vs. Emotional' or perhaps better said 'Functional and Emotional' as they clearly 'work' closely together?

Firstly, do we have evidence of value? Compellingly is the answer and multiple surveys have established a simple fact: the proportion of people who say they like a brand is strongly correlated with the proportion that uses it...with all the derived positive benefits to the brand.

Among others, the IPA has studied 1400 cases of successful advertising campaigns submitted to their 'Effectiveness Award' over the last three decades. The purpose of this analysis was to compare the profitability boost of campaigns which relied primarily on 'emotions' versus 'information.' Illustration 3.1 shows the 'emotional' campaigns performing about twice a well as those with 'rational' only content and slightly better than those combining emotional and rational. (Note 3)

ILLUSTRATION 3.1	COMPARED IMPACT OF RATIONAL VS. EMOTIONAL BRAND CAMPAIGNS

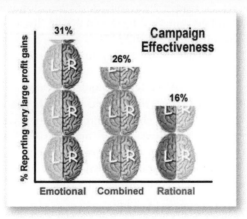

Credit – Roger Dooley; The IPA Effectiveness Awards

Beyond profit, the same conclusions apply to sales, market share, penetration, loyalty... and price sensitivity – analytics show that emotional brands excel at reducing price sensitivity, with 20% a generally accepted number for premiums which they are able to command over weak affinity brands.

Critically important to this book's purpose - the Enduring Strategic Brand, the IPA then identified a major time dimension to 'Functional and Emotional'. Emotional brand positioning and campaigns take more time to produce effects - although the good news about persevering is that they relentlessly become more productive over time (Ref. Illustration 3.2)

ILLUSTRATION 3.2	EMOTIONAL BRANDS ARE REWARDING BUT NEED TIME

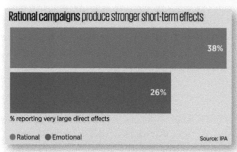
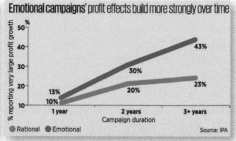

Credit – The IPA

The author of *'Brainfluence: 100 Ways to Persuade and Convince Consumers with Neuromarketing'* Roger Dooley notes that building emotional brands which sustain heartfelt and genuine relationships with stakeholders is not easy – and also confirms that it takes time. It can also be risky if the brands 'push' the emotional aspect beyond the reality of the enterprise and get damaged by the emerging disconnect. Comparatively, developing brands based on functional killer facts is simpler and less risky – but it usually doesn't go as far on impact, profits and enduringness (Note 4).

Not every brand is BMW or Nike, which both excel with their respective pervasive emotional themes of *'joy and the sheer pleasure of driving'* and *'success in sport'*; nor Coca-Cola and its masterful storytelling, which creates emotional connections through simple 'happiness' stories told in everyday's context and language. In my experience, the intent to build an enduring 'Functional and Emotional' brand is absolutely the right strategy, while being very clear on the major commitment it takes to *'hard-wire the emotional dimension into the fabric of the brand'*.

And I will steal a good representation of my point of view from Nathan King, strategist at Mekanism (Note 5): *"I find I am most attracted to the products with a benefit that is immediately clear and relevant. But the messaging will stick with me longer and make me more likely to purchase if it connects with me on a deeper level"*

A framework to build 'Functional & Emotional' brands

The big question is how to build this mutually reinforcing and winning combination of IQ and EQ into the brand? To be a brand that ideally combines best-in-class functional benefits with deep emotional fulfilment is a very big challenge – if only because it takes time. My experience is, in fact, that only Enduring Strategic Brands can achieve this and, equally, that a brand will only become a Strategic Brand if it manages to square this circle. We will consider a few brands which do this well a bit later.

Bart Michels, Global CEO of Kantar Added Value and UK Country Leader for Kantar is passionate about how to strike the balance between 'Functional and Emotional' benefits:

"A Strategic Brand is the combination of two really important things: it's a brand that is positioned well and one that is executed brilliantly.

'Functional and Emotional' are always there together
"It is a myth that these two things are distinct; that there is a functional and an emotional benefit, and that some people choose one or the other. There is no such thing as only 'functionally differentiated brands'.

"Marketers might say: 'If I deliver a functional brand, which is all about making life easy, is that a functional benefit or an emotional benefit?' It might appear as a functional benefit, because it's about doing things more simply. But the associated emotional benefit would probably be: 'I feel smart, it's hassle free.' So the functional benefit also has an emotional benefit.

"Functional and Emotional get increasingly confused in the digital world because you can target more precisely, make things easier, reduce time and cost. We mistake these as functional benefits – but we mustn't do that. The functional benefit is a combination of the practical things the brand provides to someone, which they value, and the fact that it fits with their life. It is what always gives it an emotional dimension."

'Functional and Emotional' have to be one of the same thing, enduringly
So how does this translate into the required practice of brand gurus and strategic marketers? Bart says it all comes down to category. First, understand the key drivers of choice, then understand which of these drivers are functional rather than emotional, and vice versa.

"Think carefully about what category you are in and its key drivers of choice. This will determine the best blend between your functional superiority versus your emotional superiority.

"When you get to the 'executed brilliantly' part, this is about how you bring that product to life or communicate your message. Take Volvo and safety: you could say that keeping you safe in the car is a functional benefit. But does Volvo talk about all the safety features

which it is great at? Or about something much bigger, that the car could keep what matters to you safe...whilst also letting you explore, enjoy...and THEN use technology and the safety features to underpin and reassure people that choosing Volvo is a first-class choice?

"To generalise, one could argue that people choose a car as a reflection of who they are. Choice of a car brand most often makes a statement about 'me and my life', what I do and who I am. The things it does, safety features, low emissions, etc. are mostly reinforcers of decision and sometimes 'excuses'.

"In fashion there are plenty of must-have functional benefits. Buying a Nike top, I have got to be sure that it allows moisture out but doesn't let cold in; that it doesn't disintegrate in frequent washes, that it doesn't snag when I run etc. Do I care what it looks like and how it makes me feel? Of course, as I want to look like and/or feel like an athlete – and maybe even more stylish and trim than I actually am. So you can't escape thinking about how to optimise 'Functional and Emotional'.

"Financial services is a very low involvement category. But paradoxically, people care about money. So, if you are HSBC, RBS or Barclays, you have to have a clear sense of what you, as a brand, think about money – say, 'money is the key to freedom, business success, happiness, security, a full life or just making everyday things go smoothly.' And then you have to underpin this belief with the functional: 'We have got the best innovations, most flexible rates, the best service functionality or friendly support, etc.'"

Many of us probably agree with Bart – but are we crystal clear on our brand's strategic 'Functional and Emotional' pillars and how they combine and reinforce each other? Do we understand that this is what creates the 'killer' differentiation in our category? Is the entire organisation clear about these two pillars and mobilised to make them happen, day in day out?

Brands that achieve 'Functional and Emotional'

Let's consider brands recognised for epitomising this combination of 'Functional and Emotional' and how they achieve this. Our exploration journey begins in earlier days of that idea, with the list of 2005 in Illustration 3.3 (Note 6).

This is a very diverse list of brands – from city landmarks to cartoons and pop stars – that people would never want to give up. All have the 'Functional and Emotional' combination at their heart. Let's pick a few examples:

Harley Davidson's *"We are Harley Davidson"*. Unusually in this space of excellence, Harley has had different brand promises over the years but they all consistently revolved around the idea that there is nothing like a Harley. Their current expression promises a consistent experience at every touch point, whether it's the product, the dealer, the site, or the community. A clear emotional association routed in perfectly engineered functional performance.

ILLUSTRATION 3.3	FUNCTIONAL AND EMOTIONAL BRANDS

LOVEMARKS LIST

REMO, Palm Pilot, IKEA, Singapore Airlines, A-Channel, Apple, The Statue of Liberty, Fender, Barbie, Aveda, Twinings, Where the Wild Things Are, BBC, BMW Motorcycles, Jean-Paul Gaultier, Dodge Viper, Absolut, Technics, Birkenstock, Mikimoto, The Eiffel Tower, Tiffany's, Coppertone, Toyota, Campbells, Google, Doc Martens, Ermenegildo Zegna, Bundaberg, Steinway, Virgin Atlantic, iPod, Krispy Kreme, Victoria's Secret, Becks, 42 Below, Alessi, The Simpsons, Nikon, Tim Tams, The Lord of the Rings, Borders, The All-Blacks, LEGO, The New York Times, Stella Artois, Dilmah, Madonna, Titleist, Lexus, Disneyland, mary-kate&ashley, Royal Doulton.

Credit - Stanford Management Institute Business Book Summaries.

Apple's *"Think different"* also offers an engaging functional guarantee and emotional inspiration: the guarantee that product development will always be top class, because it comes from seeing the world differently; and the inspiration that you, the customer, might then also be better able to see and experience the word differently.

As noted earlier, Nike is interesting in its bias towards emotion. Nike's, *"to bring inspiration and innovation to every athlete in the world"*, never actually mentions their products. Rather, it invites consumers into an inspiring world with no borders, not confined to sports, clothing or equipment.

Coca-Cola's *"to inspire moments of optimism and uplift"* doesn't mention products or services either. Instead it offers a lifestyle of 'happiness', one that everybody in the company would also champion. And Starbucks' lifestyle brand aspiration is in a similar league: *"to inspire and nurture the human spirit – one person, one cup and one neighborhood at a time."*

Alternatively, some brands want to be clear about fulfilling their functional role, and how this results in deep emotional benefits. For example, Marriott uses a balanced approach with, *"Quiet luxury. Crafted experience. Intuitive service"*, promising wellbeing through a consistent service and experience wherever you are.

 Or Walmart's *"Save money. Live better"*, which combines the functional benefit of lower prices with the emotional promise of a better quality of life.

This 2005 list demonstrates the special feature of 'Functional and Emotional' Strategic Brands - they endure and become increasingly successful. There are a few exceptions though, like Nokia and Palm Pilot, which lost their functional edge and differentiation over a relatively short period of time.

A zoom on building Emotional Brands

The ideal combination of 'Functional and Emotional' is not a new idea. But the intensity, the importance and the impact of this happy marriage have become much greater in recent times, alongside the massive opportunities brought by connectivity and individualisation.

Eight compelling needs for people to buy products

In 2001, Marc Gobe published '*Emotional Branding: The New Paradigm for Connecting Brands to People*'. He made the point that emotional branding originates first and foremost from the essence, purpose and values of an organisation, even more than from its products and ads. With this concept, he was one of the first to give emotional branding a strategic status. (Note 7)

ILLUSTRATION 3.4	EIGHT COMPELLING NEEDS FOR PEOPLE

1   **Need for Emotional Security** – "we are living in one of the most insecure eras in human history", so we want to be ensured, everything is fine.

2   **Need for Reassurance of Worth** – especially because we live in a highly competitive and partly impersonal society.

3   **Need for Ego Gratification** – not only "you are good enough", but also "you are special, you are the one and only".

4   **Need for Creative Outlets** – and uniqueness.

5   **Need for Love Objects** – if there is not a partnership, it is usually replaced by pets and so on, (why not).

6   **Need for a Sense of Power** – also in a sense of driving a motorbike on the open road which makes you feel powerful.

7   **Need for Roots** – especially with increasing our mobility we appreciate to know and feel our roots, our home (it can be the home inside of you, in your soul, sure).

8   **Need for Immortality** – partially because of our fear of our own mortality, partially because of our need to "leave a trace in the world" – not to die when we die physically.

Credit – Vance Packard

I have always wondered how to become better at understanding the needs of customers, i.e. what motivates someone to buy a brand now and in the future. It sounds like a dim question, as the obvious answer is 'connectedness', 'research', 'big data-led insights' and so on, all of which marketers do. I don't think this suffices and would like to motivate enterprise leaders to use psychology more and in a scientific way to better respond to these questions - as a way to better listen and make judgments.

In his research on customer motivations, researcher and author Vance Packard identifies eight "compelling needs" which make people buy products [Ref. Illustration 3.4]. (Note 8)

The ten commandments of emotional branding

So how does a brand move the needle on any or a combination of these motivators to create a strong bond? Firstly, by transforming its thinking and operating framework. Here I find Gobe's '*Ten commandments of emotional branding*' helpful, in which he transitions traditional approaches into 'Functional and Emotional' Strategic Brand tenets [Ref. illustration 3.5].

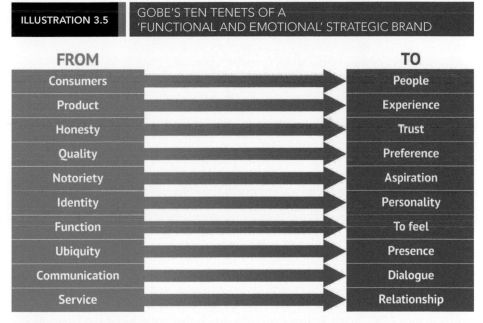

ILLUSTRATION 3.5	GOBE'S TEN TENETS OF A 'FUNCTIONAL AND EMOTIONAL' STRATEGIC BRAND

FROM	TO
Consumers	People
Product	Experience
Honesty	Trust
Quality	Preference
Notoriety	Aspiration
Identity	Personality
Function	To feel
Ubiquity	Presence
Communication	Dialogue
Service	Relationship

Credit - Marc Gobe - *Emotional Branding: The New Paradigm for Connecting Brands to People*

Embracing these guidelines will make emotions the greater foundation of people's judgment and allow new bonds with the brand. They will act as a guide to move from 'functional mainly' performance to emotional promise, such as: *"you don't buy a soap but beauty"*, *"you don't buy oranges but vitality"*, *"and you don't buy a car but status"*.

Some readers might not fully agree with this shift and I remember an interesting article some time ago titled: *"Brand building: is Function the New Emotion?"*. Remember, it is AND, not OR.

Four qualities of emotional branding

Once this shift is progressed, successful emotional branding needs to be anchored in four critical qualities and practice [Ref. Illustration 3.6]:

ILLUSTRATION 3.6	THE FOUR PRACTICES OF EMOTIONAL BRANDING

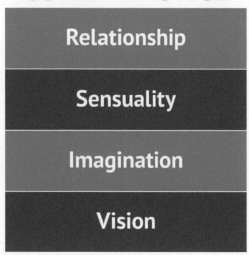

There are countless examples for each practice, including:
- Relationship – e.g. Nike being part of its stakeholders' lifestyles;
- Sensorial experience – e.g. Karl-Heinz Kalbfell's appeal to Castrol R's smell; or generation Y's appeal to the Abercrombie sent;
- Imagination – e.g. Apple's mission to invent the different;
- Vision – e.g. IBM making radical business transformations from equipment to service, data and AI.

The Science of Lovebrands

A more recent rejuvenation of this conceptual approach came from Saatchi & Saatchi and their then CEO, Kevin Roberts, in 2005, when they introduced the language of 'lovemarks'. (Note 9)

This came in for a lot of cynicism from many – and adherence from others. Whilst acknowledging with the sceptics that this approach was neither revolutionary nor that brands will disappear and be replaced by 'lovemarks' as was suggested, I have in the main stood in the supporter camp.

As I am arguing that the combination of 'Functional and Emotional' is vital to any aspiring or existing Strategic Brand, Saatchi & Saatchi's concept is helpful because lovebrands – rather than 'lovemarks' - represent the quintessence of 'Functional and Emotional'.

Love and respect

I also agree with the proposition that the strongest, longest bond with a brand (or a person) is based on both 'respect' and 'love' (Ref. Illustration 3.7). In fact, this really strikes a chord for I have forever held onto the premise that, "no respect, no love".

ILLUSTRATION 3.7	THE 'LOVEMARK' COMBINATION OF LOVE AND RESPECT

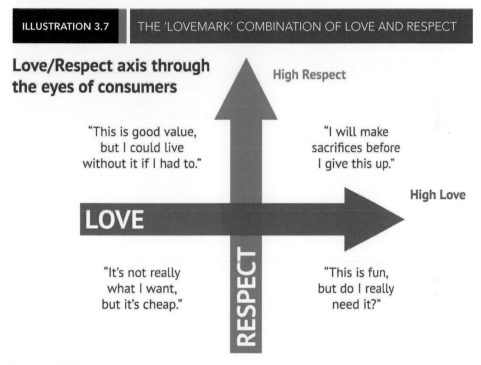

Credit: Saatchi & Saatchi

The way I use the 'lovemark' (for lovebrand) framework in practice starts with the over simplification of equating 'respect' and 'functional'. My rationale is that not doing well what you are here to do, or not performing your core role, kills respect immediately. Would you respect somebody who does not do his / her job well, has no or little role or does not have meaning or relevance?

12 attributes and actions of 'Functional and Emotional' Strategic Brands

Saatchi & Saatchi evolved and modernised some of Gobe's frameworks, including the '10 commandments', into 12 attributes and actions – which we have adapted to Strategic Brands, as shown on Illustration 3.8.

ILLUSTRATION 3.8	THE MODERN TWELVE ATTRIBUTES OF A 'FUNCTIONAL AND EMOTIONAL' STRATEGIC BRAND

BRANDS	STRATEGIC BRANDS
Brands	Strategic Brands
Information	Relationship
Recognized by Consumers	Loved by People
Generic	Personal
Presents a Narrative	Creates a Love Story
The Promise of Quality	The Touch of Sensuality
Symbolic	Iconic
Defined	Infused
Statement	Story
Defined Attributes	Wrapped in Mystery
Values	Spirit
Professional	Passionately Creative
Advertising Agency	Ideas Company

Credit to Saatchi & Saatchi – 'Lovemarks' attributes applied to Strategic Brands

Three qualities and five practices

Saatchi & Saatchi also evolved Gobe's four practices into three intangible qualities which make up a brand's emotional appeal …and five useful principles and attitudes [Ref. Illustration 3.9]

My beliefs and learning about brands are therefore well attuned to Vance Packard, Marc Gobe and Saatchi & Saatchi's frameworks on why and how to build the strongest combination possible of 'Functional and Emotional', as a vital dimension of a Strategic Brand. If you do it strategically, with determination and building on evidence, it will be transformational.

THE QUALITIES OF 'FUNCTIONAL & EMOTIONAL' STRATEGIC BRANDS

Mystery – Translated into great stories, past, present and future; dreams; myths; icons and inspirations

Sensuality – The impact from sounds, vision, touch, taste and aroma

Intimacy – The characters of commitment, empathy and compassion

THE PRINCIPLES OF FUNCTIONAL & EMOTIONAL STRATEGIC BRANDS

Be Passionate
Customers can smell a fake.
If you're not in love with your business, they won't be either.

Involve Customers
Involve them in everything, and make your own commitment to change.
Be creative.

Celebrate Loyalty
If you want loyalty, you have to be consistent.
Change is fine, but both partners must be willing participants.

Find, Tell & Re-tell Great Stories
'Functional & Emotional' Brands are infused with powerful stories which can become legends in their own time.

Accept Responsibility
'Functional & Emotional' Brands are the top of their class to devotees.
The passion can be intense. Be prepared for the reaction your Brands creates!

Credit to Saatchi & Saatchi – Lovemarks principles applied to Strategic Brands

BMW, THE EXEMPLARY STRATEGIC BRAND FOR 'FUNCTIONAL AND EMOTIONAL'

 So which Strategic Brand perfectly combines 'Functional and Emotional'? This was a hard call with fierce competition, as the earlier magnificent list showed. But we had the highest level of confidence in selecting BMW. Before explaining why and how, let's consider the iconic BMW Strategic Brand itself.

BMW: a Compelling Enduring Strategic Brand

The first reason of this choice lies in how compellingly BMW is a 'Strategic Brand', as evidenced when running the brand against the 13 Imperatives - and represented on illustration 3.10.

ILLUSTRATION 3.10	THE ENDURING STRATEGIC BRAND IMPERATIVES – BMW

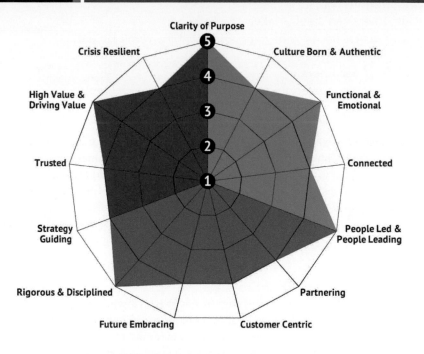

I have been closely associated with BMW for almost 25 years. I evoked earlier the extraordinary, wide-ranging, long-term partnership between BMW and Castrol. For the best part of 15 years, there were multiple expressions of brand association: on the engine, in the dealerships, on racing tracks, in the media, at industry events, and so on. Castrol's prominent association with the BMW brand was just pioneering the space of branded partnerships - more on this in chapter 6.

The Ultimate Driving Machine

I was recently the guest of Dr. Ian Robertson at BMW Welt in Munich. Beyond being Member of the Board of Management of BMW AG since 2008, in charge of Sales and Brand BMW and Aftersales BMW Group, Ian is a world-class brand leader and strategic marketer.

ILLUSTRATION 3.11	BMW FOUR CYLINDER BUILDING AND BMW WELT IN MUNICH

Credit – BMW

Over lunch on the 21st floor of the Four Cylinders, BMW's world HQ, we discussed the magic of the BMW brand. Being there again was quite emotional. I could see inside the BMW boardroom from where I was sitting, and remembered that day in 1999 when I led a Castrol delegation to present our partnership vision to the BMW Board. We were absolutely awful, failing to consider the plan enough from BMW's perspective and the meeting concluded with the Group After-Market Director saying *"over my dead body"*. Thankfully, my colleagues' passion for the brand and for a job well done turned things around later.

BMW Brand extraordinary consistency

What impressed me again throughout my day at BMW, while discussing and reviewing the brand with Ian and his colleagues, is its extraordinary coherency. It all seems a perfect dance, with every aspect of the brand naturally re-enforcing the others. And it looks so simple when it works like this, when it is natural, when it is embedded, when it is who you are. Let's hear Ian's thoughts on the BMW Strategic Brand:

"A Strategic Brand is what drives the company, rather than anything else. People often make the mistake of saying, 'we have a good idea or we have a good product and then we make a brand,' but that's not what achieves consistency and endurance.

"A Strategic Brand is what drives the company, rather than anything else. People often make the mistake of saying, 'we have a good idea or we have a good product and then we make a brand,' but that's not what achieves consistency and endurance."

"The DNA of the BMW brand has clear focus. It's what we use to attract people into our company; to motivate people within the company; to design our cars and services; to communicate to our public; to guide our dealers. That's why we have a Brand Academy, just across the street, where thousands of people every year, both within the company and our outside partners, become immersed in the brand – because it's not easy for everyone to understand.

"Part of our message is to say that BMW is the Ultimate Driving Machine. That's been our central focus for over 45 years, but as well as it being our message to the outside world, we have to look at the more complex issue of how you ingrain that concept in the people who come to work here. How do you ensure that, whatever they're designing, they have the Ultimate Driving Machine in mind?"

And you stick to it! BMW has used a number of different slogans over the years - *"We don't just make cars, we make joy"; "the ultimate driving machine"; "sheer driving pleasure"; "the ultimate driving experience"*, etc. Each of these messages has been used during different life phases and communication campaigns and their variance has given BMW a fresh look. But the magic is that they actually all say the same thing.

The emotion of "Joy"
"It's too easy to have a set of words on the wall or words in a book. What you need is an emotional context to the brand. The emotional context at the centre of the BMW brand is 'joy'. That's what we want our people to have. That's what we want our customers to experience. That's what we want our products to deliver. That's what we want our communication to say. It's consistent: we've never changed 'joy'. Joy is always there.

What you need is an emotional context to the brand. The emotional context at the centre of the BMW brand is 'joy'. That's what we want our people to have. That's what we want our customers to experience. That's what we want our products to deliver. That's what we want our communication to say. It's consistent: we've never changed 'joy'. Joy is always there.

"'Freude' is the word for joy in German. People are attracted to BMW because it is a brand which exhibits this trait. Then joy embeds other sub-elements, like 'youthfulness' [Ref. Illustration 3.13]

"This consistent approach throughout the company is the foundation of a Strategic Brand. You start with the brand and then, ultimately, you have products, you have services, you

have what you stand for. Because of this consistency, all those people behind the brand become the greatest brand ambassadors. It underpins our business and our values.

"How do you achieve this? The magic lies with consistency – our brand is something that is understood by anyone you talk to in the company, whether they are on the production lines, in the offices or in the dealerships.

"Companies have ups and downs of course but even in difficult times, we still want people to experience that motivation and excitement. You have to keep reinforcing it. So we had strategy 'Number One' in 2007, and we've just gone through the process of defining our strategy 'Next'. Now we're in the process of communicating and engaging with everybody in the company about what the strategy means and how we are evolving the business. Within that, "joy" plays a very central role.

"Hence our core remains consistent. The way in which our products are developing, the way in which the world is changing, the way in which our business models are evolving – these things will be different. But the ultimate heart of the brand is consistent."

The BMW magic of 'Functional and Emotional'

"I think people engage with the emotional context. I see a lot of 'vision-mission' statements from other companies, and some of them are bland: there is nothing emotionally hooked into it. For example, when a company says: 'We're going to be the best in this area and the biggest and most successful in that area.' So what? says Ian.

"It is emotion that makes great marketing and provides great service. The rest can be trained. The emotional context of a brand's core is essential. Going the extra mile becomes easier if you have an emotional context. One thing we are consistent on in the company is for everyone to experience the product because, ultimately, that's our business: we sell cars or services. But we also want to have that joy in the factory in Dingolfing or Regensburg or Spartanburg in North America.

"In today's world, the difference between one car and another is narrower than it's ever been and the context of the brand proposition is therefore even more powerful. Because what is a brand at the end of the day? It is a promise. It's a promise of great design, of great technology, of outstanding innovation, of great service, of employers and employees who will go the extra mile for you. All areas where our customers know we deliver strongly on our promise."

BMW stands for 'Functional and Emotional'
BMW's highest-level brand statement – 'the ultimate driving machine' – is about the combination of 'Functional and Emotional'. Let's look at each word:

'Machine' is generally seen as functional, though there is a certain amount of irony in designating a BMW car simply a 'machine'.

'Driving' is a combination of the functionality of an act and the considerable emotional evocation contained in the excitement of it.

'Ultimate' is excessively emotional, leaving space for aspiration and imagination - like the Little Prince and his sheep.

The German original and equivalent *'Freude am Fahren'* is even more emotionally loaded: *'joy and the sheer pleasure of driving'* are at the centre of the brand purpose and promise.

ILLUSTRATION 3.12	A DEEPLY 'FUNCTIONAL AND EMOTIONAL' BRAND PURPOSE

Freude am Fahren   **Sheer Driving Pleasure**

Credit – BMW

Think also about 'Efficient Dynamics', a central strategic pillar for BMW. Head of Brand and Customer Institutes for all BMW Group brands, Jörg Dohmen describes how this strategic guide for BMW's work is rooted in both 'Functional and Emotional': *"Efficient dynamics' means we are pushing the boundaries in both directions – more dynamics but less fuel consumption. So on the one hand we're working on the functional thing, the efficiency. Because a customer – rationally – does not want to spend more than necessary on fueling the car.*

But then on the other hand, we're also working on the emotional side of things, on the dynamics - the drive the customer experiences with our cars. Because our customers might be rational but they also want to enjoy driving. It's a challenge for our engineers, getting better dynamics and better efficiency at the same time, but it's also about striking the right balance across the range as a whole.

"Of course different products might concentrate on one of these elements more than the other – a BMW M2 is the most efficient car in its segment, but it's mainly about dynamics; whereas a 218i is more about efficiency, while still offering a good drive. So you can see that having a clear understanding on where each product fits along the scale gives our engineers a clear direction to their work. And we always remember that our job is never finished, because our customers' needs continue to evolve."

To Jörg's point, Illustration 3.13 shows how BMW expresses and links its brand attributes – a natural and powerful mix of rational and emotional dimensions, with joy at the centre.

| ILLUSTRATION 3.13 | THE BMW BRAND ATTRIBUTES EMANATING FROM JOY |

Design: 'THE Enduring Strategic Brand'. Source: BMW, translated from German

BMW: Countless evidences of a 'Functional and Emotional' Strategic Brand

Returning to Saatchi & Saatchi's adapted lovebrand model, does BMW engender respect from its stakeholders, whether they are employees, customers, dealers, suppliers, hosting countries, etc.?

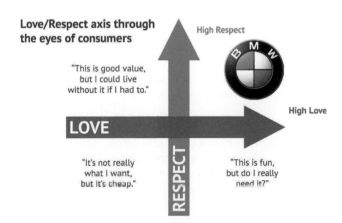

Not only do people have deep-seated respect for BMW, but they also develop considerable self-respect when they associate with the BMW brand (Ref. Illustration 3.14). This very personal involvement takes respect for the brand to a whole different level as with most other brands.

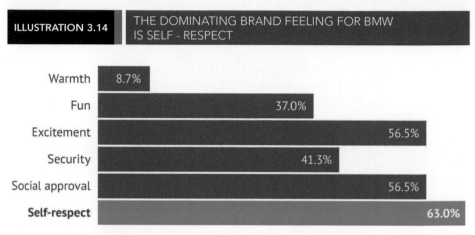

| ILLUSTRATION 3.14 | THE DOMINATING BRAND FEELING FOR BMW IS SELF - RESPECT |

Warmth — 8.7%
Fun — 37.0%
Excitement — 56.5%
Security — 41.3%
Social approval — 56.5%
Self-respect — 63.0%

Credit to Lindsey Sun, Marketing Expert

As for love, just take a look at social media; headlines are generally positive and very often using such phrase, as "*I love my BMW*". Widespread and almost excessive love for the brand can't be argued, with the only tempering that sometimes, the brand can be challenged of being 'loved by snobs'.

What about the 12 'Functional and Emotional' brand attributes and how BMW measures up on each of them? Go down the list on Illustration 3.15 and check our review. Consistently impressive, isn't it!

Finally, the BMW brand stands significantly ahead of its luxury car competitors in Saatchi & Saatchi's lovemarks top 200 ranking. Illustration 3.16 shows how they qualify BMW's intangible qualities and underpin its high ranking.

'Functional and Emotional' is owned by BMW's people

For Ian Robertson, people are everything: "*The brand context comes over time. You need to nurture it because the context in the outside world is changing fast and the promise has to evolve, while remaining clearly anchored to its core.*

"*In Germany, BMW is always number one or number two in the most desirable employer list, even higher than Google and the new players. When new employees join, you give them the introduction. They are really excited to be here. They are proud and hungry for the brand. So you are starting off with a great foundation. Now, the challenge is keeping that emotion going, because business is tough. There are ups and downs and we've got 120,000 employees all around the world – that's a lot of people.*

ILLUSTRATION 3.15	BMW AND THE TWELVE ATTRIBUTES OF A 'FUNCTIONAL AND EMOTIONAL' STRATEGIC BRAND	
BRANDS	**STRATEGIC BRANDS**	**THE ENDURING STRATEGIC BRAND BMW REVIEW**
Brands	Strategic Brands	∨ Exemplary
Information	Relationship	∨ At every touch point
Recognized by Consumers	Loved by People	∨ And desired
Generic	Personal	∨ A person - An experience (the theatre)
Presents a Narrative	Creates a Love Story	∨ People love their BMW
The Promise of Quality	The Touch of Sensuality	∨ BMW is about desire and joy
Symbolic	Iconic	∨ "Iconic BMW"
Defined	Infused	∨ Sense of status, belonging, price, joy
Statement	Story	∨ A 100 years long one
Defined Attributes	Wrapped in Mystery	∨ Technology, future, emotions
Values	Spirit	∨ The "BMW Spirit"
Professional	Passionately Creative	∨ This is the BMW promise
Advertising Agency	Ideas Company	∨ A lot from within, as employees are the brand champions

Credit - Saatchi and Saatchi attributes; assessment by THE Enduring Strategic Brand

ILLUSTRATION 3.16	THE BMW BRAND IN THE 'LOVEMARK' MODEL
Mystery	▶ Great story: Long history since 1916, used to be an aircraft-engine manufacturer ▶ Logo: Rotating propeller ▶ Slogan: "The ultimate driving machine"
Sensuality	▶ Symbol of comfort, safety and luxury ▶ Different product models ▶ Design ▶ Quality & Excellence ▶ Performance ▶ Pleasure to drive
Intimacy	▶ Emotional promotion ▶ High customer loyalty ▶ Personalisation and Customisation of the products

Credit – Saatchi & Saatchi

"We do annual surveys to gauge what our employees are thinking. The results of the emotion-based questions all come back at a very high level. The understanding of BMW is right up there. Of course there are always things people want to improve about how we do things but the perception that BMW is a fantastic brand is a big tick in the box – that's never in doubt."

Perhaps any brand could do this. But as Ian says: *"You have to create it… and then nurture it."* And this is what we've seen with structural commitments like the BMW Brand and Customer Institutes – more later on the Institutes.

The emotional power of WHY to the BMW Brand

BMW makes great, leading products – and of course a large part of the company's success is to do with its range of cars. But nobody really needs a BMW, do they? And certainly nobody absolutely needs to pay a significant premium for a car. Why this happens resides with the brand and in particular with its ability to fairly uniquely combine 'Functional and Emotional'.

Probably the main reason BMW is such a brand-led organisation is that the brand itself is actually the answer to any WHY question anybody could ask within or about BMW.

This brings us to one of my favourite guidelines in business, *'Start With Why: How Great Leaders Inspire Everyone to Take Action'*, the masterpiece on the prevalence of WHY by Simon Sinek. https://www.youtube.com/watch?v=sioZd3AxmnE. Simon starts with a fundamental question: *"Why are some people and organisations more innovative, more influential and more profitable than others? Why do some command greater loyalty from customers and employees alike? Even among the successful, why are so few able to repeat their success over and over?"*

His answer is that people like Martin Luther King Jr., Steve Jobs and organisations like BMW seem to have little in common, but they all start with WHY. They realise that people won't truly buy into a product, service, movement or idea until they understand the WHY behind it. He shows that those people or brands who have the greatest influence in the world all think, act and communicate in the same way- starting with WHY, the opposite of what the vast majority of people do.

Going around BMW, you just know that almost any individual in almost any circumstance can respond to the question: why am I here? Why am I doing this? Why am I doing it in this way? Why am I buying this car? The BMW Enduring Strategic Brand is always there to provide the answers, as one of the clearest and most impressive brands, organisations and contributors that we know.

As both Ian and Jörg say, the Brand empowers BMW's extended employee base, from engineers to ad agencies. It gives a clear purpose and sense of direction for everything. Before engineering a car part, dealing with the 'what', engineers will refer to the Brand

and ask themselves: *"Why am I engineering this way?"* Because it is in the service of the BMW brand, in the service of BMW's meaning and promise.

The BMW brand 'Functional and Emotional' combination is consistent over borders

Ian explains why international brand consistency is so important:

"When we entered the Chinese market, 12 to 13 years ago, we were dealing with a consumer base who knew very little about BMW. So we had to build that emotional base. Today, we have around 16,500 employees in China and they are great ambassadors for the brand. But the whole communication strategy has been adjusted – it has to be different to the one that we have in Germany, where we have 100 years of history. Specifically, the emotion and the youthfulness of the brand have been particularly strong in our communication, but we approach it in a start-up manner, rather than how we would in a more mature market environment like Germany, France, the UK or America.

"This adjustment – staying anchored but also flexible - has worked. BMW is right up there in the number one / number two brand slots in China these days. Does everything go right? Of course not. But the context of the brand proposition drives the success. In 2016 we sold half a million cars in China, making it our biggest market by a long stretch. This emotional context, allegiance and alignment to the brand drive our success.

"The context of the brand has international consistency. However we focus on certain topics more in some markets than in others. For example, in China we did a lot of communication regarding the history of where the brand came from, because in China, longevity is strongly valued. Clearly wherever we are in the world, we must also make sure our service upholds our brand promise: a BMW is not your average car, nor does it provide your average car service. It has to be at a different level.

"So the consistency, the anchor of what the company stands for is exactly the same in China as it is in Germany or America or South Africa, or wherever. Some companies have completely different profiles in different countries, whereas we want our brand to have consistency all around the world. The core has to be there, and 'joy' was at the core of our Chinese communication right from day one."

BMW: a Natural 'Strategic Brand' Character

'Functional and Emotional' starts with the core essence of the BMW Brand and deep purpose, culture and connectedness collide as a coherent system to build up the jewel of the crown.

BMW clarity of purpose

A lot has been evidenced by BMW's decades-long deep purpose and the power of WHY behind the brand.

Actually, a visit to their HQ and a conversation with anyone there says it all by evidence. Rich Karlgaard, publisher of Forbes magazine, wrote: *"Successful businesses engender loyalty, both among customers and employees. BMW is a great example. Its customers go beyond loyal; they are fans and evangelists for BMW's products. BMW is a purpose-driven organisation. 'The Ultimate Driving Machine' is more than a slogan for BMW. It is a timeless goal, a purpose for existence."*

Culture born and authentic BMW

Ian breathes BMW's heartfelt culture: *"I think our history says a lot about how authentic we are as a company. BMW is 100 years old, beginning first with aero-engines. Then there were high-speed dynamic motorcycles in the early Twenties; and the first cars at the end of the Twenties. By the mid-Thirties, we had cars winning big events, like the Mille Miglia. So 80 years ago, efficient performance and dynamic sportiness were already in our DNA.*

"The car I drive in the Mille Miglia every year (Ref. Illustration 3.17) has some unique features compared with other cars built in 1937: all aluminium, lightweight body – 830 kg; a six-cylinder engine; and even little things, which demonstrate a way of thinking from the engineers which you might not expect to find in a car designed back then. For example, around the gear shifter there is a gap where you can see the road; and the first time I drove the car, I didn't know why it was there. So I asked the mechanics, "Why is that gap there?" They replied: "Oh, you'll find out." And I did, when I drove the car in Italy. There was a cold, mountainous area just before Rome, with snow on the ground. Now, there is a plate welded underneath the car, which scoops the hot air off the exhaust that is running through, and that warm air comes through the hole in the floor. Suddenly you realise you have a heater! There isn't officially a heater in the car but there is heat being transferred into the car from the exhaust system, which is a really efficient use of waste heat – and to think someone at BMW was thinking about that eighty years ago!!"

ILLUSTRATION 3.17	IAN'S 1937 BMW AT THE MILLE MIGLIA

Credit – BMW

Connected BMW

Numbers don't make the whole story, but they provide enlightening insights on BMW's connectedness. BMW is the leading automotive brand on Facebook, Twitter, Instagram and YouTube - its Facebook presence counts over 19 million followers, nearly 20 million 'likes' and they have close to 11 million followers on Instagram. This Facebook clip had a reach of 24 million and 10 million views: https://www.facebook.com/BMW/videos/10154743638047269/

As analysed by the social markcting firm Syncapse, the average fan value of BMW is over $1,600, 20 times more than a Coke fan.

"Our strategy here is to offer highly engaging content which is tailored for the specific target-groups on each platform. One reason for our success is the fact that we spend a lot of time getting to know the various communities in order to better understand them – we know that authenticity and 'closeness' to the brand is very highly regarded by our followers on the various platforms.

So, for BMW, connectedness is about the brand's relevance to individuals and their lives. Let's hear Ian on some examples: *"BMW is youthful but, in essence, the average age of our consumers is mid-40s upwards. Other premium automotive brands are significantly older. When we ran the 'joy' campaign back in 2008/9, we decided to include older customers in our external communication, which was unheard of before. And it worked. I had many letters from customers, saying: 'Finally, you recognise who I am.' And I think our ability to widen our core of connectedness was good.*

"It's also about the aspiration of people who might never be customers. One day, when I lived in South Africa, I was driving a newly launched BMW and I pulled up to a traffic light. There were several guys selling sunglasses and cheap and cheerful souvenirs and their reaction was interesting: 'Wow, it's the new BMW - I haven't seen one of these before.' They would always know everything about the latest model. There was real aspiration for these guys, who might never earn enough to drive a new BMW. But they knew what we were talking about, which meant the brand communication was working – and that made me feel good."

BMW: A recurring strength of delivery

What sort of outcomes does the BMW brand produce?

BMW Enterprise's Strategy guided by its Brand

Ian was unambiguous from the very start: *"The Brand drives the company, rather than anything else"*.

Illustration 3.18 is a straight extract from BMW's corporate website. On which other home page would you see such a passionate call for brands as on BMW's?

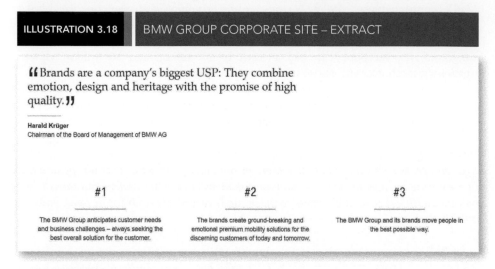

| | ILLUSTRATION 3.18 | BMW GROUP CORPORATE SITE – EXTRACT |

❝ Brands are a company's biggest USP: They combine emotion, design and heritage with the promise of high quality. **❞**

Harald Krüger
Chairman of the Board of Management of BMW AG

#1 — The BMW Group anticipates customer needs and business challenges – always seeking the best overall solution for the customer.

#2 — The brands create ground-breaking and emotional premium mobility solutions for the discerning customers of today and tomorrow.

#3 — The BMW Group and its brands move people in the best possible way.

Trusted BMW

BMW remains consistently in the world's five most reputable companies in the Reputation Institute's Global RepTrack 100 ranking, alongside or outperforming brands like Google, The Walt Disney Company, Apple, Rolex or LEGO.

Let's hear Ian's 'tough and fair' perspective on how BMW builds trust: *"Trust has to be earned, and if you look at our guiding principles within the company, trust is in there. It's not only trust in us and in our customers and our products. It's trust in each other. If you don't start with trust inside, you'll never get trust from outside. That doesn't mean that we are an easy-going company that says: 'Well, I trust you, so let's just hold hands and walk off into the sunset.' We are rigorous and challenging – but trust is a big part of that. What we say, we generally deliver on. So we think long and hard about what we say. It's not luck."*

He adds: *"Trust in the auto industry isn't as strong as it was a year or so ago. Trust is fundamental to a brand, so we are now focusing more intensively in this area, to see how we can actually improve trust continuously".*

A 'High Value and Driving Value' BMW Brand

The firm has a track record of continuous growth over close to a decade. It generates an impressive $2bn net profit per quarter, with unit's operating margin of plus or minus 8.5 per cent.

In the 2017 Global 500 Brand Finance ranking, the BMW brand is worth $37.1bn, up +6% versus 2016 and stands in 17th position in the world. Impressively, the BMW brand value represents over 25% of the enterprise market cap.

Crisis Resilient BMW

One never knows with crisis of course, but the CEO of a major company was recently reflecting spontaneously to me: *"If you look at BMW, they don't seem to have ever been part of a major crisis or scandal, unlike regrettably many others in the auto industry. And their recalls are either rare or very low profile."*

Ian's reflects on BMW's philosophy and practice when it comes to managing crises or issues: *"Not everything works out all of the time. For example, the industry as a whole is facing an ever-increasing number of recalls. Sometimes it's due to a mistake we made, sometimes it's due to a mistake someone else made. In either case, we just get on and deal with it – we solve the problem.*

"Of course we could try to push back, but as soon as you are seen to be trying to avoid a problem rather than dealing with it, you lose the customers' trust. If there's an issue with something, we need a culture where people can point that out, so it can be dealt with. Not a culture where we try to sweep it under the carpet."

BMW: a Strong 'Strategic Brand' Practice

BMW Strategic Brand performance is built on a strong practice across all five capability imperatives of a Strategic Brand. Let's examine more:

People Led and Leading People

This is where all starts in BMW. Indeed, Ian repetitively makes the point that people are guided by the brand in what they do and the way they do it - and, equally, that they are guiding the brand because *"if your employees don't buy it, why would you expect your customers to buy it? Every employee needs to be a great brand ambassador."*

"If your employees don't buy it, why would you expect your customers to buy it? Every employee needs to be a great brand ambassador."

The BMW Brand and Customer Institute - It is hardly surprising that a brand that is so remarkably coherent and consistent pays careful attention to embedding brand values throughout the organisation.

The BMW Group has 16 Brand and Customer Institutes all over the world, including two in Beijing and Guangzhou, China. This is where they educate employees, as well as agencies, suppliers and other brand ambassadors. In Munich, they train 2,500 people annually through 15 trainers - 60 worldwide.

The concept of the BMW Group Brand and Customer Institute was invented in 2002 and, since then, BMW has educated and trained about 100,000 people worldwide. I spoke with Jörg Dohmen and he passionately introduced the Institute:

The BMW Group Brand and Customer Institute

'Why a Brand Institute? - We see the Brand Institute as a tool to create a consistency of understanding for our brands. The content considers four aspects: Sensitization, Understanding, Anchoring and Transferring. Every element of the training has at least one of these goals in mind and it's very important that we explain the significance of the brands and the idea that brands create value. The other four elements within the course are a System of Branding consisting of Brand Design, Message, Product & Services and Brand Behaviour.

"System of Branding - We believe that brands need to be supported. Depending on the situation they can play many different roles and therefore we create a system of branding, from product names to the brand architecture, which includes primary and secondary design elements of the products and services.

"Brand Design – Brands appear in various elementary ways: word mark, logo, typeface. These elements are a toolbox that is used in 2-D (advertising, print flyer), 3-D (retail, fairs) and 4-D (web, apps, car displays). This is about how we express the brand beyond the actual product. For example, it might be what our headquarters building represents about the brand - so the BMW Group decided with Mr. Karl Schwanzer in 1970 to build the four-cylinder building.

"Message – Whatever you communicate towards your clients, partners, suppliers and other stakeholders needs to follow a consistent and continuous image of your brand identity. Of course there will be focal topics with regards to your brand and business plan, but the foundation will always be the brand identity.

"Product and Services – Many brands will always have certain design cues, a design shorthand that represents the brand. For example, if people see the double kidney front grille and double headlights, they think, "oh, it must be a BMW." The same unique signature also applies to services under the BMW trademark.

"Brand Behaviour - How the brand behaves and how you, as a brand ambassador, behave directly impacts on a customer's or potential customer's

experience and therefore how they feel about the brand. Everything you do carries a message and it's not simply about how you behave at work, it's also about how you are in your private life, when you're talking to your neighbor as he washes his car. You are responsible for underlining the core message of our brand.

"What does the training look like? - Training tends to last one day. We begin with an introduction to the marketplace, raising awareness of brands in general before we move onto our house of brands. We explain the brand architecture and how it relates to the BMW Group and its three automotive brands, BMW, Rolls-Royce and MINI. We then take everyone into the brand rooms, each dedicated to one brand, with special areas for the appropriate sub-brands.

"Initially, the Brand and Customer Institute focused just on managers, but today we train every employee, including new recruits. We know that we're competing with many other training programmes and sometimes an engineer says: "What I need is technology training or skill training for my engineers, not training on the brand." And I always say: "Before you go to a climbing centre to do your team-building exercise, come here for your team meeting. The experience here gives you a toolbox that will ensure your behavior is in line with the appropriate brand image and reflects the specific needs of those customers"

"Results - We know it works. We can measure our effectiveness and we average 90 per cent customer satisfaction from delegates. It's a good result but there is always room for improvement.

"We want people to see that branding is not about plastering a logo on every space you can. It starts with thinking about what kind of brand values we want to achieve in the long term and what this means for the products or services we create. We hope that they take these lessons back to their desks and use them in their daily business life.

Leadership -To Ian, the role of leadership including his own as the brand champion is also evolving: *"At the board and with my senior team, we deal with the operational stuff - because we are bringing the revenue and that's what counts. But I spend more time now challenging the way the business model is going to develop. Five to ten years ago the business model was clear: we make cars, we sell cars, we supply the parts and we provide the finance for them. That's what we do.*

"Today, a large part of strategy 'Next' is about digitalisation and this is an area where many companies make very bold statements without really knowing what they mean.

But thinking about what is right and how you shape a positive outcome for the future is something which needs careful, ongoing consideration, not a catchy slogan."

Future Embracing BMW

Ian shares how the BMW brand shapes and creates the future, is future proof and carries the organisation's transition into the future (Ref. Chapter 8) – which is by keeping to the core. *"You have to have the flexibility in your brand to be able to evolve, but also the consistency to keep it anchored. I think many companies lose their anchors. And when they do, they begin to drift.* Because it is so much a part of BMW's brand promise to be "The Ultimate Driving Machine" and provide *"the best ever mobility solution for customers"*, 'Future Embracing' is clearly in the DNA of the BMW Brand.

"Some companies who thought they were too big to fail, did fail, because they lost their core. We used to make very large, high performance engines. We still do. But we also make electric engines with zero emissions. These days everyone's talking about autonomous driving. How does that fit with the Ultimate Driving Machine? None of this is a problem if you still have your core: the technology can be laid on top. It's this ability to change whilst also staying true to ourselves which has enabled our success over the years – we've always done it and by now it's expected by our customers and our fans."

Ian shares an example on how the BMW Strategic Brand will take the enterprise into a transformed and brighter future: *"In the future, we believe individual mobility will remain prevalent and we don't think that mass transit systems are going to take over. But the utilisation of the average car in the world today is around 5 per cent. So, it's around an hour and 10 minutes a day.*

"If you took the utilisation up to 50 per cent, you would then have more movement and fewer traffic jams. Does that mean that we are going to sell fewer cars? Well, the industry today is a hundred million new car sales per annum globally, plus or minus. Are we reaching a peak? That might be the case. But the point is this: premium luxury brands represent roughly seven million of those 100 million new-car sales. And those seven million people have to earn quite a bit of money, just so they can use their premium car for a hour a day.

"If you start to sell cars by the minute, which is what we do with our car sharing service 'DriveNow', the ability to access a premium car is significantly widened. So the luxury premium offering becomes available to a much broader consumer base - you are not dealing with 7 million customers anymore, but with 60 or 70 million customers. And what is going to be the key to success? It's the brand!

It's the brand which will drive the aspiration that says: 'Do I want to take this normal volume product or shall I have a BMW, which is only going to cost me a euro or two more?' This means the brand proposition will become even more important in the future than it is today, because the brand is what will broaden our customer base considerably."

Customer Centric BMW

While I was visiting the BMW Welt Brand Institute, I could observe a BMW employee delivering a car to a customer a few floors below me in BMW Welt. It was simply stunning: he had space, a rotating floor, and was patiently taking the new owner around and inside the vehicle. Jörg Dohmen turned to me and said: *"This is the theatre!"*

"We have complete clarity when it comes to our customers – our job is to deliver our brand promise at all times, at all touch points with our customers."

"We have complete clarity when it comes to our customers – our job is to deliver our brand promise at all times, at all touch points with our customers. We continuously survey the dimensions of the promise and the whole brand is measured every year, in every country around the world. We assess ourselves against other people on the things we think are important and we steer our work to make sure that we are always raising the bar" Ian says.

"Another major aspect of customer centricity for us is how strongly a customer assumes certain things because of the BMW brand promise. When they get in a BMW, they expect all the latest technology. And why wouldn't they? If autonomous driving is the topic of the moment, BMW is going to have it of course. If you want the latest zero emission vehicles, BMW makes them. We are known for pushing the boundaries of innovation and technology - that's part of our DNA. So the customer expects these things, because the BMW promise says we will have them - so we will!"

The relationship is becoming increasingly personal: *"There is a lot of change around digital marketing at the moment, which is exciting. It opens up the possibility of communicating directly with individual or potential customers – and in a way which is relevant to them. We can target people much more specifically, building brand awareness and a very different, more personal kind of relationship. People engage with the brand far more when we use this tailored approach, because its relevance speaks more directly to that individual. It is far more effective than traditional mass marketing, where you might make a great TV commercial but you have no idea who was watching it or whether they were the right target audience. Digital marketing also interacts well with social media, supporting the dialogue we have with our customers and fans on platforms like Facebook and Instagram."*

Partnering BMW

Is BMW a real partnering company that views its partners as equals and with little or no sense of dominance? Ian: *"Partnerships are very important to BMW and we develop more every day – the important relationship with Amazon Echo being a recent one. A good reflection of our attempts to partner successfully can be found in the purchasing side and in the measures of the relationships between companies and their suppliers. BMW always comes out near the top as a good company to work for."*

Indeed, we reviewed studies and BMW comes first or second, usually head to head with Toyota in terms of partnerships. A comprehensive 2014 study feeding into the '*SuRe index rating of relationships with the supply base*' showed BMW leading in the US and second in Asia and Europe.

ILLUSTRATION 3.19	BMW LEADS ON PARTNERSHIPS ACROSS REGIONS

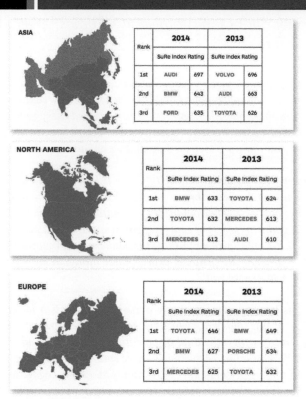

ASIA

Rank	2014		2013	
	SuRe Index Rating		SuRe Index Rating	
1st	AUDI	697	VOLVO	696
2nd	BMW	643	AUDI	663
3rd	FORD	635	TOYOTA	626

NORTH AMERICA

Rank	2014		2013	
	SuRe Index Rating		SuRe Index Rating	
1st	BMW	633	TOYOTA	624
2nd	TOYOTA	632	MERCEDES	613
3rd	MERCEDES	612	AUDI	610

EUROPE

Rank	2014		2013	
	SuRe Index Rating		SuRe Index Rating	
1st	TOYOTA	646	BMW	649
2nd	BMW	627	PORSCHE	634
3rd	MERCEDES	625	TOYOTA	632

Credit – IHS Inc SuRe index and Autonews

Rigorous and Disciplined BMW

Discipline is a way of being for the BMW brand, including the highest and most consistent quality of brand execution globally. Let's hear from Ian about how rigour and discipline starts with strategy, alignment and continuous refinement. "*It is important that the context of the brand has a consistency internationally. We don't change things. Rather, we fine tune them.*"

In an almost circular manner, this brings us back to how the BMW Strategic Brand understands and practices better than most the power of combined 'Functional and Emotional'. To return to the wisdom of Le Petit Prince: "*The most beautiful things in the world cannot be seen or touched, they are felt with the heart.*" He would probably have driven a BMW!

CHAPTER 4
CONNECTED

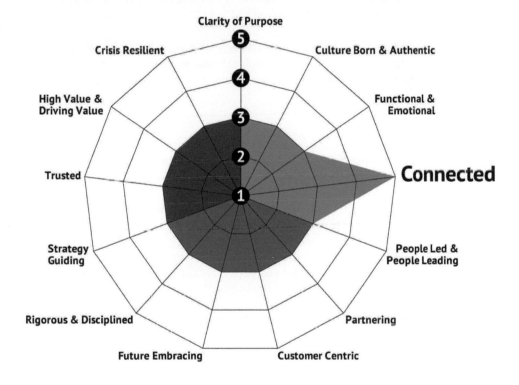

"Connection is the energy that exists between people when they feel seen, heard and valued; when they can give and receive without judgment; and when they derive sustenance and strength from the relationship"

Dr. Brené Brown, Professor at the University of Houston

For six years, between 2007 and 2013, the BP Brand team held ritual deep dive meetings on communication strategy. These featured Duncan Blake and Kathy Leech, directors of brand, advisory executive guests and myself. Our debates always involved two questions.

First – if you removed our BP logo would our communications still look and feel like BP? Internally, this is what we used to call the 'Duncan test', but it might be better explained as the 'Nike test'.

Second – was there grit in the communication, or rather, was there explicit benefits to the audience? We called this the 'Luc test', because I was fixated on the idea that we should only be talking if we had something overtly valuable and beneficial to provide (some help, a gift, an emotion) to our engaged audience.

Both these simple tests were about connectedness – apparently a simple concept that is all about how deep, personal, relevant, emphatic and impactful the relationship is between a brand and the individuals in its audience.

BP on the Street

One of the ways this concept of connectedness came to life was through 'BP on the Street', when we stopped and asked people on the street for their opinions on what we called the energy paradox (Ref. Chapter 1). The world needs more energy but that means more greenhouse gases: how should we do it? Or, renewable energy is better for the environment but more expensive: would you pay more?

We wanted to have this dialogue with society, however hard some of these conversations might become. These 30 and 60 second vox pops were turned into TV ad spots and broadcast nationally.

Duncan Blake is Global Director of Brand at BP. He believes one of the reasons the campaign was so successful is because it was authentic. *"BP on the Street was about real people. It reflected the actual debates that our target group, the opinion formers, were having on energy. We were sometimes accused of manufacturing these interviews, but we absolutely didn't. These were great times for the BP brand, it was becoming truly differentiated."*

"We took a strong point of view with a strong creative platform, we stuck with it and pushed it hard. We became quite famous for those messages in a way that a lot of competitors didn't because they kept chopping and changing their messaging. BP on the Street gave people something to be excited about, beyond the initial brand promise."

I agree with Duncan. This approach was not perfect, but neither was it some slick communication by a big corporate. It reflected the characteristics of an organisation that tried hard to be genuinely engaging and connected. And in the eyes of opinion leaders and opinion formers – our target groups, the BP Brand was indeed well connected and outrivaled others in the sector, as it showed through strong metrics (Ref. Chapter 10).

This chapter is about the transformational power of being a connected organisation in today's world. No connectedness, no Strategic Brand!

Connected brands

Consulting firm iCrossing uses a good description for connectedness: *"A way of thinking about how successful brands do marketing: focusing on audiences, not targets; engaging in dialogue, not shouting; and developing trust that is meaningful and lasting."* (Note 1)

I also like the Diageo approach that the prize of connectedness performance is to make your brand 'truly iconic' rather than 'quietly irrelevant' [Ref. Illustration 4.1]. Clearly you will be looking for the best position for your brand in the 'quadrant' and 'attributes' framework. Where would you position the brand you champion, sincerely?

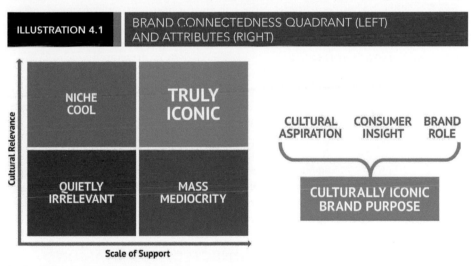

| ILLUSTRATION 4.1 | BRAND CONNECTEDNESS QUADRANT (LEFT) AND ATTRIBUTES (RIGHT) |

Credit – Diageo, Cannes Lions 2015

What are some examples of iconic connected brands? I remember a valuable contribution in *Entrepreneur* in 2012 (Note 2), which expressed the reasons for a brand's unparalleled success from the audience's perspective. It remains extremely relevant and contemporary today:

amazon Amazon – *'Get personal'*. Amazon does an exemplary job at fostering relationships with consumers by helping them make decisions through recommendations of items based on past purchases, user reviews and ratings, and suggested complementary purchases.

Coca-Cola – *'Self-happiness'*. Jim Stengel, former Chief Marketing Officer of P&G observes that everything Coca-Cola does is inspired by the idea of 'how do we promote, develop and create happiness?' They push this message across all points of customer contact.

FedEx – *'Live up to your promise'*. FedEx has elevated the brand by recognising it is not just about logistics, but about the content of the packages it transports - people's treasures, livelihoods and futures. They are thinking of their customers as humans, not just as numbers.

Apple store – *'Keep it cool and fun'*. As much as the Apple (corporate) brand gets low ratings on connectedness, Apple Stores are the opposite. Jim Stengel believes they are *"the best retail endeavour in history"*, as they want people to be inspired, and feel more confident from their store experience. How to make that happen? Hire empathetic people and don't measure them on sales.

Nike – *'Can do attitude'*. Nike has always been customer-focused, with a broad access point that makes the brand relevant to athletes as well as the everyday person. It is about self-empowerment and being your best, and the brand invites everyone to *"Just Do It"*.

Ford – *'Stay consistent'*. Ford forges a strong connection based on stability and dependability. It is perceived to be unique in offering 'concern', by behaving responsibly and caring about the well-being of customers and employees.

Airbnb – *'Belonging'*. The brand was born from and built on open connectedness. We could have selected any of the brands above, and a larger number of other non-American brands, as our Exemplary Strategic Brand for "Connected". As we will see a bit later, we have elected for Airbnb.

THE STRATEGIC BRAND CONNECTEDNESS DIAMOND

In recent years, I have been looking to some structure for getting better at building affinity - and have developed and used the connectedness diamond on Illustration 4.2.

Let's look in more detail at the six component elements in the diamond, which make up connectedness: audiences, purpose, function and emotion, engaged voice, exposure and visibility, and finally impact. When exchanging on this imperative with Syl Saller, Group CMO Diageo, Bart Michels, Global CEO Kantar Added Value and Izzy Pugh,

| ILLUSTRATION 4.2 | THE ENDURING STRATEGIC BRAND CONNECTEDNESS DIAMOND |

© THE Enduring Strategic Brand

Global Head of Culture Practice Kantar Added Value, I used the diamond as the basis of our discussion to make the link with how they approach connectedness to win.

Connectedness Diamond – Audiences [WHO]

Knowing your audience is crucial. The brand must have deep knowledge and understanding of its target stakeholders in order to connect with them. This knowledge will guide the substance and tone of the brand and the relationship between the brand and its audience(s).

In the days following the Deepwater Horizon explosion, a key audience for BP was the population of the Gulf Coast, including fishermen and local businesses which were affected. BP made considerable efforts and searched every way to reach them and explain how they could claim compensation. We had to identify the people who needed help and use the right language and tools to support them. For example, in social media we reached out to the Vietnamese community in their own language, because this was an important group on the Gulf Coast which had been affected and who didn't always understand English.

Every audience will be different, and will connect to your brand in its own way.

"Connected brands look outside their category at the wider world to understand the contribution they should be making to people's lives. At Diageo, we talk about developing a culturally iconic brand purpose."

DIAGEO

Syl Saller explains Diageo's approach: *"Connected brands look outside their category at the wider world to understand the contribution they should be making to people's lives. At Diageo, we talk about developing a culturally iconic brand purpose. Here's how we think about it:*

1. *Start with an aspiration that is meaningful to the core consumer that would earn the brand cultural distinctiveness against its category.*
2. *Understand how this translates into consumer behaviours and tensions that your brand can help overcome.*
3. *Be clear and authentic about what role the brand can play to overcome these tensions and help consumers reach their aspiration.*

SMIRNOFF *"A good example is what we're doing with Smirnoff Vodka (SV). SV is the world's biggest international spirits brand by volume: we sell 26 million cases a year in 121 markets. It's a $2bn brand. But we know there are big risks being bland, so we have to ensure this doesn't happen. We are trying to work out how to make Smirnoff a cultural icon for millennials, as this generation is increasingly defining the future for many brands because of their scale and influence. Legal purchasing-age millennials represent more of SV's volume than any other group. The breakthrough for Smirnoff came when we focused on big cultural insights instead of small ones. We looked at what matters to this generation and what makes them distinct from Generation X or their parents.*

"Millennials are the first completely networked generation. They live their lives online. They create trends, shape politics – and actively use inclusivity for positive change. We've applied this ideal to Smirnoff: our cultural mission is to move the world to be more inclusive. This is a good example of how a brand can contribute to the culture around it in a way that is authentic."

[We will be addressing the challenges and opportunities of connecting with millennials later in this chapter].

Connectedness Diamond – Purpose [WHY]

Purpose gives us the simple reason WHY we connect or interact with a brand. Get this wrong, and everything else will be wrong too. Syl Saller says it all: *"In general, marketers totally overestimate how much consumers care about brands. People don't go out for an SV evening, they go out to have a good time. So if people don't care about your brand, then make the brand the authentic champion of something they do care about. This is easier said than done – but in an image-driven category like ours, it's important to try to make brands cultural icons which transcend their categories."*

"So if people don't care about your brand, then make the brand the authentic champion of something they do care about."

ILLUSTRATION 4.3   DIAGEO BRANDS' CONNECTEDNESS

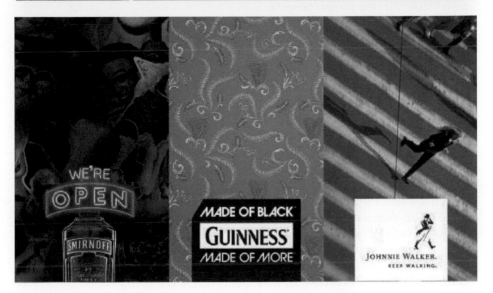

Credit - Diageo

This idea builds on Chapter 1's exploration of Brand Purpose. Here, we are moving and deepening the magic from 'Purpose' to 'Connected Purpose', which is how the brand improves the life of its stakeholders in a relevant way.

Bart Michels explains what connected purpose means to him: *"In the midst of so many other successes, Coca-Cola tried to use music and social media to connect with customers. They ran a viral campaign to create the best new dance move and people sent in videos of themselves. It got a few million views on YouTube.*

This was around the same time that Korean pop star Psy released his breakout worldwide hit, Gangnam Style. This later became the first video to hit two billion views on YouTube. Without referring to precise quantifications, the impact Gangnam Style had on Korean brands like Samsung was real.

Why was the impact of these two YouTube campaigns so different? They targeted the same audience, but Gangnam Style was amusing and tapped into something culturally relevant: it was authentic and didn't appear to have a commercial motive behind it. So connectedness is about adding value to things that people want, in their own context, and doing this authentically."

Bart evokes an absolute 'connectedness' phenomena - whereby humour remains typically very nationally cultural, Gangnam transcended borders. By the end of 2012, the song had topped the music charts of more than 30 countries. Its dance moves were attempted by many political leaders such as United Nations Secretary-General Ban Ki-moon, who hailed it as a "*force for world peace*", U.S. President Barack Obama and British Prime Minister David Cameron.

Connectedness Diamond – Functional and Emotional [WHAT]
This is when 'Luc's Test' might help to assess exactly and eyes wide open WHAT a brand brings to the customer. A brand is truly connected when it is both functional and emotional – i.e. when it does something truly useful, is easy to interact with and creates an emotional bond with the customer, whether that's a desire, a fulfilment or an association.

Most often there is no real difference between functional and emotional – for example, a brand that does something for the customer 'quickly and easily' offers both a functional benefit (being fast and efficient) and an emotional one (a feeling of simplicity, ease and comfort). We reflect more on this compelling combination in Chapter 3 with exemplary brands like BMW – but it's important to remember here how vitally intertwined 'Functional and Emotional' is with 'Connecting' to the customer.

Connectedness Diamond – Engaged Voice [HOW]
A connected brand must develop an individual voice which will make customers feel included and valued. This makes them willing to give discretionary contributions to the brand, such as loyalty and advocacy.

On engagement, story telling is critically important. Using 'brand as a story' allows to connect with the culture and needs of its audiences; and ensuring that story matters to them creates a deeper emotional connection with the customer and increases impact. When John Browne expressed his vision for Beyond Petroleum in 2000, the BP brand became a story of our future world, in which affordable clean energy would be available to nine billion people.

A connected brand should take an immersive cultural approach: to adopt the cultural symbols, practices and expectations of national cultures while remaining true to its purpose, mission and operational framework [Ref. Chapter 2 – Culture]

Wardāh *inspiring beauty* Wardah, a Halal skincare brand in Indonesia, is a good example of cultural connectedness, says Izzy Pugh. "*Wardah understands the world of the women it exists for: it celebrates the desire for adventure and discovery which drives modern women but also offers a beauty which is both unique and modest in a way that is relevant to modern Muslim women (though not exclusive to them). Global personal care brands have to work very hard to deliver something with the same authenticity – and as a result, Wardah is threatening to knock them off the top spot.*"

Connectedness Diamond – Exposure and Visibility [WHERE]
The connected brand must be highly visible and have extensive levels of engagement with its stakeholders. In the forensic digital media landscape, this engagement

and activity must cross a wide spectrum of channels. But it's also about how these channels are used: how social technologies can be leveraged to engage, communicate and collaborate with stakeholders. Once a conversation is started, a connected brand can and needs to cultivate the relationship by providing new content and being in continuous dialogue: gone are the days of one-way, one-shot messaging.

An example of this was how BP managed a 24-hour social media presence to communicate with the impacted population of the Gulf Coast after the Deepwater Horizon explosion and oil spill. When the US was asleep, we used teams in Australia and Hong Kong to ensure we were available around the clock and could post immediately, on the spot.

Channels have changed greatly with the digitalisation of society. But I remain fixated on an old but nevertheless enduring goal for brands: to aim for others to talk about the brand rather than the brand talking about itself. This is achieved when communications are channelled through ambassadors, supporters and communities. A connected brand can 'influence the influencers', which means they have a targeted approach that identifies key cultural influencers who can disseminate the brand's story. These influencers are made up of two different types: '**connectors**' as identified by Malcolm Gladwell in '*The Tipping Point*' – artists, writers, film-makers, musicians, bloggers or cultural conduits who help create culture; and **opinion formers** – consumers who are empowered by social media to take control of brands and culture themselves (Note 3). We will discuss the Utility Warehouse example a bit later.

In BP our key audience was opinion leaders and opinion formers. The rationale was that energy matters are complicated and require awareness and continual attention. If we could progress the debate with people who were involved and connected, they in turn would express their voice to society, politicians and energy-involved communities, and influence them – hopefully favourably.

| ILLUSTRATION 4.4 | MULTIPLE ESSENTIAL CHANNELS AND INFLUENCERS FOR DEEP CONNECTEDNESS |

Credit – Social Media Week

Syl Saller talks about the importance of visibility and exposure – the WHERE: *"Without looking at the world around us, we wouldn't know that 18,000 people attended the last Major League Gaming Championship. That's a stadium full of people watching someone play computer games, and a further two million tuned in to watch it online. These are the kind of adult sports events that we need to learn how to play a part in. The 'Third Place' is a culturally engaged zone and we have to change our business model to be more visible in this area. That's why Smirnoff is investing in the growth of festivals."*

Connectedness Diamond – Impact [HOW MUCH]
Connectedness is of course about impact, about making a difference, about value creation. By using big data, connected brands should measure quantitatively and qualitatively the three areas discussed above: what (function, usefulness and emotional 'brand magic'); how (quality of engagement and feedback), and where (intensity and depth of presence). Strategic Brands will also measure economic outputs to gauge their connectedness, such as net promoter scores or inclination to purchase.

Beyond these rather traditional measurements, there is more to understand and capture about connectedness: something which Bart Michels and Izzy Pugh call the 'vibrancy' of a brand.

SAMSUNG Bart explains: *"Connectedness can provide a good prediction of future growth. We use a proprietary tool called Cultural Traction™and run brand VIBE studies. In essence, the tool breaks down a brand's connectedness in four main areas: how visionary it is, how inspiring, how bold, how exciting. You use proxy measures and can therefore predict if the brand is becoming more or less popular – which means you can make predictions on whether the business will grow faster or slower.*

As a matter of fact, VIBE is a proven indicator of future brand success. I remember a 2010 to 2014 study when we looked at Apple vs. Samsung. Samsung was very active with new products, sponsorship deals and so on – and its VIBE measure turned to be positive while Apple was static. Who would have said then, but what we saw next was Samsung going from strength to strength. For the first time, it was more relevant and connected than Apple – and our vibrancy measurement picked up on this early."

Ford JAGUAR Izzy refers to a similar vibrancy analysis in the car industry. *"When we first did the vibrancy survey, tech brands bagged all the top spots and auto brands were left to languish. But over the last five years, auto brands have climbed up. Ford has made the decision to behave more like a tech brand than a car brand and has climbed 11 per cent. Jaguar also climbed 11 per cent, following its #goodtobebad campaign, which broke the rules of the performance car category and gave the brand a dark side which contrasted with its technologically slick but emotionally less intriguing German competitors. They went on to see their US sales rise by 20 per cent.*

T
T Ξ 5 L Π   *"Interestingly, Tesla took the VIBE number one spot in 2014, passing reigning leader Google and had the highest score ever measured in the previous five years, even beating Apple's 2010 metrics. It had almost double the cultural vibrancy that we would expect to see from a brand of this size. The reason for mentioning this case, even if it brings us 3 years back, is that if you only looked at traditional brand health measures, Tesla would be a niche brand, largely off the grid compared to Mercedes or other luxury brands. However, if you look at its cultural vibrancy, you see a completely different story. And consequence followed – Tesla sold over 50.000 units in 2015, nearly 60% more than in 2014...which was to be followed by over 76.000 units in 2016."*

Consultancy 'Truth' provides a good summary of what we mean by being and communicating as a connected brand and the difference with traditional marketing (Ref. Illustration 4.5). (Note 4)

ILLUSTRATION 4.5	A CULTURALLY CONNECTED BRAND VERSUS ONE 'DOING MARKETING'

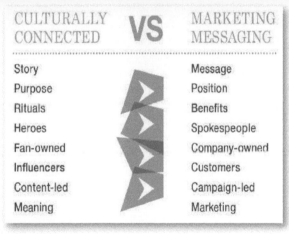

Credit - Truth, January 28, 2015 – Culturally Connected Brands

AN EXAMPLE OF A CONNECTED BRAND - UTILITY WAREHOUSE

THE UTILITY WAREHOUSE   I first learned about Utility Warehouse, UK at the European Business Awards 2014/15 when it won European Public Champion. It is a utility supplier, providing gas, electricity, landline, broadband and mobile services to over 500,000 households throughout the UK. And it has a fundamentally different way of doing business:

First, it is fully integrated: customers benefit from a single monthly bill for all their services (making it much easier for them to manage their household budget) and enjoy better customer service from a single call centre in North London.

Second, it provides its services through the Utility Warehouse Discount Club, which every customer joins to access valuable benefits, such as cash back on their household shopping.

Third, it doesn't advertise or appear on comparison sites. Instead, it works in partnership with 44,000 part-time, self-employed partners who proactively recommend them to friends and family.

ILLUSTRATION 4.6	UTILITY WAREHOUSE CONNECTEDNESS FORMULA AT A GLANCE

Credit - Utility Warehouse

This business model is entirely based on connectedness. Referring to our diamond, it starts with a simple clear purpose, grounded in understanding and dealing with customers' needs. This translates into a clear function, which is to simplify people's lives with an integrated service and save them money on commodities where spending more is a waste. Their engaged voice and exposure is entirely and exclusively human, has the tone of 'a club' and visibility through satisfied customers.

Very distinctive is the way in which a large number of people have become part of the Utility Warehouse community. Satisfied customers follow a curriculum, which starts with becoming active promoters to their friends, neighbours or colleagues, before they potentially graduate to become authorised business partners. They acquire knowledge through the Utility Warehouse 'College of Excellence' and can earn a part-time income. Some of them become champions and heroes, recognised at community events. Utility Warehouse claims to have 44,000 people providing this face-to-face, word-of-mouth marketing, who develop a community-based connection with potential clients and whose life is enhanced in multiple ways through their association with Utility Warehouse. This is an interesting connectedness formula for an emerging company which breaks the code of traditional utility firms fighting customer churn in a commoditised industry.

Airbnb

 We have selected Airbnb as our Exemplary Strategic Brand for the 'Connected' Imperative simply because connectedness is inherently everything the platform is about.

As they define themselves, Airbnb is a community marketplace for people to list, discover and book unique accommodation around the world. Whether a flat for a night, a castle for a week, or a villa for a month, Airbnb connects people to unique travel experiences, at any price point, in more than 34,000 cities and 191 countries. And with world-class customer service and a growing community of users, Airbnb is the easiest way for people to monetise their extra space and showcase it to an audience of millions. It is now so popular that someone books an Airbnb room every two seconds.

Most people know the story of Airbnb co-founders Brian Chesky and Joe Gebbia opening up their home in San Francisco to the first Airbnb guests during the Industrial Designers Society Conference in October 2007. They had a 30-year-old Indian man, a 35-year-old woman from Boston and a 45-year-old father of four from Utah sleeping on their floor. They charged $80 each a night. *"As we were waving these people goodbye Joe and I looked at each other and thought, there's got to be a bigger idea here,"* Brian said.

"They ended up with something more than just an airbed at a slightly messy apartment. They learned our favourite places to grab coffee, ate the best tacos in the city, and had friends to hang out with whenever they wanted. They were thousands of miles from where they lived, and yet they felt right at home. What started as a way for a few friends to pay the rent has transformed into something bigger and more meaningful than we ever imagined."

"Unite a community behind the universal, powerful, human desire to connect, to understand and to belong... and that belonging can take us anywhere."

Airbnb was founded in August 2008 in San Francisco, California to *"unite a community behind the universal, powerful, human desire to connect, to understand and to belong... and that belonging can take us anywhere."* Their participation grew massively and at extraordinary pace, as shown on Illustration 4.7.

| ILLUSTRATION 4.7 | AIRBNB IMPRESSIVE METRICS WERE BUILT OVER JUST A FEW YEARS |

 Total Guest Check-ins
170,000,000

 Cities
34,000+

 Castles
1,400+

 Countries
191

Listings Worldwide
3,200,000

Credit – Based on Airbnb data

Over a very short period of time, Airbnb has become one of the most powerful and loved Enduring Strategic Brands in the world, a poster child for the sharing economy. Illustration 4.8 represents one of the strongest and most consistent Strategic Brands we studied.

| ILLUSTRATION 4.8 | 'THE ENDURING STRATEGIC BRAND' IMPERATIVES - AIRBNB |

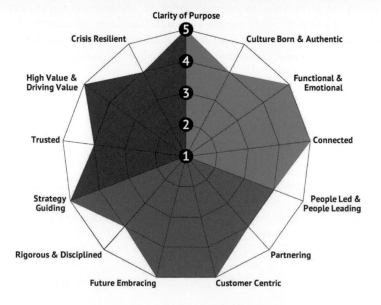

Inherently Connected Airbnb

I was privileged to meet Jonathan Mildenhall, Airbnb's Group CMO to talk about what he believes makes a Strategic Brand and how this relates to Airbnb – and to Coca-Cola, where he worked for seven years before joining Airbnb in 2014.

I was impressed how, without any prompting from me, his first thoughts immediately related to our connectedness diamond: *"First, the brand needs to have a mission that transcends its product category. Quite a lot of brands fail because they don't understand how to create emotional value outside of their product category. Looking at Coca-Cola and Airbnb: Coca-Cola's mission is to create a world of more happiness; Airbnb's mission is to create a world where all 7 ½ billion people can belong. Today this is just in homes – but tomorrow it will be across the travel industry. This mission is never going to be achieved in my lifetime, but it feels tangible, because every single home on the platform and each new person we put in someone else's home, creates a world with a deeper sense of belonging and trust. So the number one priority is to create a brand purpose.*

"Coca-Cola's mission is to create a world of more happiness; Airbnb's mission is to create a world where all 7 ½ billion people can belong."

"The second priority is to create an iconic mark that is instantly recognisable and universally understood. There are some amazing ones, like the Nike Swoosh and the Apple logo. These mean the same, whether you are in China, South Africa, Brazil or Canada.

"The third priority is to create a universal ideology. Companies like Disney are incredible at creating a universal value proposition across all sorts of different facets of their organisation. It doesn't matter if I am a South African mum, a Korean mum, or a Japanese mum, Disney's value proposition for my family is consistent.

"The final ingredient is to have a clear understanding of your human values. Think of Coca-Cola's Small World Machine in India and Pakistan, which allowed Indians and Pakistanis to connect with each other and virtually share a bottle of Coke. That had nothing to do with selling Coca-Cola but put the brand's human values out there into the world.

"It's the same with Airbnb's 'Mankind' campaign: a little baby is walking to the door and you hear Angela Bassett's voice say: "Is man kind? Are we good? Go see. Go look through their windows so you can understand their views, sit at their tables, so you can share their tastes, sleep in their beds, so you may know their dreams. Go see, and find out just how kind the he's and she's of this mankind are". https://www.youtube.com/watch?v=Dxy4IIVE8IQM. *We weren't trying to put another home on the platform or trying to sell a night, we were just putting our human values out there.*

"Finally, a brand needs the bravery, confidence and commitment to put content into the world that has nothing to do with selling the category or selling the specific aspects of the business but everything to do with promoting the human values that the brand cares so deeply about."

In less than four minutes, Jonathan distilled how Airbnb is outperforming on the five interlinked Strategic Brand imperatives of 'Connected', 'Clarity of Purpose', 'Functional and Emotional', 'Future Embracing' and 'Strategy Guiding'. Illustration 4.9 shows how the characteristics of the Airbnb brand relate to the connectedness diamond - we comment below on the power of each pillar.

ILLUSTRATION 4.9	AIRBNB PERFECT CONNECTEDNESS DIAMOND

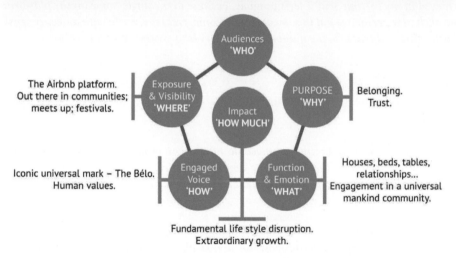

© THE Enduring Strategic Brand

As said, the fact and the matter with Airbnb is that they are all and entirely about connectedness. Let's look at how this plays out, from their purpose to even their brand logo and its 'connected' shared utilisation.

Clarity of Purpose; Functional and Emotional Airbnb

Airbnb is a coherent brand whose purpose, function and emotion is embodied by its mark. Here Jonathan shares his thoughts about the Coca-Cola, Nike and Apple marks, and his ambition to make the Airbnb logo synonymous with 'belonging anywhere'.

Coca-Cola *"Coca-Cola was one of the first brands to establish an iconic mark – with the contour bottle. That bottle was designed to remain cold and to mean the same thing all over the world. It was even the first 3D structure designed so that a blind person could feel what it was. Coca-Cola then took that 3D structure and turned it into a 2D iconic symbol, which is universally understood and symbolises Coca-Cola's* mission to 'inspire moments of optimism and happiness'. The bottle design is now 102 years old, so Coke has been practicing this belief for over a century.

NIKE "The Nike swoosh was introduced about 45 years ago and stands for speed, excellence and performance all over the world. It is consistent and inspires exactly the same thing in a young Chinese basketball player as a British soccer player.

The Apple logo is the world's most valuable mark. It doesn't mean as much culturally as they haven't spent a lot of time consistently building cultural values into the brand – but it stands for product excellence. And, like Coca-Cola and Nike, it has a coherent meaning all over the world.

"We named our marque, the 'Bélo', ourselves. It is the first four letters of the word 'belonging', but we put an accent over the 'e' so it sounds more international. Over the next decade, our job is to make this marque the universal symbol for a world of belonging.

"There are actually two different logo approaches for Airbnb. On the one hand, we have the company marque called the Bélo and on the other we have a range of community symbols that anyone in our community can apply to their homes or businesses. This is called "Create Airbnb."

"Essentially, the Bélo is protected, in the way that Apple has protected its trademark. But we also share the design to reflect how we are a community of individuals, powered by people of different backgrounds and beliefs, each with their own outlook and own story. With 'Create Airbnb', we are letting everyone create their own unique symbol under a shared identity, in a way that has never been done before."

ILLUSTRATION 4.10	THE TWO TYPES OF AIRBNB LOGOS

The Bélo   Create Airbnb

Credit – Airbnb - Left: the Bélo. Top right: the four meanings behind the logo - People, Places, Love and Airbnb. Low right: examples of unique symbols from 'Create Airbnb'.

Future Embracing; Strategy Guiding Airbnb

It's not surprising, given Airbnb's mission, that its guiding strategy embraces a bigger future. Jonathan explains:

"If P&G is about moms, Airbnb is about hosts. And historically, you had to have a home to be a host. Our launch at the end of 2016 changed this, making it possible for people to host, even if they don't have a home. This is a different sort of hosting, around an experience. For example if you have a passion for fly fishing, hiking, art culture, wine tasting or horse riding, Airbnb will make it easy for you to host others and share this passion.

"In November 2016, we had our fourth festival of hosting in Los Angeles, with over 20,000 hosts from all over the world. The big news was how we are redefining Airbnb hosting. Now, you can even earn money by hosting your passion on the Airbnb platform."

Airbnb, a community-driven Strategic Brand

Airbnb has already disrupted and transformed the hospitality sector. Now – with its unique connectedness – it aspires to be the world's first community-driven super brand, disrupting the traditional ways in which people come together.

Jonathan explains: *"What does 'community-driven' mean? What are some of the world's best community-driven brands? Examples lie outside the world of brands: the religious organisations, political parties, soccer clubs, etc. All of these communities have traditions, rituals, beliefs, and hierarchies – but without people turning up to take part (at church, on political stands, at football practice, etc.), the community cannot exist. This means that these community brands are driven by the behaviours, traditions and characteristics of the community itself.*

"Super brands like Nike, Apple and Coca-Cola are iconic, universally understood and fiercely protected by the marketers that run them. Historically they have taken on their status as icons without mobilising or involving the creative expression of the people who buy from them."

Culture Born & Authentic; Customer Centric; Partnering Airbnb

"There has never been a super brand driven by the creativity, fingerprint, energy and stories of its community. We build who we are from mining the stories in our community which we turn into marketing content.

"We want to create a community-driven super brand by unlocking the creative power of a community. This has never been done before.

"We will build our traditions in the same way that other communities have – for example in gathering the community together. We have local and regional host meet ups and the

*annual international hosting meeting like the one we had in Los Angeles. These celebrate
the business of our human community.*

*"We built the technology to allow the different Airbnb communities to talk to each other,
share problems, ask questions. Our hosts can connect with others through community
chat rooms all over the world."*

Like eBay before them, Airbnb understands that its hosts are not simply customers
but business partners. Every year, more than 5,000 hosts from over 100 countries are
invited to the company's Airbnb Open and encouraged to talk about the nature of their
work. This connects the local hosts into the global Airbnb community and also helps
the company understand how they can serve them better.

There are many other examples of the cultural connectedness made possible by
Airbnb's partnerships. Do you want to stay at the Abbey Road studios, where the
Beatles recorded (Illustration 4.11, top left)? Or at the Art Institute of Chicago, where
Van Gogh's famous bedroom has been recreated (bottom left)? Or drive an Audi to an
Airbnb location in the most desolate part of Death Valley (top right)? Or spend a night
at Grandpa Max's Rust Bucket, as a fan of Ben 10 (bottom right)?

ILLUSTRATION 4.11	AIRBNB CONNECTEDNESS THROUGH DEEPLY CULTURAL EXPERIENCES

Credit - Airbnb

Airbnb: The next level of connectedness is engagement

The idea of engagement takes brand connectedness to a different place. Jonathan: *"I
wear Nike trainers every day. I am very connected to Nike. But I am not engaged with
the Nike community at all.*

*"We want to change this at Airbnb. We want people to not only be connected to us, but to
be engaged with the brand. This is about participation.*

"We want to change this at Airbnb. We want people to not only be connected to us, but to be engaged with the brand. This is about participation."

"The need for belonging is primal. Airbnb has been successful because we've tapped into something deeply rooted in the human psyche all over the world. Ultimately, the Airbnb brand belongs to the community."

Rigorous & Disciplined Airbnb

How does Airbnb ensure that the ideas of community engagement and brand building succeed in practice? Jonathan: *"This is down to three things: first, to establish and inspire the community to practice the right behaviours and expressions of belonging; second, to enable the community to connect to each other in depth; and third, to protect the community by doing our absolute best to ensure that every home, every exchange and every interaction is safe. Inspiration, enablement and protection are the role of the company; the role of the community is to drive the involvement and engagement from there.*

"We are rigorous about measuring our impact through data. We run a weekly brand tracking study in most markets, alongside a more detailed quarterly study. We measure brand awareness, brand sentiment, consideration and how relevant belonging is in expressing itself in different markets.

"Airbnb is a 21st century brand, so we don't have to deal with a legacy of meaning in people's minds. Hence we can both build the brand and its mission of belonging at the same time. Brand tracking has shown us that the idea of belonging is already intimately tied to the brand."

"Airbnb is a 21st century brand, so we don't have to deal with a legacy of meaning in people's minds. Hence we can both build the brand and its mission of belonging at the same time."

People led & People leading Airbnb

Airbnb's mission makes the brand entirely people-led and dependent on how people in the community act. Airbnb controls less than 10 per cent of the consumer / renter experience, and not much more of the host's delivery and experience. Hence, the brand is the outcome of its users' interactions with each other, with over 90 per cent of the Airbnb brand dictated by its users, rather than corporate leadership. In short, people in the community define the brand.

So how does the Airbnb brand provide guidance for its community brand definers? Jonathan: *"We ask every host to sign our 'Discrimination and Belonging' Community Commitment from October 2016, which made it clear that if you want to be an Airbnb host, you have to aspire to these kind of values. We will use lots of carrot and a little bit of stick to make sure that our values are protected across the community."*

Strongly Performing Connected Airbnb

It is notoriously challenging to get details about Airbnb's financials because of its shareholding structure. But we have sufficient evidence from various sources showing that the Airbnb brand is both driving considerable value creation and is extremely valuable itself.

High Value & Driving Value

According to the US investment bank Cowen & Company, Airbnb should have processed $12.3 billion in reservations in 2016, an estimated 70 per cent increase over 2015. A related assumption is that the company's own revenue from these reservations might have reached $1.6bn in 2016, as Airbnb receives between 6 per cent and 12 per cent commission of the guest payment and 3 per cent of what the host receives.

On recent occasions, both in July 2015 and in July 2016, Airbnb has successfully filed for successive capital raising. It also secured a $1bn debt facility in June 2016 from a pool of banks. The July equity round of $850 million values Airbnb at $30 billion. This makes it the second most valuable private start up in the San Francisco Bay Area behind Uber Technologies Inc (Ref. Illustration 4.12, middle picture). But Airbnb spends far less money than Uber, which gives it the robust prospect of being eminently profitable.

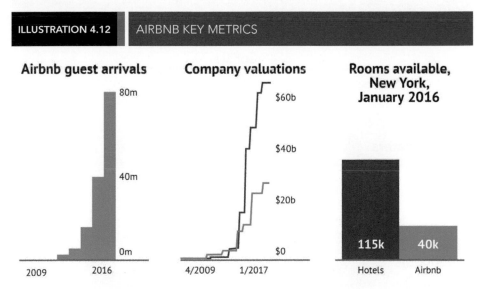

| ILLUSTRATION 4.12 | AIRBNB KEY METRICS |

Credit: Airbnb; Cowen & Company

This is extraordinary value creation from a company only founded in 2008. A lot of this value can be attributed to the Airbnb brand. Multiple surveys (Ref. Cowen & Company, Goldman Sachs) point to travellers being far more satisfied with Airbnb than with the average hotel stay (3 to 1 ratio). And in general, Airbnb attracts very strong favourability ratings. Therefore it wouldn't be surprising if Airbnb's brand value was at least similar to the highest level brand value of hotel chains – which is over $8bn.

Trusted Airbnb

Trust is inherent to Airbnb's business model: the whole company operates on the belief that people trust each other enough to stay in one another's homes - there is an interesting YouTube video from February 2016 by Joe Gebbia, one of the Airbnb founders, in which he shares his philosophy on *'How Airbnb Designs for Trust'*. https://www.youtube.com/watch?v=16cM-RFid9U

The role that trust plays is reflected through the following data points: Airbnb has hosted 123 million nights (and counting); hosts' rating of Airbnb is 4.9 out of 5; there are over 500 million connections between Airbnb and Facebook.

The Airbnb stakeholder map is by no way simple, as represented on Illustration 4.13. With 90 per cent of the brand experience in the hands of others rather than itself, deep connected trust is required with those who form the natural Airbnb community - the hosts, guests, partners and, as much as possible, with audiences that might be or are hostile – hotels, neighbours, municipalities. As noisy as it gets sometimes in a few cities, Airbnb demonstrates excellence of stakeholder management in 34,000 others.

ILLUSTRATION 4.13	AIRBNB SIMPLIFIED STAKEHOLDER MAP

Crisis Resilient Airbnb

As we discuss in Chapter 13, it is insightful to test an Enduring Strategic Brand against opposition, challenges and any ongoing or potential crisis. So, if Airbnb epitomises connectedness, how does this manifest in a crisis? Airbnb has encountered significant criticism and opposition in its time. I will use the following case from New York as an example of a main challenge it faces (though there have been similar problems in Berlin, Amsterdam, Barcelona and Quebec among others).

Following a 2011 New York State ruling prohibiting the renting of residential units for less than 29 days, New York Governor Andrew Cuomo signed a bill in October 2016 prohibiting Airbnb hosts from listing unoccupied apartments for less than 30 days. Proponents of the law – represented mainly by hotel unions and some New York City officials – say this is an issue of affordable housing and the bill is a way to oppose commercial operators to *"take thousands of units that they control, which could be rented to permanent New Yorkers, and turn them into one-night or two-night stays."* Their main argument is that Airbnb is depriving permanent New Yorkers of a place to rent, including many that were at one time occupied by New Yorkers and now are occupied by tourists.

Airbnb hosts argue, *"It is just part of the sharing economy, in that Airbnb allows people to share their homes, and has nothing to do with affordable housing. Instead, Airbnb offers opportunities to 'everyday New Yorkers' who engage in responsible home sharing, as hosts. It offers solutions to tourists and provides a material source of revenue for New York"* - an estimate of $90m a year.

ILLUSTRATION 4.14	AIRBNB SUPPORTERS PROTESTING THE LAW AND OPPONENTS RALLYING AGAINST AIRBNB

Credit - Andrew Burton/Getty Images; New York Daily News

What was remarkable – and a reflection of the deep connectedness of Airbnb's community – was the rally organised by the New York Host Clubs from the city's five boroughs. Boxes containing over 80,000 messages in support of home sharing were also delivered to Cuomo's office - Airbnb describes Host Clubs as *'host-led local organisations that drive initiatives to better their neighbourhoods'.*

Jonathan reflects on how these challenges are approached by Airbnb and its hosts: *"One of Airbnb's roles is to protect the community: in turn the community has fantastic engagement with Airbnb. There are community action networks all over the US which help Airbnb hosts to operate in the way they'd like. Here Airbnb sticks to its role, to inspire and protect the community in different cities. It's the community itself which actually drives the action and the engagement."*

The New York mobilisation for Airbnb is far from unique. In its fight with San Francisco last Fall, a 'people-to-people voting bloc' of hosts, guests and supporters knocked on hundreds of thousands of doors and attended each and every legislative hearing to defeat Measure F, a bill that would have more tightly regulated home sharing in the city. Or, after the Chicago host club made 42 visits to legislators and 1,500 phone calls to elected officials, Chicago passed a set of Airbnb-friendly regulations that allow the company to continue to operate in the city. And there are many more stories like these.

Isn't this the definition of brand connectedness, when your 'customers' become your best activists? From the beginning, Airbnb built strong relationships with its hosts, bringing them together in their own local online groups. As the platform has grown and faced greater scrutiny from city regulators, Airbnb hosts have taken unique steps as community action networks, with local chapters and volunteer teams, to attend hearings, write letters to elected officials and meet other activists locally. Anticipating a larger fight, Airbnb plans to grow its 64 local host clubs to 100 new cities around the world.

Learning from Airbnb : Just Connect!

Airbnb is showing the way with the company's intuitive understanding that your community, your customers are the best marketing asset you have. Brian Chesky, co-founder and CEO of the firm said that the best piece of advice he ever had was, *"It's better to have 100 people love you than to have 100,000 people sort of like you"*. That's how you keep connected (Note 6).

It's better to have 100 people love you than to have 100,000 people sort of like you.

Airbnb has adeptly transformed the challenge presented by a lack of control of the customer experience into the biggest opportunity and greatest success of their brand. A symbiotic relationship with their community gives Airbnb the ability to collaborate and build the brand together with their connected stakeholders. This brand is so much more than a tour operator – it's about creating the space for the personal connections that their community forms.

Of course, platforms lend themselves to this system of brand building. Using technology, they enable the exchange of value between user groups that is not directly owned by the platform itself. However, I would argue that traditional companies also have a lot to gain – particularly on growth and risk management – from building a strongly 'Connected' Brand and applying some of Airbnb's best in class principles and practices.

Deepen the connections between your brand and your audience - that's where the magic happens. That's where the joy begins. And perhaps John Lennon's beautiful words will apply to your Enduring Strategic Brand, in the way he hoped they would apply to the world: *"You may say I'm a dreamer, but I'm not the only one. I hope someday you'll join us. And the world will live as one"*

THREE OPPORTUNITIES FROM GREATER BRAND CONNECTEDNESS

So where and how to apply Airbnb's magic? We have chosen three audiences where connectedness plays a vital role but arguably only a few brands do a good job at truly connecting.

First, we will review two crucial generations: millennials and the silver generation. Second, we will reflect on global brands versus local brands, because, as I also experienced during many years of leading global branded businesses, global brands face the continuous and growing connectedness challenge versus local champions.

Millennials

Connectedness is crucial for millenials. In fact, some would label them as the connected generation. As Syl Saller mentioned earlier, this generation is defining the future of many brands because of their scale and growing influence. This is backed up by simple demographics: there are 1.8 billion millennials and by 2025 they will represent 75 per cent of the workforce. They are the first completely networked generation, unconstrained by geographies or culture.

To connect with them properly, it is important to have a thorough understanding of their needs and codes and how these differ from their parents or from Generation X. Broadly speaking, this generation could be labelled 'pragmatic idealists', with the following characteristics:

Where they come from: Children of the digital revolution; globalisation; successive crises and sharing economy
Who they are: Narcissistic although team players; non-hierarchical; educated; open minded to change; optimistic; in haste; unfaithful; engaged; entitled
How they live: In the moment (instant messaging); definitely possess but share; in community (local and global); permanent content creators; early adopters of useful technology

What are they expecting: They have very high expectations in general:
- At work, fast advancement, good salary, coaching relationship, change;
- Develop wealth and financial security;
- Make the world a better place

And what they expect specifically from brands:
- 'Useful is the new cool' and brands need to enhance their lives;
- Brands should entertain them, co-create with them, share feedback with them;
- Brands need deep authenticity: millennials are also called 'corporate hackers'; they are very sensitive 'bullshit detectors', hate brands that are about nothing more than the bottom line and/or appear to fabricate manipulative marketing.

Together with the marketing agency Foresight Factory, we ran and analysed quantitative surveys throughout 2016, which showed what millennials consider priorities for brands as having a connected character: 'reputation', 'similar to me', 'genuine'. By contrast, the priorities for baby boomers were more functional and with direct impact on 'me': 'quality', 'making me feel good', 'value for money' (Ref. Illustration 4.15).

ILLUSTRATION 4.15	TODAY'S PRIORITIES FOR SUPERMARKET BRANDS – GENERATION Y AND BABY BOOMERS

From more (1) to less (not numbered) important
Credit: The Foresight Factory; THE Enduring Strategic Brand

Clearly there is much about the millennials that calls for intimate connectedness from brands. Illustration 4.16 shows how the brand essentials for this generation relate to the connectedness diamond. Is your brand deliberately making these connected essentials central to your practice in order to succeed with millennials?

ILLUSTRATION 4.16 | CONNECTEDNESS PRIORITIES WITH MILLENNIALS

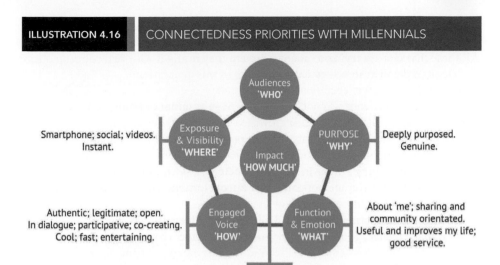

Smartphone; social; videos. Instant.

Deeply purposed. Genuine.

Authentic; legitimate; open. In dialogue; participative; co-creating. Cool; fast; entertaining.

About 'me'; sharing and community orientated. Useful and improves my life; good service.

Word of mouth.

© THE Enduring Strategic Brand

The Silver Generation

My advisory role to the UK Government's Cabinet Office helps me understand different society mega trends more deeply. One that has struck me the most recently is the staggering increase in the age of the world population – as represented on Illustration 4.17. We all know this is happening, but perhaps don't often look at the real numbers and take full consequence.

ILLUSTRATION 4.17 | 2 BILLION PEOPLE OVER 60 IN 2050

Projected acceleration of world population aging

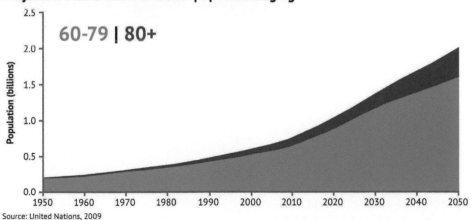

Source: United Nations, 2009

The ageing population has already impacted many industries: leisure, transportation, food, insurance, residency, health, safety, communications, the Internet, sports, retail... All these markets are trying to adapt – but are they doing it with real connectedness? Let's look in detail at some key characteristics of this generation:

Where they come from: Baby boomers are 55–69; seniors are above 70; consumer society; employment and economic growth

Who they are: Materialistic; ambitious; opportunistic; desire personal growth; have work ethic; questioning

How they live: 'Young', often in denial of their age; with purchasing power (30 per cent more than the average population in Europe); many are still working; children focused; consuming; using technology

What are they expecting from brands: Extensive information; value for money; best quality; make me feel good; 'keep me young and engage with me accordingly'.

Illustration 4.18 shows how the brand essentials for this generation relate to the connectedness diamond. While many brands are already trying to connect to the silver generation, there still remains a huge opportunity to perfect this connectedness and unlock one of the main sources of growth on earth. What about your brand?

ILLUSTRATION 4.18	CONNECTEDNESS PRIORITIES WITH THE SILVER GENERATION

Multi-channels, including traditional. Content marketing.

Audiences 'WHO'

Exposure & Visibility 'WHERE'

PURPOSE 'WHY'

Proving and ethical. Successful.

Impact 'HOW MUCH'

Informative; Precise. Feel good; Feel younger.

Engaged Voice 'HOW'

Function & Emotion 'WHAT'

Quality; Value for money. Useful and improves my life; good service.

Loyalty. Share of wallet and upgrade.

© THE Enduring Strategic Brand

Global brands, local brands

If enduring performance relies on achieving connectedness, many global brands have done a sterling connectedness job up to this point. But how can they continue to do so in face of some key trends in our fast changing world? With our BP customer-facing brands, we wrestled with the important question of brand architecture: we faced the strategic alternatives of, on the one hand, the power of global brands and, on the other, the intimacy and relevance of a local brand.

Where is the trend going? The high performing CPG brands – P&G, Unilever, Nestle, General Mills, Danone, etc. – have a stone in their shoe: the rise of local brands. In its July 9th 2016 edition, the *Economist* wrote about a study on how this manifests: the Dollar Shave Club controls 5 per cent of America's razor market; Daniel Lubetzby's fruit-and-nut bars have invaded airports and Walmart stores; Yunnan Baiyao Group is now accounting for 10 per cent of the Chinese toothpaste market; Botica Comercial Farmaceutica represents 30 per cent of perfume sales in Brazil and Ghari Industries 17 per cent of detergents in India. In the US, large CPG companies lost 3 per cent of market share between 2011 and 2015 (Ref. BCG and IRI study). (Note 5)

Illustration 4.19 represents the continuing relative decline of global brands versus local brands. It should be noted that the global market continues to grow – but this trend is a revealing indicator of how global brands are not always sufficiently connecting with their consumer base.

ILLUSTRATION 4.19	GLOBAL BRANDS' LOSS OF SHARE TO LOCAL BRANDS

Decline of global and rise of local brands, % share

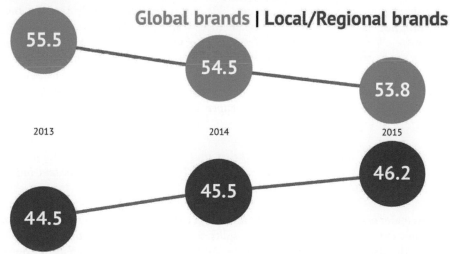

Global brands | Local/Regional brands

| 2013 | 2014 | 2015 |

55.5 · 54.5 · 53.8

44.5 · 45.5 · 46.2

Source: Kantar Worldpanel - GFK - IMRB - 2015 - FMCG

Picture 4.20 nails the point by showing how the leading brand in any market is local, with a continuing trend in this direction.

ILLUSTRATION 4.20   NUMBER ONE BRANDS ARE LOCAL BRANDS, UNIVERSALLY

Credit - Kantar World Panel 2016

There are multiple reasons for this shift: a greater trust in smaller brands, an appeal for craft versions of products, extra convenience through proximity trade, targeted innovation, environmental or societal considerations, and so on. But what all these come down to is cultural connectedness.

Two years ago, Martin Sorrell, Group CEO WPP cleared his calendar for two weeks to visit around 20 Chinese companies. He reminded me recently that on media consumption habits, Chinese are in advance – and also: *"Chinese companies have become much more competitive. So if you take the yoghurt category - Yili and Mengniu, it's not Nestlé versus Danone, it's Nestlé or Danone versus the local competition. In fact, Danone is linked up with Mengniu. So, Procter shouldn't worry about Unilever and Unilever shouldn't worry about Procter. They should be more worried about that little company in India that's doing the one rupee sachet of shampoo and will swamp the market.*

"And the reason they're being successful is that they're starting to think about their business as brands, connected to their customers. The same thing would be true in India, Brazil and Russia".

So can major brands hear, understand and adapt to local customer cultural aspirations? Can they develop the required *"speed, agility and dexterity of a start up"*, to quote Tim Cofer, Mondelez Chief Growth Officer? Can they, in effect, do what Yili has done in China – as related by the Kantar WorldPanel in Illustration 4.21?

| ILLUSTRATION 4.21 | BEST IN CLASS LOCAL CONNECTEDNESS- YILI IN CHINA |

BUILDING CONSUMER TRUST THROUGH INNOVATION

It is no surprise that the majority of brands seen on this map are local champions, developing products which effectively identify and celebrate the cultural appetite of the people buying them.

2015 saw home-grown brands Colanta and Yili rise to the number one spots in Colombia and China, fending off other beloved local brands.

Growing its CRPs by 5% in 2015,

Chinese dairy brand Yili is a masterclass in innovative thinking from the boardroom to the billboard. Its chairman, Pan Gang, led the management team on a tour around Europe to visit Yili's multinational peers, trade bodies and academic groups.

Together, they challenged their own creative techniques and exchanged ideas around corporate culture, precision management and food safety, in a global context

Meanwhile, its marketing department leveraged the brand's extensive portfolio to build mental availability and drive growth. The premium UHT brand, Milk Satine, registered growth following a nationwide marketing campaign which used popular Chinese singer, songwriter and actress Wang Faye as the brand ambassador.

QQ Star, Yili's flavoured milk drink sponsored the reality television show Dad! Where are we going? popular among its target audience: children and

parents. This resulted in an impressive 14% value growth for the brand.

Driven by fresh thinking at the top and brilliant execution on the ground, Yili retained its solid reputation among Chinese consumers and rose to the top of the country ranking for the first time. Yili boasts exceptional rates of penetration (88.5%) which means that it is bought by nine out of 10 Chinese urban households.

Credit -Kantar WorldPanel

Think how it goes in practice for a global brand: it can get off to a good start, with local connected teams on the ground getting the correct cultural vibes - differences in taste, needs and wants, economics etc. It then often gets more challenging, as any required adaptation to the offer, the design or the communication will go through the debating and the convincing of corporate and matrix management. At best, the connected 'locals' will eventually win the case...but it will take time - and there is often the case of losing it.

The question becomes: with the fast growing digitally led individualisation, is connectedness (or lack of connectedness) going to change business models? The *Economist* analysis argues that CPG firms might increasingly become more like big pharmaceutical companies, which acquire small firms or join up with them, handle marketing, distribution and regulation, but attempt to protect their brand.

Can disciplined 'glocalization', the mix of globalisation and localisation, be the structural solution? McDonalds is very often cited as the benchmark, being fierce at protecting its consistent customer experience and branding, while adapting to sub-groups (national or others) through local menus, varied advertisements etc.

Similarly, Diageo's Syl Saller remains determined and encourages global brands with her mantra, *'Global campaigns shouldn't compromise to meet everyone's desires.'* Her formula is clearly the sweet spot of impact and value generation, and guides the work of global brands to develop offers and communication that combine a global idea with culturally connected executions.

'Global campaigns shouldn't compromise to meet everyone's desires.'

BUILDING REAL CONNECTIONS

For all three audiences, connectedness means two things. First, it's about cultural connectedness as a deep understanding of where they come from and how to fulfil their needs. Second, it's about the physical connectedness, using the right channels, the right tools and the right intensity to engage meaningfully with them.

The ultimate form of application of Airbnb's recipe will be to get your customers or stakeholders connect for you, do part of your 'marketing', be your advocates, act as your campaigning community; they are entirely connected to your brand. And for each of them and through their own channels of communication, it will work!

It takes me back to the Deepwater Horizon crisis, somewhat discontent. Many of our branded dealers, the business people who ran the BP service stations and retail outlets, asked then how they could help more. As you can imagine, we had extensive exchanges and ran joint campaigns but our plans turned out to mainly be about protecting them. In hindsight, it was an inadvertence not to use and benefit from their impact more than we did.

These local business people were embedded in the local Gulf Coast or broader US communities, sponsoring the local sports teams, exchanging news with locals as they refuelled their cars and trucks, etc. Their community-connected presence had what the corporate brand didn't have: they could have been our strongest local advocates reinforcing the understanding of the situation and the respect for BP's gigantic efforts in their localities. It was largely a missed opportunity that I wish I had forced through more, as deep connectedness in crisis is best practice.

Never again such blind spots…thanks to Airbnb!

CHAPTER 5
PEOPLE LED AND PEOPLE LEADING

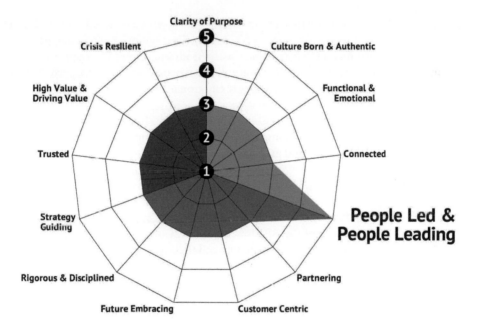

"Great companies make meaning. A company has a name but its people give it meaning."
Richard Pascale, business consultant, author and professor

I feel very privileged to have met, worked with and developed strong relationships with extraordinary people. And to have witnessed the unique impact people make on others, on organisations – and of course on brands.

One late afternoon in October 1994, at Burmah House in Swindon, John Ellicock and I were talking. John was a Board member of the Burmah Castrol group, in charge of Europe – a man I have always had great respect for. Along with HR and a few others, we spent the best part of the day discussing the role of a Castrol Country Chief Executive. This had followed a multi-month selection process, which I had just survived. Ultimately, John handed a file to me and said solemnly: *"From now, you are the brand!"* This was his way of saying that he had decided to appoint me as CEO of the Castrol Brand in France – and the document was my contract.

Castrol One of my first actions as CEO was to visit a regional team and some of their customers in Normandy. The regional director had prepared a breakfast presentation and, in the grand Castrol tradition, showed a couple of films of the brand engaged in motorsport. They were all about people, enthusiasm, performance, winning - and I found them overwhelmingly emotional.

I was 37-years-old and had been continuously involved in branded businesses before. But these two separate events gave me goose bumps: this brand would be under my skin forever, turning my blood red and green, its two colours.

Never before had I felt so deeply that a brand is the people and the people are the brand.

I would never forget this and when BP acquired Castrol, I stayed at BP for the people. I then remained a member of the BP Downstream ExCo HR Committee for over ten years, where we cared for about 75,000 people and their leadership globally.

"Your people are your product"

This observation by Richard Branson, the founder of Virgin says it all on the intrinsic link between brand and people. I believe this relationship plays in two ways, with the brand both leading people and being led by them.

People Leading
A Strategic Brand acts as people's guide, and becomes their ultimate reference framework, providing boundaries and, most importantly, space to take decisions on a continuing basis. As elicited in Chapter 2 and represented in Illustration 5.1, the brand journey starts with culture, from which purpose and values are derived. Strategy is then developed in tune with the organisation's soul. These form the brand foundations and the anchors for people to make judgments and act - ideally doing the right thing without needing to be told.

People led

With a neat symmetry, every employee is a brand ambassador. There can be no Strategic Brand if people in the organisation do not stand behind it - every person must embody and epitomise the brand. Michael Kouly, President and CEO at the Cambridge Institute for Global Leadership says: *"The culture of a company is the sum of the behaviours of all its people"*. This relationship between employees and brand translates into an authentic daily expression of the brand. It is a genuine, unconstrained inside-out. No slick marketing here, just normal people projecting the human face of the organisation to the world.

ILLUSTRATION 5.1	THE PEOPLE LED INSIDE-OUT VIRTUOUS CIRCLE

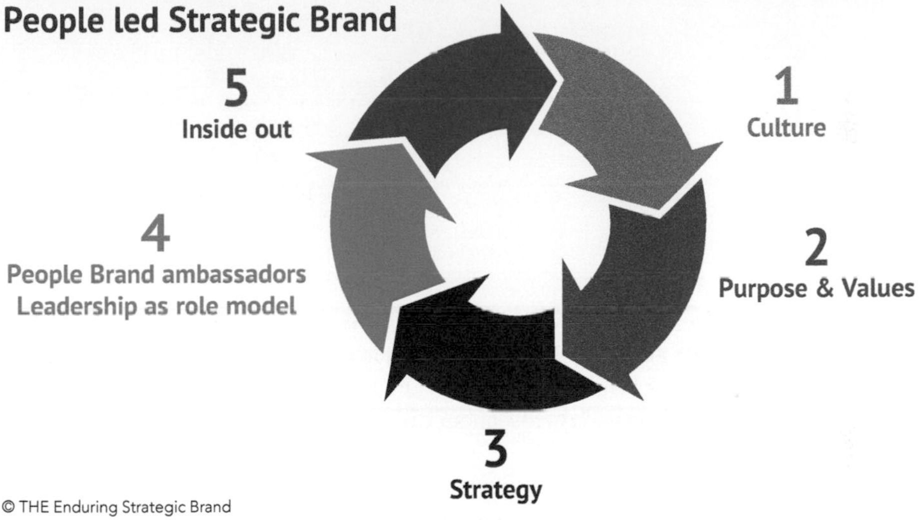

People led Strategic Brand

5
Inside out

1
Culture

4
People Brand ambassadors
Leadership as role model

2
Purpose & Values

3
Strategy

© THE Enduring Strategic Brand

In practice, a 'People Led' Strategic Brand organisation is truly 'One Company', structurally networked and operating through cross-functional task forces. Similar to a honey bees' hive, it has structured communication, complex construction, environmental control and defense and division of labour. It attracts and develops the best talent, and is driven by purpose and satisfaction rather than short-term profit.

The two themes of 'People Leading' and 'People Led' are deeply symbiotic. As 'People Leading' has been largely discussed in chapters 1 and 2 – purpose and culture, the vast majority of what follows will be focused on 'People Led' and notably on the organisation and leadership needed to build Strategic Brands.

Four main groups impact the Strategic Brand

Four main groups make up the human network of any organisation as it relates to its brand: its plural stakeholder base; its extended workforce; and two important individuals - the CEO and the CMO.

ILLUSTRATION 5.2   THE STRATEGIC BRAND PEOPLE INVERSED PYRAMID

The Strategic Brand Inversed Pyramid

Organisation's stakeholders, extended work force, promoters

Organisation's workforce

CMO

CEO

© THE Enduring Strategic Brand

We will reflect consecutively on each. How do they make or break a Strategic Brand? How are they behaving and how should they act? How does a CEO appoint their CMO and against which profile? What enables a CEO and his/her CMO to work in tandem and succeed with their brand mission? How about turning the CMO into a transformational 'Chief Value Officer'?

ORGANISATION'S WORKFORCE: THE BRAND ASSOCIATES

Nobody is more important to the Strategic Brand than each employee, the very people who make the brand come alive for your stakeholders and customers. A Strategic Brand is the best way to connect employees to your products and services. Without that connection, employees will undermine the expectations set by your offer and communication.

Tony Hayward comments: *"When I took over at BP, we had allowed Beyond Petroleum to go too far into the 'renewable world', where it became disconnected from what 90% of the people in BP were doing every day. The task was therefore to reconnect many thousands of people to a brand that they could relate to. Your brand has to link to what your workforce does. We made it real."*

Greg Welch, Senior Partner at Spencer Stuart based in Chicago, has recruited many of the most recognized CMOs in the USA. He talks about the Strategic Brand as a rallying cry inside the company. *"In many large companies, it is important that every person feels good about the brand and becomes an ambassador, whether they be in finance, in customer service or in the store. In order to have a brand-led organisation, you need to make sure that all people are positive ambassadors for the brand. So job one of a Strategic Brand is the idea of creating a rallying cry inside the company."*

Apply best strategic marketing to build internal engagement with the Strategic Brand

By applying many of the principles of external practice to internal communications, associates can be offered a much better understanding of the Strategic Brand which almost unavoidably leads to deeper engagement.

I have come to rationalise the brand 'inside' best practice around eight principles:

1. Choose the right moment - Turning points are ideal opportunities for a brand restatement, by clearly and vividly articulating what makes the company special.

bp
BP seized the opportunity when it merged with Amoco, ARCO and Castrol and launched 'Beyond Petroleum'. This break with the past gave employees from each of the original companies a new and distinctive identity. A survey taken after the launch of the internal branding campaign showed that 76 per cent of employees felt favourably toward the new brand, 80 per cent were aware of the brand values and 90 per cent thought the company was going in the right direction.

New leadership is another opportune moment for internal rebranding. Staff expect to hear from a new leader right away and are usually open to new ideas at such times. Carly Fiorina exploited this window when she took over Hewlett-Packard.

2. Link internal and external marketing – Associates need to live and hear the same messages that are sent out to the marketplace. At most companies, however, internal and external communications are mismatched.

WPP's Martin Sorrell comments: *"We estimate that over half of our work is aimed internally rather than externally. Get the internal communities on your side, all your employees and suppliers aligned with what you want to do and your other stakeholders supportive. Brand building is not just about externalities, it's about internalities and getting your people to live the brand."*

IBM When it comes to execution, the most effective way to link internal and external marketing campaigns is to create external advertising that targets both audiences. IBM used this approach when it launched its e-business campaign. It took out an eight-page ad in the *Wall Street Journal* declaring its new vision, a message directed at both customers and internal stakeholders. This is an expensive way to capture attention but, if used sparingly, it is a powerful form of communication.

NIKE At Nike a number of senior executives are called "Corporate Storytellers." They deliberately avoid stories of financial successes and concentrate on parables of "just doing it", reflecting and reinforcing the company's communication and ad campaigns.

3. Bring the brand alive for employees – The goal of your internal brand development is to create an emotional connection to your company that transcends any one particular experience. In the case of employees, you also want the connection to inform the way they approach their jobs, even if they don't interact with customers.

As John Hayes, former American Express CMO for over 20 years, shares in chapter 7, *"it is not just one department who is worried about the brand – the brand stewards are just about every employee, to deliver the service experience every day to the 118 million card customers"*

Designed to invite associates into the reality and emotion of the brand, a professional internal brand campaign takes very similar forms to a consumer campaign – it includes a set of stages that start with research and continues through the planning and execution of the communications strategy. It should be a joint Marketing and HR Department responsibility.

4. Don't preach - One of the reasons employees scorn internal marketing materials is that they are usually developed from on high and therefore seem out of touch with day-to-day business realities – or even worse are patronising. Brand leaders should draw on research to identify what employees are actually thinking - and how they express it - and then develop materials that reflect employees' own language.

bp When BP rebranded, it created a film for employees that broke the conventions of the form by using rank-and-file employees, rather than managers, to explain the brand vision. Rather than reading from scripts, they articulated genuinely their own hopes and aspirations for the company.

5. Emphasise beliefs and purpose rather than intentions - Beliefs and purpose reveal much about what the company is at its core. Such beliefs shouldn't change over time.

Intentions describe how business objectives will be achieved. While intentions are necessary, beliefs are more inspiring to employees as they give something to care about. They should be the focus of internal campaigns, which means that before choosing a course of action, employees will consider how it serves their belief and purpose.

6. Make the communication medium part of the message - To capture the attention and imagination of your audience, you will have to surprise and intrigue—and the same old memos and dry presentations will accomplish neither. Indeed, the form of the message can say as much as the content.

When BP wanted to instill confidence in the newly merged company, it gathered hundreds of facts and stories from all the divisions and listed them in a huge document that became known as *The Scroll*. You didn't have to read the whole thing to get the point. The symbolism of the almost biblical presentation gave it gravitas, and when the document was posted throughout the company, it became an object of pride.

7. Design materials to fit the purpose – BP's *Scroll* worked because the point was volume—the cumulative impact of the stories, not the details of each one. But if you're counting on people actually using the materials you send out in their day-to-day work, they should be designed with ease of use in mind. An enormous book, no matter how beautiful, will almost certainly be left on the shelf and its contents easily forgotten.

When IBM wanted to communicate why the Linux open-source movement was important to the company, it issued a little pamphlet, something like Chairman Mao's little red book, which people would carry with them to meetings.

8. Have fun and be joyful - In an effort to be thorough, companies often create internal communications materials that are self-important or just plain boring. This can be avoided if you inject joy and a little humour or style.

When Volkswagen relaunched its brand with the "Drivers Wanted" ad campaign over a decade ago, the company created a film to explain the brand vision to staff and dealers. Forgoing the usual speeches and beauty shots of cars, the film took the form of a whimsical journey of two young people setting out on a Saturday morning to do some errands, intercut with slogans that captured the new spirit of the brand. The film was a phenomenal success, communicating the brand in a way that no PowerPoint presentation ever could—and it even became the basis for the first commercials in the television campaign.

INSPIRING PEOPLE AT RBS

There are multiple exemplary brands on the 'People Led and People Leading' imperative. Although not perfect, a revealing indicator is how good it is to work for a company. In October 2016, *Fortune* magazine published its annual report of the 25 best global companies to work for, with Google, SAS Institute, Gore Associates, Dell and Daimler Finance as the top five and Hyatt and Mars not far behind (Note 1). We studied all these cases and found considerable evidence of symbiosis between associates and their enterprise brand.

RBS However, we chose Royal Bank of Scotland (RBS), the third biggest UK bank as a brand case instead. Not that RBS is a finished article but because the bank is on a fascinating journey as it works to re-establish its reputation following a taxpayer bailout in 2008 and aims to become "the most trusted bank by

2020". And its story offers a slice of realism – for this is a space where many other companies find themselves.

RBS: A people-driven approach to brand

A critical step in RBS's journey was the appointment of David Wheldon as its first ever Group CMO in the summer of 2015. CEO, Ross McEwan commented: *"The creation of this position sends a clear message about how we want to do business and move the bank on to a new footing. Last year we set out to make RBS the number one bank for customer service, trust and advocacy and have already made progress in becoming a simpler and fairer bank that puts the needs of customers at the core of everything we do."*

A Brand leader with purpose
David is also President of the World Federation of Advertisers and Chair of the Marketing Group of Great Britain and we have known each other for a long time. Here is how he reflected on his appointment as we were talking recently: *"I am not an expert in financial services. I was hired because I am an expert in brand and we are going to be a brand-led bank. It is that notion that the brand is the destination, because it's the brand that builds relationships and reputation."*

David firmly believes that brand, strategy and people are very closely linked; *"If I look in my trajectory, people got confused about business strategy and Strategic Brands, as though they were separate things and actually - they're the same. As a marketer, you need to be aware of this: you've got to use the right vocabulary in the right place. And if you don't put the word 'strategic' alongside 'brand' and do not prioritize people, you're probably going to get marginalised."*

In a service-led industry like banking, the people must embody the brand. They are its most important ambassadors. For David, the RBS people are intrinsically tied to the notion of Strategic Brand: *"We're going to make this the place where anybody who does this kind of thing wants to work. We've got very engaged colleagues - they will help create very engaged customers and build loyalty. And when we have got more engaged customers, they will buy more from us. That's how we will become number one. And if we do all of that, they might even advocate for us."*

Slowly, deeply, systematically
But how to make this happen? David acknowledges that a fundamental part of building a Strategic Brand is to partner with HR and works closely with Elaine Arden, the Chief HR Officer, RBS Group - more of this later. Here are some primary principles he follows:

Brand essence - David uses three simple pillars of common purpose, common values and common language to align everybody around the goal and the vision. *"We have* *to create an emotional connection to our people internally. It builds confidence and excitement and then only can you follow that externally."*

"And you go slowly. If there is anything I have learned, it is that this takes longer than you think - because we have got to share what we're doing and take everybody with us. We have got to get levels of confidence up, because we've only got one chance to get this right."

Leadership - David stresses the importance of being a full member of the executive team to provide the required breadth of leadership, as he experiences now at RBS.

I agree wholeheartedly with David and when at BP, there was one thing I insisted on during my over 10 years as Group Vice President - that was to sit in the Downstream HR Executive Committee, where most leaders and people are nurtured. That gave me the reality of people and leaders and the ability to contribute through the lens of the brand.

Systematic training - Marketing and HR have developed a training system of how RBS works, called 'Determined to Lead', which is a systematic approach to delivering better service. David admits: *"The young version of me would have sneered at that. Now I go: That's fantastic, that's the operating system that we are going to attach to."*

Rewards - Delivering better service must be supported with the right kind of employee rewards and remuneration system and David acknowledges that this has changed. *"In a bank, we can't reward people like we used to - so we are changing that. Of course, investment bankers still get paid more than most people but it gets more balanced.*

"For the frontline staff in RBS branches, we have removed sales incentives and focused our colleagues on serving customers well. They get paid fairly in accordance to this priority and we develop and train them, so they are professionally equipped to take on whatever is coming in the world. We also strive to make it a stimulating and nice place to work, celebrate success and say 'thank you' for the good things they do.

"And we point out things that they might learn and give them a real ability to show up and pursue who they are and what they want to do."

Consistency -The complexity in this strategy lies in implementing it into other areas of the business – for example in the corporate bank where employees expect to be incentivised on what they sell. However, David says that they are increasingly measured on what they do and how they do it as well as the straight financial performance delivery.

Draw outcomes - Is it working? David admits that when this new approach was first introduced in the retail bank, a lot of people thought sales figures would plummet - but this is not the case. And *"customer satisfaction has gone through the roof "*.

Brand and HR as One in RBS

Responsible for 90,000 people worldwide, Elaine Arden understands better than most the requirement for the partnership: *"David and I are working together so well because the strategy, the purpose and the vision are all about the customer…and customers are delivered through our people. The imperative of the right interaction is ensuring there is a strong connection between everything we put externally - our brand communication - and how we live this internally"*. Elaine comments on joint principles which she and David apply:

Principled – *"When I first met Ross McEwan, he was working in an Australian bank, CBA. And he described to me how they had transformed from nowhere to being number one for customer service. And he said: "When we reflected on what made the difference, it was care for the customer. And if you are trying to emphasise care for the customer, you have to demonstrate care with your people. And not just the people who interact with the customers, but people everywhere in the company and how we interact with each other - with care."*

Simple – Elaine's 20-year career in HR has taught her that intellectual and complex behavioural change programmes don't stick. She prefers a practical approach: *"When we are looking at service behaviours across the organisation, we focus on a few practical ideas like 'take ownership and follow up' or 'be proactive.' We train people on it, have dialogues about it, allow people to call each other out on them. We keep it simple. There are consultancies all over the place keen to run complicated programmes for front-line and internal service people but actually it comes down to a few core human behaviours."*

Support – Elaine has a team of over 100 performance coaches working with the senior leaders of the bank to effectively practice their skills. *"This is really specific. We literally write down the coaching goal and then observe the individual and give them feedback. It's incredibly practical."*

Measure – RBS builds up four simple core behaviours, which will be measured in appraisals as well as the annual staff survey. And their most senior few hundred people are measured on how they've led these core behaviours. *"One of the tenets in the leadership model is the power of consequences; both positive and negative ones. Because no consequences, no attention. And we will be fixated on measuring if anything happens as a result"*

Continuity – Elaine admits that she is very protective of the 'foundation stones', as she calls them, and does not allow them to be, *"tinkered with or tainted with or refreshed and renewed too often."* She explains: *"We defined four simple values (Ref. Illustration 5.3) and ran day-long events with over 10,000 people, trying to translate them into 'what will I do about them'. It took two years before we had high recognition of 'I know what the values are'."*

ILLUSTRATION 5.3   RBS BRAND PEOPLE CENTRIC VALUES

Our values

We have a single, simple purpose – to serve customers well.

This is at the core of our ambition to build a bank known for its consistent, high quality customer service.

We want to be trusted, respected and valued by our customers, shareholders and communities.

We have put a common set of values at the heart of how we do business. Our values are not new, but capture what we do when we are at our best:

Serving customers

We exist to serve customers.

We earn their trust by focusing on their needs and delivering excellent service.

Working together

We care for each other and work best as one team.

We bring the best of ourselves to work and support one another to realise our potential.

Doing the right thing

We do the right thing.

We take risk seriously and manage it prudently.

We prize fairness and diversity and exercise judgement with thought and integrity.

Thinking long term

We know we succeed only when our customers and communities succeed. We do business in an open, direct and sustainable way.

All this comes together in Our Code.

Credit – RBS

"Some people in head office got bored and were pushing to change some words. We went: 'No, because it takes years and we should focus on embedding, simplifying or connecting them better. Haven't we learned that the amount of happiness or value you think you get from tweaking or changing in comparison to actually getting greater embedding across 90,000 people is minuscule?"

David and Elaine are at pains to point at that they are still at the beginning of the journey. *"We are already doing great work in some places, but we're not doing it consistently well everywhere. When the different parts come together it can really start to work. It's the behaviours and actions that are the most difficult but this is what drives the most performance. It's a bit of an experiment in holding our nerve but this is how you turn around organisations, this is how you change behaviour."*

As we heard from both David and Elaine, CEO Ross McEwan is central to their joint brand journey – but are all CEOs as inspired?

THE CEO AS BRAND CHAMPION

While everybody in an organisation is vital to a brand, the CEO makes or breaks a Strategic Brand. As John Ellicock told me when I became CEO, Castrol France: *"the CEO is the brand"*.

It was Apple's Steve Jobs who brought the concept of CEO as brand to a new level, imbuing computers with his own personality and sense of aesthetics. As he said, *"A lot of times, people don't know what they want until you show it to them. It was an idea that made us want those products before we knew what they were"*.

This strong identification between CEO and brand can play out well on the bottom line. Because when it works, it's a thing of beauty, it's about connection. Who got excited about buying a computer before Jobs's passion made us want to be first to touch the latest Apple product?

John Browne also imbued the BP Strategic Brand, building trust and authority and bearing the idea of 'doing the right thing', especially with Heads of States and Governments. Consequently, he guided the build of the best Exploration & Production portfolio in the sector at the time.

A personal selection of iconic leaders to their organisation's brand

I have been fortunate to meet and work closely with a number of Strategic Brand CEOs – and some of them have become friends.

For the power of evidence, let me signal out just a few of the 'big' leaders whom I believe deeply equate to their organisation's brands:

 Dr. Shoichiro Toyoda, Fujio Cho and Tekashi Uchiyamada deeply epitomise the Toyota brand – and we are discussing how in Chapter 2.

The President of the International Paralympic Committee, Sir Philip Craven imbues the movement's brand values of determination, equality, inspiration and courage. When talking to him, you feel like the most important person on the planet; together with his deep humanity, he demonstrates outmost determination, a case in point being when he decided to exclude the Russian team from the Rio Paralympic Games in the name of inspiration and equality.

Jeff Immelt powerfully lives and projects the GE growth values of external focus, clear thinking, imagination and courage. I have seen him tirelessly sharing his vision with others and mobilising people. I have observed his readiness to take accountability for tough choices and humility for deep learning.

Sir Frank Williams fascinates with his courage, an absolute imperative in Formula One. Over a couple of decades, he took the highest risks in changing the team's motorists from Renault to BMW, BMW to Toyota, Toyota back to Renault and then Mercedes. It was not because the previous option was not good; it was because it was not good enough in the circumstances.

Each of them in their own way is the Brand!

Global iconic leaders for their brands

The CEO as 'the brand' can be upmost for brand visibility. CEO mentor Martin Roll, calls it the *"romance of leadership"*, explaining, *"Media and customers want to attribute the success and failure of brands to some top executive."*

ILLUSTRATION 5.4	EXAMPLES OF CEO RANKINGS

TOP 10 BEST CEO REPUTATIONS

Reputation Management Consultants (RMC) 2015	Fortune Magazine December 2016
Tony Hsieh (Zappos)	Mark Zuckerberg (Facebook)
Richard Branson (Virgin)	Jeff Bezos (Amazon)
Mark Zuckerberg (Facebook)	Mary Dillon (Ultra Beauty)
Marc Benioff (Salesforce)	Larry Page (Alphabet)
Mary Barra (GM)	Satia Nadella (Microsoft)
Larry Page (Google)	Brad Smith (Intuit)
Russell Simmons (Def Jam)	Jen-Hsun Huang (Nvidia)
Tim Cook (Apple)	Cheng Wei (Didi Chuxing)
Arianna Huffington (The Huffington Post)	Rodney Sacks (Monster Beverage)
Elon Musk (Tesla)	Jack Ma (Alibaba)

Credit – Reputation Management Consultants; Fortune Magazine

Contemporary CEOs are center of attention and of greatest influence to their enterprise brand and, in a wider sense, to society. Illustration 5.4 provides measures of their individual impact, as reflected by various surveys.

The truth is that putting a human face on a company adds connectedness. We can identify with J K Rowling's struggling to publish her Harry Potter novels. We feel a part of her story and have a human connection to the woman who gave life to one of the most successful franchises in the history of publishing. Every enduring brand has a story, and making that story about someone gives us something we can deeply and emotionally relate to.

The key role of a Strategic Brand CEO

Similarly, employees feel inspired when they are working for a person, not a concept. Stories about Walt Disney and Steve Jobs still energise the workforce of their companies giving employees a real sense of purpose in their jobs. They set the tone.

"Brand is about walking the talk, so if you've got a CEO who is not behaving consistently with the brand, you've got a big problem."

Tony Hayward reminds us first principle for success: *"Brand is about walking the talk, so if you've got a CEO who is not behaving consistently with the brand, you've got a big problem. I was a big advocate of the relaunching of BP in 2000 with 'Beyond Petroleum'. I was one of John's key lieutenants. By 2005, I realised it had gone off track, and was disconnected from what most of our people did day-to-day and it didn't resonate with me any more. The journey to bring it back was straightforward because I wanted the brand to reflect what I felt. I think with 'all of the above' (Ref. Chapter 10) we got it to a place where it resonated again with people. Everyone could connect with this idea, whether you were in renewables or producing oil in the Gulf of Mexico. It reflected the company.*

"If you want to change culture, change the people - a brand shouldn't be the cold stuff of an organisation. A brand should represent how you think about the world, what you do when you wake up in the morning, what you do every day, it should be a guide."

If you want to change culture, change the people - a brand shouldn't be the cold stuff of an organisation. A brand should represent how you think about the world, what you do when you wake up in the morning, what you do every day, it should be a guide. And that's where 'Beyond Petroleum' started – but then we went wrong. I remember giving a talk to newly recruited Amoco employees just after the merger. They were business unit leaders and I was describing BP through its brand. It was not about advertising, it was about how the brand represented the way we think about our business, how we conduct our business, and how I believed it was the pole star."

The individual versus the brand: being a Strategic Brand CEO

Being a Strategic Brand CEO requires the ability to embody the organisation's culture, purpose, mission and values. You must be an absolute role model for the organisation – while also being authentically yourself.

When talking about my time at Castrol and BP, I say that my blood flows in the brand colours, because this metaphor describes the way that I lived the brand. Tony used similar language about BP, saying: *"When you have spent 25 or 30 years in a company, like me, you assimilate a lot of what the company is about over time. If you cut my head off, what would flow would be yellow and green. Undoubtedly, a CEO has the ability to impress on the brand components he or she fundamentally believes in. But what he or she believes in would have been shaped by 25 years of experience - in my case in BP: what I've done, what I've experienced, places I've been to. It might have been different if I was someone from outside."*

Tim Stevenson, former CEO of Burmah Castrol and current Chairman of Johnson Matthey, talks about the responsibility of the CEO in terms of being a caretaker. I recently asked him how 'being the brand' influenced his own personality. Did it lead to the conscious act of doing things differently because it was in service of the Castrol brand and that was more important?

"I remember our chairman Jonathan Fry saying, before he appointed me: 'When you become Chief Executive of Castrol... before you answer, think hard, it will age you.'

"What he meant was that the pressure of the role was substantial and came with a huge sense of responsibility, of being a temporary caretaker of a great tradition. Any major strategic decisions you made, in terms of how the business was to be run, needed to be taken with considerable care for the quality of the brand and its future. And that was a considerable pressure which, combined with all the responsibilities of a very substantial job, a global company and lots of travel, puts a lot of strain on you as an individual.

"What major effects did it have on me? Probably two: one was the need, when making big decisions, to stand back and see them in the context of the history of the company, where the company had come from and how it had got there.

"Second, I had to think hard about the characters, dispositions and outlooks of the people that I put in the most senior positions in the company. Whether they were the sort of individuals who would understand what Castrol as a brand was all about and would treat it in an appropriate way."

And here we come to the crunch: the ultimate goal is to marry excellent performance with being a Strategic Brand CEO, making both mutually reinforcing.

The founder CEO versus the corporate CEO

It's not a coincidence that many of the Strategic Brand CEOs ranking high on reputation are also founders - Virgin's Richard Branson, Facebook's Mark Zuckerberg, Zappo's Tony Hsieh, Google's Larry Page.

The trick is ensuring their Strategic Brand lives, breathes and thrives as their leadership changes. John Seifert points out that many of these founder brands go to talk with leaders of 100-year-old brands. *"If you ask the CEO of American Express, he's inundated with requests from new economy. Because they want to understand the lessons and learning of brand and trust building over generations. They are not naive to the fact that their model could easily be replicated and made irrelevant if somebody who is more trusted, more enduring or whatever figures it out."*

Castrol One company that has managed the difficult transition from founder to corporate leaders is Castrol. Tim believes that Castrol's tone was set many years ago by its charismatic, persuasive founder, Charles Cheers (CC) Wakefield, who founded the business in 1899 at the age of 39 selling lubricants for trains and heavy machinery. There is a famous photograph of him exercising with his staff on the flat roof in Wakefield House in the middle of the morning. Tim recounts: *"In the 1930s this was remarkable, ahead of his time, but I think it set a tone. There was in a sense part of the culture that you were employed by someone who minds about employees and is going to look after you - and being fit and healthy is part of that."*

In the new century, Wakefield took a personal interest in two new sporty contraptions – the automobile and the aeroplane. The company started developing lubricants especially for these new engines, which needed oils that were runny enough to work from cold at start-up and thick enough to keep working at very high temperatures. Adding a measure of castor oil did the trick nicely. They called the new product "Castrol."

Having helped invent a new kind of motor oil, CC Wakefield pioneered a way of getting customers to notice the product: sponsorship. The Castrol name appeared on banners and flags at competitive aviation events, auto races and at speed record attempts. When a Castrol-sponsored event won, ads heralded the victory, mentioning that the winner had done it with Castrol. The world land speed record was broken 23 times in the 1920s and 30s, 18 of them with Castrol in the engine.

Tim also believes that telling these stories about the founder was a way to keep the brand living and plays a critical role in strategic decision-making. *"Our chairman Jonathan Fry was a built-in marketer for the brand. At any opportunity, he would get up and tell the story about Wakefield. I remember him in meetings, when we were talking about the Formula One sponsorship, he said: "Before we go any further in this conversation, let's all ask ourselves, what Charlie Cheers Wakefield would have done - would he have spent this money or not? " We all thought: "he'd have spent the money". And then our strategy director was saying: "how do we assess what value we're getting out of it?" Of course, it's very difficult to put metrics on a sponsorship of that sort and the strongest answer was,*

"Well, that's what Charlie Cheers would have done and it worked for him, so we'll do it."
Clearly, the history of the company and the strength of the brand played an important part
in strategic decision-making at that time."

The risks of the CEO as prevailing Brand Ambassador

However, using CEOs as chief brand ambassadors for a company comes with risks. What happens when the personal relationship between the CEO and the customer is called into question? Similarly, when company leaders get in trouble, employees see it as a personal betrayal.

For both external stakeholders and employees, the opportunities and risks associated with a CEO who is a brand ambassador can be compounded by the fact that the 'best CEOs' stay in their post a long time [Ref. Illustration 5.5)

ILLUSTRATION 5.5   HOW LONG A CEO STAYS IN THEIR POST

18%	37%	31%	14%
2-7 years	7-12 years	12-17 years	17-20 years

So what does this say about the relative risks and rewards of building a brand around a company's leader?

I have already written about the circumstances surrounding John Browne's resignation in Chapter 1, suffice to say that in 2007 his motivation to resign was deeply branded: *"to save BP from embarrassment,"* and therefore protect the brand and the people.

The type of leaders who feel comfortable as brand ambassadors often don't entertain the idea of succession planning. Employees, customers and investors want the company to outlive the 'big leader'. In fact, they expect it. But many strong leaders aren't contemplating leaving, so they resist grooming a successor.

How do you succeed Steve Jobs? Is Tim Cook instilling a similar brand energy in Apple? Who will succeed Paul Polman at Unilever as the incarnation of 'Sustainable Living'? Or Ratan Tata at Tata & Sons, Richard Branson at Virgin, Mark Zuckerberg at Facebook?

If an organisation wants to outlive a high profile leader, its reputation has to be based on more than just that one person's personality. It must be rooted in all 13 Strategic Brand imperatives in a comprehensive and balanced manner. CEOs can be the face of a company, but not its full heart and soul.

Zappos' Strategic Brand CEO taking an inside-out approach

One of the best examples of a 'People Led' Strategic Brand organisation is Zappos, the online shoe retailer famous for customer service, partly because it attracts the best talent, driven by purpose and satisfaction.

Zappos Zappos' CEO, Tony Hsieh believes that companies who care about their bottom line should make their employees feel like a family.

Returning to David's earlier points about the challenge in incentivising RBS staff beyond financial bonuses, Hsieh offers all new hires $2,000 if they decide to quit after the initial five-week training programme. He told Business Insider: *"We want to make sure that employees aren't just here for paychecks and truly believe this is the right place for them…We've always prioritised company culture and how we treat employees."* (Note 2)

Hsieh's customer loyalty team answer phone calls 24/7 from customers. They are not held accountable for call times and not rewarded for upselling. What they care about is going above and beyond for every customer. Some customer care stories have become folklore. Their longest phone call with a customer lasted six hours while she looked at thousands of pairs of shoes. When a loyal customer revealed she'd forgotten to mail back a pair of shoes because of death in the family, she was sent flowers.

Hsieh's track record for transparency is just one example of a CEO embodying the brand values. Early on as leader, he used Twitter to personally respond to customer compliments and complaints. He encourages everyone on his team to do the same, clearly demonstrating one of the brand's core values of 'building open and honest relationships with communication and be humble.'

At Zappos we are all about blurring lines. Our goal is to hire employees whose personal values match our 10 core values, so every employee is automatically living the brand, at home, in the office and in social media. You can't force employees to be like a family – they actually need to want to do it themselves.

Hsieh is the perfect illustration of a CEO who believes in an inside-out approach to the brand. In a CNN interview about workplace happiness and the bottom line he said, *"rather than focus on work-life separation, we focus on work-life integration. At Zappos we are all about blurring lines. Our goal is to hire employees whose personal values match our*

10 core values, so every employee is automatically living the brand, at home, in the office and in social media. You can't force employees to be like a family – they actually need to want to do it themselves."

He also has a refreshing marketing perspective on social networking which chimes with the idea of a people-led Strategic Brand. *"For us, Twitter, Facebook, YouTube, blogs, etc. are all ways we can connect with our customers and employees. We're not looking at them as marketing channels, more as connection channels, the same way we view the telephone as a great way to connect."*

Hsieh doesn't believe that the notion of 'happy customers' and 'happy employees' should be classified as a quirky business metric. *"The reason why we aren't seeing more companies in corporate America focus on these things (yet) is because the payoff from a financial perspective is usually two to three years down the road. Many companies are focusing on the current quarter or current year at best. The good news is that information is moving faster and companies are becoming more transparent whether they like it or not. As a result, the lag time between brand and culture is becoming less - in the long run I think the 'good guys' will win."*

The CEO–CMO tandem is critical to the Strategic Brand

WPP's Martin Sorrell has a clear view on the role of a CEO and a CMO to the brand: *"Brand is leadership, leadership, leadership. If the CEO absolves himself or herself of the responsibility for the brand, you have a problem. If they delegate, it says 'this is not important enough for me'.*

"The CEO should be the brand guardian and have a brand vision – and then have a CMO who shares that vision and is given the power to implement it. But 50 per cent of the CEOs in the FTSE 100 are ex-CFOs. Brands need to be differentiated by tangible factors, such as product performance and price, but also intangibly – because they make the consumer feel better and the brand says something about them. And you need to create that from the top."

The CEO should be the brand guardian and have a brand vision – and then have a CMO who shares that vision and is given the power to implement it.

Spencer Stuart's Greg Welch reaffirms his belief that a symbiotic relationship between the CEO and CMO is vital to a Strategic Brand. *"When I sit back from my ringside seat and evaluate which companies are doing well, which C-Suites are rowing in the same direction, which brands are winning in the market, the common thread I often find is a naturally marketing-centric CEO. The CEO and CMO of the Target Corporation in the US are a good example - over generations of leaders in these roles, you have a marketing oriented CEO and a world-class CMO. And the CEO sets the tone for the CMO to thrive.*

When I evaluate companies and say: Why is Company A doing well and Company B is not, I often find at the root of the healthy ones that the CMO has an honest and open working relationship with his peers. They are all on the same page and there are no hidden agenda".

RBS's David Wheldon reflects on his own relationship with CEO Ross McEwan: *"I believe that the CEO of a service company is the brand director, is the ultimate owner of the brand and must cherish it more than anybody else. I say to Ross: 'you represent the brand, you are the brand'. So when you're talking to people and bringing your direct, honest, cool and calm voice in the crisis we're in, this is perfect, because that's what the brand is'.*

"You also have to be brave enough to say when things don't work. So I tell him the truth, when things are going wrong, and I think most CEOs suffer from people not telling them the truth. It is about building on the human side of the truth although anchoring it into the business performance. It takes a while to build that trust, but if you were talking to him he'd probably say it was about finding the right person to do the job."

As brand focused some CEOs might be, they have a lot of other things to do and simply can't give justice to nurturing, growing and yielding the brand. They need a strategic CMO in unison, to provide undivided attention to lead on this. Think of amazing such tandems discussed in this book: Ross McEwan and David Wheldon at RBS; Paul Polman and Keith Weed at Unilever; Brian Chesky and Jonathan Mildenhall at Airbnb; Jeff Immelt and Beth Comstock – more recently Linda Boff at GE; Thomas Bach and Timo Lumme at the IOC; Gini Rometty and Jon Iwata at IBM. Think of the primordial impact as Strategic Brand leaders of Ian Robertson at BMW, John Hayes at American Express, Nina Bibby at O2, Syl Saller at Diageo - and I can't name them all.

REFRAMING THE CMO'S CENTRAL ROLE IN THE ORGANISATION AS 'CHIEF VALUE OFFICER'

Greg believes the CMO should be the heartbeat of an organisation: *"Somewhere the heartbeat of the company needs to pulsate. I believe the heartbeat, the centre of the brand in most companies, needs to sit with the CMO. This needs to be a loud, consistent, colourful voice. I also use the words 'disciple' or 'orchestra leader' to illustrate the idea that someone needs to be the architect, the owner and the keeper, the shepherd of that brand. And I think the CMO is the best person to do that.*

"For example, if I am a CMO at Apple, I'd get incredible latitude to be successful as an executive in the company and drive the business because of what I already know about marketing, technology infrastructure, customer relationships, the P&L, customer acquisition. Although it's a difficult job, I think it's a great place from which to lead."

"I want all my CMOs waking up thinking about the customer and the brand. And feeling that their mission is: "if I own the customer I'm going to be successful". Whereas a CEO, obviously, has other things they need to be entangled with, so I don't think there is a conflict of interest in any way."

What type of CMO should a CEO appoint?

The world is changing fast and, as ever more crucial the CEO - CMO tandem should be, we will observe next that the CMO role is often getting increasingly unclear and disconnected from the value heart of the enterprise.

In chapter 12 – Value, we are making the case that brands need to be at the heart of the company's value creation model – and that each brand has its own specific business model.

In this midst of this upheaval, who is your CMO for the modern age? How to advise CEOs to frame precisely and be to the point on the profile of their ideally suited CMO? Symmetrically and as a CMO, where and how can you create most value and thrive personally?

Who is your CMO for the modern age? How to advise CEOs to frame precisely and be to the point on the profile of their ideally suited CMO? Symmetrically and as a CMO, where and how can you create most value and thrive personally?

As a CEO, who is my ideal CMO?

How does it come that Linda Boff at GE is not a marketing lifer; nor is Michelle Peluso at IBM, Stephen Odell at Ford and nor was I? Why is that Jonathan Mildenhall at Airbnb, David Wheldon at RBS, John Hayes at AmEx are world class discipline-born strategic marketers? And irrespective of backgrounds, we all have the same mission to transform the brand.

I am spending considerable time reflecting with CEOs, CMOs and Search firms on this question. And have come to believe that, in modern strategic marketing, the Enduring Strategic Brand CMO should ideally be that of 'Chief Value Officer', someone who can profoundly influence sustainable value generation and growth. As a case in point, the recent Coca-Cola move to create a 'Chief Growth Officer' role in lieu of a CMO is revealing - an opportunity to wish the very best to Francisco Crespo in this new position.

Over the final pages of this chapter, I will outline what a Chief Value Officer - CMO might look like and a framework for CEOs to select their ideal CMO - and for CMO to approach their role more strategically.

Is the CMO role being 'dumbed down'?

Against all evidences of their ever-growing importance, CMO and Marketing's role in organisations seems increasingly unclear. There are multiple factors moving marketers far and fast away from their traditional comfort zone. Illustration 5.6 summarises some of the transformational factors in the business environment which are leading to a rethink.

ILLUSTRATION 5.6   DUMBED DOWN…AND HEIGHTENED EXPECTATIONS

© The Enduring Strategic Brand

CMOs should be naturally placed to take a hard look at these unprecedented challenges, identify the strategic responses and turn them into transformational opportunities. But too often it seems that their important role is overlooked – and a raft of surveys reflect the fact that the majority of senior marketers sense a continuing 'dumbing down'.

So let's examine how our companies and CEOs can get the best from strategic marketing and what senior marketers can do to make their offer more compelling.

Heightened expectations
It starts with being much clearer about what CMOs can bring to value creation and how they can play an essential role as 'value' partners for their CEOs (Ref. Chapter 12 – Value).

In numerous studies today's CMOs say that their jobs have become 'relentless' as the pace quickens and the expectations of what they can contribute to corporate achievement intensify. A survey of marketing leadership described in the *Harvard Business Review* (1) reports an increase by 20 percentage points of the need for marketing's greater influence on strategy development. But the question is: are CMOs in a position to deliver this influence?

Theoretically, they should be. As the article's authors point out, when *"marketing demonstrates that it is fighting for the same business objectives as its peers, trust and communication strengthen across all functions and… enable the collaboration required for high performance."*

Yet, in practice, such demand on senior marketers can translate into counter-productive and competitive responses, with increasing silos built as barriers and ghettos.

CMOs have to be constantly asking themselves *"What is my impact on the business?"* This is undoubtedly a wide remit for marketing leaders, since it requires having a vision that sees well beyond marketing department borders as well as earning the trust and confidence of the CEO. This may need different structures but, at the very least, it requires deeply strengthened capabilities and practices, as well as heroic acts of collaboration, team building and time management.

Growing uncertainties about what marketers stand for

In practice, success in gaining board and executive committees acceptance remains slow. Surveys consistently show there is a disconnect, often associated with deep frustration, between the marketer's vision of the company's future and the route pursued. Arguably, one of the key reasons is that too many spend the majority of their time fulfilling traditional marketing, caretaking and hygiene tasks. This is not surprising, since the speed of communications today means that these activities are much more complex and therefore important, demanding and absorbing than before.

Consequently, the average CMO tenure in their roles remains low, between three and four years [Ref. Illustration 5.7]. The same Spencer Stuart study for 2016 even showed the average tenure dropped from 44 to 42 months. In contrast and pointing to success, think of a few of the names mentioned earlier and how long Ian Robertson, Beth Comstock, Jon Iwata, John Hayes, Keith Weed and others have been in their role for - therefore having the opportunity to lead brand transformation.

ILLUSTRATION 5.7	AVERAGE CMO ROLE TENURE

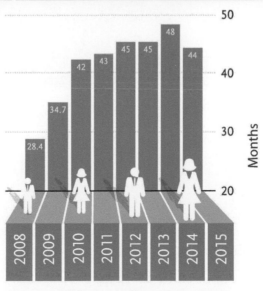

Average CMO tenure through the years

Credit – Spencer Stuart

Meanwhile, CMO roles are in danger of becoming diluted and confused, with the Chief Technical Officer's intervening in the marketing sphere through big data and digitalisation, the emergence of chief customer or Chief Customer or Chief Experience Officers, Corporate Communication spreading their wings and HR's aspirations towards the people brand - just to name a few.

But there is a compelling business and personal case for CMOs to raise their game to become indispensable to the creation of business value. And ultimately, it is this cohort of strategic marketers that CEOs will truly come to depend on and reward.

The big question is: are CMOs up to it? It all depends on how strategically clear they can become about their own role in the context of their particular business. They should own and champion a number of aspects of the company's core activities, but not everything, as we'll detail now.

From marketing to strategic marketing: the natural territories of CMOs

Strategic marketers need to equip themselves to better champion the six key organisational focuses outlined in illustration 5.8. It is time for the sharpest, bravest and brightest marketing leaders to restate their leadership.

ILLUSTRATION 5.8	THE CMO'S SIX NATURAL TERRITORIES

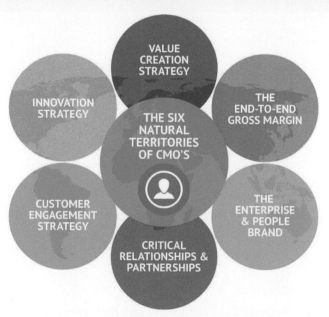

© The Enduring Strategic Brand

CMO territory 1 - The value creation strategy.

Value creation both internally and externally should be at the heart of what a modern marketing leader does. The best marketing brains focus their efforts on the organisational objectives and results that are fundamental to the enterprise's performance and sustainability (Ref. Chapters 8 & 12).

The implications:

Be deeply a strategist - A Spencer Stuart survey among more than 160 senior marketing leaders in 2014 assessed what skills the CMO needs both today and in the future to be successful. Over half said it was having a strategic mindset, with even more saying it was a critical future skill, and this was by far the top choice rather than being strong at idea generation or analytics. (Note 3)

Be deeply a leader rather than a doer - This transition is not easy in a hyper-connected world where the expectation is that the marketing leader should know and resolve everything instantly to mitigate any reputational risk. But, as Egon Zehnder mentions in its C-Suite Perspectives on CMOs, they should be "*an orchestra conductor rather than a field general*". (Note 4)

CMO territory 2 - The end-to-end gross margin.

As the value creation strategy is formed, the CMO needs to take an end-to-end perspective of top line value generation. Not only top line, since it is all about the profit and loss (P&L) and net performance, but a natural territory is certainly to 'own' the end-to-end gross margin.

The implications:

Be deeply the chief growth officer – So, are CMOs showing their CEOs that they can think, talk and work holistically with the balance sheet and profit and loss metrics? Or are they still concentrating too much on brand equity or commercial key performance indicators - vital though they are – making them feel remote and self-serving to colleagues?

Be deeply a generalist leader & influencer - Success will be based on becoming more able to speak the language that resonates across the organisation. This is a position that has to be strongly fought for. Marketers who make an impact are those who are actively engaged in the actual delivery of value, fully integrated into the overall business strategy, plan and implementation (Ref. Chapter 10).

CMO territory 3 - The enterprise and people brand.

More than ever before, the Strategic Brand is the organisation's pole star. It encompasses its essence and purpose, its values and beliefs, its character and ambitions, its value proposition and expression (Ref. Chapter 1).

However, surveys reflect that a large proportion of CEOs still regard the brand essentially as a logo and a marketing artefact, often a cost. The whole purpose of '*THE Enduring*

Strategic Brand' is to advocate that this changes and the vital role of CMOs to lead on this change.

The implications:

Be deeply the champion and guardian of the brand - There is no more compelling imperative for a CMO than to oversee the development and management of the Strategic Brand. Managing the brand with a small 'b' is traditional marketing; building an Enduring Strategic Brand is the highest level of strategy. And it shouldn't be a top priority only in consumer goods companies - heed the words of a CSMO whose brand was generating the biggest revenue globally and went through the Gulf of Mexico crisis (Ref. Chapters 11 & 13)!

Be deeply an empathetic and inclusive leader and colleague - Embarking on a Strategic Brand journey without an apparent burning platform to force the issue can throw up massive hurdles. There is great need to walk in other people's shoes in order to grow the brand influence. It starts with replacing marketing jargon with those that everyone can recognise, value and feel part of. In BP, I learned this the hard way with the upstream unit and even replaced the word 'brand' with 'reputation', 'license to operate' or 'access'.

Take deeply things from others' perspective - Marketers need to improve the effectiveness of the dialogue with their financial colleagues by talking analytically about optimised resource allocation and measuring returns. They should also build the necessary cooperative relationships with IT colleagues, by being able to embed technology in marketing-driven business and articulate its impact on performance. And we've already discussed the vital partnership with HR so that the Strategic Brand plays its key role in motivation, recruitment and retention as well as 'inside-out' projection.

CMO territory 4 - Critical relationships and partnerships.

Technology has made the world one of unlimited connectivity. Winning is increasingly about building alliances and eco-systems. Success in key markets relies on deep, trusting relationships in business, as represented by 'Guanxi' in China (which roughly translates as relationships or connections) and 'Wasta' in the UAE (which roughly translates as connections, clout or who you know).

The implications:

Be deeply a relationship strategist - There are simply too many relationships for the CMO and marketing team to manage - so the CMO should become more systematic. For example, draw up a chart of the relationships and partnerships that are critical to your value mission and strategy. This contact map should start with the clearest understanding of who the single ultimate 'customer' target group is. And from there, with a motto of "fewer but deeper" be ruthless about investing all the necessary efforts to build partnerships with selected priorities and delegate other interactions to other parts of the organisation.

It's easier said than done. Because, it is not only about managing a stakeholder map, but also about understanding and leveraging networks of influence. And it is about developing the necessary expertise to excel in the practice of building and managing deep partnerships that have the potential to strategically transform value creation (Ref. Chapter 6).

Be deeply globally focused – Many people talk about cultural differences but few manage to develop a deep enough scientific understanding of how they work in a global system (Ref. Chapter 2). Marketers are in the unique position of being able to understand the changing landscape of growth patterns across the world and not only manage the effects within the company but foresee any discontinuities. For example, they should be the ones to deal with any changes in market resilience when major upheavals take place within financial systems and markets.

CMO territory 5 - The customer engagement strategy.

Marketing has always been identified with the voice of the customer. But now, it moves to a whole new level, as total customer engagement becomes one of the few sources of competitive differentiation in a frenetically connected world (Ref. Chapters 4 and 7).

The implications:
Be deeply the resonant voice for customers in the new era - Deeper customer relationships transform rich insights into hard benefits. The right offer with the right delivery is the beginning of a strong story. So what is needed to become better brand storytellers –internally as well as externally? How can the CMO encourage seamless integration in the relationship between the enterprise and its customers? How to understand and participate with digital networks to sustain brand relevance (Ref. Chapter 7)?

Be deeply the internal and external integrator - As the McKinsey Quarterly points out, *"As more advanced marketing science and analytics take hold, they are making it increasingly natural for marketing to go beyond messaging and to shape the substance of the business, particularly the experiences of customers, the delivery of functional benefits and the drive to develop new products and services"*. (Note 5) Amazon is the blueprint of excellence for this, as it internalises customer needs and expectations into function and merges marketing, technology and operations into a single offer and service.

CMO territory 6 - The innovation strategy.

How much leadership, let alone involvement, do CMOs have in the innovation strategy? Obviously, innovation can't be done in isolation and it flourishes where there are both formal and informal connections with a wide assortment of people both internally and externally. So what is the role into combining these perspectives and ideas (Ref. Chapter 8)?

The implications:
Be deeply about big insights, including from big data - It is not about big data per say, but big insights. As the Marketing 2020 Study says, *"Over-performers have the edge*

in extracting big insights from big data. They blend data, knowledge and intuition to get a clear point of view on their business and their brand(s)". (Note 6) Marketers are the natural owners of big insights and should bring them consistently to cross-functional teams, to inform, shape and provide a direction to the innovation pipeline. It will help to break down functional silo mentalities and transform the relevance and effectiveness of the innovation strategy. To do this, CMOs and their teams almost need a digital reboot, certainly a considerable skill set on (big) data handling and interpreting, so they grab the opportunity and minimise the risks.

Be deeply about content marketing and selected new ways of working -The 21st century is about content, reality and substance. Our practice should provide the edge to focus on hard benefits and excellence in execution, while leaving aside the difficult to monetise 'nice to have' ideas. With society's needs as our starting point, marketers can design storytelling and communication with a publishing and broadcasting mindset, to initiate, develop and be part of the relevant and important conversations.

Are these six natural territories of the CMO too ambitious for the real world? Not, if they, as the marketing pioneers in your organisation, get the balance right to achieve the best outcomes for the enterprise's unique set of circumstances. In other words, if CMOs are clear on which of these territories they should own (Ref. Illustration 5.9).

ILLUSTRATION 5.9	WHICH TERRITORIES SHOULD THE CMO 'OWN'?
THE VALUE CREATION STRATEGY	▶ Be deeply a strategist. ▶ Be deeply a leader rather than a doer.
THE 'END TO END' GROSS MARGIN	▶ Be deeply the Chief Growth Officer. ▶ Be deeply a generalist leader & influencer.
THE ENTERPRISE & PEOPLE BRAND	▶ Be deeply the champion and guardian of the brand. ▶ Be deeply an empathetic and inclusive leader & colleague. ▶ Take deeply things from others' perspective.
CRITICAL RELATIONSHIPS & PARTNERSHIPS	▶ Be deeply a relationship strategist. ▶ Be deeply globally focused.
THE CUSTOMER ENGAGEMENT STRATEGY	▶ Be deeply the voice of what resonates for customers in the new era. ▶ Be deeply the internal and external integrator.
THE INNOVATION STRATEGY	▶ Be deeply about big insights, including from big data. ▶ Be deeply about content marketing and selected new ways of working.

© The Enduring Strategic Brand

The right CMO for the enduring enterprise priorities

Every organisation has their own set of circumstances, priorities and needs. Hence, CEOs and senior marketers need to have mutual and total clarity on what business territories the CMO will 'own', 'lead', 'influence', or keep a 'watching brief' on, as reflected in illustration 5.10.

ILLUSTRATION 5.10	THE CMO'S LEADERSHIP FRAMEWORK

OWN
The CMO applies full integrator leadership and accountability in the areas they "own"

COORDINATE
The CMO leads and organizes the activities in the areas they "coordinate"

INFLUENCE
The CMO intervenes and contributes to the strategy and activation of areas they "influence"

WATCHING BRIEF
The CMO actively decides areas where their organisation will not contribute and only be a receiver

© The Enduring Strategic Brand

One size, doesn't fit all

By having this clarity, CMOs will become true and appropriate integrators. By ceding control in the 'watching brief' areas, they will gain power and pace in the 'own' and 'coordinate' spaces, to the benefit of the company and their own.

Very few senior marketers reach this sweet spot. It demands fighting against the power of daily life as well as tradition and organisational expectations. It demands earning this authority - but those who reach strategic clarity about their role as CMO win because they are able to associate with the main objectives and successes of their enterprise, with value creation and therefore have a profound impact on the business. This is how you become an Enduring Strategic Brand CMO…and, being at the heart of value creation, the Enterprise 'Chief Value Officer'.

Defining the type of CMO to fit a specific organisation

Optimising the combination between the CMO's natural territories and their leadership framework in the context of a specific organisation defines the ideal profile of a candidate - which is precisely what a CEO needs to select their best suited CMO.

Here are six examples of CMO profiles (Ref. Illustration 5.11). So CEOs, which CMO type do you need? And CMOs, which type is best fitted to who you are and want to become?

ILLUSTRATION 5.11	YOUR CMO – CHIEF VALUE OFFICER TYPES
THE LONG-TERM BUILDER	Obsessed with a vision
THE TRANSFORMATIONAL INNOVATOR	Obsessed with transforming the biz model or offer
THE EMPOWERING PARTNER	Obsessed to get the best from all stakeholders
THE GUARDIAN OF THE TEMPLE	Obsessed with coherence & long-term reputation
THE CUSTOMER GURU	Obsessed with the customer experience
THE GROWTH CHAMPION	Obsessed with business growth

© The Enduring Strategic Brand

The long-term builder – Obsessed with a vision, they deliberately own the 'value creation strategy' by delegation of the CEO and the 'enterprise & people Strategic Brand', while they coordinate the 'critical relationships & partnerships' and the 'innovation strategy.'

The transformational innovator – Obsessed with transforming the business model or offer, they are unchallenged owners of the 'innovation strategy'. They also own the 'value creation strategy' to propel the company into a competitively advantaged future. They coordinate 'critical relationships & partnerships', as innovation can't be a lonely act anymore.

The empowering partner - Obsessed to get the best from all stakeholders, they passionately own the three engagement territories of the 'customer engagement strategy', the 'enterprise & people Strategic Brand' and vitally, the 'critical relationships & partnerships'. Their engagement focus leads them to be much less involved in other territories.

The guardian of the temple – Obsessed with coherence and long-term reputation, they own the 'enterprise & people Strategic Brand' and 'critical relationships & partnerships', who they passionately want to associate positively with the enterprise. They coordinate the 'customer engagement strategy', as the third key stakeholder group. They influence the 'value creation strategy' and 'innovation strategy', so the enterprise substance is coherent and deepens its reputation.

The customer guru – Obsessed with the customer experience, they are the owners of the 'customer engagement strategy', the 'innovation strategy' and vitally, the 'critical relationships & partnerships' that are required to ensure the consistent development and delivery of the value proposition at the highest standards.

The growth champion – Obsessed with business growth, they undoubtedly own the 'end-to-end gross margin' and the 'customer engagement strategy' and coordinate 'the enterprise & people brand' and 'innovation strategy'.

These are only snapshots of carefully defined archetypes of Strategic Brand CMOs as 'Chief Value Officers'. Those organisations who can recruit the individual who is going to be 'fit for purpose' are best placed to significantly improve performance in the future.

THE Enduring Strategic Brand CMO

To meet the challenge of appointing your most suitable Enduring Strategic Brand CMO and 'Chief Value Officer' if you are a CEO - or being one if you are the CMO - there is a vital need to strengthen skills and knowledge on what it takes.

To do that, CEOs and CMOs might want to step back in their respective roles and assess both their organisation for the CEO, and themselves for the CMO on where strengths and critical gaps lie. A very first step could be to examine the following seven practical questions:

- What is the CMO role in relation to organisational strategy? What should it be in the Enterprise specific context?
- What are our main sources of growth? What should they be for a sustainable future? How should the CMO be involved to ensure we are on the right growth path?
- Are we mobilising their /our expertise as content creators and storytellers, to produce a simple and compelling Strategic Brand story that resonates consistently internally and externally? If not, how to make this happen?
- Have we carefully analysed the state of the different relationships we /I do or should manage? Could we / should we be doing a better job of prioritising them? How do we move the potentially transformational ones to become strategic partnerships?
- Do we all live and breathe stakeholders' and customers' needs and satisfaction in unison? Is the CMO entitled to strategically carry the customers' flag and if not, how to make this happen?
- Does our company have the most profitable sources of innovative ideas that will bring competitive differentiation? How can we be better?
- And above all, what are the critical personal skills that need to be developed further to grow the confident 'Chief Value Officer' the organisation needs?

Once this done, the CEO and CMO should align on what to 'own', 'coordinate', 'influence' or keep a 'watching brief' on. It's easy to get distracted by short-term pressures and the ever-changing world around us. This approach will empower the CMO to focus on the stuff that really matters and better serve the enterprise and the CEO.

To return to David Wheldon's earlier comment, the best marketers always put the word 'strategic' alongside 'brand.' So let's expand the club of the winning CVO's - Chief Value Officers!

CHAPTER 6
PARTNERING

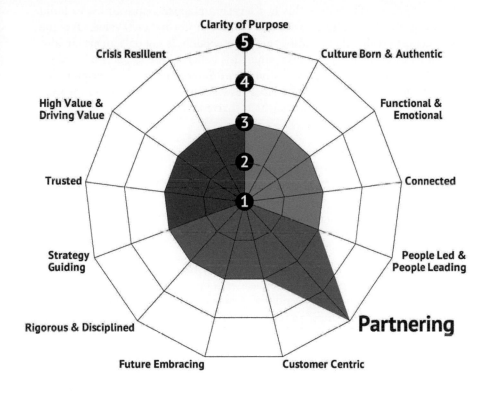

"Chains do not hold a marriage together. It is threads, hundreds of tiny threads, which sew people together through the years."

Simone Signoret, actor

In earlier chapters, we noted that a brand is a relationship; and a Strategic Brand is a partnership. Today, more than ever, relationships define Strategic Brands. The opportunities from transforming relationships into proper partnerships are game changing. I spent my whole career working on dissolving boundaries, simplifying interfaces and building the power of 'WE' between the brands I served and their stakeholders. I have been inspired by the strategic transformations which arise from successful deep partnerships - although more often than not, I have been disappointed to observe either the failure of these partnerships or the lukewarm survival of floundering co-operations.

Partnerships, and in particular branded partnerships, offer the sweet spot of access, invention, growth, and efficiency – this is a largely untapped opportunity, to build unique advantage for the involved parties and create transformational value. Over the years, I have come to realise that building these partnerships is not only an art but also a science that requires high levels of discipline. This belief led me to publish 'Strategic Partnering: Remove Chance and Deliver Consistent Success' in 2013, a 'recipe book' that advocates for partnerships and describes how Brands can move from forming relationships into being Strategic Brands which thrive through transformational and defining partnerships. (Note 1)

I have already mentioned a memorable day in Munich in 2004. BMW and Castrol were discussing a global co-operation for the joint development and marketing of advanced lubricants. This was to include brand association, to be defined. When you think of the BMW brand, its purity and clout, you might expect it would never accept any co-branding – and certainly not with a lubricant company.

It was 10pm, after a full day of discussions and negotiations. Inspired by Torsten Lindau, one of the best strategic cooperation leaders I have ever met and the person in charge of strategic partnerships between BP and the German auto manufacturers, we all rushed out from our smoky meeting room to a BMW car on the company's parking lot and looked under its bonnet.

For the first time ever in our respective sectors, a premium energy brand was to be intimately associated with a premium automotive brand. What's more, the energy brand would sit at the very heart of what makes a BMW a BMW - in its engine, where a Castrol-branded filler cap would feature the partnership. Over the many years to follow, this joint signature supported material sources of value to both brands and was overtly visible in the varied areas of Research and Development, Marketing and Customer offers, After Sales and Motorsport.

As a result of their strategic partnership, BMW and Castrol jointly developed advanced product formulations saving an estimated $500m on otherwise required development costs. Castrol's marketshare with BMW's global network rose to over 90 per cent. BMW benefited from a global, consistent, high quality and immaculately executed after-sales lubricant marketing programme. The joint brand programmes had a positive impact on each brand's loyal customers.

| ILLUSTRATION 6.1 | EXAMPLES OF THE BMW – CASTROL BRANDED PARTNERSHIP |

Even the Strongest Heart Needs Protection

Credit – BP plc and Castrol ads.

A large part of BP's Downstream business is predicated on developing advanced and efficient fuels. The other industry which is most involved in this sort of work is the automotive sector. Irrespective of this, relationships had been challenging for decades, with each sector trying to push accountability and investment on to the other for meeting the regulator's mandates on fuel efficiency. In 2002, BP attempted to change this ill-formed approach and develop partnerships with a few auto companies, selected for their partnering and trust potential – competence, judgment, benevolence and integrity [Ref. Chapter 11]. In 2003 a wide-reaching partnership was developed with Ford Motor Company, notably in Europe, and is still active. As represented in Illustration 6.2, this partnership took multiple forms and covered many areas, including a strong jointly branded marketing association.

| ILLUSTRATION 6.2 | EXAMPLES OF FORD – BP JOINT BRANDED MARKETING |

Ford and BP Growing Together for Their Customers

Credit – THE Enduring Strategic Brand from BP and Ford ads.

Ford and BP developed a highly trustful relationship, integrating their product portfolio strategies, co-developing advanced fuels formulations, combining aspects of their supply chains, creating new marketing offers, co-marketing and co-branding. Business and brand benefits, both efficiencies and top line, reached hundreds of millions of dollars.

While overseeing the development of these partnerships over many years, one of most important things I have learned is how different they are from one another: each partnership had its own core objectives, character and priority expressions. As such, in the automotive sector, our partnership with BMW was very different from the one with Ford, which was in turn very distinct from our relationship with Toyota.

One of the iconic pathfinders of broad-range branded partnerships is Intel Inside. In 1990, despite an already established reputation as a quality producer of microprocessors amongst OEMs, Intel needed to differentiate itself from its competitors. To do so, it decided to market its product with extensive Intel Inside 'ingredient' branding. In 1991, Intel launched the co-op programme in which manufacturers placed the Intel inside logo in their advertising and other marketing material (Note 2).

ILLUSTRATION 6.3	THE ICONIC IBM – INTEL BRANDED PARTNERSHIP

Results were impressive: the campaign focused the entire organisation around the brand. Intel gained the confidence of the end consumer that they represented quality and reliability and, by 1995, 94 per cent of European PC buyers were familiar with the Intel Inside® logos, against 24 per cent in 1991. Having linked with premium brands like IBM and Compaq, Intel created the lasting impression that they made something worth paying more for. This was a win-win situation, as it also contributed directly to PC makers' campaigns: from 1991 to 1997, Intel and PC makers together spent US$3.4 billion on advertising with the Intel Inside logo; over US$2 billion of this came directly from Intel. By 1998, Intel controlled 90 per cent of the world's share of PC microprocessors; and in 2001, it was listed the sixth most valuable brand in the world, with a value estimated at US$35 billion.

A key element of this magic relates to some principles behind Intel's strategic alliance with IBM: neither partner was deeply dependent on the other, yet there were considerable respective benefits from the partnership; net of pluses (major brand boost) and minuses (aspects of brand dilution), each party's brand has benefited dramatically from the partnership.

PARTNER, PARTNER, PARTNER!

There are no business practices more important than strategy and partnering. In my book '*Strategic Partnering: Remove Chance and Deliver Consistent Success*', I describe best practice at each stage of a partnership's development in order to avoid falling into the numerous pitfalls that exist. To keep from duplication, '*THE Enduring Strategic Brand*', focuses only on the brand aspects of Partnering.

Because why would you want to do it all alone? Can you be best at everything? Do you possess an infinite amount of resources, authority, capabilities, knowledge, reach or reputation? If you said 'no' to any of these questions, then how can you access what is missing? You can of course buy – through M&A or services from suppliers – or hire what you need. But can you get the best for everything and be truly differentiated through these traditional approaches? Will you achieve a best-in-class result from a mundane relationship with a procured service?

The solution is partnerships, which are about bringing together different organisations that complement or complete each other's mission, enabling focus, excellence and flexibility to deliver jointly the experiences their audience seeks, at the quality they expect.

What we have found is we are really good at five things. So if somebody else can provide those other 13, we would consider partnering with them.

Ross McEwan, Group CEO of RBS, explains in an interview to PwC (Note 3): "*At one stage, our organisation was in 18 products in the international investment community. What we have found is we are really good at five things and those are the things our customers are open to. They value our expertise in those areas; they never saw us as being great at 18 things. So if somebody else can provide those other 13, we would consider partnering with them. I think that's where the point about doing all things for all people comes in – and I don't think you can.*"

His thoughts are echoed by Teo Spierings, CEO of Fonterra in New Zealand: "*We follow the guiding principle of focusing on our own strengths and growing those hard and fast, and then partnering in areas where we are possibly not as good.*"

As reflected in Illustration 6.4 from PWC's 18th Annual Global CEO Survey, the encouraging news is that CEOs are largely convinced that partnering is strategically an ever more important imperative.

ILLUSTRATION 6.4	CEOS STRONG MOTIVATION TO ENTER PARTNERSHIPS

51% of CEOs will enter new alliances in the next 12 months

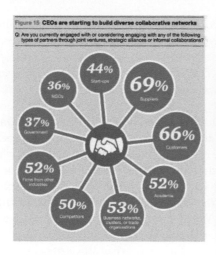

Credit – PwC 18th Annual Global CEO Survey

We will expand more on this later in the chapter – but the real question is HOW, meaning how an organisation develops the complex and extensive capability to truly perform at partnering.

In the Fourth Industrial Revolution, Partnering is the way society works

Professor Klaus Schwab, Founder and Executive Chairman of the World Economic Forum (WEF) – Davos, writes on how partnerships are simply becoming the way society operates: *"A world of customer experiences, data-based services and asset performance through analytics requires new forms of collaboration, given the speed at which innovation and distribution are taking place... When firms share resources through collaborative innovation, significant value can be created for both parties as well as for the economies in which such collaborations take place* (Note 4).

SIEMENS +

"One such example is the recent collaboration between the industrial giant Siemens, which spends around $4 billion a year in research and development, and Ayasdi, an innovative machine-learning company" he adds.

While Siemens has 343,000 employees to Ayasdi's 100, this mutually beneficial partnership enables the start up to validate its software while working with real world data, while Siemens is benefiting from early insights from Ayasdi's novel approach to analytics.

Klaus Schwab continues: *"Such collaborations, however, are often far from straightforward. They require significant investment from both parties to develop firm strategy, search for appropriate partners, establish communication channels, align processes, and flexibly respond to changing conditions, both inside and outside the partnership. Sometimes, these collaborations spawn entirely new business models, such as city car-sharing schemes. This is only as good as the weakest link in the partnership chain. Companies need to go beyond marketing and sales agreements to understand how to adopt comprehensive collaborative approaches. The Fourth Industrial Revolution forces companies to think about how offline and online worlds work together in practice."*

The best partnerships flourish from a mutual understanding of the future. For BP and Ford, this was about a shared contextual understanding that the future would be lower carbon, and the purpose of both companies was connected to that future.

Klaus Schwab believes the need for partnerships extends beyond innovation into good leadership: *"In the Fourth Industrial Revolution, to develop contextual intelligence, decision-makers must first understand the value of diverse networks. They can only confront significant levels of disruption if they are highly connected and well networked across traditional boundaries... It is only by working in collaboration with leaders from business, government, civil society, faith, academia and the younger generation that it becomes possible to obtain a holistic perspective of what is going on. This is critical to develop and implement integrated ideas and solutions that will result in sustainable change.*

Pankaj Ghemawat, of the Stern School of Business at New York University, has calculated that America's top 1000 public companies now derive 40 per cent of their revenue from alliances, compared with 1 per cent in 1980.

"This principle is embedded in the multi-stakeholder theory (what the World Economic Forum communities often call the Spirit of Davos). Boundaries between sectors and professions are artificial and are proving to be increasingly counterproductive. More than ever, it is essential to dissolve these barriers by engaging the power of networks to

forge effective partnerships. Companies and organisations that fail to do this and do not walk the talk by building diverse teams will have a difficult time adjusting to the disruptions of the digital age."

In fact, Klaus Schwab describes a future that is already with us. Pankaj Ghemawat, of the Stern School of Business at New York University, has calculated that America's top 1000 public companies now derive 40 per cent of their revenue from alliances, compared with 1 per cent in 1980.

Partnering builds the Strategic Brand as a unique relationship

As I have said earlier, Brand and Partnering are two sides of the same vital coin: a relationship. Meanwhile, we are experiencing a transformation of brand relationships as the partnerships between customers and brands become democratic. Uber transformed the roles of driver and passenger, Airbnb transformed the roles of host and guest...

Dr Nick Udall, founder of Nowhere, says: *"In today's world, successful brands need to co-create with partners and value chains. This is creatively exciting but requires a different type of leadership. It is no longer about leadership within boundaries or through hierarchy, but about holding spaces where people can come together at new and novel intersections, stand in their difference, step into the unknown, and hold the tension of not-knowing long enough for new patterns of thought and action to emerge. This also requires leaders to embody stories that inspire us to step forward, and disrupt us so we can let go of our preconceptions and habits – both essential and central for catalysing innovation and change."*

The *Harvard Business Review* of 9th May 2016 published an analysis entitled *"Build Your Brand as a Relationship"*, by Mark Bonchek and Cara France, in which the authors argue that brands have gone through various mental models over time. (Note 5)

The first mental mode was '**the brand as object**' i.e. the brand is something applied to what you make.

This then moved from a feature to a '**perception**', from an object to an '*idea*', a singular idea or concept that you own inside the mind of a prospect. In this view, a brand is not something you make, it's something you manage. Apple is a strong leader of this '*perception*' model.

The prevailing existing model is about brand as an '**experience**', where the brand is the container for a stakeholder's complete experience with a product or a company, which is no longer managed over time but delivered at every moment – Amazon might be considered an exemplary brand of the '*experience*' model.

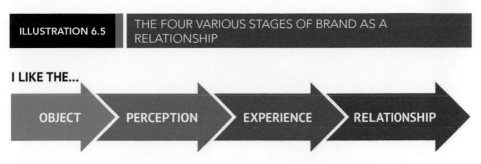

According to the authors, the emerging model is the brand as a **'relationship'**. The essence of their thesis is for organisations to redefine current relationships, which are mainly transactional and one directional, and make them more collaborative, symmetrical and reciprocal. So in the hospitality industry, move from *host/guest to citizen/citizen* – e.g. Airbnb; in taxi and livery services, move from *driver/passenger to friend/friend* – e.g. Lyft and their tagline *"your friend with a car"*; in financial services, from *card issuer/card holder to club/member* – e.g. AmEx; or in amusement parks, from *operator/rider to cast member/guest* – e.g. Disney. This approach opens up a multitude of transformational opportunities for the future in asking ourselves: how do we redefine *doctor/patient, teacher/student, manufacturer/buyer*, etc.?

In this context, the space and opportunities for Brands are boundless.

The era of co-

I believe we have already entered the era of co- (the reduced Latin form of "with"). And although it's just the beginning, here are seven 'co-s' already reshaping the modern enterprise and redefining its brand:

1. *Cobot* - or co-robot, intended to physically mesh with humans in a shared workspace;
2. *Co-opetion* – the ideal mix of competition and cooperation;
3. *Co-construction* – the transformation of a relationship, for example a partnership between teaching staff and their students;
4. *Co-working* - combining a shared working environment with an independent activity;
5. *Collaborative* (economy) – or shareconomy, collaborative consumption or peer economy, based on peer-to-peer transactions often via community-based online services;
6. *Co-determination* - the cooperation between management and associates in decision-making, with less hierarchy. This is growing in importance, particularly with Y and Z generations;
7. *Co-operative* – the voluntary association of people to meet their common economic, social and cultural needs and aspirations.

ILLUSTRATION 6.6   SEVEN PILLARS OF THE CO-SOCIETY

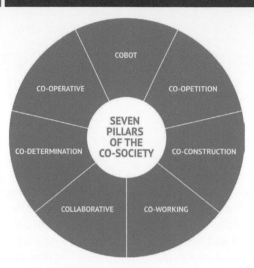

Credit – THE Enduring Strategic Brand from Les Echos data, December 2016

In the Fourth Industrial Revolution, the era of 'relationship' and co-, the Strategic Brand doesn't have functional only relationships; it develops and holds collaborations and partnerships with its stakeholders. All interactions are practised in the spirit of mutual advantage – or they are not entertained at all. There is a genuine desire to begin relationships by seeing things from someone else's perspective, and to give and receive.

All interactions are practised in the spirit of mutual advantage – or they are not entertained at all. There is a genuine desire to begin relationships by seeing things from someone else's perspective, and to give and receive.

The Strategic Brand develops collaborative interactions with its stakeholders. It knows it's impossible to do everything alone, so it creates deep partnerships and rich ecosystems to innovate and deliver its services. It knows that others praising your brand is much stronger than your own advertising. The 'Partnering' Strategic Brand delivers much higher returns because of the meaningful contribution of resources from others to its activities.

So, how do you play well, win and lead in the emerging new form of society and enterprise? How do you build the capability to partner at scale and in depth? Let's explore these questions and look at how to approach partnerships, the role of brand in partnerships and the impact of partnerships on developing and building 'relationship' brands. We will also explore the impact of ecosystems on brands, as these are arguably the most advanced and fastest growing forms of collaboration.

THREE MAIN TYPES OF PARTNERING BRANDS

As represented in Illustration 6.7, brands practise three main types of partnerships: 'capability', 'joint offer' and 'branded'. These are not mutually exclusive but rather complementary, and each represents an evolution or expansion of the previous type.

ILLUSTRATION 6.7	THE 'CAPABILITY', 'JOINT OFFER' AND 'BRANDED' PARTNERSHIP TYPES

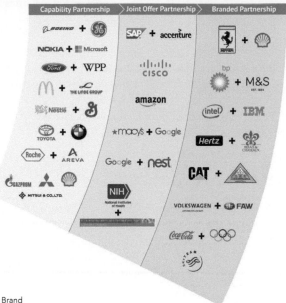

© THE Enduring Strategic Brand

Type 1 – Capability Partnerships

This form of co-operation is the most frequent to date. In essence, these partnerships aim to improve or enhance the branded business of one of the parties, while also bringing business benefits to the other party. In practice, partner B brings a critical capability or resource (technology, finances, an entire functionality, a rare skill, a higher security of supply or reduced risk) to partner A, which requires this asset for staging and executing its strategic offer. Partner B's benefits are: further learning, knowledge application, growth, direct financials, etc. Partner A's benefits are of a different nature: enhanced growth, transformed offer, greater efficiency and lower costs, etc.

Thousands of examples include: GE and Boeing cooperating to optimise the development, fitting and maintenance of GE's engines into Boeing's aircrafts; WPP bringing their A-team and full suite of marketing services to build the Ford brand; the global cereal partnership of Nestle and General Mills, which is celebrating its 25-year anniversary and is as important as ever; Mondelēz and Facebook renewing their global strategic partnership to leverage and innovate around consumer insights; Vera and RFA (Richard Fleischman and Associates) announcing a strategic partnership to equip hedge funds and investment management firms with industry leading encryption and data security; Innate Pharma and Sanofi in a research collaboration and licensing agreement for new bispecific antibodies using technology and tumour targets; Serimax and Technip entering into a strategic partnership for pipeline welding; in fintech, J.P. Morgan developing a white-label partnership with OnDeck Capital, using their technology to quickly approve small business loans within hours instead of weeks; Starbucks partnering with Barnes and Noble and United Airlines to grow business, and with Pepsico and Kraft to expand distribution.

Hertz We talked to Michel Taride, Group President Hertz International, about strategic partnerships: *"Hertz has a long history of partnerships. Because renting a car is only one piece of the travel chain, partnerships give us the ability to offer a seamless travel experience. A simple example of this is booking your airline ticket at the same time as your car rental, both at a preferred price, customised for the needs of that particular trip or customer.*

ILLUSTRATION 6.8	EXAMPLES OF HERTZ PARTNERSHIPS IN THE TRAVEL CHAIN

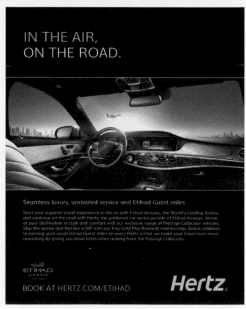

Credit – Hertz International

"We have been strategic partners with Air France for 28 years; we have status matched our loyalty programs (a Platinum Customer of Air France will be a Platinum Customer of Hertz) with preferred rates, preferred treatment and fast-track options at key Air France destinations around the world.

"Another motivation is economical; partnerships are a cost-effective way of reaching vast populations of travellers with targeted communication, marketing and sales efforts, using our co-operations as a key channel to distribute, market and promote our products and services.

"Because we are a global company with a strong brand, we partner with big travel operators, airlines, hotel chains, resorts like Disneyland Paris, loyalty programmes, credit card companies and car manufacturers. Specifically, OEMs see us as a wonderful test-drive for customers without any commercial pressure, and with freedom of experience. Often our partnerships are long term, such as our major relationship with 'AAA', the American Automobile Association, with Marriott, or with our historical partner American Express. These partnerships also tend to be global, such as our relationship with Relais & Châteaux."

Most partnerships are type one – mutually beneficial relationships – but in most cases, they don't have a boundless potential for transformation.

Type 2 – Joint Offer Partnerships

These are fast developing and world-shaping co-operations. Partners or ecosystems contribute their individual capability and excellence to create new joint solution offerings or business models. For example, smart grid technology, 'the energy internet', requires multiple companies to come together to develop intelligent energy management solutions. Involved parties include utilities, developers of automation software, providers of intelligent electronic hardware systems, expert testing companies, etc.

Book and music shops are being replaced by Amazon and its supply and logistics ecosystem. When the Apple Watch was first launched, I remember Tim Cook declaring, *"In a few years, people will say: How could I have ever thought about not wearing this watch?"*; in the same breath, he admitted there were *"limited functionalities"*, which a very dynamic network of apps developers would soon make much richer.

There are many transformational 'joint offer' partnerships operating at considerable scale: Apple and IBM combining IBM's analytics and computing with the user experience of iPhone and iPad, to bring a new class of apps and connect business users to big data and analytics on their iOS devices; Spotify and Uber co-operating to welcome you in your hired car with your favourite playlist; Macy's and Google partnering to allow shoppers to use Google search to check if the items they want are in stock, so they can order them for immediate in-store pick-up; Cisco and Accenture creating a 'one team' alliance, called the Accenture Cisco Business Group (ACBG), which is a transformational collaboration in which a single team is able to deliver all of the underlying technology as well as the business-process transformational services.

Joint Offer Ecosystems

Companies such as Cisco link their future success to their ability to partner. Their vision and commitment to partnering is to enable boundary-less collaboration with other market experts to deliver customers a choice of best-in-class solutions.

ı|ıı|ıı To that end, Cisco has developed a multifaceted partnering program (Ref.
CISCO. Illustration 6.9) and built a global ecosystem of partners that includes integration, channel, technology and industry solution companies as well as service providers. Together they provide a range of consulting, resale, outsourcing, services and technology integration solutions. Partnering companies include Accenture, Apple, AT&T, Fujitsu, Johnson Controls, Microsoft, Tata Consulting and Wipro just to name a few.

ILLUSTRATION 6.9	CISCO COLLABORATION ALLIANCE AND PARTNER ECOSYSTEM

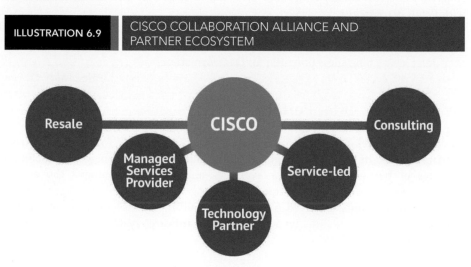

Credit – Data from Cisco corporate site

Brands are no longer defined by single company boundaries but by the latest sophisticated customer experience or by the customer 'relationship'.

Equally, brands are no longer defined by products but by highly relevant functionalities - every aspect of the integrated customer experience is expected to be perfectly executed. Experiences are increasingly provided by ecosystems, a trend Josh Feldmeth, the Interbrand North America CEO, confirms in a study called 'The Alpha of Cohesiveness' (Note 6): *"The strongest brands are built through the most cohesive business systems."* But success comes down to immaculate delivery – and Klaus Schwab rightly warns, *"The outcome is only as good as the weakest link in the partnership chain."*

 Josh uses the example of Apple to show how the powerful and comprehensive Apple branded ecosystem drives considerable value, pointing to *"Apple's brilliant functionally-integrated model, where software, hardware and other touchpoints are connected by a level of interoperability that justifies the Apple premium and discourages defections.*" In effect, Apple creates an environment where "it all works" between an iPhone, iPad, MacBook, iCloud, App Store, Airdrop, Apple TV, etc.... Examples of other companies with strong cohesion of their ecosystems are Amazon, Google, GE, Nike and BMW among others.

amazon.com Prime In the case of Amazon – and in particular Amazon Prime – products are linked with value-add services like video, music and cloud services, and delivered through convenience logistics and personal recommendations.

Josh concludes that cohesiveness drives demand and value. This is represented in Illustration 6.10, where the majority of the fastest growing brands have highly cohesive ecosystems which deliver seamless, frictionless and responsive brand experiences at all touchpoints, e.g. Google, Apple, Microsoft, Honda and Toyota.

ILLUSTRATION 6.10	COHESIVENESS OF ECOSYSTEMS

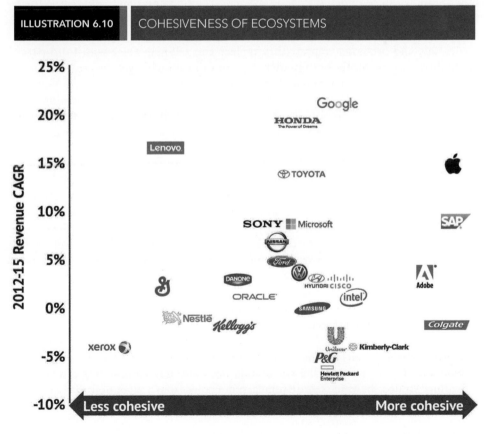

Credit - Interbrand

A very fast growing form of co-operation is with developers, who feed Apple or Google App stores; and idea-based micro-organisations that 'invent' for bigger companies - for example molecules for pharma or application softwares for banks. Attracting the best represents big battlegrounds between major companies and requires sophisticated partnering management.

Strategic Brands therefore need partnering to build high quality cohesive ecosystems derived from and stabilised by a co-operative approach. In turn, they will be the main attraction point to peer companies, smaller firms or developers in search for partners.

Type 3 – Branded Partnerships

Branded partnerships can have the most impact. This is when two or more brands associate and jointly act and communicate, to provide their positive brand halo to the other brand(s). In so doing, they boost awareness, affinity and mutually accrue their respective fan and follower groups, their communities and their 👍s, leaning on the simple idea that *"the friends of my friends are my friends"*. They provide their own credentials and promoter impact. They replace the self-help voice with third-party credibility. They enable the optimisation of communication budgets by providing new already largely paid-for channels and marketing outlets.

This is a 'marriage' of brands, in which two or more different brands bring their qualities, resources, friends, knowledge, energy and vision together to enhance their offering.

I have already cited BMW–Castrol, Ford–BP, IBM–Intel as strong examples of the branded partnership. Other examples include Michelin and Harley-Davidson and their more than ten-year-old partnership to develop and market an exclusive jointly developed tyre range, co-branded 'Scorcher'. This brings Michelin's image of technical expertise to Harley, and Harley's legitimacy to Michelin in the cruiser bikes segment. Bonne Belle and Dr. Pepper developed and co-branded a lip balm flavour that was famous for decades among teenage girls. BMW i8 and Louis Vuitton designed luggage to fit the car model perfectly – and, from an image standpoint, added another element of exclusivity to BMW and increased awareness and favourable brand association for Louis Vuitton.

GoPro and Red Bull, two action-packed and fearless lifestyle brands, are pairing in co-branding campaigns, including 'Stratos', in which Felix Baumgartner jumps from a space pod with a GoPro strapped to him, redefining human potential, which is a feature of both brands.

Genius and Spotify ally their complementary services – streaming and music collection – into a co-branding of collaborative playlists called 'Behind the Lyrics', supported by lyrics back stories and convenient functionalities.

GM and IBM co-developed and recently introduced OnStar Go, 'the auto industry's first cognitive mobility platform' where IBM Watson brings its personalised understanding of drivers' personalities to make life in their cars more enjoyable, safe and convenient. OnStar Go will also favour brand partners such as ExxonMobil for gas, Mastercard for on-the-go payments and iHeartRadio.

Snapchat and Square also partnered to create Square's Snapcash, with each party providing credibility in their respective area of strength, creating significant revenue and brand enhancements.

You don't need to belong the digital aristocracy to transform your business through branded partnerships. For many years BP tried to turn its retail sites into the best combination of fuelling and convenience. Not being a grocery expert, the attempts had mixed success and delivered low returns. M&S were interested in giving scale to their 'Simply Food Stores' format.

In 2004, BP and M&S agreed a partnership and opened their first shop in Hammersmith, London. It would be co-branded and M&S would operate the forecourt shops. This is a type three partnership where M&S and BP bring their respective expertise and assets to each other; they market a joint offer to customers; and they marry their brands on the sites.

Early days were certainly not easy. But 12 years later, the partners operate 248 sites in the UK, the forecourt business performance has been transformed…and BP announced in December 2016 its intention to replicate the model in other markets.

ILLUSTRATION 6.11	EXAMPLES OF BRANDED PARTNERSHIPS IN ACTION

Credit – Companies corporate sites

Sponsorships

Other major types of branded partnerships include sponsorship and brand ambassadors. A company sponsors a sport, club, art or social cause and publicly associates with it, allying it to what their brand stands for. Examples include O2 or BMW partnering with rugby, Toyota with the Olympics and Paralympics, and BP with the Paralympics. For BP, this partnership expressed the purpose, values and behaviours of a diverse and inclusive global organisation which needed to overcome and recover from adversity, as it strove to 'do the right thing' and reach 'frontier achievements'.

Brand ambassadors

Similarly, a brand ambassador's name brings new significance to the brand. Chanel No 5 took on a different meaning with Marilyn Monroe, as did Guess with Gigi Hadid, Nespresso with George Clooney, Tag Heuer with Leonardo di Caprio, and Aston Martin with James Bond. Jaguar's recent introduction of Professor Stephen Hawking as the latest British Villain is fascinating for the brand.

David Beckham and Arsene Wenger were long-time brand ambassadors of Castrol; and UK track and field athlete Jessica Ennis, US swimmer Nathan Adrian and US track and field athlete Sanya Richards-Ross were BP's. BP and Castrol are part of the same house of brands, but their brand ambassadors suitably represent their different characters and significance.

The Hertz exemplary branded partnership with Disneyland Paris

Hertz Michel Taride shares his experience about Hertz's branded partnership with Disneyland Paris: *"We have been partners for 20 years. One of the reasons we decided on this partnership is that we felt the Hertz brand needed to be warmer, closer to families, more fun and appealing to the young – and Disney would help us achieve this strategic goal.*

"We didn't see our partnership with Disney Resort as a way to drive local business traffic, putting a location there and adding a few thousand transactions a year. It was truly about the brand, how we use Disney in our communication and promotional activity, how we include some of their characters to look warmer and funnier. We spent a lot of time discussing characters, because Disney does an outstanding job in not compromising their brand and is very selective in terms of who they work with, how their partners can use their characters, how often and when."

This is one of the reasons why we like long-term partnerships: you can create the trust and goodwill needed to leverage those agreements and make them ever richer throughout the group.

"We use Disney extensively in our internal and external communications, making them part of our products and putting them on our website, while we are on theirs. We access thousands of Disney passports to enter the park, which we use to reward our loyal customers and hold family parties at one of the Disney resorts. These are a lot of fun and

ILLUSTRATION 6.12	EXAMPLE OF HERTZ AND DISNEYLAND PARIS BRANDED PARTNERSHIP ACTIVATION

Credit – Hertz International

special because it is rare to invite kids to a corporate event. We are also able to incentivise our own staff and intermediaries like travel agents, etc.

"Beyond a number of traditional commercial partnerships, Disney has about a dozen 'strategic alliances', typically multi-year agreements managed by a dedicated department. Hertz is one of Disneyland Paris's historical strategic partners; our well-established global brand gives them a way to promote their resorts and characters, as do Nestle, Visa and others. Another interesting aspect is how you penetrate the Disney ecosystem in search of mutual advantage and synergies: they are, of course, a resort but they also have brand license, movies and many other activities. For example, we were featured in their 'Cars' movie. This is one of the reasons why we like long-term partnerships: you can create the trust and goodwill needed to leverage those agreements and make them ever richer throughout the group."

Brands are and should continue to look to partnerships to enhance their image and impact, boost favourability in a cost effective and synergetic manner and, to put it simply, stand out in a crowded digital world.

Risk - Reward - The usual considerations around the C-suite table

Haven't we all been in these sorts of conversations: prove the value and what about the risks?

Value
Having seen the evidence through repeated delivery, I am absolutely clear on the considerable value of branded partnerships. And I believe the returns outweigh the investment ten times or more.

However, having being party to dozens of agonising discussions with C-Suite colleagues on 'proving the investment' business cases on all sorts of partnerships - business, new ventures, sponsoring like F1 or Olympics etc. - here are a few thoughts from my experience:

1. **Compatible cultures and connected purposes** are required between partners.
2. **Clarity of sources of value** is indispensible, if only to ensure that the partnerships serve the brand and its business model well.
3. **Approaches to measurements** are much better now than they were before, especially when using big data – for example to track a customer journey from awareness to decision. A clear base line and a few quality KPIs should be developed to track progress against the aspired sources of value.
4. **Mid- to long-term commitment** is a requirement to success. Whatever people hope and think, the early days will not be a partnership. Only time well used will improve the profile of delivery, as the joint work deepens, and is represented on Illustration 6.13.
5. **Disciplined management** is required to run the branded partnerships systematically, pre-emptively and ambitiously.

ILLUSTRATION 6.13	PROFILE OF VALUE CREATION FROM PARTNERSHIPS

Strategic Partnering Aims at 'Transformational' Value

'Improved' joint work delivers 2; 'Enhanced' 3 to 4; Transformed 10+

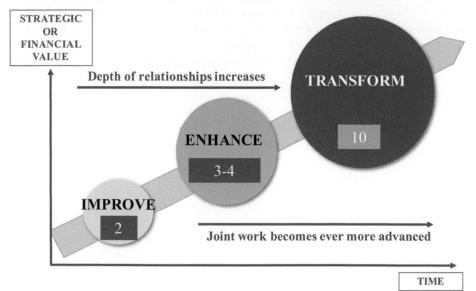

© THE Enduring Strategic Brand

I would venture that C-Suite conversations on partnerships should certainly continue to include elements of 'prove' but that these should be directed more towards the essence of the partnership and the processes needed to reach and deliver their transformational value.

Risk

What about brand dilution? What about changes of strategic direction by one of the parties? What happens if a scandal hits a branded partner?

These are valid questions and, as I have said, ultimate care needs to be taken to select the right partners. Then, just like in a marriage, partners need to manage the hard times as well as the good ones. If I think about the Ford and BP strategic partnership, Ford went through a very difficult financial period in 2008 / 2009 and had to break some of our joint Brand commitments. In 2010, the BP brand was badly tarnished, and there were risks to Ford's image given the public profile of our association. Thanks to a deep belief in the partnership and strong leadership on both sides – an opportunity to thank here Lewis Booth, John Fleming and Stephen Odell of Ford Motor Company – the alliance endured and went from strength to strength in Europe, its native region.

A GREAT PARTNERING CASE – AND AN INVITATION TO CEOS AND CMOS

There is one partnering example I would like to single out here, and it's one which BP, American Express, IBM, Ford and GE have in common: their long-term strategic partnership with Ogilvy & Mather. Rather than telling BP's story, which I have eluded to already, I will instead provide the perspective of John Hayes of AmEx and Shelly Lazarus, Chairman Emeritus of Ogilvy & Mather. Their words highlight the benefits of trusting your agency as a partner, rather than as a mere supplier.

John: *"At AmEx, the brand is about creating a sense of belonging – and with clients, this is membership. The stronger the brand, the deeper the relationships, the greater value to those involved, the more stability. It is part of AmEx's strength that it deepens its relationships over time.*

"Ogilvy helps AmEx go to market every day [type 1 partnership above] *and the depth of our partnership is represented by our shared responsibility. Our best partners understand what drives our business and we work together in driving growth. One of the reasons Ogilvy has been the core agency for American Express for so many years is because they truly understand that it is not about transactions but about driving the core of our business metrics. They don't see themselves as a service provider but as a partner in shared outcomes. On that basis, a true partnership can fully be developed because it is predicated on real success."*

The vast majority of brands don't operate like this anymore; they are more transactional, preferring zero-base marketing, slicing and dicing costs, and involve procurement much more. Is the relationship between AmEx and Ogilvy a model for the future?

At AmEx, the brand is about creating a sense of belonging – and with clients, this is membership. The stronger the brand, the deeper the relationships, the greater value to those involved, the more stability. It is part of AmEx's strength that it deepens its relationships over time.

John: *"Procurement is a key part of every business. But the real difference is between being a cost or an investment. Ogilvy has worked hard on demonstrating the return on investment, how that investment improves the top line, identifying the relevant metrics, what growth we are looking for; and then mapping back to see the work we are doing and the respective accountabilities against the growth objectives. It takes some shared risk, because if something is an investment for growth, the question has to be: 'What is your partner risking if they are benefiting from some of the upside growth?' And as much as that agency's risk doesn't have to mirror exactly the risk profile of the company, there has to be some evidence of it.*

"Tactics on their own don't grow a business, while only the long-term development of the brand or the consistent customer experience isn't going to deliver that business day-to-day, quarter-to-quarter. It's not either/or: a useful partner should be able to help with both – and the challenge and opportunity is finding that balance in the future. I am optimistic because if you understand the real makings of a business, you understand what this combination is and you will succeed."

Shelly agrees: *"American Express and Ogilvy have been inextricably linked since the early 1960s, at almost the very beginning of the American Express card, when David Ogilvy's next door neighbour was Howard Clark, the CEO of American Express.*

"We were invited to every meeting. I even used to go to the HR meetings where they would rate people up; because they cared what the agency thought. I have never seen such a deep partnership.

"So we grew up together. We weren't just called in to do the advertising but rather we were a partner from the start of the conversation about the business strategy. That made everybody in Ogilvy completely invested: it was their business, there was total ownership and anybody who was talented at Ogilvy wanted to work on the American Express Account team. If you ask creative people a big enough question, you get a pretty interesting set of answers. Together we created: 'Don't leave home without it'; 'Do you know me?'; 'Membership has its privileges'; 'Portraits'; 'Realise the Potential'; 'The Membership Effect', etc.

"As in all great partnerships, there is care for each other and loyalty. Another best practice is that the partnership is global: American Express understood that their brand was global and that the partnership had to go around the world, not just be at headquarters.

"On the financial relationship, I remember a famous meeting after somebody within American Express had said: 'We think we are paying Ogilvy too much money. We should figure out country by country how much work is actually being done relative to what we are paying them.' Lou Gerstner, then President of the Card Division, was there, and I remember the meeting started with Argentina and went through things like: 'They did four posters and three letters to acquire card members...' Within four minutes, Gerstner said: 'Let's stop this: this is a waste of time and money. Let's just agree to pay one amount of money and assess on delivery.' Of course we are tracking hours and so on. But there is something very compelling about agreeing on how much money it will take Ogilvy to get AmEx to the targeted brand and business place and expect our best people, wherever they do business, to deliver the best possible solutions. It is a contemporary model and should be used more.

"Here is how Lou Gerstner was thinking about this: 'You want to be one of the three most profitable clients in any professional services firm, because that is where the talent goes. Professional services firms put their best talent against their most profitable clients. If you are not getting the best people, then move on.' As a matter of fact, the better the people are in an agency, the more they have the right or the opportunity to say where they want to work. They could say: 'I would really like to work on American Express because they are asking the big questions, you can do great work, and they don't torture you on how many hours.' Clients in general don't appreciate what a differential that is to the quality of the work they get. An hour of labour is not an hour of labour, and it is difficult to put this in a procurement approach and measure increments of quality."

In BP, we have thoroughly enjoyed and benefited from this partnerial agency model. If you want the best combination of tactics and long-term build, the best people everywhere and the big solutions to big questions – what you need is a true Strategic Partnership. I would do it again any time.

OUR EXEMPLARY STRATEGIC BRAND FOR PARTNERING - IBM

IBM is our selection as the Exemplary Strategic Brand for Partnering because they do it naturally and their brand is impressively coherent on this imperative. As shown in Illustration 6.14, our review found IBM's brand system to be driven by an overwhelming 'Purpose' (5) which is deeply owned by 'People' (5), 'Future Embracing' (5), and both built on and improved with 'Partners' (5).

ILLUSTRATION 6.14   'THE ENDURING STRATEGIC BRAND' IMPERATIVES - IBM

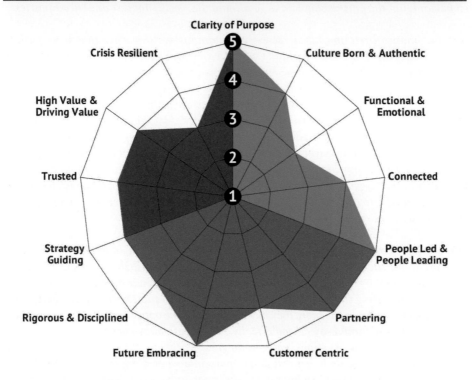

In 2002, as part of putting forward my case in BP to create a dedicated Strategic Partners/Accounts business, I recommended that the BP Downstream ExCo visit Armonk IBM's corporate offices. John Manzoni, our determined and progressive CEO, and the executive team returned persuaded that it was a good idea!

Partnering is fundamental to IBM's Culture and Purpose

We had a fascinating conversation on partnering with Kevin Bishop, an IBMer for 31 years and the VP, 'IBM Brand System and Workforce Enablement' - IBM's Chief Brand Officer for over 3 years until the end of 2012. *"Partnering is fundamental to our DNA. It is central to what we do because it starts from the early founding ideas about why IBM exists and who we serve.*

"Everything about IBM comes back to our founding principles and why we exist, expressed by our founder Thomas J Watson in the organising idea that: 'IBM exists to make the world work better, to make the world a better place; we make tools that make things work better; and what every business needs is more people who think.' [Purpose and values]

With our purpose come our core values – about which Lou Gerstner said: 'You can change everything about IBM, except its values.' And this is what we have done throughout our history: we have changed our products, the countries we operate in and our business model but we have remained true to the same core values. This is all part of what it means to be a modern corporation. This has been reinforced by the fact that we have only had nine CEOs in a 105-year history. Internally, we have always sought to be explicit about what these values are:

- *Dedication to every client's success – [Customer Centric];*
- *Innovation that matters – for our company and for the world – [Future Embracing]; and*
- *Trust and personal responsibility in all our relationships – [Trusted].*

"We have reframed our brand values in modern language but the underlying ideas remain absolutely the same – [Connected and Rigorous and Disciplined].

You see this in our external brand engagement with customers, such as 'Solutions for a Small Planet', 'e-business', 'on-demand business', 'Smarter Planet', and now 'outthink' – these are all variations of the same organising idea, something which connects people around 'how can I make the world work better?', but with modern expression.'

ILLUSTRATION 6.15	EXAMPLES OF IBM EXTERNAL BRAND ENGAGEMENTS AT KEY TRANSFORMATIONAL TIMES

IBM PC

"Little Tramp advertising campaign for PCs."
John R. Opel, 1981

OUT THINK

"This era will redefine the relationship between man and machine."
Ginni Rometty, 2016

E-BUSINESS

"Every now and then, a technology or idea comes along that is so profound, so powerful, so universal that its impact will change everything."
Lou Gerstner, 1997

ON-DEMAND

"Future growth will come from meeting customer demands for 'a new business design'."
Sam Palmisano, 2003

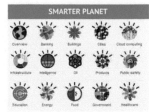

SMARTER PLANET

"Our planet is becoming smarter. This isn't just a metaphor. I mean infusing intelligence into the way the world literally works."
Sam Palmisano, 2008

Credit – THE Enduring Strategic Brand, using IBM ads

"For example, with 'Smarter Planet' we asked, 'How can we use interconnected instrumentation to get new intelligence to make something work better?' Now, with cognitive and augmented intelligence, the question is: 'How can you use this new set of tools that never existed before to help with problems you could never work on before at scale?' This idea brings up a whole set of new problems that you can work on, for example how you can understand patients' illnesses.

"We do this with those we call the forward-thinking people, the people who are frustrated with how things work today and think they could work better. This leads us directly to the idea of partnership; if, from the start, we are bringing new technological capabilities to forward-thinking people, we partner with them – with our clients – to work on solving their problems." [Partnering and Future Embracing]

With IBM Watson, 90 per cent of innovation comes from partners

'THE Enduring Strategic Brand' team studied IBM Watson, a textbook case for partnership types 2 and 3, which acts on a global scale with major importance and impact. In essence, Watson is a cognitive technology that processes information more like a human than a computer, by understanding natural language, generating hypotheses based on evidence and data, and learning as it goes. The expert community agrees that lots of cognitive technology exists – but that it doesn't do much by itself, because *"90 per cent of the innovation will come from partners"*; in IBM's case, the Watson ecosystem.

ILLUSTRATION 6.16	IBM WATSON'S AREAS OF PARTNERSHIPS

Credit – IBM

IBM Watson partners with tens of the best global and many smaller specialist organisations to make the world healthier, more secure, more engaging, more efficient and more personal. It does this in almost all areas of interest for society and business:

- Cognitive healthcare - e.g. Teva, Pfizer, China hospitals, Medtronic
- Cognitive learning - e.g. Pearson
- Cognitive vehicles - e.g. General Motors OnStar
- Cognitive communication - e.g. Vonage Partners, Call centre technologies
- Cognitive retail - e.g. Reflexis Systems, Honest Café
- Cognitive finance - e.g. Thomson Reuters
- Cognitive industry - e.g. Shaeffler on IoT
- Cognitive hospitality - e.g. Connie, Zumata
- Cognitive fashion - e.g. Grech, Marchesa; and many others.

Of course IBM partnerships don't stop with Watson. IBM also have partners for cloud solutions and analytics, among other areas of activity. What is striking is the line up of IBM's huge recent partnerships: with Apple to market custom cloud apps; with Twitter, to develop the tools to analyse tweets; with Tencent to support access and growth in China; with Facebook, to sell more personalised and targeted Facebook ads and IBM marketing cloud services; with SAP to offer SAP's database as a cloud service, etc.

ILLUSTRATION 6.17	IBM LEADS WITH ALL TYPES OF PARTNERSHIPS

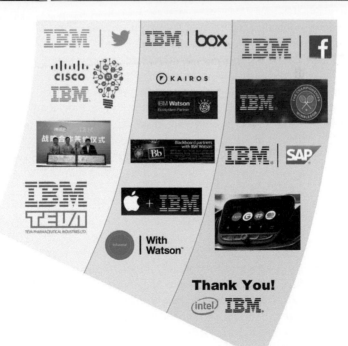

© THE Enduring Strategic Brand

IBM and 100 years of partnerships

As Kevin says, this continues a tradition and systemic practice of partnering by IBM. *"When we had our 100-year anniversary in June 2011, we selected 100 stories as '100 icons of progress' from across the world to reflect what IBM was about. The first category was 'advancing the science of information' and featured our partnerships with Columbia University, the National Science Foundation and others.*

"A second theme was around 'making the world work better'. We had many partnerships with different types of clients, one of which was Citibank, who also had their own 200-year anniversary. On this occasion, Citibank talked about being an IBM customer for 100 years and of our ongoing partnership to reinvent what the bank is. We had NASA who talked about IBM being on every space programme and putting somebody on the moon. And we featured the Broad Institute (with MIT and Harvard) who combined genomics and Watson to do research on cancer and why tumours resist drugs.

"A third theme was about 'reinventing the modern corporation', about equal pay for equal work, about equal opportunity based on talent and expertise, about employing people of colour and with disabilities many years before there was any legislation around that. Each of those stories meant us partnering with government entities. And we have been partnering with Ogilvy for over 20 years, who brought some of their best creators and thought talents to IBM."

The 100 icons stories are an inspiring read (you can find them online - http://www-03.ibm.com/ibm/history/ibm100/us/en/icons/). Indeed it is impressive how long-held IBM partnerships at scale have been pioneers in the world and reshaped entire activities. You will find additional examples of IBM partnerships there including: with Malta, developing the first nationwide smart energy and water grid; with Bharti Airtel, creating a new business model for telecom that would fast speed growth on the Indian market; with the All England Tennis Club, innovating the Wimbledon fan experience; with Guangdong hospital, setting up a smarter healthcare management system; with American airlines, a six-year project to develop the first online reservation system that was widely adopted and extended to other sectors... and there are so many others.

IBM's 'secrets' to Partnering

What is IBM's 'secret'? Could Kevin give us a few of the company's best practices for succeeding with partnerships? *"Ideally, partnering is part of your DNA, because our three core values are about others and about relationships. Publicly we make it an explicit part of our culture - expectations are clear with everybody that it's important. Partnering needs to be imbued with empathy and always be a win-win union, being equally dedicated to the success of any type of partner: clients, academic and research institutions, our distribution channels, the communities that we work in, etc. We feel we have to understand the other's point of view and they have to be successful with it.*

"We actually have a piece that 'teaches' our clients to be better clients, to become partner clients. It says: if you are bringing the problem even before you get anywhere near the technology, we bring the best of IBM forward. If you merely tell us 'I want to buy this box, or that piece of software or this number of hours of time', we will try to do a great job but it won't be as good.

Ideally, partnering is part of your DNA, because our three core values are about others and about relationships. Publicly we make it an explicit part of our culture.

"For well over 30 years we have had a 'business partner charter'. This means you have clear expectations about how we work with, train and brief partners and what we expect in return. Formal training is also important. You need a model of practice, of steps to develop your partnership that goes into details and provides sufficient granularity on how to partner well.

"You have to look at the whole problem. For example, we were struggling with the supplier of automatic cash machines into Russia. We sat down with some of our partners and drew a value map of who was doing what and the respective returns. We realised we had missed key aspects of the customer's value map and their problem, which had nothing to do with technology, the software or the transaction processing - it was simply getting the cash into the machines without people being mugged. And we didn't have the right partnerships in our community to address this.

"A complex question arises when capable organisations find it hard to partner. Like any relationship you have to meet people on their own ground and respect their boundaries. Equally, part of our practice is to bring our knowledge and experience and suggest how they can get increased benefit by working in a more collaborative manner. A good example is with standard initiatives like Linux or the new Partnership on Artificial Intelligence, where it is in nobody's best interest for each person to have their own proprietary standard. Lots of organisations start with a closed view. It has been our experience that you have got to begin by meeting people on their own brand, trust that and then try to bring knowledge, broaden their aperture to work more openly and more collaboratively. It is about making the cake bigger together, as opposed to fighting to divide a smaller cake."

A highly personalised brand 'owned' by the IBMer

Partnering starts and finishes with people. The foundation for success in IBM is the personalisation of the Brand and how everything rests in the hearts and minds of their people [People led and People leading and Authentic]. The following two facts are good examples of this.

The brand is the IBMers

First, unlike companies like BP, Unilever or others, the core values are not 'IBM Values' but 'IBMers Values'. Sam Palmisano, former IBM CEO, explains in Illustration 6.18 how the brand, its values and the in-depth people orientation process gives IBMers space and boundaries, and allows them to make the right judgments and decisions.

ILLUSTRATION 6.18	THE IBMERS VALUES

IBMers values:

- Dedication to every client's success.
- Innovation that matters - for our company and for the world.
- Trust and personal responsibility in all our relationships.

"If there's no way to optimize IBM through organizational structure or by management dictate, you have to empower people while ensuring that they're making the right calls the right way. And by 'right,' I'm not talking about ethics and legal compliance alone; those are table stakes. I'm talking about decisions that support and give life to IBM's strategy and brand, decisions that shape a culture. That's why values, for us, aren't soft. They're the basis of what we do, our mission as a company... You've got to create a management system that empowers people and provides a basis for decision making that is consistent with who we are at IBM."

Sam Palmisano, Harvard Business Review Interview, Leading Change When Business is Good

This is a universal idea which plays into Thomas J Watson's belief that *"the IBM spirit, the IBM heart and the IBM language are the same in all tongues in all countries."*

The second fact occurs if you look at Kevin's job title for what was effectively global brand leadership: rather than CMO or Brand Director, his job title was 'Brand System and IBMer Enablement'. This is about looking at brand and people as one of the same, it is about the brand lived through the people. Kevin remembers the conversation he had on his appointment to the role: *"It was very simple. The Group Chief Marketing and Communications Officer didn't put on the white board 'corporate voice, corporate image, corporate thoughts, corporate colours, imagery, brand police,' etc. He wrote: 'What does it mean to think like IBM? And what does it mean to perform like IBM?' IBM's brand strategy is firstly to be a great company – and then they will be a great brand. Hence brand management is not about managing how we look or sound but rather about how we think, act and perform as an organisation."*

So who are these IBMers? *"Many people who apply to IBM don't just want to work on cool technology or earn a good salary; they want to work with others on meaningful* problems. We have always been big on assessment processes through a combination of interviews and exercises; we look mainly at personality behavioural traits as well as the explicit personal and professional skills that the jobs require. So we ask 'Are people curious? Are they social and open? Are they willing to express their point of view, backed up by facts and evidence? Are they willing to look to others and ask questions of them to make sure that they've understood properly?' Our processes reinforce those things. For example, people join as a group and go through stages of leadership training and development as a group: so 30 years into my IBM career, I am still friend with two people who were on my initial induction training and have multiple contacts through the company and the world from the continuous professional development I have enjoyed.

"In the last 10 years we have acquired a lot of companies and outsourced entire activities, which has made it more difficult because lots of people didn't go through that personal selection. We have reengagement programmes to help them understand what it means to be an IBMer.

The IBMers are the brand

"The primary source of experience of and differentiation for IBM is whether IBMers actually live up to our values and our corporate character. In my time, we used some simple but powerful communications to explore the nature of character - things like what is it that makes James Bond, Bond? There are around 30 Bond books written by three different authors, something like fifty films with nine different Bond actors. And yet you always know what is James Bond and what is not, how he looks, sounds, thinks and performs. We looked at Bond with groups, large and small, in every country of the world and established that he always goes into a casino, has the gadgets, talks to the villains, pursues the girls and is cheeky to his boss. We would discuss what it means to look, sound and perform as Bond. This is what IBM is about: we are not about having people in uniforms – but there is something consistent about how IBM looks, sounds, thinks and performs – about how we show up as experts to solve your problem, how we behave as a team and at the same time value our individuality, which is our character.

"We 'treasure wild ducks' at IBM, because we need a diversity of ideas and opinions. Someone might be contrarian or difficult but he or she could also be the source of a breakthrough idea. And even if they are not, they might be the one who does the job well, who makes whatever it is you are building rigorous enough and good enough quality. The brand is lots of people, is every IBMer – and the brand system is workforce enablement.

The brand is lots of people, is every IBMer – and the brand system is workforce enablement.

"We have great confidence in the leadership team because, as IBMers, they look at fundamentals. If you read the financial papers these days, there are two completely different schools about IBM: those who just play stock markets and beat us up for our revenue growth and PE ratios; and others who look at a company's fundamentals and make investments for the long term – including Warren Buffet. In times of massive change like now, when the whole of our leadership is seen as not driving enough revenue *growth, you have to keep doing the right thing under fire. This is what Ginni [Rometty, CEO of IBM] is doing, and it echoes the fact that we've only had nine CEOs in 106 years. Of those, only one CEO came from outside, and that was Lou Gerstner.*

"Every CEO has been humble and collaborative. We don't have a cult of personality here, with a key founder or a key player. The CEO expresses their role as being the steward of a great company and a great brand. In his book 'Who Says Elephants Can't Dance?' Lou Gerstner wrote, 'When I joined, I didn't know what it meant to be an IBMer. And now I will always be an IBMer. I am an IBMer for life.'"

A long-term guiding brand to build trust...and feed partnering

This extraordinary brand formula generates outstanding Strategic Brand results:

Strategy Guiding and Crisis Resilient

Kevin: *"We are in the technology business – and of course we invent new technologies – but our Brand and values guide and drive us to apply technology to problems that are worth solving in order to make the world work better. We don't just care about innovation but about innovation that matters to the world. We are a for-profit entity, but what we work on needs to be a problem that people care about.*

"When faced with something messy, we come back to the Brand and its values to assess the diverse interests in balance across our four main stakeholder groups – employees, customers, communities and shareholders. For example, we went through a time of crisis during the global banking meltdown, when we nearly couldn't fulfil our financial obligations. We actively discussed the issues across our group of leaders – and in this case we decided to over serve our employees, or we would lose them and would not be able to serve our customers in better times. At other periods, the result might be to put other groups ahead. These discussions are explicit, and we try to stay true to what we are and believe. If companies don't have this guiding light and these roots, it must be really hard as a management team or a client team or as a non-executive set of directors to make good and understandable choices.

"At the moment we are not driving revenue growth because the whole industry is changing. Instead we are putting the investment into making the transformation, because the change will really matter to society. We are placing big bets on Watson and artificial intelligence. Ginni has tremendous backing from the board and from our clients to do that, and we are now starting to get growth in these new businesses, which is needed for the whole company. This is the same approach we have employed at other major turning points, such as when new strategic plans were presented during the Thirties or the Fifties, but in a modern context. It is a business imperative first for the company – and therefore the mark and reflection of a great brand. Ginni might still feel vulnerable sometimes – but who we are, our values and our brand build confidence in the plan, transition, evidence and delivery of all those milestones and that we will get the expected return."

Trusted

There are many manifestations of how strongly trusted IBM is, even by looking at the number, importance, quality and outcomes of its partnerships. 'Trusted' is at the pinnacle of IBM's purpose, as its third value is 'trust and personal responsibility in all relationships'. Kevin explains: *"This applies to how we work with colleagues, our clients, suppliers, partners, academic institutions, all the many types of people that IBM collaborates with in order to work on difficult problems that are worth solving, and be successful in delivering great outcomes."* IBM ranks a commendable 28th in the global Reputation Institute ranking, with a clear upwards trend.

High Value and Driving Value

The average of the 2016 IBM Brand's valuation by Brand Z, Interbrand and Brand Finance is around $60bn and its average global rank is 13th, which is of course a plaudit for what is essentially a B2B and B2G brand. As for driving value, the IBM brand clearly opens doors. Despite the natural ups and downs in absolute numbers, as we have seen recently while the company was going through reinvention and not driving revenue growth, the ROS ranges consistently between 16 per cent and 18 per cent.

With IBM, all brand imperatives converge and contribute to partnering. Not a day passes without IBM announcing a new major partnership of one of the three types we have described. This approach is reflected in the quote by John R Opel, former President, CEO and Chairman: *"As long as IBM has been in business, IBM people have viewed themselves as partners in the business, with a proprietary interest in everything we do and how we do it."* This is a good way of saying 'Partners Inside, Partners Outside' – and rings true to Lou Gerstner's belief in 'Inside-Out'.

Let's leave the last words on our Exemplary Enduring Strategic Brand for Partnering to IBM's CEO Ginni Rometty who demonstrates why the IBM Strategic Brand will continue to impact and transform the world…in partnership.

You make the right decision for the long run. You manage for the long run, and you continue to move to higher value. That's what I think my job is. **Ginni Rometty**	What forebodes well for a long-term partnership: the two teams, the engineers, the designers, the consultants, they've worked beautifully together **Ginni Rometty** **(with Tim Cook on Apple partnership)**	What has always made IBM a fascinating and compelling place for me is the passion of the company, and its people, to apply technology and scientific thinking to major societal issues. **Ginni Rometty**
Your value will be not what you know; it will be what you share. **Ginni Rometty**		To me, I learned along the way, you know, culture is behaviour. That's all it is; culture is people's behaviours. **Ginni Rometty**
You define yourself by either what your clients want or what you believe they'll need for the future. So: Define yourself by your client, not your competitor. **Ginni Rometty**	We believe this era is 'man and machine' – and in fact I know we say artificial intelligence, but it is really augmenting our intelligence. Artificial Intelligence is to conduct 'supervised learning', not overtake human smarts. **Ginni Rometty**	Clients say, 'What's your strategy,' and I say, 'Ask me what I believe first.' That's a far more enduring answer. **Ginni Rometty**

CHAPTER 7
CUSTOMER CENTRIC

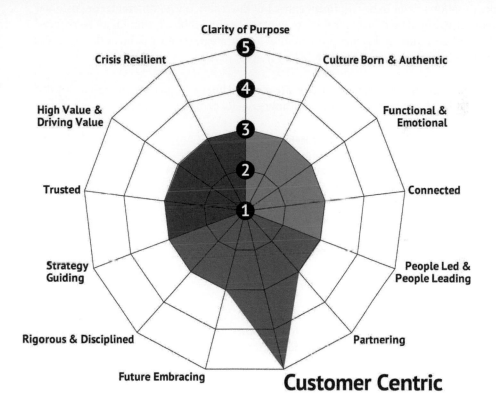

"We see our customers as invited guests to a party, and we are the hosts. It's our job every day to make every important aspect of the customer experience a little bit better"

Jeff Bezos, Amazon

If we reflect on the experience of customers across a variety of industries, I think we can safely say we are not there yet. Transport and utilities are generally awful at customer service and focus very little on the consumer, if at all; some hotels try hard, but legacy weighs heavily; online commerce has its extremes, from Amazon's excellence (which we'll examine later) to frequent online brand disasters. Few organisations are consistent high performers in customer service, able to deliver a satisfying end-to-end customer experience repeatedly.

Hardly any executive or marketer would disagree on the importance of customer centricity, yet the majority of brands are still not executing this properly. Indeed, many organisations claim to be customer centric but the reality is very different. For customer centricity should be a *"way of being"*, to quote O2's Nina Bibby. It should not be reduced to the idea of tools and tactics but a cultural and strategic guiding light, as the examples of O2, American Express and Aldi in this chapter illustrate.

The benefits of customer centricity are extraordinary – growth, margins, loyalty, innovation… and getting it right is the holy grail for Strategic Brands.

When I meet with B2B or B2G colleagues, they often claim that there is a lot to learn from the big B2C FMCG companies in respect to strategic and operational marketing and developing a brand. This is true in many respects but less so in others. In BP and its Strategic Accounts business, our team needed to develop the highest level of customer centricity in dealing with the best of B2B / B2G organisations to reach strategic partnership status. This is perhaps a brand discipline where B2C can learn from B2B – at least this is what I observed from my BP experience and by looking at other partners' brands. Let's consider customer centricity in greater depth.

Customer Centricity

There are many different definitions of Customer Centricity, although in general they are all aligned behind the same core idea. Here is the definition we are using in *'THE Enduring Strategic Brand'*:

"A way of doing business with your customer (or stakeholder) that provides a great experience at every stage in the relationship, from awareness to purchasing and beyond, in order to drive repeat business, customer (or stakeholder) loyalty, customer (or stakeholder) advocacy and profit."

If we focus the definition on customers for now (rather than on other stakeholder groups), a customer-centric company does more than offer good customer service. Rather, customer centricity is a culture, a mindset shared throughout the organisation – not just in marketing or sales – which translates into a consequent strategy based on putting your customer first and at the core of the business. Both Amazon and Zappos are prime examples of brands that are customer centric and have spent years creating a culture around the customer and their needs.

Marc de Swaan Arons is CMO and Executive Board Member, Kantar Vermeer and the master minder of the important 'Marketing 2020' study. (Note 1) He tells us about a case in point: *"One of the projects I'm most proud of was for the CEO of a big European dairy company. He was a cigar chain-smoking chairman who sat in the back of a Mercedes, driving to all the farmer-cooperatives in Germany and Holland. We once had a 'Marketing and Insights' Conference. The theme was 'Customer Immersion' and he was on the stage, with nobody knowing what he would talk about. He began by telling the audience about a slightly overweight Dutch housewife, who he introduced as Anya, how she had a job, how she was a homemaker, how she was trying to be a good wife and how difficult it was. Over the first five minutes, people were giggling and smiling because they had never heard him talk like this. He spoke for 20 minutes; after 10 the room was completely silent. They had realised that this CEO Chairman, this cigar-smoking man in a pin-stripe suit removed from reality, actually knew a customer far deeper than they ever did. They discovered he had spent 24 hours with Anya, went shopping with her, went to her work and spent time in her home while she cooked, used the company's product, and parented. This was real immersion, both functionally and emotionally; he had connected to this customer and spoke about her with an elegance, insight and care that touched everybody in the room."*

Customer centricity is both a cause and a result. It is a cause because it drives many Strategic Brand imperatives, such as 'Authenticity' and 'People leading'. It is a result because achieving true customer centricity requires everything that makes up a Strategic Brand: simple and clear 'Purpose', being 'People led', a 'Disciplined' and Consistent' execution, a 'Collaborative' approach, and so on.

Let's consider some research in this area.

A few data points on Consumer Centricity

Performance
Customer-centric companies are 60 per cent more profitable than companies that are not focused on the customer - Deloitte.

Companies able to identify and maximise the value of their best customers have the potential to increase sales by 17 per cent - Dr. Peter Fader, Wharton Business School

Increasing customer retention by 5 per cent increases profit by 25 to 95 per cent - Bain & Company

It takes 12 positive experiences with a brand to make up for one unresolved negative experience - *"Understanding customers"* by Ruby Newell-Legner.

Consumers tell twice as many people about poor experiences than positive ones - White House Office of Consumer Affairs.

| ILLUSTRATION 7.1 | REWARDS OF CUSTOMER CENTRICITY AND RISKS WITH A LACK OF IT |

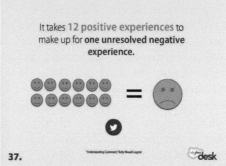

Credit – Gartner Group; Ruby Newell- Legner; Salesforce desk

Impediments

Using data to inform decisions is at the centre of customer centricity. However, executives view the flood of incoming data as part obstacle and part opportunity, with 61 per cent of CMOs admitting they still have a long way to go in using big data properly - CMO Council and SAS

A lack of clear ownership of the customer is holding companies back from a true customer focus. 48 per cent of marketers are only moderately confident in the ability of their organisation's core touch points to reach and engage with the customer – CMO Council

For most marketers, customer centricity is an aspirational goal rather than a reality because: 70 per cent of companies have suboptimal or no ability to integrate customer data between online and offline sources; 80 per cent don't apply customer value scores; and 74 per cent can't recognise customers in real time – Axciom and Digiday

Creating a happy customer is not a marketing-only endeavour – customer service, product development, R&D teams, operations and IT all play a role. However, only 12 per cent of B2B marketers said that functional teams were strongly aligned around a holistic customer experience strategy – SAP and CMO Council

According to consumers, customer service agents fail to answer their questions 50 per cent of the time - Harris Interactive

Opportunities

63 per cent of CEOs see rallying their organisations around the customer as one of the top three investment priorities in 2017. Nine out of 10 US CEOs say they are strengthening their customer and client engagement programmes this year - PwC

90 per cent of marketers say that customer individualisation is a priority: they're learning that the more personal the approach, the greater the chance of a positive response - Teradata

58 per cent of marketers say that by far the most important characteristic to establish a truly 'digital native' culture is to be customer centric, ahead of data-driven (40 per cent) and well ahead of any other criteria - Econsultancy

Customer service is a key component of a customer-centric strategy. 86 per cent of consumers say they would pay more if they could guarantee superior service. 89 per cent who had recently switched from a business to its competitor did so because of poor service - Harris Interactive Survey

Banks and other financial institutions have significantly enhanced their customer focus, increasing the number of customer-centric jobs by 52 per cent in the last year – Seek's Employment Market Report

Enterprise brands, like multichannel retailers, are asking their customers to set their own preferences: brands today are 62 per cent more likely to give their subscribers the ability to set their own preferences for branded communications than they were in 2013. Further, they are 89 per cent more likely to allow them to select the type of messages that they receive and 48 per cent more likely to give options for how often subscribers want to receive those communications – Experian Marketing Services

45 per cent of B2B marketers feel their levels of customer centricity are good, if not high. And 45 per cent believe their customers would say that customer centricity levels are good to high – SAP and CMO Council

The opportunities from being customer centric seem straightforward – the big question is how to achieve proper customer centricity and do it in the digital age.

10 KEY TENETS OF CUSTOMER CENTRICITY

Every marketing agency, many professors and plenty of brands have their own view of Customer Centricity, particularly when it comes to the moving context and inherent changes that digital brings to execution. The purpose of '*THE Enduring Strategic Brand*' is not to repeat those things, but to share the thoughts and learning of practitioners - how can we progress towards true and real customer centricity in practice?

In my observation, many organisations have an incomplete customer centricity approach. Customer centricity should be treated as a science, as a comprehensive system. Companies are often missing the foundations, such as 'Culture' or 'People led', and are therefore failing, at least in part, as they are unable to build on these. Here are the ten tenets of customer centricity as we see them:

1. **Culture and mindset** – Customer centricity is foremost a culture and a mindset.
2. **Purpose led** – There is no successful customer centricity that is not driven by deep purpose.
3. **Total experience design** – For any product or service, unparalleled focus is needed to design a total and consistent experience at every touch point. Dissect every detail of the customer journey to achieve excellence and consistency. Executives and leaders should spend considerable time in the field and online, going through the customer journey.
4. **Trends integration** – Integrate societal and behavioural trends early in the experience through continual (re)design, so your customers move seamlessly from one point of success to the next.
5. **Customer as a partner** – The customer should be viewed as a partner, with a relationship driven by mutual advantage and held day after day across all touch points.
6. **Cross-functional teams** – Sales, Marketing and Aftersales are one, ideally also combined with R&D. In a broader way, a customer centric organisation operates through cross-functional teams, leading continuous customer-fed improvement and innovation.
7. **Decision on the frontline** – Customer centric brands empower the frontline through brand values, behaviours and capability development. Organisations are flat, practising an inverse pyramid. Leaders are enablers, in service of cross-functional teams and measured on their success on the frontline.
8. **Magnet for talents** – In a customer centric organisation, people need to feel like they are the CEO of their own area. They need to be true talents – and the organisation should be focused on attracting the best.
9. **Unparalleled growth** – Customer centric brands achieve unparalleled sustained and sustainable growth. Performance management focuses on inputs, following Peter Drucker's guidance that *"the only correct and effective way to increase the value of a company is the creation of customers"*; and that *"employees should be able to realise their value by making decisions"*.
10. **"We are the Platform"** - A customer centric Strategic Brand is vital to prevent disintermediation of the enterprise in the 'uberisation' of the economy. The Strategic Brand leads the platformisation opportunity, rather than getting platformised as second tier.

We will use these ten tenets later in this chapter to assess the customer centricity readiness and practice of brands, and to review three exceptional brands which are different in style: O2, AmEx and Aldi. Would you want to run an objective self-assessment of your brand against this framework?

The Customer Centricity Cycle

As I said earlier, winning and enduring customer centricity results from a comprehensive and systematic process, which in effect turns the ten tenets into an operational model.

Hence, I have got used to approaching customer centricity as a 'cycle' system as shown on Illustration 7.2. Experience suggests how important it is to operate this cycle in sequence, building strong foundations ahead of operationalization.

In Chapter 4, 'Connected', we looked at how essential it is for a Strategic Brand to be deeply connected, in particular with its customers – but connectedness on its own is not enough. In Chapter 6, we talked about partnerships. Achieving a partnership with your customers creates a balanced, high quality relationship, which delivers the highest possible value over time. This is the area where I believe B2B has much to teach B2C.

ILLUSTRATION 7.2	THE CUSTOMER CENTRICITY CYCLE

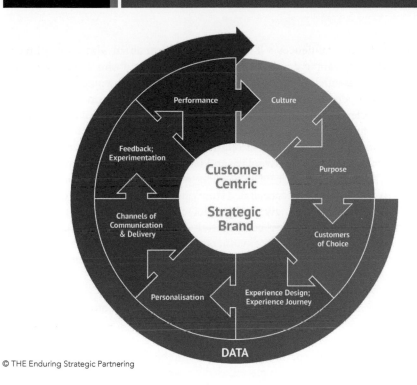

© THE Enduring Strategic Partnering

Customer centricity is the combination of connectedness with a mindset of partnership. Using Chapter 4's 'Connectedness Diamond' as a basis, the Customer Centricity cycle should follow the sequence captured on Illustration 7.2, and described below:

1. Culture and mindset – The very first imperative for developing and building Strategic Brand Customer Centricity is to be culturally fit for it. Everybody in an organisation – not just those in marketing or sales – needs to understand what it is and takes to be customer centric. For example, quality of listening to a customer should be at the highest level. Customer centric organisations are passionate that *"without the customer,* *they cannot succeed in business. These organisations want to see the world through the customer's eyes."*

2. Purpose – Many of this book's contributors believe that everything is driven by an organisation's purpose, i.e. why you are here, what difference you are here to make and why your brand is important. When it comes to a partnering customer relationship, your purpose and how you act on it are paramount. Doesn't Simon Sinek intimate that *"people don't buy what you do; they buy why you do it."*

Achieving a partnership with your customers creates a balanced, high quality relationship, which delivers the highest possible value over time.

3. Customers of choice / Audiences – It is critical to be clear about who your ultimate customers are, who you want to develop a relationship with – and who you do not. The clarity of selection is essential – I suppose an historical form of this would be 'customer segmentation'. This understanding defines the organisation's focus on providing an inspiring total experience, and delivering a lifestyle platform which will delight their target customers. I have witnessed organisations trying to be everything to everybody but don't believe this approach supports the long-term build of a Strategic Brand. At some point, they lose clarity, competitive advantage and fall into head-to-head competition.

In the early 2000s, Starbucks accelerated store openings and added a broader food menu. This made it increasingly feel like McDonald's or Dunkin' Donuts, while these two chains were in turn adding competitively priced premium coffee drinks to their offer –making Starbucks' high prices vulnerable. Eventually, Starbucks redesigned both its food offer and its stores to match the preferences of its core customer targets and recreate white space with McDonald's.

So, culture, purpose and the selection of audiences are the three foundations of customer centricity.

4. Customer Journey / Total Experience Design – With the three previous foundations in place, next comes strategy. I am single-minded on what it means: framing, shaping and enabling for immaculate execution, supporting the proposition that *"strategy is execution"*.

amazon At this stage it's vital to design and test with precision and clarity the total experience and customer journey of any service or product. My repeated observation is that 'value proposition' design is one of the activities which most companies find the hardest to do well. Amazon is the archetype of excellence, with every micro-step of a customer's journey considered from any potential start point.

NIKE Marc de Swaan Arons comments: *"At Nike, somebody once made a chart which described all the factors contributing to a customer's decision-making. This journey was about getting somebody off the couch, knowing where to run, the music (because 90 per cent of runners use music), the planning in terms of training schedules, seeing progress in preparation or performance. There are 10 such things; these aren't directly about shorts or shoes but they are about Nike's purpose of 'unleashing the athlete in everyone'. After that, Nike made the strategic choice of saying that as a brand, they could credibly play a role in each of these other touch points and, for example, be the first to create and offer an easy-to-use online running planner. Then came NikeiD, which is not about the generation of direct income but about building brand loyalty and usage. Of course, it did both. It took deep customer centricity for Nike to take a step back and say: 'What does life look like?'"*

The type of relationship we want to have with our selected audiences is a major driver to the design of our service and experience, meaning that 'outside-in' elements – customer needs, white spaces, and societal shifts – are of course very important. But 'THE Enduring Strategic Brand' approach to customer centricity begins with 'inside-out' – brand, culture, DNA, heritage – and being clear about the type of relationship and experience we want and can provide, while being true to who we are and not trying to be what we are not.

5. Personalisation – This is the first phase of activation and implementation. Nowadays, the extraordinary availability of data enables a service, experience or relationship to be adjusted and adapted to the personal journey of each individual customer, making it personalised. This is one of the bases of Amazon's success and personalisation is spreading across all sectors, from pioneer Oakley for sunglasses to unexpected Bank of America for personal cards.

6. Channels of Communication and Delivery – This is how the offer is communicated or made available to the customer, and includes sales people, digital channels or physical shops – though today, digital channels are often dominant. Increasingly, these are in the hands of third parties and a delivery service ecosystem. Each and all of these touch points must be fully consistent with the brand.

7. Feedback and experimentation – The modern age allows extensive direct or indirect feedback through multiple channels. This feedback should be collected, built into big data and translated into insights, to lead directions of continuous improvement or transformation. Equally, the feedback will guide experimentation and be a large source for testing innovation.

Marc de Swaan Arons comments: *"This is a world of everyday feedback in which a big 'C' for change in marketing is taking place: you don't need market research anymore when you have feedback every day!"*

8. Performance Performance is measured throughout the cycle, and assessed at the end of it. There are a number of usual output performance measures to customer centricity - e.g. growth, margins, profit. Equally important are three other measures which I have always used as leading indicators for enduring growth, longer-term renewal and development of performance:

- Loyalty, i.e. repeat purchase
- Net promoter score (critical given the impact of customers' input today – we'll explore this later in relation to Aldi)
- Strategic Brand key metrics.

The cycle then begins again with culture. And although culture doesn't change (Ref. Chapter 2) it can evolve, improve and adjust to better fit customer centricity.

It is my belief of what is required – the ten tenets and the customer centricity cycle. But let's see whether this system works against three brands that are well known for their customer centricity – O2, American Express and Aldi.

O2 BRAND: A CULTURE AND MINDSET OF 'CUSTOMER AS A PARTNER'

O2 The O2 brand, with its 25 million customers, epitomises the 'Culture' of customer centricity. Just look at how their three clear values of 'Trusted', 'Bold' and 'Open' are expressed from the customer's perspective, from 'YOU'. For example, 'Trusted' is defined with this partnerial phrase *"If it's good for you, it's good for us"*.

At O2, what we say is that we are not a business that runs a brand, we are a brand that runs a business

Nina Bibby is Chief Marketing Officer at O2. We had an energising conversation about Enduring Strategic Brands: *"At O2, what we say is that we are not a business that runs a brand, we are a brand that runs a business. That to me is what a 'Strategic Brand' is: the backbone of the business, central to its purpose, how it creates value and how it delivers its products or services, in short the way it actually imbues the spine of the business. At the top table, O2 is thought about almost as a person. As we make decisions on the executive committee, brand is always there in terms of 'this is the O2 way of doing things, that's how we would operate – or not.'* [**2. Purpose led ✓**]

"The brand can only be sustainable and effective in the long term if it is at heart a customer champion. This has always been true but particularly now: in our world of transparency, customers will very quickly perceive a disconnect between what the brand is reported to do and what it delivers.

"O2 is emphatically a customer and brand led business and there are five principles at the heart of the 'customer centricity' idea." [**1. Culture & Mindset ✓**]

ILLUSTRATION 7.3	O2 AS A CUSTOMER CENTRIC STRATEGIC BRAND

O₂

1. Culture & Mindset — 4
2. Purpose Led — 5
3. Total Experience Design — 4
4. Trends Integration — 4
5. Customer as a Partner — 5
6. Cross Functional Teams — 4
7. Decision on the front line — 4
8. Magnet for Talents — 3
9. Unparalleled Growth — 3
10. We are the Platform — 3

Scale 1: Low to 5: Very Strong

O2 - Customers as partners

"The first principle of customer centricity is 'partnership' and 'partnering with customers'. This is a relationship of equals, not a parent-child or adult-child relationship, but adult-adult. In today's digital world, this idea is very important. The old communication model of parent-child – i.e. company versus customer, 'us and them' – which we operated for many years, can't survive today. Of course, the partnership has to be meaningful for the customer, and this depends on how determined you are to understand what is important to them. This will also make it long lasting. A partnership must be built on a clear value-exchange: as a business, we are here to make a profit, but it works both ways. We will only create value from our customers if we create value for our customers. [**5. Customer as a Partner** ✓]

O2 - Equality

"The second principle is: 'O2 values all of its customers equally.' In many industries, as in mobile, when you are trying to acquire customers, there is a huge temptation to keep giving better and better deals to new customers. But this results in your existing customers thinking they are paying more to subsidise the new ones. O2 was one of the first mobile phone companies to commit to allowing our existing customers to get access to the same deals as new customers. It sounds obvious but it is amazing how many companies still don't do this. [**5. Customer as a Partner** ✓]

O2 - Freedom

"The third principle is: 'we want our customers to feel they are in a hotel not a prison.' It's easy for a subscription-based business to make customers feel trapped, so we introduced different innovations over time so they could leave. We introduced 'O2 Refresh', which enables a customer to leave their contract early by only paying off their phone. Many customers told us that they wanted to use Wi-Fi calling: whilst some of us were worried

that this would hurt our revenues, we thought that if it was what customers wanted, we should enable it, so we developed 'TU Go' to make it possible. Ultimately it's delivering great service which attracts and retains customers – and, at heart, O2 is a people, personal and customer service brand, which strives to achieve this: in 2016 we were voted as having the best customer service by Ofcom for the seventh time in a row. [**5. Customer as a Partner** ✓]

O2 - Partnerships for innovation

"The fourth principle is: 'we partner on behalf of our customers to innovate.' We seek out relationships with third parties to innovate on behalf of our customers in a way that we wouldn't be able to do alone. This includes sponsorships which for us means true partners including AEG for the O2 arena, LiveNation [with 19 O2 academies around the country], and rugby where we have been partner-sponsor for 21 years. [**4. Trends Integration** ✓]

O2 - Inspiration

"The last principle is: 'try to make a difference to our people and society.' This may sound trite but we can't expect to inspire our customers if we can't inspire our colleagues. This means that any big launch starts with our colleagues. In 2014, we launched the £1 lunch on a Monday beginning with lunch in the O2 canteens. When we launched the Rugby World Cup 'Rose Army' campaign in 2015 to get the whole nation excited and recruit the 'Rose Army' of 100 England Superfans, the first 10 recruits were our colleagues. We are a service business. It's not the advertising which delivers the brand but our colleagues on the frontline, in the shops and on the phone. And it's important to look for opportunities to give back to society. [**8. Magnet for Talents** ✓]

O2 - Measurements

"Beyond our culture, O2 is sustainably customer centric because we quantify investments and paybacks. I use econometric modelling to input everything we advertise and promote, and for our services like Priority, the biggest digital loyalty program in the UK, I look at what drives consideration, loyalty and recontracting. We bring a lot of rigour to understanding the outcomes of our investments and align our numbers with our CFO." [**9. Unparalleled Growth** ✓]

AMERICAN EXPRESS BRAND – A 166-YEAR-OLD
BRANDED CUSTOMER CENTRED SERVICE

The American Express brand is a benchmark Enduring Strategic Brand (Ref. Illustration 7.4), and we recounted an example of its partnering practice in Chapter 6 – 'Partnering'.

Customer centricity is intrinsic to the AmEx brand as it is, by its nature, continuously redefined by the service experience it delivers every day to its 118 million card customers. The company expresses its customer focus mindset through its first value, *"customer commitment"*, and through its operating principle: *"We offer superior value propositions to all of our customers."* [**2. Purpose led** ✓]

Everybody is an AmEx brand steward

John Hayes is immediately clear on the importance of the brand: *"We talk about the brand frequently because there is a universal understanding that it is fundamental to our business success. It is not just one department which is worried about the brand, but the entire company. The brand stewards are just about every employee within the company - everyone feels a certain responsibility to uphold the tenets and values of the brand.*

It is not just one department which is worried about the brand, but the entire company. The brand stewards are just about every employee within the company.

So our definition of what the brand stands for doesn't change from location to location or from person to person or from business unit to business unit; it is interpreted for that particular constituent but it's universally discussed, understood and turned into reality within the company." [**1. Culture & Mindset** ✓]

ILLUSTRATION 7.4	AMERICAN EXPRESS AS A CUSTOMER CENTRIC STRATEGIC BRAND

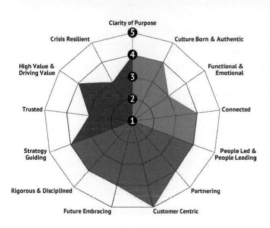

1. Culture & Mindset	4
2. Purpose Led	5
3. Total Experience Design	5
4. Trends Integration	4
5. Customer as a Partner	5
6. Cross Functional Teams	4
7. Decision on the front line	4
8. Magnet for Talents	4
9. Unparalleled Growth	4
10. We are the Platform	4

Scale 1: Low to 5: Very Strong

AmEx Customers are members

Any insight into AmEx starts with the sustainability of its performance - +3 per cent CAGR revenue growth and ca. +4 per cent CAGR net income growth over the past 9 years. How successfully the brand has come through the financial downturn and continuing industry transformations is the reflection of an enduringly high performing organisation [**9. Unparalleled Growth** ✓].

John Hayes explains: *"From a brand standpoint, the most important thing is creating a relationship with depth. At AmEx, we call this 'membership', which means a sense of belonging, a sense that one could rely on the AmEx brand for many things. AmEx also looks to create a relationship with prospects, a desire to be part of the franchise.*

"My definition of marketing versus sales is that marketing is designed to build this desire in the marketplace while sales is there to convert that into business; if the desire to experience the products and services of that particular offering is strong, it is easier to convert from a sales standpoint, and this therefore makes everything more efficient. [**6. Cross Functional Teams ✓**]

"The brand is at the core of creating that desire in the marketplace. What has made American Express as successful as it is, in terms of its ability to offer both value and innovation, is its level of customer focus. You can't be a highly successful branded company without being customer focused. That means understanding what your customers want today but also anticipating what they are going to want and where they might be looking for value tomorrow - and understanding how that might relate to the value of your brand and the value of what you offer. American Express is strongly focused on this – and this includes recognising that it can't do everything by itself and looking to partnerships to provide high levels of innovation." [**4. Trends Integration ✓**]

AmEx - Trust, security and service

I asked John about AmEx's magic to its enduring success in a highly competitive sector. *"The core tenets of the brand, meaning the relationship, are trust, security and service - these aren't purely functional, they also have an important emotional element.*

*"***Trust*** is fundamental to sustainability when you are in the business of money and financials. You earn the trust of your customers over time, based on your behaviours. And over time you might also earn a reputational trust that extends beyond your existing customer base.*

*"***Security*** is also earned and we started delivering security early on with our freight forwarding business, when we moved people's valuables around the US. Regardless of what industry we are doing business with, security remains paramount to how people think about and value American Express. The simplicity of doing business with the company in every aspect of that security is also central to the brand.*

*"***Service*** is the core of the value delivered by the brand. While today this service mindset applies in the payments and travel business, who we are altogether is the 'service of American Express'.*

"Those three related pillars make up the American Express brand. There is a considerable emotional part to each tenet and in their combination because AmEx often helps customers solve something they can't do by themselves. Therefore a lot of the emotion comes from the customer experience: getting this right is fundamental to the brand and, more generally, to building a successful brand today. [**5. Customer as a Partner ✓; 3. Total Experience Design**]

AmEx - Respected and special

"Communication is secondary if the way you are doing business enables your customers

to feel 'respected and special', which are the two most important effects of the American Express brand. There are many things that the company does, particularly in its service delivery, to ensure you feel these things.

An example is 'Small Business Saturday', in which individual small businesses, which are not large enough to promote themselves in any meaningful way on their own, become much more visible when they come together with others. It's a win for everybody when the sellers, buyers and American Express get together around that day's special deals."

AmEx - Leadership and principles-based environment

"Customer centricity starts with a leadership which truly believes that how customers are treated is important to the welfare of the business. American Express has a great history to this day of leaders who believe in making people and customers feel respected and special. This is pervasive throughout the business and anchors the company's cultural ethos of 'we value treating people well, whether it is our employees or our customers, because in order to get employees to treat customers well, we have to treat our employees well. Our employees have to feel respected and special.'

In order to get employees to treat customers well, we have to treat our employees well.

"Finally, it is important to have a principles-based environment, as opposed to a rules-based environment. It's difficult to treat customers constructively across the board in so many situations and at such scale with only a set of rules. What you need to do is establish the principles by which the company will operate and give people the freedom to service those customers and make decisions according to those principles. We do lots of training and education at all levels of the company. When someone joins us from outside, there is a process they enter that helps them understand the brand values. Then that conversation continues through the lifetime of that employee." [**7. Decision on the front line** ✓]

ALDI BRAND – A PURPOSE-DRIVEN EXPERIENCE FOR CUSTOMERS AS PARTNERS

In preparation for this 'Customer Centric' chapter, '*THE Enduring Strategic Brand*' carried out qualitative and quantitative research to test and identify the attributes which drive the Net Promoter Score (NPS), a critical reflection of customer centricity. The Foresight Factory, a marketing consultancy that specialises in trends and foresights, ran the research with the simple overarching question: "*What makes consumers love and recommend a brand?*" And we worked out insights from the data with Christophe Jouan, CEO and Co-Owner (Note 2).

Net Promoter Score

The research was conducted in 2016 across a number of countries, including the US, China, the UK, Germany and Sweden, in the supermarket, banking, technology and 'best of brands' categories. A split analysis was also run between the baby-boomer, Y and Z generations. Rather than detailing the methodology here - which is available on the Foresight Factory site, here are the study's conclusions.

Looking at the UK example, Illustration 7.5 shows what drives NPS and therefore is core to customer centricity - a mix of functional attributes like 'value for money' and 'best quality'; and more emotional ones like 'genuine', 'inspires me' or 'makes me feel good'.

| **ILLUSTRATION 7.5** | WHAT INFLUENCES BRAND ADVOCACY IN THE UK |

☺ POSITIVE	☺ NO CLEAR RELATION	☹ NEGATIVE
▶ Value for money	▶ Reliable	▶ Exclusive and personalised
▶ Best quality	▶ Good customer service	promotions
▶ Innovative	▶ Convenient	▶ Reward my loyalty
▶ Genuine	▶ Easy to use	
▶ Inspires me	▶ Pay flexibly	
▶ Makes me feel good	▶ Good reputation	
▶ Cool and impressive	▶ Fun and entertaining	
	▶ Help achieve goals	
	▶ Reflect my personality	
	▶ Environmentally friendly	
	▶ Treats workers well	

Credit – The Foresight Factory

Aldi's customer centricity 'magic'

The German retailer Aldi came out particularly strongly in the research. Aldi [Nord and Süd] run over 10.000 stores in eighteen countries, notably in Germany, the USA and the UK. They are growing fast – as a case in point, they announced a $1.6bn investment in US expansion in February 2017. Here we focus on Aldi UK, recognising that very similar observations apply to its other markets.

In the UK, Aldi has more than doubled its market share in the past four years to over 6 per cent, overtaking Waitrose and more recently Co-op to become the UK's fifth largest supermarket chain.

Aldi claims a *'no-nonsense approach to running its business'*. Whereas other food retailers have more elaborate displays, additional services and promotions to draw customers into the business, Aldi's core purpose is to *'provide value and quality to our customers by being fair and efficient in all we do'*. [**2. Purpose led** ✓]. The model is driven by the three values of *'simplicity, consistency and responsibility'*. Lean production, including the fact that 90 per cent of their products are ALDI exclusive brands, ties in closely with these values, and savings are passed back to consumers.

Aldi's customer centricity 'magic' seems to lie in the fact that they have moved the customer-to-supermarket relationship from being purely functional to something more akin to an 'alliance'. That is, consumers feel strongly that Aldi is on their side and will help them out, as opposed to being simply a supermarket. [**5. Customer as a Partner** ✓] This makes Aldi a formidable, albeit low profile, Customer Centric Strategic Brand.

ILLUSTRATION 7.6	ALDI AS A CUSTOMER CENTRIC STRATEGIC BRAND

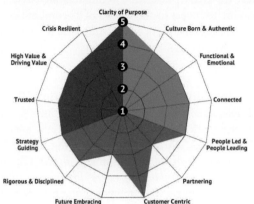

1. **Culture & Mindset** — 5
2. **Purpose Led** — 5
3. **Total Experience Design** — 5
4. **Trends Integration** — 4
5. **Customer as a Partner** — 5
6. **Cross Functional Teams** — 4
7. **Decision on the front line** — 5
8. **Magnet for Talents** — 4
9. **Unparalleled Growth** — 4
10. **We are the Platform** — 4

Scale 1: Low to 5: Very Strong

From the research, Aldi had by far the highest proportion of strong brand advocates amongst its customers compared to all its competitors – close to 70 per cent, compared to 48 per cent on average of all supermarkets in the researched countries. This was confirmed by a strong 48 per cent of positive comments on social media, well above par and a major rise from their 2012 27 per cent. Our brand attribute research explains what underpins this strong performance, as shown in the diagnosis in Illustration 7.7.

ILLUSTRATION 7.7	ALDI BRAND DIAGNOSIS: ALL CUSTOMERS

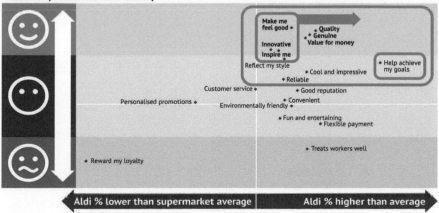

Credit – THE Enduring Strategic Brand and The Foresight Factory

Aldi - Genuine; helps achieve my goals; quality and value for money

To explain the illustration: the higher the elements on the vertical axis, the more positive they are in terms of generating brand advocacy for supermarkets. Horizontally, the further these elements are to the right, the better Aldi compares with its competitors. Altogether, Aldi gets strong results, with most attributes higher than average. The busy top right quadrant reflects a strong competitive position for the most important criteria behind active NPS, with 'genuine' and 'help achieve my goals' powerful and differentiated assets. These are areas in which Aldi should continue to invest to stay ahead of its competition. Areas of improvement, i.e. important criteria for consumers where Aldi does not have a real differentiation, are: 'make me feel good', 'inspire me' and 'innovative'.

Aldi - Brand simplicity

So how has Aldi achieved this position of strength? Broadly speaking, because of their customer centricity. The Aldi Brand is simple, so simple that it comes first routinely in the global Brand Simplicity Index run by the marketing consultant Siegel+Gale, ahead of Google, Ikea or Amazon. Here are Siegel+Gale's words when announcing the 2017 ranking: *"Discount supermarket chain Aldi once again takes the top spot in the Global Brand Simplicity Index. Its formula for success? Uncomplicated offers, low prices, high quality products and great customer service. Consumers also appreciate the transparent price comparisons to competitors, which provide confidence that they're getting the best deal."* (Note 3)

ILLUSTRATION 7.8 THE ALDI BRAND FIRST FOR BRAND SIMPLICITY GLOBALLY

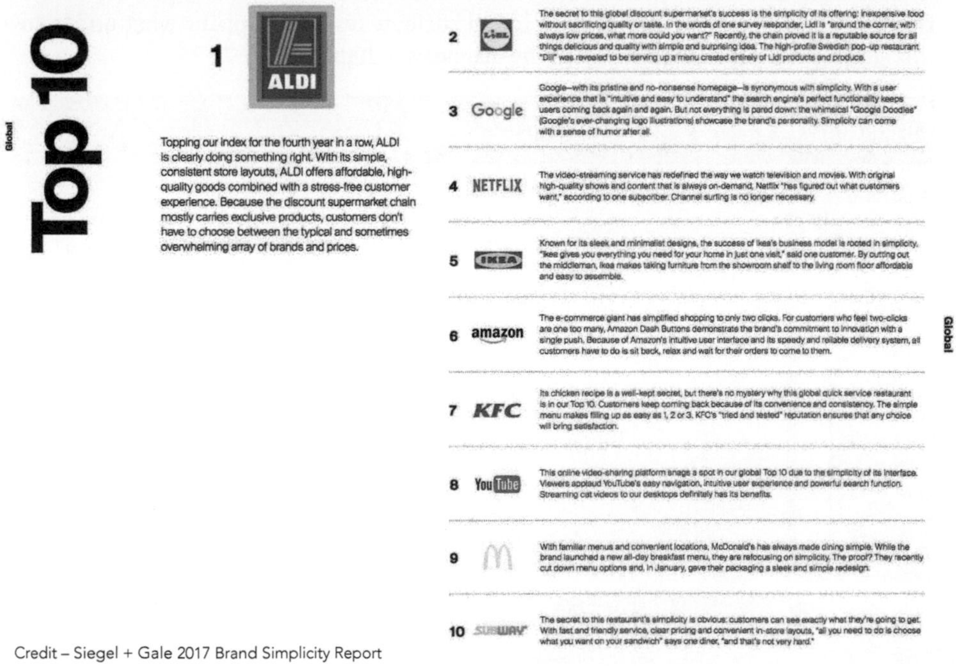

Global

Top 10

1 ALDI

Topping our index for the fourth year in a row, ALDI is clearly doing something right. With its simple, consistent store layouts, ALDI offers affordable, high-quality goods combined with a stress-free customer experience. Because the discount supermarket chain mostly carries exclusive products, customers don't have to choose between the typical and sometimes overwhelming array of brands and prices.

2 LIDL — The secret to this global discount supermarket's success is the simplicity of its offering: inexpensive food without sacrificing quality or taste. In the words of one survey responder, Lidl is "around the corner, with always low prices, what more could you want?" Recently, the chain proved it is a reputable source for all things delicious and quality with simple and surprising idea. The high-profile Swedish pop-up restaurant "Dill" was revealed to be serving up a menu created entirely of Lidl products and produce.

3 Google — Google—with its pristine and no-nonsense homepage—is synonymous with simplicity. With a user experience that is "intuitive and easy to understand" the search engine's perfect functionality keeps users coming back again and again. But not everything is pared down: the whimsical "Google Doodles" (Google's ever-changing logo illustrations) showcase the brand's personality. Simplicity can come with a sense of humor after all.

4 NETFLIX — The video-streaming service has redefined the way we watch television and movies. With original high-quality shows and content that is always on-demand, Netflix "has figured out what customers want," according to one subscriber. Channel surfing is no longer necessary.

5 IKEA — Known for its sleek and minimalist designs, the success of Ikea's business model is rooted in simplicity. "Ikea gives you everything you need for your home in just one visit," said one customer. By cutting out the middleman, Ikea makes taking furniture from the showroom shelf to the living room floor affordable and easy to assemble.

6 amazon — The e-commerce giant has simplified shopping to only two clicks. For customers who feel two-clicks are one too many, Amazon Dash Buttons demonstrate the brand's commitment to innovation with a single push. Because of Amazon's intuitive user interface and its speedy and reliable delivery system, all customers have to do is sit back, relax and wait for their orders to come to them.

7 KFC — Its chicken recipe is a well-kept secret, but there's no mystery why this global quick service restaurant is in our Top 10. Customers keep coming back because of its convenience and consistency. The simple menu makes filling up as easy as 1, 2 or 3. KFC's "tried and tested" reputation ensures that any choice will bring satisfaction.

8 YouTube — This online video-sharing platform snags a spot in our global Top 10 due to the simplicity of its interface. Viewers applaud YouTube's easy navigation, intuitive user experience and powerful search function. Streaming cat videos to our desktops definitely has its benefits.

9 — With familiar menus and convenient locations, McDonald's has always made dining simple. While the brand launched a new all-day breakfast menu, they are refocusing on simplicity. The proof? They recently cut down menu options and, in January, gave their packaging a sleek and simple redesign.

10 SUBWAY — The secret to this restaurant's simplicity is obvious: customers can see exactly what they're going to get. With fast and friendly service, clear pricing and convenient in-store layouts, "all you need to do is choose what you want on your sandwich" says one diner, "and that's not very hard."

Global

Credit – Siegel + Gale 2017 Brand Simplicity Report

Aldi looks at things from the consumer's side, offering quality at affordable prices in a format that displays a genuine, rather than a fabricated, character. [**5. Customer as a Partner** ✓]

Aldi - From culture and purpose to actions

We deepened our analysis of the Aldi brand into the connections between its actions and brand attributes. Our findings on 'actions to outcomes' brand building are summarised in Illustration 7.9. One of Aldi's key pillars is to provide maximum convenience to consumers – simplicity and quality of product selection, modest and efficient store size,

ILLUSTRATION 7.9	ALDI'S BRAND ATTRIBUTES, ACTIONS AND TRENDS

BRAND ATTRIBUTES, ALDI'S ACTIONS AND TRENDS (1)

BRAND ATTRIBUTE	ALDI'S ACTIONS	FACING THE TRENDS
Help me achieve my goals	**Budget balance** - With many consumers concerned about living costs and their household budgets, Aldi's provision of good-quality consumer goods for reasonable, low prices - more on this below - can play a large part in helping consumers reach their goals.	**Maximising Behaviour**, which gained prominence in the economic turmoil that followed the recession, plays a part here: many consumers still have squeezed household economies and Aldi's low prices help them reach their financial goals without compromising on food quality.
Value for money	**Quality for less** - Through focusing on just a few (or even just one) brands per product, Aldi keeps procurement costs down and ensures best quality. E.g. rather than offering a wide array of olive oil brands, one or two kinds are offered - this means that Aldi's purchaser can focus on finding the olive oil with best value for money and, since Aldi will buy all their olive oil from that producer, they receive a discounted price. These savings are passed on to the consumer	As above, this plays into **Maximising Behaviour** and consumers' strife to maximise their ratio of goods to money spent. Aldi's explicit emphasis on providing *quality* goods for affordable prices also touches on **Everyday Exceptional** - consumers want a reason to celebrate and treat themselves, meaning a brand can doubly benefit if they combine money-saving measures with high-quality and desirable products.
Convenient Reliable Innovative	**Convenience** - Aldi has implemented a range of innovations, which make their stores more convenient for consumers. Many of these are focused on speeding up consumers' route through the store: the tills are wider to accommodate more products, own-brand products have large barcodes on a number of places to enable quicker scanning and rather than holding up the queue behind them while packing, consumers pack their wares at the store entrance. The end result is a quicker trip to the store and valuable time saved in the consumer's day.	This particularly touches on our upcoming **Functional Trust** trend: consumers do not prioritise traditional CSR efforts - as we know - as much as they appreciate a brand, which makes their life easier and delivers a good product. Aldi's conscious effort to redesign their stores to speed up the consumer's path to purchase appeals to this, as well as to our upcoming trend **Cult of Immediacy**. The 21st century consumer is busy and impatient - helping them complete their shopping quicker is thus highly appreciated.
Good customer service	**Service offer** - Convenience in the form of increased speed of service and reducing unnecessary choice between brands - by focusing on only a few per product and ensuring good quality of those available combine to increase consumer experience.	As above, **Functional Trust** is particularly important here. Additionally, advising consumers is easier when there are fewer brands to choose from, making sales assistants' jobs easier.

BRAND ATTRIBUTES, ALDI'S ACTIONS AND TRENDS (2)

BRAND ATTRIBUTE	ALDI 'S ACTIONS	FACING THE TRENDS
Make me feel good	**Healthy Offer** - Aldi has also committed to helping their customers achieve healthier lifestyles through offering a wide range of low-sugar or sugar-free alternatives, multi-buy offers on vegetables and by only having healthy treats displayed at the tills.	Aldi's drive to promote healthier snacks and alternatives also fits into societal trends such as **Society of Sobriety.**
Genuine	**Simplicity** - Aldi has made a commitment to simplicity, demonstrated through having 1,500 grocery lines vs. main retailers having 50,000 products in large stores.	Simplicity meets multiple trends, notably those contributing to perceived good customer service: **Cruise Control, Managed Transparency** and **The Me Me World.**
	Connectedness - Many Aldi stores in the UK have made a point of including local or regional produce, e.g. in the form of beer from local breweries and meat from local farms (69% of products are British sourced). This helps them stay grounded in their community and plays to local pride.	The trend **Pursuit of Real** describes consumers' interest in and search for "genuine" products, often defined as local, micro-produced or "craft" goods. This fits well with Aldi's promotion of local and regional brands and products.
Inspire me	**Indulge and be surprised at lowest price** - This results from a combination of complementary actions: Aldi's fruit, vegetables and fresh meat weekly deals; 'special buys'; cheap but award- winning wines, dry-aged steak and cut-price lobsters; and healthy alternatives and snacks continuously available help inspire consumers to be happier and healthier.	This is in line with the **Society of Sobriety** mind-set.
Good reputation	**Commitment** - The commitment to money-saving – 10% to 15% cheaper than equivalent products, quality and the simplicity of overall experience have helped Aldi retain a good reputation among consumers and position them as being on their customers' side.	Aldi's expressed desire to achieve the highest possible savings and pass these on to the consumer acts as a positive influence on their operation: consumers feel that Aldi is on their side and, as above, is helping them achieve their goals. Here again **Functional Trust** is evident.

Credit – The Forsight Factory and THE Enduring Strategic Brand.

innovative designs of carts, alleys, tills, bar codes and packing. [**3. Total Experience Design** ✓] For example, Aldi uses simple innovations to speed its customers' passage through their store – own-brand products have large, numerous bar codes for quicker scanning and customers pack their bags at the store entrance to free the tills for the next shopper.

Aldi and trends

Finally, the research considered trends and tested the likelihood of the fast-growing millennial customer group to become strong brand advocates. The research highlighted millennials' strong desire for 'good service'. Far be it from this book to deliver consultancy – but rather to learn from the experience of exemplary brands. Nevertheless, if the importance of 'good service' is deemed to grow – as represented by the vertical arrow in Illustration 7.10 – and since Aldi is undifferentiated in this area, the retailer might

ILLUSTRATION 7.10   ALDI BRAND DIAGNOSIS: ALL CUSTOMERS

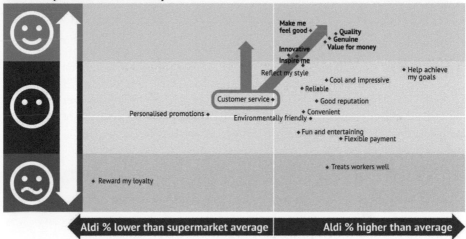

Good for supermarket brand advocacy

Make me feel good • • Quality / • Genuine Value for money
Innovative •
Inspire me
Reflect my style • • Help achieve my goals
• Cool and impressive
• Reliable
Customer service • • Good reputation
Personalised promotions • • Convenient
Environmentally friendly •
• Fun and entertaining
• Flexible payment
• Treats workers well
• Reward my loyalty

Aldi % lower than supermarket average | Aldi % higher than average

Credit – THE Enduring Strategic Brand and The Foresight Factory

consider ways to improve and drive this and other societal and consumer trends in its favour.

Aldi is growing quickly: they have rapidly increased their online offer alongside the fast opening of new shops in convenient locations, with a plan to grow from 652 shops in the UK in 2016 to 1000 by 2022. The fast innovation in the customer service area, both off and online, presents Aldi with both a challenge and an opportunity.

Aldi is redefining the relationship between price, quality and experience. They believe that they can offer all three; price and quality no longer need to be trade-off.

Bart Michels offered a strong perspective: *"In UK retail, Aldi is redefining the relationship between price, quality and experience. They believe that they can offer all three; price and quality no longer need to be trade-off. They are therefore disrupting the traditional model of lower price meaning lower quality and positioning themselves instead as the smart choice of 'lower price (vs. competitors) and higher quality'. This sort of repositioning is a characteristic feature of Strategic Brands. Another way in which they are changing the model is their redefinition of local. Supermarket brands are often defined locally, but Aldi combines a feeling of Britishness – with fresh UK produce and its sponsorship of Team GB at the Olympics – with cheap German products that perform well."*

PLATFORMISATION AND THE ROLE AND IMPORTANCE OF BRANDS

While, O2, Amex and Aldi all demonstrate best practice customer centricity in today's world – what do customer centric organisations of the future look like?

amazon Let's consider Amazon as an example of how a single brand can put immense pressure on other retail and service brands. Specifically, does Amazon already put pressure on Aldi - or will do so, with its fresh food offer? Whether you like the online retailer or not, taking them through the ten key tenets of Customer Centricity test, they arguably receive 5 out of 5 on each of the 10 criteria, as presented on Illustration 7.11.

ILLUSTRATION 7.11	AMAZON AS A CUSTOMER CENTRIC BRAND

amazon

1. Culture & Mindset	5
2. Purpose Led	5
3. Total Experience Design	5
4. Trends Integration	5
5. Customer as a Partner	5
6. Cross Functional Teams	5
7. Decision on the front line	5
8. Magnet for Talents	5
9. Unparalleled Growth	5
10. We are the Platform	5

Scale 1: Low to 5: Very Strong

Amazon's brand promises are to have the world's biggest selection of products and be the world's most customer-centric company. As Jeff Bezos explains: *"Our focus is on customer obsession rather than competitor obsession, eagerness to invent and pioneer, willingness to fail, the patience to think long -term and the taking of professional pride in operational excellence."*

"Our focus is on customer obsession rather than competitor obsession, eagerness to invent and pioneer, willingness to fail, the patience to think long -term and the taking of professional pride in operational excellence."

There is no doubt that Amazon excels in this area – and customers agree: Amazon has over 120 million accounts in the US, gained 19 million more Prime members in the country in 2016, was recently inducted into the customer service hall of fame...and more.

Shareholders also like the model, with Amazon together with Apple, Alphabet, Microsoft, and Facebook now among the 10 world's largest listed companies by market capitalisation. As sector leader, the Amazon brand is permanently redefining what customer experience should be and challenging retail and service brands. Other platforms are also pressing hard on their respective sector leading legacy brands. Are they the future of customer centricity?

Major sectors get 'platformised'

In less than 10 years, and as pictured on Illustration 7.12, iTunes and then Spotify have redefined the record industry; Netflix is doing the same with the DVD industry; Lendingclub is making dents into banking; Whatsapp is terminating fixed phones; Uber is seriously questioning the auto OEMs model; Amazon and Alibaba are redefining shopping; and Airbnb, hospitality. Meanwhile Cisco and GE are redesigning industry while Google and IBM are revolutionising health, communication, education, etc. In each case – and these are only among the most visible examples of a much bigger wave – the customer is at the centre of the transformation, receiving a better, faster, cheaper, on-demand, personalised end-to-end solution.

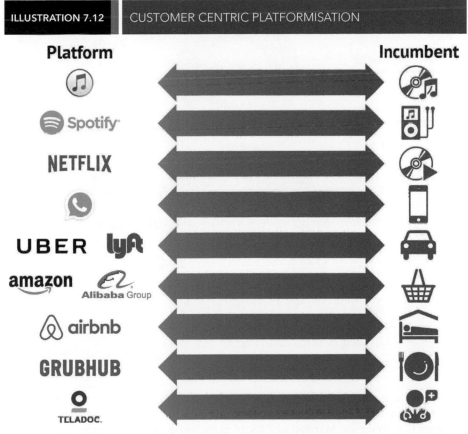

ILLUSTRATION 7.12   CUSTOMER CENTRIC PLATFORMISATION

Platform   Incumbent

Spotify

NETFLIX

UBER   lyft

amazon   Alibaba Group

airbnb

GRUBHUB

TELADOC.

Credit – THE Enduring Strategic Brand

Customer centric platformisation

What was once designated the "uberisation" of the economy is now more generally referred to as platformisation: the online connection of users and providers enabling the exchange of value among them. Arguably, this development is only just starting and will go faster and much deeper across many more sectors in the coming years. As will disintermediation, which removes the direct link between brands and their users.

Just take the sharing economy and its impact on the traditional rental sector as an example: according to a PWC analysis, and as shown in Illustration 7.13, five main sharing economy sectors generated $15 billion of global revenue in 2013, 5 per cent of the 10 sectors studied. In 2025, these sharing economy sectors are predicted to generate $335 billion of global revenues, rivalling the size of the sectors they are disrupting – and their brands (Note 4).

ILLUSTRATION 7.13	THE MAJOR RISE OF THE PLATFORM-BASED SHARING ECONOMY

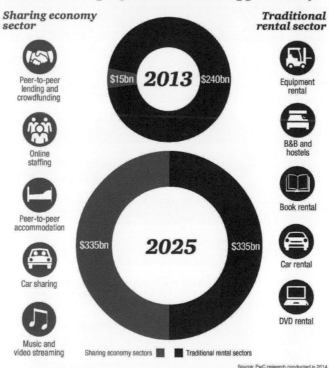

Sharing economy sector and traditional rental sector projected revenue opportunity

Credit – PwC

In this context, our key question is on the role of a Strategic Brand: is it still important today to build a strong brand like Deutsche Grammophon, Sony, Warner Bros., Motorola, GM, Walmart, Marriott or RBS, to name just a few strong incumbents?

Disintermediation – The growth of online intermediaries

Hertz We learned from Hertz's Michel Taride about partnerships in Chapter 6. Here we extend our conversation into platformisation and disintermediation: *"In the travel chain, there are two main trends. One is with aggregators, who apply a 'vertical' model. These online travel agents offer an integrated travel solution, including airline tickets, hotels, a car rental and other things for one price. Because car rental is less than 10 per cent of the full revenue of travel, there is less focus on us than on hotels, for example.*

"The second trend, and this is especially true in Europe, is brokers who apply a cross-sector 'horizontal' model. They are essentially technology companies, often backed up by major companies or private equity houses who aggregate the car rental supply and then market, calling themselves car rental companies. They don't own a single car or location, but they spend a lot of money on online marketing, search engine optimisation, natural search and paid search. They put a lot of pressure on us to provide the lowest prices because they tell the leisure traveller: 'It doesn't matter where you travel, we have all the car rental supply you want. You don't need to go through the car rental companies' websites, as we have aggregated it all.'

"As a matter of fact, the car rental market is extremely fragmented: there are thousands of car rental companies involved and fed by these brokers, even very small, local ones. It is a true strategic issue: on the one hand, they are an important distribution channel, but at the same time they compete against us, B2B and B2C. As a customer you can either go to Hertz.com or to the site of one of these brokers. There you would see pages of car rentals, from Hertz to anybody else, from known to unknown brands.

"These sites guide a customer's selection towards pricing. In our company, we change retail prices three billion times a year in the US, three million times a day in Europe. The brokers apply the latest generation technology and human-free algorithms to 'guerrilla' pricing. They spend a lot of money marketing prices online – and are growing significantly.

"From a brand standpoint, the risk is to become a commodity; by losing direct contact with customers, people are led to believe it's all about price and you can be compared instantly to anyone. There is no doubt that the brand is still a reassurance and customers are often ready to pay some price premium for a well-known brand, but only to a certain extent. This 'price power' is not strong enough to support what we need as operators to do our job properly, to run the physical supply, buy cars, maintain vehicles and rental locations, etc.

"So we need to reflect our real work and continue to improve and differentiate the customer's experience, so they come directly to us rather than to anyone else for a different, rewarding, simple and competitively priced experience. And the brand is at the centre of achieving this."

Hertz's strategic response to this challenge includes segmentation of needs, CRM, service differentiations, experience management, brand portfolio including value brands, pricing policy, capacity management, etc. We won't say more here both out of respect to

Hertz's plans and because it would be too specific for our purpose. But Hertz's experience serves to stress the fact that nowadays, any brand, even the very best like Hertz, are subject to both the opportunities and challenges presented by platformisation and/or disintermediation - and that developing a Strategic Brand must be at the heart of the response.

Brand response

Faced with these challenges, most Strategic Brands have the potential to come out on top, because they hold the relationships and should have developed strong barriers to disintermediation – and because their 'Future Embracing' nature will dynamically support the evolution.

Here are some key practices for consideration:

1. **Identify the mechanisms of disruption** early, as well as the potential or incoming disruptors;
2. **Recognise that most 'platformisations' are not revolutions** but rather surfing on existing dynamics to provide different ways of packaging, communicating and serving customers through existing assets;
3. **Develop clear strategies and capabilities** that can rival those of the disruptors;
4. **Disrupt yourself** by bringing platformisation and disintermediation into your branded model;
5. **Understand and use their own formula:** obsessed with talents, investing in their core skills, sacrificing immediate financial rewards like dividends to the longer term of establishing mastery, paying endless attention to detail, going early and fast. These platforms are playing '*blitzscaling*' (lightning war), to borrow the phrase of PayPal's former COO Reid Hoffman, so they acquire lots of customers fast and for the long term.
6. **Nurture a strong purpose and sense of identity** in service of a cultural obsession for customers.

Ideally, the incumbent brand and market leaders would reinvent the terms of their leadership, maintaining the ability to shape and remain prominent in their business sector and ecosystem. This should start with strategic clarity in the role and position of the brand, anchored into what it stands for and does best.

Becoming the 'super competitor' in a sector, ala Google or Amazon, is one answer and of course the ideal position – but this will only be possible for a few brands with extensive and very distinctive capabilities.

Another way to success is to develop into a first-tier ecosystem player, joining forces with others through strategic partnering associations, ala IBM, to provide a fully integrated innovating solution (Ref. Chapter 6 - Partnering).

A third way applies to very big customer bases and revenue pools, like automobiles, banking, energy or consumer packed goods, where a sufficient degree of differentiation and search for excellence across a cohesive ecosystem of supply, mass manufacturing and distribution, ala Citi Bank, will protect incumbency and secure a brand's position in the oligopoly.

However you do it, the journey must start with strategic clarity for the customers. And strong nerves - 'blitzscaling' over a significant period of time is cash demanding, which means most platforms and disintermediators usually have an Achilles heel: their financials. In 2016 Uber lost over $2.5 billion, Spotify lost $175 million in 2015, while Twitter hasn't yet established a sustainable economic model. And they need corporatisation, such as sales and branding, early - as customers demand perfect service and products, these companies are forced to rapidly scale up to a larger operation from the start-up mode where they could afford to get things right only 90 per cent of the time.

INSPIRATION FROM STRATEGIC BRANDS ON CUSTOMER CENTRICITY

Let's steal some learnings from a few of 'THE Enduring Strategic Brand' selected exemplary brands to strategically move to or consolidate as a leader, based on customer centricity in our digital world.

WORLD ECONOMIC FORUM Klaus Schwab: *"Platform strategies, combined with the need to be more customer centric and to enhance products with data, are shifting many industries from a focus on selling products to delivering services… an end-to-end approach from service acquisition to delivery."*

John Hayes: *"AmEx is built on platforms and in fact is an ecosystem of buyers and sellers organised around a win-win principle. What is powerful is that it is not merely a transaction, but rather a full relationship with and through the ecosystem, something rather hard to replace with a transactional opportunity."*

Haier Zhang Ruimin: *"We at Haier are no longer the ones directing things. We are the glue binding everything together… because the rapid evolution of user preferences represent a huge source of pressure."*

Jonathan Mildenhall: *"Airbnb is the world's first community driven superbrand. If Airbnb only controls approximately 10 per cent of the user experience, 90 per cent of the Airbnb brand is then dictated by its users, not its corporate leadership."*

Mark Fields: *"We want to be known as a brand that will help people be mobile – and when we say be a mobility company, we mean mobility at its highest level. The definition is allowing people to live, play and work where they want… and to do this, our approach is to first disrupt ourselves."*

Never before have the Strategic Brand and Customer Centricity played such a defining role in a company's success, in society, and in the economy.

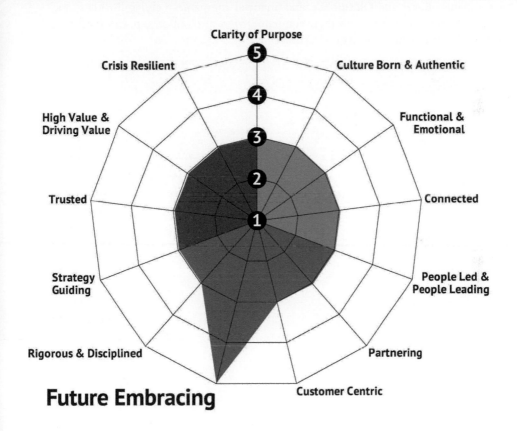

Future Embracing

"Everything needs to change, so everything can stay the same"
Don Fabrizio, Prince of Salina - The Leopard

All of us – Boards, CEOs, CMOs and leaders - need to embrace the future as a priority. For history is littered with the gravestones of brands that failed to look to the future and we do not want to join them in the brand cemetery. To name a few: Kodak, Nokia, Woolworths, Pan Am, Lehman Brothers, Marconi, Rover, Nova magazine, Tower Records, Polaroid, Moulinex, Zenith Electronics, Borders, Blockbusters, Enron, Oldsmobile etc.

You'll note from this list of brands that the pitfalls of failing to embrace the future are not restricted to tech companies. Yes, Kodak, Polaroid and to a large extent Nokia collapsed because of their ingrained inability to adapt to fundamental disruptive changes in their industry. But so too did high street retailers Borders, Blockbusters and Woolworths, car companies Rover and Oldsmobile, and financial companies Lehman Brothers and Enron. For very different reasons these companies were also out of step with the future and paid the price with their lives or fortunes.

ILLUSTRATION 8.1	EXAMPLES FROM THE BRAND CEMETERY

Sony Betamax

Polaroid Camera

Pan American World Airways

We don't need to tell you about the pace of change in today's world, albeit to say that keeping sight of your Enterprise Brand Pole Star in an increasingly destabilising future is one of the most important acts a leader can undertake.

Enduring Strategic Brands embrace the future and have the capacity to learn and change. Their leaders largely focus on everything that does not exist yet while their teams deal as much as possible with what already exists. This is how they build sustainable success.

To be able to see the path ahead in a way that others might not is a competency that all Strategic Brands should develop within their organisation. This is not about gazing into a crystal ball; this is about building the future as a capability, a platform for growth.

From the car revolution to the mobile revolution

A couple of years ago, I spoke at a Barclays Senior Marketing Forum organised by David Wheldon, then Barclays Managing Director – Brand, Reputation Citizenship and Marketing. This gave me the opportunity to listen to Facebook's talented Nicola Mendelsohn, who delivered a compelling address about the future.

As I started to write this book, I thought that it would be interesting to talk to Nicola again and get her perspective on how her predictions are coming true and what being a 'Future Embracing' brand means. We are in the midst of the Fourth Industrial Revolution – and she believes that the mobile is the most important and on-going transformational invention following the car a century ago.

f Nicola: *"The theme of the 2016 World Economic Forum in Davos was the Fourth Industrial Revolution and Davos 2017 has built on it. We looked at what lessons had been learned from the previous industrial revolutions that we have seen: steam, mechanics, electricity, automation and now digital, mobile and telecom. The revolution which has had most impact on our modern age is probably Henry Ford's mass manufacturing of cars. Not only did Ford make it possible for everyone to be able to travel, but the mass production of automobiles helped in the creation of cities, of grouping people together and of the organisation of shopping in the way we know it today. The impact of great technology on how our lives work is not only about the short term but the medium to long term. I think the same is true of the mobile phone.*

Not only did Ford make it possible for everyone to be able to travel, but the mass production of automobiles helped in the creation of cities, of grouping people together and of the organisation of shopping in the way we know it today.

"Not being a future-teller, I don't know how the mobile might change the physical organisation of the world. But the speed of this revolution has been much quicker than the ones before. If you think about televisions, it took 67 years before they reached a billion people, while mobiles did this in five years. After 10 years, two billion people on the planet have a mobile phone: the opportunity for the entire world to be connected online is within reach. We are not there yet, as 4.5 billion people are still not connected – but there is that potential. At Facebook, our mission is to make the world more connected, so that people can share more. That level of connectivity around the planet has never happened before.

"Increasingly more time is being spent on digital media versus traditional media, which is a considerable shift. This has disrupted all businesses and verticals profoundly, including

our own. This sort of disruption brings fear and challenges – but it also brings great opportunities. Standards of living have risen around the world; there are jobs today that didn't exist two or three years ago; small businesses now have the same opportunity to use advertising as large businesses. So there are incredible opportunities emerging, although they require different ways of thinking and different mindsets."

THE ENDURING STRATEGIC BRAND SUPERPOWERS

Further globalisation, digitalisation, 'uberisation' and other sorts of disruption mean that organisations today are facing continuous changes and transformations at a faster pace than ever before. An anecdotal example is what now happens in just sixty seconds, as shown in Illustration 8.2:

ILLUSTRATION 8.2	IN AN INTERNET MINUTE….

- 763,888 people use Facebook
- 69,444 hours watched on Netflix
- 150 million emails
- 1,389 rides on Uber
- 51,000 app downloads
- $203,596 in sales on Amazon
- 65,900 videos and photos posted
- 38,052 hours of listening on Spotify
- 972,222 swipes on tinder

Credit -Nicola Mendelsohn's Marketing Society Conference Presentation November 2016

WPP's Martin Sorrell places brand development in the context of considerable changes, for example those on media consumption: *"In the UK, traditional newspapers' circulation figures and advertising revenue are down steeply. On the other hand, look at what Jeff Bezos is doing with the Washington Post: he has people looking at what you and I are downloading, what content we are interested in on the web. He has editorial people that are developing and providing that online content and as he offers the strong content that people want, they will pay for it.*

"Google is our biggest media investment on behalf of clients at around $5 billion in 2016. And Facebook, by 2018 will probably be our second biggest - and wait and see what happens with people like Snapchat, etc. There is though, still a tremendous weight of spending on traditional media. For example Fox/NewsCorp/Sky are our second biggest media investment with approximately $2.25 billion every year.

"We are in transition and the Googles of this world are disrupters – they offer very powerful one-to-one communication. But they also know that the established media still has very significant capability. And data shows that engagement with traditional TV and newspapers is still better than with online media.

In this context, Strategic Brands must possess two related superpowers:

Superpower 1 - See, shape and create the future

An Enduring Strategic Brand must be a pioneer in its sector. It must be all antennas out and be disciplined to analyse and make strategic judgments on strong or weak signals and on-going trends. It must give an organisation the confidence and guidance to proactively find and lead transformations and innovations. Because of the current tendency for 'first in takes it all', an organisation's ability to lead transformation places it in the winning position. The GE and Amazon brands are benchmarks for this superpower.

Superpower 2 - Be future proof and enable the organisation's transition into the future

A brand has to do more than just live through the changes. It has to carry the organisation through its transformation, using change to create a different access and support base, and providing all stakeholders with stability and confidence during the transition. In short, an Enduring Strategic Brand must be stable and have the longevity to 'brand any future'. The IBM brand is a benchmark for this superpower.

Nick Udall describes the uniqueness of being 'Future Embracing' and the importance of taking an agile approach to strategy, adapting as you go along:

"The world is becoming ever more volatile, uncertain, complex and ambiguous. Boundaries are blurring, technology is changing the game, consumers are gaining ever more power, and more and more things are becoming interdependent. You can't navigate these forces with a static strategy anymore i.e. a plan for getting from A to B. Most people aren't really aware or honest about where they are now (A); and as soon as you try and described B, everything changes and it is out of date. The challenge is to learn to work with emergent strategy, which is counter-intuitive to most business leaders and their stakeholders, but is very familiar to creators, innovators and entrepreneurs.

The way of working is about feeling into sensing the empty spaces of the future, that you can bring your difference to and monopolise i.e. uniquely claim, shape and make your own. Then you need to innovate your way there, knowing that it (your understanding of the space) and you (your sense of who you are and what you are capable of doing) will change with every step you take.

Ultimately, the only thing you can hang onto into an uncertain world is your sense of self, your identity – core purpose and core values. Knowing who you are enables you to stand still when you get lost in the forest, so you can deepen your listening, expand your senses, and notice the fragile, subtle and momentary clues that are all around you to help you find the optimal way forward"

From a brand standpoint, BP's Beyond Petroleum fitted brilliantly into the first superpower space as it was predicated to support the transition to a low carbon economy. It had the potential to grow into an Enduring Strategic Brand as the transition progressed – but it did not have enough of the second superpower, meaning a strong enough foundation from which to create that future, particularly as the brand was insufficiently driving strategy (Ref. Chapter 10).

Similarly, GE's Ecomagination, which focuses on cleaner technology innovation, was a brilliant way of representing and communicating GE's commitment to a lower carbon world. When it was launched in 2005, the dedicated Ecomagination business and branding were extremely successful and had a big impact. Ten years later and irrespective of its success - Deb Frodl, global head of Ecomagination, recently declared that GE gained $232 billion in revenue from its clean tech investment - it could be argued that Ecomagination should have been more than a satellite and instead been taken up by the whole of the GE brand and business from the start.

Future enabling Facebook

Facebook is a naturally 'Future Embracing' brand: it creates the future and inherently enables the transition into it. I asked Nicola Mendelsohn what thoughts she would share with those who want to develop or manage a 'Future Embracing' brand, and her views can be summarised as:

1. Always be on a mission
2. Follow your customers
3. Communication will continually change
4. Be ruthless about your focus on the future.

She explains: *"First you must have a brand purpose, a mission and a role in people's lives into the future – but this mission must also be something which connects to where people are today. Facebook is a mission-driven company: our mission is to make the world more open and connected, so that people can share more. Through programmes like 'Free Basics by Facebook' we are helping the 4.5 billion people without access.*

"Next, a brand should disrupt itself by following the consumer - understanding what they are doing and their reactions, where they are spending their time and how they want to be communicated with. You bring those learnings right up front and early; you think mobile first from the beginning, not as an afterthought; and suddenly, you are able to do personalised marketing at scale. We are often asked: "Why is the advertising not more specific to me?"

"You bring connections together among people and then they can share things with those they care about in a new way. This will continue changing – we have moved from the written word, to photographs and now to moving imagery and immersive videos. You

can expect major shifts to visual communication – these supercomputers we call mobile phones, which we carry in our pockets, are actually fabulous production and photographic studios. In a world inundated with information, a picture tells a thousand words and helps you edit more quickly. This has massive implications for communication and is why at Facebook we invest in different forms of visual communication. Just look at Instagram: it is 5.5 years old and now has half a billion users. It was born mobile, it was born visual, and it caught that trend.

You can expect major shifts to visual communication – these supercomputers we call mobile phones, which we carry in our pockets, are actually fabulous production and photographic studios.

"Finally, an organisation must understand and apply new technology. The story of how in mid-2012 Mark Zuckerberg got the whole of Facebook to transform from desktops to being a mobile first company is well known publicly – as is his admission that he should have done this earlier. We stopped what we were doing, refocused and went from 0 to 49% of our revenue on mobile in 18 months.

Today, mobiles represent 84% of our total ad revenue. I bet the next big platform will be virtual or augmented reality (AR). Artificial intelligence (AI) is already in all our lives – for example when the bank phones you and says: 'There has been some spending and we are checking if everything is OK'. Facebook could use AI to read out what the words are on a picture; we could enable 250 million visually impaired people on the planet to technically see the picture and have a much-enhanced Facebook experience."

Mark Zuckerberg couldn't have predicted the future better: in October 2016, for the first time ever, the majority – 51.3% – of all global internet links were made on mobiles versus 48.7% on desktops. Only three years ago, the ratio was three to one for desktops. Zuckerberg's admission that he should have focused on mobile earlier demonstrates that it is not only first mover advantage that counts – ruthless focus can get you there too, although being late to the game makes it harder and riskier.

SEEING THE FUTURE

As Nicola is suggesting, a brand (and therefore also a brand's strategic marketing team – Ref. Chapter 5) has a vital role to see and understand the future. And she mentioned that the theme at Davos 2016 was 'The Fourth Industrial Revolution'. In the following pages, we will share some of the cross-category shifts which are already taking place and are forming the future, which understanding is fundamentally important to brand development. We will then be more specific on what this means for brands in a few selected categories, although these short insights are in no way a substitute for a deeper look. I would encourage everyone to read *'The Fourth Industrial Revolution'* by Professor Klaus Schwab, the Founder and Executive Chairman of the World Economic Forum (WEF). (Note 1)

The Fourth Industrial Revolution

Professor Klaus Schwab comments first on the 'Future Embracing' company and brand: *"The first imperative from the Fourth Industrial Revolution is the urgent need to scrutinise oneself as a business leader and one's own organisation. Is there evidence of the organisation's and leadership's capacity to learn and change? Is there a track record of prototyping and investment decision-making at a fast pace? Does the culture accept innovation and failure? This ride requires a hard and honest look."*

Let's benefit from the thinking of Professor Klaus Schwab and the WEF team – and the substance in the next pages is largely credit to their research.

Systemic changes

As pointed out earlier by Nicola, technological innovations are transforming the world in every respect and at a formidable pace and scale. Uber, Airbnb and Alibaba scarcely existed less than a decade ago and are now mammoth leaders in their respective sectors. The iPhone was launched in 2007; there are now well over 2 billion smartphones on the planet. In 1990, the big three automobile manufacturers in Detroit had a combined revenue of $250 billion, a market value of $36bn and 1.2 million employees. In 2014, the three biggest companies in Silicon Valley had the same revenue – ca $250bn – but were worth $1.09 trillion, around 30 times more, and employed 137,000 people, almost a tenth of the automobile manufacturers. Seven of the 10 largest listed companies in 2016 did not appear in the 2006 ranking. And if the three largest social media sites were countries, they would come first, fourth and tenth in the top ten populations, with Facebook having almost the same number of people as China – as shown on Illustration 8.3.

ILLUSTRATION 8.3	SYSTEMIC TECHNOLOGY–LED TRANSFORMATIONS

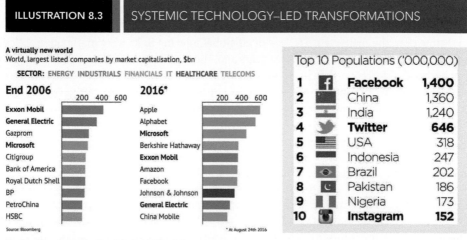

Credit – Bloomberg; The Fourth Industrial Revolution

Drivers

Professor Klaus Schwab's report points to three main drivers of this transformation, all linked to the power of digitalisation and information technology:

- <u>Physical:</u> autonomous vehicles, 3D printing, advanced robotics and the appearance of revolutionary new materials.
- <u>Digital:</u> the Internet of Things (IoT), the invasion of billions of sensors and linked devices everywhere in the economy and our lives, remote monitoring, blockchain and bitcoin and, of course, sharing economy on-demand platforms like Uber or Airbnb.
- <u>Biological:</u> probably less visible to the general public, the manifestations are immense, such as the fast exploration of millions of genetic variations, the consequent ability to edit human genes and, soon, the synthetic biology which will enable us to write DNA. This is revolutionising medical knowledge and medicine – just think of engineering a pig's genome to grow organs suitable for human transplantation – but it will also impact agriculture, nutrition – and on a philosophical level, will interrogate our perspective of humanity itself.

Tipping points

The 21 tipping points in Illustration 8.4 were published in a WEF report at the end of 2015 and show the framing drivers described above as concrete realities. The table includes the percentage of respondents who expect that the tipping point will have occurred by 2025. Against each of these, *THE Enduring Strategic Brand* added examples and evidence of the shifts already happening or on their way.

ILLUSTRATION 8.4	FOURTH INDUSTRIAL REVOLUTION TIPPING POINTS EXPECTED BY 2025		

Tipping Points Expected to Occur by 2025	%	Today's Evidence of Shift
10% of people wearing clothes connected to the internet	91.2	514 million smart watches in 5 years
90% of people having unlimited and free (advertising-supported) storage	91	Already existing free storage offers up to 50 GB
1 trillion sensors connected to the internet	89.2	50 billion devices connected to the Internet by 2020
The first robotic pharmacist in the US	86.5	'Rethink Robotics' released Baxter received overwhelming response
10% of reading glasses connected to the internet	85.5	Glasses are already on the market today
80% of people with a digital presence on the internet	84.4	The 3 largest social media sites have 1 billion people more than China
The first 3D-printed car in production	84.1	GE's LEAP jet engine incorporates a fuel nozzle produced by 3-D printing
The first government to replace its census with big-data sources	82.9	The volume of business data worldwide doubles every 1.2 years
The first implantable mobile phone available commercially	81.7	Digital tattoos perform useful tasks. Computers + antennas can be smaller than a grain of sand
5% of consumer products printed in 3D	81.1	3-D printers shipments almost double each year
90% of the population using smartphones	80.7	2 billion people have a mobile within 10 years
90% of the population with regular access to the internet	78.8	Today, 85% of the world's population is less than 2 km from a mobile tower
Driverless cars equalling 10% of all cars on US roads	78.2	Tesla already running semi-autonomous cars
The first transplant of a 3D-printed liver	76.4	Peking University implanted a 3-D printed section of vertebra
30% of corporate audits performed by AI	75.4	IBM Watson already performing better functions than humans
Tax collected for the first time by a government via a blockchain	73.1	In 2015, the first virtual nation, BitNation, was created
Over 50% of internet traffic to homes for appliances and devices	69.9	Nest already offering internet-connected thermostat and smoke detection
Globally more trips/journeys via car sharing than in private cars	67.2	Largest retailer doesn't own a shop (Amazon); largest hospitality firm doesn't own a room (Airbnb)
The first city with more than 50,000 people and no traffic lights	63.7	The city of Santander in Spain has 20,000 sensors
10% of global gross domestic product stored on blockchain technology	57.9	Smartcontracts.com provides programmable contracts to do payouts between organisations
The first AI machine on a corporate board of directors	45.2	Concept Net 4 passed an IQ test better than most 4-year olds

Credit – Data by the World Economic Forum; Interpretation by THE Enduring Strategic Brand

So what do tipping points 4 and 14 mean to med. tech. and pharmaceutical brands? Or tipping point 1 to clothing brands? Or tipping points 7, 13, 18 and 19 to the auto industry? And tipping points 9, 11, 12 and 17 to the telecom sector? This is without even analysing the major impact they will have on the running of governments, the financial sector or companies at large. And when it comes to brands, understanding these major trends has a considerable impact on what they should be and how their superpowers are developed now and into the future.

Monumental impacts

Brands should embrace the key impacts of the Fourth Industrial Revolution as they plan for the future:

Impact on Economy - There are many debates about the impact of the Fourth Industrial Revolution on the economy. Here is a moderately optimistic perspective: global growth would sustain at around 3.5% p.a., a doubling of global GDP over 20+ years, driven by new offerings, fast emergence of middle-class groups in developing countries and highly digitalised productivity. The effects of population ageing and social disruptions would probably abate a potentially higher growth scenario.

Impact on Work - There are equally ferocious debates about this highly sensitive subject – but everyone agrees that new technologies will dramatically change the nature of work with considerable depth, breadth and speed. It is also widely agreed that there are two main competing effects at play: a technology-led destruction of labour, at the same time as the creation of more jobs in response to new and more demand. This will mean labour substitution and transformation of skills at pace. It will impose a rethinking of the developing economies model, as 're-shoring' of manufacturing into mature economies occurs, based on robots rather than humans – all deeply challenging and unsettling, of course. And it will only become more complex. Professor Nick Bostrom, director of the Future of Humanity Institute at Oxford University talks about the intelligence explosion in his book, '*Super intelligence: Paths, Dangers, Strategies*'. This is when machines much cleverer than us begin to design machines of their own. (Note 2)

Impact on Business - There are numerous symptoms of change, one example being the reduction in the average lifespan of a corporation listed on the S&P 500 from 60 to 18 years. This statistic brings to life the extraordinary acceleration of change and what it means in reality for many businesses. In the past, you may have had 30 years to adapt to changes; today you have 13 months. Take this urgency and root the future into who you are.

Across industries, the four main effects will be:
1. Customer expectations shifting from products to experiences; from ownership to access; from groups to 'me personally', although informed by peer-to-peer sharing; from company-generated to user-generated content; from later to real time (think Nike+, Apple's iTunes).

2. The enhancement of product performance through data – for example, sensor-led equipment monitoring, predictive maintenance and, in general, the optimisation of asset performance and lifetime value. These dynamics open up the way for new business models, such as value-in-use pricing (think GE's Internet of Things).

3. Collaborative innovation becomes the norm in a customer experience world, with multiple parties bringing their skills into the end-to-end service. But succeeding with these collaborations is challenging and forces companies to fundamentally change their approach and practice (think Haier platformisation - Ref. below and Apple Watch – Ref. Chapter 6).

4. New operating models are required and or emerging, to operate faster and in tune with the technology potential. Examples include platforms (Ref. Chapter 7), where ownership is replaced by access (think Amazon Kindle, Spotify or Airbnb); or fully automated manufacturing replacing traditional operations (think 3D printing or AI).

To survive and thrive, companies need to continually strengthen their agility and speed, in the service of innovation. The shape of business might change – with large organisations increasingly organising their ecosystems into a number of innovative SMEs or start-ups. We have already seen this with initiatives like Unilever Ventures, the venture capital and private equity arm of Unilever and other equivalent set up.

Impact on Government - The regulatory landscape will evolve considerably. It will combine on the one hand more legislation to shape how researchers, businesses and citizens develop the effects of new technologies, some of which present dangers we need to avoid; and on the other hand, a shift of power away from government to loose networks where citizens use technology to voice their opinions, coordinate their efforts and possibly circumvent government supervision. Because digital technology knows no borders, the trend will probably accentuate the central importance of cities (and regions) as innovation hubs, rather than nations. Indeed, 'Connectography', an influential book by Parag Khanna, states that mega-cities will become the centres of global demographics and economic activity, with around 50 megacities dominating the world and mattering more than most of the world's 200 countries. (Note 3)

Impact on Society and the Individual - We will not comment here on the monumental issues of security and new forms of warfare. Rather, let's look at how societies and companies approach and deal with six major dynamics:

1. The possible opposition between the new modernity and traditional and non-secular beliefs, with the high risk that some groups fight progress with extreme ideologically motivated violence.

2. The rising inequality from the substitution of capital for labour, between those who lead innovation and hold the required high technical capabilities and the current middle class pushed to lower-skill labour and individualisation of work – the agency MBO predicts 40% of the whole US workforce will be self-employed by 2020. This has already translated into major political manifestations of 'winners vs. losers' or 'forgotten people' – e.g. Donald Trump's election in the US, Brexit in the UK – with more to come.

3. The meaning of growing individualisation, the 'me – me' society, and the emergence of new forms of community, not driven by space but by personal projects, values and interests (Ref. Airbnb 'belonging' strategy in Chapter 4).
4. The redefinition of what it is to be human, if only through what some technologies really mean for humans, such as control of AI, life extension, designer babies, memory extraction etc.
5. The transformation of human connections, whereby our obsessive interaction with digital, high tech and mobiles deprive people of human connectedness and, as a result, of empathy, deep reflection or substantial thinking. Isn't it the case already that 44% of teenagers do not 'unplug' from technology, even when with family or friends?
6. As big data and technological interconnectedness collide, the meaning and practice of privacy and private information has changed: on the one hand the use of data is the key to success in the modern economy; on the other hand, this could have a potentially huge negative effect on individuals.

When I think of my previous executive roles at BP or elsewhere, I don't believe we were embracing the future deeply enough, in order to shape it or guide our brand. Now I find it easier, as I have been able to step back into strategic advisory roles. From this perspective, I don't think any brand can be successful without learning about and building pro-actively on these major ongoing changes.

Professor Klaus Schwab explains the critical importance of engagement and how to approach the Fourth Industrial Revolution appropriately: *"We are at a point where the desire for purposeful engagement is becoming a major issue. This is particularly the case for the younger generation... It is in our power to address the challenges and enact the changes and policies needed to adapt (and flourish) in our emerging new environment... I believe we must adapt, shape and harness the potential of disruption by nurturing and applying four forms of intelligence: contextual (the mind), emotional (the heart), inspired (the soul) and physical (the body)."*

We must adapt, shape and harness the potential of disruption by nurturing and applying four forms of intelligence: contextual (the mind), emotional (the heart), inspired (the soul) and physical (the body).

This is exactly what our Enduring Strategic Brands are about, what they are eager to provide and what they must achieve.

What does it mean in practice for brands in transforming industries?

I believe this is all infinitely relevant to brands, so how do we make the link between the ongoing Fourth Industrial Revolution and building our Strategic Brand in practice? Let's look at how these systemic changes are transforming the reality of a few specific sectors - we were greatly helped in this research by Christophe Jouan, of the Foresight Factory.

Brands in Automotive

A car is already a computer on wheels, with electronics representing roughly 40% of the cost of a vehicle. Many other things are changing, such as moving from the combustion engine to fuel cells and/or electricity; developing autonomous vehicles; transitioning from car ownership as we know it to access-on-demand cars and part-time sharing; generalising multi-channel paths to vehicle purchase, rather than dealers only; and fundamentally redefining the core approach to mobility, especially in cities.

ILLUSTRATION 8.5	THE FUTURE OF MOBILITY AND AUTOMOBILE

Alternative fuel vehicles will make up a third of all new car sales in developed markets

THE TESLA EFFECT

Tesla joins Apple, Google and Coca-Cola in Top 100 list of best global brands

Tesla's Model 3 Reservations Rise to Almost 400,000

Model 3 is Elon Musk's iPhone moment

Tesla made electric cooler through premium vehicles which have quick to charge and long lasting batteries.

The path to purchase is digitalised – but policy will determine the fate of dealerships

36% of Gen Y either have already or are interested in buying a car online without going to a car dealership

INDUSTRY QUOTES

"...we will **have multi-channel approached** that will be **usable for the i-products** and, in time, other products as well."
**Ian Robertson,
Sales & Marketing Director, BMW AG**

"We want people to **start buying cars over the internet.** It is a potential half step away from our traditional channels"
**Dan Akerson, CEO,
General Motors, October 2013**

Source: FF Online Research | Base: 1002 online respondents aged 16+, GB, 2016 May

Urbanisation will promote smaller, cleaner options transport options

Today's Cars Are Parked 95% of the Time

Global urbanisation

45%   55%   62%

Continuing urbanisation will put pressure on air quality in cities to improve and stop posing a serious threat to health

1.23m   3m

Global road traffic   Global ambient air
deaths 2013   pollution deaths 2012

WHO Ambient Air Pollution Report, Global, 2016
UN, Department of Economic and Social Affairs, World Urbanization Prospects, 2014

Peer and corporate mobility systems will encroach upon urban spaces where public transport fails

The City of Alamonte Springs Florida has partnered with Uber to pilot a programme which integrates Uber into the public transport system. The city provides a 20% discount on all Uber trips that both begin and end in the city limits and a 25% discount that cover the last mile journeys to or from the SunRail station.

The car brands you see today will not be the only brands of tomorrow

INDUSTRY QUOTE

"The automotive industry is **not afraid of them [apple] making a superior car.**"
Wolfgang Ziebart, JLR

Importance of brand/model when buying a car | Net: selected

TOTAL	**48%**
No Car	34%
1 Car	51%
2+ Cars	54%

Source: FF Online Research | Base: 1002 online respondents aged 16+, GB, 2016 May

Mobility won't be the only transport system – but individual car ownership will fall

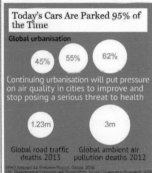

In March 2016, Audi launched its mobility service, Audi at Home, in Hong Kong, enabling residents of Kerry Property's Dragons Range properties to rent Audis on a per hour or daily basis by registering with their driving license and credit card and book via a smartphone app.

Credit – The Foresight Factory and THE Enduring Strategic Brand

So what is a car brand of the future in the context of this revolution? Where will profitability be achieved – in manufacturing a car or developing and licensing software? Will tech companies redefine, corner and/or replace car companies' integrator roles, with Google, Apple, Uber, Lyft or even Zoox breaking in to change the rules of the game? Or will car companies join the tech sector - like Ford who created a Smart Mobility subsidiary as a separate limited liability company (LLC) to develop software and tech-services in the same way Apple does?

Bill Ford, Executive Chairman and Mark Fields, President and CEO of Ford Motor Company provided a fascinating perspective in the 2014–15 FMC sustainability report: (Note 4) *"Without question, we are embarking on one of the most transformative periods in our history. We understand that the winners will be the innovators, the disruptors and those willing to break with tradition and find new solutions. That's why we are pushing ourselves even harder to think, act and disrupt like a start-up company. We are driving to be both a product company and a mobility company. Our vision is nothing less than to change the way the world moves. At Ford, we view this as the ultimate opportunity. In fact, it is as big an opportunity as when our founder put the world on wheels more than a century ago. Henry Ford believed that a good business makes excellent products and earns a healthy return. But he proved that a great business does all that while creating a better world. That is what continues to drive us each day."*

Mark Fields continues: *"We want to be known as a brand that will help people be mobile – and when we say be a mobility company, we mean mobility at its highest level. The definition is allowing people to live, play and work where they want… and to do this, our approach is to first disrupt ourselves… This means to be less about the 'thing' we sell and more about usage."*

Brands in Retail

With immediate online access, winning in retail today and tomorrow is less about the shop or control of the shopping experience than about the consumer's need and how it is fulfilled. As Werner Reinatz beautifully put it in the March 2016 issue of The Harvard Business Review: *"In the future of retail, we're never not shopping."* (Note 5) Indeed, consumers increasingly shop as soon as their need emerges, using Amazon or one of the many other online merchant sites. Moreover, many different products are now purchased automatically, using rapidly expanding online functions like Amazon Dash, or 'intelligent products' messaging, such as the automatic reordering of washing soap from Amazon, provided in the Whirlpool Smart Kitchen Suite app. And subscription-based platforms are transforming retail, for example Netflix for video, Spotify for music, Zipcar for transportation and the Dollar Shave Club for razors.

With the continuous expansion of these models and experience enhancements, such as online product personalisation, augmented reality (AR) improved retailing and autonomous delivery, to name just a few, physical stores as a main source of brand experience and loyalty are becoming less relevant, if not superfluous. So what about retail brands? Our point of view is that a brand has never been more important - so brand first! Be simple, create a consistent experience across multiple platforms

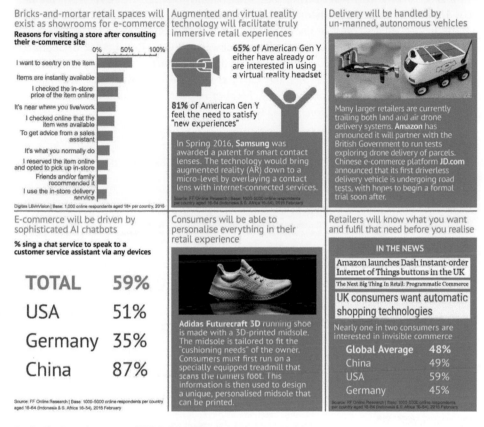

ILLUSTRATION 8.6	THE FUTURE OF RETAILING

Credit – The Foresight Factory and THE Enduring Strategic Brand

throughout the customer journey, online and offline, and be the most relevant to inspire *'customers always on shopping'*. (We have explored how ALDI continues building its brand successfully in Chapter 7)

Brands in Financial Services & Banking

Disruption comes from every direction and a multitude of challenger banks, non-traditional players and fintechs are addressing every line of the banks' business with focus, agility, new products and services at lower costs. This applies to lending, including peer-to-peer; payment services – cross-border, clearing etc.; retail banking; blockchain and bitcoin; wealth management and even the relationship world of investment banking, where 'robo-advisory' algorithms provide portfolio tools at a fraction of current transaction costs. What are the future prospects of high street bank branches, which were once so critical to the relationship and loyalty with a banking brand? Today, most transactions are available on mobile and 48% of global bank customers use the Internet weekly to manage their money?

Of course, major transitions take time. Many fintechs will default, while mega-banks are already reacting, including by acquiring fintechs - over $20bn was invested in 2015, compared to $4bn two years earlier. But what conclusions can we draw from the fact that 18% of US millennial customers have switched their primary bank over the past 12 months, compared to just 3% of people over 55? I recently attended a Marketing Group of Great Britain dinner where Ross McEwan, CEO of Royal Bank of Scotland, was the keynote speaker. He candidly observed: *"If we don't change the fundamentals and improve for our customers, then our business will be eaten away. But if we evidence capability, confidence, trust and integrity, I would be reasonably confident that we can largely prevent disintermediation."*

ILLUSTRATION 8.7	THE FUTURE OF BANKING & FINANCIAL SERVICES

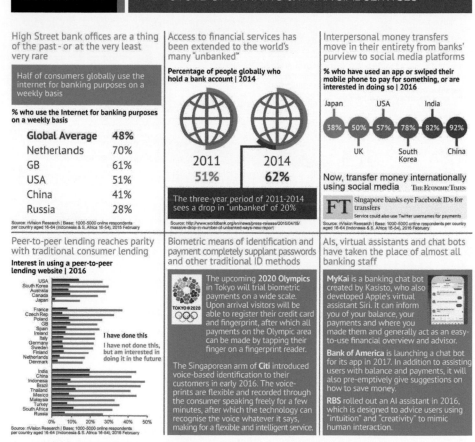

Credit – The Foresight Factory and THE Enduring Strategic Brand

Brands in Healthcare

I take a particular interest in this sector, as a Non Executive Director of a wonderful and deeply branded NHS Foundation specialist hospital in the UK – and working with the Department of Health to address the major financial challenge posed by the growing demand for care and cost of ever improving treatments.

The healthcare industry is transforming through the development of new diagnosis approaches and therapies, the digitalisation of patient records and the development of wearable and implantable devices, which provide a wealth of real-time patient information. What does this mean for the biggest med-tech and pharmaceutical companies' brands, which mainly define themselves in relation to their next blockbuster equipment, device, molecule or drug finding?

ILLUSTRATION 8.8	THE FUTURE OF HEALTHCARE

3D printers in pharmacies will allow for truly personalised pills

Spritam, from company Apricia, is the first 3D-printed drug to be approved by the FDA. The drug is used to treat epilepsy, and through 3D printing the tablets are made more porous and thus easier to swallow as they dissolve more quickly on contact with water. It began shipping to pharmacies in the USA in 2016.

The majority of care delivery will be provided by AI and robots

Zora was launched in 2015 by the Belgian company QBMT as the "first care robot". Zora has been deployed in care centres, schools and hospitals where she assists the elderly, autistic children and in-patients. The robot is small, just 57cm high, and mobile - she can walk, dance and do exercises, as well as read the news or discuss the weather. If an incident occurs, for example someone falls or has an epileptic fit, she can alert a human care assistant.

Doctors will spend more time interacting with patients remotely than face-to-face

Interest in "an online health appointment service that allowed me to receive remote health advice from a healthcare professional via a video link/video call/webcam"

Global Average	44%
China	72%
USA	43%
GB	41%
Sweden	39%
Germany	28%

Source: FFonline Research | Base: 1000-2000 online respondents per country aged 16+ (China 16-64), 2016 October

AI diagnosis tools will significantly reduce medical mistakes

IBM's Artificial Intelligence system, Watson, is to be trialled in 21 hospitals in China in 2016 to assist in diagnosing and treating cancer. According to CA: A Cancer Journal for Clinicians, 12,000 cancer diagnoses are made every day in China.

We will see the emergence of the first pharma company that does not produce pills

Projected revenue from VR/AR software in healthcare in 2025 | USA

 $5.1 billion

Expected users of VR/AR in healthcare in 2025 | USA

 3.4 million

Source: Goldman Sachs Global Investment Research. Virtual and Augmented Reality: Understanding the race for the next computing platform. IDC

The majority of medical education will take place in digital/virtual environments

In March 2015, VR company Next Galaxy announced a partnership with Miami Children's Hospital to develop Virtual Reality medical courses focusing on CPR and life-saving procedures. The VR applications allow users to walk around, use Voice Commands, gestures and Eye Gaze Control in order to interact with the scene. Real-time feedback is given when mistakes are made.

Credit – The Foresight Factory and THE Enduring Strategic Brand

Brands in Pharmaceutical

There is a very intriguing brand future in Pharma and my Strategic Brand question and challenge to the sector is - which major pharmaceutical brand will lead the industry transformation by becoming largely a consumer brand? The prize is considerable (Ref. Chapter 12 – Value) as, looking at the top 100 companies by market cap in the world, 18 are from the pharmaceutical industry but only one comes in the top 100 brands by value - J&J, whose value is arguably more driven by its FMCG business.

Beyond the brand valuation revealing insight, here are a few facts and trends driving change:

- Demographics – The world is becoming older and sicker, with considerable potential growth ahead, notably in developing markets.
- Government and peer scrutiny – Normative stakeholders are ever more intervening, notably about compliance, quality and drug prices. Pressure on prices lead to massive consolidation across the customer base.
- Digital revolution - The industry shows numerous signs of being on the brink of disruption to embrace an e-health revolution.
- Advancing science – The conjunction of biology, new generation genomics, big data and precise diagnoses are redefining the outcome.
- Intensifying competition – Changing demands from patients apply a strong pressure on traditional business models. Giants without roots in pharma are entering, such as IBM, Amazon, Samsung, Google, Apple and technology start-ups.
- Patients – The role of patients is transforming as they are much more connected, empowered, informed about their genetic profile, about diseases they have or might face in the future.

Smart patients - The changing attitude of patients represents a major shift: they are behaving more and more like consumers, embracing prevention, prediction and dedicating more time, energy and money to staying healthy. Patients want to be empowered, in control, proactive and reliably informed. They expect and demand more than just medicines – for example, masses of people are looking for graphic guides for their journey towards health and away from sickness. They simply want a different and closer relationship with pharma and this is both a major business threat and opportunity for incumbents.

These forces are reshaping the competitive landscape and pharmaceutical companies have the opportunity to shift from looking at diseases, drugs, and treatments only, to rather consider patients and how to help them to take greater control over their condition. It would mean moving from almost purely B2B to largely B2C (or B2B2C) by, like integrators and platforms, developing and offering services and solutions, devices and technology and personalised treatments that build millions of relationships over billions of pills.

Strategic Brand needed - There are evidences of this evolution starting to take shape, primarily led by small to mid-size tech companies. But no major pharma corporate brand seems to be decided yet on a radical brand pivot that would make patients' holistic quality of life its purpose. Arguably, success would require developing a Strategic Brand for at least three reasons:

➤ Major pharmaceutical companies have hundreds of drug names across the globe, so they need a strong and clear Strategic Brand to change the relationship and get patients to recognise them.

➤ The biggest threat might not come from established pharma companies but from Google, Amazon, Apple and similar. They have very strong brands and consumer connections, with a foremost competency to interact with patients. Many of the companies in our brand cemetery made the fatal mistake of believing competition lays much closer to home.

➤ The final reason is that for years, the industry has blamed the regulatory agencies and environment for its inability to create real proximity with patients and lead the conversation. This is now required by patient pull, giving brands the space and incentive to lead the shift.

None of this is easy. But the most effective 'Future Embracing' companies are those that see competitors on the horizon outside of their own industries. So go first and strongly…to 'take it all'.

I will now examine two brands which are doing exactly this – GE, in industrial B2B and B2G and Haier, in Consumer Goods. Both are seeing and shaping the future and taking the lead in the transition to the Fourth Industrial Revolution world.

GE, A B2B AND B2G 'FUTURE EMBRACING' STRATEGIC BRAND

Of the ten highest global market caps in 2006, only three remained in 2016 – and GE was one of them. Valued $35.3 billion, the GE brand celebrates its 125th anniversary in 2017. But don't get it wrong, it is not the same GE, as the enterprise was uniquely able to foresee the future early and walk into new industry leadership positions.

I was talking recently with John Rice, GE's Vice Chairman and CEO of GE Global Growth Organisation based in Hong Kong. I have already referred to the partnerial relationship between GE and BP (Ref. Chapter 6) and feel privileged with a long held friendship with John, a pioneer of that relationship. John: *"In the 20th century, we were a big financial service business, contributing to 40% of our earnings; and a consumer business with media, white goods, light bulbs and so on. 21st century comes with the global financial crisis and major questions about the combination of financial services and industrial".*

Embracing digital industrial
"You could say: this combination has always worked, so let's keep doing it. Or, this world is going to change and you have to separate the two. At the same time, you see the early signs of the move to digital and recognize that the combination of digital and industrial is likely to happen. And you have to decide if we are going to be in the middle of it, helping it happen or we're going to be overtaken by the tsunami. We choose the former"

Over a very short period of time and through major disposals – NBC Universal, GE Appliances, GE Capital - and acquisitions - Alstom, Baker Hughes -, GE has deeply reshaped its portfolio and centered its identity on selected industrial platforms - turbines, jet engines, oil & gas services, power systems and healthcare equipment. All these areas are suffused with increasingly interoperable sensors, data analytics, software controls and digital automations. This gigantic analytical power - GE only is expected to generate a million terabytes of data per day by 2020 - is used both for GE's manufacturing operations and the management of its customers' industrial assets.

A 'Culture' and 'Purpose' led GE brand

I asked John about GE's magic to see ahead and transform a 125-year mega and complex organization in such depth and at such pace. The obvious answer probably lies in the essence of the GE brand itself, 'Imagination at work'.

John goes further *"It is a cultural strength and we continuously test this culture in quick easy 10-question surveys we run to assess whether we're moving in the right direction: Do people believe in our digital strategy? Do they think we're customer focused enough? Do they think we're simple enough? Do people have the space to experiment, a key aspect in our culture but a harder one to protect in big companies?*

A big part of our ability to move also comes with helping everybody understand the 'WHY'.

"A big part of our ability to move also comes with helping everybody understand the 'WHY'. How do you get 300,000 people to buy in? In lots of companies that have been around for a while, there's an institutional bias to the 'what' and 'how' and not enough time is spent on 'why' at the beginning. As we invest and have to make sacrifices to fund our digital efforts, it became easier if people could answer 'why it has to work'; and 'why it's key for us'. I am not naive enough to think that all 300,000 people have totally bought into all of our strategies but a lot of them have and I think the progress we make is because we really do have leaders and teams that get it - and are ready to execute, because they understand 'why'. And it's the brand and it's your reason for being."

A 'Customer Centric' and 'Strategy Guiding' GE brand

As said, I have worked many years with GE across multiple areas and I remember two of their obsessions: be a 'technology company', notably cross-pollinating innovation throughout their portfolio; and base their value proposition on outcome sales. The combination of both resulted in looking to sell based on life time costs for their customers rather than the straight equipment – using a simple example, how would GE reduce BP's cost per megawatt produced in our wind farms by optimizing every aspect of the design, running and maintenance of the assets?

In the early 2000's, it was becoming harder to sustain productivity at the past average rate of 4%, because process improvements by nature were slowing down. With the 'why' question being 'customer productivity', GE's response to this customer centric concern was: digital industrial. Incidentally, they can now get up to 20% more electricity from the same wind hardware than in the start of the decade.

Digital industrial means obtaining operating information and developing analytics to optimize asset performance [the internet of things]; changing product design and building greater quality ones at pace [through 3D printers and digital fabrication]; automating manufacturing and operating processes; combining analytics-based and physics-based analysis to predict and influence machine behaviour and industrial processes.

A 'Connected' and 'Partnering' GE brand

These multiple applications of the Industrial Internet – which some call Industry 4.0 require an operating platform. And GE, with a leader and integrator vision, is developing the Predix platform – with Jeff Immelt admitting that GE would be *"a top 10 software company by 2020"* (Ref. Illustration 8.9).

ILLUSTRATION 8.9 THE PREDIX ECOSYSTEM

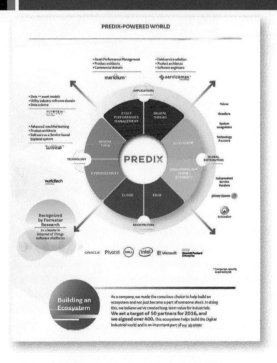

Credit – GE Corporate Site

John: *"We are developing Predix as the operating system for the Industrial Internet – providing a platform to connect industrial equipment and use the applications to analyze data and guide actions. It is an open-system, cloud-based where we are inviting all to participate, including competition. We have partnerships with many companies [over 400 end of 2016] including some that aren't in our industries, because we believe that it is the way to create the industrial standard equivalent to the operating systems in the consumer internet."*

GE, an Exemplary Future Embracing Strategic Brand

As we just established, the GE brand has a fully coherent system and evidence to make it 'Future Embracing'. And John's observations confirm it plays its dual role of 'seeing, shaping and creating the future', as well as 'being future proof and enabling the organisation's transition into the future'. The review of the remaining Strategic Brand Imperatives also concludes on a very strong GE Strategic Brand, as represented on illustration 8.10

ILLUSTRATION 8.10	THE ENDURING STRATEGIC BRAND IMPERATIVES - GE

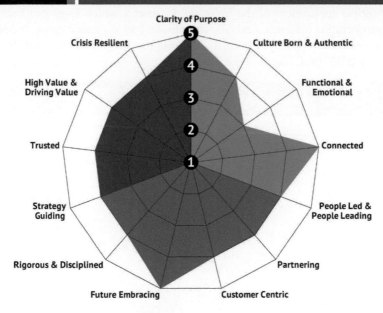

I asked John his perspectives on the brand and what the ongoing transformation of GE meant - for example could Predix become the brand? John: *"The brand is our reason for being; it holds our culture strength and represents the why; it is our credibility and allows us to meet with leaders in any country; it makes people care because of what we know; it represents our 'GE store', which is our fairly unique set of horizontal capabilities across our multi-industry businesses and one of our major competitive strengths".*

"And we want GE to be known for setting the standards for the whole plan for digital industrial through Predix. Our digital work will be known as Predix, which will be a kind

of brand, like IOS, or Android. And Predix could be associated to GE in a similar manner to how IOS is associated with Apple"

There is little doubt the GE brand will continue evolving and notably in its expression, to reflect the 'flow created by machines sensing, predicting, and responding to their unique environments' - and with a 'digital first' stance. But if we were to predict, it will keep leaning on its deeply anchored Strategic Brand Imperatives to continue shaping the future and leading the transition into it.

HAIER, A B2C FUTURE EMBRACING STRATEGIC BRAND

Haier Like Nicola Mendelsohn and in the face of globalisation and individualisation, I am absolutely convinced that a Future Embracing Strategic Brand starts with 'followings its customers', whoever the customer is. In other words, 'Future Embracing' is fully intertwined with 'Customer Centricity', linking the preceding chapter 7 to this one. All anticipations described earlier on the future of the Automotive, Retail, Financial Services, Healthcare and Pharmaceutical sectors are indeed customer driven.

Everything is 'Future Embracing' at Haier! The enterprise has devoted its whole raison d'etre to restlessly transition into the future with formidable intent, pace and agility, guided by placing the customer at its core and driving everything this $38 billion company does to make progress from their perspective.

The Haier Group

A quick introduction: the Haier Group Corporation (Haier) is a Chinese multinational consumer electronics and home appliances company headquartered in Qingdao, China. Its main product lines are air conditioners, mobile phones, computers, microwave ovens, washing machines, refrigerators and televisions. The company was nearing bankruptcy when CEO Zhang Ruimin took the helm in 1984 and in a relatively short period led the Haier brand to gain the world's largest market share in white goods, with about 14 per cent of the overall retail volume.

In 2015, Haier achieved a global revenue of 188.7 billion yuan ($27.3 billion), a 6 per cent CAGR in the last 9 years. Its total profit reached 18 billion yuan ($2.7 billion), a 20 per cent year-on-year growth rate and a 33 per cent CAGR in the last 9 years. Among other developments, the Haier Group acquired General Electric's appliance division in 2016 for $5.4 billion. [High Value & Driving Value]

Beyond these facts and figures, the Haier brand story is extraordinary. It is an Exemplary Strategic Brand, continuously engaged in a succession of radical 'Future Embracing' transformations that serve a deep 'Brand Purpose' (5) and achieve ultimate 'Customer Centricity' (5) and Brand 'Connectedness' (5). Let's go through these phases of visionary change.

ILLUSTRATION 8.11 | HAIER AS A 'FUTURE EMBRACING' STRATEGIC BRAND

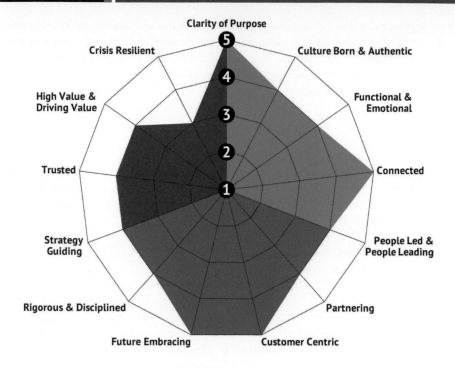

From commodity to brand

One of Zhang Ruimin's first 'Future Embracing' foundational acts was in the very early days after receiving a customer letter complaining about a faulty refrigerator. He called people from quality control to the warehouse where there were 400 units. They inspected them one by one and pulled out 76 problem fridges. In a time when these refrigerators would have sold nonetheless, he lined them up in the street and destroyed them with a sledgehammer. His message was clear: any product leaving the warehouse for delivery would be first rate.

Zhang Ruimin always understood the importance of a brand. The Haier corporate site describes the first step of strategic development following the 76 fridges episode as the *"Brand Building Strategy"* phase: *"It was at the beginning of the reform and… at the time, household appliances were in short supply, which led many companies to strive to expand in scale. Focus was put on quantity at the expense of quality. Instead of following this trend blindly, Haier made quality a priority, putting a comprehensive quality management system in place. 'Either not in it, or in it for the win', as it was put. When finally there was an oversupply in the household appliance market, Haier was already well positioned to win with its differentiated quality."* The brand had been formed. (Notes 6 and 7)

From volumes to branded quality

From the inception of its revival, Zhang Ruimin changed Haier's business model to solving problems for customers and embraced branding on the basis of superior quality. This purpose translated into Haier's primary brand value – *"Rights and Wrongs: users are always right, while we need to constantly improve ourselves"* – a value which never changed through the various phases of the company's strategic transformations [Purpose; Culture born]

For Haier's employees, this meant *"users are always right, and deserve the best and multiple choices, hence we need to constantly improve ourselves and realise achievement by establishing innovation out of change."*

These deep brand purpose and culture gave Haier its 'Future Embracing' character. Over the last 30 years, the company continuously disrupted itself and came to epitomise Customer Centric 'Future Embracing'. Here are Haier's successive reinventions, as shown on Illustration 8.12.

ILLUSTRATION 8.12	HAIER'S SUCCESSIVE PHASES OF 'FUTURE EMBRACING' REINVENTION

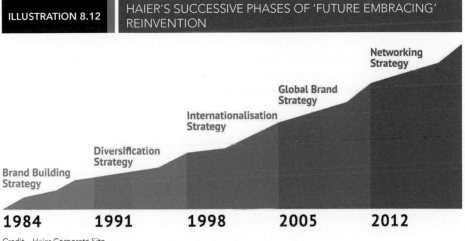

Credit – Haier Corporate Site

From product to service responsiveness

In 1991, Haier observed that competitors had caught up, quality was readily available and other brands were becoming well known. So it made a new jump into innovative 'Great Service' with its 'Star Service' offer, whereby employees would provide the highest levels of service responsiveness. This drove a new form of customer responsive innovation to serve distinctive consumer needs. An example was the launch of a vegetable washing machine after a service technician had visited a farm and reported that the family washing machine had become faulty after being wrongly used to wash vegetables. Another example was the launch of a small washing machine, 'The Little Prodigy', initially developed to offer the daily and discreet washing of underclothes [Functional & Emotional].

This jump into service responsiveness led to an organisational transformation, by which Haier got rid of middle management, with front line staff and service technicians bringing ideas from the customers directly to top management. Equally, the silos between departments were blown away – we'll describe this in more detail below. [Connected]

From service to customer intimacy

In the early 2000s, when good service had become the norm across the household sector in China, Haier decided to shift its emphasis again, from customer responsiveness to customer intimacy. In short, Haier's goal was to anticipate what customers wanted rather than drive this need from direct observation or feedback. This required a complete re-engineering of the way work was done, and Haier moved from their previous lean but still rather traditional model to the so called ZZJYT – Zi Zhu Jing Ying Ti – system.

Haier decided to shift its emphasis again, from customer responsiveness to customer intimacy. In short, Haier's goal was to anticipate what customers wanted rather than drive this need from direct observation or feedback.

This broke up the company into a bottom up structure of several 'anticipatory' (rather than retrospective) independent ZZJYT units. [People led] Their slogan was *'zero distance to the customer'*; in essence Haier cultivated new ideas rather than acting after customer responses to their offerings. At this point, Haier even stopped advertising, on the basis that it was far better to meet consumers directly online [Strategy Guiding].

As shown on Illustration 8.13, typical 'first tier' ZZJYT must face the market directly, understand customer needs and provide customers with the right products. Each unit has the character of a small start-up group and is typically composed of sales, R&D, marketing and finance, with each department talking directly to customers and coordinating among themselves continuously. The units are not permanently assigned but formed to a purpose through internal competition.

For example, when Haier launched a three-door refrigerator – two doors on the side and a freezer door at the bottom – they invited employees to compete for the role of leading the ZZJYT by submitting their plans on how the product could be built and best succeed. The young Pu Xiankai was selected to lead the business because of the imaginative way he described the product; two years later it is generating $1.5 billion in revenue. To achieve this, Xiankai selected his ZZJYT members and oversaw the related 'community of interest', made up of people inside and partners outside, who helped his team to deliver the value chain. This customer centric organisational model goes well beyond 'open innovation' and 'project team' structures practised in other companies; its deeper, wider, systemic, cross-company nature makes it pure and fast [Rigorous & Disciplined].

ILLUSTRATION 8.13   RE-ENGINEERING HAIER FOR ZERO DISTANCE TO CUSTOMERS

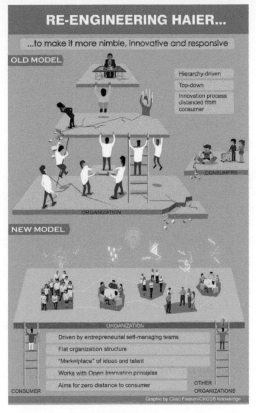

Credit - Chao Fansen, CKGSB Knowledge

Haier's primary value of *"The customers are always right while we need to constantly improve ourselves"* demands that each employee develops *"the two spirits of entrepreneurship and innovation".* As in the three-door refrigerator case, Haier encourages each employee to move from being managed to becoming CEO of their own area, to drive new value from innovation and create new users. Haier has therefore become a magnet for the most capable engineers and business people. [People leading]

Delivering customer intimacy from global brand building

Haier 'Future Embracing' ethos is further evidenced in that the company anticipated how digital would transform the terms of delivering customer intimacy very early on and used this to further its branded transformation. Here is how the company describes the move: *"The Internet Age brings with it segmentation of marketing. The production-inventory-sales model of traditional businesses can no longer meet the personalised demands of users, and a firm has to transform from self-centred product selling to a user-centric sale of services, i.e. a user-driven 'on-demand manufacturing and delivery' mode.*

The Internet has also given rise to the integration of global economies... and therefore Haier has consolidated global resources in R&D, manufacturing and marketing to create a global brand."

The production-inventory-sales model of traditional businesses can no longer meet the personalised demands of users, and a firm has to transform from self-centred product selling to a user-centric sale of services, i.e. a user-driven 'on-demand manufacturing and delivery' mode.

The business model Haier applies to create customers in the Internet Age is the so-called *"Win-Win Model of Individual-Goal Combination"* (aka the "Rendanheyi Win-Win Model"). Here, 'Individual' refers to the employees' two spirits of entrepreneurship and innovation; 'Goal' relates to users' value. In the model, each employee creates value for users (goals) in different ZZJYTs to fulfil their own values (individual).

As an example, 670,000 people took part in an online conversation following Haier's question: *"What do you want from your air conditioning?"* A concept emerged, *"Cool, not cold"*, which became the tagline for the Tianzun ('Heaven'), Haier's advanced household heater/air conditioner/air purifier, released in 2014. But there was more to the "cool" concept than temperature: consumers wanted air which was not dry or dusty, an appliance which wasn't noisy, which prevented bacteria, had attractive and convenient design, remote activation via the internet, etc. Even using the customer phrase *"cool, not cold"* in the Chinese communication campaign, rather than the creation of a professional marketer, reflects the principle of *"customer service leadership"* through a multi-layered approach to consumer insight.

Equally impressive was the cross-functional nature of the appliance's development and launch: while the marketing staff digested the insights from Haier's online customer interactions, manufacturing was already considering what this would mean for production, procurement was speaking directly to suppliers about sourcing feasibilities, and after-sales service was developing plans for follow-through. Representatives of each ZZJYT function conducted conversations directly with customers, adding a responsive dimension to the company's consumer insight capabilities. Because they worked closely together from the start, managers from all these functions moved forward in concert, addressing any possible disconnects as they arose. This allowed products to be developed very quickly and go to market as soon as they were ready, instead of waiting for each department to throw its work 'over the wall' to the next one.

We would be incomplete if not noting at this stage Haier's perfect 'Future Embracing' enabled 'Customer Centric' scorecard, as represented in Illustration 8.14 [Customer Centric].

ILLUSTRATION 8.14   HAIER AS A 'CUSTOMER CENTRIC' STRATEGIC BRAND

Haier

1. Culture & Mindset	5
2. Purpose Led	5
3. Total Experience Design	5
4. Trends Integration	5
5. Customer as a Partner	5
6. Cross Functional Teams	5
7. Decision on the front line	5
8. Magnet for Talents	5
9. Unparalleled Growth	5
10. We are the Platform	5

Scale 1: Low to 5: Very Strong

...implementing the development strategy of a networked enterprise is embodied in three dimensions: border-free enterprise, manager-free management and scale-free supply chain... to continuously create value for customers.

Networking Strategy

More recently, an iteration of the now famous "Win-Win model of Rendanheyi" is taking Haier's core principle of customer service leadership and customer centric organisation to a new level through its 'Networking Strategy', a radical decentralisation, disintermediation and debureaucratisation. The base idea is to extend the ZZJYT to open up cooperation not only with customers but also with innovators around the world, including competitors and members of the supply chain. *"The new model finds its expression in networking, with the market and enterprise demonstrating features of networking. From Haier's perspective, the way of implementing the development strategy of a networked enterprise is embodied in three dimensions: border-free enterprise, manager-free management and scale-free supply chain... to continuously create value for customers."* In practice, Haier has established a user-centred ecosystem for co-creation and winning together, which adds value for all stakeholders [Partnering]. The organisational structure remains based on ZZJYT but each ZZJYT has evolved into a networked platform, an open node distributed on the Internet with a flat structure free from hierarchical organisation.

No more inside versus outside the company

In an interview to strategy+business, Zhang Ruimin explained: *"I want to turn Haier into an internet-based company, a company unrestricted by borders...We believe that there is no 'inside' the company versus 'outside' anymore. Whoever is capable, come and work with us. We now have a lot of entrepreneurs at Haier who don't work inside the company... and in the long run, there won't be any company employees to speak of – only the Haier platform... You might find yourself working together with a group of people you didn't know yesterday, and after tomorrow you'll all go your separate ways. People come together for special projects, after which they disperse."*[Crisis resilient] (Note 8)

I want to turn Haier into an internet-based company, a company unrestricted by borders...We believe that there is no 'inside' the company versus 'outside' anymore.

Using the air conditioning unit we mentioned earlier as an example, Ruimin added: *"We concluded that the AC unit should be able to test the cleanliness of the air and be controlled intelligently... If a home appliance can't communicate with the internet, it shouldn't exist... We then brought in Samsung and Apple to help us meet users' requirements... We at Haier are no longer the ones directing things. We are the glue which binds everything together... Nowadays, we make users part of the R&D process. Even after the product is successful, we go back for constant revisions in which we invite users to participate, and also competitors, as we did for the 'cordless home appliance'. It means we don't keep absolute secrets like we did in the past."* [Trusted]

Among the other effects of this transformation, the number of employees has decreased by 45 per cent compared to its peak headcount. But Haier's platforms have provided over 1.3 million job opportunities for society as a whole.

In May 2016, the State Council of China praised Haier for its exemplification of *"mass entrepreneurship and innovation"*, the exact same words of *"the two spirits of entrepreneurship and innovation"* used by Haier's to describe its 30-year-old brand culture.

BUILDING A 'FUTURE EMBRACING' STRATEGIC BRAND

In summary, have Facebook, GE and Haier shown us what makes them so compellingly 'Future Embracing'? My belief is 'yes' and the main suggestion is that they are Exemplary Enduring Strategic Brands and epitomise the two 'Future Embracing' superpowers through the best practices elicited below.

See, shape and create the future
1. Follow your customers - Haier, IBM, GE, Amazon, Facebook and other Future Embracing brands consistently do this [Customer Centricity]
2. Be all antennas out and disciplined at analysing and acting on trends - Nicola took deep notice and consequence of Davos' Fourth Industrial Revolution [Connected]
3. Be ruthless about your focus on the future -Haier took the most radical decisions, including organisational ones. [Rigorous & Disciplined]

4. Partner, as you neither can see nor create the future alone - IBM consistently develops partnerships to create the future, by combining their technology and their partners' application expertise. [Partnering]
5. Disrupt yourself - Facebook took time to disrupt itself with the mobile …and came close to have to deeply regret it. [Strategy Guiding]
6. See far away, act now - IBM, GE have a long-term point of view…but fasten immediate execution into that future. [Strategy Guiding]

Be future proof and enable the organisation transition into the future

7. Always be on a mission, so it becomes cultural - IBM's 'Think' has this inherent capability. [Culture]
8. Be deeply purposed and strengthen culture accordingly - E.g. Haier's " two spirits of entrepreneurship and innovation". [Purpose & Culture]
9. Be bold and transformational at pace, faster than others - E.g. Facebook's mobile transformation. [Strategy Guiding]
10. Break the inside walls - Haier shortened their lines of command to create a direct link between markets and leaders. They empowered people to engage and lead into the future. [People led and People leading]
11. Break the inside – outside walls - Transparency, Inside-Out and Outside-In are just a way of being for Haier [Culture & Transparency]
12. Develop a brand culture of fast adoption of technology - This is mobile for Facebook, AI for IBM and Amazon, IoT for GE, digital innovation for Haier [Culture and Strategy Guiding].

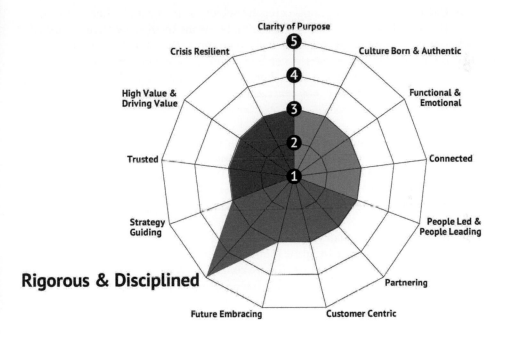

"Discipline is the bridge between goals and accomplishments. Affirmation without discipline is the beginning of delusion"

Jim Rohn, entrepreneur and business philosopher

What do a Danish digital learning company, a Spanish food retailer and a French aeronautical supplier have in common? Clio Online, Grup Ametller and Figeac Aero seem very different in terms of industry, ambition and scale – but they all share one particular attribute, one of the key elements of a Strategic Brand: they are run with 'Rigour and Discipline', leading to spotless execution.

It is this quality execution that separates them from competition, that defines their differentiated brand in the eyes of their stakeholders and customers and, indeed, in the eyes of the judges of the European Business Awards (EBA). (Note 1)

For they are all EBA winners, which judges over 33,000 organisations across 33 countries each year, in order to select a handful of best practice businesses.

Clio Online is an educational company helping 85 per cent of schools across Denmark to empower teachers in their jobs, saving them 24 per cent of time in their lesson preparation. It all began in 2006 when three friends had an idea about how they could make teachers' lives easier by tapping into technology. Today, Clio Online's turnover exceeds 10 million euros. I like the way founder Janus Bern Sorensen describes his company's purpose: *"600 years ago Gutenberg invented the printing press and changed the face of book publishing; we're trying to do the same with digital learning."*

Figeac Aero, the French aeronautical subcontractor, is another stellar example of a company run with 'Rigour and Discipline'. Founded in 1989 from personal savings of 18,000 euros, today the company is one of the biggest *"partners of major aeronautical manufacturers"* in the world, with customers including Boeing and Airbus and a fast growing 250 million euros turnover.

Grup Ametller, a Catalan food company, has created the largest independent fresh produce company in Spain in just 14 years. 'Rigorous and Disciplined' attention to integrating its processes to guarantee quality and economy has created 1700 jobs and a retail brand with 12 new stores and three restaurants.

For the last eight years, sharing the same beliefs as the European Business Awards (EBA), I have been involved in every possible way – as a partner, supporter, judge, prize-giver or even chair of their conference. The EBA has always been among the most rewarding days in my business calendar: I emerge exhilarated, inspired and excited by the absolute best of European business – in fact, by the best of business globally.

BEST OF EUROPEAN BUSINESS AND BRANDS

The EBA is a fantastic initiative founded in 2007 by Adrian Tripp. Its reputation across Europe is now well established. In the 2016/17 awards, they engaged with over 33,000 organisations representing a combined turnover of over €1.0 trillion euros, employing over 2.7 million people and generating over 60 billion euros profit.

Adrian describes their purpose: *"The European Business Awards is built on the ethos that an innovative, strong and thriving business community makes a more successful and prosperous Europe. We believe that from unemployment to climate change, from conflict to poverty, it is business that has one of the biggest roles to play in helping tackle the major challenges faced by the region and globally. Creating stronger, more successful, innovative and ethical business communities will help address all of the challenges above, and many more. Each year, the EBA recognises some of the exceptional talent and capability we are lucky to have in Europe. Europe needs more companies like these and we hope the EBA gives inspiration to an ever greater number of them."*

ILLUSTRATION 9.1	EBA AWARDS CEREMONY, MILAN 2016

EBA 2015/16 Gala Celebrations
Winners and Finalists celebrate their success in the EBA Final in Milan

Source: EBA

Why talk about the EBA here? Because over the years, the inspiring quality of the businesses and the winners has reminded me of an important lesson: the best businesses are not necessarily about the most innovative idea; they are not always about the latest tech or the breakthrough invention. Rather, the vast majority are about 'Rigour and Discipline', traditional businesses executed immaculately. Whatever they do, it's these businesses' consistent, systematic, embedded, determined execution, with ultimate attention to detail, which differentiates them from their competitors and defines their brand.

I have experienced hundreds of these perfectly run businesses, and found that they share ten similarities:

1. **Operate in well-known, traditional sectors** but grow and transform their sector through operating excellence, taking the experience to a different place. Innovation is continuous improvement, with rapid but evolutionary application of technology and digital.
2. **Run by extremely involved, committed people,** who practise the highest levels of engagement. Associates talk and act like leadership, and there is a shared sense of ownership. People come first.
3. **Team leadership rather than individual,** although often these are founder businesses in their first, second or third generation which have cultivated and anchored the founder's culture and values over generations to be shared by all in the team.
4. **Leadership embodies a listening and learning style.** Leaders are role models driven by a deep sense of duty to the institution.
5. **Customer centric.** No effort is spared listening to customers, their needs, issues, objectives and relationship with the organisation.
6. **Consistent ethos of continuous improvement,** to build deep capability and excellence over time. Any mistake is treated as an opportunity, which is integrated into a company's shared knowledge and processes. This ensures it doesn't happen again – but also results in continuous improvement.
7. **Authenticity throughout the company.** Associates live the organisation's purpose and delivery model and are the best cases of inside-out.
8. **Joy.** The enthusiasm, belief, entrepreneurial spirit, and 'can do' attitude provide a communicating energy within and out of the organisation.
9. **Profit is an outcome, not the key action driver.** Immediate profit is never valued above doing the right thing for the longer-term build of the brand and the business.
10. **Staggering profit and growth.** Success and compelling metrics are a key requirement in participating in the EBA. Double-digit returns and growth over years are common among candidates and, of course, winners.

These companies are not necessarily slick: they are not elaborate or flashy. But as I have mentioned, there is joy. I remember the first ever EBA won by a Croatian company, Belmedic – for best European 'customer focus' – in 2016. Their table of 10 ladies at the gala evening was noisier than the other 600 guests put together!

Are they Strategic Brands? Most of them are – and there are even some of the most accomplished Strategic Brands among them, though you may not know of them. In short, they epitomise novelist George Eliot's great observation: *"Genius at first is little more than a great capacity for receiving discipline."*

RIGOROUS AND DISCIPLINED EXECUTION

'What doesn't kill you makes you stronger.' As is often the case with the best learning, my understanding of immaculate operations comes from failed attempts.

I remember 2002, when I moved from leading BP Downstream's strategy to help turning it into reality for BP's B2B businesses. I was passionate about the opportunities these Air, Marine, Fleet, LPG, Castrol B2B and other such businesses could gain from clearer customer segmentation, more advanced offers and transformed routes to market. I wanted them to become less asset and product driven, and rethink their model around customers – so, less push and more pull.

At this time, we met all over the world to try and thrash out a solution – seven of us around the table, myself and the CEOs of these businesses. To put the scale of this meeting in perspective, if these BP divisions had been independent companies, almost each of them would have been listed in the FTSE 100. What would happen if Air BP focused more on individual customers such as British Airways, rather than primarily on its assets in different airports? Could we develop a BP Fleet end-to-end solution and partner with Fedex and other global major energy users? In these meetings, many of my colleagues insisted we got the basics right first – focusing on the 'Rigour and Discipline' in the management of our assets, service and brands – before we considered these attractive business options. Otherwise we would end up with a nice sauce over badly cooked food.

They were right about the sequence – and did a great job at establishing the basics. Over a period of five years, these businesses were turned into undisputed world leaders in their categories and became fit to step into advanced value added business models.

Another example of this 'Rigour and Discipline' comes from the BP Strategic Accounts business, which I founded and ran for over 10 years. The purpose of this Division was to create real and lasting partnerships with the best organisations in the world. For example, BP's partnership with Ford began with the intent that we would develop joint 'technology to market' solutions. We agreed to share tech secrets to develop a better joint energy + engine performance. From there arose another 10 streams of cooperative activities, but the key point is that the strategic partnership was immaculate in its execution because it was grounded and run with a deeply shared 'Rigour and Discipline'.

Stephen Odell, Executive Vice President , Global Marketing, Sales and Service, Ford Motor Company, with whom I had a close and trusting working relationship for many years, talks about the complexity of making the Ford Brand what it is and how it requires ultimate 'Rigour and Discipline':

"Ford is an awesome aggregator: we deal with suppliers, we deal with the dealers, we deal with third parties, we deal with distributors, we deal with partners and we find a way of aggregating all of that capability and bringing it together into a very complex product that

has to perform at a very high level on a number of factors, including safety. And it is how we perform this task that helps to define the Ford brand."

A true partnership results in mutual dependency and reliance. It only takes one wrong execution to destroy the long-built trust, confidence and reliance on your partner. The management and perfect execution of these critical tasks was crucial for Ford – and our business needed to be able to deliver this excellence day after day, year after year.

Of course, 'Rigour and Discipline' was also essential in our retail business: *"Retail is detail"*, as often said. From a brand standpoint, the way to make Beyond Petroleum work on the forecourt turned into *'a little better'* strategy, which was largely predicated on its day-to-day consistent execution across our network. A humble promise in words, a huge promise in practice! This saw us dissecting every act of a visit to a BP petrol station - ergonomic petrol nozzles, cleaner toilets, faster queues, more parking, a friendly 'hello'. We were down in the trenches making these details work because that's how we delivered our brand promise and this rigour would define who we are.

No 'Rigour and Discipline', no Strategic Brand

Entrepreneur and writer Jim Rohn also says, *"Success is nothing more than a few simple disciplines, practised every day."* So many bright ideas get killed and so many good asset-based businesses never reach their potential because of imperfect translation and execution.

More important every day
Rigour, discipline and consistency are considered pre-requisites today – but there's a downside to this. It means they are hardly ever talked about. They are not glamorous and they don't create heroes.

The key thesis in this chapter is that thoroughness in execution, while hard to achieve, is not only essential to building an Enduring Strategy Brand but will continue to place the brand above its competitors in the future almost by itself.

As an engineer who started his career in production – where quality is absolutely mandatory – I have always insisted that extreme 'Rigour and Discipline' are the core foundations of the brand and business, especially at every touch point with customers. As a consumer, I am infuriated when respect, service and effort are not exhibited by a brand, whatever their sphere of activity. I am sure we all have our own, but my worst customer experiences have unfortunately come from my country of origin, with BNP Paribas and Air France ('Air Chance' for many – I am probably not the only deeply frustrated traveller to have broken two of their counters in my time…)

Both the bank and airline have good assets and a respected product offer, yet the cultural absence of intent and effort, of the required rigour required for customer relationships, fails their brands. Instead, if you focus on this first - and it starts with leadership - it will be the best thing you could do to build your Strategic Brand – because *"talent without discipline is like an octopus on roller skate,"* says Author H. Jackson Brown.

Implementation is strategy

In all honesty, my determination to get this right has not always been well received. There have been multiple times around exec and board tables when my 'strategy' presentations were about the way to do things, the how, the discipline formula, rather than the brilliance of promising futures – and sometimes I was rebuffed as *"not strategic enough"*.

There was a particular meeting in 1998 when we presented the Castrol Europe strategy to the Group CEO and got hammered for it. Rather than focus on the visionary nature of our strategy, we wanted to use the meeting to anchor and get support on the tricky stuff, and build the 'Rigour and Discipline' of how we would achieve our objectives. Our boss at the time was not very interested – he didn't want to get down into the trenches and what he perceived as details.

I see this all the time, how a brand and strategy so often fail because not enough importance is given to the details. The skill of leadership and management is not simply to create the vision but also to help solve trickier issues. I am from the school of thought that *"implementation is strategy"* or, more precisely, that there is no real strategy without great implementation. Hence I remain convinced that the how something is achieved must be at least a key aspect of the brand and business strategy, if not over and above others.

"Be your own best customer, live your customer lifestyle."

So, keep at it even if you are not popular all the time! I like to follow environmentalist Milena Glimbovski's advice to *"be your own best customer, live your customer lifestyle."* If I were an investor, a key metric for leadership would be the proportion of their time they personally spent in the field whether that's in the aisles of their supermarkets, on flights with crews, in a customer service call centre, a bank branch or a petrol station.

The 'Rigour and Discipline' brand house

The mental image I have always held for 'Rigour and Discipline' is one of a three-level house, with a foundation, ground level and top floor [Ref. Illustration 9.2]. Each represents a different level of impact and importance of 'Rigour and Discipline' to a brand.

House necessary foundation - survival

The foundation represents a pre-condition for two parties engaging in any business or transaction and potentially repeating it. No foundation – no house, no real brand. In today's world of good quality brands, stakeholders and consumers take well-delivered and consistent functionalities for granted – and when this doesn't happen, it's a major breach.

ILLUSTRATION 9.2   THE BRAND 'RIGOUR AND DISCIPLINE' HOUSE

© THE Enduring Strategic Brand

BRITISH AIRWAYS I am writing these lines on a BA flight and get what I expect: a disciplined standard service from the crew. Nothing to raise emotion, but a very acceptable experience. They deserve my business!

House ground level – incentive

The house's ground level includes the hall, kitchen, etc. and is an important place. 'Rigour and Discipline' is more than a required background, it is a key value added and positive contributor to the relationship and experience. Alongside other brand dimensions, excellence plays a full role in a customer's or stakeholder's choice, support and loyalty. It is part of the vernacular of the brand and takes its fair share in the brand positioning and communication. Many luxury brands will be 'living' at this level of the house. The overall execution and consistent feel of luxury in the experience are important.

In BP, our 'convenience' shops in petrol stations were also ground-floor inhabitants. If their product offer, access, pick up of goods, payment, parking and general convenience were all designed and executed consistently well, that sort of rigour was a differentiator and brand builder.

House top floor – differentiation

The roof of the house contains the living and playrooms, the places for fun and relaxation. Here 'Rigour and Discipline' are THE differentiator.

amazon An undoubted leader in this space is Amazon. A business partner recently summed it up: "*I don't like Amazon but I can't not use them.*" Amazon has built its dominance on an unrivalled supply chain that delivers at or above expectations again and again. Amazon internalises all aspects of a customer journey, including the most challenging ones – complaints, returns etc. – to make their resolution simple. To use a common phrase in the marketing lexicon, Amazon epitomises the 'frictionless experience', where people not only get what they want and don't need anything else, but also value the brand for what it removes: hassle, complexity, stress, time losses. In the upper level of our excellence house, 'Rigour and Discipline' is THE brand maker and lives in accordance with business magnate Stephan Persson's approach to business: *"Loyalty is not won by being first. It is won by being best."*

"Loyalty is not won by being first. It is won by being best."

LLOYDS BANKING GROUP   If you visit Lloyds Banking Group Headquarter in Gresham Street in London as I did recently, you get welcomed by two gigantic posters aside the elevator cases saying: Our purpose - *'Helping Britain Prosper'*; Our mission - *'Best Bank for Customers'*; Our values – *'Putting customers first'*, *'Keeping it simple'*, *'Making a difference together'*. And when you leave the escalator on the 8th floor, other posters are here to celebrate 250 years of the brand and *'Helping Britain Prosper'*. From the lobby to the corridors, you are with the brand – and as Andrew Bester, Group Director and Chief Executive of Commercial Banking puts it: *"our whole effort is to get Lloyds Black Horse to gallop faster"*

"The brand is a big thing for Lloyds Banking Group. Around the ExCo table we spent an estimate of 5% of our entire time talking explicitly about the brand. If you now take the broader discussion on purpose, values and what we are trying to do on culture going forward, this probably moves up to around 20% of our time. With one of four accounts in retail banking in the country, the commercial business, where we provide in excess of 20% of funding to the economy and our other activities, we touch literally every person in this country every day.

"By providing the essence of what we're trying to do, the brand is a critical framework for people within the organization who manage all these touch points, to know why they're doing what they are doing, what they should be doing and how they should be doing it. And it is particularly important given that our vision is being the 'Best Bank for our Customers'. For example, a mortgage clerk would know that by giving that mortgage they would contribute to supporting jobs in the building industry.

"By providing the essence of what we're trying to do, the brand is a critical framework for people within the organization who manage all these touch points, to know why they're doing what they are doing, what they should be doing and how they should be doing it.

"It is critical to remain anchored at the core through the brand, as even if our purpose has not changed for 250 years, what does and will continue to change ever faster is actually the way we do it and notably digitalisation. Having this stable purpose will help to understand and support why each of us is changing some of the ways we do things. Because we all need to remain very alert these days against the disintermediation risks, both on the way the services are delivered and the costs at which they are delivered"

Our conversation over lunch with Andrew crystalized a conviction in me: real 'Rigour and Discipline' with brands can only come if it flows naturally from a deeply shared purpose – in other words, 'Rigour and Discipline' is not imposed to people, it is self-generated from their individual will, belief and respect in the brand.

The 'Rigour and Discipline' house is here to help work out which type of brand you are or would want to be. I am always impressed how, from the many winners of the EBA to Amazon to the Lloyds Banking Group, many brands increasingly have 'Rigour and Discipline' as their definer.

Are these boring and obvious realities? That may be – but it is vitally important to an Enduring Strategic Brand. To succeed in taking 'Rigour and Discipline' from a good intention to a systematic reality in the way the brand operates day-to-day across all the organisation's activities is incredibly challenging and requires the best of culture, purpose, leadership, practice and incentive.

Rigour and Discipline to Brand Development and Management

A lot of organisations are increasingly disciplined in the way they manage and project their brand. There is considerable focus on consistency and effectiveness of delivery, as the context and reality of stakeholder and customer requirements change with digital, individualisation, globalisation and platformisation – and strategic marketing money is usually very constrained.

Techniques and practice evolve. It is not our purpose here to detail what these are but to guide on an attentive awareness of all the areas of brand building represented on Illustration 9.3.

An example of useful aggregation of good practice was a weeklong event in London in November 2016 on the topic of effectiveness – 'Effectiveness Week' (EffWeek). (Note 2) The event included a summit at BAFTA for two days, when top marketers shared their challenges on improving their accountability and capability, and held 20 satellite events where brands, expert practitioners and industry bodies reviewed and celebrated best-in-class examples. Who would have thought that metrics, analytics, tools and processes would one day be as popular as creativity!

EffWeek was instigated by IPA, and masterminded by Deborah Parkes. Testament to the fact that we live in an evidence-based world, 14 marketing industry associations agreed to collaborate to the project including: the IPA, AMEC, DMA, MRS, IAB, WFA, ISBA, PRCA, BCMA, CMA.

The fact alone that EffWeek took place tells us a lot about business today – everyone understands that evidence-based decision making is the only game in town, and that

ILLUSTRATION 9.3   AREAS OF BRAND RIGOUR AND DISCIPLINE

Credit – The IPA

everyone in an organisation needs to apply 'Rigorous and Disciplined' focus on what propels their brand. Here are a few examples:

Pulse testing decision-making – Vodafone shared how they had been unhappy for some time about the basis on which decisions were being made on marketing investments. They wanted to drive more reliable accountability, suspecting that less than optimal decisions were being made based on 'bad data', and wanted more control over the levers. Having weighed up a number of approaches (econometric and attribution type models) they concluded that there were flaws in all (correlation vs. causation or too long term in nature) and built a new system that is basically Pulse testing. This has revolutionised their media investment across all their channels.

Behavioural change anticipation – Government Communication Services talked about the dashboard that they have developed to give them better visibility on the top 25 campaigns that the government runs each year. By devising a way of understanding early indicators of behavioural change, they can predict effectiveness and tailor spend against certain projects more accurately to ensure that taxpayers' money is well spent.

Understanding emotional connections – John Lewis Head of Marketing and Brand, Rachel Swift, shared how they have isolated 'emotional connection' in their metrics and now know, after years of tracking, its impact on ROI for the business. Dialling up on creativity is a clear strategy to engage better with consumers, and because they can now measure and explain this, their colleagues have become totally supportive.

PEPSICO **Data for growth** - PepsiCo's VP Insights and Analytics, Europe and Sub Saharan Africa and Global Executive Innovation Practice, Tim Warner, described the systematic journey that they had embarked on to create an environment where data can be fully leveraged – where it becomes a strategic asset and the fuel that drives more effectiveness and growth. He observed that the insight function needs to be focused on equipping business leaders to answer the most important growth questions. This starts, he said, with knowing very clearly what these questions are.

DIAGEO
Cascading learning – Diageo talked about improving marketing accountability by driving cultural change around 'evidence'. Ed Pilkington, marketing and innovation director, Western Europe said his mantra is '*I don't know what I don't know*' and to encourage others in the team to be open to learning and experimenting to continuously improve. He advised that cascading learning is a big focus for Diageo, and individuals are invited to attend training sessions and access evaluation stories from around the business on their intranet.

Failing; testing efficiency – Google and Monster shared their companies' commitment to 'test and learn' and how they are making it OK to fail – as long as you fail fast! To them, this liberates the workforce to be evidence driven and excited about improving everything that they do by scrutinising every detail. Alison Lomax, Head of Brand Solutions at Google UK, said that having read Bill Gates's '*Business at the speed of thought*' in 1999, she had been convinced that businesses needed to use technology to create 'a central nervous system' for faster feedback loops. What has changed since is the massive reduction in the cost of data storage, which increases processing power and capacity and supports the proliferation of digital data points and tracking tools. It is now possible to run hundreds of tests a year, without needing to scale headcount or other overheads to accommodate such an approach. So, rigour within business is the easiest it has ever been.

Data infrastructures are a must – Thomas H Davenport, Professor at BABSON Babson College, MIT talked about the four eras of marketing analytics and gave the audience a snapshot of how businesses will drive better performances through technology and leveraging data – and warned that those who are not yet building the infrastructures necessary will be overtaken in the blink of an eye. His message was clear: be rigorous in all processes – collate data on customers that will allow you to personalise your offerings to them in the future.

There were plenty of other rich learnings about how to continue raising to a more 'Rigorous and Disciplined' brand development and management. And it was interesting to observe how a number of our Exemplary Strategic Brands practise a large combination of these advanced approaches - the best are getting even better.

To put it simply, 'Rigour and Discipline' is the start and a major part of the finish of an Enduring Strategic Brand. And this gives it an important place in the 13 Imperatives.

THE OLYMPIC BRAND

 We have selected the Olympic Brand as The Enduring Strategic Brand for 'Rigour and Discipline' for three main reasons:

- Although the Olympic Brand provides no tangible practical product or service at first sight, and its main stakeholders are people involved in sport as well as society at large, there is something very special about the value and impact of a complex brand like this. The brand is very representative, as it's challenging, elaborate, global, B2C + B2B + B2G, human, emotional, political and intermittent.

- Its global consistency is impressive, though this comes more from self-discipline than an imposed rigour. I have learned a lot about how to build impressive Strategic Brands from the discipline of the Olympic Movement – and I hope readers will find their example helpful.

- Finally, for the last 15 years, I have been fascinated by the Olympic and Paralympic ideals and the roles they play, each in their own way, in society. These include respect, emotion and a desire to serve.

I actually had a fourth reason: aren't Strategic Brands very much like successful athletes – don't they require absolute 'Rigour and Discipline'; don't they need deep purpose and to partner intimately with their ecosystem? Aren't brands and athletes all about people? And isn't performance and winning their ultimate destination? The answer to these analogies is probably yes…and will hopefully make the following story enjoyable.

Is the Olympic brand – represented by the five rings – a Strategic Brand? Can the Olympic brand teach us about Strategic Brands in modern society and modern marketing? How is the Olympic Brand such a powerful 'Rigorous and Disciplined' Brand? The answers lie in the 13 Strategic Brand Imperatives, which we discuss below.

ILLUSTRATION 9.4   THE ENDURING STRATEGIC BRAND IMPERATIVES - THE OLYMPIC BRAND

Rigorous & Disciplined Olympic Brand

Having seen the Olympic brand in action, what makes it the epitome of 'Rigorous and Disciplined' includes a combination of two things:

- A self-driven distributed discipline guided by the shared ownership of purpose and deep respect for the Olympic ideal and brand
- In its complex circumstances, a more rigorous practice of brand management than many other commercial organisations

I will always remember the manifestation of brand-led self-discipline as explained by Lord Paul Deighton, former CEO of the London Organizing Committee for the 2012 Olympic Games (LOCOG), who I worked closely with at the time: *"On building the teams to deliver and manage London 2012, the key thing for us was to develop people's confidence and trust that we had the basic competence to deserve to be the holders of the Games 'magic dust'. Once people realized how precious this was, they would relieve us of it if we were not doing an excellent job or they certainly wouldn't join in. Once they realized we were doing a good job, they were happy to partner up with us because we could take them to a very special and positive place"*

Let's explore how every Imperative contributes to a system of 'Rigour and Discipline' for the Olympic Brand.

Self-disciplined Extraordinary Olympic Brand

Lisa Baird, Chief Marketing Officer of the United States Olympic Committee (USOC), talks about the rigour and self-discipline required to manage such a complex and extraordinary brand: *"The Olympics is managed as a brand. But it is different because it's not directly controlled in the way an enterprise might be. The Olympic brand is more of a Movement and has a near ubiquitous presence and global recognition. The International Olympic Committee (IOC) plays an essential role as the brand's central organisation, but they do not set the direction in every detail, because it's a movement rather than a single entity.*

"The biggest impact on the brand comes from the organising committee of each Games (OCOG). Of course, there are legal agreements between this OCOG and the Olympic Movement / IOC, but how each organising committee executes their Games is very much down to them. Then you have the athletes, who stand for and represent the brand, but can't be directed in the same way that you might control brand champions in a company. Finally, there are very few traditional tools that are effective in boosting or projecting the Olympic brand. For example, advertising to say how good the Olympic brand is, doesn't work.

"But the Olympic brand is powerful [Ref. Illustration 9.5] – and perhaps powerful brands are not controlled from the centre but rather owned by everybody around the organisation. It has clarity of meaning and purpose; it has one of the most powerful logos in the world;

it continues to remind people what it stands for, with ideas like the refugee team in Rio; it shapes the Games through positive stories and relationships; it has the right broadcasters around the world, who invest in making the brand as strong as possible. These are the things which make it an extraordinary brand."

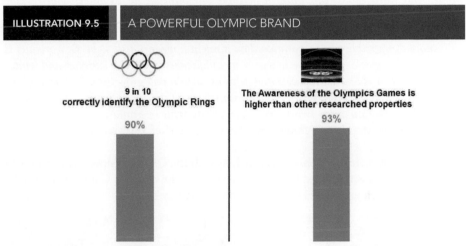

ILLUSTRATION 9.5   A POWERFUL OLYMPIC BRAND

9 in 10
correctly identify the Olympic Rings

90%

The Awareness of the Olympics Games is higher than other researched properties

93%

Credit: - IOC Proprietary Research, Sponsorship Intelligence (2016)

This discipline results into a consistently highly rated wide range of brand attributes represented on Illustration 9.6 - which have continued to strengthen on the back of the Rio Olympic Games

ILLUSTRATION 9.6   INSPIRING OLYMPIC GAMES

Attributes of the Olympic Games

Are wide ranging and consistently scored high

Including the Olympic Values of "Friendship", "Excellence" and "Respect"

Have Strengthen since London 2012

— London 2012
— Rio 2016

Data source - IOC Proprietary Research, Sponsorship Intelligence (2016)

I spoke to Timo Lumme, who I have known for years, and is Managing Director of the IOC Television and Marketing Services, which also includes the IOC Global Sponsorship Programme. Timo and his marketing team, Melinda May, Daniela Negreda and Ben Seeley, agree about the uniqueness of the Olympic brand

Applying a franchise model

Timo and team: *"The Olympics is managed as a brand, although it is not rooted in a corporation or a single product. But as the brand has grown, we've needed to employ new mechanics which correspond to the approach and language of brand marketers in today's world. And we reinforce this through multiple disciplines – for example, with regular research.*

"It is more comparable to a corporation than it might appear at first sight. Our product is the Olympic Games and we have to ensure its uniqueness in regular summer and winter celebrations. This is one of the facets that helps us sustain and grow the brand around the world, with 206 countries or teams, and various types of sports. It means a fresh product rollout or reinvention every two years, which is powerful in brand management terms. And we have an extensive programme of other activities [Ref. Illustration 9.7]

As a partner, I remember extensive discussions with the Olympic Movement on how to ensure continuing activity and share of mind between the Olympic Games, which is the purpose of the rich and varied programme mentioned by Timo.

ILLUSTRATION 9.7	OLYMPIC BRAND ACTIVITY FRAMEWORK

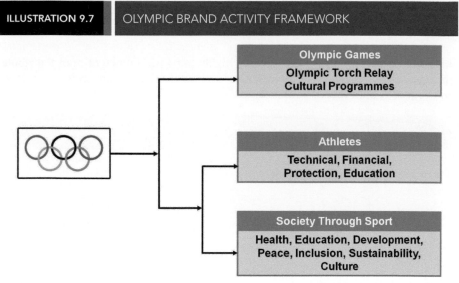

Credit – THE Enduring Strategic Brand based on IOC data

"If you go back 35 years, the IOC was in the middle of a boycott crisis, its coffers were empty and it did not have a balanced relationship with the organising committees. Over time, the IOC has reclaimed control of managing key aspects of the Games – such as the television images and having a structure of reviewing and approving the organising committee's plans. With the IOC, we can apply a well-developed but continually evolving franchise management model. This was tested to its limit in Rio, but still got through the most difficult of circumstances. In a sense, this is owning, developing and controlling the brand's own IP and means of production.

"The IOC gives a structure to how we oversee and manage our brand, whether it is handled directly or granted to third parties, such as organising committees, commercial partners, broadcasters, or licensees."

From Direction, to Command and Control, to Partnership

"All this has evolved and continues to do so. Over a 30-year period, the first 10 were marked by a realisation that there needed to be greater coordination and consistency in our actions and their implementation – that some areas required control. The next 10 involved a command-and-control set of regulations. Over the past few years, we've moved towards working more in partnership. This is certainly something Olympic Agenda 2020 is propagating: how we go from control to expanded value creation.

"In short, when dealing with organising committees or sponsors, we work within a framework which is governed by Olympic brand management principles. These guidelines are not designed to be restrictive but to create value. The better we can protect the brand, the more value those five rings retain. Then we can continue to raise funds and reinvest them back into sport.

"We have both the resources and the legal standing to protect our brand, and required disciplines to do so, such as IP protection. We may be the only brand that has a treaty to protect its IP: the Nairobi Treaty is focused on protection of the Olympic rings and was signed by 50 countries. And our legal department has a strict and broad-spectrum IP protection registration programme, which ensures protection for the remaining 156 countries.

"When it comes to the host city, we require them to pass legislation about protecting the Olympic emblem. Often, this is housed in a sort of Olympic law – that was the case for Rio and London.

"This means we will work with local communities pragmatically, enabling them to engage better with the brand."

Some might argue that the IOC doesn't – and can never have – the ability to control the brand and organisation from their headquarters in the same way that P&G or Coca-Cola might. But this is for the very best reasons, which exemplify the Olympic brand's 'Rigour and Discipline'. Its distinction comes from the fact that its brand philosophy for life, its shared sense of values, its execution and the protection of the five rings are greater than in most organisations. As Lisa Baird says: *"The Olympics is part of a higher purpose. Its power lies in this higher order. What would happen if a brand didn't exist, like, say, Apple? Perhaps Samsung would be more powerful, or maybe other new brands would emerge. Now, what if the Olympic brand ceased to exist? What would happen? Would our world be a poorer place? Would we be worse off? It's very important to think in these terms about a unique brand like the Olympics."*

High Value and Driving Value Olympic Brand

In July, at the height of the London 2012 Games, a CNN article asked: *"Is the Olympic brand worth more than Google?"* (Note 3) To our knowledge, the IOC does not run brand valuations. However, with the world importance of the five rings, valuation agencies do so and, at the time, Brand Finance valued the brand at $47.5 billion, behind only Apple ($70.6 billion) and at parity with Google ($47.4 billion).

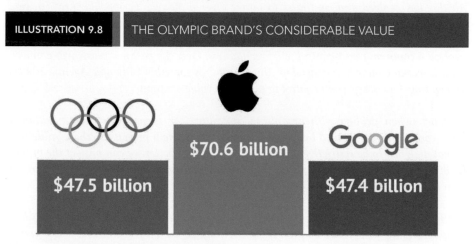

| ILLUSTRATION 9.8 | THE OLYMPIC BRAND'S CONSIDERABLE VALUE |

Credit – CNN, July 25, 2012 - Based on Brand Finance Data.

More recent valuation work has confirmed the extraordinary worth of the Olympic brand. Post Rio 2016, the average value of the assessments we collected from various institutes was $60 billion. This puts the Olympic brand within the 10 most valuable global brands – and interestingly worth more than each of its TOP sponsors, brands like Toyota, Samsung, GE or Coca-Cola.

This high value has a direct effect on how the Olympic brand creates and drives value. Its unique platform can probably be defined as 'engagement marketing', a well-known approach to helping companies maintain an interactive and on-going dialogue with consumers and create measurable preference and loyalty. In the case of the Olympic brand, this plays out at considerable scale – and builds into three main sources of value:

Broadcast and TOP sponsoring – First, the International Olympic Committee (IOC) agrees major long-term broadcasting agreements, such as the one sealed in May 2014 with NBC Universal. This agreement covers the period 2021 to 2032 and is valued at $7.65 billion, plus an additional signing bonus of $100 million to be used for the promotion of Olympism and Olympic values between 2015 and 2020. Then come the TOP sponsoring partnerships: there are currently 13 TOP global partners, such as Coca-Cola, McDonald's, GE, Visa, etc. The scale of these agreements never stops growing – in March 2015 Toyota announced a record deal for any IOC sponsorship to date: if you include early rights, independent sources estimated this contract around the

$1 billion mark for the 10-year period. January 2017 saw another landmark agreement with Alibaba committing until 2028 and for a value estimated over $600 million by independent industry sources.

Games sponsoring – The second benefit is seen by the organising committee of each Games – LOCOG in London, Rio 2016, POCOG in PyeongChang and Tokyo 2020, each raising considerable funding from local partners in order to set the Games up. For example, LOCOG, led by Chris Townsend, raised the best part of $2 billion to benefit the London Olympic Games. Tokyo 2020 already has over 40 sponsors, in addition to the 13 TOP partners, with the 'whole of corporate Japan' raising their hand to be involved and contribute.

Sponsors' value – Finally, beyond the financial benefits for the Olympic movement, major value is created for the sponsoring partners, such as the following:

Coca-Cola One of the TOP partners is Coca-Cola, which perhaps spends more on sports marketing than any other company in the world, and has been a partner of the Olympic Games since 1928. Said Stu Cross, former VP of worldwide sports marketing Coca-Cola: *"We have to constantly market our beverages in a way that creates the impression that there's more than just the liquid in the package, that Coca-Cola refreshes the spirit. The Olympics does that for us. All that fun and excitement, and its global nature, culminates in an image that makes people pick Coca-Cola versus a lot of other choices they have out there."*

P&G The Olympic Movement gets results for brands. Procter & Gamble's iconic and emotive 2016 campaign *'Thank You, Mom – Strong'* was seen by billions and was a game changer, developing brand usage and loyalty internationally – and increasing sales by hundreds of millions.

VISA *"The Rio 2016 Olympic Games provided an unparalleled opportunity to promote the VISA brand on the world stage"*, said Chris Curtin, Chief Brand & Innovation Marketing Officer, Visa Inc. A partner since 1986, Visa celebrated its three decades of Olympic Games sponsorship around the Rio Games, with an inspiring look back on how a global brand, the changes in the way we pay and some winning moments of the Olympic Games can become intertwined – and how their close combination can be to everybody's benefit -https://usa.visa.com/dam/VCOM/global/visa-everywhere/documents/visa-and-the-olympic-games-timeline.pdf

Trusted; Functional & Emotional; Crisis Resilient Olympic Brand

The Olympic brand engenders a high level of trust. From experience, reviews and conversations, we believe that the 'WHY' society trusts the Olympic brand lies largely in its strong positive and enduring 'Functional and Emotional' contributions.

In their report *'How do we know that Rio 2016 was a success'*, the Olympic Movement eluded to some of these unique contributions: *"Universal and Inclusive"*; *"The only global event in a troubled world where the whole world comes together"*; *"Hope"*, with the first-ever Refugee Olympic Team. (Note 4)

"Universal and Inclusive", "The only global event in a troubled world where the whole world comes together"; "Hope."

It is no surprise that there is hardly another brand that combines such high levels of 'Functional and Emotional' bond. Who has not had goosebumps seeing vintage images of Olympic Games, or supporting their national team or favourite athlete?

But it isn't all plain sailing. It is challenging to run the Olympic movement – not just the IOC but every part of the organisation. Take the concerns in the run up to the Rio 2016 Games – would it be safe? Would the stadiums be completed in time? Would the Games bankrupt the city? And beyond these were other issues on a larger scale: the Olympic brand's handling of the Zika virus, the alleged touting of tickets, the international doping scandals, including the challenging case of Russia, non-participation, corruption, etc. These issues have led some to argue that, rather than creating a "legacy of heroic sporting glory", the Olympic Games has largely become a media franchise which doesn't sufficiently honour the brand and its ideals.

Any individual challenge or crisis, or a combination of them, tests the trust in the Olympic brand. The way it has sustained these challenges and continued to prosper through them makes it different – and from that standpoint, makes the Olympics very much a Strategic Brand.

I have had a long association with the Olympic movement and haven't always liked what I've seen. The IOC's relationship with money has not always been to everybody's taste – and every gesture counts: I remember the grand Olympic Club at the Vancouver Games in 2010 with some discomfort. Governance should also evolve to epitomise best global practice and display high ethical standards of behaviour. And the Olympic Games will continue to face challenges like doping for a long time.

But over the course of my independent and occasionally challenging relationship with the Olympic Movement, I have been convinced of the great importance, positive impact and formidable nature of the brand.

Timo and team: *"In the face of threats, the IOC is more proactive, to reaffirm the positive benefits of the brand, as opposed to being held hostage by other forces or external entities. The Olympic Movement has seen times of war when the Games have been cancelled; there have been terrorist attacks; there have been moments when people felt the Olympic Games were being used by certain political regimes for their own ends; or pressure groups have led boycotts, etc. But through all this, the Olympic brand has been resilient and continued to appeal to people and businesses. This means we are now more able to think about the*

future with, for example, the creation by our current President of 'Olympic Agenda 2020',
our strategic roadmap.

"It's better to pre-empt change: this makes the brand 'future-proof'. Or at least, the brand
must remain flexible, relevant and credible as well as sustainable, so that in our rapidly
changing world, it can weather any storm.

"Take the issue of the Russian athletes and the doping scandal before Rio 2016. From a
practical point of view, the impact – if any – on the brand was small compared to the
positive effect of the Olympics. But this is no reason to be complacent. To give the Olympics
greater credibility, positions must be taken in the fight against doping. It's important to
be on the front foot. What was difficult in that particular instance is that many people
were trying to put the Olympics Movement on the back foot – and to some extent, they
succeeded.

"In a broader sense, there are existential threats to the notion of Olympism. You will not
solve illegal doping in a day. But people should see that we are committed to addressing
these matters in the most robust way. It is the strength of the brand that gives us that
confidence to take action, to have a conversation about trying to meet such challenges.

It is the strength of the brand that gives us that confidence to
take action, to have a conversation about trying to meet such
challenges.

"The Olympic brand is about keeping the idea of Olympism alive all year round. It is about
celebrating the uniqueness of the Olympic Games in many different geographies; it is about
the athletes; it is about the implementation of our social development plan through sports
strategy; it is about credibility, about having acceptable and progressive benchmarks of
governance, of transparency; it is about being recognised as an organisational entity that is
not only trying to do the right thing but which actually lives by its values and acts according
to (and sometimes even better than) societal and corporate norms.

 "Returning to the challenges we face: I think we need to be bold. Since Thomas Bach
became President of the IOC three years ago, he has met with over 140 Heads of State.
According to anecdote, these Heads of State have told him that, given all the negative things
that are happening in the world today, they regard Olympism as something positive, as a
beacon of hope. Although the last thing we want to do is to blow our own trumpet, this
should encourage us to have a conversation based on positivity."

Olympic Brand - Culture Born and Authenticity; Clarity of Purpose; Strategy Driving

So where do all these areas of extraordinary performance and resilience come from?
Undoubtedly from the deeply held sense of what Olympism stands for. Timo and

team: *"Olympism is described as a philosophy of life, which places sport at the service of humankind. This is a paraphrase of one of de Coubertin's 19th century quotes, the founder of the modern Olympic Movement. (Note 5)*

ILLUSTRATION 9.9	THE PRINCIPLES OF OLYMPISM

Fundamental principles of Olympism
(from the Olympic Charter – 1896)

OLYMPIC CHARTER

IN FORCE AS FROM 2 AUGUST 2015

Olympism is a philosophy of life, exalting and combining in a balanced whole the qualities of body, will and mind. Blending sport with culture and education, Olympism seeks to create a way of life based on the joy of effort, the educational value of good example and respect for universal fundamental, ethical principles.

The goal of Olympism is to place sport at the service of harmonious development of humankind, with a view to promoting a peaceful society concerned with the preservation of human dignity.

The practice of sport is a human right. Every individual must have the possibility of practicing sport, without discrimination of any kind and in the Olympic spirit, which requires mutual understanding with a spirit of friendship, solidarity and fair play.

Credit – International Olympic Committee – Olympic charter – Fundamental Principles 1, 2 and 4 (Note 5)

Timo adds: *"The Olympic vision, symbolised by the Olympic rings, is about 'building a better world through sport.' This is underpinned by values, which de Coubertin put in long, florid prose, but which we summarise as: 'Excellence, Respect and Friendship.' This is brought to life through our three missions: ensuring the celebration of the Olympic Games; putting athletes at the heart of the Olympic Movement; and promoting sport and the Olympic values in our society."*

ILLUSTRATION 9.10	THE OLYMPIC BRAND ESSENCE

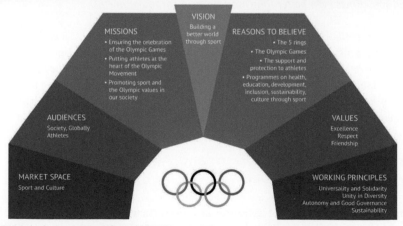

Credit - THE Enduring Strategic Brand from Olympic Movement Data

Hence, the Olympic brand is culturally driven, clearly purposed and authentic. And its core is defined by a 120 year legacy.

As any great brand does, the IOC runs regular surveys on the Olympic brand, whose details are not public but broad outcomes are. The report following Rio (Ref. IOC News Rio 2016, visibility & awareness) quoted that *"the awareness and appeal of the Olympic Games remains the highest amongst all the measured sports and entertainment events surveyed"*

Further more, the IOC shared a proprietary research ran by Sponsorship Intelligence 2016, whereby a range of brand attributes were benchmarked against best in class brands. This survey helped establish that *"The Olympic rings outperform other key global brands surveyed across these attributes"* (Ref. Illustration 9.11). Without being in the know of which benchmark brands were used, the striking conclusion is that the five rings surpass best brands for each of the individual attributes, which then turns into a formidable brand when you combine all the attributes.

ILLUSTRATION 9.11	THE OLYMPIC BRAND OUTPERFORMS OTHER LEADING GLOBAL BRANDS ACROSS MAJOR BRAND ATTRIBUTES

Range of High-Ranking Attributes of the Olympic Rings

GLOBAL

DIVERSITY

INSPIRATIONAL

EXCELLENCE

FRIENDSHIP

OPTIMISTIC

INCLUSIVE

Credit: - IOC Proprietary Research, Sponsorship Intelligence (2016)

People Led and People Leading Olympic Brand

The Olympic brand is strong at naturally guiding people. Timo and team: *"The guiding principles of Olympism concretely inform what we do. For example, in the IOC corporate structure, they inform our annual and corporate plans. They also inform our relationships with stakeholders – because everything we do is governed by the Olympic Charter.*

"It is the moral compass by which we work, because only by doing that can we stay true to the brand.

"Take the example of negotiating a broadcast agreement. Your deal might be better if you give exclusivity to a given party. But we insist that a certain amount of coverage is made available to the widest possible audience at no cost. And that's been a fundamental tenet of our broadcast rights since the age of television in the late 1950s. In the 1990s, Rupert Murdoch made a big financial offer, which was turned down in favour of continuing with a partly public service broadcaster. The financial bid was higher but didn't correspond to our guiding principles.

"And that continues even in today's fast-paced media landscape. For example, the ongoing tension between free TV and pay TV: many sports have migrated to pay TV but we want to stick to our fundamental values by finding a balance where a minimum of 200 hours of free-to-air coverage on a free-to-air platform is provided."

At the heart of the Olympic Movement stand the athletes. They are the brand's ambassadors – and if any of them deviate from Olympic values and expected behaviours, there are huge negative consequences. Just look at the rejection of the American swimmer Ryan Lochte following his false statement about being robbed at gunpoint during the Rio Olympics. On the positive side, athletes as role models have considerable impact – remember how Jesse Owens shattered Hitler's aim to use the 1936 Games as an example of the "new Aryan man". His lap of honour with the German silver medallist Luz Long became a symbol of the triumph of sportsmanship over Nazi ideology.

Lisa describes the people dimension of the Olympic brand:

"The positivity about the Olympic Games is also what the athletes achieve together, which makes the brand meaningful. And this phenomenon occurs every two years.

"This is not easy in practice: it is never easy to get everybody in a company behind a brand. On the one hand, the athletes are at the heart of Olympism and their forum is the event itself, the Olympic Games. But on the other, they feel they don't get sufficient recognition or reward from the Games. So it's a conflicted part of the Olympic Movement, which needs to evolve further.

"Nevertheless, it is the athletes who make the brand. I think the Olympic Games give the world heroes. In a simpler time, the world had heroes and prophets and intellectual gurus. And maybe some Nobel Prize winners or country leaders will still emerge to become heroes, but that's rarer. I think Olympic heroes fill that void: we are a civilisation and civilisations need heroes."

Connected and Future Embracing Olympic Brand

In the face of an increasingly complex and challenged world, the Olympic brand has both a role and a duty to be 'Connected' and 'Future Embracing'. A post Rio survey showed a strong and positive connection to the Olympic brand through the Olympic Games across genders and generations (Ref. Illustration 9.12). It is also a legitimate pride for the Olympic Movement that half of the world's population watched the Rio Olympic Games coverage, 206 NOCs participated and 45% of the athletes were women.

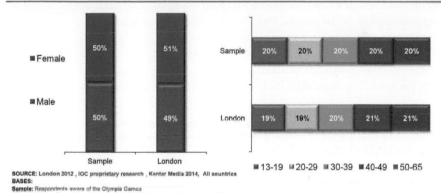

| ILLUSTRATION 9.12 | THE BRAND TALKS TO EVERYBODY |

Olympic Games fan base is balanced
All countries sample vs. All Olympic Games fans

London

Female — Sample 50%, London 51%
Male — Sample 50%, London 49%

Sample: 20% | 20% | 20% | 20% | 20%
London: 19% | 19% | 20% | 21% | 21%

■ 13-19 ■ 20-29 ■ 30-39 ■ 40-49 ■ 50-65

SOURCE: London 2012 , IOC proprietary research , Kantar Media 2014, All countries
BASES:
Sample: Respondents aware of the Olympic Games
Olympic Games Fans: Respondents aware of the Olympic Games & rating appeal of it at 6 or more out of 10

Now the brand is looking to the future by extending its role in using sport to improve people's lives.

Timo and team: *"Looking at the broader brand of Olympism, there is a strong notion of promotion within society. Sport is part of the sustainable development goals of the United Nations. This has helped politicians realise that sport is a glue which holds society together and creates a common language.*

"We have 7 activity streams directed at society at large. These range from peace in sports, as demonstrated by the Olympic Truce that's signed at the United Nations before every Games, to development through sport and many other humanitarian programmes in partnership with the UN which use sport as a catalyst for getting kids healthy or practise sports in refugee camps, etc. We also have a stream called inclusion through sport, to get more women into sport and which also relates to our important relationship with the Paralympic Committee (Ref. Illustration 9.7).

"The whole area is being reviewed with a new 2017 strategy. The road map will also include a brand building plan for Olympism in action and Olympism in society in the future."

Partnering and Customer Centric Olympic Brand

My own experience of partnering with the Olympic Movement has not always been smooth. It can be tough: there are boundaries and many legal requirements. I remember intense debates as Timo and I finalised a multi-country activity plan in London in winter 2009. This was a meaningful and mutually valuable outcome, a mark of fabric, I suppose.

Timo and team: *"We liken our commercial partnerships to a sort of marriage. Ultimately you have to look at the quality of a relationship after the first blush of romance, assess whether you share values, whether your prospective partner walks the talk. We also assess whether we want to be involved with a company in a particular field of activity and then look at the sort of company they are in their sector, how they are perceived and how they, for example, treat their customers. Obviously, some of this is subjective when there are real-life decisions to be made with commercial context – so this is an area where we use our guiding principles to ensure that we remain faithful to the core brand values."*

The Olympic Movement has a considerable partnership footprint, from the 13 TOPs (Ref. Illustration 9.13) to thousands of other commercial and non-commercial organisations. Some of these relationships, like Coca-Cola, are close to a hundred years old.

ILLUSTRATION 9.13	OLYMPICS 13 TOP PARTNERS

Lisa mentioned earlier another core pillar which both nurtures and communicates the Olympic brand to hundreds of millions people – and this is media. Timo and team: *"Before 1960, in the pre-television era, the Olympic Games used distribution, mainly print, radio, word-of-mouth, town hall gatherings, cinema and so forth to reach people. When television came along, it was a real rocket boost to the modern Games because they were able to reach so many more millions of people in the four corners of the world in a visual way. But it also created a financial model. Now we've entered the third phase of 'mediatisation', the digital revolution, whereby we are actually able to connect, engage and reach our audience directly.*

"The commercialisation of the Olympic brand started in a structured way in the 1980s, most markedly with the advent of the TOP programme. This meant having an organised approach to broadcast rights as well as getting big corporations involved with sponsorship. The virtuous circle was that through their promotion, these corporations enabled the brand to be distributed more broadly to many more people.

"In these earlier times, we were able to control the messaging. The IOC registered the five rings around 25 years ago, so the process of promotion was ultimately protected. There was a framework within which we were able to manage our brand, but we were also able to manage it in terms of how we created relationships with third parties.

"The digital world is fragmented and less controllable. We've moved from a B2B world to a B2C world, in that we don't go through intermediaries, like broadcasters or sponsors, but talk directly to the consumer.

"What is a brand? Ultimately, it is the relationship you create with people, based on their perceptions of you. We feel comfortable having that conversation with people directly because we believe in the power of the Olympic brand. And in turn when we create these relationships, the conversation continues to nurture the brand and gives us feedback, notably through digital media.

"What is a brand? Ultimately, it is the relationship you create with people, based on their perceptions of you. We feel comfortable having that conversation with people directly because we believe in the power of the Olympic brand."

"The Olympic Channel will be a new means of engaging with people and connecting them, not just to the brand or a logo, but to the essence of what we stand for. That's going to be a big part of the future."

The Olympics is an extraordinary brand, and sets the direction for many other organisations. Its very nature means it is representative of the wide-ranging opportunities and challenges for any brand – and in particular for those wanting to become 'Rigorous and Disciplined' Enduring Strategic Brands. As Timo said, the Olympics' vision is all about 'building a better world through sport'.

Strategy without tactics is the slowest route to victory.
Tactics without strategy is the noise before defeat

Sun Tzu

Creating a Strategic Brand is not an easy journey. I know this too well, from when we created Beyond Petroleum, that the difficulty lies in ensuring the strategy is connected to the brand throughout the entire organisation.

In this chapter, we will explore how a brand can drive strategy in practice, for as BMW's Ian Robertson says, *"A Strategic Brand is what drives the company, rather than anything else...It's what we use to attract people into our company; to motivate people within the company; to design our cars and services; to guide our dealers"*

Shelly Lazarus helped build many of the world's most famous brands and reflects on how brand and strategy are linked, *"A brand is a great organising principle and everything comes out of your understanding and your beliefs about what the brand is. While really the brand doesn't determine what the strategy is, the deep understanding of the brand does keep you in a place, in a group of territories that have to be consistent with the brand".*

I have found the relationship between the enterprise brand and strategy a continuous interrogation over my whole career. At Castrol, the brand was driving strategy. And at the risk of overgeneralising - at BP, strategy was driving the brand.

BP AND UNILEVER

We will be using the respective journeys of BP and Unilever to investigate 'Strategy Guiding'. The two organisations have much in common: their brand have been purposed on the transition to a more sustainable planet - for BP, the three journeys of 'Beyond Petroleum'; for Unilever, the three pillars of 'Making Sustainable Living Commonplace'. They are truly global and both play a leading role in crucial sectors - energy and consumer goods. Their restated brand journey started under the helm of iconic business leaders, John Browne and Paul Polman.

They are also different in many ways, if only that BP launched 'Beyond Petroleum' in 2000 and Unilever its 'Compass' nine years later. Analysis of the changing language alone reveals the shift – at the beginning of the millennium, sustainability was mainly Corporate Social Responsibility (CSR) whereas by the late 2000's, it had to be good business at scale.

Using the evidence of each brand, we will reflect how placing a 'Strategy Guiding' Brand at the heart of decision-making with enough perseverance and commitment creates transformational results.

Sustainability
It's a persuasive argument. We should leave our children an equally welcoming planet to the one we enjoyed - while ensuring our enterprises perform competitively.

For over ten years, I oversaw multiple aspects of BP's attempt to marry sustainability and financial delivery – BP's 'SuMo' strategy (sustainable mobility), dozens of lower carbon strategic partnerships, BP targetneutral, the World Business Council for Sustainable Development (WBCSD) and more. I stood at the centre of the progressive and collective learning that, in the course of ten years, moved sustainability from the CSR space to a value added way of doing business. And I was privileged to work alongside Toyota's Dr. Toyoda and Mr. Cho, Unilever's Paul Polman, Tata Sons' Ratan Tata and other enlightened world business leaders.

If your brand purpose is about sustainability, linking brand and strategy remains a massive challenge. Because demand and reward from society is loose. Who is ready to make a purchase decision let alone pay significantly more on environmentally friendly solutions? Which market analyst is absolutely beyond doubt that progress on the sustainability agenda should equate a higher stock price?

  Ask Nestle and General Mills with their recent revenue target misses, mainly from their healthier offerings and fresh-food divisions.

Or Indra Nooyi, the CEO of PepsiCo who tries hard with PepsiCo's 'good for you' products …and finds that consumers mostly want their favourite chips, Lay's, Doritos and Cheetos.

"Everybody is looking for this transformation, and yet the big wheels of commerce don't support it", said former PepsiCo President Zein Abdalla.

Let's consider why pioneering BP hit a ceiling with its brand-guided 'Beyond Petroleum' strategy, a development that many enterprises might recognise. And how Unilever continues showing the way to most with its 'Sustainable Living Plan' and a method that many brands might want to embrace.

THE BP BRAND AND STRATEGY - 2006-2010

First, let's step back to Chapter 1, where we left the BP brand in the wake of formidable changes.

Where was the BP brand in 2006?

At that point, BP had arguably developed into a textbook Strategic Brand: it had a clear and differentiated purpose and vision; it was progressing a number of 'Beyond Petroleum' programmes; it was fostering growing trust with and from its stakeholders; and it benefited from strong branded leadership. Lord Browne declared at the time: *"In a global marketplace, branding is crucially important in attracting customers and business. It is not just a matter of a few gasoline stations or the logo on pole signs. It is about the identity of the company and the values that underpin everything that you do and every relationship that you have."*

External fortunes

By 2006, the outside world had taken notice of our hard work and bold ambitions for the brand. In 2002, *Management Today* magazine voted BP as Britain's most admired company, with Lord Browne crowned its most admired leader. This was the first time that one company received both top awards. In 2005, *The Financial Times* ranked BP seventh in its global most respected company list. These were among a number of clear indicators demonstrating how BP was achieving its goal of being one of the world's great branded companies. And this had an impact on the bottom line, with, for example, sales of fuels and lubricants consistently increasing above market growth throughout 2004.

BP is first and foremost an upstream energy developer and supplier in a highly commoditised category. Could effective branding make a difference? *Fortune Magazine* thought so, recognising BP as one of the 10 most improved brands from 2001 to 2005 in terms of brand equity value (Note 1). Young & Rubicam's Brand Asset® Valuator research – the world's oldest and largest brand database – in conjunction with Stern Stewart's Economic Value Added analytics, quantified that the value of BP's intangible assets (which included its brand) increased by more than $7 billion during this time period, while the intangible assets of its larger energy rivals declined in value.

Internal uncertainty

But there were weighty signals that the internal reality was different. As Ogilvy's John Seifert reflected, the situation reminded him of Jan Carlzon, the customer service guru at SAS Airlines and author of *The Moment of Truth*. In the mid-80s, Carlzon pioneered the notion that great customer service is about the 'moment of truth' when an employee takes accountability irrespective of their particular role, so that everything becomes about the customer problem.

John Seifert comments: *"In John Browne, we had a visionary leader who was constantly thinking ahead of the actual operationalization of the promise. It was challenging for the BP organization to sufficiently live up to it in the short or medium term and realise the full scope and benefit of the vision. But if you looked at it from the 20, 30, 50-year basis, you will probably agree that BP created enormous value in a wider societal context even if it hasn't been able itself to fully enjoy the fruits of that. Sometimes, companies are great agents of change, but their timing isn't as elegant as it might need to be."*

The brand was not consistently 'Strategy Driving'

He continues: *"In the 2006 or 2007 period, the excitement of 'Beyond Petroleum' had started to wane. And there was just a lack of enlightenment on how to align the business strategy to the company's point of view. We were not stepping up enough to the next things of development that were going to live up to the promise."*

Indeed, many of the activities of 'Beyond Petroleum' were not economically competitive – notably those in alternative energy; they were sporadic rather than systematic. The performance engine of the company, its upstream division, was far from convinced of the brand purpose, as they tried to remain competitive in a $20- to $40-a-barrel world.

One event had amplified much of BP's self questioning - on 23rd March 2005, a major explosion occurred at BP's Texas City Refinery, the third largest facility in the USA, killing 15 people. BP came under harsh scrutiny, which was compounded by a large leak in an Alaskan pipeline the following year.

These serious issues tested BP's brand and culture. In truth, we faced these challenges squarely, dealt with them transparently, stayed the course and acted in full keeping with the BP brand. We were consequently able to maintain BP's prominence as the trusted leader in its industry. Nevertheless, these events raised questions on BP's priorities - had we truly integrated Amoco, Arco etc. to create a single operating company? Were our operations and safety processes robust and systematic enough? Was the significance of green and future energy overplayed in proportion to operations and technology?

Brand status

The BP situation was typical of many organisations: an inspirational vision, a deep purpose…with the major challenge of turning these aspirations into a credible reality at scale.

As shown on illustration 10.1, a number of key Brand Imperatives were under developed at that time. Notably 'Authentic' - as the brand purpose was not culturally natural to many, 'People led' –as the purpose was not owned by essential parts of the organisation and 'Driving Value' – as the purpose was certainly not a short-term money maker.

ILLUSTRATION 10.1	THE ENDURING STRATEGIC BRAND IMPERATIVES - BP 2006

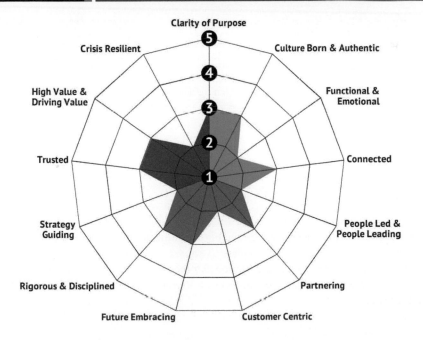

Don't get me wrong, many aspects of BP were running well and we were notably discovering and developing some of the best oil and gas basins in the world, as well as shaping a first-class downstream portfolio. But despite laudable business successes and favourable perception with most external audiences, the 'Beyond Petroleum' brand purpose was a long way from guiding and driving strategy.

Major change of societal context

In 2007, the industry entered a period of structural unbalance between supply and demand, which prompted a radical transformation and magnified the debate within BP. Fast demand growth in China and other developing economies could not be matched by global production, notably as multiple producing countries were in a period of significant instability.

Illustration 10.2 shows how Lord Browne's era was one of relative balance between supply and demand for oil. From time to time geopolitical events would create a short-term disruption or industry short-term excess, but this would not be structural (left handside graph). In 2007, and as BP changed its Chief Executive - which I will talk about in greater detail below -, demand started to exceed offer materially and structurally. This significant unbalance would last over six years, making every drop of oil a coveted asset (right handside graph).

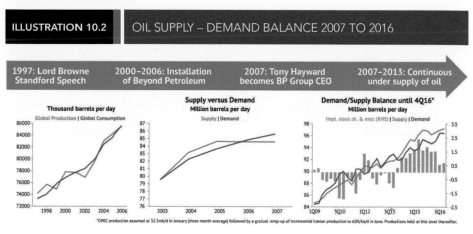

| **ILLUSTRATION 10.2** | OIL SUPPLY – DEMAND BALANCE 2007 TO 2016 |

Credit – EIA Supply and Demand data; Askja Energy, based on IEA data

Consequently, the pricing dynamics changed dramatically and this would have big impact on the brand context. As graph 10.3 shows, we went from a period of relative stability between $20 and $40 a barrel in John's times, to an era of massive price increases which reached unprecedented absolute levels (over $140 a barrel) over a sustained period of time.

ILLUSTRATION 10.3   PRICE OF OIL PER BARREL, 1970–2014

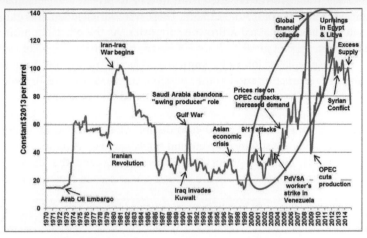

Credit – US Department of Energy February 9, 2015

Between 2006 and 2008, society's perspective and priorities on energy changed dramatically. In John's era, security of supply and affordability were not at the top of the agenda. This gave space for the third pillar of public consideration, the environment, while science was establishing the link between energy consumption and the rising risks of climate change. It had made Beyond Petroleum connected, relevant and inspiring.

All of this shifted dramatically from 2006 onwards, when security of supply and energy poverty emerged as society's top concerns. Conversations about the environment almost vanished. This was a less natural territory for Beyond Petroleum (Ref. Illustration 10.4).

ILLUSTRATION 10.4   THE DIFFERING SOCIETAL CONCERNS DURING LORD BROWNE AND TONY HAYWARD'S ERAS AT BP

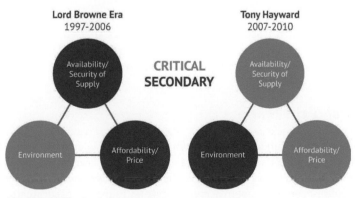

Credit – THE Enduring Strategic Brand

The perfect storm

On 1st May 2007, John Browne resigned from BP due to private and personal matters, forfeiting a leaving package of around £15.5m. There were varied judgments among staff, but I was sad and have remained a Browne supporter. As the official communication stated, this was "*a tragedy for BP*". Tony Hayward, head of the BP Exploration and Production Division replaced John with immediate effect. A month later, John Manzoni, head of Refining & Marketing and another possible successor to Lord Browne, left BP. Iain Conn, already a BP main Board Director, succeeded him.

As BP's new CEO, Tony Hayward faced considerable challenges - deep integration of some legacy companies was still incomplete and safety standards seemed not uniformly embedded. Moreover, financial performance was lagging, and the share value was decoupling from Exxon's and others in the industry, as shown in illustration 10.5.

ILLUSTRATION 10.5	SHARE PRICE OF BP (BLUE) VS. EXXON (GREEN)

Credit – Yahoo UK & Ireland

At a time when every barrel of oil was worth a fortune, extraordinary assets in the BP portfolio remained unfructified. BP employees were destabilised by the loss of their historic leader and divided on the shifting focus of international oil and gas companies towards security of supply in a very high price environment.

The BP brand challenge

In the context of these fundamental transformations, it was critical for the brand to authentically represent BP's core business strategy, and confront – through deep engagement and constructive dialogue – the world's increasingly complex energy demands. Would Beyond Petroleum accommodate and support this dramatic change of context? Would it survive the loss of its founder?

Would Beyond Petroleum accommodate and support this dramatic change of context? Would it survive the loss of its founder?

Tony Hayward recalls his feelings when he took over - *"A brand needs to reflect what people in your organisation do every day. In BP, we had allowed Beyond Petroleum to go way too far into 'a renewable world', where it became disconnected from the activity of 90% of people and this was a major problem. Because then people, who are the company's biggest emphasis, are walking around, not relating to what the company is promoting."*

Tony wanted the brand's inspirational position on a lower carbon future to be changed to reflect the company's day-to-day reality of production, performance and safety. And he appointed me, a convert to Beyond Petroleum, to do this as Group Chief Sales & Marketing Officer!

A brand needs to reflect what people in your organisation do every day.

That began the most challenging and energising three-year journey for the brand team, that I was privileged to oversee. We would go through major internal debates about whether to keep or lose 'Beyond Petroleum' – a brand whose essence to many people, both inside and outside BP, had become associated with alternative energy. Duncan Blake, BP Director of Brand remembers: *"There was a tension: a number of senior figures wanted to talk more about our core business, about oil and gas. I wouldn't say that they didn't want to talk about the future of energy at all, but not with the same emphasis. On the other hand there were people who could see the amazing equity that BP had built up through its successful positioning from 2000 to 2007. And we knew that this was important to society and people wanted to see, hear and believe in a brand that was tackling the energy paradox."*

The BP brand vision and essence

Tony Hayward was a pragmatist and recognised that BP held a position of trust, influence and authority in the mind of its main stakeholders, including governments, oil and gas resource holders and customers. We, the Strategic Brand team - and I will single out Board Member Ian Conn for his inspirational leadership and Brand Directors Duncan Blake and Kathy Leech for their expert resolution - were very conscious of this status.

For the team, this was a task to evolve rather than change the brand, while remaining true to its essence. For us, success would mean ensuring that the market and the realities facing BP would not change the core brand agenda. We therefore needed to be able to represent BP's commitment to society on how it would contribute to the world's energy needs in practice – and to find better ways of doing so in the future. Or we risked losing the brand's essence, losing Beyond Petroleum and its considerable positive significance and franchise.

Recontextualise the Brand

We spared no effort and began with a deep strategic reconsideration of the enterprise mission. How could we project BP's commitment to making every effort to supply more energy, while being true to the Beyond Petroleum three journeys – including the path to a low-carbon economy? How could we be resolute 'hard hat' people (as we sometimes called our upstream colleagues) and remain true to the brand essence?

In this societal and internal context, we created a framework for the next phase of Beyond Petroleum: it would be powerful, involving, pragmatic, linked, engaging and guiding. And that framework helped us to navigate and to build on Beyond Petroleum, to create our new expression and communication.

A brand substance that creates deep convergence

With the benefit of hindsight, it looks easy and even obvious now – but in fact, we worked hard to reach a response. And we found it in the brand itself, in its three journeys -it was 'energy diversity'. We even dared to add 'no energy' to our energy diversity mix.

Energy diversity would mean that BP was committed to all forms of energy, which would help supply, and combine both carbon and low-carbon options. Wasn't this exactly the essence of 'Beyond Petroleum' and what our businesses did in reality – and often uniquely! Wouldn't we have the three societal drivers for energy bundled in one reality: 'energy diversity'? Wouldn't the brand be able to guide and echo the enterprise strategy and thus strengthen its position as a Strategic Brand? Wouldn't the BP enterprise reinforce its thought leader role in redefining the industry agenda once again? For all of us in the brand team, the answer to these questions was absolutely yes.

A brand that creates value to each business

The message of diversity…also reflected a reality. Take exploration and production: we had a message that said 'carbon and non-carbon products living in harmony'. Another one that said 'more oil, more gas equals more energy, equals more diversity'. All of these messages were true to Beyond Petroleum, and to the situation, the context, and the strategy of each of our businesses.

Duncan Blake remembers: *"Balancing these different views, led us to the idea of 'energy diversity' or 'all of the above', as a way to reintroduce oil and gas back into the communication while retaining the spirit of Beyond Petroleum".*

Aligning brand and strategy

Duncan adds *"It was a really important moment, a break-through that re-aligned brand and strategy. And at that time, the world was looking for every drop of energy it could find, whatever the form, and therefore energy security through diversity (which was the substance of our messaging) and the related 'icon' campaign were absolutely in tune with society's needs."*

Sticking purely to the management principles of a Strategic Brand, we diligently worked the components of the essence of 'Beyond Petroleum' and restated them in the new context, as represented in Illustration 10.6 on the evolved BP brand bridge. Never before had Beyond Petroleum bridged the gap between society's needs and BP's business realities so earnestly.

ILLUSTRATION 10.6	THE EVOLVED BP BRAND BRIDGE - 2008

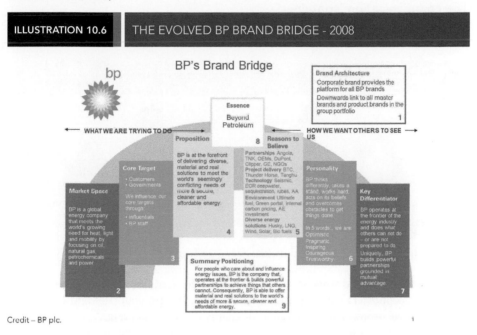

Credit – BP plc.

At this point, we were yet to reflect the restated brand in a new mission statement and in communication. It could not be slick, corporate or arrogant. The language had to be fresh and humble, clear and simple to understand – and it had to have an impact.

The brand promise
The idea was "all of the above" – a proposition of energy diversity as a progressive yet practical way to a more responsible and secure energy future. This became not just a BP

ILLUSTRATION 10.7	ENERGY DIVERSITY 'ALL OF THE ABOVE' REFERENCE AD.

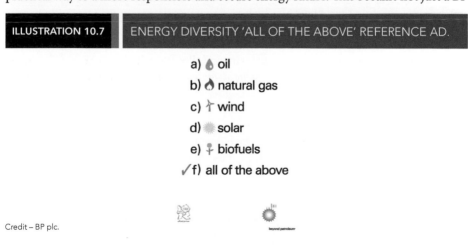

Credit – BP plc.

brand proposition, but part of the political vernacular that both sides of the political spectrum – and even our competitors – could actually agree on.

The communication 'container'

The creative container we selected represented plural energy through icons. It was simple, versatile, and would prove appealing.

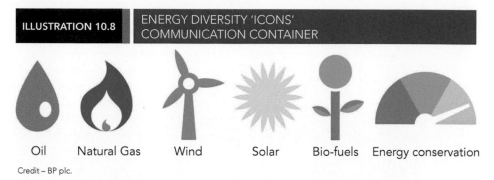

ILLUSTRATION 10.8	ENERGY DIVERSITY 'ICONS' COMMUNICATION CONTAINER

| Oil | Natural Gas | Wind | Solar | Bio-fuels | Energy conservation |

Credit – BP plc.

BP brand activation - internal debates and external praise

Despite having reached what appeared a brand sweet spot, internal debates remained fierce, with supporters and challengers within each groups, countries and businesses. Why would BP project itself as a leader for energy diversity (although it was one) when the priority was to supply much-needed oil and gas? Why would 'hard hat' engineers welcome representation by icons rather than with rigs or high-tech imaging?

I remember one particular meeting with BP's ExCo team when we discussed the core message and icon's language for the first time. Many around the table, notably in exploration & production, were carrying the immediate and major challenge of operations, with strong beliefs in technology and production. What I retain from this animated debate is how the icons were objected as "flowerpots", with some executive participants pointing their fingers to the bin.

We developed a target contact map of seventy top leaders whose opinion we believed was critical to the way forward. We were trying to follow Sun Tzu's guidance: *"Victorious warriors win first and then go to war, while defeated warriors go to war first and then seek to win"*. By involving people in the dialogue, we were aspiring to create committed brand advocates.

Duncan Blake remembers: *"When we created 'Beyond Petroleum', there were those in the company, who felt uncomfortable with it, because they looked at it in a literal sense - I do petroleum and I don't want to go Beyond Petroleum. And yet, there were many who were incredibly motivated by it and grasped that it was about a longer-term journey. With the 'icons' campaign, a number of people initially branded the whole thing, 'the flowerpots'. But we kept going and after a while, I think most of them were won over."*

Positive notes

I remember the first focus groups we ran on the combination of Beyond Petroleum, energy diversity, 'all of the above' and icons. The entire brand team was petrified. Had we missed the pulse? But the response was universally positive with unexpected levels of favourable feedback. As Duncan says: *"It was one of those moments, when you see something, and you just know it's going to work and make a big difference. It's probably happened three or four times in my career but I just knew that this was absolutely going to be superb and powerful for BP".*

I remember many small encouragements - in the autumn 2008, when our executives received an unexpected compliment from the Chairman of Shell, *"on the quality of BP's advertising and its positive impact"*; a meeting with the BP Secretary General, who in the midst of a heated debate on the brand admitted that *"his children loved the advertising"*; Tony intervening with BP Investor Relations saying: *"We should consider a strong linkage to the current external PR campaign because it seems to be going very well. Even my wife approves it".*

The Brand team won a Helios Award – an important internal award. And what was remarkable in 2008 and 2009, was that the Helios Awards themselves were amazingly 'on brand', which was a big signal within BP.

The brand activation brings positive surprises

We were ultimately entrusted to do what we thought best, despite the "flower pots". We underpinned the link between 'energy security' and 'availability through diversity' in multiple and straightforward visual messages – and went out to communicate the message to the world.

ILLUSTRATION 10.9 ENERGY DIVERSITY 'ALL OF THE ABOVE' ACTIVATIONS

Credit – BP plc.

"All of the above" went on to define the energy conversation, and even took centre stage in the battle of presidential politics in the US.

In September 2008, candidate Senator John McCain proclaimed, *"Attack the energy problem on every front"*, and the following month issued his *"All of the above - nuclear, wind, tide, solar, gas, coal"* energy plan. BP's brand language on energy had entered political rhetoric.

Similarly, in 2012, Barack Obama borrowed our language to describe energy including. *"All-of-the-above approach to reduce foreign dependence"* and *"All-of-the-above energy; enough natural gas for 100 years."* More recently, Hillary Clinton subscribed to an 'All-of-the-above' energy policy in her 2016 presidential campaign.

| ILLUSTRATION 10.10 | US PRESIDENT CANDIDATE SENATOR JOHN MCCAIN ADOPTS ' ALL OF THE ABOVE' |

Credit – YouTube

This balanced approach of promoting "energy security through diversity" was a potent leadership platform in a post 9/11 world – and ultimately transcended the BP brand itself as the language leak into political rhetoric demonstrates.

BP brand outcomes

Technically, the brand impact was amazing and BP almost solely owned the positives in the category. In 2009, over a third of our peers' communication in the US was attributed to BP, often more than to the advertiser company itself. The example on Illustration 10.11 reflects this situation, with Shell print advertising between July and September 2009 showing a 9 per cent attribution to them and 31 per cent to BP. And our positioning and message appeared clear to our audiences, well more than our peers.

ILLUSTRATION 10.11   CLARITY OF BRAND ASSOCIATIONS IN THE US

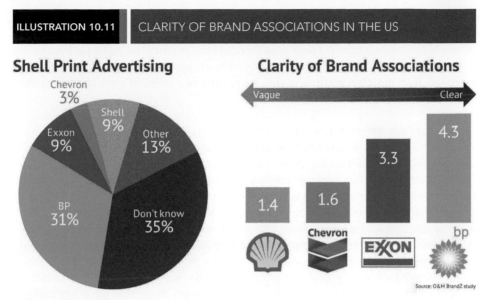

Credit: BrandZ brand study

Ultimately, the brand communication attracted significant favourable and positive feedback compared to our competitors, as reflected on Illustration 10.12.

ILLUSTRATION 10.12   BP COMMUNICATION IMPACT IN THE US VERSUS COMPETITION

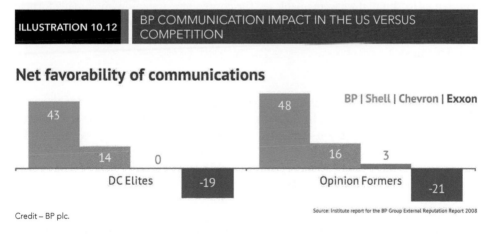

Credit – BP plc.

The BP brand as the enterprise strategic compass?

It took a while before the brand provided an internal compass. It was a long march to give it a deeply strategic importance again in the new context. In fact, we lived through thirty months of ups and downs, ambiguity and day-to-day close navigation. The brand team exhibited passionate resilience to find ways to make it happen– and they got it right at the end.

Head down

From his early days as Group CEO, Tony Hayward had decided that there was no way BP would be *"leading from the back"* and therefore the priority was to fix performance, progress safety and address some basics of the company. Once these would have improved, it would then be time to step back, express a point of view and frame the future.

It is not that Tony did not believe in Beyond Petroleum. He had declared on the 4th June 2007 in Berlin: *"At BP, we like to say we are moving Beyond Petroleum. It was not, and is not, a denial of our core business. Rather, it is about three things – producing more fossil fuels more efficiently today, making better use of fossil fuels and beginning the transition to a low carbon future. BP is proud to be in the oil and gas business. We, and our competitors, do a good job serving millions of customers every day, providing energy for the essential things of life. Beyond Petroleum is an affirmation that BP aims to conduct its business on a sustainable basis, both today and for the long term. And the most critical issue for us is climate change. Everyone in our industry must face up to the fact that fossil fuels are responsible for 60% of greenhouse gas emissions. So, increasingly, Beyond Petroleum is about concrete action, by making the right investments to prepare for a low carbon economy – one in which carbon emissions are restricted."*

But BP was not going to aspire to anything high profile just yet. Instead, the enterprise would keep head down and focus on operations and safety until we had recovered. And in many ways, Tony trusted us, *"the experts"*, to do the right thing for the BP brand and expected us to 'shout' if we were unable to. The consequent ambiguity took many forms and the following couple of anecdotes will perhaps help give a sense of this 'yin and yang' – which many senior marketers might recognize part of their past, present and plausible future.

Hiatus on BP's vision

Brand investment, particularly in 2008, became the lowest that we ever had. There were a number of reasons for this. The first was a big internal saving programme to restore profitability versus competition – and that was absolutely fair. And the brand team took it on to produce the highest impact form the reduced investment.

The second was that some colleagues were seeing a risk. The position and performance of the brand was strong and started to overtly define the company's point of view before it had been corporately restated. Let me give you an example - in 2009, the whole company, and everybody around us, became increasingly impatient for a BP enterprise narrative. Remember we had lost our iconic leader John Browne and we were on air with our brand messaging, responding to the energy challenges with 'all of the above'. Governments, other companies, even the BP Board started to phone and say: *'Is this BP's vision, is this the enterprise point of view? Can we take it for granted? Because we like it.'* I remember being asked these questions around the world, once even by members of the GE Board. But for months – I should say years – we could not say yes formally because the company wasn't prepared to go there… until early 2010.

Alignment

By then, the company's performance, its internal simplification and integration and progress on safety, gave more space for a strategic perspective. On 5th February 2010 Tony gave a speech in front of the London Business School that, for the first time in three years, stated a BP point of view… centered on 'all of the above.' Here are some of the highlights and we have included ads from the campaign to evidence the sound alignment:

"Energy security will dominate politics and policy for the next 12 months and considerably beyond. So what delivers energy security? I believe the key factors are diversity, competition and efficiency.

ILLUSTRATION 10.13	ENERGY DIVERSITY FOR ENERGY SECURITY AND A LOWER CARBON ECONOMY

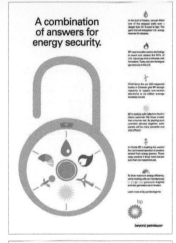

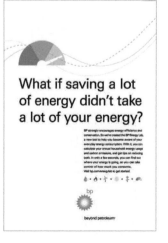

Source – BP plc.

"BP's projections suggest we'll need around 45% more energy in 2030 than we consume today - and double what we consume today by 2050. That's going to require investment of more than $1 trillion a year – every year. How do we meet that demand sustainably? Certainly there will need to be changes in the energy mix. We need more low-carbon energy. And we need to use energy more efficiently. But the main point is that there is no magic solution, and we will need a wide mix of energy types in 20 years time...."

The energy of the future will be more than oil...The critical point is that it will be a diverse mix....We believe in a broad and sustainable mix that embraces oil, gas, coal and renewables, producing and using them all with innovation and efficiency.

ILLUSTRATION 10.14   ENERGY DIVERSITY IN ...ITS DIVERSITY

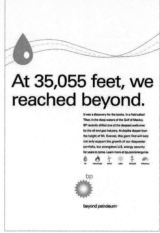

Source – BP plc.

His speech ended like this… *"As well as ensuring that we don't leave future generations with the prospect of rising sea levels, we need to ensure that we keep the lights on in the next decade. If we can meet both these challenges, as I believe we can, then we will truly have delivered energy security."*

Once again the brand was becoming a compass. And for the brand team, it was celebration day…and a relief - the vision set in the brand restatement was the company's Pole Star again.

ILLUSTRATION 10.15	THE ENDURING STRATEGIC BRAND IMPERATIVES – BP Q1 2010

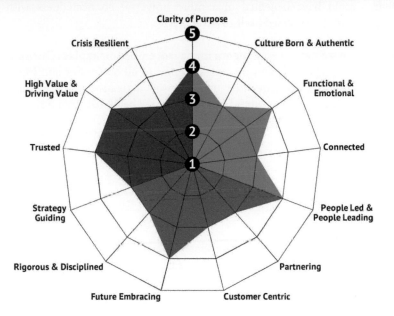

More than ever, the evolved BP brand remained true to the company's character of "caring and doing the right thing", "performing at the frontier" in "open dialogue with others". The four values of the company – Progressive, Responsible, Innovative and Performance Driven – would epitomise the culture and dovetail with the brand.

Tony Hayward believes that the achievement for the BP brand during this time period of 2007-2010 was a fact of: *"We made it real. We made it connect to the reality of where society was, rather than of where society might be in 50 years time. We made it connect to the reality of our workforce, not where the workforce of BP might be in 50 years time. And that was the main thing we did, but it was quite bold and it allowed everyone to get it, in the way they hadn't quite got it before."*

What does this story tell us? As much as Beyond Petroleum proved resilient and was valuably restated, what did we learn from these years?

Practice 1 - Strong brand purposes are enduring. As much as a lot changed to BP's context, the three Beyond Petroleum journeys proved resilient, guiding to, enabling and supporting the brand restatement.

Practice 2 - Hard test the brand against extreme scenarios. When developing your brand purpose and enterprise point of view, test it hard against all possible scenarios for your businesses – Beyond Petroleum turned out to be strongly challenged in an 'oil short' economy.

Practice 3 - Cross audience clarity and connectedness. Ensure your brand purpose is clear, relevant and connected to your internal and external audiences – Beyond Petroleum would have benefited of a more universal connectedness with critical audiences …until it expressed itself as 'diversity'

Practice 4 - A systematic, performance managed, embedment plan. Once established, the brand is not negotiable and there is a request to all businesses and individuals to develop, activate and measure their own relevant activation plan for the common purpose – Beyond Petroleum would have immensely benefited from a more thorough implementation plan developed in the early days.

Let's now turn to Unilever, a Strategic Brand that continues getting strong 'traction' on a brand purpose-led strategy of sustainability.

UNILEVER, FROM AMBITION TO IMPLEMENTATION

Things happen to Strategic Brands, probably more than to others, because they are meaningful, impactful and hold more promise than most.

Branded response to a world scale takeover bid

On the 17th February 2017, Kraft Heinz made a takeover offer for Unilever to the astounding amount of $143 billions. Following Unilever's strong rejection and only 2 days later, the three Brazilian billionaires [3G] and US investor Warren Buffett leading the proposal withdrew their bid. The joint statement by Unilever and Kraft Heinz said: *"Kraft Heinz has the utmost respect for the culture, strategy and leadership of Unilever."*

I have been impressed with the extent to which Unilever's response was branded and let's note a few ways it was - you know by now how much I believe in testing a brand in extreme circumstances.

The first obvious take away from these events was the evidence of immense desirability of the Unilever enterprise and its portfolio of brands in every account.

There was an instinctive rejection from Unilever of the takeover deal and media reported comments such as, *"the idea to be owned by these guys [3G] is revolting to management, the board and many of its stakeholders".* Why was that - because the brand, culture and strategy are very widely polarised between the two groups.

Paul Polman manages growth for the long term by investing in brands, committing resources to develop the company's product range and promoting environmental sustainability. Didn't he tell investors early in his tenure to steer clear unless they were prepared to sacrifice short-term profits for long-term sustainability? And when you visit Unilever's corporate site, it first claims *"Making Sustainable Living Commonplace".*

In contrast, 3G acquires companies, applies draconian cost and investment frugality through their zero-base budgeting method, cuts workforce radically and consequently optimizes operating margins in the short term. Their corporate site pitch is *"A platform for performance".*

The attraction for 3G was compelling – with 13 brands over $1 billion sales per annum and a strong footprint in emerging markets, Unilever's operating margin is close to half that of Kraft Heinz 's. The calculus was that if you applied 3G's management discipline to Unilever's portfolio, notably slashing costs by combining the two packaged food businesses, a considerable premium would yield short-term. Unilever's objection to this logic was one about the longer term, in that cutting costs might work if you can be satisfied with no growth – Kraft Heinz growth was close to zero in 2016, compared with +3.7% for Unilever.

These two businesses have a radically different brand philosophy and deeply mismatched strategies. By going back to the company's brand roots and its unique culture, Unilever's answer could only be an offended 'no'.

That Unilever will leverage the event to accelerate its own margin improvement and brand-pruning programme is another story. But its own version of zero-based budgeting is held consistent with the brand and related strategies.

I have interacted with Unilever for a long time, and so it was a pleasure to reflect recently on brand and strategy with Keith Weed, the Unilever Group Chief Marketing and Communications Officer – our main conversation occurred before the Kraft Heinz take over offer. As I said earlier, there can only be a few strategies as challenging as the ones related to sustainability, so my main question to Keith was: *"what is Unilever's winning formula?"*

Briefly introducing Unilever

Keith: *"We have the corporate Unilever brand and the 400+ consumer brands that live underneath it, such as Knorr, Magnum, Dove and Lipton. Our brands are available in over 190 countries and reach two billion consumers a day, generating sales of €52.7 billion in 2016. 58% of the company's footprint is in developing and emerging markets"* [vs. 37% for P&G and 43% for Nestlé].

ILLUSTRATION 10.16   EXAMPLES OF WORLD-CLASS UNILEVER GROUP BRANDS

Credit – THE Enduring Strategic Brand from Unilever Data

Unilever's logo is a visual expression of the enterprise commitment to make sustainable living commonplace. It was introduced in 2004 and designed by Wolff Olins around the idea of "adding vitality to life". Each icon, from the hand to hair, fish, and heart represents its corporate values or one of the company's sub-brands.

ILLUSTRATION 10.17   EXAMPLES OF UNILEVER BRAND SYMBOLS AND THEIR MEANING

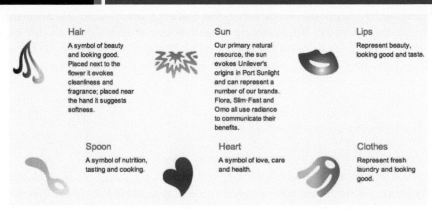

Hair
A symbol of beauty and looking good. Placed next to the flower it evokes cleanliness and fragrance; placed near the hand it suggests softness.

Sun
Our primary natural resource, the sun evokes Unilever's origins in Port Sunlight and can represent a number of our brands. Flora, Slim-Fast and Omo all use radiance to communicate their benefits.

Lips
Represent beauty, looking good and taste.

Spoon
A symbol of nutrition, tasting and cooking.

Heart
A symbol of love, care and health.

Clothes
Represent fresh laundry and looking good.

Credit – Designed by THE Enduring Strategic Brand, from Unilever data

By all accounts, Unilever is a strong Strategic Brand, as seen in Illustration 10.18 and analysed below.

ILLUSTRATION 10.18	THE ENDURING STRATEGIC BRAND IMPERATIVES – UNILEVER

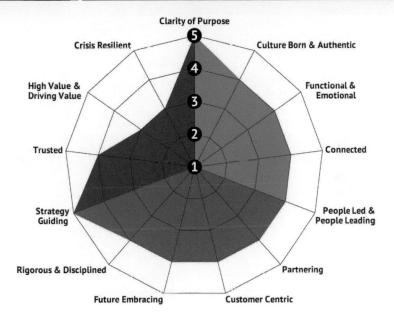

Doing well by doing good

Clarity of Purpose

Unilever's purpose comes up immediately in any conversation with Keith: "*We have a single clear and uniting purpose for Unilever, and that is to make sustainable living commonplace. This is a play on 'making cleanliness commonplace', which was the ambition of our founder Lord Leverhulme when he started producing Sunlight soap back in the 1880s. So we have always had this purpose at the heart of our business. It feels disingenuous to talk about 'designing' our brand point of view as it has grown up through the DNA of our business. How we articulate that vision of making sustainable living commonplace is through our business model, which is to grow the business while reducing our environmental footprint and increasing our positive social impact.*"

Culture Born & Authentic

As we learned from BP, the primary challenge to embed the brand purpose was about culture.

When Paul Polman succeeded Patrick Cescau on 1st January 2009 as CEO of Unilever, he set out 'The Compass' - the strategy underpinning Unilever's determination to build a long-term sustainable business. In 2010, the 'Unilever Sustainable Living Plan (ULSP)' was launched, with the aim of doubling the group's size while reducing its overall environmental footprint and improving its social impact.

ILLUSTRATION 10.19   THE UNILEVER VISION IN ITS CONTEXT

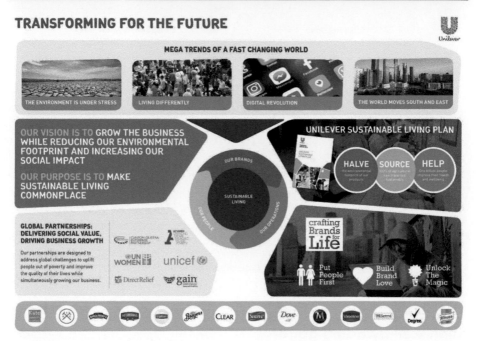

Credit – Unilever

Keith explains: *"The USLP commits to:*
- *Helping more than a billion people take action to improve their health and well-being by 2020*
- *Halving the environmental impact of our products by 2030*
- *Enhancing the livelihoods of millions of people by 2020.*

ILLUSTRATION 10.20   THE THREE PILLARS OF THE UNILEVER SUSTAINABLE LIVING PLAN

Credit – Unilever

People Led

Though Unilever was not the first company to make sustainability a goal, Paul would need all his personal leadership skills, resilience, determination and clarity to build a true internal culture behind a concrete sustainability plan. From talking to him, and those close to him, I believe he finds his determination in a hard-headed pragmatic belief that in a world of finite resources, running a business sustainably is vital for long-term growth, can mitigate risk and reduce costs. He inherently believes in the enterprise vision *"to grow our business, while decoupling our environmental footprint from our growth and increasing our positive social impact"*. In short, doing the right thing for both humanity and the enterprise is mutually reinforcing and beneficial. [Future Embracing]

High Value & Driving Value

This bold vision meant Paul and his team took the heat, day after day, quarter after quarter. The company missed its sales targets in six out of eight quarters in 2013 and 2014. On a personal level, I knew there were rumblings from within Unilever; and as a business colleague, I observed the worries of some investors, such as this one saying early 2015: *"I do not have an issue with Polman talking about sustainability... but the results have not been that strong."*

It was not easy – but Paul and his team persevered, and it is wonderful to see his transformational efforts bring growth and bear structural fruits. Keith reports: *"Six years into the Unilever Sustainable Living Plan we can be clear that this vision is a positive economic differentiator. In six years, our share price has risen steadily and the Total Shareholder Return is 220%."*

ILLUSTRATION 10.21   UNILEVER PLC SHARE PRICE 2009 – 2016

Credit – Unilever

Keith continues: *"We have strong economic evidence relating to our Sustainable Living brands, which are actually leading Unilever's growth. In 2015 our Sustainable Living brands grew 30% faster than the rest of our business and delivered nearly half our growth. They also grew faster than they did the previous year."* Unilever's strategy has also brought significant efficiencies: water, waste and energy efficiencies have saved over €600 million since 2008.

Our review backs up Keith's view: in 2016, underlying sales growth was 3.7% and core operating margins lifted to 15.3 per cent. Emerging markets (58% of group sales) continued with higher than average growth, although they obviously create volatility from quarter to quarter, notably India and Brazil. Markets and analysts now consider Unilever a "safe haven investment" in a volatile economic context.

Keith also believes there is another, non-financial performance marker which is indicative of progress: *"Unilever was ranked number one in its sector in the 2015 Dow Jones Sustainability Index. In the FTSE4Good Index, it achieved the highest environmental score of 5. It led the list of Global Corporate Sustainability Leaders in the 2016 GlobeScan/ SustainAbility annual survey for the sixth year running. And in 2016, for the second year, Unilever was ranked the most sustainable food and beverage company in Oxfam's Behind the Brands Scorecard."*

Unilever, an Exemplary Brand for the 'Strategy Guiding' Imperative

There were certainly some similarities between BP's and Unilever's Strategic Brand pillars. Where they were different was the way in which Unilever went to execute the brand purpose through a systematic strategy and activation plan. Keith remembers: *"Of course there have been challenges to implementing that plan along the way, but the brand purpose has always remained firmly at the centre of the business model. The plan encompasses every brand and every market. One of the challenges has been recognising that each of the brands is on a different journey to find their own social purpose within the USLP, and what their defining contribution is. A number are still in development but our top five brands (Knorr, Dove, Dirt is Good (laundry), Lipton and Hellmann's) are now all Sustainable Living brands.*

Of course there have been challenges to implementing that plan along the way, but the brand purpose has always remained firmly at the centre of the business model. The plan encompasses every brand and every market.

To be called a Sustainable Living brand, a brand must meet rigorous criteria which show it has integrated sustainability into both its purpose and its products. The purpose delivers a specific social benefit, while the products contribute to at least one of the goals of the USLP.

For example, Knorr is tackling malnutrition in Nigeria –in which almost one in two women of reproductive age and 72% of children under five suffer from anaemia – by adding iron to its bouillon cubes and promoting healthy cooking. Dove has a very clear mission around improving the self-esteem of women and girls with its Real Beauty campaign, now over a decade old. The 'Dirt is Good' campaign for our laundry brands encourages more outdoor play for children. 100% of the tea for our Lipton tea bag blends is now certified sustainable by the Rainforest Alliance. Hellmann's is committed to sustainable sourcing and reducing environmental impact. Having the single Unilever brand point of view to hold all of this together, has been key to our success."

Without being rocket science, the combination of clear principles, a plan and thorough execution makes Unilever a world-class 'Exemplary Strategic Brand'.

Six best practices making Unilever a 'Strategy Guiding' Brand

I will comment on what I believe are six best practices and how they apply to the corporate Unilever brand and Dove.

Practice 1 - A non-negotiable enterprise brand purpose, with an embedment plan

Once developed, determined and firmed up, the brand is not up for debate any more and there is no opt out. Each business and person does not hold the 'if' but rather the 'how' question. How will 'I' contribute to the brand ULSP purpose and make it value accretive to our strategy and endeavours in an enduring way?

Practice 2 - Deployed rather than central: consumer brands turn the vision into reality

Consumer brands make up most of Unilever's business. The cross-brands' horizontal groups, such as innovation, sourcing and operations, have an important role to play in the brand purpose - but Unilever is clear that deploying the brand purpose into its businesses is the only way to have impact and therefore continues to extend the sustainability plan to a growing number of brands [Authentic].

In contrast, in BP, although we ran some truly valuable business-led initiatives (Ref. Chapter 1), we lacked the consistent deployment across all businesses and therefore a sufficiently strong ownership to gain proper and consistent impact.

Practice 3 - Brand purpose activation in the business interest of the brands

The reality of strategic activation is of course complex, in particular on how to make each particular brand's social purpose a natural fit to that brand - rather than a directive imposed at corporate level. Unilever was always clear that its purpose was not about morality but about business. As Keith explained earlier, instead of being blindly determined to impose a one-size-fits-all formula to each consumer brand, the Unilever brand point of view acted as a framework to all brands. *"There is no debate and it has to happen but it is down to each brand to identify their Sustainable Living Plan role and the contribution they can make"*

As a true house of brands, Unilever respects the purity of a key brand architecture principle: to give space to brands, allowing them to form their own character and to compete on the markets with no limiting inhibitors or compromise. [Customer Centric; Rigorous & Disciplined]

Keith cites Dove as an example of a Sustainable Living brand. Says Dove: *"We encourage all women and girls to develop a positive relationship with beauty, helping to raise their self-esteem, and thereby enabling them to realise their full potential. In 2005, we developed the Dove Self-Esteem Programme (DSEP) to make real changes to the ways women and girls perceive and embrace beauty... and build a healthy body image. Specifically the objective was to reach 15 million girls globally by the end of 2015, with educational interventions lasting at least an hour."* [Functional & Emotional]

There is no trade-off between sustainability and profitable growth.

Keith is encouraged by growing signals of connectivity: *"Through a unique research project we also have clear evidence that consumers reward brands that deliver social benefit as well as product performance and affordability. Our research showed that 54% of consumers want to buy more sustainably, and many already are. It also showed that consumers want it all – high-performing products, at the right price and with a purpose that they can connect with. There is no trade-off between sustainability and profitable growth."* [Connected]

Practice 4 - Clear and transparent objectives and measures

Each brand has its own function and develops clear objectives as part of the broader Unilever USLP; progress is measured and published transparently under the group umbrella. [Trusted] I would encourage you to review the USLP performance update against the ambitious targets it sets, which are available online and depicted in Illustration 10.22 using the Dove example - it is an interesting read.

ILLUSTRATION 10.22   UNILEVER PERFORMANCE REPORTING OF ITS USLP

USLP BIG GOAL	USLP BIG GOAL SUB-CATEGORY	DOVE CONTRIBUTION & OBJECTIVE	DOVE REPORTED PROGRESS
Improving Health and Well-being — By 2020 we will help more than a billion people take action to improve their health and hygiene.	Health & Hygiene "By 2020, we will help more than a billion people to improve their health and hygiene"	Improve self-esteem Objective: reach 15 million girls globally by the end of 2015... for at least an hour"	Dove reached its target one year early – helping 15.8 million young people by 2014. By 2015 it had increased to 19.4 million.

Credit –THE Enduring Strategic Brand from Unilever corporate site data

Dove comments: *"We accelerated the reach and quality of the Dove Self-Esteem Project, developing cost effective, impactful implementation strategies. We reached 56% of young people with teacher-led programmes...The main contributors to our success were our partnership with the World Association of Girl Guides and Girl Scouts; scaling our digital presence; and the project's growth in new geographies."*

Practice 5 - Reality of action owned by people

There is always a huge cultural challenge with a non-traditional strategy. Achieving a true inside-out cultural evolution can feel like a never-ending crusade and could take two generations to fulfil – but Unilever is clearly making progress. In 2016, Unilever was recognised by the Glassdoor Employees' Choice Awards as one of the Best Places to Work in the UK, in seventh place and the only FMCG company in the top ten. Satisfaction rating scores result from a range of key workplace factors, including, "embedding, across the business, strong values in sustainability". In the LinkedIn Top Attractors list of the most sought-after companies, Unilever ranks first in the FMCG category and eighth globally. [People Leading]

Practice 6 - Partner, partner, partner

I don't believe anyone could succeed with a sustainability strategy without collaborating. At BP, I remember working hard with partners on a wide range of energy-saving initiatives, such as fuel-efficient engines and driving practice campaigns. Similarly, at Unilever, Dove's partnership with the World Association of Girl Guides and Girl Scouts (WAGGGS) has been spreading its message of self-esteem to millions more girls for over a decade. [Partnering]

In general, partnerships are preconditions for progress, with three vital sources of value: access, capability and resources. Unilever has hundreds of such partnerships - to enhance livelihoods, they need a trusting access to farmers to improve agricultural practices. They join NGOs, UN agencies and other organisations and companies to help transform health and hygiene. They co-operate with public, private and NGO sectors to increase preparation for and lessen the impact of disasters. They work with others – such as the WFF on deforestation and the Global Foodbanking Network – to reduce their environmental impact, improve lives and support zero waste. The Unilever Foundation is an epicentre of partnerships with NGOs.

At the end of 2015 and under the UN banner, 193 world leaders agreed to 17 "Global Goals" for Sustainable Development – Ref. Illustration 10.23 – with the aim of ending extreme poverty, inequality and climate change by 2030. Unilever was prominent in setting this coalition and committed to it in a branded way.

ILLUSTRATION 10.23   THE GLOBAL GOALS FOR SUSTAINABLE DEVELOPMENT

Credit – Unilever

The next phase in global leadership for the Unilever brand

For brands anchored in sustainability, the context was set at the end of 2015 after the COP 21 agreement in Paris. As Christiana Figueres, Former UNFCCC Executive Secretary, explained: *"We have spent years creating a new vision and now, I argue, we have to work two or three times as hard to make the new reality as laudable as the vision we created. That is going to be much harder."*

It is strange how history repeats itself. I remember going through a wave of similar discussions between 2005 and 2010, when the debate shifted from CSR to business, from vision to action. Unilever is already in the rare and commendable position to have made that transition successfully and to be in the midst of action at scale. From past experience and also as a more generic reflection for other brands, I believe this enviable position triggers the following three dilemmas:

Clarity of branding and brand roles: push / pull

By putting its consumer brands out in front, Unilever remains a relatively 'small' brand by itself. The Dove brand alone is valued $5.3bn, compared to $4.3bn for the Unilever corporate brand [Ref. Brand Finance]. At the same time, Unilever's profile is considerable and fast growing, with recent events raising its profile even further.

Keith tells us: *"Gradually over the past three years we have started to make the corporate Unilever brand more consumer facing through our 'Bright Future' campaign, which is focused on helping people to understand that they can make small changes to build a brighter future for generations to come. Among other things such as the increased visibility of the Unilever logo on packaging, it has contributed to a significant growth in awareness of Unilever's brand."* [Connected]

'Bright Future' is an inspiring platform: *"We believe there has never been a better time to create a better future for our children - a world where everyone has enough food to eat and no child goes to bed hungry. Where every child lives to their fifth birthday and has the right to a happy childhood. Where every home has enough water to drink and to wash, cook and clean. And where everybody can enjoy life today while protecting the planet for future generations."*

What will the economic role of the Unilever brand become in the future? How will the link with its consumer brands evolve? How will the 'push – pull' combination play out between corporate and consumer brands? We debated the same thing at BP, particularly in regards to Aral, a 'star' consumer brand in Germany while BP was our 'star' corporate brand.

Focus on few and big

The nature of sustainability driven strategies is to have infinite reach; they are emotionally draining and a constant moral challenge – 'how do you say no?' Demands for help come from everywhere every day. And as the strategy is deployed into multiple brands, multiple geographies and multiple teams, the initial strategic clarity and focus might loosen, with everybody starting to do their own thing guided by short-term benefit perspectives.

How will Unilever remain focused on making a big difference in few selected areas rather than a multitude of smaller impacts? How will it take on the continual challenge to be ruthless and 'say no' elsewhere? Because the Unilever and its consumer brands will only be known for something if it is simple, consistent over time, big and connected.

Sustainability full cycle end-to-end progress

Usually, the first wave of strategic and performance progression on sustainability plans comes from significant internal improvements of the enterprise's own operations: energy, waste, water, etc. But by far the biggest potential comes from how the company's products are used by its customers.

In the oil and gas sector, 10 to 20 per cent of CO_2 emissions come from operations, and the balance from customers using the products (Ref. Illustration 10.24, lower image). A similar pattern applies to Unilever, with an estimated 61% of greenhouse gas footprint driven by consumers - although numbers vary according to the product usage. So, how can water usage be reduced while incentivising five hand washes per day? How to reduce greenhouse gases (GHG) while championing showering and better nutrition? In fact, GHG emissions from Unilever products have grown by 6 per cent since 2010, while their factory sites emit 39 per cent less. (Note 1)

ILLUSTRATION 10.24 | 'OWN' VERSUS 'CUSTOMERS' GENERATED EMISSIONS

Our greenhouse gas footprint (2014–2015)

There is a variety of oil and gas resource users

80-90%

of CO$_2$ emissions from oil and gas products are from their use by consumers

Around 80-90% of CO$_2$ emissions from oil and gas products are from their use by consumers, with the remainder generated during their extraction and development.

Unilever is committed to a full value chain approach, *"as the most meaningful reflection of the true impact of its business"*, and transparent performance reporting. This is the only credible approach for a truly responsible brand – but it's a challenging one. As we learned in BP, it will take breadth of thought about systems and relationships to frame, guide and support the profound behavioural changes to deliver the desired end-to-end progress.

Uniting consumers, regulators and enterprises is one of the most challenging aspect – and the area in which the strongest Strategic Brand can and will play a vital role. As Keith says: *"We need to start thinking about brands as citizens too, with a responsibility to promote, share, create exposure and help to make change."*

Translating the brand into strategy

Let's conclude with Keith talking about Unilever's magic formula, the symbiosis between brand and strategy: *"The brand point of view rigorously informs and guides strategy because the brand purpose is so intrinsic to the business model. We have always been clear that this was not something that we were doing because it was a moral obligation or a nice thing to do. We were always clear that this was an economic strategy – and that is now paying off. The corporate purpose remains constant, though the expression may change."*

As Unilever demonstrates, a true Strategic Brand is connected both inside and outside the organisation with purpose. For many companies, it is an incredibly challenging journey as they experience points of disconnect between how the brand is perceived by the external world and the reality within the business. So how can we do this well?

Let's use BP's and Unilever's combined best practice to guide and execute strategy starting with the brand – Illustration 10.25 summarizes the key learning from this chapter.

| ILLUSTRATION 10.25 | BEST PRACTICE OF A 'STRATEGY GUIDING' STRATEGIC BRAND |

➤ Hard test the brand purpose against extreme scenarios for the business

➤ Ensure clarity, relevance and connectedness with internal and external audiences

➤ Once established, make the brand purpose non negotiable and develop immediately an embedment plan

➤ Deploy across each and all brands and businesses rather than hold centrally

➤ Activate in the business interest of each brand, for them to determine

➤ Performance manage through clear and transparent objectives and measures

➤ Embed the reality of action so it is owned by people

➤ Partner, partner, partner

Finally, let's recall our Strategic Brand champions' guidelines on how to live and translate brand purpose into strategy and make this discipline the way of doing business:

Lord John Browne - *"In a global marketplace, branding is crucially important in attracting customers and business. It is about the identity of the company and the values that underpin everything that you do and every relationship that you have."*

Ian Robertson - *"A Strategic Brand is what drives the company, rather than anything else…It's what we use to attract people into our company; to motivate people within the company; to design our cars and services; to guide our dealers"*

Shelly Lazarus - *"A brand is a great organising principle and everything comes out of your understanding and your beliefs about what the brand is. The deep understanding of the brand keeps you in territories that have to be consistent with the brand".*

Tony Hayward - *"When you have a brand for a global corporation that does not reflect what 90% of your organisation does every day, I'd say, you have a major problem. Because you have people, who are the company's biggest emphasis, walking around not relating to what the company is promoting."*

Keith Weed - *"Of course there have been challenges to implementing that plan along the way, but the brand purpose has always remained firmly at the centre of the business model. The plan encompasses every brand and every market. One of the challenges has been recognising that each of the brands is on a different journey to find their own social purpose within the USLP, and what their defining contribution is."*

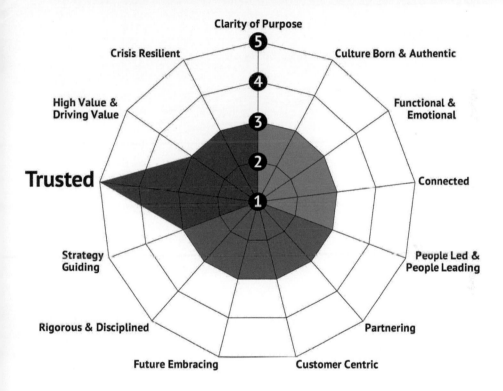

The best way to learn if you can trust somebody is to trust them
Ernest Hemingway

Trust is one of the most precious assets to a brand in today's world, a consequence of consumers' extensive access to information and reflecting the political and social climate. Although trust is integral to brands, it isn't necessarily well understood or always managed effectively as such.

As reflected on Illustration 11.1, society's trust in institutions has been declining markedly over the last decade. So what can brands do to earn trust and benefit from a positive contrast with the main authority figures?

ILLUSTRATION 11.1	ACCEPTANCE OF AUTHORITY FROM INSTITUTIONS IN GREAT BRITAIN

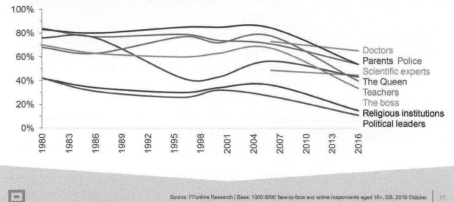

Credit – The Foresight Factory, October 2016

Needless to say, there is a strong link between trust, an Enduring Strategic Brand and strategic value creation, something that I've talked about extensively with Shelly Lazarus. Shelly serves on the boards of General Electric, Merck & Co., New York-Presbyterian Hospital, the American Museum of Natural History, the World Wildlife Fund and others - so who better than her could comment: *"When people have trust in your brand, you have license to operate broadly and deeply, to extend across categories, and this is a huge gift"*.

More later from Shelly but what are some brand views?

Ford's global trend and future manager Sheryl Connolly believes that building trust has never been more daunting, but that, *"The brands that develop relationships built on trust are at a competitive advantage."*

Probably more than most organisations, BP needs high levels of trust from all stakeholders. It manifests into long-term, trusted relationships with governments like Azerbaijan or Trinidad and Tobago, as BP operates their natural resources and in countries like the US where BP supplies their defense fuels. This is why, following the oil spill in the Gulf of Mexico, internal conversations were hardly ever, *'how do we restore the BP brand?'* but rather, *'how do we rebuild trust?'*

As for me, I have taken a major learning over time, which I believe applies fundamentally to trusted Enduring Strategic Brands and has become a calming, strengthening guideline to life: *"Do the right thing, always"*.

"Do the right thing, always".

TRUST MATTERS FOR STRATEGIC BRANDS

As many organisations have experienced, lack of trust in a brand has a massive negative impact on the enterprise value. As detailed on Illustration 11.2, VW, Target, McDonalds, the FIFA, Maggi noodles have all faced the down side of not having enough of stakeholders' trust or the trauma of having lost it, with the subsequent drain of brand and business value.

ILLUSTRATION 11.2	EXAMPLES OF REAL OR PERCEIVED TRUST BREACHES

Volkswagen drops 23% After admitting diesel Emissions cheat

Bloomberg, September 21, 2015 - Martin Winterkorn, who has led VW since 2007, was forced to halt sales of the cars on Sunday and issue a public apology, saying he's "deeply sorry" for **breaking the public's trust** and that VW would do "everything necessary in order to reverse the damage this has caused."

Target profit falls 46% on credit card breach and the hits could keep on coming

Forbes, February 26, 2014 - As customers seek to **regain confidence** in one of the nation's largest retailers, Target, the company is paying a hefty price for the credit card data breach that spilled information on as many as 110 million customers. Its profit fell nearly 50% in the fourth fiscal quarter of 2013 and declined by more than a third for all of 2013.

Coca-Cola, Visa and FIFA Adidas are responding to the FIFA corruption scandal

Associated Press, May 28, 2015
Companies like Coca-Cola, Visa and Adidas have in recent months shown a growing willingness to voice their concerns publicly about FIFA's string of scandals, which have spanned from past allegations of corruption to the abuse of laborers building World Cup venues in Qatar... "As a sponsor, we expect FIFA to take swift and immediate steps to address these issues within its organization", the statement reads. "This starts with rebuilding a culture with strong ethical practices in order to **restore the reputation** of the games for fans everywhere."

McDonald's faces declining sales In asia after china food scandal

LOSS OF TRUST
CMR survey data suggests Chinese **consumers trust** in, and desire for, KFC and McDonald's has been falling since hitting a peak in 2010, with the decline accelerating since the 2012 food safety scare.

Maggi withdraws all noodles in India after state bans and lead scare

FOOD SAFETY
The Guardian, June 5, 2015
"The trust of our consumers and the safety of our products is our first priority."

Credit – THE Enduring Strategic Brand, form various media extracts

Trust is more important than ever. A 2016 Readers Digest survey in the US found that trust continues to be a major factor in consumer decision-making, with 78 per cent of the survey participants stating they would choose a brand that's been identified as more trustworthy over another brand with equal quality and price. In addition, the study reported that 67 per cent of US adults surveyed pay more attention to trusted brands, and another 67 per cent would be willing to pay more to support trusted brands. (Note 1)

There is much at stake! The 2016 Edelman Trust Barometer surveyed over 33,000 respondents in 28 countries, with 68 per cent of respondents choosing to buy products from trusted companies and 48 per cent refusing to buy from distrusted companies. Similarly, 59 per cent actively recommended trusted brands and 42 per cent criticised distrusted ones (Ref. Illustration 11.3 and Note 2).

ILLUSTRATION 11.3	CONSIDERABLE IMPORTANCE OF TRUST

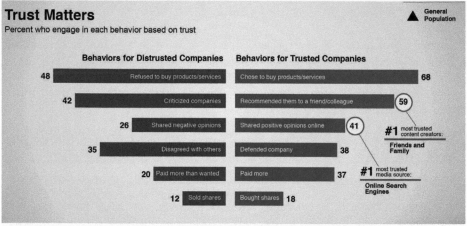

Credit - Edelman Trust Barometer, 2016

In the new reality of consumers' rising influence through digital, 75 per cent of respondents declared taking 'moment of truth' decisions in terms of purchase after having conversations with their peers. As they communicate about brands, others play pivotal roles in recommending brands, reassuring and giving confidence or reversely pointing to risks   (Ref. Illustration 11.4).

Should we make trust a standard item in our Board and C-Suite meetings? Should investors make trust barometers a companion to their three-year discounted cash flow model? I would certainly advocate for their immense relevance as leading indicators to future performance.

ILLUSTRATION 11.4   TRUSTING PEERS INFLUENCE CHOICES

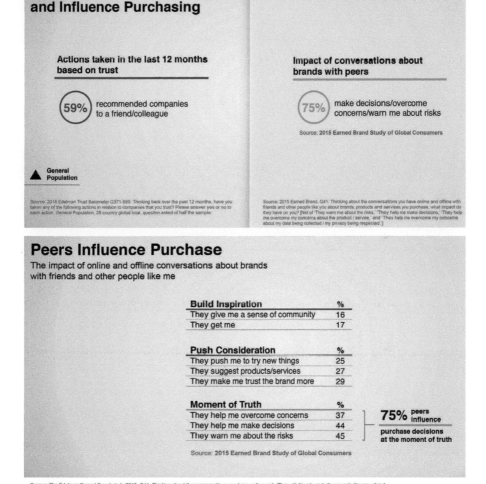

Peers Recommend Companies and Influence Purchasing

Actions taken in the last 12 months based on trust

59% recommended companies to a friend/colleague

Impact of conversations about brands with peers

75% make decisions/overcome concerns/warn me about risks

Source: 2015 Earned Brand Study of Global Consumers

▲ General Population

Source: 2016 Edelman Trust Barometer Q371-589. Thinking back over the past 12 months, have you taken any of the following actions in relation to companies that you trust? Please answer yes or no to each action. General Population, 28-country global total, question asked of half the sample.

Source: 2015 Earned Brand. Q41: Thinking about the conversations you have online and offline with friends and other people like you about brands, products and services you purchase, what impact do they have on you? [Net of 'They warn me about the risks,' 'They help make decisions,' 'They help me overcome my concerns about the product / service,' and 'They help me overcome my concerns about my data being collected / my privacy being respected.']

Peers Influence Purchase

The impact of online and offline conversations about brands with friends and other people like me

Build Inspiration	%
They give me a sense of community	16
They get me	17

Push Consideration	%
They push me to try new things	25
They suggest products/services	27
They make me trust the brand more	29

Moment of Truth	%
They help me overcome concerns	37
They help me make decisions	44
They warn me about the risks	45

75% peers influence

purchase decisions at the moment of truth

Source: 2015 Earned Brand Study of Global Consumers

Source: The Edelman Earned Brand study 2015, Q41: Thinking about the conversations you have online and offline with friends and other people like you about brands, products and services you purchase, what impact do they have on you?

Credit - Edelman Trust Barometer & Edelman Brand Study

Insightfully for strategic marketers, Illustration 11.5 demonstrates the growing divide in the level of trust between the general population and the informed public (otherwise known as opinion formers). Countries like France, the UK, the US and Spain have seen this gap widen sharply over the last four years – which could be at the root of Brexit in the UK, the election of Donald Trump in the US, the rise of the extreme right in France and the emergence of Podemos in Spain. Too many politicians forget that the political world is another market whose customers need to be given an all-encompassing choice. Both governments and business need to remember that every voice (and vote) matters.

| ILLUSTRATION 11.5 | A GROWING DIVIDE IN PERCEPTION BETWEEN AUDIENCES |

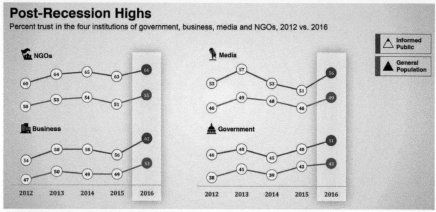

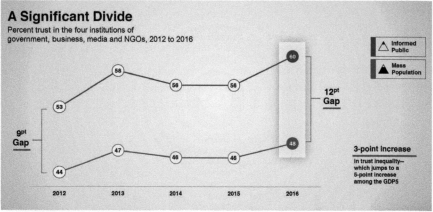

Credit - Edelman Trust Barometer & Edelman Brand Study

THE WHY, WHAT AND HOW OF BRAND TRUST

Trust is not declared, but earned. Here are a few questions to penetrate the art and science of building and maintaining a trusted Brand:

Trust is not declared, but earned.

Risk – reward balance of trust? - There are serious consequences to the breakdown of trust in an organisation. As Warren Buffett says: *"It takes 20 years to build a reputation and five minutes to ruin it. If you think about that, you'll do things differently".* So why develop and lean on such a vulnerable asset? How can we understand and manage the risk – reward balance better?

Invest in trust? - A couple of years ago, I was a keynote speaker at the annual Future Foundation conference and asked to consider: "How much should you invest in trust?" At first I thought it a daft premise: you can't invest in trust, it is about who you are, it's not something that can be fabricated. But on reflection, this is a very good question.

How trust manifests and creates value? - Can trust in a brand have a defining, positive and lasting impact on an organisation and its performance? What does this look like: how does brand trust manifest and what are its sources of value? What are the tradeoffs and risks in building a trusted brand?

How to build and maintain brand trust? – The killer question is how do you build and maintain a trusted brand? What about CSR and other investments, which arguably also anchor brand trust?

What does a trusted brand look like?

First, we must define trust. I have always believed that there are four types of trust. Let's talk to Kevin Murray, author of *The Language of Leaders* and *Communicate to Inspire*, about trust and leadership: (Note 3)

"A brand is about relationships. And relationships are the engines of success. Therefore, when you think about a brand, you are thinking about how you build, sustain and thrive in all the organisation's relationships. When companies think about their brand, it needs to be about a lot more than the image they project to the world and rather about the relationships which they need to succeed into the future.

Ten years ago about 80% of the balance sheet was made up of tangible assets; today, it is the opposite, with more than 80% of most balance sheets made up of intangible assets

"Relationships immediately bring you to the idea of 'reputation' and 'trust', to the territory of intangible assets. Ten years ago about 80% of the balance sheet was made up of tangible assets; today, it is the opposite, with more than 80% of most balance sheets made up of intangible assets: goodwill, brand, reputation, trust – all the things that you can't see. Ultimately, the trust in the brand and its reputation provides the organisation with its license to operate, which is probably the most valuable effect of any brand.

"Hence trust has enormous value. It is worth trillions of dollars in today's economy. Trust within the company, among colleagues, among employees, between leadership and employees, between divisions, between suppliers and the company – that trust is the oil that allows the enterprise to operate externally and internally.

"If you don't have trust, all you have in its place are rules and regulations. Regulation is cost heavy compared to trust, which lubricates relationships, enables things to happen, speeds things up, liberates partnerships, collaboration, co-creation – all that we need today.

"So the idea that brand is something that the CMO handles and can be projected to the world is a dangerous misconception. Trust is not something you can manufacture: it is an outcome of being trustworthy and the main question becomes, 'How can we be more trustworthy?'

"Trust has three dimensions. The first is competence: 'Can you do what you tell me you will do? Will you deliver your promise?' The second is judgment: 'Have you got a track record of making well judged decisions?' The third is character: 'Do you have integrity? Are you only in this for yourself? Will you rip me off?'"

Four types of Trust

The Trust Quadrant in Illustration 11.6 shows four different types of trust which I believe form overall trust. The only variation from Kevin's framework is the addition of 'benevolence' as an essential character trait of a trusted brand. As Theodore Roosevelt said: *"Nobody cares how much you know, until they know how much you care."* Benevolence means a brand recognises that trust has mutual advantages; that it sees its own success in protecting you to advance your goals or improve your life. Because some brands might have considerable integrity but not care very much if at all.

ILLUSTRATION 11.6	THE 'TRUSTED' QUADRANT - FOUR TYPES OF TRUST	
	CAPABILITY	**CHARACTER**
OUT	COMPETENCE	BENEVOLENCE
IN	JUDGEMENT	INTEGRITY

© THE Enduring Strategic Brand

Among the four, two types of trust are of a functional nature, 'competence' and 'judgment', and two are emotional ones: 'integrity' and 'benevolence'. A truly trusted brand needs to have all four.

The **Walt Disney** Company   Disney is a trusted brand. Arguably Disney is uniquely 'competent' on its purpose; people have confidence in its 'judgment' and consider the organisation to have 'integrity' – while the perception of Disney's 'benevolence' is particularly strong.

amazon Who would distrust Amazon's 'competence' and 'judgment'? Doesn't Amazon also express a high level of 'benevolence' in its own way, by integrating every step of the customer journey into core functionality, so the customer's needs are fulfilled simply? Some might question the online retailer's 'integrity' but overall, Amazon is a high trust brand.

Before a series of incidents adversely affected the brand, BP's brand measures reflected a high level of trust in the 'competence' of the company; and with Beyond Petroleum, deep trust in its 'judgment' and 'integrity', especially when compared to peers. Benevolence was split between audiences – the general population's trust was low (as for the whole sector), with a perception of an imbalance of power and greed.

Exceptions to the rules of Brand Trust?

An interesting debate arises about a few companies who are successful despite not fulfilling all these trust types. For example, Goldman Sachs, Exxon Mobil or Ryanair.

RYANAIR Robert Jones is strategist at Wolff Olins, visiting professor at the University of East Anglia and author of '*Branding, a Very Short Introduction*'. Robert told me: "*Ryanair became Europe's biggest airline with none of the attributes of a traditional brand-led business, without even a single logo used consistently. Yet Ryanair unquestionably had a brand. Ryanair's operational efficiencies created a very clear brand in people's minds: they knew exactly what to expect and what not to expect from the airline. Its brand was an external idea, out in consumers' minds, rather than an internal managerial driver. The Ryanair brand was not, in that sense, a cause – but it was very successful at brand as effect.*

In the last three years, Ryanair has adopted some of the traditional principles of branding. It now has a chief marketing officer, Kenny Jacobs, who has introduced an internal mantra, 'Always Getting Better', and an external slogan, 'Low fares. Made simple'. Under Jacobs, Ryanair has dramatically improved its customer experience. But Ryanair still resists the idea of being brand-led. It's a practical, operational business, not a high-brand business like Virgin. It measures the experience it offers, not the brand. Its brand is the effect of what it does, not the cause."

So, a brand can potentially be successful without fulfilling all four areas of trust. Ryanair, Goldman Sachs and Exxon Mobil attract extremely high levels of trust for their 'competence' and are successful brands…but cannot be considered trusted brands. And we would strongly argue that incomplete trust is a considerable vulnerability and major risk into the future.

Illustration 11.7 positions the brands discussed in this chapter for the type of trust they engender…and you might want to test yours against these axes.

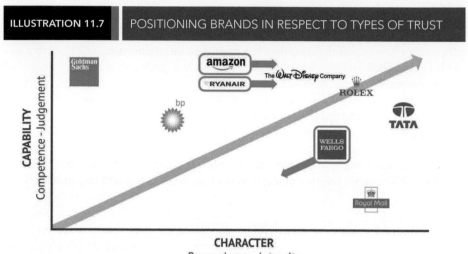

| ILLUSTRATION 11.7 | POSITIONING BRANDS IN RESPECT TO TYPES OF TRUST |

© THE Enduring Strategic Brand

HOW TO BUILD TRUST - A MODEL

How might and should enterprises build a trusted brand and therefore generate more future sustainable value? There is a science to building trust.

My experience is that using the trust model below in the context of your own organization will help enhance your brand trust and its value generation. As Stephen M.R. Covey, author of 'The Speed of Trust', says: *"Contrary to what most people believe, trust is not some soft, illusive quality that you either have or you don't; rather, trust is a pragmatic, tangible, actionable asset that you can create."*

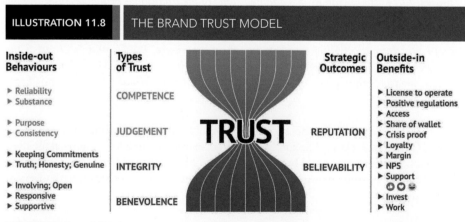

| ILLUSTRATION 11.8 | THE BRAND TRUST MODEL |

© THE Enduring Strategic Brand

Let's examine the trust model diagram from left to right, from inputs to outputs, from building trust, to building reputation, and ultimately gaining support. On the left-hand side, each of the four types of Trust emanate from behaviours and traits that reflect:

- WHO the brand is - e.g. keeping commitments, telling the truth
- WHAT it does – e.g. substance, purpose
- HOW it lives / communicates – e.g. involving and supportive.

I have always admired organisations which combine the following simple guidelines:

- WHO: "Be yourself" ["*Because everyone else is already taken*" said Oscar Wilde];
- WHAT: "Always do the right thing";
- HOW: "Say what you do; do what you say".

Moving to the centre of the Trust model, high levels of the four types of trust result into a strongly trusted brand, which at a strategic level, generates a strong 'reputation' and 'believability' in the brand.

On that basis, stakeholders will actively manifest their support with their own means (right-hand side). In B2C, Trust will attract loyalty and margin across sectors and geographies. In B2B, it will open markets and earn share of wallet and better pricing. In B2G, it will provide license to operate and more favourable regulatory contexts. In society, it will attract media support, encourage shareholder investment and persuade people to work for the brand.

Ultimately we want Trust to result in active support. As the research from the Reputation Institute shows in illustration 11.9, it is 'Enterprise and Brand' which drive willingness to support, more than 'Products and Services'. To which entrepreneur and author Lisa Gansky says wonderfully: "*A brand is a voice and a product is a souvenir*"

ILLUSTRATION 11.9	ENTERPRISE AND BRAND ARE DRIVING SUPPORT

REPUTATION INSTITUTE

Companies Will Benefit from Telling Their Company Story
- Enterprise Drives **60% of Willingness to Support**

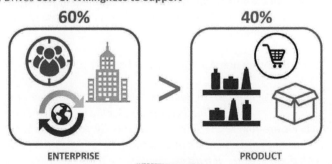

ENTERPRISE > PRODUCT

SUPPORTIVE BEHAVIOURS
RECOMMEND COMPANY • SAY SOMETHING POSITIVE • GIVE THE BENEFIT OF DOUBT • TRUST TO DO THE RIGHT THING • BUY PRODUCTS • INVEST • WORK FOR COMPANY • WELCOME TO THE NEIGHBOURHOOD • RECOMMEND PRODUCTS • RECOMMEND AS AN INVESTMENT

Credit – The Reputation Institute

WHO: "Be yourself";
WHAT: "Always do the right thing";
HOW: "Say what you do; do what you say".

Shelly Lazarus makes a strong link between Trust, the Enduring Strategic Brand and strategic value creation:

"At a time past, if you talked to American Express card members, they would actually say: 'All things being considered, I'd just do business with American Express rather than anyone across any category'. Maybe not mayonnaise, but across almost any category, you could think of. When people have trust in your brand, you have license to operate broadly and deeply and this is a huge gift.

It also makes a massive difference in times of vulnerability because one day, bad stuff is going to happen. So let's build up the goodwill beforehand and be ready to act as a trusted brand in the circumstances: be out in the open and admit a mistake; come forward and admit to everyone that you did something wrong; that some people did something wrong and are no longer part of the organization; operate a full recall, as in the masterfully led Johnson & Johnson Tylenol case in 1982; and be ahead, so you don't let the media come after you and accuse you".

Perrier Perrier's drawback over 25 years ago is a case in point. The French sparkling water brand was tarnished by a contamination issue. Perrier, which stands for 'natural purity' seized the initiative and held their hands up to the public to explain the problem. *"Firstly, we might have a small level of impurity; so we will remove all our bottles from the shelves immediately; and we won't market again until our purity has returned to perfect and we have a systemic assurance of quality."* This message was advertised so extensively that many people, myself included, were worried that this incident would tarnish the brand forever. Actually, it didn't, for the very reasons Shelly highlights.

One of the most critical insights about trust is that it is earned not claimed.

As Shelly says, *"If you take a strategic perspective to being a trusted brand, know that you earn trust by behaviour and not by claiming it. It comes right out of the ethics, the values, the principles and the behaviours of the company. Only your audience can conclude that you are to be trusted...and they know."*

I asked Shelly to spontaneously name a few Trusted Brands:

Johnson&Johnson *"Johnson & Johnson, which is why, when the trust was violated, this became so significant. Volvo is another, with everything they do to ensure your safety. Disney undoubtedly. Amazon is becoming a trust brand, because it is one of these companies that can go to lots of different places and bring their consumers with them because of trust.*

Since the financial crisis, if you asked consumers in the United States to rank bank brands based on trust, the number one brand was Wells-Fargo, year after year and by a wide margin. It was a matter of character and behaviour: they were looked at as non-Wall Street, care about people, small businesses, didn't have all the fancy stuff that the people in New York had. And so, when they violated trust, the way they did with the fake accounts scandal that was revealed in October 2016, it was lethal. They failed on the first rule of a trusted brand: 'tell the truth and tell it fast'.

And I know people who have an account and called the Wells-Fargo number to just check that they didn't have extra accounts they would not know about. And the call centre said: "Why would you think we would do that?" And the customers said: "Have you been reading the newspaper?" All meaning Wells Fargo doesn't seem to have informed their own people broadly enough."

Measuring Trust

Reputation is the outcome of trust, which means we can reasonably measure brand trust through reputation. Using advance regression analysis, multiple studies have demonstrated the almost perfect correlation between a trusted Strategic Brand and a strong reputation.

We have borrowed measures from a few different sources and surveys: The Reputation Institute, Readers Digest, The Good Relations Group Tripple G rating, BrandSpark International etc. (Note 4) - Illustration 11.10 shows the outcomes of two of them.

| ILLUSTRATION 11.10 | REPUTATION INSTITUTE AND READERS DIGEST 2016 RANKING |

Reputation Institute 2016 Global RepTrack® 100

Rank	Company	RepTrack® Pulse Score
1	Rolex	78.4
2	The Walt Disney Company	78.2
3	Google	78.1
4	BMW Group	77.9
5	Daimler	77.7
6	Lego	77.4
7	Microsoft	77.0
8	Canon	76.9
9	Sony	76.7
10	Apple	76.6

Credit - The Reputation Institute 2016 Global RepTrack ® 100; The Readers Digest 2016 Trusted Brand ® Survey.

Rolex, Disney and Google top the 2016 reputation list, with BMW, Daimler and Lego close fourth to sixth. The key characteristic of these brands is the consistent high level of trust with customers across all 15 markets studied. What is also fascinating is how strongly these high trust levels correlate to the key Imperatives of the Strategic Brand: for example, high quality products - *functional excellence;* open communication – *authentic;* strong vision for the future – *future embracing;* caring about employees – *people led and people leading,* etc.

Another key take out from the study is that the aggregated reputation index increases year on year, meaning that companies can't only maintain strong reputation and trust, but need to constantly strive to improve them. Standing still means going backwards. There is particular scope for companies to improve their corporate narrative that can both raise public awareness in general and increase knowledge about what the company really stands for.

Lastly, companies in the survey with the highest levels of reputation and trust receive active support from more than half of respondents, sometimes rising to an extraordinary 80 per cent, as trust continues to grow.

Avoid the 'cover up' CSR trap to build Trust

Do not fall into the trap of thinking that CSR investments will act as a shortcut for building trust. A lot of CSR is historically used as a tactical excuse to balance the wants of shareholders, customers, employees, suppliers and local communities. However, unless CSR is intrinsically connected to the core purpose and is central to the business, like for example, Unilever's Sustainable Living Plan, it is not worth the investment. As CEO, Paul Polman says, *"If it doesn't build the business, I think it is unsustainable."*

"If it doesn't build the business, I think it is unsustainable."

CSR is rarely done well
Experiences with BP and other organisations over the years have shown me how vulnerable and largely ineffective most CSR activities are – unless they manage to meet the following criteria:

- Be genuine – if not, at worst, they will appear as pure self-interest; at best, as enlightened self-interest;
- Emanate directly from the company's purpose and values;
- Be strategically aligned with the business, contributing to its objectives;
- Be central to the organisation, rather than nice to have at its periphery;
- Be owned and championed by many rather than few;
- Not used to distract from a negative impact on society, or a way to repair a reputation – these are major causes of CSR backfiring;
- Establish the tangible impact of the investment - have a performance managed existence and demonstrable value creation model
- Add value beyond money through embedded volunteering which provides intelligence to your cause;
- Be long term rather than short-lived or opportunistic.

CSR is usually not done well

Here are some of former BP CEO John Browne's thoughts on 'The Death of Corporate and Social Responsibility' from his book 'Connect' (Note 5): "CSR – or 'Environmental, Social, Governance' (ESG), as it is known in the investment community – has failed in its main purpose of building a stronger relationship between business and society. It has proven to be irrelevant to a company's reputation in the face of corporate scandals. It is a small, uninspiring answer to a problem that requires a big-picture solution. Inside business, executives view CSR as a fluffy, largely irrelevant cost centre. For civil society groups, it is meaningless propaganda that fails to achieve their goals. Neither side is satisfied. As one of the earliest CEO proponents of CSR, I feel well placed to call for its final demise.

The criticism from people inside and outside business centres around one crucial shortcoming: CSR is fundamentally disconnected from a company's core commercial purpose and activity. This has four main flaws: First, CSR ambitions are rarely realised because they lack the active participation of the big-spending commercial functions such as production and marketing. Second, centralised CSR teams tend to take too narrow a view of the relevant external stakeholders. Third, CSR focuses too closely on limiting the downside. Companies often see it only as protecting their reputations, perhaps to get away with irresponsible behaviour elsewhere. Finally, CSR programmes tend to be short-lived."

John cites Unilever's Paul Polman, who equally paints a discouraging picture of the status quo - "This is how CSR works in most companies – and I'm not trying to be cynical because it's better than not doing it at all. The typical CSR executive is 55-years-old; he wants to work for another three years on something less stressful. There are some good projects going on in the company, which make it into the first three pages of the annual report. They maintain relationships with some very safe NGOs. It is about giving an ambulance away. It's about opening a hospital and it's about linking it a little bit to the business. But it's merely post-rationalisation. It's definitely not the business model. In reality it's very much separate from the business.

The disconnect between CSR and commercial operations means that companies with superb CSR records can also be hugely damaging to society. Howard Davies, the Chairman of Royal Bank of Scotland, cites a handful of investment banks which, in the run-up to the financial crisis, "had very good CSR on the one hand but who had completely lost touch with what the core of their business was doing for the economy and for society". An even more damning indictment of CSR is the story of Enron, the energy company which collapsed in the US's largest ever bankruptcy and corporate corruption scandal. Up until the moment that allegations emerged of concealed debts and exaggerated profits, Enron was widely lauded as a CSR champion..."

Improve society with your brand strategy

This doesn't sound the death knell of CSR but we come back to the absolute need that CSR is done well. The Edelman Trust Barometer provides a strong incentive, as 81 per cent of respondents said they believed a company could engage in activities that

BOTH increased profits and improved economic and social conditions. Here are a few examples:

Unilever's Sustainable Living Plan - As John Browne notes: *"When Unilever want to change the way they source ingredients to ensure security of supply and an improved life for farmers, they instruct their procurement team, not the CSR department"*

Airbnb's Disaster Response - During and directly after a natural disaster, temporary housing for relief workers and those who are displaced can be hard to find. Airbnb activates its community to support local and national efforts in addressing this need. In partnership with local, regional, federal and global relief agencies, Airbnb automatically contacts hosts in the impacted and surrounding areas asking if they have extra space to share with their displaced neighbours. Hosts who respond choose to list their spaces free of charge, and Airbnb waives all booking fees. Guests and hosts in the area also have access to Airbnb's 24/7 customer support.

Toyota's Approach to the Olympics and Paralympics - Toyota's societal drivers behind their commitment are to serve Japanese society through putting their weight in support of Tokyo 2020; make the world a better place through encouraging the practice of sports; enhance inclusivity through embracing the Paralympic cause; transform mobility through learning from and associating with sports. But it is the way Toyota commits that commands admiration - rather than bidding for Tokyo 2020 only, they committed to a minimum of 10 years; rather than selecting markets for their partnership with the International Paralympics, they applied for all 206 countries, a first ever; instead of making their participation an add-on, they are committed to making sports an integral part of who they are.

BP's Target Neutral - This is a scheme to neutralise emissions by funding projects that help to offset CO_2. The scheme struggled in its early days as it was mainly positioned as CSR, led by corporate. I remember BMW telling us: *"Our objective is not to offset the CO_2 of our vehicles, but to reduce emissions as much as possible through technology."* Today, the scheme is thriving, thanks to former colleague Andrea Abrahams. The main difference is that Target Neutral is now strategically embedded in the organization - it has been adopted and leveraged by key BP businesses as part of their solution offering. Rather than standing alone, it has become an important part of an end-to-end scheme to 'reduce, replace, offset' emissions.

I am not a 'corporate idealist', I am a 'corporate realist': CSR and societal marketing is a good thing when done well.

Fourteen ways to build and protect a Trusted Brand

Building on the elements we've explored above, including the trust model, the advice from Shelly Lazarus and our review of CSR, here are some thoughts on how I have tried in practice to build, maintain, protect and enhance a trusted brand:

1. <u>Be strategic and deliberate on building Trust</u> - only by applying the Brand Trust Model consistently will you create the right input – trustworthy behaviours, resulting in trust that in turn yields reputation and positive actions towards the brand. A simplified version of the Brand Trust Model is shown in Illustration 11.11:

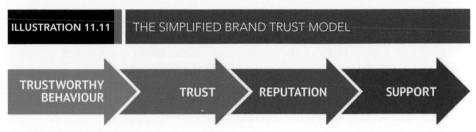

ILLUSTRATION 11.11 | THE SIMPLIFIED BRAND TRUST MODEL

| TRUSTWORTHY BEHAVIOUR | TRUST | REPUTATION | SUPPORT |

© THE Enduring Strategic Brand

2. <u>Never breach the four main pillars</u> of <u>trustworthiness</u> – deliver on your promise; be genuine in what you stand for and say; stand out from the crowd; deliver a consistent experience.

3. <u>'Look at yourself in the mirror in the morning'</u> – said Jack Welch. Rather than writing lots of rules or detailed legalese, this is a simple way for you and your associates to check if you are proud of what you are doing.

4. <u>Live according to your brand purpose</u> – the most trusted brands are fully consistent with their mission and therefore don't risk being misunderstood or misrepresented – this is the main filter of 'doing CSR well'. The examples of Rolex, Walt Disney, Google and BMW are shown in Illustration 11.12, with more cases in Chapter 1.

ILLUSTRATION 11.12 | HOW BRANDS DRIVE TRUST AND REPUTATION FROM DEEPLY LIVING THEIR PURPOSE

EXAMPLES OF GLOBAL BRAND PURPOSE AND STRONG REPUTATION   REPUTATION INSTITUTE

"We exist to assure that our customers are always first."   Strong 78.4

"We exist to create magic in the world."   Strong 78.2

"We exist to make information universally accessible -- while doing no evil."   Strong 78.1

"We exist to inspire people on the move and to shape tomorrow."   Strong 77.9

Credit – The Reputation Institute Global Rep Trak

5. <u>Focus</u> - be selective of what you do, and do it well. Don't be idealistic - you cannot solve all the world's problems. But you can make a huge difference and your organisation can be known and valued for its chosen areas, which you might even 'own' reputationally.

6. <u>Put execution and the 'little things' first</u> - rather than putting huge amounts of effort into grand marketing schemes, address the day-to-day problems your stakeholders might have at all levels of the organisation. With the pervasive nature of social media today, doing these small things will go a very long way.

7. <u>Trust</u> – the assumption that trust does not exist contributes considerably to the high cost and high complexity of doing business.

8. <u>Nurture relationships through a series of basic best practices</u> - be loyal to one another; never judge – first seek to understand; laugh with others; take issues directly to the source; express genuine appreciation; help others with critical tasks; 'people are not problems: problems are problems'; smile frequently; start with 'how can I serve you?'

    As General Colin Powell said: *"The day soldiers stop bringing you their problems is the day you have stopped leading them. They have either lost confidence that you can help them or concluded that you don't care. Either case is a failure of leadership."*

9. <u>Build referrals and online communities</u> – *"By creating a community, you create trust,"* says BlaBlacar, a ride-sharing service company based in France. They built trust with their online community using six pillars: declare [your personal details], rate [your experience], engage / commit [by pre-paying your ride], be active, moderate [by validating information], and link [with other social media engagements]. They have reached unprecedented levels of digital trust. (Note 6)

10. <u>Always tell the truth</u> - avoid falling into advertising 'beautiful lies'. By wanting 'sexy' ads, some brand stories are magnified, modified and idealised – to the point where they risk misrepresenting the truth and reality of the organisation.

11. <u>Place content over communication</u> - *'Facts talk louder than words'* – therefore, prove the truth through action. It is generally accepted that 90 per cent of an organisation's trust and reputation is determined by what the organisation does and 10 per cent by what it says. Because as Henry Ford said: *"You can't build a reputation on what you are going to do"*

12. <u>Say what you do, do what you say – and be who you are</u> – one of my favourite guidelines, largely inspired from the ISO norms but wonderfully powerful and practically helpful.

13. Reduce unbalance of power – this is one of the greatest challenges to trust: corporate and major companies can look impersonal, dominating and like 'Big Brother' to individuals. From 2005, led by CEO Sam Palmisano, IBM empowered its employees to engage in Web 2.0 dialogue through blogging and social networks, generating trust by developing meaningful relationships with stakeholders.

14. Be consistent across all audiences - don't segment trust! For example, being courted as a business class traveller but neglected as a family holiday standard traveller is disastrous. Providing all stakeholders with a consistent experience is a big challenge for enterprises – but it's a must for building trust.

Perhaps you will want to test these 14 tenets against the inspiring story of an extraordinary global company from India, Tata - because Tata has Trust at its core and is a world-class example of well-executed CSR at scale.

OUR EXEMPLARY STRATEGIC BRAND FOR TRUST: TATA

This is: Tata's logo:

Leadership with trust

This is: Dr. Mukund Rajan's email signature. Dr. Rajan is Chairman - Tata Global Sustainability Council, and Chief Ethics Officer, Tata group:

This is: Tata's mission statement: *'To improve the quality of life of the communities we serve globally, through long-term stakeholder value creation based on Leadership with Trust.'*

This is: The way Tata's mission and vision permeate throughout the organization, with the example of a Tata Motors presentation – you will find a multitude of similar examples across the Tata businesses.

MISSION

"At the Tata Group, our purpose is to improve the quality of life of the communities we serve. We do this through leadership in sectors of national economic significance, to which the Group brings a unique set of capabilities."

(www.tata.com)

VISION

"The Tata name is a unique asset representing **LEADERSHIP WITH TRUST**. *Leveraging this asset to unify our companies is the route to long-term success and delivery of returns to the shareholder in excess of the cost of capital."*

Uniquely to Tata, Trust appears at the centre of everything Tata Group stands for and does - trust is utterly Tata's culture.

Uniquely to Tata, Trust appears at the centre of everything Tata Group stands for and does - trust is utterly Tata's culture.

And as Tata also appreciates the strategic importance of the brand, trust and brand are inextricably linked. No wonder it is an Exemplary Strategic Brand that we can be inspired by.

For many years I led BP's 'Sustainable Mobility' and represented the group at the World Business Council for Sustainable Development. On a number of occasions I was fortunate to observe former Chairman, Ratan Tata's personal commitment to preserve the environment. He was always keen to consider every possible option – I remember his leadership in exploring the Jatropha tree as a source of bio fuels or for hydrogen mobility. I believe his mantra is the union of environment + development + business. This long leadership legacy probably explains why Tata was ranked number one for Asia by the 2016 Sustainability Leaders Survey - for its efforts in advancing sustainable development (along with Unilever in Europe).

Tata challenged, as no Brand is immune

Just before writing this chapter, a major challenge to Tata reached the public domain. On the 24th October 2016, the Tata Sons' Chairman, Cyrus Mistry, was deposed and replaced temporarily by Ratan Tata, the iconic former Chairman for 21 years. Reasons behind his departure included strategic differences on how to deal with the lossmaking steel business at Port Talbot in the UK and a concern on the risks of eroding the group's ethical principles relating to a commitment to Japan's NTT DoCoMo.

Over the following months, Mr. Mistry fought back with a hard-hitting public campaign built on multiple accusations that pointed to *"the risk of major write downs in Europe"*, to *"Mr. Tata's pet projects like the Tata Nano"*, to *"an aggressive and risky foreign expansion"* and *"a distorted governance"*.

A rescue package for Port Talbot was agreed early December 2016, a major relief for its 8,000 workers. Conversations with DoCoMo are ongoing with a different approach. On the 13th January 2017, Natarajan Chandrasekaran, head of Tata Consultancy Services, was anointed the seventh Chairman in Tata's 149-year history.

It is not our purpose here to assess Mr. Mistry's allegations nor to detail the three-month public debate, which Ratan Tata qualified as, *"turbulent, wasteful and destroying"* in a letter to staff, but rather to reflect on Brand Trust, because these events have the critical dimension of Trust at their very heart.

The DoCoMo story is revealing. In 2008, NTT DoCoMo bought a 26 per cent stake in Tata Teleservices for $2.7bn, aiming to participate in the huge opportunity of the Indian market. The purchasing contract included a 'stop-loss' clause that obliged Tata Sons to buy back its stake at half the investment value in 2014 if performance targets were not met...which they were not. Consequently, DoCoMo's new management exercised the exit clause. This execution was subsequently blocked by the Reserve Bank of India and then the Finance Ministry. Among other arbitration and legal actions, DoCoMo accused Tata Sons of having misrepresented the situation to the Indian authorities to avoid the payment, which Tata denied.

Over the months, Ratan Tata is commented to have become increasingly unhappy with these developments and his entourage remarked: *"Mr. Tata is a man of his word. If he makes a commitment, he'll keep it"*. Ratan Tata apparently wrote a letter to Mr. Yamada, his former counterpart at DoCoMo, saying that this difficult issue would not have arisen if both had still been in command. Rightly or wrongly and it is certainly not for us to say, the previous Tata Chairman was perceived to have departed from the 'ethos of the group' on his dealing with DocoMo, Port Talbot and other cases...

Every major company will face business challenges and respond in its own way. Their response will both be guided by who they are, and what their brand values stand for ... and these actions will further define their brand. As illuminated below by Dr. Mukund Rajan, Tatas' way is guided by Trust.

A short introduction to Tata – a house of brands

In 1868, Jamsetji Tata founded Tata as a trading company in Mumbai, India. A first industrial venture was in textiles but it quickly broadened its activities. Today Tata is multinational, employing over 660,000 people with combined 2015-16 revenues of $103.5bn and market cap. of $116bn (31/03/2016). Roughly two-thirds of the Group's activities are now outside its home market, following a smattering of acquisitions in the 2000s like Tetley, Teleglobe, General Chemicals, Brunner Mond, Jaguar-Land Rover and Corus Steel.

The Tata group comprises over 100 independent companies operating in more than 100 countries across the six continents. It is a true conglomerate, with activities spreading across communication & ITeS, consumer & retail, defence & aerospace, financial services, manufacturing, infrastructure and services. Tata holds multiple global leadership positions: among the top ten vehicle manufacturers, the second largest IT services company by market cap, the second largest tea company, etc.

Tata is a house of brands, as represented in the kaleidoscope of the group's brands in illustration 11.13, which we will discuss in more detail later. In 2016, Brand Finance valued Tata's multi-brand portfolio at over $23bn.

ILLUSTRATION 11.13 | EXAMPLES OF TATA GROUP'S BRANDS

Tata Sons is the principal investment holding company and promoter of Tata companies. It is a distinctive company in that 66 per cent of its capital is held by philanthropic trusts, which support charitable causes in spaces such as education, health, livelihood generation and art and culture.

Tata 'walks the talk', spending in excess of $200 million annually on CSR. Over 70,000 Tata employees from across the globe have registered to participate in TATA's volunteering initiatives, 'Tata Engage', and contributed over 1.2 million hours of their time to social causes last year.

Tata as a Strategic Brand

As we have ongoing exchanges, I remain impressed with Dr. Mukund Rajan, especially his calm confidence on every subject we touch. My sense is that he is guided by strong principles and embodies the notion that if you want your brand to have the values of virtue and trustworthiness, then lead by example and be virtuous and trustworthy yourself.

In *'THE Enduring Strategic Brand'* system represented in Illustration 11.14, Tata receives a strong rating on all 13 imperatives. The assessment is based on Tata's unique impact in India and the conviction that the brand is building a strong resonance elsewhere and will therefore be able to replicate a consistent image and message beyond Indian borders. This view is reflective of the words of the MD of Tata Teleservices, Mr. Srinath, that *"Our core values are universal."*

ILLUSTRATION 11.14 'THE ENDURING STRATEGIC BRAND' IMPERATIVES - TATA

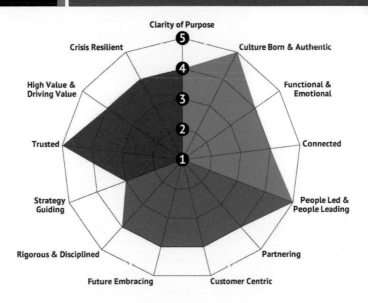

The Tata brand is particularly distinctive for having the strongest ratings in the combination of 'Culture Born and Authentic', 'People Led and People Leading' and, of course, 'Trusted'. Let's explore the idea of being 'Trusted', which is at Tata's core.

Trusted Tata

In Morgen Witzel's excellent book '*Tata, The Evolution of a Corporate Brand*', the author reveals that Tata executives spoke, *"with quiet passion about the importance of trust. People trust Tata because of heritage and because they continue to believe in their mission."* (Note 7)

"Trust has been the essential pillar for the way in which the group has been viewed by stakeholders over generations," concurs Dr. Rajan who qualifies his perspectives on each of the four types of trust.

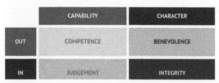

Integrity – *"There is a shared sense that Tata is a trusted brand, a corporate group that you do business with, whose products and services are truly intended to deliver value for customers, and who will never renege on a commitment.* Tata is seen as a group that not only has a commitment to doing good business, but is also in the business of doing good."

Benevolence; with Purpose – This idea is at the heart of Tata, guided by the Group's founder Jamsetji Tata's early philosophy that *"in a free enterprise, the community is not just another stakeholder in the business, but is in fact the very reason for its existence".*

Dr. Rajan continues: *"This profound statement found resonance with our unique ownership structure. The sons of the founder each endowed charitable trusts with their equity holdings in the holding company of the Tata group, Tata Sons. As a result, around two thirds of the ownership of Tata Sons still vest with charity today. This notion of trusteeship was articulated by former Tata Chairman, J R D Tata, who said: 'The wealth created by Tata is held in trust for the people and used exclusively for their benefit. The cycle is thus complete. What came from the people has gone back to the people many times over.' This unique ownership structure gives Tata employees a sense of higher purpose about the work we do and its virtuous cycle, which engenders trust in the Tata brand."*

Judgment – *"For years before the 1990s, economic context was strongly controlled and this bred corruption. Tata refused to indulge in that kind of behaviour and therefore our growth was slower. The then Chairman of Tata,*

Jehangir Tata, who served for 53 years from 1938 to 1991, would repeatedly state that he was satisfied with our rate of growth, because we would not cut corners. We paid a price for a brand built on trust and for a significant period of our history we were not able to grow as fast as our competitors. But when circumstances changed, we built on trust and grew much faster than others"

CAPABILITY	CHARACTER
OUT COMPETENCE	BENEVOLENCE
IN JUDGEMENT	INTEGRITY

Competence; with Customer Centricity – *"That we all think we are serving a higher purpose by working at Tata shows up in crises like the terrorist attacks at the Taj Mumbai on 26 November 2008. As many as 11 employees - a third of the hotel's casualties - died helping 1,500 guests escape. Their ultimate dedication like that of so many Tata lifers, reflects a sense of higher purpose to help make the world a better place."*

Trusted Tata is built on people, authenticity, discipline of brand and partnering

As might be expected, Tata's basis for trust starts with people.

People led & People leading

Dr.Rajan: *"Leaders in an organisation need to speak with one voice on the importance of values, because the rest of the organisation takes its cues from the language and the actions of leadership. This is critical. I cannot think of one speech by Mr. Ratan Tata in all his years as Chairman, where he did not emphasise the importance of our value system.*

"When new people come into the organisation, we communicate our values, code of conduct, and the anecdotes which help people to understand the way in which our organisation responds to crises and challenges. This storytelling is critical because new employees need to believe that our values live beyond paper.

"Often, the reality of support is revealed during specific crises. In the 1970s the steel industry was dominated by the public sector. We had the privately run Tata Steel and the Jamshedpur plant named after our founder, Jamsetji Tata. Jamshedpur was a thriving, well-planned city thanks to his vision. A new Industry Minister emerged on the scene who wanted to nationalise Tata Steel and make it part of an already large public sector. The entire township, the employees, the unions and the local citizens turned out in support of the company, saying they would resist any government moves to nationalise Tata Steel. The government eventually dropped its plan. These moments when you face an almost existential challenge, demonstrate the impact of a brand created from a value system that people have faith in.

"Things will from time to time go wrong. We can never assume that a hundred per cent of your organization will line up to every single value a hundred per cent of the time. So, in times of controversy, it is important to respond transparently, and demonstrate your active

commitment to doing the right thing. An example of this is how we dealt with a scam that we had in the early 2000s with one of our financial services companies. We went beyond what any other Indian corporate would have done, to make all the relevant disclosures to regulators. We prosecuted the company's senior management and the managing director eventually went to jail. It was a grievous violation of our code of conduct – and we wanted to demonstrate our upset and that we would take action against those who were guilty.

One of Tata Brand's greatest achievements is the connected meaning it enjoys with all stakeholders.

Authentic, Connected & Customer Centric

As I have said before, authenticity – and being connected – is contradicted if a brand behaves differently with different audiences: if it is one thing to customers, another to employees and a third to shareholders. One of Tata Brand's greatest achievements is the connected meaning it enjoys with all stakeholders – as reflected in Illustration 11.15. Each core facet of the Tata Brand speaks powerfully and coherently to each key audience, while having specific relevance.

ILLUSTRATION 11.15	FACETS OF THE TATA CORPORATE BRAND RELATING TO VARIOUS STAKEHOLDER GROUPS					
	Consumers	**Employees**	**Financial Community**	**Politicians**	**Media**	**Country at large**
Service to the community	Sense of emotional warmth and community	Positive identification, works to support people like me	Creates stability and long-term value	Useful partner in nation- building	Constant source of stories about social programmes	Serves the people, aids those in need
Trust and integrity	Low risk to the consumer	Employer who will keep its promises	Low risk, safe and secure investment	Honest, incorruptible	Honest, incorruptible	Honest, incorruptible
Fairness and responsibility	Low risk, and fair treatment if a product is defective	Employer who is willing to talk and will deal fairly	Transparency, will be honest and not devious	Effect uncertain	Tries to deal fairly with everyone	Tries to deal fairly with everyone
Innovation and entrepreneurship	Superior to what competitors offer	Go-ahead company, opportunities for advancement	Opportunities for growth	Comes up with new products and services for the good of India	Constant source of stories about new products and ideas	Provides things that India needs
Global aspiration	Pride, company as good as any in the world	Company people can be proud to work for	Opportunities for growth	Helps raise India's profile abroad	Helps raise India's profile abroad	Source of national pride
Quality and value for money	Good for the consumer	Deals honestly with customers so makes employees feel proud	Efficient business, well run	Effect uncertain	Provides things that people want/need	Products and services can be trusted
Perception of 'goodness'	'Halo' effect goodness rubs off on the consumer	'Halo' effect goodness rubs off on the employee	Effect uncertain	Recognition of past services; 'halo' effect?	Tries its best to live up to its principles	Has India's best interests at heart

Credit – Tata, the evolution of a Corporate Brand, Morgen Witzel

Dr. Rajan explains how Tata strives to reach this position: *"We are always learning. We try to ensure that the local leadership is well integrated into the community. In many cases, especially where we make acquisitions, we hold onto and integrate the existing management into our way of thinking and value system."*

The MD of Tata Chemicals, R.Mukundan expanded on this idea: *"Our average time for integrating a new acquisition is now fifty days."* When he was told that the minimum time for integration is at least a year and that three years is usually recommended, he argued: *"We look for companies whose values fit with Tata's own and whose cultures can understand each other."*

Dr. Rajan agrees: *"Alignment of values and stability of management have given the workforce confidence that Tata is a group that intends to do the right thing, that we are patient and invest in training and teaching. This has been meaningful as we cascade our values.*

"But in each market, we also demonstrate our willingness to learn. For example, when we were refreshing our code of conduct, we found we had to articulate the clause on whistle-blowing carefully. A number of whistle-blowers tend to prefer anonymity. Our policies needed to reassure people that their identity would be secure, that they would not be acted against vindictively and that they should have the courage to come forward with their concerns. But we had strong conversations with our colleagues in Europe because of the behavioural legacy from the world wars, where informants were looked down upon. We were told to avoid any negative connotations, of seeming to encourage people to squeal and tell tales about their colleagues. We needed to position the policy so that people understood our common goal: if we all want the company to succeed, the local community to benefit and stakeholders to get value, it is important that when someone spots a problem, they raise it – so that the company can grow stronger.

"The wider point here is to always be willing to learn, to embrace the multicultural environment, and be willing to deal with feedback. You need to carry everyone with you. It doesn't mean you are a noisy democracy but that you are very sensitive to perspectives."

Rigour and Discipline of Brand
"In any large organisation, you need systems and processes, as well as checks and balances. You need a support structure in which people are vested with the responsibility to resolve dilemmas, to investigate issues, and to report back on whether the organisation is living up to their values. We have compliance related officers, but also 'ethics counsellors': people who are available to employees with grievances, concerns or dilemmas.

"The brand is something you can hang your hat on; we had a reputation, but we did not have a brand."

The same rigour applies to developing the Tata Brand. Brand development began in earnest in the early 1990s when Ratan Tata said: *"The brand is something you can hang your hat on; we had a reputation, but we did not have a brand."* As discussed earlier, this is the opposite of most situations, where building a brand aims to create a sustainable reputation. Though Tata already had an established reputation it still needed to create a true brand.

The Tata brand overtly defines itself as a House of Brands, some of which bear the Tata name and others don't, including several global brands the group acquired after 2000. Dr. Rajan explains: *"We have a long history of nurturing and supporting non-Tata named brands, which we created or acquired. Examples include the Taj, which represents our hospitality business and was created in 1903; Lakme, our cosmetic range created in 1952; Voltas air conditioning, Rallis agrochemicals, Titan, a watch brand created in 1984; and Vistara, our new full-service airline with Singapore Airlines. Brands do not necessarily carry the Tata name. Each brand needs a unique relationship with its customer base. We don't want to interfere with these brands unless it becomes essential to defend the larger values for which our group stands. Jaguar-Land Rover (JLR) is an example of this: it was a struggling company when we acquired it in 2008 but had a huge reservoir of goodwill amongst consumers across generations. Instead of impinging on this established relationship, we put the group's weight behind the company's turnaround, used our capital for new product development and ensured effective management for the Jaguar and Land Rover brands to send a strong signal that they are here to stay and succeed."*

A strong Partnering Ethos

Today, Tata has a joint venture with Singapore Airlines named Vistara. Here is the story of this partnership:

"In the early 90s, we were approached by Singapore airlines for a joint venture in India. The Indian government encouraged it for two reasons. First, India was trying to cement a strong partnership with Singapore as part of a new 'Look East' policy; and second, the government felt that Tata, which pioneered Indian aviation with the international carrier, Air India before it was nationalized, was well placed for this venture. Air India was in fact nationalised in the wake of Indian independence but the government retained our Chairman, Jehangir Tata as Air India's Chairman until 1977.

"India then had a series of coalition governments through the 1990s. One of these coalitions introduced a law that no foreign airline could hold equity in an Indian carrier effectively blocking the Tata-Singapore Airlines joint venture. In the late 90s the BJP party came to power and wanted to re-privatise Air India, which by that time had been run into the ground. The government ran a bidding process and we were shortlisted. But then they sat on our application and in the early 2000s, we decided to withdraw.

"Our Chairman at the time, Ratan Tata, wrote one of the sternest letters I have seen to anybody in government, explaining that since the early 90s we had been held back at every stage in our efforts to re-enter the aviation space. He told the government that after almost a decade of trying, we would now pull back. So for 13 years after this, there was no conversation with Singapore Airlines. But finally in 2013, the policy was amended again, permitting foreign airlines to acquire equity in domestic Indian carriers, thus allowing Singapore Airlines to again consider investing in India. The first company they approached for a joint venture was Tata.

"Because when people develop trust, it survives generations. There was no reason why Singapore Airlines should return to Tata in 2013; there was no commitment, no legally binding contract. But they had a strong sense that Tata was a partner they could trust. Many years after our initial plan, we finally agreed and co-created Vistara. This story illustrates the value of building a bond, where people want you to succeed, believe in you, and have faith that you are the right type of business with decent people for them to work with."

Trusted Tata creates long-term value across its stakeholder groups

There are substantial core benefits resulting and emanating from trust - and notably that strategy is led by the brand beliefs, as Dr. Rajan explains compellingly:

Strategy leading

"Two elements have usually helped us to make the right calls: long-termism and balance of interest.

"In a broader sense, and as a group, we always try to take a long view in the businesses we invest in. If a business seems to be floundering, we don't react in a cowboy fashion and shut it down overnight or sell it off. We are patient investors and try to support these businesses as much as possible.

"We do whatever is necessary: sometimes the economic cycle is awkward, so we have to use our financial power to hold out; sometimes the management may need help or to be replaced. We don't make knee-jerk reactions based on short-term signals. We always take the long view.

We observed this approach in action in the UK when on 7th December 2016, Tata made a commitment to secure jobs and production at Port Talbot and other steelworks, bringing an end to eight months of uncertainty.

"As to the second point about balance of interest: our mission is 'to improve the quality of life in the communities we serve globally, through long-term stakeholder value creation based on leadership and trust'. In the short-term, there may be choices that will impact a particular group of stakeholders. That's when you have to use the wisdom of experience. That's what we mean by balancing interests.

"An example is when a business is not doing well during an economic cycle and you have to consider, for instance, an employee separation scheme. This is obviously not great for the employee stakeholder group, but it is important for the investor stakeholder group or lenders. On other occasions, the business may be challenged and you have to retain knowledge workers, which means you are unable to pay a dividend. We did this last year at Tata Motors. Our Chairman was explicit: at this point of time, we simply do not have the capacity to pay dividends. If you are a short-term investor, please take your money elsewhere.

"A business is continuously faced with challenging decisions. Our philosophy takes the long view and in the short term makes the choices that create the best balance of interest across our stakeholder groups, with the prospect that when the challenges end, everyone can recover towards sustained profitable growth."

High Value & Driving Value

The obvious question about the trusted Tata Brand is: 'Does all this create value?' Yes, in numbers: the 2016 net profitability was $5 billion; and Brand Finance has valued Tata's multi-brand portfolio at over $23 billion in 2016. At the same time, Interbrand pegged Tata as the most valuable Indian Brand, 97 per cent more valuable than its closest Indian competitor.

By no means is this easy, as Tata competes in many different sectors, some of which are cyclical, in mature industries or extremely battled. Continuing focus needs to be given to temporary or underlying underperformance at some businesses. Tata's approach to these realities imbues its values and trust-based approach, including its 'balance of interest' and long-term approach.

Dr. Rajan: *"There are significant advantages to building our brand on trust. We have attracted some of the most talented managers in the country. Our approach has also earned us a powerful reputation with our lenders. We get some of the best interest rates in the market because people trust us with their money. We have a large base of dedicated, long-term shareholders, many of them retail investors, who buy Tata stock because they trust our commitment to deliver healthy returns over a period of time. They believe that Tata will not cheat shareholders. We are called a 'widow' stock.*

"Being trusted gives you enormous staying power. Over the last 100 years, for every decade of our existence, we have held onto our number one position in the market. And when times changed, like they did after 1991 when the Indian economy opened up, we were able to become the fastest growing corporate. Today we are the largest Indian corporate by every measure, whether it is top line ($103.5 billion in 2015-16), bottom line, number of employees (660,000), number of markets (over 100), and so on.

Staying true to our values might have meant slower growth at certain times but it has helped to create a very powerful brand, particularly during times of crisis."

Embracing the Future

With a capital investment of $35 billion over the last three years, Tata is always looking to the future. It just delivered new plants like Tata Steel's new 6 million ton per annum steel facility in India, new products like Jaguar's XE and new technologies like the Tata Consultancy Services Ignio platform, the world's first neural automation system for the enterprise.

Crisis Resilient, Functional & Emotional

Closing the circle, how does the trusted Tata Strategic Brand face crisis, such as the succession issue evoked earlier, and how does it help the organisation to win over the challenge? Dr. Rajan: *"When you hold a position of trust with your stakeholders – your customers, shareholders, lenders, value chain partners and employees – many want you to succeed. We have been facing a deeply challenging situation [as referred to before, public debates following the deposition of former Chairman Cyrus Mistry]. At times like these, the foundation of goodwill uniquely supports your brand."*

Trust at the Centre of Tata's Global Strategic Brand Campaign

The Tata Brand has a clear point of view that customers everywhere are looking for authentic brands, which have credibility and consistency, and which it feels good to engage with. Tata summarises this as *"no longer what you buy, but what you buy into"*. Hence, the group is pursuing a global Strategic Brand campaign in which the corporate brand reinforces and also benefits from the individual brands' campaigns to create a multiplier effect. Tata is committed to this long journey.

"No longer what you buy, but what you buy into."

Dr. Rajan: *"It started with seeking to understand internal perceptions, so the brand messages are in tune with the employees' views. We then identified the key drivers of brand equity, tested and ranked them with external stakeholders across multiple audience types and, finally, following considerable internal debates and validation of proof points for different messages, agreed on the three brand messaging corridors: 'Tata is Global'; 'Tata is Trustworthy'; 'Tata is a Good Corporate Citizen'.*

At the heart of the campaign are our employees, who will be our best brand ambassadors and will communicate to all other stakeholders that Tata is a successful, pioneering global enterprise with the community at its heart."

Trust, a Culture and Way of Being

The ultimate question of our Brand Trust Model is 'Do you believe?' *'THE Enduring Strategic Brand'* believes in the Tata Brand!

Tata brand's trust system is robust and strongly embedded. As a source of inspiration to other brands, Illustration 11.16 represents a simple pyramid diagram that captures how the bedrock of 'People', 'Authenticity', 'Discipline' and a 'Partnering' ethos underpins the deeply trusted Tata brand.

ILLUSTRATION 11.16 | THE HIERARCHY OF PILLARS SUPPORTING TATA'S TRUSTED BRAND

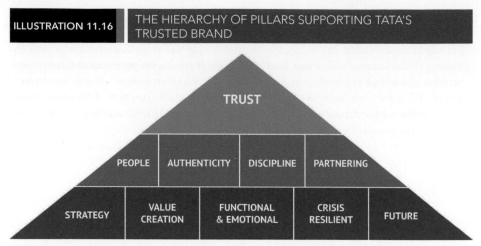

© THE Enduring Strategic Brand

Tata's trust culture is deeply part of the company's fabric and a way of being. What's more, we feel confident that by 2025, Tata will achieve its informal goal to touch the lives of a quarter of the world's population and emerge as one of the 25 most admired brands in the world.

Because we have trust in the power of their trust!

CHAPTER 12
HIGH VALUE AND DRIVING VALUE

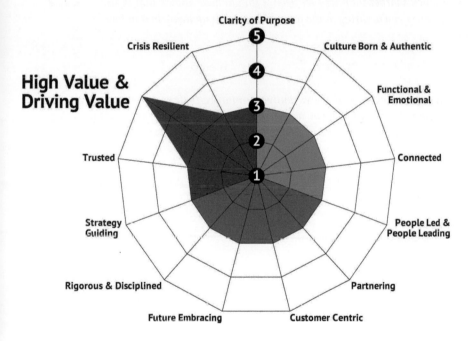

People know the price of everything and the value of nothing
Oscar Wilde

If you spend 34 of your 36-year career leading branded businesses and being accountable for the bottom line, the intimate link between brand and value creation may become second nature. Even when I was head of strategy or BP group chief sales and marketing officer, my portfolio included multi-billion-dollar businesses and, with them, the imperative to grow and deliver financial performance through building and leveraging the brand. I find an almost physical thrill in building a sophisticated brand or offer and translating it into exceptional financial value.

However, this connectivity is not always as obvious as it sounds to everybody. RBS's David Wheldon says that the constant consideration of value remains a key challenge for many marketers: *"Now that I sit at the RBS Group Executive Committee table, my understanding of business is much sharper than it's ever been. I should have known that before – because in marketing, unless you're sitting at the top table, you end up living in a bubble."*

The value challenge to the Strategic Brand

"When you see the issues around the executive committee table or a board, you have a better appreciation of the value that you are supposed to deliver from brand and marketing, and you have to deliver this in a context which makes sense to people.

"Looking back, I can see those moments when I think 'I can't believe I used to go into meetings and say "A, B and C". Now I see brand or marketing people coming and having the same approach and I say to myself: "that's not how you need to position it". People have to anchor things much more commercially. Once upon a time I wouldn't have bothered with the commercial anchor because I thought, 'Can't you see, how brilliant this is?' Now I've learned.

The brand and marketing industry is in a kind of crisis and has lost its sense of purpose. The reason it isn't taken more seriously is because it's not serious enough.

"I do think the brand and marketing industry is in a kind of crisis and has lost its sense of purpose. On the one hand, people say: "Marketing should be taken more seriously." And I reply: "No, the reason it isn't taken more seriously is because it's not serious enough."

The value imperative from the Strategic Brand

At Castrol we engineered and marketed engine lubricants which were sold at a higher price per litre than best champagnes. This meant that the brand and its marketing were everything, as Tim Stevenson, former Castrol CEO explains:

 *"The brand was behind everything we did, as the following story illustrates: one year Tom Crane, our CEO in the US, suddenly started*

to see sales slow down markedly. We were sufficiently worried about the impact on Tom's bottom line to experiment with his marketing budget. We had a big annual media budget in order to pump the brand and get the product out into the market. I can picture us sitting around the conference table in Tom's office in Wayne, New Jersey, talking about whether we could risk cutting the media budget for a three-month period. The analogy we used at the time was to imagine a vehicle going towards a gap the size of the Grand Canyon: you're going along the flat and then you come to big chasm in the ground, and on the other side of the chasm the land carries on flat again. I said: 'Well, if we go over the gap really fast we can get across it, land on the other side, and nobody will notice that we've taken three months out of the advertising budget.'

"That turned out to be wrong: towards the end of the three-month period, sales perceptively dipped as a result of having cut the marketing budget. This tells you that the brand was there and it was essential – we had the technology to keep the brand alive in the technical sense, pushing and promoting it in order to keep it in the forefront of people's minds – but support for the brand was crucial. That was a revealing reminder of some branded marketing fundamentals."

It was exactly the same paradigm with BP Ultimate, the BP performance fuel. We experienced similar symptoms and effects with our marketing investment as Castrol. BP Ultimate's brand with its supporting technology platform attracted a 15 per cent gross premium over quality fuels - which, when you consider fuel volumes and the impact on margin, represents massive dollars.

These two straightforward examples remind us how critical it is to be absolutely clear on the link between brand and value creation, inputs and outputs – in short, the 'brand business model'. And equally, to echo David Wheldon, how vital it is to express this in 'commercial' terms, so it is supported by colleagues around the board and executive tables, as a proven important part of how the organisation conducts business and performs - Nina Bibby talks about how this alignment gets formed at O2 in Chapter 7.

The value OF and FROM the Enduring Strategic Brand

I absolutely and intuitively believe that the Strategic Brand and Value make the perfect and necessary marriage. But the 'courtship' between them is challenging. So I have distilled this into two central questions which we will explore in the coming pages: what is the **value OF a brand** and why is it important; what is the **value FROM a brand**, i.e. how does it create value?

The Value OF the Strategic Brand

As its main custodian, how do you know that you are making real strategic progress on building your brand? CMOs measure many things – awareness, satisfaction, connectivity, presence, pulses, etc. – but how do they know that these measures are reflective of the right ingredients for value creation, for and from the brand? And how can they tell their story simply and convincingly to the multiplicity of stakeholders, especially those with a financial mindset?

To achieve this, I have settled on the use of a rather simple and crude tool: to repeatedly, consistently and independently measure the intrinsic value of the brand. Hopefully, this measurement will show that the brand's value is high and continuously growing. The goal and gauge, therefore, become simple: to strive for a 'high and growing brand value'.

The Value FROM the Strategic Brand

How do we prove the hard value brought by a brand to the business, whatever the nature of that value, in such terms that the financial market, CEOs and CFOs are all able to rally behind it? Which CMO has not had and doesn't continue to have the most ferocious debates with their CFO colleagues, similar to Tim Stevenson's story, on how much to put into the brand, especially in times of downturn?

WPP's Martin Sorrell, reminded me recently how acute the challenge remains: *"The Economist says that 'brands are the most valuable thing that companies as diverse as Apple and McDonald's own, often worth much more than property and machinery'. WPP's Millward Brown estimates that brands account for more than 30 per cent of the stock market value of companies in the S&P 500.*

"Brands have to be tended like garden plants, they must be constantly nurtured, fertilised, invested in and developed. A long-term approach for long-term success. If you invest in brands, you succeed. For example, you'd do three times better investing in the top 10 brands in our BrandZ survey every year, than you would do investing in the MSCI World index. People who invest in brands generate higher top-line like-for-like growth, which is the biggest determinant of total shareholder return.

"Unfortunately, this is not always what happens. A number of factors explain this – low 3 to 3.5 per cent worldwide GDP growth, little or no inflation, little pricing power, high focus on costs, short life expectancy of CEOs, CFOs and especially CMOs.

"If you look at the S&P500 over the last few years – and this is driven by post-Lehman risk-aversion and short-termism – they're now distributing more than 100 per cent of their profits as dividends and sharebacks. Companies lack the confidence to invest in the future."

When one does succeed in proving the importance of investment in the brand, this becomes hardwired into the financial reality and value creation imperatives of the organisation.

Value OF and value FROM

So, we have two basic requirements about value for a true Strategic Brand: the first is that its own intrinsic value is independently measured, and hopefully this measurement demonstrates that it is an ever more valuable key asset.

The second is that the business model that links brand to value generation is made crystal clear, is accepted by everyone and turned into reality, so that investing in the brand is not sporadic but a business imperative which, in turn, protects and drives enterprise value creation and growth.

HIGH VALUE OF A STRATEGIC BRAND

Castrol EDGE That Castrol's lubricants sell for a higher premium per litre than champagne is a clear example of the power of Strategic Brands adding value to the business. Similarly, in the drinks sector, the high value of brands was well instantiated by Smirnoff's $1 billion acquisition by Grand Met (now Diageo) in 1985, when Smirnoff's tangible assets were just $100 million.

Brand-driven value build at Diageo

DIAGEO Today, Diageo is highly regarded as a global company that understands the value of Strategic Brand building. Group CMO Syl Saller, is very clear that her brands, from Guinness to Johnnie Walker and Smirnoff to Tanqueray, create higher shareholder return (Note 1): *"Purpose-driven brands are empirically proven to create higher return. At Diageo, we've long recognised the value of purpose – the purpose of Johnnie Walker is to 'celebrate personal progress'; the purpose of Smirnoff is to 'bring inclusivity to a divided world'; and Diageo's purpose as a company is to 'celebrate life every day, everywhere'. People celebrate with our spirits because of their quality but they identify and resonate with the purpose of our brands."*

Syl echoes David Weldon's point that marketers need to anchor their craft more commercially (Note 2). *"Marketing needs to be the growth engine of the business, and if marketers aren't business people, that will never happen. You can't be credible without discipline. And you can't find growth without a bit of magic."*

Marketing needs to be the growth engine of the business, and if marketers aren't business people, that will never happen.

Syl talks from a position of high believability based on track record. As we are writing these lines, Diageo is reporting sales growth of 14.5% to £6.4 billion in the second half of 2016. This is also an organization which spends $2.5 billion a year in advertising and marketing, with an exemplary clarity on the balance between short-term investments to support sales and long-term build of the value of their brands. This is all done with the rigour and discipline of thorough measurements and valuations, using leading-edge financial approaches - of which deployed ROI type econometric analysis and zero-based budgeting (ZBB) are just examples.

How to measure the value of a Strategic Brand?

There are multiple ways and practices to measure the value of a brand. A number of blue chip companies, notably FMCG, have their own internal practice. The big four also offer this service, as well as some of the leading global marketing agencies.

Omnicom's Interbrand, WPP's BrandZ and Brand Finance are three specialist players in this industry. Their methodology differs to a certain extent, and for this reason, their brand valuations can vary. However, I am less concerned with the differences between these three brand valuation companies than motivated by the importance of brand valuation itself, as a strategic tool for shareholders, boards and CEOs, CMOs and both the finance and marketing departments.

In his recently published book, *'Brandfather'*, founder of Interbrand John Murphy recalls a series of big ticket, high profile mergers and acquisitions in the 1980s, including Smirnoff by Grand Met (Diageo) and Rowntree by Nestle, that began to shine a bright light on the value of intangible assets in the City. As a brand expert, John spotted a business opportunity in carving out a new expertise to give a value to brands when both City bankers and accountancy firms at this time were mystified. (Note 3)

Subsequently, John and his Interbrand team created a brand valuation methodology that assessed over 40 brands belonging to Ranks Hovis McDougall as it faced a hostile bid from an Australian company. Despite the bid falling away, RHM management decided to include a £650 million brand valuation on its balance sheet – the first time this had happened outside an acquisition. Since then, the fact that brands have a value has become a familiar concept.

John says: *"Our individual brand analyses produced all sorts of insights into which brands could be stretched further, those which were receiving too much promotional support and should probably be placed on a care and maintenance regime and milked for profit, those which might be extended internationally, possibly through licensing arrangements, those which should be abandoned, and so forth. We started to realise, accordingly, that our brand valuation methodology was a very valuable [strategic] marketing tool."*

However, I suspect that even more marketers could use brand valuations as ammunition to help them build and grow Strategic Brands – and use them in a deeper and more strategic manner.

David Haigh is the founder and CEO of Brand Finance. (Note 4) I asked him to reflect on why we should measure the value of a brand, how it works and the strategic and financial value it creates. I have combined my own experience and beliefs with David's thoughts, so we provide an integrated 'brand valuer–brand developer' perspective.

Why measure the value of a brand?

The opportunities which arise from quality brand valuation are rich and multi-form, including numerous strategic and performance sources of value, such as balance sheet strengthening, brand and enterprise strategy, assurance on brand management practice, etc.

Assurance of appropriate brand management

We often see companies that have invested heavily in their brands in the past and created strong brand equity produce high growth and strong margins. When they become complacent and reduce their brand investment a few years later, their brand equity measures wither.

Tim Ambler, former senior fellow at the London Business School and author of 'Marketing and the Bottom Line' used to describe the brand as a *"reservoir of cash flow, earned but not yet released to the income statement."* The brand as a reservoir image emphasises the critical point that if you don't keep filling it up, then not much will come out after a while. With regular brand valuation, you will know if and how well you are filling the reservoir!

"Reservoir of cash flow, earned but not yet released to the income statement."

Brand value and share price

Brand Finance has established a direct link between brand value and share price. Following the 10th Anniversary of its 'Global 500' brand valuations table, which ranks the top 500 brands in terms of value across the world, they decided to go right back to the beginning. They looked at the brands whose value was either 30 per cent or more of the enterprise value and, on that highly representative sample of strong brands, tracked the share price performance of those companies between years 1 and 10. They discovered that the cumulative share price had doubled and largely outperformed the S&P 500 - by over 50 per cent, as shown on Illustration 12.1.

This certainly illustrates the power of strategic insight from brand 'valuation', and I will come back to this in terms of straight value creation impact later. If high brand value means outperformance, why don't we make brand value a key metric for investors more systematically?

Brand valuation versus brand measurement

There is valuation of brands…and there is measurement of brands. Our world still does much more measurement than valuation, and my experience is that it is worth and important to do both. David Haigh makes the point that one leads to the other: *"The reason for having a brand is because it is shorthand for a particular product, service or type of delivery. Brands are a trigger for a decision and you cultivate brands so that people respond quickly in making that decision. Brands affect behaviour, so if you have a very*

ILLUSTRATION 12.1   HIGH BRANDS PERFORMANCE VERSUS S&P 500

Share Price Correlation Study

Performance of Global 500 brands relative to the S&P from 2007-2017. There is a clear correlation between BV/EV and stock performance as well as brand strength.

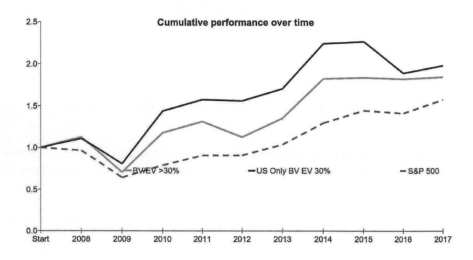

Credit: Brand Finance

strong brand, people will pay more, they'll be more loyal, they'll go out of their way to find it, they'll come back more often, they'll recommend it to their friends: there are so many different behaviours that come from strongly branded entities or from strong brands.

"For this reason, you measure how people are feeling about your brand against a number of different yardsticks, and see how it translates into higher value. All these measurements ideally lead to one point: how is a brand considered by its audiences, how does that change their behaviour against a number of different objectives – and then how does that translate into a financial value?"

Marketers measure their brands but do they use metrics which truly reflect the enduring impact and strategic reality of a brand? What are the insights and how do we improve on what the measurements are and then tell us? Are they more often than not, part of the marketer bubble rather than reflecting real strategic performance cycle and value creation?

Brand valuation – Three key measures

I believe there are three key brand valuation metrics: 1) the brand value; 2) the brand strength; and 3) the ratio 'brand value to enterprise value'. Each brings a wealth of strategic insights on how to develop the brand and where to take the branded business further. Let's explore:

Key Metric 1 - Brand value

The brand value is a number, the end product of a continuous process of business actions. A professional valuation – a repeated, like for like, routine measure of the value of the brand – and the background of the valuation are a good proxy for how well the brand is doing in achieving its potential to influence behaviours and decisions. I have used brand valuations again and again, and recommend using them more. Because once you understand the links between actions and brand valuation, you can improve.

Illustration 12.2 shows the top ten brands in the Brand Finance 2017 global ranking. Isn't it fascinating and what does it mean strategically that Apple's brand loses 27% this year while Google's brand value jumps 24%? Or that Samsung is coming back strongly after the Galaxy Note 7 crisis?

ILLUSTRATION 12.2	WORLD LEADING TEN BRANDS - 2017 RANKING

Credit: Brand Finance

These studies not only look at the variations year on year but also over longer periods of time - which is very insightful. David: *"As you can see from the Global 500 2017, the ranking is dominated by tech and mobile brands – Google, Apple, Samsung, Amazon, Microsoft, Verizon, AT&T, China Mobile. Compare this with the table in Illustration 12.3 which shows the market capitalisation of the world's most valuable public companies - and how this varies from 2006 to 2016: technology and data is the new oil."*

ILLUSTRATION 12.3	CONSIDERABLE CHANGES IN COMPANIES' VALUE IN THE LAST TEN YEARS

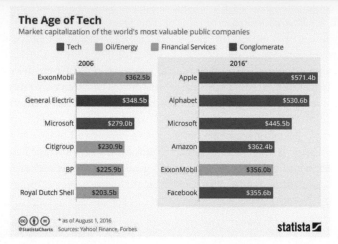

The Age of Tech
Market capitalization of the world's most valuable public companies

■ Tech   ■ Oil/Energy   ■ Financial Services   ■ Conglomerate

2006		2016*	
ExxonMobil	$362.5b	Apple	$571.4b
General Electric	$348.5b	Alphabet	$530.6b
Microsoft	$279.0b	Microsoft	$445.5b
Citigroup	$230.9b	Amazon	$362.4b
BP	$225.9b	ExxonMobil	$356.0b
Royal Dutch Shell	$203.5b	Facebook	$355.6b

* as of August 1, 2016
@StatistaCharts   Sources: Yahoo! Finance, Forbes

statista

Credit: Statista, Yahoo! Finance, Forbes

The track records of each individual company are equally interesting, as shown on Illustration 12.4 – the main take out being that brand value growth has been simply extraordinary.

Note that changes happen fast: following five years leading the valuation ranking, Apple has fallen to second place behind Google in 2017 and is closely followed by Amazon. Something we could have foreseen the direction of by using the 13 Strategic Brand Imperatives system.

ILLUSTRATION 12.4	CONSIDERABLE VALUE GROWTH OF THE TOP STRATEGIC BRANDS

Brand Value Over Time

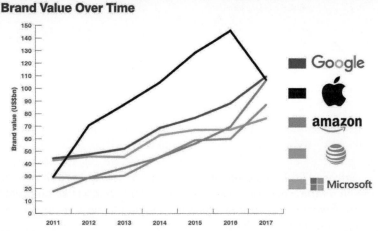

Credit: Brand Finance

David makes the valid point that: *"A lot of simple measures (resulting from a sophisticated valuation process) can build on brand valuation. From there, you can see your progress, you can report it, you can share it with shareholders, etc. – all of which is strategically and financially contributive and important to the enterprise."*

Key Metric 2 - Brand strength

One of the components of brand valuation is 'brand strength'. There are lots of different ways of measuring brand strength. In the abstract, it is extremely relevant because a 'strong' brand is the leading indicator of stronger financial performance in the future.

I like the brand strength measure because it is the closest measure to intrinsically assessing a Strategic Brand, even more than brand value itself - which has some element of scale associated with it. The 2017 ranking is shown on Illustration 12.5, with Lego reaching first place ahead of Google and Nike.

ILLUSTRATION 12.5	WORLD-LEADING BRANDS FOR BRAND STRENGTH – 2017 RANKING

Brand	BSI Score
LEGO	92.7
Google	92.1
Nike	92.1
Ferrari	91.9
VISA	91.5
Disney	91.3
NBC	91.3
pwc	90.9
Johnson&Johnson	90.1
McKinsey&Company	89.9

Credit: Brand Finance

Brand strength is an insightful gauge: if you see that your company is doing well on brand equity and on a variety of other measures, it is certainly going to be outperforming the market a few months and years down the track. Brand Finance uses its own proprietary brand strength measure, as do its industry peers.

David explains how measuring brand strength involves looking at a brand like a financial investor. *"We look at a balanced scorecard of measures that investors would be concerned about. First there is the quality and level of investments going into the brand, i.e. inputs. Second, there are the brand equity measures: 'How well known is the brand? How relevant is it to people (external and internal)? What are the attributes people understand, think and value? How strong is the brand preference?' And then there are the output measures: margin growth, sales growth and so on.*

"We produce a balanced scorecard that takes those three buckets into account: 25 per cent to the inputs, 25 per cent to the outputs and 50 per cent for the leading indicators in the brand equity section. That is, in our view, the way a financial investor would look at the brand asset. So a score is developed which might say 'this brand across those series of measures is a $X billion brand'.

But then, it is important to look underneath the score to understand if this is a brand that is being heavily invested in and growing in brand strength? Or if it is a brand that is being milked and gradually declining in brand strength? Are there any other considerations to take into account?"

Key Metric 3 - Ratio 'brand value to enterprise value'
The ratio of 'brand value to the overall corporation market value' is also extremely pertinent. It reflects how important branding is to that business.

NIKE's 40% and H&M's 37% (Ref. Illustration 12.6) are certainly a tribute to extraordinary brands outperforming in extremely competed areas. Reversely, Chevron's 9% - with other oil & gas companies like Exxon Mobil not being distant, shows the relatively low importance given to brands in the energy sector.

ILLUSTRATION 12.6	HIGH AND LOW RATIOS 'BRAND VALUE TO ENTERPRISE VALUE'

Brand name	2017 BV / EV
Nike	40%
H&M	37%
Pepsi	36%
JD.com	36%
Mercedes-Benz	36%

Brand name	2017 BV / EV
Ping An	5%
Chevron	9%
Spectrum	10%
General Electric	10%
Visa	11%

Credit: Brand Finance

Isn't it essential to rationalize that in some cases, close to half the value of an enterprise lies in its brand - or inversely a tiny fraction of it? Take BMW whose ratio is over 25% - no wonder that brand is BMW's obsession, as observed in Chapter 3; or that brand connectedness is managed extremely tightly by McDonald's, as referred to in Chapter 4.

An example of strategic insight: when brand value is high in relation to enterprise value, this might indicate that the financial market has undervalued the enterprise. Therefore, you should consider acquiring it, as the value of the company is low but the value of the brand is high within it – which is promising. That's the modus operandi for Warren Buffett, who has a tendency to target companies that are distressed or undervalued in the short-run, but where there is evidence that their strong brands has the potential to recover the value. He then grows them for the long run into the future. There have been quite a lot of transactions in the last few years – notably, Cadbury – where the company had been fundamentally undervalued in relation to the importance of its brand.

Using brand valuation as a major source of strategic guidance

I am often asked the following questions on brand value, brand strength and brand share of market value - how can C-suites, CEOs and CMOs use the high value of a Strategic Brand as ammunition or as a guide to actions? How can it help marketing departments answer the ROI question? Do you believe brand valuation helps give CMOs a voice in the boardroom? How is this field changing? What advice would you offer to CMOs at the beginning of this journey to ensure their Strategic Brand's value is understood and acknowledged by the financial market and CEOs/CFOs? What is the easy part of this and what is harder?

Based on experience, here are a few strategic benefits stemming from brand valuation

Guidance 1 - Brand valuation informs brand strategy
Brand value can be used as a major source of strategic insight. I have developed the simple matrix in Illustration 12.7 on brand strategy, which relates brand value to brand strength.

Let's explore a couple of examples.

'Expand brand' strategy - If you have high brand strength but not such a high valuation (top left quadrant of the matrix), this indicates an opportunity to grow. Let's take Ferrari: its brand is given a consistently high brand strength rating (Ref. Illustration 12.5). Ferrari used to belong to Fiat, before it was spun off as an IPO. Their performance in the IPO was successful and their rating was extremely high with financial investors.

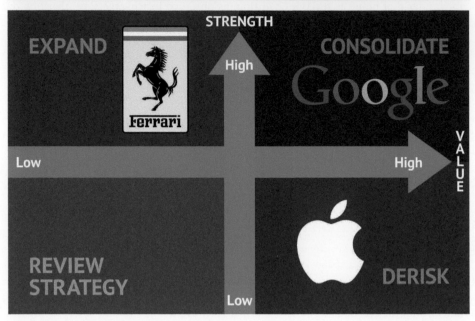

ILLUSTRATION 12.7   ANALYSING BRAND VALUATION VS. BRAND STRENGTH

© THE Enduring Strategic Brand

Why? Not just because people like driving around in Ferraris - but also because investors see the massive growth potential in expanding the core business or getting into a number of different areas which Ferrari could diversify into. The previous CEO, Luca di Montezemolo, wouldn't diversify into other areas or disproportionately grow the business, as he took the view that Ferrari was a luxury niche brand which wouldn't make more than 7000 cars a year. He fell out with Sergio Marchionne, the Chairman of Fiat Chrysler Automobiles, Ferrari's parent company, whose view was to make the most of the brand equity.

There are lots of similar cases: very often acquisitions are driven by the investors' view that there are far more places and unexploited reservoirs of value and growth than already exploited, which brand valuation underpins and justifies with numbers and insights.

'De-risk brand' strategy - If you have high brand value but not a very high brand strength (bottom right of the matrix), this can indicate one of two things. The company has high brand value because their financial performance remains strong – but if their brand strength is lower than others in the same market, they are vulnerable to a future fall. Or, if they were to strengthen, they could be even more valuable. It's for management to decide which one of those it is, and then act upon it.

Apple is very much the extreme of this case. Its extraordinary market value and brand valuation are based on the anticipation that the brand will continue its track record of being a trendsetter in branded and excellence-driven technology. But new technology is less differentiated and under considerable competitive pressure - for example the iPhones; and true innovations take time to break through - for example the Apple Watch. Management understands the required de-risk approach very well, and have taken steps, including the brand's fast investing in services, apps and a tightly held Apple branded lifestyle ecosystem.

Guidance 2 - Brand valuation informs business strategy

If a company has strong brand valuation and measurements, the CEO and CMO can build on this strength to undertake actions and investments with confidence.

The brand valuation can strengthen the marketer's armoury by providing them with the required information and evidence to make a robust case to the board.

Such real actions guided by insights drawn from the brand valuation and its underlying measurements might be: create a new distribution network, change the visual identity, invest in a new advertising campaign or do something different in PR, change the product or the prices. And a virtuous circle will kick in, with customers weighing up the options, changing their point of view and their behaviour to the brand – all feeding back into the next brand valuation.

Q8 David cited the example of Q8 in the oil sector. *"Q8 was a classic oil company, owned by financiers, which had an old visual identity. The marketing and communication people felt it was time for a refresh. But the finance people were challenging: 'What's the point? The existing identity is perfectly good. Let's not waste hundreds of millions of dollars to rebrand our Q8 network when it is just money down the drain.'*

"What the marketing and communication department needed to do in this instance was to demonstrate that by making an investment in the visual identity, response of consumers would be positive – more people would come into the stations, they would buy more often and spend more. And then show that those behaviours would only arise if they completely revamped the brand. In such cases, you model it and show the financial result, for example that a $100 million might be making $20 or 30 million extra a year. It doesn't take many years to pay that back, and therefore it's worth doing. And you can track it all the way through."

AON Another example is sponsorship. AON, despite being a massive company, was relatively unknown outside its closed world and its brand was very much undervalued - a typical case of 'low brand value/low brand strength', guiding to 'review strategy' (bottom left of Illustration 12.7). This position meant a clear opportunity and the decision to sponsor Manchester United football club put the undifferentiated insurance brand on the map worldwide. Says the AON's CMO Phil Clement: *"Our 'We are United' global campaign has more than doubled the company's awareness."*

V-Power So did Shell with its investment in Formula I and sponsorship of Ferrari, to build and support its value added fuel brand, V-Power.

This is nothing new of course – but perhaps an invite for the consistent use of an enduring and rigorous brand valuation tool to unpick the underlying threads behind its variations.

Guidance 3 - Brand valuation offers ROI data

Variations in the brand value can help assess the return on investment in the brand, as the evaluation brings quantitative robustness to the CEO and CMO with their board or Exec colleagues. This common language is particularly helpful with CFOs, who will relate to and appreciate the quantitative approach. O2's Nina Bibby comments: *"I know exactly how much things cost, what they deliver in terms of increase in customer satisfaction, recommendation and retention. For example, I can quantify how much it would cost me to acquire a new customer versus holding on to this one, or bring econometric modelling to things we advertise, promote, drive consideration, drive recontracting, etc. All things we discuss and get aligned on with our CFO."*

Guidance 4 - Brand valuation offers competitive intelligence

Valuations glean deeply strategic insights on master facts and direction of travel for Strategic Brands, providing interesting dynamics on competitors, as well as on sectors and geographies.

Looking at the sector picture 2007 to 2015 on Illustration 12.8, it is no surprise that the technology sector's consolidated brand value has grown by a factor of 2.5, while the bank sector's consolidated brand value has grown by 45 per cent – and this almost entirely in China. So what is the future view? Is there a possibility for some enterprises to break from the trend through their brand?

ILLUSTRATION 12.8	BRAND VALUE DYNAMICS BY SECTOR

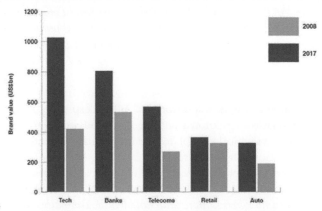

Brand Value Total for Top 5 Sectors (2008 and 2017)

Credit – Brand Finance

Guidance 5 - Brand valuation offers market intelligence

Equally, a geographic market perspective provides invaluable information and incentive for traditional brand owners to focus and invest strongly in their brands, because competition is strengthening.

ILLUSTRATION 12.9	MOST VALUABLE BRAND BY GEOGRAPHIC ZONES

Most Valuable Brands by Region

North America:	Africa:	Middle East:
Google	MTN	STC
US$109.5 billion	US$2.9 billion	US$6.2 billion
South America:	Europe:	Asia:
PEMEX	BMW	SAMSUNG
US$8.5 billion	US$37.1 billion	US$66.2 billion

Credit – Brand Finance

The key fact is that Chinese brands and their value have increased markedly, and are continuing to do so. David comments: *"China now has very strong fundamentals: they are the second biggest economy in the world; their 1.5 billion people are becoming increasingly wealthy – there are more billionaires and millionaires in China than anywhere else – and the wealth is trickling down through the middle classes. China's financial resources are massive; and there has been a change of behaviour: historically, the Chinese have saved and not spent, but now they are seriously beginning to spend."*

A simple figure - Brand value in China is up ten-fold in 10 years. Specifically, the number of Chinese brands represented in the BrandZ Global Top 100 increased from one in 2006 to 14 in 2015. China is now the second centre of brand value growth after North America.

David adds: *"Moutai is a brand of baijiu, a Chinese liquor, which has suddenly become the number one drinks brand, overtaking Johnnie Walker. Chinese people are spending lots of money, and their preference is to buy Chinese brands, which are consequently rising and becoming more valuable. And the Chinese are now thinking: 'We generate a lot of wealth and demand, why don't we buy brands abroad and make more of them?'"*

Management Today Magazine (Note 5) estimates that Chinese new investments in Western companies were worth well over $30 billion in Europe alone in 2015, and Chinese foreign direct investment (FDI) in the UK now totals more than $100 billion since the year 2000 - to the point where the EU is considering protectionist regulations.

For example, Gieves & Hawkes from Savile Row, one of the most respected clothing brands, was taken over by a Chinese entrepreneur, the Trinity Group. There are now 400

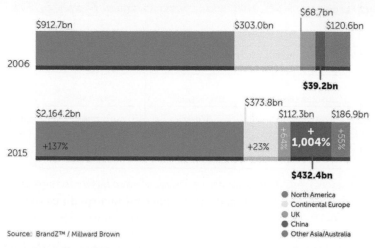

ILLUSTRATION 12.10

A MASSIVE INCREASE OF CHINESE BRAND VALUE
OVER 10 YEARS

Brand value growth velocity shifts to China

The number of Chinese brands represented in the BrandZ™ Global Top 100 increased from just one in 2006 to 14 in 2015, and the total Brand Power of Chinese brands increased 1,004 percent.

Source: BrandZ™ / Millward Brown

Credit: Brand Z / Millward Brown

shops in China and they are booming. There are plenty of other examples, too many to mention here – from Qingdao Haier's $5.4bn acquisition of General Electric Appliances to Anbang Insurance's $14.3bn bid for Starwood Hotels (Note 6). This pattern spans all sectors – Chinese Investment Corporation owns 10 per cent of Heathrow Airport, Dalian Wanda's Wang Jianlang owns 20 per cent of Atletico Madrid.

David adds: *"For some time, the concept of 'Made in China' has been transformed from white-label manufacturer to brand owner and builder. The Chinese are rapidly getting into professional branding because they have decided that branding is important. And they're progressing in creating a whole range of standards around measurement and management of brands, as well as establishing specialised brand research and development institutions. It is possible, if not likely, that in 10 or 20 years you'll find the Chinese are leaders in brand management science, in the same way that they are now for manufacturing. They've worked out that the way to capture added value is to add marketing and branding – and they're determined to find out how that works."*

It is possible, if not likely, that in 10 or 20 years you'll find the Chinese are leaders in brand management science, in the same way that they are now for manufacturing.

In summary, we argue to constantly eye to grow the value OF your brand and leverage the strategically insightful brand valuation, both as "the thermometer" and "root cause analyst". Don't be disconcerted by the fact that the actual figures from Brand Finance may differ from BrandZ or Interbrand - brand valuations are not just a number but rather a structure for insights and making sensible decisions. Indeed, professional valuations are about scenarios, strategies and tips, far more than an absolute number, as helpful as the number itself may be.

Driving value **FROM** the Strategic Brand

We move to the second thread on brand value, this arising FROM the Strategic Brand – as it can, should and will deliver much sustainable benefit by itself.

Leaders for Strategic Brand

Extracting the full value inherent to Strategic Brands starts with leadership. David explains – *"There is still no general recognition among management that brands and marketing directly impact not only the value but also the stability of their businesses.*

"Many CEOs and CFOs talk about whether a particular brand has a good or bad reputation – but reputation is not an asset on its own, it is attached to a brand, be that Vodafone, Rolls-Royce or VW.

"The reputation of the brand drives the performance of the business. Until CEOs and CFOs truly accept that, the industry will remain underinvested and the way in which you can use brand reputation as a means of managing your business will not be fully optimised. It is still not quite there – except for Enduring Strategic Brands that are established, considered, developed and managed as such already.

"Many people who run companies spend a lot of time talking about brand, saying how important it is. But they don't necessarily follow through with putting the resources, the organisation and themselves fully behind it. We need to move towards a general culture in which brands and reputation, the way you manage and optimise them, are as important as nailing strategy, as important as getting your OPEX or funding strategies right, or any other major aspect of business performance."

We need to move towards a general culture in which brands and reputation, are as important as nailing strategy, as important as getting your OPEX or funding strategies right.

Of course there are many exceptions, especially in the FMCG and luxury sectors - and we are referring to a number of these as Exemplary Brands in this book.

Mega trend behind brands

Despite not all CEOs valuing branding, awareness of the importance of the corporate brand is growing across most, if not all, sectors, and will continue to do so. Unilever,

P&G and Mars were fairly silent in the past. They are now very much visible and outspoken on overarching purpose, endorsement and reassurance.

Sectors like utilities, aeronautics, cement or steel were historically unbranded. Branding is now increasingly considered, as both an assurance of quality and a means of competing in an increasingly competitive world. The steel sector is over-serviced with massive over-capacity; so are cement and concrete. A strong brand gets more than its fair share of the demand and has a greater chance of surviving.

A variety of key sources of value from Enduring Strategic Brands

The case for transformational value creation from strong Strategic Brands is made throughout this book. There is much literature on this but in order to make it simple and applicable to real life, I have consistently operated in consideration of eight output value threads or sources of value (SoV), represented on the octagon in Illustration 12.11:

1. Stock price
2. Profitability
3. Growth
4. Efficiency
5. Transformation
6. Licence to operate
7. Access
8. Shield.

ILLUSTRATION 12.11	THE SOURCES OF VALUE OCTAGON FROM ENDURING STRATEGIC BRANDS

© THE Enduring Strategic Brand

Some of these sources of value, or combinations of them, have been prevalent at different times in my career.

Castrol As Business CEO in Castrol, the combination of profit margins, growth and access was absolutely what we were building the brand for. The Castrol brand main, enduring and transformational role was to establish a major and differentiated access to new markets and stronger channels; retain and acquire more consumers and higher quality customers; and command premium unit margins.

bp At BP during 'peace time', the magic combination of sources of value from the brand was licence to operate, access and transformation. Licence to operate came first, as BP needed the active support and cooperation from governments to exploit the resources they owned. And, of course, we needed strong and high quality access and the ability to carry and support transformation for all involved parties.

In each and every role, 'efficiency' as a source of value was a must, an imperative business requirement and the basis for credibility. This is a discipline Indian companies are usually zealous for.

It is vital to be clear about what combination of core and enduring sources of value you are building the brand for, so the brand can be at the centre of the enterprise agenda and performance generation. I learned over time how to develop and express brand strategies and then rally colleagues accordingly – although I only managed to do this reasonably convincingly later in my career. Hence, I would guide CEOs, CMOs and their colleagues to form this clear view early – and stick to it.

SoV 1 - Company Value and Stock Price

Scott Goodson, the author of *Uprising*, asks the right question: *"When Tata Motors of India bought Jaguar and Range Rover from Ford, what did they buy? Factories? Raw Materials? Employees? No, Goldman Sachs and Morgan Stanley helped Ford sell the brands to Tata for $2.56 billion and the brands were worth more than all the other ingredients combined."* Likewise, when Grand Met acquired Smirnoff for $1 billion as we noted earlier, or Kraft bought Cadbury for $19.5 billion, or the Four Seasons Hotels Inc. sold itself to Bill Gates and Prince Al-Waleed bin Talal for $3.8 billion. The list goes on with Budweiser, Volvo, SsangYong and many others, all acquired for their brand or house of brands.

We mentioned earlier the distinctive financial performance of stocks with strong brands. The graph in Illustration 12.12 provides another piece of evidence for this, as it shows a 102.6 per cent growth of aggregated stock value for the 100 highest brand value companies in the WPP BrandZ TM ranking between 2006 and 2015.

David Haigh takes the argument further: *"Solactive AG in collaboration with Brand Finance launched equity indices in 2016, namely the Solactive BrandFinance® European Leaders Select 30 Index and Solactive BrandFinance® European Leaders Low Risk 30 Index.*

ILLUSTRATION 12.12	OVER 100 PER CENT STOCK VALUE GROWTH FOR STRONGEST BRANDS

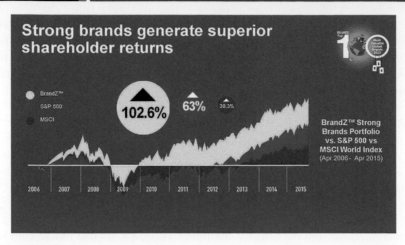

Credit: BrandZ TM Ranking

These indices will be used as a basis for investment products and target investors, who will be putting at first one or two billion into them. These investors will be seeking exposure to companies with a strong brand value relative to enterprise value, while displaying specific dividend yields and volatility features. This is a unique concept, since the indices focus on an intangible asset that can generate competitive advantage and benefit a company's performance. They recognise that brand value can be associated with pricing premiums, greater customer loyalty and market share. These factors can have an impact on a company's profitability and, all things being equal, more valuable brands can be expected to generate more cash flow.

The observation is that over the last 10 years, this is precisely what happened: this group of strongly branded companies with certain characteristics outperformed the others – and are expected to outperform in the future. In short, these indices seek to capture this performance premium."

This is only one way among many others to substantiate the fact that Strategic Brands are considerable value generators, if only because these brands can potentially attract a large amount of money for their enterprises.

SoV 2 - Profitability

As we reported earlier, Apple has topped global brand value for the last five years until 2017. What does this tell us about Apple's ability to command high margins and therefore profitability? The story starts with a number: Apple's historical gross profit margin remains consistently around the 40 per cent mark, a phenomenal number in a very competitive market. This is absolutely the Strategic Brand at work.

Indeed, whatever the announcement from Apple, there is always a shared, unifying strategy at play – and that is the pursuit and protection of high unit profit margins. Viewed through the unemotional prism of *"how much money do I make from every unit sold?"*, there's a perfect congruence between the diversity of new iWatch bands, the content-focused reboot of the Apple TV, and the launch of the large iPad Pro. Apple isn't here to sell the most of anything; its overarching goal is simply to generate the greatest possible profit with a boundary that each unit's margin doesn't go under a set level. It's a beguilingly simple approach to a difficult and challenging market. And for this, it builds and leverages its Strategic Brand to "command" that people queue all night in front of the shops to be the first to buy the brand's latest expensive kit.

Take an example of brand consistency in their response to the following challenge: when confronted with stagnating sales, as Apple has been with the iPad in recent times, others would usually look to stimulate demand by cutting prices or adding features and enhancements at the existing price. In other words, they would erode their unit profit margin in the hope of producing a larger absolute profit through a greater sales volume. That's how most price wars start and these often turn out to be devastating to most of their participants. That's why Apple resolutely refuses to engage in them – and instead has developed the brand muscles not to have to fight in the pack.

Apple's brand answer to iPad stagnation was to go further upmarket. Instead of slashing iPad prices to counter competition from Samsung and the rest of the Android hordes, Apple stepped into a higher price bracket and equipped the iPad Pro to become its first 2-in-1 device. More generally, Apple is building a strong branded ecosystem to create an ever more 'sticky' relationship with its customers and strengthen its pricing power.

SoV 3 – Top line growth

Continuing with our Apple example - at a portfolio level, Apple leverages its brand to grow high-margin services fast, such as iTunes, the various App Stores, Apple Music, Apple Pay, Apple Care and licensing revenue. Analysts used to gloss over services, instead concentrating on Apple's huge hardware numbers, but the segment is becoming increasingly important and attracting more attention as the company leverages its enormous installed user base.

A striking figure: in the first fiscal quarter of 2017, Apple reported a services sales value of $7.17 billion, representing an 18-percent year-on-year growth. Looking at full year 2016, services sales accounted for 11% of group net sales, as they reached $24.3 billion - a 22% growth compared to 2015. That measures against a total reported group revenue decrease of 8%.

And if you compute back, gross margins on service revenue can be estimated at around 59 per cent, with further estimates for the App Store of 90 per cent, Apple Care of 70 per cent and iTunes of 30 to 40 per cent – whereby group average gross margin in 2016 was 39.1%. Talking of growth, Apple Music is estimated to have generated $2.0 billion in revenue and 20 million paying subscribers worldwide as of end 2016.

Strong brands are generally recognised as a key – if not *the* key – engine of growth. Just take the fast-growing middle classes in India, China, Brazil, Russia, South Africa, Indonesia, Nigeria and many others: these consumers buy brands, often premium brands. The fact that so much is now online and purchased over the phone, means consumers must have considerable trust in who they are buying from – rather than in what they are buying.

So the case is made but the challenge remains: how to build definitively, maintain and continue growing a Strategic Brand in ways that obviously and clearly generate growth? Remember our brand value–brand strength matrix, the top left quadrant 'high brand strength–lower brand value'. Combine it with Marc de Swann Arons 'Way to Play' approach '*to map the market in a new way and reduce your market share from 85% to 3%*'(Ref. Chapter 7)- there is phenomenal growth potential for Strategic Brands here.

'To map the market in a new way and reduce your market share from 85% to 3%.'

SoV 4 - Efficiency

I have always believed that if a Strategic Brand is the father of value, it is the mother of efficiency. Efficiency is an absolute must, a pre-condition to everything in our modern economy.

From 2008–10, when BP owned its sector brand space with 'All of the Above', the return on every dollar invested in communication was massive – arguably allowing a financially challenged BP to squeeze its investment for a while. The brand team didn't like the reduction but it was tolerable because of the brand's strength – and the fact that our industry peers' communication would accrue largely to BP.

With regards to growth efficiency, a Strategic Brand builds loyalty and therefore reduces costs of acquisition (Ref. O2 in Chapter 7); it builds authority and therefore reduces costs of channels (Ref. Airbnb in Chapter 4); it spreads more easily and therefore requires reduced investment (Ref. Haier in Chapter 8), etc. I have found that brand owners often underplay the efficiency angle, although it is very dear to most CEOs and CFOs.

As Martin Sorrell was mentioning earlier, questioning the efficiency of building and leveraging a brand is more frequent than ever, as the enterprise interrogates the investments in brand, their cost effectiveness and their return. As a balancing act, there are continuously improving methods and tools in modern marketing to assess brand investments – and there need to be, given the daily evolution of the digital channels. We are referring to zero base marketing budgeting and other similar methodologies. In Chapter 9, we discussed the valuable initiative undertaken by the IPA at the end of 2016 in the UK, "Marketing Effectiveness Week", where 14 industry associations and their members, leading marketers and four learning centres reviewed and shared insights, tools and techniques of modern marketing efficiency, particularly in the context of the proliferation of commercial and communication choices.

SoV 5 – Transformation

Take a sector that is in a period of challenge and change. To rely on a strong brand during such times makes life a lot easier.

In the cable, TV and broadband sector, a number of players came into the market, like NTL and various others, and didn't do particularly well nor were they particularly liked. On the other hand, there was Virgin, which is a very small player in that market – but whose brand is liked. Two big players bought Virgin Media specifically because they wanted its brand; because they felt that if they did so, they could create a much bigger, more stable and more robust concern; that customers would respond well (which they did). So, in a highly dynamic industry, where people were going bust and rearranging things, reliance on the Virgin brand helped dramatically.

I was talking recently with the Head of Sky Digital and he was expressing a similar enthusiasm - it is the Sky brand that galvanizes and guides the teams through the hard choices of complex and fast transformation in a very highly competitive area.

There are plenty of other instances in different sectors, of brands painting over the cracks during times of massive structural change and allowing things to move smoothly. We have singled out the IBM brand in Chapter 6 and GE brand in Chapter 8 as exemplary in supporting major enterprise transformations.

SoV 6 - Licence to operate

This is an ever more important source of value from brands and a major *raison d'être* for corporate brands –because of two main trends in the world economy and its organisation: the fast-growing importance and intervention of governments and regulators in the economy; and the increasing scale and impact of deeply regulated sectors in the world order.

There is therefore a compelling role for the so-called B2G (business to government) brand.

BP could not do business without a strong licence to operate and the same extends to all resources businesses, such as energy and mining – but also to sectors like automotive, which is deeply regulated on emission levels and future mobility like autonomous driving. Or pharmaceuticals, a massively regulated sector where drug evaluation and release most often depends on governmental agencies. Or banking, which is driven by detailed and continuously evolving rules on their robustness, offers and management practice.

These are just few examples, with more reflected in Illustration 12.13.

ILLUSTRATION 12.13   THE 10 MOST REGULATED INDUSTRIES

The McLaughlin-Sherouse List: The 10 Most-Regulated Industries in 2014

1,130 the median industry   number of restrictions

Industry	Number of restrictions
Petroleum and Coal Products Manufacturing	25,482
Electric Power Generation, Transmission, and Distribution	20,959
Motor Vehicle Manufacturing	16,757
Nondepository Credit Intermediation	16,579
Depository Credit Intermediation	16,033
Scheduled Air Transportation	13,307
Fishing	13,218
Oil and Gas Extraction	11,955
Pharmaceutical and Medicine Manufacturing	11,505
Deep Sea, Coastal, and Great Lakes Water Transportation	11,279

 **MERCATUS CENTER**
George Mason University

Source: RegData 2.2 from RegData.org.

Credit – Mercatus Center, from Regdata.org

The role of brand in these sectors is huge – and still under played. Apart perhaps a few defence enterprises, hardly any company has developed time and time again a truly B2G Strategic Brand that makes a major difference to their enterprise's licence to operate. Perhaps BP came close and I have seen the defining impact this has when it does exist.

SoV 7 - Access

The majority of my upstream colleagues at BP did not really connect to the word 'brand', even less to investing anything in it. But they always admitted how useful it was to be called BP to get access to almost anybody they wanted, in particular to government officials.

bp   Apart from inherently being a B2G business, BP is mainly a B2B business and its customers are airlines, marine ship-owners, chemical groups, fuel and lubricants distributors, jobbers, retailers etc.

Actually, B2B is the prevalent model for most enterprises in the vast majority of economic sectors - including the B2B2C businesses. In new markets, the access to the best B2B intermediates and best operators is essential – and the quality of this access is actually led and largely defined by the brand.

SoV 8 - Shield in adverse or crisis situations

There are two main types of crisis: contextual challenging times, such as the 2008 global financial crisis; and own-built specific crises, such as the recent Volkswagen emission scandal.

On the former type, e.g. the 2008 financial crisis, no category was spared as customers and consumers spent more cautiously and consciously. But brand valuations, and notably brand strength indices, demonstrate that stronger brands not only survived but also continued to perform well above their peers with less powerful or influential brands (Ref. AmEx in Chapter 7 or Tata in Chapter 11). Moreover, the Strategic Brands' speed of recovery and further expansion after the crisis was much faster than their peers, as people regained confidence and wanted to spend again on what really appealed to them. So, a Strategic Brand will have better resistance during a crisis and much faster growth following one.

On the own-built crisis, let's hear David Haigh about Volkswagen and Malaysian Airlines: *"The Volkswagen brand is fantastically strong. Arguably, the company may suffer deeply financially from the emissions set back but the fact is that demand for their cars remains high. In this instance, the blame for the scandal must be put on the management, not on the brand. It's the brand which will hopefully carry the company through - because VW is a quality enterprise.*

"Malaysian Airlines is a company whose brand is fundamentally weaker. It was a low-power brand; then they had two crashes, neither of which were really their fault. As a result of these two disasters, people stopped flying Malaysian Air. Now, I think if that had been BA, BA probably would have survived because of their strong brand."

EACH AND EVERY ONE OF THE 13 STRATEGIC BRAND IMPERATIVES IS A VITAL VALUE DRIVER

In consideration of these eight sources of value, any brand needs to develop clarity on its priorities among them in respect to strategic value generation – hence there are a number of key questions related to the value FROM brands. What are the enduring priority sources of value which the brand should develop? Is it to support growth and profitability, like many FMCG brands? Or carry the organisation through its required transformations, most needed by technology brands? Or help establish a useful regulatory context, which corporate brands often aspire to achieve?

This question on value priorities links to Chapter 5, where we advocate that the CEO selects their CMO with a profile best fitted to the core enduring objectives of the organisation. Of course, one could say "all of the above" – and there is some validity in wanting the brand to be serving all sources of value. But in reality, there are and should be priorities: like people, brands are better at some things than others.

Getting to a clear 'brand value model'

Once these strategic value priorities are set, how do we go at delivering these objectives for the organisation? What is the model by which the brand will be able to lead to the desired strategic value outcomes, again and again?

As David Wheldon says, the answer to this 'brand business model' question is often loose - many marketers lose their edge and find it challenging to make this 'brand value model' crystal clear, straight, well understood and adhered to by the organisation. No effort should be spared in achieving this sharpness and then embedding and performance managing the consequent 'brand value model' throughout the organisation.

This is where THE Strategic Brand is different – because, as shown in the matrix on Illustration 12.14, there is a direct link between the Strategic Brand Imperatives and the Brand ability to deliver the core organisational value objectives in a strategic and enduring manner.

Simply said, the Strategic Brand Imperatives are the 'inputs' to the enterprise business model and, once they are established, invariably drive the delivery of the desired performance 'outputs' and objectives – Case made?

ILLUSTRATION 12.14	HOW THE 13 STRATEGIC BRAND IMPERATIVES CONTRIBUTE TO EACH SOURCE OF VALUE TYPE

SOURCES OF VALUE

13 IMPERATIVES	Stock price	Profit	Growth	Efficiency	Transformation	Licence to operate	Access	Shield
Clarity of purpose								
Culture born & authentic								
Functional & Emotional								
Connected								
People led & leading people								
Customer centric								
Partnering								
Future embracing								
Rigorous & disciplined								
Strategy guiding								
High value & driving value								
Trusted								
Crisis resilient								

Major value linkage | High value linkage | Moderate value linkage

© THE Enduring Strategic Brand

I believe this matrix provides a useful connection between the 13 Strategic Brand Imperatives (as input) to the Eight Sources of Value (as output). No surprise that this link is nearly universally strong (dark and mid-blue) and at the strongest level for most (dark- blue). Building a true Strategic Brand is vital if you want the brand to be central to the organisation's agenda, priorities and enduring performance delivery…and reversely, a true Strategic Brand will be your biggest and most natural value driver.

Three cases on how Strategic Brand Imperatives deliver value

Rather than commenting on each of these links, we have selected a few which seem central to many organisations' interrogations, challenges and aspirations – they certainly have been for me. They link to various chapters of this book and explain how developing the brand imperative creates the value.

Case 1 - People Led and People Leading

As discussed in Chapter 5, no brand can get close to being a Strategic Brand without being successful with the 'People' Imperative because it contributes vitally to each and all sources of value - the 'People Led & People Leading' line in the matrix is uniformly dark blue.

In 'THE Enduring Strategic Brand', we ground the strength of BMW (Chapter 3), Zappos (Chapter 5), IBM (Chapter 6), Tata (Chapter 11) and others in their People Imperative. Let's briefly look at Google, which ranks number 1 in the 2016 FORTUNE 100 best companies to work for. (Note 7)

Google Google has been on the list for 10 years, and 2016 marks the seventh time it has been at the top, thanks to its ability to spark the imagination of its talented and highly compensated workers, and by adding perks to an already dizzying array of freebies. Last year it enhanced healthcare coverage by offering virtual doctor visits, second-opinion services and breast-cancer screenings at headquarters. One Googler explained, *"The company culture truly makes workers feel they're valued and respected as human beings, not cogs in a machine. The perks are phenomenal - from three prepared organic meals a day and unlimited snacks, artisan coffees and teas, to free personal-fitness classes, health clinics, on-site oil changes, haircuts, a spa truck, a bike-repair truck, nap pods, on-site laundry rooms, and subsidised wash and fold."*

The list is endless but the results across Google's workforce speak for themselves (Ref. Illustration 12.15) - which other organisation could claim that 95 per cent of their employees "are willing to give extra to get the job done"?

ILLUSTRATION 12.15	BENEFITS FROM 'PEOPLE LED AND PEOPLE LEADING' AT GOOGLE

- ▶ We have special and unique benefits here – 97%
- ▶ I'm proud to tell others I work here – 96%
- ▶ People here are willing to give extra to get the job done – 95%
- ▶ I am given the resources and equipment to do my job – 95%
- ▶ Management is honest and ethical in its business practices – 95%

Credit - 2016 Fortune 100 Best Companies to Work For - Great Place to Work Institute

In a broader sense, the performance, results and achievements of a Strategic Brand that is both truly 'People Led & 'People Leading' are unparalleled. One measure of this is voluntary turnover which, as represented in the *'Great Place to Work'* report, is roughly half the amount in the 100 best companies to work for compared to their peers. When it comes to delivering any and all of the core sources of value, what can be more important than holding onto and getting the best out of your carefully selected, strongly developed team talents? I relearned this during the heart of BP's 2010 Deepwater Horizon crisis, when the already low employee churn even halved then – and the loyal and mobilized BP team contributed massively to the resolution and rebuild of the company.

ILLUSTRATION 12.16	LOWER STAFF TURNOVER WHEN 'PEOPLE LED AND PEOPLE LEADING'

100 Best Companies Voluntary Turnover by Industry

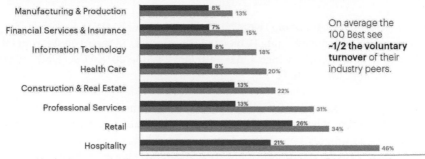

Source: "100 Best" data provided by Great Place to Work® Institute, Inc. Comparative data provided by BLS. "100 Best" data includes PT & FT turnover; BLS data includes the same in addition to turnover for temp/contract workers.

Credit - 2016 Fortune Best Companies to Work For - Great Place to Work Institute

Examples from Strategic Brands benefiting the Enterprise's people equation are plenty. We are impressed with Unilever who has become one of the most in demand employers since it placed 'Sustainable Living' at its heart, with job applications shooting up by 65%.

Case 2 - Clarity of Purpose and Simplicity.
In Chapter 1, we noted that a key manifestation of a true Strategic Brand Imperative is 'simplicity', especially of its purpose. In Chapter 7 and others, we have shown how companies like Aldi, Google, Netflix, McDonald's or IKEA are focused on developing and delivering uncomplicated offers, low and transparent pricing, high-quality products and great customer service.

Clarity of purpose and simplicity pays off - 64 per cent of consumers are willing to pay more for simple experiences. Simplicity gets shared - 61 per cent of consumers are more likely to recommend a brand because it's simple. Simplicity outperforms - data from the past six years shows that a stock portfolio comprised of the simplest publicly traded brands in the Global Top 10 outperforms the major indexes by over 400 per cent (Ref. Illustration 12.17).

ILLUSTRATION 12.17 | VALUE FROM SIMPLICITY

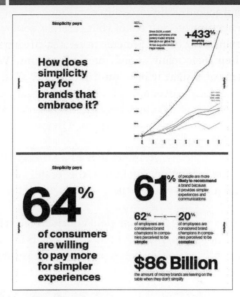

Credit: Siegel + Gale - 2016 Simplicity Index Report (Note 8)

Case 3 - Customer Centricity.

As explored in Chapter 7, Customer Centricity is not just an attitude; it's not simply a matter of making verbal commitments to "put the customer first" or "provide outstanding service". It's about culture and literally building your business around the needs, preferences and actions of your customer, whoever your ultimate customer is, on an on-going basis.

When you truly become customer centric, you gain the unprecedented power to transform your business and achieve new growth. Illustration 12.18 shows a few outputs from cross-company studies – and we noted more in Chapter 7.

ILLUSTRATION 12.18 | VALUE FROM CUSTOMER CENTRICITY

▶ **Deliver 60% more profits than peers**
By being customer-centric companies
Deloitte & Touche 2015

▶ **Increase sales by 17%**
By identifying and maximizing the value of best customers
Dr. Peter Fader, Pennsylvania's Wharton School of Business

▶ **Increase profits by 25% to 95%**
By increasing customer retention rates by 5%
Frederick Reichheld, Bain & Company

Credit: Deloitte, Dr. Fader, Bain & Company

Add to these performance metrics the ability to identify and target at-risk customers with timely offers in order to retain their business, and this all builds into why customer centricity is so powerful economically.

In today's world, companies can collect preference-related customer data and behaviour like never before, filling their many siloed internal systems. Within this wealth of information lay nuggets of insight which can drive greater Customer Centricity and help to transition the company to become a Strategic Brand that commands outstanding performance.

Case 4 - Trusted and Reputation
In Chapter 11 we discussed the 'Trust' Imperative of a Strategic Brand and established the link between trust and reputation. Looking at the 'brand value model' matrix, trust shows up as a major input – dark-blue, to the vast majority of the sources of value.

No surprise surely that trust and reputation yield considerable value. Illustration 12.19 represents how a 5 per cent improvement in reputation results in an 8.5 per cent increase in active recommendation - a major impact, especially for those organisations for which 'net promoter' scores are vital. (Note 9)

ILLUSTRATION 12.19	TRUST ENGENDERS HIGH LEVELS OF POSITIVE RECOMMENDATION

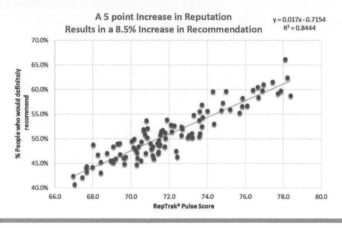

The Impact of Reputation on Support Has Increased

A 5 point Increase in Reputation
Results in a 8.5% Increase in Recommendation

$y = 0.017x - 0.7154$
$R^2 = 0.8444$

Credit – The Reputation Institute, RepTrack 2016

By 2005, BP had established a high level of trust within society (at least high for an energy company). After the Texas City refinery explosion that year, BP's recovery was helped considerably by its Strategic Brand - the trust it had engendered extended to the belief that this was truly incidental and BP would do the right thing. This was invaluable to the on-going concern and its vital license to operate.

A Brand is All about Value

We could expand the detailed analysis further and infinitely strengthen the evidence-based correlation between the Strategic Brand and enduring strategic performance delivery. Over the years, I have come to this simple conclusion: performance is the mother of legitimacy. If and as the causality between brand and delivery is clearly established, it places the brand at the centre of the company's agenda. Spending the necessary time to firm up the 'brand business model' and building the Strategic Brand accordingly will prove transformational to the organisation's performance and to all those involved.

CHAPTER 13
CRISIS RESILIENT

Next to doing the right thing, the most important thing is to let people know you are doing the right thing

John D Rockefeller

Tuesday, the 20th of April 2010 is a date that will forever be etched in my consciousness. We all remember some 'public' moments in our lives as if they were yesterday. For me these are General De Gaulle's death, President Kennedy's assassination and 9/11 when I was in Singapore.

But it is this April Tuesday in 2010 that will always remain the most emotional for me.

Very early in the morning, I took a call from a member of my team who told me there had been an explosion on one of our rigs in the Gulf of Mexico. I was in the UK and the time difference meant that this was all happening the night before in the US.

Immediately, I heard from the Gulf of Mexico strategy performance leader, James Dupre, who said there had been a big incident, that the incident management team was engaged and a number of crewmembers were still unaccounted for. The first priority was to locate these missing workers. There were a lot of uncertainties and unknowns at that time.

That day, the Deepwater Horizon offshore oil drilling rig exploded in the Gulf of Mexico, around 40 miles south east of Louisiana, costing the lives of 11 people, injuring 17 others and leading to one of the worst oil spills in United States history.

| ILLUSTRATION 13.1 | THE DEEPWATER HORIZON RIG |

Credit – Getty Images

It was a terrible day for the families and friends of the deceased workers – and my thoughts will be with them forever.

BP would never be the same again. We nearly saw the end of our great company. Ultimately, we watched it shrink by a third; saw the brand tarnished like no other in history and endured six years of difficulties with little to no space to act in the US. What had seemed impossible before the incident became the norm.

But in that moment, early in the morning, our priority was the safety of the workers. As a conservative step, the brand team stopped all UK advertising and we started thinking about communication plans for the US. Everything was dependent on how the situation would develop. Flights from the UK were severely disrupted by the Icelandic volcanic eruptions so we watched and planned from London, knowing that our Gulf of Mexico team was doing everything in its power to rescue the people on site.

What I didn't yet anticipate was how long we would be in crisis. For me, it would mean weeks in the same office space in Houston at BP's Westlake 4 building, 3rd floor, where Tony Hayward, group CEO, Bob Dudley, future group CEO and a dozen other people, including Bernard Looney, current Chief Executive Upstream, led the core of the response. And it would mean many more months in the US, thinking, living and breathing the crisis.

BRAND CRISIS

What do BP, Samsung, Toyota, Siemens, VW, Toshiba, AIG, FIFA, Wells Fargo and so many other brands have in common - crisis.

Crisis management has become a new normal for every business today – from the most complex and potentially dangerous crises to the seemingly benign. I never imagined I would be so deeply involved in helping to manage the extremes of this crisis that nearly wiped BP out, one which was certainly a cataclysm for the brand.

Although I was on site, I won't focus on the sequence of events themselves, the engineering steps to shut the well or the political play. They have been documented elsewhere and continue to have deep, emotional consequences for many people. Rather I will illustrate the role of crisis in developing and testing a true Enduring Strategic Brand through my own first-hand experience. I'll also take a perspective on the brand at this critical moment in BP's history, running through the sequence of brand communication steps to raise the question: what can we learn from this extreme case of crisis management? Isn't crisis the most revealing time to assess if a brand is truly a Strategic Brand? What should we do now to prevent a potential crisis? And, if a crisis does happen, how could we build a brand in peacetime to make the organisation 'too good to fail'?

These questions are somewhat similar to an extreme bank stress test – ensuring that a brand is as prepared as possible to respond to and then recover from a crisis.

I will first refer to the brand aspects of Volkswagen's recent emission scandal and contrast it with the Johnson & Johnson Tylenol crisis, as a way of considering and building a brand so that it becomes the main line of defense for hundreds of organisations involved in similar crises each year. Then, I will come back to and run through the brand aspect of BP's Gulf of Mexico disaster.

Because, one thing I know for certain after being in the eye of the storm during BP's most difficult time, is that no brand is 100 percent immune or ready for a crisis. And it is amazing how quickly a brand's circumstances can change. Even the most respected organisations and brands are vulnerable to unexpected events.

THE VW EMISSIONS CRISIS

On 12 January, 2017 Volkswagen agreed to plead guilty to three felonies and pay $4.3 billion in penalties to settle a US Department of Justice investigation into the Diesel Emission Scandal.

This penalty includes a criminal fine of $2.8 billion, the second largest criminal environmental settlement in US history after BP's Deepwater Horizon case. This fine comes on top of the $15.3 billion that Volkswagen agreed to pay in a partial civil settlement with US federal, state governments and car owners in June 2016, plus an additional $1 billion announced in December 2016 related to the 3 litre engine models. It's a punishing $21 billion fine for Volkswagen after 15 months of continuous battle.

Sequence of events

On 3 September, 2015, Volkswagen admitted to the Environmental Protection Agency (EPA) that it had installed illegal 'defeat devices' in its 2.0 litre diesel engines to circumnavigate the US emission tests. This software could detect when diesel engines were being tested, changing the performance accordingly to manipulate the results. A couple of weeks later, on 18 September, the regulators revealed the VW scandal to the world, also known as 'emissionsgate' or 'dieselgate'. A fast sequence of events followed: on 23 September, VW's CEO Martin Winterkorn resigned. He accepted responsibility for the emissions scandal, while claiming no personal wrongdoing. He also declared he was stunned that misconduct on such a scale was possible in the Volkswagen Group. Matthias Mueller, the former boss of Porsche, was named the new CEO of the Volkswagen Group on 25 September.

The new CEO vowed maximum transparency as the company investigated the diesel violations and committed to improve the group's governance and compliance practices. Since 2008, 11 million cars from the VW Group were fitted with the defeat device. On 22 April 2016 Volkswagen reported its largest annual loss in history.

ILLUSTRATION 13.2   VW SHARE PRICE THROUGH THE CRISIS

Key moments in VW emissions scandal
Share price (€)

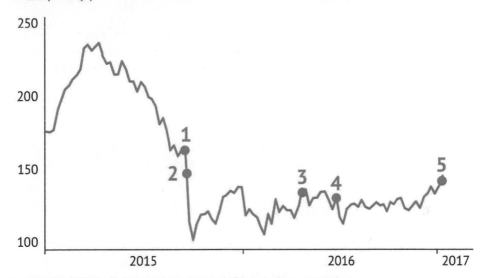

1. **Sep 18 2015** US Regulator reveals VW emissions cheating
2. **Sep 23 2015** Chief executive Martin Winterkorn resigns
3. **Apr 22 2016** VW reports its largest annual loss
4. **Jun 28 2016** VW agrees to pay up to $15.3bn in US civil settlement
5. **Jan 10 2017** VW agrees to $4.3bn US criminal settlement

Credit – Thomson Reuters

The major shake-up included the departure of such iconic leaders of the group as Ulrich Hackenberg, Audi's technical director and Michael Horn, the CEO of Volkswagen Group of America. The scandal also led to a major reconsideration of the culture, the brand and the group's strategic plans. In June 2016, Matthias Mueller promised the biggest-ever change process, with a key focus on the turnaround of the underperforming Volkswagen brand. Culture change included, as an example, that Volkswagen independent brands and regional operations would obtain greater autonomy, moving away from the previous top-down model, where almost all decisions were made at the headquarters in Wolfsburg.

On 22 June 2016, Volkswagen announced a new strategy, 'TOGETHER – Strategy 2025', with details on how it would transform the core business. One key feature is the development of 30 new pure electric vehicles and a pledge to reach annual unit sales of 2-3 million e-cars by 2025, an equivalent of 20-25 per cent of total sales.

ILLUSTRATION 13.3   VOLKSWAGEN 'TOGETHER - STRATEGY 2025'

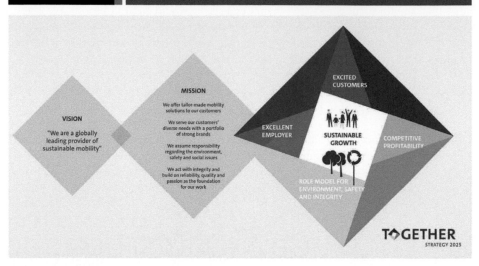

Credit – Thomson Reuters

I will not go into further details about the sequence of events to settle the scandal in the US, nor the continuing exposure of the Volkswagen Group to more claims and related compensation costs, both on-going and on the horizon in Europe, Korea and other markets. Rather in reflecting on the 'Crisis Resilient' Strategic Brand Imperative, I will focus on four learnings I certainly took from the Volkswagen scandal.

1. Lean on your brand's position as your reservoir of goodwill
2. Make the most of your customers' vote of confidence
3. Develop a crisis management strategy early
4. Put your culture under the microscope

Lean on your brand's position as your reservoir of goodwill

I knew the Volkswagen Group well, having partnered with them for over 25 years. The Board of Management member for Procurement, Francisco Garcia Sanz, has been a close and dear colleague for a long time - he was actually made responsible for supervising the "systematic processing of the diesel issue". I had periodic but regular interactions with the former Chief Executive Martin Winterkorn, as well as with many other senior executives of the group.

I always had a strong respect for the enterprise and its leadership – set in the essence of the VW brand, a passionate belief in technological perfection. Ferdinand Piech was a formidable engineer and when he handed over the reins to a successor, he selected Martin Winterkorn, at the time the head of Audi, for the very same reason.

I have seen Martin Winterkorn in action multiple times, restlessly chasing technical excellence. I remember major dealer events or annual global sourcing meetings, where rather than spending his time with other attendees, he would circle around the vehicles, talking with the engineers and asking detailed questions to check that what he had in front of him was absolutely to the highest standard of technology. This passionate quest for technology perfection lies in the Audi brand tagline: "*Vorsprung durch Technik*", which can be best translated as "*Advancement through Technology*" – although Audi USA uses "*Truth in Engineering*". Each of the 12 brands of the group benefited from and contributed to this technical excellence.

Hence my biggest challenge to the Volkswagen Group's response to the emissions scandal is that it simply was not branded! By this I mean, of course they used their logo, but they didn't embrace their Strategic Brand. In times of crisis, organisations should lean on their strength and make the most of their differentiated positioning and correlated reservoir of goodwill.

VW's response was complex and went into many tangents, including future electrical vehicles – which, as attractive they might be, are not where the positive reputational capital lies. VW's plural points of view didn't simply and obviously talk into the heart of the brand's unique sweet spot of technical excellence, leveraging the considerable related reservoir of goodwill.

I would have liked to see – and would have advised them to adopt a simple, humble but confident narrative: "*Yes, we have cheated. It was in pursuit of our core purpose, which is technical excellence for customers and society. We made a big mistake and are deeply sorry. We will respond, repair and improve based on the best technical solutions we can develop. We will lean on our technical expertise to first focus on fixing all the cars involved and in the future we will continue to develop the best performing cars of all types for our customers, in full compliance with all laws and regulations.*"

Make the most of your customers' vote of confidence

There was some great news in this crisis for Volkswagen, which was their customers' phenomenal vote of confidence. Sales have been remarkably resilient as a result of the group's technological excellence, reputation and brand positioning. While sales of the 12 group brands including Audi, Porsche, SEAT, Skoda and Volkswagen had fallen by 2 per cent in 2015 to 9.93 million vehicles, the group sold a record 10.3 million cars in 2016, from the eye of the cyclone, almost 4 per cent more than in 2015.

This sales performance crowned the Volkswagen Group as the world's largest carmaker for 2016, ahead of Toyota with its 10.1 million sales. While the crisis did impact the US and South America, with a 25 per cent decrease in sales and Germany with a 3 per cent decrease, this was more than made up for by a 12 per cent increase in the company's biggest market – China.

We researched hundreds of testimonies to better understand the resilience of the Volkswagen Group performance and they all point to the same conclusion: the simple brand positioning of technological excellence as well as customers' enduring trust that the Volkswagen Group cars are among the best in the world – and this is what protected the brand during its worst-ever crisis.

Develop a crisis management strategy...early

As the VW Group crisis developed in the US, I recognised the considerable similarities, - in particular the US Department of Justice (DoJ) actions, with what we experienced with BP's Deepwater Horizon. I very much hoped that the carmaker would use all learning from the BP experience to inform its actions. If they had done so, they would have taken a strategic position from the very early days of the crisis and been in a better position to anticipate some of the manoeuvres by the DoJ in particular.

Indeed, 18 months into the crisis, as I write in March 2017, these events are identical to what happened to BP. For example, at the point of highest pressure in the settlement negotiation and pre-settlement announcement, the FBI arrested Volkswagen executives. Human pressure at this particular point is a common tactic and used to dramatise the situation. We had exactly the same at BP, including the arrests of some of my dear colleagues at their homes, being handcuffed in front of their children on a Saturday morning.

The learning for brands is to spend days and nights very early on in a crisis, sketching the likely scenarios ahead; imagining what the detailed milestones will look like, from civil to penal, from early settlements to potential personal arrests; and developing a broad desired position for 18 months later. It is vital to draft this early, using others' experience and accepting the fact that you can't possibly anticipate every detail. From this exercise, a clear enduring point of view should be developed, which I describe as the 'crisis management strategy'. And then, the enterprise needs to be consistent in communicating and acting against the pillars of this point of view, at scale and repeatedly with all stakeholders.

This is taking some control, the best defence against all opposers and the unavoidable and inevitable groups of plaintiffs -and the best defence for the brand's reputation, now and in the future. A brand in crisis must see ahead. It needs a point of view early. It must stand firm on what it means and represents. It must be transparent. It needs to do the right thing. It should humanize every part of the response.

A brand in crisis needs a point of view early. It must stand firm on what it means and represents. It must be transparent. It needs to do the right thing. It should humanize every part of the response.

And the enterprise must ground everything in the brand. This requires stable, confident leadership, who are resilient and passionate about getting it right.

Put your culture under the microscope

There has been a lot written about the internal culture of Volkswagen, which allegedly is at the root of the Emissions scandal. The thesis is that the top-down, centralised, authoritative culture and leadership practice placed huge pressure on the engineers and supposedly led them to hide their inability to deliver their technical objectives. Instead, they developed a defeat device to reach the goals, which fell very short of the company's required ethical standards.

From my personal experience, there is no doubt that there were strong personalities and demanding technical experts at the top of the group, setting very ambitious technical objectives for themselves and for their teams. There is also no doubt that the organisation was centralised and as the new Chief Executive admitted himself, that often, *"Germany knew better than Sao Paulo for Brazil"*. However, the stance by the media, describing a 'dictatorship', seems well too caricatured and not necessarily the exact reality.

The Imperative assessment on Illustration 13.4, reveals a strong Volkswagen Strategic Brand, although with weaker aspects on 'Culture and Authenticity', 'People Leading' and if we had added it, 'Joy'. With hindsight, it reminds us how critical it is to be strong on all 13 imperatives to be a true, low risk and enduring Strategic Brand - and to take action on the lower score imperatives, to avoid the risk inherent to them.

ILLUSTRATION 13.4	THE 'ENDURING STRATEGIC BRAND' IMPERATIVES - VOLKSWAGEN

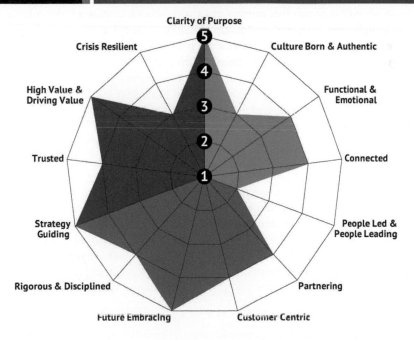

THE JOHNSON & JOHNSON TYLENOL CRISIS

Tylenol was the most successful over-the-counter (OTC) product in the United States with over one hundred million users and the leader in the painkiller field with 37 per cent market share. During the fall of 1982, cyanide was added to Tylenol capsules and seven people died as a result.

Johnson & Johnson unexpectedly faced an unprecedented crisis where one of its most trusted products was killing people. And here is how they turned what could have been a disaster into a textbook branded crisis management best practice. (Note 1)

Crisis and strategic response

The news of the deaths first came to J&J from a Chicago news reporter. CEO, James Burke immediately took accountability and convened a seven-member team with the aim of developing a response strategy. No crisis management plan would have been appropriate to tackle a tragedy of the scale of the Tylenol poisoning, so where could they find guidance? The company turned to their credo for help: *"It was the credo that prompted the decisions that enabled us to make the right early decisions that eventually led to the comeback phase,"* said David R. Clare, President of Johnson & Johnson at the time.

The credo was written in the mid-1940s by Robert Wood Johnson, the company's leader for 50 years. He believed business had responsibilities to society and that long- term sustainability and business success would come from this responsibility. This extended *"to consumers and medical professionals using its products, employees, the communities where its people work and live, and its stockholders."* Observing the credo, Johnson & Johnson would work through the crisis for the public interest and Burke's team emerged with a very simple crisis strategy framework:

- Protect the people
- Save the product

This ultra-simple strategy was translated into three strands of actions: protect and remediate; rectify and communicate.

Protect and remediate

The company undertook immediate, significant actions to protect the public. Through mass communication, they alerted consumers across the nation to not use Tylenol until further assurance could be provided. They conducted a national withdrawal of every capsule, even though there was little chance of discovering more cyanide capsules. They stopped all production and advertising of Tylenol. In taking these actions, Johnson & Johnson demonstrated that they would not put the public's safety at risk, whatever the cost to the company.

The remediation plan included support, counsel and compensation to the victims' families. This help continued even when it was established that Johnson & Johnson was not directly responsible for the product tampering, which had significant positive impact on public's opinion.

Rectify
Working with FDA officials, Johnson & Johnson developed a triple sealed packaging, which included some technical firsts that would make a repeat of the sabotage impossible. They changed the tablets themselves so that they were harder to tamper with. They also applied new inspection procedures to their processes, such as a final control before shipment. These practices became industry standards for OTC medications.

All response actions were communicated formally, so that as many people see them as possible.

Communicate
Johnson & Johnson used significant amounts of paid advertising and sought for earned media to communicate their strategy during the crisis. The campaign began with national alerts warning the public not to use Tylenol and continued with daily messages. A 1-800 hot line was set up immediately to respond to enquiries. A disciplined and systematic media relations plan followed, through several press conferences held at J&J corporate headquarters and broadcast nationally. Chief Executive, James Burke participated in selected high profile shows, such as '60 Minutes'.

J&J used every available channel at scale to counteract what was described as *"the highest US news coverage since the assassination of President John F. Kennedy"*. At first, the media made the story deeply emotional and sensational, focusing on the tragedies of Mary, Adam, Stanley, Theresa and others who had died and linking their names to the Tylenol brand, *"until now, a trusted consumer product"*. Print media headlines were equally devastating, including *'Tylenol, Killer or Cure'* or *'The Tylenol Scare'*. An extraordinary 90 per cent of the American population had heard of the Tylenol case within a week.

ILLUSTRATION 13.5   TYLENOL CRISIS MEDIA ACTIVITY

Johnson & Johnson leaned heavily on advertising, as its PR capability was then limited. It called for establishing a positive, if possible partnering relationship with the media, something that few organisations know to do well in peace time - to be ready just in case. On the other hand, Johnson & Johnson culture and brand were consistently at the heart of the leadership's response and this had a strong and positive impact.

Outcomes

Through its 'protect', 'remediate' and 'rectify' actions, Johnson & Johnson won the functional battle of 'forgiveness'. People were made aware of actions and developments and felt that the company was placing them ahead of the company's interests. Tylenol's sales rebounded as early as within a year of the crisis although the cost of the recall plus other losses exceeded $100 million. As reflected in Illustration 13.6, the rebound of J&J's stock was even more positive. While the Johnson & Johnson share price plunged close to 20 per cent during the early days of the crisis (point B), it returned to pre-crisis levels 43 days into the crisis (points A & C) and raised a further ca. 10 per cent by January 1983.

ILLUSTRATION 13.6	JOHNSON & JOHNSON SHARE PRICE SEPTEMBER 1982 – FEBRUARY 1983

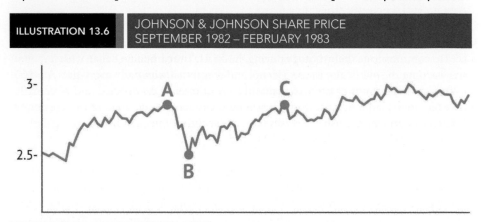

Source: Yahoo! Finance – September 1982 to February 1983

Credit – Thomson Reuters

Johnson & Johnson also won the battle of 'sympathy'. Its continuous focus on and communication about public safety anchored the brand. They made everything very human. As the incident was soon attributed to tampering by hostile parties, the company later became seen as a victim as well.

Today Johnson & Johnson and Tylenol have completely recovered their reputation and market share. And the fundamentals of crisis handling and response, although 35 years-old and with a completely different communication landscape, remain best in class. This strategy and actions should guide any brand considering its crisis plan or facing a similar reality. (If only Johnson & Johnson had applied the same excellent response to the Motrin "phantom recall" in 2009!)

THE BP DEEPWATER HORIZON CRISIS

As Volkswagen and J&J evidence, during times of crisis, the heart and soul of the brand is exposed like no other time in the business's history. If the brand is just a 'shell', a logo or a piece of TV advertising, a crisis will see it crumble.

Turning back to the BP Gulf of Mexico crisis, I completely agree with Tony Hayward when he says, "*BP, as a Strategic Brand, was our pole star*".

The inner core of the BP brand informed our people and our culture, inspired us to "do the right thing", and united us as a team, working 24/7 for 88 days during the most challenging time of our business lives as we tried to shut the leak. And it carried on guiding us for many years after the oil stopped flowing, as we continued the work to contain and then repair the damage from the oil spill.

The Strategic Brand, "biggest savior in times of crisis"

Outside of America (more of this later), Tony Hayward believes that, "*the BP brand was our biggest savior. Everyone knew that BP was a good company doing the right thing, conducting operations safely and responsibly. And through its actions and its brand, we had earned tremendous trust, with governments and societies all over the world - and that held us through enormously big stakes throughout the summer 2010.*"

"The BP brand was our biggest savior. If we had not had that brand, then we would have been punished outside of the US, in a different way but we would have been punished."

He adds: "*If we had not had that brand, then we would have been punished outside of the US, in a different way but we would have been punished. We were widely supported, I met a lot of government heads in that five or six months before I left BP. Everyone was saying: 'we can't believe what America is doing to your company, it's not what you deserve'.*"

Let's explore firstly the sequence of events, followed by the story of the brand in crisis.

The first 88 days' dramatic events

20 April 2010 was going to be wonderful for BP in the US. It was the day the Olympic and Paralympic Team USA made its traditional visit to Washington DC. Hundreds of the best US athletes were coming to the federal capital to meet the President and connect with politicians and communities in the city.

Events - The day that changed everything for BP

As an important partner of the US Olympic Committee, BP was fortunate to be central to the celebration: athletes appeared at local BP fuel stations; BP joined the White House

Rose Garden reception and so on. We also hosted the main evening reception for the athletes in the Supreme Court Chamber, a considerable honour for our company. The BP Olympic & Paralympic team, which I was privileged to oversee, had put considerable efforts into preparing for these events.

Senator Hatch spoke with great conviction about the importance of sponsors like BP and how they helped to support Olympic dreams, and received a vigorous round of applause from the athletes and attendees.

There was universal endorsement of the partnership with BP and great excitement about its potential. Although information was limited at the time, once we learned of the tragedy of the Deepwater Horizon rig explosion, the excitement in the room went down.

Nobody knew yet that we were heading to a unique combination of events, which remained centre stage in the media and public eye for an exceptionally long time. Unlike most crises, which tend to break quickly and then subside almost as fast, the oil spill was a slow motion and multi-threaded disaster.

Events - 88 days of a multi-fronted crisis

Oil began to flow into the waters of the Gulf of Mexico on 22 April, 2010, when the platform sank. The flow didn't completely stop until 15 July, 2010. Those 88 days were extremely tense, punctuated by a number of failed attempts to shut the well – all technical firsts and each of them better than the previous one. It was a dramatic, disappointing shock to the neighbouring communities and the whole of the US when these attempts failed.

Then there was the fate of the people directly involved, not just the bereaved families but the communities in the Gulf region - the fishermen, shrimpers, tourist professionals and many others – including the oil industry itself. How could these people recover when the season was lost and they were unable or limited in their ability to do their job and earn a living? What was the future of their environment, and when and how would the Gulf Coast from which they made their living be restored? What did the future hold for their industries now that a massive premium had been placed on security of operations?

There was also the political theatre: the efforts of the Obama Administration to avoid repeating the political fiasco of Hurricane Katrina; the obsessive attempt by some in Congress to make a political point by launching a series of investigations and bring BP to its knees; the competitive posturing of the Gulf region's local politicians and so on.

There was the judiciary process, with a multitude of lawsuits initiated at all levels, including State and Federal, civil and criminal. One striking milestone: on 2 June 2010 Attorney General Eric Holder declared that he was investigating the disaster for both civil and criminal infractions.

After a well publicised failure to stop the leak in late May - "the top kill", the Obama administration unleashed its wrath on BP. Our shares plunged and the company came very close to bankruptcy, as described later. A major stabilising act was required and took the form of a meeting with President Obama at the White House, where a $20 billion fund was agreed to compensate victims of the oil spill.

This complex, multi-fronted response would last for weeks until the oil flow was stopped on 15 July. It took months to complete the clean-up and restore the impacted economy and it took years to settle the core litigations.

My own remit did not escape the multiplicity of fronts and deep scrutiny. For example, on Tuesday 17 August 2010, US Congress sent a formal request seeking information on our communication spends since the crisis start - more about this later. How many times have I took Henry Ford's words as an encouragement: *"When everything seems to be going against you, remember that the airplane takes off against the wind, not with it"*

Illustration 13.7 summarises some of the most dramatic events in the first three months of the crisis, which felt like both the shortest and the longest time of many of my BP colleagues' and indeed my own life. I will relate the key brand milestones against these events later and notably with Illustrations 13.14 and 13.21.

ILLUSTRATION 13.7	OPERATIONAL AND CORPORATE EVENTS TIMELINE

2010 Operational Crisis Timeline		2010 Political & Corporate Timeline	
Date	**Activity**	**Date**	**Activity**
April 20th	Explosion on the Deepwater Horizon drilling platform	April 30th	First class action lawsuit against BP and the platform owners by Louisiana shrimpers
April 22nd	Platform sinks, rupturing the pipe Attempts to activate the blowout preventer fail	May 10th	Cost of leak already assessed well above previous estimates
May 2nd	Drilling on relief well begins; 200 boats to tackle the spill	May 28th	President Obama states that BP would "pay every dime" for the damage caused
May 8th	Containment dome fails	June 2nd	Attorney General Eric Holder declares he is investigating the disaster for both civil & criminal infraction
May 10th	Oil dispersant begins to be sprayed in the Gulf	June 9th	BP's share slips further, a 40% drop to pre-crisis levels
May 30th	Top kill operation fails	June 16th	White House Agreement for a $20bn escrow fund
June 4th	First containment cap; oil flow reduced	June 17th	Tony Hayward appears before a congressional committee investigating the disaster
June	Continuing massive technical and clean up efforts	June 30th	President Obama directs officials to draw-up a long term plan to help the region get back on its feet after the spill
July 12th	New cap inserted with further reductions in oil flow	July 27th	Tony Hayward is replaced by Bob Dudley as Group CEO
July 15th	Cap retrofitted and oil stops flowing	July 27th	BP takes a $32.2bn charge against earnings for the damage
August	Relief well successful and the well is permanently shut in		

And there was BP, in the eye of this storm, dealing with the fallout, its first task to plug the well and stop oil spilling into the Gulf waters; then to address the needs of the people directly impacted by the disaster, while facing attacks and challenges from every corner. Everybody wanted a sacrificial lamb.

Events - Shutting the leak and mitigating the consequences of the spill
In the first three months, BP first focused its work on shutting down the well. We brought in internal and external experts from around the world, worked closely with

the Coast Guard and the US government, and developed short-term and long-term engineering fixes.

The second main stream of immediate activity was to mitigate the impact. We began oil collection efforts on the surface at considerable scale, created a massive claims process across the five Gulf States, introduced community centres in 25 key locations, partnered with wildlife foundations to help the impacted animals and collected environmental samples of all sorts to monitor the impact on the ecosystem.

While these real actions were not sufficient to counter the volume and intensity of criticism, BP's collective belief was that being as action-orientated and problem-solving as possible – despite the skepticism – would make a difference to its ongoing efforts and, ultimately, prove defining. In many ways, pastor and author Charles Swindoll's words could have become our common motto: *"Life is 10 per cent what happens to me and 90 per cent of how I react to it"*

Events - An unprecedented response

'Living the brand' through the shared mission of *"Commitment and Actions"*, BP's priority from day one of the crisis was simple: *"Do the right thing and honour our commitments."* – more on this later in the brand story.

BP's response reached an unprecedented scale and included:

- $14 billion to support the clean-up, restoration and recovery
- A $20 billion fund for the Deepwater Horizon Oil Spill Trust, in agreement with the US Government, so those impacted could be quickly and fairly compensated
- The mobilization and support of 48,000 response workers (twice the seating capacity of Madison Square Garden).

ILLUSTRATION 13.8	BOATS, PLANES, WORKERS CLEANING BEACHES, COMMAND CENTERS AND WILDLIFE EXPERTS INVOLVED IN THE RESPONSE

Credit – BP corporate site

- 6,500 vessels (23 times the size of the active US Navy fleet) and over 100 aircraft to serve on the clean up
- BP helped to survey 4,300 miles of shoreline (five times the length of California's coastline)
- A $1.2 billion donation to fund the largest scientific study of the Gulf ecosystem ever conducted
- Nearly $200 million invested to fund tourism promotion efforts for the Gulf Coast States.
- $82 million for the testing and promotion of Gulf seafood.
- $1 billion pledged in early restoration projects along the Gulf Coast, provided to the National Fish and Wildlife Foundation to establish the Recovered Oil Fund for Wildlife.

ILLUSTRATION 13.9	RESOURCES AND ASSETS DEPLOYED IN THE SURFACE RESPONSE PLAN

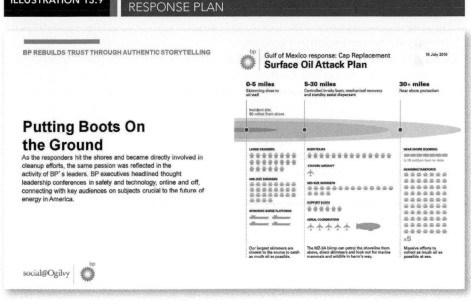

Credit – BP

Every aspect of the Deepwater Horizon disaster was studied by a wide array of experts in complex industrial processes and accidents. BP has led the way in learning from this tragic event. And now it is applying those safety lessons across the company, while sharing them with others across the globe.

Ultimately, it was an incredible response on the ground. Tony observes that no one has ever fought against our actual response to the crisis and he doesn't think anybody will. *"Its scale, its comprehensiveness, our willingness to accept responsibility, embrace and to do all of it. It was an unbelievable response: 10,000 vessels, 50,000 people. People objected to the fact that it [the oil spill] had happened in the first place but not to the response."*

Events – A well-rehearsed crisis response plan

So how did we do it? BP had a well-rehearsed crisis response plan, with a crisis response governance structure that was both regional and global.

Tony elaborates: *"If you have this structure in place, you can do that. We just scaled it and we kept scaling it… The biggest challenges were not the lines of communication nor the ability to work well but pulling together 50,000 people in a very short period of time. And only a large global organisation can do that, because we sucked in BP people from all over the world, from our contractors and their contractors. It was the fact that we had a governance structure for crisis management and clarity of accountability that made it possible.*

"What we found was, it was expandable, we could just keep scaling it. When it became clear that we were not just dealing with a spill in Louisiana but we were also dealing with one in Alabama, Mississippi and Florida, we replicated what we already built in Louisiana to deal with those in Alabama, Mississippi and Florida."

Events - The day when BP almost died

Some days were even more tense than others on the 3rd floor of Westlake 4. And there certainly were such days very early in June 2010, when the inconceivable almost happened – when BP almost disappeared as a company, when a company everybody had thought was 'too big to fail' teetered on a precipice.

The spill had already wiped billions of pounds off the company's value. Amid rumours that BP was seeking bankruptcy protection for its US division and that President Obama might force the company not to pay a dividend, BP's share price plummeted, falling to $36.52 on June 1st, nearly 40% below its pre-crisis levels.

Tony and I reminisced about these days recently, notably the 7, 9 and 10 June, when we could hardly trade anymore and bankruptcy was so close. Tony: *"It started on the Memorial Day weekend, right after the top kill failure. The market said: 'Maybe they can't fix this!' And that's why CDS (BP's credit default swap, the cost of insuring the company's debt) blew up to 1500 and there was no liquidity available for our vital short-term needs of credit".*

I remember one particular occasion talking with Tony then, when he openly shared with me how bad the situation was. How could he remain so calm? Tony: *"Honestly, I don't think I can describe it. I had tremendous faith in the firm. I think if this had happened three or four years earlier, it would have been very different because the company wasn't performing in the way it was then. I always believed we would fix it and that we had a balance sheet that would get us through. I simply believed, I guess".*

Events – Saving BP

Two particular events ultimately saved BP. The first followed the top kill failure, when the Obama administration had unleashed its wrath on BP and we were teetering on the edge of bankcrupcy. A major stabilising act was required and took the form of a meeting with President Obama at the White House, on the 16th June, where a $20 billion fund was agreed to compensate victims of the oil spill.

The second was on the 15th July when a containment cap was retrofitted over the leak and the flow of oil was completely stopped. From then, the recovery phase could start.

BP faces the biggest brand storm ever

As far as brand and communication were concerned, the crisis evolved on an hourly basis. But I do remember a number of pivotal moments when the mood changed and we had to make a step change in our response.

Brand storm - Change of mood

In the early days of the crisis, from around 20 April until the 8 May, the focus of the media was not on the BP brand but on Transocean, the rig owner and operator. During this phase, we were criticised but there was some positive coverage around what BP was doing, especially around Tony Hayward's response. The coverage focused on how we were supporting Transocean with every possible resource, trying to stop the flow of oil and doing whatever was required to support communities. We believed the media coverage at that time to be quite balanced and fair.

But then it started to deteriorate.

There was a pivotal day on 13 May when the focus on BP started to take a negative perspective. That day I remember Transocean filed a petition in the Federal Court in Houston to cap their overall liability relating to the incident. It was extraordinary because at the same time BP was just focused on fixing the operational issues. The two companies were taking a very different approach.

I was working late in the UK office on a revised messaging strategy, as there would be a point when it would be badly needed. I received a call from Tony's executive office around 1am. *"We're losing the media battle, can you join us in Houston?"* I flew over later that morning and we held an emergency strategy meeting to plan the brand communication going forward right after I landed.

Brand storm - A media tsunami

We then faced unprecedented levels of negative media coverage. This tragic incident was a major story in the media for months until the leak was sealed and the clean-up and recovery were well underway. BP was in the middle of an unrelenting, 'always on' news cycle.

Some images literally "killed BP" and I will mention two in particular. The first was the visual from our own subsurface ROV cameras of oil flowing from the broken well into the Gulf waters, over 5,000 feet below sea level - this became a continuing feature on some channels, notably on CNN, which displayed it on the screen 24/7. The second was a picture of an oiled pelican, which was published on the front page of many papers on the same day and deeply touched people around the US and the world.

ILLUSTRATION 13.10	OILED PELICAN, OIL SHEEN OVER THE GULF WATERS, OIL FLOW FROM THE WELL, TAR BALLS IN WATER AND A RESCUED TURTLE

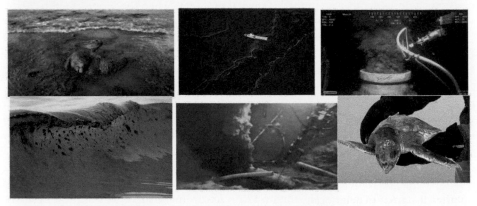

Credit – Top left to right: Getty, 2010; Reuters; BP / Bottom left to right: AP, 2010; BP; Wildlife Trust

Coverage of the crisis required a significant amount of technical and scientific expertise. Consumers were introduced to a series of new terms and concepts as the media tried to cover the efforts to contain the spill and formulate reliable estimates of the extent of the environmental and economic damage. Hence the news media found themselves with a complicated, technical and long-running saga that did not break down along predictable political and ideological lines. And they were reporting to an American public that displayed a ravenous appetite for the spill story.

Brand storm – Unprecedented media coverage and public interest

The spill generated unprecedented media metrics. For over three months after the explosion, the oil spill remained by far the most dominant story in the mainstream news media, accounting for 22% of the news as a whole as shown on Illustration 13.11– almost double the next biggest topic. The Pew Research Centre states that *"while most disasters are covered by the media as 'one week wonders', the Gulf of Mexico oil spill was a slow-motion disaster that exceeded the usual media attention span by far"*. (Note 2)

The activities in the Gulf – the cleanup and containment efforts as well as the impact of the disaster – was the leading storyline, accounting for 47% of the overall coverage. Next was attention to the role of BP (27% of the coverage). The third biggest storyline was Washington-based, the response and actions of the Obama Administration (17%).

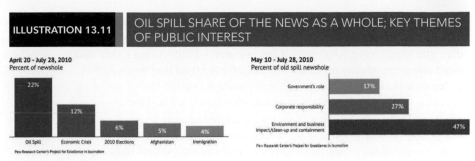

Credit – Pew Research Centre

The Gulf saga was first and foremost a television story. It generated the most coverage in cable news (31% of the airtime studied). CNN devoted considerable attention to it (42% of its airtime) and, as noted earlier, at any point in time and whatever story they were running, featured a square at the bottom of the screen that filmed the oil gushing from the spill camp.

The so-called 'BP spill' made the roster of top stories five times in 14 weeks in social media. During those weeks one theme resonated: skepticism towards almost all the principals involved in the story.

If anything, public interest in the Gulf saga even exceeded the level of mainstream media coverage, as represented in illustration 13.12. According to surveys by the Pew Research Center for the People & the Press, between 50% and 60% of Americans said they were following the story "very closely" during these 100 days. That surpassed the level of public interest during the most critical moments of the healthcare reform debate.

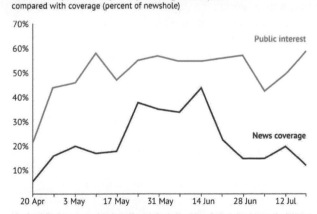

Credit – Pew Research Centre

Kathy Leech, was Director of Brands, BP America at the time. She is clear as to why the story ran and ran and its impact. *"You've got a slow summer when there isn't a lot of other news; you've got evocative pictures of pelicans and dolphins on the beach; and the news just seized this, and unfortunately took this as such a big issue that they vastly over-represented the harm to the Gulf.*

"Suddenly there is no one going to the Gulf anymore because people think that every square mile is covered with five feet of oil, which was not the case. Which means you then have all the stories about devastated tourism. Then it is the seafood industry that goes down because no one is eating Gulf seafood anymore.

Hence there was a major macro-economic impact on five states in the country in the height of what is their high season. No wonder this was huge news: it was political, economic and social and fed the simple and appealing narrative of: 'big oil companies or big companies, in general, cannot be trusted."

Brand storm – It got simply terrible for the brand
In marketing terms, you can't exactly describe this as unprecedented brand awareness, nor was it a brand-building moment, to say the least – although certainly a defining one!

Throughout the crisis, the BP brand was vilified across a wide spectrum of daily news, business, political, entertainment and cultural touch points, including the de-facing of our brand identity.

Against this onslaught, there was virtually nothing BP could say to make anyone feel better about the brand. Internally, we asked ourselves what does the BP brand really mean in this reality and what does it actually stand for in such times, so it acts properly

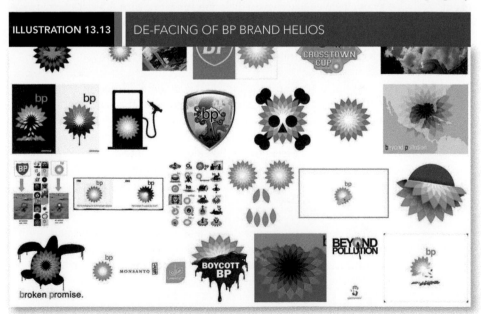

ILLUSTRATION 13.13   DE-FACING OF BP BRAND HELIOS

and usefully? Certainly, an important answer was that the people of BP would be ultimately judged on how well they 'lived the brand' through their actions. Or at least, this was what they deeply believed and hoped… and they lived the brand passionately.

The BP Brand in crisis defined by its people and culture

As we've already seen with J&J, most people and organisations in crisis return to who they are, what they know - and their deep culture, purpose and values drive their actions. From the genesis, and throughout the heat of the crisis, nobody in BP was thinking about "branding" per se, but what everybody actually did, through his or her actions, was absolutely true to the brand. And this is precisely what I mean by the notion of a truly Strategic Brand.

Most people and organisations in crisis return to who they are, what they know - and their deep culture, purpose and values drive their actions.

Culture - Drawing on BP values to "do the right thing"
Without a thought for who was ultimately accountable or for the consequences of their actions, the people of BP took responsibility immediately for plugging the well, for the clean-up and stepped up to provide as much assistance as possible to all those affected by the explosion and spill.

BP's people, starting with the CEO, committed themselves beyond imagination *"to do the right thing"*. They tried to do the impossible *"at the frontier"*. [Ref. Chapter 1]. And they were always available to engage, have a dialogue and work with those impacted and wider society. I was there – and never thought I would see the BP brand lived so deeply; that I would see such a profoundly branded response, even if our crisis communication was not always perfect in the heat of the moment, to say the least (more on this later).

We were not the only ones driven by *doing the right thing.* Thousands of people, companies and organisations from all origins joined forces in the same spirit. I want to signal out Admiral Thad Allen, the National Incident Commander of the Unified Command for the Deepwater Horizon oil spill, President Obama's appointee to lead the crisis response. Despite his 24/7 access to the President's red line and probably under considerable pressure to execute *"putting the boot on the throat of BP"*, I can't name a single time when the greater interests did not drive Admiral Allen's judgment and decisions.

Culture - Translating the brand culture into a framework of actions
BP's brand purpose was translated into a framework of 'commitments and actions', which is simply summarised in the next picture. This brand framework was to endure and act as a guide for our teams over a number of years after 20 April 2010.

Framework of 'commitments and actions'
Live the brand.
Take responsibility.
Do the right thing.
Keep people informed.
Share our learning.
Committed to America.

Culture - The BP family: a united front

The people of BP stood strong for those who were impacted by the disaster, and for the company. Even in the US, where their families were challenged not only at work but also in their schools, in their communities, they provided the most admirable branded response. The best evidence is that staff turnover during the crisis was around one tenth of BP's normal already low attrition.

Tony and I discussed the way the company came together like never before: *"The tougher it became, the more tightly bound the BP family became. So, the greater the adversity, the greater the feeling of BP against the world... That feeling of everyone supporting each other, everyone battling this thing. Certainly, if you were in America like you and I, it felt like you were against the world. Someone would tell me a story about how they had flown halfway around the world, left their family. It was a unique moment in terms of a united company. Everyone could see that we were trying to do the right thing. We weren't hiding behind words but trying our upmost to be fully accountable and responsible in the crisis. It was a rallying cry."*

Kathy remembers an overwhelming sense that, *"we had to do the right thing, we had to clean up our own mess. What the company did so well, was to so quickly organise people and then empower them by saying: 'Look, it is clear you are not going to be fully expert at what you'll be doing, for example you are going to run a community centre, but just do the right thing. And we trust you to do that.' And that's what people did. They could have stumbled and stopped but they didn't. They just did the right thing. And they did it incredibly selflessly and under unbelievable circumstances. It was 'we do what we have to do, we have each others' backs and we go for it."*

And this is what an Enduring Strategic Brand does – to borrow from Kathy's earlier analogy: a Strategic Brand doesn't tell, it shows. Our people were the best reflection of BP 'the Strategic Brand', doing the right thing, trying to make it right.

She believes that one reason the BP brand survived these tumultuous events was because it reacted to the crisis in a way that was consistent with its purpose: *"If a company is to hit a crisis and it needs to tap into its employees and its partners in a way that has them operating at levels they have never operated before, you have to have a larger purpose. It is more than fixing the company, it is about putting things back the way they should be or improving things. It is about a higher societal purpose."*

The BP Brand Response Strategy

As discussed about the VW and J&J crisis, I have always believed that crisis management is like chess: you need to see very far ahead before acting. And this is what we tried to do with the BP brand in crisis.

Brand response strategy - A Strategic Brand shows, it doesn't tell

If there is learning about what we did, it is that we didn't do things randomly. We developed a brand messaging strategy that endured over the different stages of the crisis, from 10 May during months if not years and this was as follows:

- Information advertising – *"Honouring our commitment to keep people informed"*
- Clear stages of messaging – *"Relevant and helpful content"*
- Seven pillars of response and restoration, to help people orientate easily -
    – Response: *'Claims'; 'Beaches'; 'Cleanup'; 'Wildlife'*
    – Restoration: *'Economic'; 'Environmental'; 'Health & Safety'*
- Tone – *"Servant BP"*; humble, factual, committed and caring

This framework was all about what was happening and what BP was doing to honour its commitment. As summarised in Illustration 13.14, we evolved the brand communication substance in stages according to where the crisis developed, and to best serve the needs and requirements of those impacted.

| ILLUSTRATION 13.14 | SUMMARY OF KEY CRISIS BRAND COMMUNICATION STAGES |

Before GoM Energy security & diversity	Stage 1 Apology	Stage 2 Response	Stage 3 Restoration commitments	Stage 4 Restoration progress	Stage 5 Best Summer Fully open for business
WHEN	Jun '10	Jun–Sep '10	Sep '10–Feb '11	Mar–Aug '11	Sep–Oct '11

Credit – Based on BP data and advertisements

If there is learning about what we did, it is that we didn't do things randomly. We developed a brand messaging strategy that endured over the different stages of the crisis, from 10 May during months if not years.

Kathy remembers: *"Many times I have said to people, 'What you really have to understand is the scale of this. What did we know about community centres? And within a couple of weeks, we stood up in about 25 of them. There were more boats out there than on D-day! And the company came in and against expectations, said: 'how can we make you whole?' So, our employees, each one of them was incredibly courageous and committed, made it happen. If you come back to the idea of a Strategic Brand, we showed, we did the right thing."*

Based on Kathy's arguments, a series of clips were developed combining information, updates and community connectedness, as reflected in Illustration 13.15.

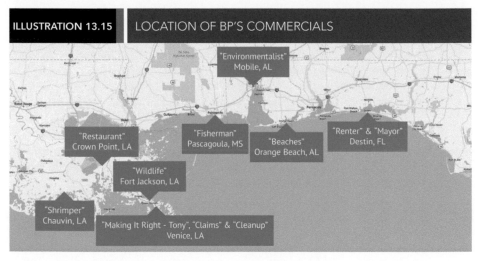

Credit – Based on BP data

Brand response strategy- A Strategic Brand is human and authentic

Illustration 13.16 is an example of BP's response communication. The ad ran from end July and featured a BP employee, Fred Lemond - a native from the Gulf region - involved in tracking and cleaning up the oil before it reached the shores. You might note the way the framework was applied: 'informational', 'relevant', the seven pillars - here 'cleanup' and 'human'.

Indeed, and although our strategy was about being helpful, we wanted to humanise BP as a company. Rachel Kennedy Caggiano was SVP Digital Influence, Ogilvy at the time. She recalls, *"the strategy became: how do we tell the stories of all the people who are involved and put faces to the people at BP, rather than exist as a big, faceless hated corporation."*

ILLUSTRATION 13.16 EXAMPLE OF BP'S RESPONSE COMMUNICATION: FRED

I grew up on the Gulf Coast. I know these waters.
And I'm doing everything I can to clean them up.
- Fred Lemond, BP Cleanup Operations

Making This Right

Beaches
Claims
Cleanup
Economic Investment
Environmental Restoration
Health and Safety
Wildlife

BP has taken full responsibility for the cleanup in the Gulf. And that includes keeping you informed.

Searching For And Cleaning Up The Oil
Every morning, over 50 spotter planes and helicopters search for oil off the coast, heading to areas previously mapped with satellite imagery and infrared photography. Once oil is found, they radio down to the 6,000 ships and boats of all sizes that are supporting the cleanup effort and working to collect the oil. These are thousands of local shrimping and fishing boats organized into task forces and strike teams, plus specialized skimmers mobilized from as far as the Netherlands.

We have recovered more than 27 million gallons of oil-water mixture from the Gulf. Other methods have also helped remove millions of additional gallons of oil from the water. We've deployed more than 8 million feet of boom to protect beaches and sensitive wildlife areas.

Hurricane Preparedness
In the event of a hurricane, our first priority is keeping people safe. In coordination with the Coast Guard and local officials, we may suspend operations temporarily but have organized to resume them as soon as possible.

Our Responsibility
We have already spent more than $3.2 billion responding to the spill and on the cleanup, and none of this will be paid by taxpayers. We will work in the Gulf as long as it takes to get this done. We may not always be perfect but we will do everything we can to make this right.

For information visit: bp.com
restorethegulf.gov
facebook.com/bpamerica
twitter.com/bp_america
youtube.com/bp

For assistance, please call:
To report oil on the shoreline: (866) 448-5816
To report impacted wildlife: (866) 557-1401
To make spill-related claims: (800) 440-0858

Credit and authorisation – BP plc.

Here is a summary feedback from focus groups on this ad, run on 14 July in Tampa (Florida) and Chicago (Illinois): *"Fred is likable. He's from Florida and I like that. It's real people, not just someone from corporate with a suit. It seems like someone like me is helping to clean it up. All those ships you see and all the different techniques. I like the helicopters searching all over, the infrared. They're showing what's happening, taking responsibility, and I appreciate that. How come they only show you the bad stuff on TV, not this good stuff? Show me what they're going to do next, in 6 months from now. He used the word "I" a lot, so I felt like he was taking initiative himself and pushing BP along with him".*

And here is what these focus groups were saying about BP after viewing 'Cleanup': *"Anything they say on their behalf is better than nothing. I never get tired of them saying that BP has taken full responsibility. I want to hear how they're making things right. Eventually, I will come around and forgive them but I'll wait and see. They should continue to inform the public, an informed public is less scared. As I've seen the commercials, my impression has changed, I now believe that they care and really are trying to get ahold of this - before I didn't. They're doing more than I thought. I do get concerned that they don't stay solvent, I'm afraid they'll go under. The media forgets that the people who are working on this need to be commended, they tend to point the finger and place blame."*

Brand response strategy - Investing $250m in brand communication

As evidenced by the focus group, we absolutely needed to get our voice heard and act to protect our brand. We were utterly committed to doing the right thing but the feedback was overwhelming skepticism. We had to find ways to let people know that we were being responsible with our actions. We needed to restore trust in our company and somehow find a way of breaking through a single-mindedly adverse media environment.

Over the course of just a few weeks, we invested $250 million talking to the US. I remember when President Obama explicitly requested that BP stop talking through advertising right after the failure of the top kill...and I took the decision that day to double the weight of communication. Everyone else was absorbed with the direct consequences of the failed top kill and to secure liquidity for the company's survival and I ended up probably not being very popular for this decision at the time...but was not sacked either.

There was a particular reason why we needed to communicate BP's brand and its commitment heavily, despite the President and his Administration's deep objections. I asked Tony Hayward recently about this spend and the risk with government. Tony: *"We spent $250 million over a few weeks talking to the US, The feedback I got at the time from a lot of people was that it was effective, and it was very important that the company's voice was heard. There was no other way to get BP's voice out there, than by paying for the space. There was no objectivity in the coverage of any of the news channels. There was simply no space for our voice. So the only means to be heard was paid advertising. And of course, we built one of the biggest social media programmes in history, although I suspect we would start with this and do even more today."*

Kathy agrees that we had to talk loudly, as we were in a unique position from a brand perspective. *"We were unable to tell our story because the news media was so negative. So, bringing them behind the curtain and telling them, look, here is what is happening; we had such a mountain to climb but until we started advertising, no one was telling our side of the story."*

This action did not come without its profusion of challenges. I recall when the US Congress sent a formal request in August asking for detailed information on our corporate advertising and marketing spending related to Deepwater Horizon oil spill and relief, recovery and restoration efforts. This was extremely tricky, as we could see the questions leading to a potential story, that *"BP is investing vast sums of money to restore its own reputation rather than taking real action for the shrimpers or the hotel owners and restore their livelihood"*. This was absolutely not the case and we also had a responsibility to help impacted people through communication and share BP's brand side of the story with the public.

"We spent $250 million over a few weeks talking to the US ... and it was very important that the company's voice was heard."

Of course, we took considerable care to provide the numbers as requested with fully auditable data down to the penny. And we included additional clarity on how we spent the money on such topics as sharing information with Gulf Coast residents about the cleanup efforts, supporting specific business sectors, advertising the procedures for OPA claimants or fulfilling our commitment to inform the American people during the recovery process. That unsolicited additional transparency would hopefully make it harder to vilify.

To our great and positive surprise and as a major exception to consistent practice of the political and media circles on every other BP matter, there was little challenge or finger pointing and no major public and media references to this submission.

The BP Brand Response Practice

Commentators' assessments of how BP handled the crisis from a brand and communication standpoint were very varied, ranging from 'outstanding' to 'terrible'. There were certainly plenty of low points but let's first surface a few of the better aspects for consideration.

Brand response practice - Telling BP's side of the story on all channels
This is what was done specifically in the first phase of 'response', to inform people in the Gulf and more broadly in America in the face of the crisis:

- BP discontinued all previously planned and currently running global advertising efforts.

- Through newspaper and television advertising, BP took on the responsibility of keeping people continuously informed on the status and progress of our efforts to plug the leak and mitigate its impact.

- Crisis communications were set up to provide information to citizens affected by the spill, including physical sites across the Gulf Coast and 24/7 hotlines for claims information, injured wildlife and cleaning requirements in the water, on land, and more.

- Multiple social media channels and teams across all time zones were set up and mobilised through Facebook, YouTube, Twitter and Flickr to provide answers in real time for those affected in the Gulf and the general public.

- BP's support of a wide range of small businesses dependent on tourism, fishing etc. was communicated factually and practically, to enable their own support of the recovery process in their communities.

We needed to engage with multiple audiences in ways that were sensitive to their concerns. And we needed to give people ways to stay informed about the ongoing activities, using content that could let them judge for themselves whether BP's efforts were authentic and truly serving the needs of all those impacted by the spill. There were no efforts spared, no channel left unused, no stone unturned.

ILLUSTRATION 13.17	ALL COMMUNICATION CHANNELS WERE MOBILIZED

Paid	Owned	Earned
TV	bp.com	Press
Print	Spillcam	
Digital	Facebook	
Radio	Twitter	
Search	YouTube	Social media
	Flickr	

Brand response practice – Listen, listen …and listen

We listened and learned what stories mattered most. Using social and search data, BP gleaned insights for creating content designed around things people really cared about.

This helped to create authentic connections between BP, the Gulf citizens and the wider American public and provided an environment where people would listen.

We launched an initial series of videos featuring BP employees who were Gulf residents and were working at the heart of the recovery effort (for example Fred). The community began to experience the story of progress from the people actually living it. This honest, human point of view revealed a personal side to BP's efforts, and focused new attention on the diverse and relatable group of people working to restore the Gulf.

Brand response practice - Rigour and discipline

Not a single mistake would be allowed. Any inappropriate word, number, picture, feature in one of our communication would make headlines in all the media outlets that were so closely following us, and crucify BP. We would also lose the ability to continue putting our voice out there through the only impactful channel available to us.

Owing to the fantastic team of BP brand professionals and our agency partners, I don't remember a mistake, despite the considerable scale and extent of the effort. How many times and for how many nights did we review each TV ad, print ad and social media posting? How many hundreds of focus groups did we run across the country, sometimes on a daily basis?

Brand response practice – The right organizational set-up

Like the operations team, we had to consider all our group communications and brand capabilities and direct all possible resources towards the crisis.

All organisations have different structures for their brand and marketing teams. Our capability was both located in the HQ in London and deployed in regions. BP also had regional and country corporate affairs, government relations and press offices. All these teams would be central to crisis management.

We also had a large number of brand leaders and product marketers in the individual businesses operating within the frameworks and boundaries set by the central team. We needed most of these people to stay focused on their business and relationships because they were critical touch points of our brand with society.

One of our most important businesses was US retail – thousands of branded BP retail sites across the country. The nation's anger was often directed towards these BP branded 'corner shops', mainly independent owners and operators, and it was our duty to support them during this challenging time. The overarching theme of our joint communication was to remind Americans that the BP stations were neighbours and pillars of the community – and we did this through the 'Locally Owned / Locally Operated' platform. I have already commented in Chapter 4 - 'Connected' - how I believe we should have gone further on joint communication with BP's jobbers and dealers.

During the crisis, we kept the deployed structure mostly intact and resourced the 24/7 central response efforts from the corporate team at HQ, a number of handpicked individuals across the global business and our partnering agencies.

Brand response practice - The war room

In early July, as it became apparent that the crisis response would only grow in scale and pace for many months to come, we set up a 'war room', a single physical location on the 22nd floor of Westlake 1, Houston, for all teams involved in communication including legal. They would lead our coordinated attempt to share accurate information about our efforts and progress to mitigate the oil spill and repair its impact. One wall was covered with nine TV screens each tuned to a different channel, so the team could keep up to date with what the news channels were reporting, another wall showed feeds from how BP was responding to the oil spill. A third wall had our brand strategic response framework, continuously guiding the team's actions. And the big operations table in the centre was the human hub.

During the crisis, Kathy was our brand 'woman on the ground'. I remember calling her at home and asking her to pack a bag and get on the first flight to Houston. At the time, her son Neil was 10 months old and we thought it would just be for three or four days. Then I had to ask her to stay over the weekend...and we realised it was going to have to be long term.

Although sad to be away from her young family, Kathy now recalls these challenging months as some of the most meaningful in her career.

"I have never worked so hard and learned so much. There was hardly any politics. If I needed to get something approved, I turned around and said: 'Please approve this.' And if it was not released in five minutes, I would turn around again and say 'I need it now'. I would march down to the lawyers and say: 'I'm shooting this commercial tomorrow; can you look at this?' So all the barriers that are so irritating in normal life, were just gone, we were all on a shared mission, and there was just no nonsense. We were doing what we had to do, we had each others' backs and we went for it. I felt very privileged to be a part of it."

Kathy believes the war room was extraordinarily important to our continuing efforts despite not initially being a believer. *"But after about two days in the war room, I thought: 'Yes, this is exactly right.'"*

From the very early days, we ensured that we were operating 24/7 by setting up centres of crisis communication all over the world – in New York, West Coast, Hong Kong, London and Sydney. Rachel Kennedy Caggiano, who led setting up a massive social media response to the disaster, recalls: *"We would have team leads in each of the offices and a hand over process, so when the East Coast of the United States handed over to the West Coast, a physical call would always happen. And you needed to organize the same thing when you had people in New York and in Hong Kong, exactly 12 hours apart. They would say: 'I just finished this and now I am handing it over to you.' So, we ensured that there was a very good process for transferring the knowledge from one office to another in real time".*

Brand response practice - World scale social media in four hours

Kathy makes the point that this information campaign was a safe way for people to listen to us…and release their anger. She remembers social media, where if anyone dared to say something that was not negative about BP, let alone positive, *"they got jumped on by all the trolls in our channels"*.

The crisis plunged us into a steep learning curve about many things, one being social media. Before Deepwater Horizon BP didn't have a meaningful presence on Facebook, Flickr, Twitter or YouTube.

This changed dramatically and Rachel remembers: *"It was exceptional, because we went from what was nothing to having a presence at scale in less than four hours. Within the next 48 hours, we had established a process of 80 people around the world working around the clock. The logistics involved the coordination I mentioned earlier between London, New York, DC, Houston, Chicago, San Francisco, Hong Kong and Sydney. It was massive and we had to establish what were best practices and standard operating procedures at the time. There were many hostile people voicing their concerns in social media; and it shouldn't be downplayed what a massive undertaking that was to interact with them all."*

Indeed, everyone was working around the clock to make it happen. Kathy reminded me recently about the pressure I'd put them under to ensure we were up and running quickly and then operating at scale, to the latest detail and 24/7: *"You and I were working on ads until about midnight. And you stopped by the next morning as I was sitting with the Ogilvy social media team and said: 'Kathy, how are the social media channels going?' And I responded: 'Luc, I was with you until midnight and I don't have the social media channels up for you. I can probably get them up for you tomorrow.' You looked at me and said: 'Hmm, you have two hours.' And you just wished us all good luck and walked out and I remember putting my head down and going 'What do I do now?' And of course at that time we didn't even have the passwords, Brunswick, the PR firm, were holding onto them, because they were supposed to be developing social media. I have to say, we didn't make it in two hours but within four hours, we had all four channels up. And you were quite pleased."*

Let's explore social media as a major and distinctive pillar of crisis leadership.

The BP Brand Social Media Response

Rachel points out that setting up our social media presence was a lot more than simply developing these platforms.

Social response – Purpose driven

Actually, we were determined to develop and stick to a very clear purpose and strategy for our channels - which endured a full couple of years:

Says Rachel: *"What we really did was establish a news bureau for the Gulf and BP. At the time the media wasn't covering the situation in the best way: they got the facts wrong a lot of the time, they were rushing to get news out, they didn't understand a lot of the nuances of a very technical situation. Later, they left and got disinterested while people in the Gulf still needed information. We created our own media, our own news desk to help balance the information out there and improve its quality and comprehensiveness."*

A critical step was to listen really well. BP's social listening, search marketing and content management efforts became core to our brand communications plan.

Social response – Value driven

Social listening tools were deployed to better understand what issues mattered most to the communities. Through advanced search efforts, it became possible to garner insights on key issues that informed the communication content plan, and then helped target responses where the dialogue and debate were happening – both online and offline. Illustration 13.18 is an example of infometrics provided to the communities and people impacted in Louisiana.

ILLUSTRATION 13.18	INFORMATION PROVIDED TO PEOPLE IMPACTED IN LOUISIANA

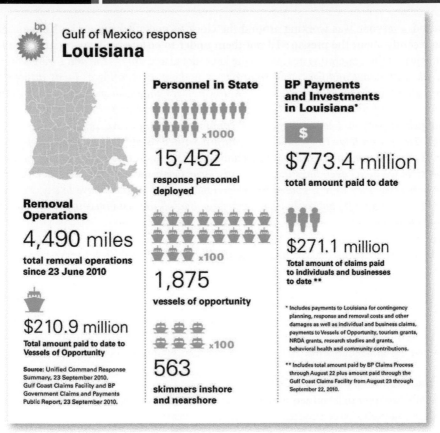

Credit – BP plc.

On a daily basis, Rachel and her global team would analyse Google searches that people were performing and use that information to guide the types of content that we would create that day or the next. *"So, we were able to say: 'People are having doubts about this; or they need more information about that; or they have more questions about this; or they are really interested in this aspect,"* she says.

The data was fed into content creation on a rolling basis. Our Google paid search data was also a constant source of intelligence that helped us optimise every single hour in the day and direct people to the right places for information Technically, BP was praised for pioneering new search techniques, starting as simply as buying early the top Google and Yahoo! search terms like "oil spill" and also building up sophisticated search algorithms.

Social response – Impact driven.

The scale of this data was massive and days with millions of impressions on BP's social channels were not exceptions. Kathy comments: *"It was the first full-scale crisis that took advantage of social media, which we saw happen again later with Arab Spring, for example."* Illustration 13.19 shows a few metrics by way of illustration.

ILLUSTRATION 13.19	SOCIAL MEDIA METRICS AS OF END OCTOBER 2010

Channel	Metrics	w/o 4 Nov - Total
facebook	Total Impressions for week Cumulative impressions	1,802,919 80,000,000
You Tube	Cumulative views Most Viewed Video 53rd most viewed YouTube	8,200,000 679,476
twitter	Tweets for the week Total Tweet Reach	2,524,000 67,000,000
flickr	Total Views	195,000
Search	Total Weekly Impressions Average position	102,963,698 1.35

- Reached social media **milestones** of 80,000,000 impressions on Facebook, 3,300 published tweets on Twitter, and more than 1,000 photos on Flickr.
- Has become a **reference news source** on BP and GoM topics for media related followers, politicians and interested parties
- Tells **BP's story** through multiple posts each day and live "Facebook Chats"
- Provides real time **monitoring of hot topics**; track bloggers, media and public sentiment; capture emerging stories early
- Proactively **monitors important BP corporate or GoM events** in a focused way through deep dive reports; gathers insights to intervene early in the debate

Credit – BP plc.

Here are a few more numbers on the scale of BP's social media activities at the time:

➤ BP's online community had 430,000+ Facebook fans, 67,000+ Twitter followers, and 9,500+ YouTube subscribers

➤ BP's content reached more than 545 million people (more than the population of the US and UK combined).

> ➤ We published thousands of pieces of content: 10, 000 posts, 18,000 tweets, 500+ videos

> ➤ We earned: 200,000+ shares and likes, 25,000+ retweets.

It's easy to forget in today's world where social media is part of the fabric of life, that back in 2010, just 47 per cent of 'online' American adults used social networks - Ref. Pew Research -, compared to 65 per cent of the entire American adult population in 2015.

Social response – People led

Considerable efforts were made to build empathy, using our employees who were closest to the community's biggest concerns. For example, the community wanted direct access to BP decision makers - hence, Mike Utsler, CEO, BP's Gulf Coast Restoration Organization hosted four candid Facebook Q&A sessions on the progress made in the Gulf between September 2010 and the two-year mark since the Gulf incident.

Our social media channels also played a critical role in taking some of the pressure from our employees on the ground. As Rachel says, *"It gave people a place where they could be mad at us. It was a place, where we could actually respond, rather than them going to the petrol stations and throwing paint on BP employees or whatever. They could actually express their anger in a way that made them feel listened to and I think that was a very healthy outlet for them."*

Social response - An extraordinary moment

Kathy, Rachel and I all recall one moment during the crisis when we knew beyond doubt that our efforts with social media were making a difference. It was the day when we were about to try plugging the well using water pressure. We were all sitting in the war room watching the story unfold on CNN and their commenters were making some factual errors, mistakenly reporting that the gauges were for 'air pressure', not 'water pressure', and that the device was going to explode. Very alarming indeed, so our media colleague was on the phone to the CNN producer yelling, *"You're getting it wrong, you're getting wrong…"* For whatever reason, the CNN producer wouldn't believe what he was hearing, so we tweeted the accurate information clarifying that the gauges were for water pressure, not gas pressure. Still on the phone, we told the CNN producer to look at what BP had just tweeted. The CNN presenter, Wolf Blitzer pulled the tweet up live on air and said, *"It looks like BP is watching this show and listening to us and they've just clarified that…"* At that moment, BP's Chief Executive Bob Dudley walked into the room, watched the end of the scene and said *"I'll never underestimate the power of social media again."*

It was an extraordinary moment and a brief glimmer of light during a very tough time. I remember we all stood up and applauded. A few weeks later, Bob told me that if it hadn't been for the brand and our concerted efforts on social media, he believed the company would have died.

Rachel believes that our efforts on social media also reflected our inner core as a Strategic Brand. *"If we talk about BP as a company trying to do the right thing, opening ourselves up on social media so that we could reach, and be reached, in less formal and more intimate ways in such dire times, it says a lot about the culture of the company. It reflected the personality of a company that was trying to do the right thing during an awful crisis."*

A few weeks later, Bob told me that if it hadn't been for the brand and our concerted efforts on social media, he believed the company would have died.

Punishing Tony Hayward and 'British Petroleum'

But, of course not everything went perfectly in the crisis communications efforts. I am not talking brand here because there was a reasonable alignment on its essence, role and the $250m plan, but rather earned media communication – which also has a major impact on the brand.

There was internal challenge and disagreement on the content, staging and tone of BP's voice and we didn't see eye to eye with all of BP's advisors at this time.

Crisis communication – Different views

So that we are clear, communications were split in two main parts, working in close co-operation: on the one hand, day-to-day press & media; and on the other, brand, social media and global business coordination. Andrew Gowers, Head of BP's press office was leading the former and I was running the later. People often - and rightly so from the outside - look at this as one programme, but I believe there is significant merit in considering each separately, as we have done so far.

One particular event sticks in my memory. We were flying back from London to Houston on Sunday 23 May, after the first 36 hours away from Westlake since the start. There were four people on the corporate jet – Tony Hayward, Alan Parker (the Chairman of Brunswick) Andrew and I. We spent most of the night debating the communications strategy going forward and I remember major differences of views between Alan Parker and me, with both of us raising our voices. We couldn't agree on long term versus short term - I should rather say from my perspective, long term AND short term.

Alan was very much into immediate political tactics and I wouldn't have them if not part of a longer-term point of view and positioning for BP and the BP brand. Alan also wanted Tony to be essentially 'always on' with media, while I was advising a much more selective approach. In hindsight and I know many in BP agree with this, Alan's options largely contributed to Tony's fall. And it is a reminder of the importance of choosing external advisors well, as they need to embrace the heart of the company's culture and ways of working, even and probably especially when it is in crisis mode.

As an example of the debates we would have, I recall being formal on June 1st: *"Every time BP assesses the chances or odds of success, and then fails, it destroys credibility. People should not estimate the odds. Bob Dudley was pressed on this point on 'Face the Nation' and said the LMRP cap approach is less risky and less complicated than the Top Kill was. That begs the question—'if it is less risky and less complicated, why didn't you do this approach first?' My suggestion with each attempt is to a) remind people we are simultaneously working on several approaches; b) do not assess odds of success. Because if it does not succeed, this only undermines credibility again."*

Back to our night debate on the flight and although Tony remembers it *"as extremely helpful"*, to be honest, I lost most of that battle…for the moment. It was okay because I was not here to score points, but do the best possible job for the Gulf and the BP brand under the circumstances. But I was concerned that the 60-second ad that we had already produced showing Tony in BP's 'NASA-type' command center apologising and directing massive resources to shut the leak, was dropped on 24 May. On the 25 of May, Purple Strategies, a DC based political campaign agency, joined us to help with some of our future communications. The first piece of creative we developed was an ad also featuring Tony that would instead be filmed 'on the beach' the following weekend. From this point, we ran a dual agency model for the crisis, with Ogilvy and Purple. Looking back and as challenging as it was to operate with two very different agencies, the response work we jointly developed over the months and years was effective and essentially on BP's brand character - credit to all.

Crisis communication – 'Killer' missteps

On Sunday 30 May, we flew to Venice, Louisiana where Tony would provide a report on the clean-up efforts and shoot the new clip. Tony had almost lived a whole day already, as he'd spent a long time in the very early morning with our operations team in the 'Hive'. This was the room for monitoring our remote operating vehicles on the seabed, where you could often meet Energy Secretary Steven Chu and other prominent figures. The Hive was situated on the other side of the corridor in West Lake 4, 3rd floor.

There were a lot of reporters in Venice and this is the infamous moment when Tony said: *"There is no one who wants this over more than I do. I would like my life back."*

Tony was exhausted after a very complex succession of days, including the failed 'top kill' attempt. He had just finished a series of long formal interviews as well as the shooting of the film. I remember he took a short call from his family just before…and then the phrase fell from his mouth. This is not an excuse for what he said but some relevant background that I have seen no one else refer to before.

By this point, there was already erosion in Tony's believability as the oil continued to leak into the Gulf of Mexico. Comments from Barack Obama in a TV interview on June 8th exacerbated this when he said that Tony, *"wouldn't be working for me after any of those statements"*.

Two days after Tony attended a hearing in Washington, he was seen on a yacht off the Isle of Wight where his son was taking part in a yacht race. This again made headlines around the world. Tony hadn't seen his son for three months and was on the boat for six hours…but this was certainly a major lapse. The then White House Chief of Staff, Rahm Emanuel criticised him, saying the boating incident has *"just been part of a long line of PR gaffes and mistakes".*

This all added up to make Tony's departure one inevitable consequence of the Deep Horizon oil spill and he resigned as CEO of BP on the 27 July 2010.

Like many in BP, I hated it when this all happened and it was very damaging. But there is another less known or told side of Tony's story in those times: he led the effort to shut the leak; he mobilized and ran a 50,000 people response; he ultimately committed $50 billion to 'doing the right thing'. And because of this, I recall multiple cases of standing ovations for Tony within BP and in closer circles outside the company.

Bob Dudley, then Head of BP's Gulf Restoration organization, replaced Tony as BP Group CEO. Bob had spent his childhood in Mississippi and proven a connected leader and very effective voice for BP with US media over the recent months.

Later, Tony told the BBC Money Programme that events would have been very different if we had managed to stop the oil spill earlier. *"If we'd been successful in killing the well in the first week of June, then so many things would've been different. Not least I'd probably still be the CEO of BP.".*

He also reflected that his comments about the spill and the reaction to them, contributed to the anger towards him. *"If I had done a degree at Rada [The Royal Academy of Dramatic Art] rather than a degree in geology, I may have done better, but I am not certain it would have changed the outcome,"* he said.

More recently, Tony and I were reflecting on how deeply the BP brand was punished in the US, in contrast to its resilience elsewhere. And Tony recalled, *"It's ironic. I had been in the White House just a week before the Deepwater Horizon explosion, talking with President Obama and Carol Browner, his energy director about how to help them with the climate bill. We were the only company truly trying to be progressive. And also, because of what we were doing on the ground in our day-to-day operations and how we had responded with Hurricane Katrina, they all recognized what BP had done in America's time of need. But all this came to nothing because of US politics. We could have had the most powerful brand in the world, it wouldn't have made a major difference: once the Republicans decided it was an opportunity to bring down Obama, which they decided early on, it became politics."*

Kathy reflects on the damage to our brand when President Obama referred to the company as British Petroleum, not BP. *"Suddenly it was a foreign company that was messing up on American soil. And that made it worse. And the President was constantly on air talking about "putting his foot on the neck of British Petroleum to make them do what he wants them to do…"*

The brand redemption – 2011 onwards

When the leak was stopped in July and the well finally closed in August, BP's commitment to the Gulf Coast restoration remained absolute.

Redemption - Branded communication in support of the Gulf Coast

The brand communication continued at meaningful levels, with social media acting as the repository of all what was happening in the Region and paid and earned media acting in support of the Gulf Coast restoration.

If BP's story was a fairy tale, this is where it would end. But of course, rebuilding and restoring the brand continued way beyond our short-term response to the crisis. I am deeply proud of BP's enduring commitment to the region and of the outcomes of all the efforts made by the tens of thousands of people involved: the beaches and marshes were cleaned of not only BP's oil but of many years of other oil debris and massive remainders of Hurricane Katrina. Fishing waters were reopened and nets were fuller than ever, by virtue of the fishing hiatus. Every consecutive year since then has seen record tourism in the region, largely owing to communication campaigns run by BP to promote the tourism in the Gulf Region. This TV, print, radio and social media campaign introduced the rest of America to the "sugar sands", cuisine and entertainment of the Gulf Coast, and was the first time that tourism advertising had been done at scale and for the entire region. Prior to BP's efforts, many of the small towns would create small radio or print campaigns which essentially competed against each other.

ILLUSTRATION 13.20	BP COMMERCIAL ON SUMMER 2011 IN SUPPORT OF TOURISM IN THE GULF

BP's commitment to community engagement through traditional advertising, social media and marketing tools undoubtedly made a major difference. It actually reached an estimated 4.3 billion people.

Redemption - The BP Brand takes steps to recover

Gradually BP achieved significant brand redemption. Favorability measures showed a rapid renewed trust, with the following highlights:

- Brand favorability came back to pre-crisis levels very fast in most places in the world. In a number of markets, favorability even went above pre-crisis levels by mid-2012, as opinion leaders and opinion formers believed BP would be a leader for safe energy
- Germany was an exception, where the BP brand had always been second to BP's owned Aral and was seen negatively in the light of the spill
- In the UK, BP's home market, the brand regained second place ahead of all but Shell within months. But it remained below its pre-spill favorability levels for years.

The US remained the main challenge. However, the continuing approach to comprehensive community engagement, the connections to general public and opinion leaders, to media and even to our strongest critics played a valuable role. They enabled a fast restoration of brand favourability, once at a low 19 during the spill up to 39 in September 2012, showing steady improvement to regain pre-spill levels of 45. The BP brand took another positive step in H1 2013, regaining second position on trust and favorability within the peer group, although still below its pre-crisis leading levels. It was interesting that the highest brand scores were in the Gulf region, where people could see BP's commitment for themselves.

In May 2012, Christopher Helman wrote in *Forbes Magazine* that, *"The scope of this turnaround ranks among the more incredible corporate comeback stories in business history."* Of course, nothing was perfect, but if it hadn't been for a series of PR missteps and gaffes, I would have tended to agree with Mr. Helman. These errors did occur in reality though and overshadowed a lot of the rest, which leaves me with some anger about a few things and mostly that Tony was not more protected.

Even with all these "actions" taken together and the noticeable progress made, this was not and would not be sufficient to rebuild BP's brand equity. Everybody in BP knew that we needed to do more to gain recognition for the company's commitment and actions. The need to earn the redemption for the BP brand was clear and this is what the company as a whole, and the brand teams specifically, were determined to undertake... under the paralyzing constraint of major and high risk legal litigation that would go on until mid-2016.

"The need to earn the redemption for the BP brand was clear."

"What does not kill you makes you stronger." This would be true if we remained determined to change and leverage the unique learning from the crisis. And if the organisation remained true to what the BP brand meant – and what it would always stand for: 'do the right thing'.

'Do the right thing'.

Redemption – Deeply considering the brand, culture & values

The company was determined to not leave any stone unturned and to do everything possible to ensure that this incident would 'never happen again'. The journey started with culture and values: were we greedy, reckless, cutting corners etc., as many had alleged during the crisis? Did we need to deeply transform our culture and beliefs? How would we restore trust and demonstrate that we were operating safely and responsibly to create long-term value for our stakeholders? What would BP's brand territory be for the next generation and how would it be expressed?

ILLUSTRATION 13.21 INTERROGATING THE FUTURE BRAND TERRITORY AND EXPRESSION

| Energy mix | GoM response & restoration | Progress on restoration (without bringing People back) | One Year After | BP gets it: Gulf restored & Safety actions | Target Territory & Expression Container |

Credit – Based on BP data and advertisements

This soul-searching took multiple paths over the course of a year. We all wanted to get this right. Ian Conn, our Executive Board Director and a dedicated team, championed this effort to deeply interrogate BP's culture and values. The Brand team travelled the world and held 10's of workshops across the organisation and with external partners and audiences.

The outcome was quite amazing. Contrary to the original theory that our culture might need a dramatic shift, BP's core values were largely reaffirmed by people. In fact, BP's deep culture would be the strongest ally in the enterprise's future progress and underpin the company's transformation on how to run its business and operations safely going forward. At the end, the enterprise values were largely restated with some adjustments and re-expressed in a somewhat evolved form.

We also looked at how BP would serve and therefore be connected to society. At a time when the world was badly in need of every bit of oil and gas it could find, the Deepwater Horizon incident, followed closely by the Fukushima nuclear disaster, put security of supply and safety even higher up on the global energy agenda. It was BP's perceived duty to play a leading – although humble – role and share its learning on safety.

Redemption - Restating BP's brand purpose, culture and values

Accordingly, BP developed a brand statement built on three pillars that were made public: "What we do", "What we stand for" and "What we value". In tune with the brand's past and the company's culture and strategy, the brand essence reflected BP's commitment to "deliver energy in better ways".

ILLUSTRATION 13.22	BP PURPOSE, CULTURE AND VALUES RESTATEMENT

"What we do
We find, develop and produce essential sources of energy. We turn these sources into products that people need everywhere. The world needs energy and this need is growing. This energy will be in many forms. It is, and will always be, vital for people and progress everywhere. We expect to be held to high standards in what we do. We strive to be a safety leader in our industry, a world-class operator, a good corporate citizen and a great employer. We are BP."

"What we stand for
Above everything, that starts with safety and excellence in our operations. This is fundamental to our success. Our approach is built on respect, being consistent and having the courage to do the right thing. We believe success comes from the energy of our people. We have determination to learn and to do things better. We depend upon developing and deploying the best technology, and building long-lasting relationships. We are committed to making a real difference in providing the energy the world needs today, and in the changing world of tomorrow. We work as one team. We are BP."

"What we value
Safety, Respect, Excellence, Courage and One Team."

Credit – Based on BP data - Corporate site

I will not tell you how many versions of this enterprise brand statement there were, until it exactly and truly reflected our promise and expectations!

Redemption - Inside-Out brand content & communication

Subsequently, we developed a brand expression and communication 'container' that represented real people, experts and operators, working together to improve the better, safer and technology-driven ways by which energy was made available to society. The communication would be strictly Inside-Out, showing BP employees from the front line in action. The stories would be practical and the look and feel deeply humble.

The brand played a considerable role in communicating our restated purpose and values within the company. In a true 'Inside-Out' approach, internal audiences would be our main focus for as long as it took until we were One BP behind our beliefs and communications.

There was considerable debate about BP's brand voice, particularly regarding several key questions:

- On strategy, how far would we and could we go in the 'safety' space? As committed and hard-working as BP was, by communicating about our commitment to safety, wouldn't we build huge expectations and risk over- promising and under-delivering? What if another incident happened, while we were getting to the roots of every aspect of safety and undergoing the transformation?
- How far would we and could we differentiate the US from the rest of the world in our communications, given how different the brand context was there. But, also as we are living in an always-on globally connected village, how could we keep brand coherence across borders?
- How much space was there for an authentic communication campaign, when during the five years following the Deepwater Horizon incident, BP lived under the immense pressure of multiple, continuous and oppressive litigation in the US? At stake in this legal battle was the future of the company, how its actions after the spill would be judged and consequently how many more billions of dollars would be paid as the result of any settlement or judgment. In many ways, Judge Barbier, the Federal Judge for the Eastern District of Louisiana, who had been appointed in August, 2010 to hear the cases related to the Deepwater Horizon spill, was a key audience for any BP communication.

And as we considered all of these strategic questions, BP was being run under strict legal control and was affected by the cadence of regular judgments and rulings upon it, most of which were adverse in nature.

From now on, the BP brand would always be held accountable for reflecting its commitment through its mission and values. I continue following BP's brand progress very closely but it is not my role and here is not the place to comment on what continues to happen, as it belongs to BP. But I appreciate BP's resolute commitment to play its part in meeting countries' and the world's energy needs safely, responsibly and with deep care for people.

Nothing, not even a truth distorting Hollywood film featuring Mark Wahlberg, should and will ever take away the dedication of people deeply living a brand that wants to do the right thing.

Nothing, not even a truth distorting Hollywood film featuring Mark Wahlberg, should and will ever take away the dedication of people deeply living a brand that wants to do the right thing.

A STRATEGIC BRAND CRISIS FRAMEWORK

These notes on the three crises at Volkswagen, Johnson & Johnson and BP have led me to adopt a 16-point practical guideline, for every brand to test their robustness and resilience to a potential crisis in peacetime and or approach crisis management when it strikes:

1. **Protect and remediate** – Facts talk louder than words and the brand should focus first on how the enterprise protects people or assets. Act very fast, with determination. Do not hesitate to put more resources in remediation than required, so the outcome is with you as soon as possible. Let everybody know and believe that every effort is made to remedy the root cause of the crisis - Tylenol did all this masterfully.

2. **Accept accountability and say sorry early** – Together with a genuine apology potentially made many times, the message should be focused on the organisation's willing accountability to protect and remediate for the strongest immediate benefit to society. BP was unambiguous on this.

3. **Establish facts first** - Don't rush to communicate on the substance of 'why' things went wrong. Rather, establish the hard truths about the crisis before taking a position. Once you have your robust version of the facts, although it might be incomplete, you must stick to it without being misleading.

4. **Be objective in assessing the nature of your brand crisis** – Be clear if the main interpretation of the events will be on a lack of competency, on the company's character or both? Tylenol was about the former and therefore, the company would be judged on how it remediated and prevented other occurrences. VW's crisis was on character and pointed to issues of culture. BP was both, with a perception of a reckless culture and technical inability – the later because of the timespan of the oil spill and successive failures to plug the leak. The two types of crisis require a very different approach.

5. **Develop a clear, far reaching strategy early** – The response strategy needs to look far ahead on what is likely to happen and place any action and communication in the service of improving that likely journey. BP and VW should have fully integrated DoJ 's usual 'recipe' and acted accordingly from the start.

6. **Under promise, over deliver** –This is one of the most challenging guidelines to turn into reality. In the case of BP, if we had under promised saying that the relief well was how we would stop the leak but that it could not be finished until August, we would have over-delivered and avoided criticism when other methods failed. But, given how unacceptable this timing would have been, we would probably have lost control of the engineering processes.

7. **Develop a simple, enduring proactive message** – J&J was single-minded on supporting society. BP was equally clear, with 'making it right' and what this meant. It is unclear what VW's message stood for, except for the electric vehicle plan 'diversion'.

8. **Act and communicate in tune with your 'true' brand** - Build on who your brand is; leverage your reservoir of goodwill. BP didn't lose about a quarter of the US population who kept faith in the brand throughout. VW could always count on

their customers, who kept buying cars based on trust in their technology. Both brands could have done a better job at acting truly in line with their brand anchor: BP counter-intuitively as an environmental champion and VW as a technology leader.

9. **Position every action and communication for the benefit of wider society and those impacted**– J&J did this perfectly. BP was deeply committed to do this, although the scale and length of restoration made it difficult to convince everybody.

10. **Be fully transparent... and make sure you are perceived to be so** – Share all bad news upfront, as nothing is more damaging than appearing to hide anything. Suspicion takes over, media is determined to uncover secrets and stakeholders only see the brand through a lens of mistrust. J&J was meticulous at sharing, staging, and pre-empting facts and news so people felt included.

11. **Be authentic** – Your people and, if possible, other external voices will bring a sincere and human authenticity to your messaging. There should be nothing looking slick, over engineered and self-serving. J&J and BP did this well from early on.

12. **Communicate heavily** – Your voice and how loud the brand talks are critical. Develop clear channel strategies and operate on real time, 24/7.

13. **Protect the CEO and select your best spokesperson(s)** – Tony Hayward was exposed too much. Matthias Mueller was left vulnerable at the start - on one occasion after a long day and flight, 40 reporters bombarded him unexpectedly with questions and led him to say, *"we didn't lie"*, which subsequently revealed a lie. James Burke, J&J's CEO played the perfect role, and was supported by a well-choreographed team.

14. **Develop your brand reservoir of goodwill in peacetime** – A Strategic Brand will do this, building a 'crisis resilient' brand. BP and VW had big reputation reservoirs, which saved them but of course were not sufficient to counter the scale of their respective crises.

15. **Develop critical partnerships and processes in peacetime** – Day-to-day partnerships should be developed with key journalists in key media. And before crisis hits, partnerships should be established with advisors who will be culturally well-integrated key aides during a crisis. In that respect, I want to acknowledge Ogilvy's CEO, John Seifert for being a textbook supporter throughout the crisis and beyond.

16. **Develop tools and processes in peacetime** – Crisis management planning is a well-practiced discipline. Just strengthen it and put the brand at the top of what needs to be protected and leveraged. Tony Hayward mentioned the invaluable importance of BP's plan and how it was possible to scale up almost as required.

Considering these guidelines in peacetime will help develop a more resilient brand in periods of crisis as well as a more impactful brand for all times. In my experience, a major 'crisis test' is an extraordinary approach to strengthen and transform a brand into a true Enduring Strategic Brand - so let's do it!

THE ENDURING STRATEGIC BRAND
CONCLUSION

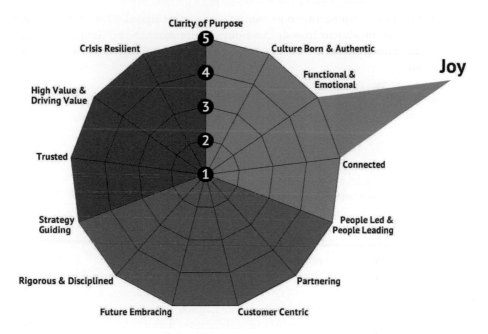

Strive not to be a success, but rather to be of value.
Albert Einstein

There is a fourteenth imperative to Strategic Brands that we have come to realise as we wrote this book. It is Joy.

Joy has a positive energy that can sweep into a brand and an organisation and create a path ahead, a sense of momentum for the future. And it was Joy that we needed at BP to redeem the brand from its lowest point after the Deepwater Horizon crisis in 2010. Our partnership with the Olympics and Paralympics created that positive energy and inspired and re-inspired our people again when they most needed it.

Joy from BP's Olympic and Paralympic partnerships

As it happens, BP's commitment to London 2012 – was signed off in 2008, two years before the Gulf of Mexico tragedy. And our commitment to the Games themselves, and the athletes in particular, was as unwavering as our commitment to the recovery in the Gulf.

ILLUSTRATION C.1	A 360-DEGREE PARTNERSHIP BETWEEN BP AND TEAM USA

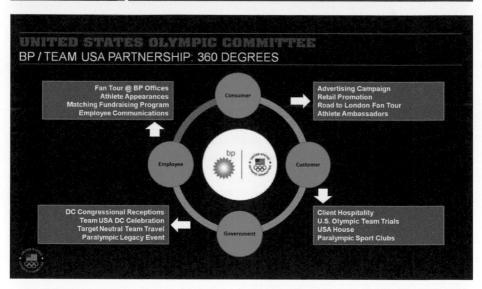

Credit – US Olympic Committee

This took of course a particular dimension in the US. There, we focused on nine courageous athletes (60 globally). I remember asking Scott Blackmun, the CEO of the US Olympic Committee (USOC) his advice and he wisely suggested we select outstanding athletes, who like BP, had overcome deep adversity, fought back and strived for excellence. They all shared the character traits that personified BP at its best, which created powerful internal engagement among our employees to the brand.

ILLUSTRATION C.2   NINE EXTRAORDINARY US BRAND AMBASSADORS

Credit and authorisation – BP plc.

And the same inspiration captured the hearts and minds of our external stakeholders. We took fans behind the scenes, transporting them into the athletes' real lives from the first day of training to the London Games, with photography, graphics, news bulletins, even augmented reality.

ILLUSTRATION C.3   SOCIAL MEDIA 'BEHIND THE SCENE'

Credit and authorisation – BP plc.

Social media played a key role. During the US Olympic and Paralympic trials, live status Instagram updates were posted to BP Team USA's Facebook and Twitter pages to give fans exclusive coverage and provide compelling behind-the-scenes footage. BP held social media training sessions, so the athletes could share content on their own channels with their own networks. By harnessing the power of their existing fan base, we extended the reach of the stories and grew the community even more.

Here are some of the results from our US partnership (Ref. Illustration C.4):

- Awareness of BP's sponsorship reached 18% among target audiences – (the number tripled from the beginning of the programme), surpassing other major USOC partners including Citibank (14%) and BMW (7%).
- Perception of the BP brand leapt from a negative 2.6 before the Games to a positive 5.9 during the Games – the second largest gain of all major Olympic sponsors aside from Visa, according to a YouGov poll.
- Sentiment of fans was overwhelmingly positive. Facebook interactions were 82% favourable and the earned value of these interactions reached over 39 million people.
- A Lolo Jones post celebrating her fourth place finish in the 100m hurdles garnered the most engagement of any post by a USOC sponsor with 91,000+ 'likes', 2,300+ 'comments' and 1,300+ 'shares'.
- Our Team BP athletes medal count: 7 gold, 3 silver, 1 bronze and 3 world records.

ILLUSTRATION C.4	BP BRAND PERCEPTION IN THE US IN RELATION TO LONDON 2012

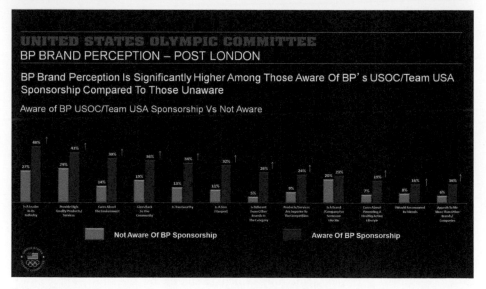

Credit – US Olympic Committee

And we brought the spirit of the Olympics and Paralympics alive in many other countries. In the UK, Duncan Blake, BP Director of Brand remembers: *"In our ad in 2012, we had Jessica Ennis-Hill running along a beach, Stef Reid running through a field of biofuels and William Sharman jumping over statues in the British Museum, all to bring to life the contribution that BP was making to the Games. It was probably the first time that I've felt an ad was right the first time I viewed the edit with the agency; the music, the voiceover, the images were all spot on"*

ILLUSTRATION C.5   STEF REID IN BP'S LONDON 2012 FIRST AD CAMPAIGN

Credit and authorisation – BP plc.

Meanwhile, there was no case that we would treat the Olympics and the Paralympics differently. During the Paralympic Games, we created the 'every day BP 4:00pm' in the Park. This consisted of two to four Paralympians from all around the world sharing their story each day with the audience. The BP 4:00pm became famous with an increasing number of people wanting to watch these ultimate human expressions of courage, determination, optimism and Joy.

So it is at this point in talking about the Olympics, Paralympics and the BP Brand that this story comes full circle - from the birth of 'Beyond Petroleum' in 2000, to the brand restatement in 2007 to adapt to a changed world, to the Deepwater Horizon crisis in 2010 and finally to the undertaking of a slow recovery marked by our commitment to London 2012. As Duncan Blake says: *"Our London 2012 partnership was most successful in terms of improving morale. It enabled BP to tap into the magic of the Olympics, but also into something wonderful that was happening in the UK. It helped the people of BP to regain some confidence and pride. And it certainly helped the brand to turn a corner."*

THE STRATEGIC POWER OF JOY - THE 14TH STRATEGIC BRAND IMPERATIVE

When I started writing *THE Enduring Strategic Brand*, the perspective was clear: 13 Imperatives were the building blocks of a Strategic Brand. As the work progressed, considering many brands and selecting a number of them as sources of best practice, a common thread surfaced, something which is shared by the most enduringly successful brands: 'Joy.'

And with Joy comes 'positive', 'happy' and 'optimistic'. As we said at the beginning of this chapter, Joy is a form of positive energy that imbues organisations with purpose, bringing people together for the good of the business, their stakeholders and colleagues.

Brands with Joy

What does BMW have in common with Airbnb, with the International Olympic Committee and many others? Success and Joy – or, rather, success through Joy. Here are some thoughts of a few of our exemplary brands on the subject of 'Joy':

BMW – Ian Robertson: *"The emotional context in the centre of the BMW brand is 'Joy'. That's what we want our people to have. That's what we want our customers to experience. That's what we want our products to deliver. That's what we want our communication to say. It's consistent; we have never changed 'Joy'. We haven't said: 'Enough Joy, now, we'll do something else.' "*

Ian explains how a campaign can be used as a temporary expression of something that is embedded in BMW: *"We ran the 'Joy' campaign globally in 2009. The world was in a terrible mess because of the economic downturn and we decided that it would be good to lift our own people internally – as well as people externally. While the 'Joy' campaign came to an end after a year in the rest of the world, in China it went on for three years. And our Joy never started or stopped with a particular campaign, it is always there."*

The International Olympic Committee – Timo Lumme: *"Since Thomas Bach became President of the IOC in September 2013, he has met with over 140 Heads of State. According to anecdote, these Heads of State have told him that, given all the negative things that are happening in the world today, they regard Olympism as something positive, as a beacon of hope"*

Airbnb – Brian Chesky: *"It's better to have 100 people love you than to have 1,000,000 people like you."* Love comes from striving to bring someone Joy – as Brian says: *"If you want to create a great product, just focus on one person. Make sure that one person has the most amazing experience ever."*

And Toyota wants to be: *"Rewarded with a smile - the greatest reward possible."*

It's not only about 'our' Strategic Brands: a lot of different research has identified and ranked 'Joy' or 'Happy' brands and here are a few frequently mentioned:

Just consider their taglines: 1979 *"Have a Coke and a smile"*; 2000 *"Enjoy"*; 2009 *"Open happiness"*.

Johnnie Walker's recently introduced the tagline *"Joy will take you further"*, which has touched over 300 million people.

Amusingly, Andrex comes top of any 'Joy' brand ranking and has been communicating happiness through its brand icon, the Andrex puppy, for over 40 years.

Target, the US retailer, *"uses its charm to put customers in a good mood"* and even introduced the 'Oh Joy!' Target collection.

Do we also have Joy in our brand? Are people in our organization living with Joy? Do we project Joy? Do we offer and provide Joy? And if Joy is important today, I predict it will become even more so as millennials increasingly dominate the global share of wallet.

If your answers are 'yes', the impact will be amazing both inside and outside the company. Internally, as Allison Rimm, author of *The Joy of Strategy*, says: *"Promoting Joy on the job is an easy way for an organisation to protect their greatest asset."* (Note 1) Externally, as Insead's L'Oréal Chaired Professor of Marketing, Pierre Chandon, says: *"A brand that creates emotional Joy is a rare thing."* He argues that when this occurs, an emotional attachment is created to the brand itself, which leads it to be better remembered, better liked and chosen more often - a good example is that 75 per cent of Zappos' customers are repeat customers.

The Science of Joy

Would you believe there is a science of Joy? Firstly, we learned in chapter 3 how Joy and happiness live in our left pre-frontal cortex. And I find the following five- point framework helpful when thinking of a brand's relationship with Joy: (Note 2)

1. **Joy and Happiness as start and end point** – Zappos' founder Tony Hsieh, who has written a book called *Delivering Happiness*, began by focusing on culture and employee happiness, *"where employees get so much out of it that they would do it for free."* He then shifted the focus to *"creating enjoyment and fulfillment for employees towards delivering happiness to both customers and the greater public".* Similarly, BMW has Joy at every internal and external touch point. Target is designed for happiness.

2. **Back to the Joy of our childhood** - LEGO can attribute its resurgence from the mid 2000s to the way in which it focused on the LEGO builder's delight without compromising Joy. One key practice was to bring creative and non-creative people together to develop products the market would love. Coca-Cola and Campbell's are two other brands which use nostalgia to their advantage.

3. **The Joy of belonging, being respected and being part of something bigger** - J.Crew succeeds by engaging customers in an ongoing dialogue about style. Prius and Tesla drivers feel they belong to a group of front-runners, those who protect the environment through smart technology choices. Airbnb is predicated on 'belonging' and its recent extension of communities offers the Joy of belonging to literally everybody.

4. **The Joy of escaping routine** – The local and welcoming presence of both McDonald's and Starbucks offers many people, from mothers to independent workers, a break from their usual routine, and a joyful escape. Starbucks claims: 'mini break, maximum happy'; while McDonalds 'brings moments of Joy to 24

cities across the globe'. Joy from escape can of course take many other forms -an Apple iPod provides musical Joy, Skype provides Joy in connection.

5. **The Joy of success… and of projecting success (status)** - As Professor Chandon explains: *"The brands of the products we use are how we show people who we are."* This is also about status. Nike sees everyone as an athlete and helps them to feel like one through "Just Do It." Nike's challenger, Under Armour has a fitness community of over 165 million on apps like MapMyFitness where users can share their achievements. Dove makes every person 'more beautiful than they think'. BMW makes people feel successful.

For many, the ultimate incarnation of Joy is Christmas. Let's apply the five point framework: the festive celebration is indeed about Joy, from start to finish. It brings back the Joy of childhood, makes you feel like you are part of something bigger, and offers the Joy of escape. It also gives the perfect excuse to watch the most joyful film of all times, *'Miracle on the 34th Street'*. Think about it - isn't Christmas the ultimate Enduring Strategic Brand? And if so, isn't the Christmas brand a compelling proof point of the osmosis between Joy and a Strategic Brand?

Joy, the 14th Enduring Strategic Brand Imperative

So transformational it is, I want to elevate Joy to a Strategic Brand Imperative. A lot of people might think – it feels more tactical and not so much a 'foundation'. This is what I want to change and that Joy is approached and built in in a truly strategic manner.

Strategic Brands are systems. And Joy gives a brand a considerably greater chance of being a Strategic Brand. Think of your organisation's brand - or yourself as a brand - being joyful and creating Joy: wouldn't Joy create emotions with the people you interact with (*'Functional and Emotional'*)? Wouldn't it be easier to connect with them (*'Connected'*)? Wouldn't it be simpler to partner with them (*'Partnering'*)? Wouldn't Joy help build trust and being trusted (*'Trusted'*)? With Joy, wouldn't people rally and support in case of a crisis or a challenge in your life (*'Crisis Resilient'*)? Wouldn't Joy drive value in simplifying access and interfaces (*'High value & Driving value'*)? Altogether, wouldn't Joy largely define and considerably strengthen the brand?

And if you want to make a start: Emojis are a contemporary example of the infinite appeal for Joy. They bring amusement and emotion to our continuous online exchanges. They also provide a true ability to understand how your followers feel about your brand, organisation or persona. So what is a good emotional territory for your brand and what is your Emoji?

Credit - Meabh Quoirin, CEO and Co-Owner, Foresight Factory

A BRAND IS A PERSON, A PERSON IS A BRAND: YOUR PERSONAL BRAND

There is a critical area of business that many people pay too little attention to – their own personal brand. Here's a challenge. Can you take a holistic view of yourself as if you were a packet of soap? What are your brand values? How do you behave with different stakeholder types - are you consistent? Does your attitude and behaviour mean that people want to 'buy' you again and again and again?

I am yet to meet a leader who is absolutely articulate and consistent in the management of his or her own brand - and I believe it's a lost and latent opportunity.

Indeed, beyond using the 13+1 Brand Imperative system to the benefit of your organisation's brand, you could apply it to your own personal brand.

You are the most important brand of all

People are brands. Think about Henry Ford, Kiichiro Toyoda, Steve Jobs, Warren Buffet, Bill Gates, Richard Branson, Jeff Bezos, Jack Ma or Elon Musk. Many of us would probably be able to sketch the brand of these founders and recognise how it has fundamentally defined their enterprise brand. And you don't have to be a founder to have a powerful personal brand - Bill Allen, Andy Grove, Lou Gerstner, Jack Welch and Indra Nooyi are probably leaders we all know and have a view about without having met them... which is nothing different than saying that they are a brand.

The more value and the greater the experience you bring to others, the stronger your brand. Like other Strategic Brands, your personal brand is both about what you do and who you are. Doesn't Jim Stengel, former global head of marketing for Procter & Gamble, tell us that brands which centre their businesses on improving people's lives resonate more with consumers – and outperform their category competitors? So is your role contributing to improve the life of people around you to outperform your peers? What is there to learn from Ivan Menezes, CEO of Diageo as he says: *"I define my purpose as fulfilling the potential of people and business."*

My own brand journey

I hate talking about myself. But my personal brand is the only practical case I can use with no constraint to explore the point.

I had a brand at work. Many of the traits I displayed were close to the real me; some were significantly different. As I became more relaxed over time to behave as myself, I found that the perception of what was not me before remained in the hearts and minds of colleagues - first impressions stick.

I received considerable help and feedback over the years, as you do in large corporates and which I'm grateful for: personal coaching, annual 360 appraisals, DiSC, Meyers & Briggs, VIA survey, ITIM cultural awareness etc. These helped me to become clearer on my purpose, culture and values, strengths and areas of improvement.

But it took many years to change my approach from focusing on WHAT I was doing to leaving more space for the reality of WHO I was. Or to use marketing language, to parallel action with perception, to combine push and pull.

It takes huge confidence to simply be yourself, authentic and comfortable in your own skin.

One of the reasons was that achieving this is not easy. It takes huge confidence to simply be yourself, authentic and comfortable in your own skin. It also takes to work on style, so there is no "loss in translation" of the real YOU because of how it is represented - *a similar risk as 'a great brand but a confusing ad'.*

I learned that performance gets only appreciated if it is connected coherently to your own authentic brand.

Another deep reason lay in the belief that by simply doing a better job and delivering more of the WHAT, others' perception would improve automatically. It does of course – but only to a certain extent and I learned that performance gets only appreciated if it is connected coherently to your own authentic brand. Because otherwise, you don't know what you don't know and 'buts' can be on the way: *"But he did not develop people enough"*, or *"But he was not giving time for the greater good"*, or…

'Entrepreneuring' your Personal Brand

When I talk to, and in some cases coach executives, very few of them truly build and live their personal brand. This is missing a significant opportunity.

Business, brand and leadership expert, Kevin Murray, author of *'People with Purpose'* (Note 3) agrees: *"Too few leaders and managers consider their own strengths, beliefs and values… Seldom in life do we take time to think about the kind of person we are, how others see us and what impact our behaviour has on others. We can all rise to the special occasion but does that carefully crafted self-image always follow up in our dealings with others?"*

Kevin cites Philip Nevill Green, Chairman of Carillion plc and Baker Corp: *"As a leader, you're being scrutinised all the time and people will micro-analyse your every behaviour. If you are not living your values in the way that truly demonstrates what you believe, people will see it and you will lose credibility. It goes with the turf of being a leader."*

This research is interesting: a YouGov survey found that 94 per cent of managers responded that they were honest at work, with only 63 per cent of employees agreeing. 90 per cent of managers said they consistently did what they said they were going to do, with 54 per cent of employees agreeing. On living the values, the split was 91 per cent against 53 per cent.

This is therefore an invitation to every leader to step back and think: am I creating my brand? Am I on top of who I want to be and how I want to be perceived? And – most importantly – am I being myself? The 13+1 Brand Imperative system will be helpful in achieving this.

Actions speak louder than words… Being a leader means looking, acting, walking and talking like a leader. Countless times, leaders forget that they are in a fishbowl and are being watched all the time.

Says Kevin: *"Actions speak louder than words… Being a leader means looking, acting, walking and talking like a leader. Countless times, leaders forget that they are in a fishbowl and are being watched all the time. A look of frustration here, a preoccupied walk through an office without speaking to anyone, a frown of frustration when someone is talking – all of these send powerful signals that staff take away and dissect for meaning... Equally, there is nothing more corrosive than the conflict between saying one thing and doing another... And leaders who clearly love what they are doing, who show it in everything they do, in every expression, are hugely infectious."*

Consciously, systematically and authentically building your own brand in a way that gives you the confidence to be yourself has the power to transform people's perception of you.

Applying 'THE Enduring Strategic Brand' system to your personal brand

There are three main areas where applying the 13+1 Brand Imperative system might make a major difference to your personal brand.

1. **Your (perceived) personal brand versus the real 'YOU'**
   Using some of the tools mentioned above – DiSC, Meyers & Briggs, VIA survey and self-reflection –, develop first a deep understanding of your true self in each and all of the 13+1 Brand Imperative spaces.

   Using coaching, 360 degrees and other feedbacks, measure and understand your brand as perceived by others. There will be areas of alignment and differences or gaps between the real 'You' and your brand - how people perceive you (Ref. Illustration C.7, left radar).

   Kevin: *"Be yourself better. Authenticity as a leader is crucial. Followers will not commit if they do not trust you and believe that you have integrity... When you are clear with yourself about the things you really care about, you cannot help but talk to them with passion. The ability to draw on and display that passion and commitment, consistently and predictably, counts for more than skills at oratory, and communicates more effectively than even the most perfectly crafted words. You have to be true to yourself, but you also have to learn to 'perform' yourself better."*

   And it will take you to Chef Geoffrey Zakarian's advice: *"Determine who you are and what your brand is, and what you are not. The rest of it is just a lot of noise"*

2. **Your brand versus the organisation's brand** – Having understood the real 'YOU' and your (perceived) brand, now apply the 13+1 Brand Imperative system to the organisation's brand. As before, this will point to areas of alignment and differences (Ref. Illustration C.7, right radar)

   If you cannot demonstrate that your purpose and values fit with those of the enterprise, you should seriously ask yourself whether you want to belong to the organisation for much longer. I have seen remarkable people fail, or at least not fulfill their potential, because of the mismatch between their and the organisation's cultures.

ILLUSTRATION C.7	YOUR (PERCEIVED) BRAND VERSUS YOUR TRUE 'YOU'; AND VERSUS YOUR COMPANY BRAND

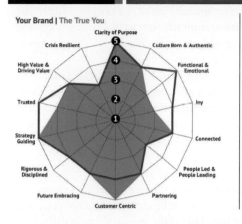

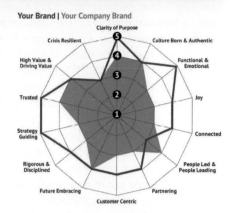

3. **Your brand versus other people brands** – Finally, reflect on people's brands around you: your boss, your peers and your team. When you consider them, use systematically the 13+1 Brand Imperative system. Doing so will help you with your connection with these individuals – and it might also inform your own understanding of how they perceive you, meaning your personal brand from their perspective.

The 13+1 Brand Imperatives = A more Strategic Personal Brand

We believe that '*THE Enduring Strategic Brand*' system can be used in its entirety with your personal brand – so how do you leverage it usefully?

WHY/WHO – The **Why of 'YOU'** and **Who 'YOU' are** should be where your brand emanates from: the clarity of your purpose; your culture and values and their authentic expression; your character and your Joy; and your inherent way of interacting and connecting with others.

HOW – The how Imperatives help you think through the following questions: what sort of leader are you? How stakeholder-centric are you in the way you operate with others? Are you naturally drawn towards mutually beneficial relationships? Do you look backwards to the past or forwards into the future? Do people see a discipline or a rigour in you – or something more random?

WHAT – You will finally be able to test your impact: does 'Who' you are guide your actions, rather than the influences coming your way? Are you somebody people trust? Are you seen as an achiever? And finally, to what extent would others help you out of a challenge?

The real 'You' versus your (perceived) Brand, versus the Enterprise Brand

As a matter of example, let's interpret briefly the 13+1 Brand Imperative system for the individual brand depicted on illustration C.7, assuming it is 'YOU'.

The left handside radar represents the real 'YOU' - light blue - versus your (perceived) brand - dark blue line. Ideally, the real 'YOU' perfectly overlaps with your brand. In areas where there is a higher 'YOU' than your brand - in this example, *Customer Centric* – you are either over self-rating or have an opportunity to improve your brand by showing more of self.

In the areas of a lower 'YOU' than your brand and where the gap is significant – in this example *Functional & Emotional*, you get a mix of messages: on one hand, congratulations that your (perceived) brand is stronger than the real 'YOU'; on the other, it requires attention and active management given the risk of disappointment when the real 'YOU' expresses itself and does not match strong perceptions and expectations – *'Oh, I thought she was emotional'*

The right handside radar represents your brand versus the organisation's brand. In this example, the respective *'Purpose'* and *'Culture'* are sufficiently close that your and the enterprise brands can probably live together. This said, the significant difference on *'Strategy Guiding'* for example makes 'YOU' appear rigorous at acting in line with the brand, whereby the organization seems to take a more flexible approach. This will become clear in your mutual dealings, for the better or worse, and certainly requires consideration.

Being eyes wide open on the importance of your personal brand and using the 13+1 Brand Imperative system will hopefully help you be more confidently showing rather than telling and become both more authentic and compelling to your audiences.

Celebrity brands

As a proxy for top personal brands, we researched which public figures people most wished were still alive. No surprise to find Jesus Christ, John F Kennedy, Martin Luther King and Walt Disney, as well as Princess Diana, Robin Williams and John Lennon in this selected group. One of the most frequently named figures is Nelson Mandela and our Strategic Brand system assessed his brand to be extremely strong. And if there is a business leader that we could all learn from in terms of the sophisticated management of his personal brand, that would be Steve Jobs.

The Donald Trump Brand

Rather than any of the extraordinary leaders just mentioned, we thought to reflect on Donald Trump's brand during the 2016 US Presidential election. Whether we like him or not is a different question and all our upcoming comments are purely technical about brands – they represent neither political nor personal opinions.

The motive for this choice lies in that 'Trump' has everything of a brand, as controversial it might be for some; and that his electoral success arguably resulted from the shrewd management of the 'Trump' brand

From a Strategic Brand standpoint, the US elections appear the victory of a 'character and emotion' led brand – Trump, over a more 'functionality' driven brand - Clinton.

Simplicity of the Trump brand essence

The Donald Trump Brand essence and messaging appeared simple and consistent, built on the following pillars of Culture and Purpose:
- An authentic strong character with obvious imperfections
- A deal maker culture
- A rallying cry from an inspiring collective purpose, *"Make America great again"*.
- A black and white view of what he is in favour of and against.

Rightly or wrongly, by comparison, Mrs. Clinton brought considerable positive functional expertise but appeared to many being less authentic and driven by a narrower purpose: 'me' and 'win'.

The Trump Strategic Brand

One of Trump's key strengths has always been his high awareness that he is a brand and illimitable desire to be one. Well before his campaign, didn't he use to say, *"if your business is not a brand, it is a commodity"*.

"If your business is not a brand, it is a commodity".

We applied the Strategic Brand Imperative system to the Trump brand (Ref. Illustration C.8). Let's review some key take out:

ILLUSTRATION C.8	THE ENDURING STRATEGIC BRAND IMPERATIVES – DONALD TRUMP

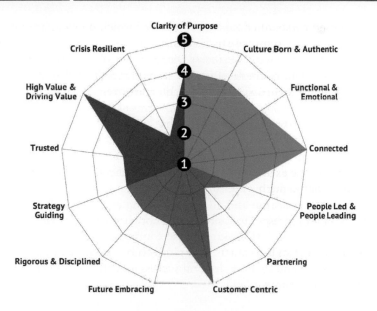

High Value (5) – Extraordinary: Donald Trump is President of the United States! And he has been a successful businessman - although some argue a generous view is being presented of his businesses.

He applies high sensitivity in his perception of what people are thinking about current events, making his brand extraordinarily connected, 'customer/voter' centric, emotional and believable to its target audiences.

Connected (5) – The brand purpose *'Make America great again'* arose from high connectedness with his target groups (male, white, middle class etc.), taping into their nostalgia, needs and pride. Inversely, he largely ignores those he does not relate to in priority (women, the gay community, minority ethnic groups).

From a reach point of view, he also made scientific use of all channels during the election, sidestepping the lens of traditional news reporting by tweeting directly real-time messages on policy from @therealDonaldTrump to his 23m followers.

Customer Centric (5) – Aligned with 'connected', he was extraordinarily consistent on addressing his target audiences, his 'customer voters'. He has a good sense of what people want to 'buy'. And as he might want to be elected again, he will push for making progress in the priority areas for these audiences.

Functional & Emotional (4) – Donald Trump imbued considerable emotion and played deeply into people's sentiments (5). His purpose was highly emotional, addressing what his voters resent they have lost and want back – grandeur, qualified employment, community life and a purposed political system. He generated equally strong although very different and polarized emotions from his opposition.

Trusted (4) – People who voted for him believed he would do what he said. Inversely, his non-voters were very opposed and skeptical.

The 'Trump' brand had a simple purpose that was represented in a personal, non-traditional way which appeared authentic to his audiences.

Purposed (4) – *"Make America great again"* is a clear, simple, and emotional brand purpose. Claiming change management, this collective purpose translates into opposition to the establishment, free trade and abortion rights, and support to immigration regulations, the fossil fuel industry and the use of torture - many things that his audience agrees with.

Culture & Authenticity (4) – He appeared deeply real as a person. He is not perfect or slick but rather is impulsive, thin-skinned and combative. He failed in business...then succeeded. He has an immigrant wife. His family is behind him...

Rigorous & Disciplined (3) – He looked undisciplined. But brand experts might argue he was extremely coherent being himself. This said and over the longer run, being extraordinarily reactive with his emotions might break the discipline.

The next months and years will reveal the extent to which the brand is able to deliver its purpose in getting policies, real actions and outcomes approved and executed.

Strategy guiding (3) –This is a main cause of Donald Trump's election. He committed to actions consistent with his brand and its purpose (5). His first weeks in office seem to have surprised people in that he was doing what he had said and signing executive orders along his commitments. If people resent what he is trying to do, he is consistent on realizing what he campaigned for. But he probably won't be able to do it all by some distance (2).

Future embracing (3) – He is a businessman and has a sense of the future. In the same breath, he is transactional and short-term result orientated. It will be down to his team to lead into the future.

The Not Enduring Trump Strategic Brand
As much as 'Trump' has clearly been a Strategic Brand in election time - and potentially holds many ingredients to continue being one, it can't be considered an Enduring Strategic Brand with confidence. Gaps in character, partnering (2), people led (2) and crisis resilient (2) look significant and introduce high risks to the sustainability of his brand.

People led & People leading (4&2) – He appears an instinctive people leader, grounded in his own confidence and straightforwardness (4). He is described as hierarchical, command and control, low delegator and rarely inclusive. He has appointed big personalities in his cabinet but would probably dispose of them if the alignment were not there - similar to how he let go many campaign advisors (2).

Partnering (2) – He would probably give away a lot for those he believes he can or should work with. With those 'non elected' by him, he will probably give nothing. This selectiveness has alienated people during the campaign and might do the same with Congress, some countries and other essential constituencies.

Crisis resilient (2) – His brand looks vulnerable and is likely to suffer - or even perhaps collapse under deep challenge, especially if he can't deliver to his committed voters. This single major exposure gives place for a significant risk that events or discontinuities might occur.

Given these vulnerabilities and if you are Donald Trump's friend, please invite him to run through the Enduring Strategic Brand Imperatives system. Believe it or not, this would be game changing for him...and the world.

The transformational advantage of Enduring Strategic Brands

As I come to conclude '*THE Enduring Strategic Brand*', let me be very clear.

This is a strategy book, not an overview of theory or tactics. It is not meant to improve but to transform. It is written from the frontline by C-suite practitioners for their peers, board members, CEOs, and CMOs, who all share the highs and lows of driving value creation, day in, day out.

Mainstream realities are clear. Despite its transformational power, the Brand is rarely at the very core of an organisation's strategy. Actually, very little research and only few articles, reports or agencies associate the words brand and strategy and focus on the long-term development of a Strategic Brand as a way of being.

Meanwhile, disruption is the new normal – and business leaders are faced with spiraling challenges and complexity to grow and sustain their brands in the brave, new world.

Through sharing candid and unique interviews with over 40 C-suite leaders – and analyzing 20 Brands from BMW to BP, Airbnb to TATA, we have tried to show that the best performing organisations are built on Strategic Brands.

This wealth of experience and exemplary practice point to what it takes to build and grow a Strategic Brand. It provides an effective system of 13+1 vital Strategic Brand Imperatives. Combining these framework and experiences, you will be guided to build the Enduring Imperatives of your Strategic Brand - what will remain true and appropriate for ever, irrespective of the massive and fast changes of channels, technology and tastes.

It will empower your enterprise to outperform competitors and sustainably deliver the best shareholder returns.

I have to admit that I would have benefited from the strategic framework of '*THE Enduring Strategic Brand*' when in post. So let me make it a rallying cry to step back and get into the strategy of brand, as it will transform what you do - an exhortation to build your Enduring Strategic Brand into the ultimate weapon of success for your enterprise and your own.

Practical steps and immediate benefits

So the potential value from '*THE Enduring Strategic Brand*' is to capture and leverage the guidance coming from the 13+1 Brand Imperative system and the best practices revealed by the Exemplary Brands discussed throughout the chapters.

Your first step might be to self-assess your organisation's brand strategically using the 13+1 Brand Imperative system, with free access on www.thestrategicbrand.net/brand-system. For example, Haier was diagnosed in Chapter 8 as a 'Future Embracing' Strategic Brand, as shown on Illustration C.9.

ILLUSTRATION C.9	ASSESSING YOUR ORGANISATION BRAND USING THE 13+1 BRAND IMPERATIVE SYSTEM – THE HAIER EXAMPLE

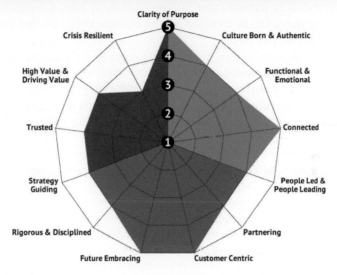

Once this diagnosis has been made - *'THE Enduring Strategic Brand'* provides in each of the 13+1 Imperative chapters an extensive number of lenses, criteria and best practices from best-in-class organisations. These best practices have often been codified in a repository of experience – but the real richness comes from reviewing the brand stories themselves where an individual organisation can collect directly the most relevant learning for its own priorities.

For example and continuing with the Haier case, Haier's Customer Centricity was assessed against the tenets of customer centricity, a test you might also want to run for your own brand (Ref. Illustration C.10)

ILLUSTRATION C.10	BRAND DIAGNOSIS FOR THE 'CUSTOMER CENTRIC' IMPERATIVE - HAIER

Haier

1. Culture & Mindset	5
2. Purpose Led	5
3. Total Experience Design	5
4. Trends Integration	5
5. Customer as a Partner	5
6. Cross Functional Teams	5
7. Decision on the front line	5
8. Magnet for Talents	5
9. Unparalleled Growth	5
10. We are the Platform	5

Scale 1: Low to 5: Very Strong

I would love to think that the wealth of strategic insights and experiences provided by world-class practitioners in each chapter of this book would be of some deep meaning and provide invaluable transformational guidance to build your Enduring Strategic Brand.

My personal take from 'THE Enduring Strategic Brand'

I felt compelled to write this book. I have such a passion for brands – after so many years of practice and learning and so many conversations with leaders and friends in business, government or academia.

And with seeing so many aspects of brand change in our globalised, individualised and digitalised world while many fundamentals remain the same, I had to get this book off my chest.

Rather than with my own words, let us conclude with twenty-four quotes which stand powerfully at the heart of '*THE Enduring Strategic Brand*':

1. **Strategic Brand** – *"A Strategic Brand drives the company rather than anything else. You have to have the flexibility in your brand to be able to evolve but the consistency to have it anchored.*

    In today's world, the difference between one car and another is narrower than it's ever been and the context of the brand proposition is therefore even more powerful." - Ian Robertson, Member of the Board of Management of BMW AG

2. **Strategic Brand** - *"A Strategic Brand acts. It shows. It doesn't tell. And we (BP in the Gulf of Mexico) showed, we did the right thing."* – Kathy Leech, Executive Director of Corporate Brand Marketing, Comcast NBC Universal

3. **Strategic Brand** -*"Everything is digital – we are now in the Fourth Industrial Revolution. We are no longer doing 'digital marketing', but brand and marketing in a digital world -and marketers need to embrace technology to keep ahead."* – Keith Weed, Chief Marketing and Communications Officer, Unilever

4. **Clarity of purpose** - *"A good Strategic Brand needs to be associated with a big idea. So, we were in the business of not just producing shareholder value, but about projecting the future. That was the big idea. That was the clarity of purpose."* – Lord John Browne, Former CEO of BP

5. **Culture born and authentic** - *"We work in an environment that is changing dramatically and need to stick to a number of fundamental values, which have been the strengths of the company in the past and are not incompatible with new*

technologies. That is the difference between a company that always searches for the latest trend and forgets the past, and a company that is based on solid foundations, is inspired by the past but remains agile, flexible and completely adaptable." – Didier Leroy, Executive Vice President, Member of the Board of Directors Toyota Motor Corporation

6. **Functional & Emotional** - *"It is emotion that makes great products. It is emotion that makes great marketing. It is emotion that provides great service. The rest can be trained. Hence the emotional context of a brand's core is essential." –* Ian Robertson, Member of the Board of Management of BMW AG

7. **Connected** - *"There has never been a super-brand that has been truly driven by the creativity, fingerprint, energy and stories of its community. We build who we are from mining the stories in our community – which we turn into marketing content. We want to create a community-driven super brand by unlocking the creative power of a community. This has never been done before."* Jonathan Mildenhall, CMO Airbnb

8. **People led & People leading** – *"Every generation of IBMers has the chance and the responsibility to reinvent our company. This is our time." -* Ginni Rometty, President and CEO of IBM

9. **People led** - *"At Zappos we are all about blurring lines. Our goal is to hire employees whose personal values match our ten core values, so every employee is automatically living the brand, at home, in the office and on social media. Rather than focus on work-life separation, we focus on work-life integration." -* Tony Hsieh, CEO Zappos

10. **People Leading** - *"American Express has a great history of leaders who believe in making people and customers feel respected and special. This is pervasive throughout the business... because in order to get employees to treat customers well, we have got to treat our employees well; they have to feel respected and special."* John Hayes, former CMO, American Express

11. **Partnering** - *"A world of customer experiences, data-based services and asset performance through analytics requires new forms of collaboration, given the speed at which innovation and distribution are taking place... When firms share resources through collaborative innovation, significant value can be created for both parties as well as for the economies in which such collaborations take place." –* Professor Klaus Schwab, Founder and Executive Chairman of the World Economic Forum

12. **Partnering** - *"Partnering is fundamental to our DNA. It is central to what we do because it starts from the early founding ideas about why IBM exists and who we serve." –* Kevin Bishop, former VP, IBM Brand System and Workforce Enablement

13. **Customer Centric** - *"If it's good for you, it's good for us." -* Nina Bibby, Chief Marketing Officer, O2

14. **Customer Centric** – *"Every player in every market needs to go back and say: what is really our market? For example, what is the market that Skype, FaceTime, Airbnb or Uber are addressing and challenging? So they reinvent their segmentation...and try to map the market in a new way, which we call 'Way to Play'. The question is: 'What is the market, the customer, worried about?' The headline of the outcome is 'Your market share just reduced from 85% to 3%. Guaranteed!' And there is no greater news, given the opportunity it creates."* - Marc de Swaan Arons, CMO Kantar Vermeer

15. **Customer Centric** - *"From a brand standpoint, the risk (of disintermediation) is to become a commodity; by losing direct contact with customers, people are led to believe it's all about price and you can be compared instantly to anyone. There is no doubt that the brand is still a reassurance and customers are often ready to pay some price premium for a well-known brand, but only to a certain extent."* - Michel Taride, Group President Hertz International

16. **Future Embracing** – *"I want to turn the company into an internet-based company, a company unrestricted by borders... We believe that there is no 'inside' the company versus 'outside' anymore. Whoever is capable, come and work with us. We now have a lot of entrepreneurs at Haier who don't work inside the company... and in the long run, there won't be any company employees to speak of – only the Haier platform... You might find yourself working together with a group of people you didn't know yesterday and tomorrow you'll all go your separate ways. People come together for special projects, after which they disperse."* - Zhang Ruimin, CEO Haier

17. **Future Embracing** - *"A big part of our ability to move comes with helping everybody understand the 'WHY'. How do you get 300,000 people to buy in?...As we invest and have to make sacrifices to fund our digital efforts, it became easier if people could answer why it has to work; and why it's key for us."* - John Rice, Vice Chairman GE

18. **Rigorous & Disciplined** - *"Perhaps powerful brands are not controlled from the centre but rather owned by everybody around the organisation and lived in a way that is coherent with the direction of travel and what is expected from the entity itself. I think this is true of the Olympic brand."* – Lisa Baird, CMO US Olympic Committee

19. **Rigorous & Disciplined** - *"At headline level, a Strategic Brand is the combination of two really important things: it's a brand that is positioned well and one that is executed brilliantly. You need to be very clear about who your customer is, what they need, why this is interesting to them, how it changes their life, what they are looking for rationally, emotionally and quantifiably."* – Bart Michels, Global CEO Kantar Added Value

Strategy Guiding - *"The brand point of view rigorously informs and guides strategy*

20. *because the brand purpose is so intrinsic to the business model. We have always been clear that this (Sustainable Living) was not something that we were doing because it was a moral obligation or a nice thing to do. We were always clear that this was an economic strategy – and that is now paying off."* – Keith Weed, Chief Marketing and Communications Unilever

Trusted - *"When people develop trust, it survives over generations. There was*
21. *no reason why Singapore Airlines should return to Tata in 2013; there was no commitment, no legally binding contract. But they had a strong sense that Tata was a partner they could trust. Many years after our initial plan, we finally agreed and co-created Vistara."*– Dr. Mukund Rajan, Chief Ethics Officer, Tata Group and Chairman, Tata Global Sustainability Council

'High Value & Driving Value' - *"The Economist says that 'brands are the most*
22. *valuable thing that companies as diverse as Apple and McDonald's own, often worth much more than property and machinery'. WPP's Millward Brown estimates that brands account for more than 30 per cent of the stock market value of companies in the S&P 500...*

"You would do three times better investing in the top 10 brands in our BrandZ survey every year, than you would do investing in the MSCI World Index."- Sir Martin Sorrell, Group CEO WPP

High Value & Driving Value – *"Marketing needs to be the growth engine of the*
23. *business, and if marketers aren't business people, that will never happen. You can't be credible without discipline. And you can't find growth without a bit of magic."* - Syl Saller, Chief Marketing and Innovation Officer Diageo

Crisis Resilient - *"The BP brand was our biggest savior. Everyone knew that BP was*
24. *a good company doing the right thing, conducting operations safely and responsibly. And through its actions and its brand, we had earned tremendous trust, with governments and societies all over the world -and that held us through enormously big stakes throughout the summer 2010...If we had not had that brand, then we would have been punished outside of the US, in a different way but we would have been punished. Rather, we were widely supported."* Tony Hayward, former CEO BP

As Facebook's VP EMEA Nicola Mendelsohn told me: *"Today, there is no single vertical that has not been disrupted."* So how do we rewrite the rules in an era of disruption? The answer is for everyone to put a 'disruptor' hat on. *"The best way to predict the future is to create it,"* said Peter Drucker.

There is no more compelling way to do this than by developing an Enduring Strategic Brand, your Enduring Strategic Brand. Because the world will never be the same without it!

THANK YOU WHOLEHEARTEDLY!

You are life guides and role models, deep friends or dear colleagues, extraordinary leaders and brand epitomisers...I mean all of the above. You have influenced my life more than you will ever realize and are the entirety of *'THE Enduring Strategic Brand'*. Thank you wholeheartedly!

Elaine Arden
Elaine Arden has been Chief HR Officer of RBS plc since 2010 during a time of immense change in the Bank and financial services more generally. Elaine is a graduate of Strathclyde University, a fellow of the Chartered Institute of Banking in Scotland and a member of the Chartered Institute of Personnel & Development.

Lisa Baird
As the Chief Marketing Officer of the United States Olympic Committee, Lisa Baird has helped the Team USA brand grow into one of the most recognized, admired and successful sports brands in the world. Baird's commitment to innovative marketing has seen her named to the board of trustees of the Women's Sport Foundation and the board of directors of GK Elite, the world leader in gymnastics and cheerleading apparel and uniforms. Prior to joining the USOC in 2009, Lisa held senior marketing roles at the NFL, IBM, General Motors, and Proctor & Gamble. She has been awarded with both the WISE Woman of the Year and Sports Business Journal Game Changer honors.

Andrew Bester
Andrew Bester joined Lloyds Banking Group in July 2012 as Group Director & CEO of Commercial Banking. He is the Executive Sponsor for the Group's Inclusion & Diversity programme and the Group Ambassador's Programme, the Chairman of Lloyds Development Capital (LDC) and sits on the Board of the Global Financial Markets Association. Previously, he has held a variety of executive roles at Standard Chartered Bank, notably in Asia as well as at Xchanging Plc and Deutsche Bank. Andrew is an Advisory Board Member of the University of Cambridge Programme for Sustainability Leadership and a member of The Prince of Wales's UK Corporate Leaders' Group.

Nina Bibby
Nina Bibby is the Chief Marketing Officer at O2 (Telefonica UK). Prior to that she was CMO at Barclaycard, SVP of Global Brand Management at IHG, and Commercial Strategy Director at Diageo. Nina has an MBA from INSEAD. She is a non-executive Director of Barratt Developments plc, sits on the Board of the Marketing Society and on the MGGB Council. She is a member of WACL.

Kevin Bishop

Kevin Bishop enjoyed a 31-year career in IBM marketing, sales and channel management, rising to lead the IBM Brand System and Workforce Enablement from October 2009 to December 2012. While being the "Chief Brand Officer" IBM's Brand Value increased by ca. 16% to over $75,5 billion (ref. Interbrand - September 2012). In addition to his line roles, Kevin was Chairman of IBM UK Trust, IBM Partnership Executive for the University of Cambridge and a Liveryman of the Worshipful Company of Marketors. Kevin is a true brand leader; a generative, systematic and narrative thinker; and an effective leader of change. He lives and works in New York, consulting on strategy, marketing and the management of major anniversary programs for major corporates and non-profits.

Duncan Blake

Duncan Blake is Global Director of Brand at BP. He has worked on the brand since the launch of the Helios and Beyond Petroleum in 2000, building differentiation through a strong brand identity and successful global advertising campaigns such as 'BP on The Street' and 'Energy Icons'. He led global communications to support BP's sponsorship of London 2012 and is proud to head up BP's worldwide partnership with the International Paralympic Committee.

Lord John Browne

Lord Browne of Madingley, FRS, FREng holds degrees from Cambridge and Stanford Universities, and numerous honorary degrees and fellowships. He joined BP in 1966, was appointed to the board in 1992 and was Group Chief Executive from 1995 - 2007. He has served on the boards of Intel, DaimlerChrysler, Goldman Sachs and SmithKline Beecham. He is presently Chairman of L1 Energy, the Chairman of the Trustees of both Tate and the QEII Prize for Engineering and Chairman of the International Advisory Board of the Blavatnik School of Government at Oxford University. He serves on a variety of other advisory boards.

Marc de Swaan Arons

Marc de Swaan Arons has been CMO and Executive Board Member Kantar Vermeer since 2014. From 2001 to 2014, Marc was Executive Chairman of EffectiveBrands, a global marketing consultancy he founded in 2000 with offices in New York, London, Amsterdam, Singapore and Tokyo. He started his career in various senior marketing positions in Unilever over 10 years. A global marketing consultant and brand expert, Marc has worked directly with some of the worlds' most prominent Chief Marketing Officers and global brand leaders, is a frequent keynote speaker and has appeared in multiple media. In 2010, he published 'The Global Brand CEO: Building The Ultimate Marketing Machine'. And over recent years, he also co-led the 'Marketing 2020' study.

Lord Paul Deighton

Lord Paul Deighton is Chairman of the Board of Heathrow Airport Holdings, guiding Heathrow through its next phase of development and supporting its vision of giving passengers the best airport service in the world. Following a career at Goldman Sachs,

Lord Deighton delivered the 2012 London Olympic Games to international acclaim as CEO of LOCOG (London Organising Committee of the Olympic Games}. He subsequently became Commercial Secretary to the Treasury, responsible for the UK's National Infrastructure Plan.

Jörg Dohmen

Jörg Dohmen heads the Brand and Customer Institutes for all BMW Group brands, running 5 distinct training programmes at 16 locations worldwide. Following studies in Business Management and International Management in Germany and France, Jörg's career began with the Ford Motor Company Cologne and he has stayed in the automotive industry ever since. He left Ford to become Marketing Director at Land Rover Germany, before moving to the BMW Group, where he has held a number of management positions within the sales and marketing division.

Tom Fadrhonc

Following a career in Telecommunications in New York and Washington. Tom Fadrhonc spent 12 years with Nike in Europe and the US in the Football division and subsequently as Country General Manager and member of the Europe Middle East and Africa Leadership Team. Since 2008, he is associate partner of itim International, advising teams in businesses, sports and education.

David Haigh

David Haigh, the CEO and founder of Brand Finance plc, qualified as a Chartered Accountant with Price Waterhouse in London. He worked in international financial management and moved into the marketing services sector. He then went on to set up a financial marketing consultancy where he worked as a director for five years, before moving to Interbrand as Director of Brand Valuation and leaving in 1996 to launch Brand Finance.

John Hayes

Most recently, John Hayes was Chief Marketing Officer of American Express overseeing American Express' marketing efforts worldwide shaping the company's products, strategy, sales and operations for the past 21 years. Over this time John's work has resulted in many of the most innovative marketing programs in financial services. More recently, he took responsibility for many of Amex's new digital business lines forging many of the key relationships in this area. Prior to American Express, John was President of Lowe and Partners and also held senior positions at Geer DuBois, Ammirati and Puris, and Saatchi and Saatchi Compton.

Tony Hayward

Tony Hayward is Chairman of Glencore plc and Chairman and Founder of Genel Energy plc. He was Group Chief Executive of BP from 2007 to 2010, having previously served as Group Treasurer and Chief Executive of Exploration and Production. He studied geology at Aston University in Birmingham and completed a PhD at Edinburgh University.

Jack Hollis

Jack Hollis is Group Vice President and General Manager of the Toyota Division at Toyota Motor North America (TMNA), where he is responsible for leading all sales, marketing, market representation, and all guest experience and retention activities for Toyota regional sales offices and distributors. Hollis also maintains a role as Global Marketing Advisor for Toyota's Global Olympics Sponsorship. A graduate of Stanford University, Hollis earned his bachelor's degree in economics. He was also a member of Stanford's NCAA National Baseball Championship team and the Cincinnati Reds for two seasons.

Robert Jones

Robert is a strategist at Wolff Olins, visiting professor at the University of East Anglia, and author of 'Branding: A Very Short Introduction'. In 25 years at Wolff Olins, Robert has worked with over fifty organisations, including Aviva, Barclays, Camelot, Skype, Oxfam, Tate and the National Trust. He leads on new thinking and learning at Wolff Olins, and has created a free online course on branding, with UEA - the first course on the FutureLearn platform.

Christophe Jouan

Christophe Jouan is CEO and Co-Owner of The Foresight Factory, a consumer analytics company, specialising in trends. More specifically, the Foresight Factory is pioneer and a leader of consumer analytics and new data techniques, providing expertise in modelling new routes to the future. Christophe develops and provides strategic vision and leads structural and organisational change. Over two decades, he has been helping businesses globally to put trends at the heart of their decision making, as well as passionately shared deep knowledge on trends through multiple public speaking events.

Rachel Kennedy Caggiano

Formerly with Ogilvy & Mather, Rachel Kennedy Caggiano was head of content for North America, specializing in working with iconic brands such as American Express, Ford, Nestlé, All-Clad, Molson Coors, Moët Hennessy and BP. A founding member who helped spearhead the rapid growth of the agency's content and social media offering, she was named a "trailblazer" in PRWeek's 40 Under 40 in 2013 for her work leading a team for BP during the 2010 Gulf of Mexico oil spill.

Shelly Lazarus

Shelly Lazarus is chairman emeritus of Ogilvy & Mather and served as chairman of the company from 1997 to June 2012. During her 40-plus years with O&M she has worked in every product category and helped build many of the world's most famous brands. Sought after for her branding expertise as well as business acumen, Lazarus serves on the boards of a number of corporate, non-profit, and academic institutions including The Blackstone Group, The Defense Business Board, FINRA,GE, Merck, New York-Presbyterian Hospital, the World Wildlife Fund, Lincoln Center, and Columbia Business School.

Kathy Leech

Kathy Leech is an award-winning branded communications leader who is expert in developing and executing brand and reputation strategies across multiple platforms. She is currently Executive Director of Corporate Brand and Advertising for Comcast. Prior to Comcast, she led the US-based advertising and social media response efforts for BP during the 2010 Gulf oil spill. Kathy currently lives in Philadelphia with her husband and two sons.

Didier Leroy

Mr Leroy began his career in the automotive industry in 1982 with Renault. He held a number of senior positions at their production plants over a 16-year term and worked closely with Carlos Ghosn. Mr Leroy joined Toyota in September 1998 to start Toyota Motor Manufacturing France and he became CEO of Toyota Motor Europe in 2010. In June 2015, he was the first non-Japanese to be promoted Executive Vice President of Toyota Motor Corporation and Member of the Board of Directors. He is also the Chief Competitive Officer of TMC with the mission to boost the global competitiveness of Toyota worldwide.

Timo Lumme

Timo Lumme is the Managing Director of IOC Television & Marketing Services, the marketing department of the International Olympic Committee (IOC). Timo is responsible for the sale of all broadcast rights to the Olympic Games, the negotiation and sale of Worldwide Olympic Partnerships as well as the management of the IOC's global sponsorship programme known as TOP. His responsibilities include the development and implementation of the IOC's strategic marketing plan and oversight of Olympic marketing programmes worldwide. Timo is a qualified lawyer and speaks five languages (Finnish, English, French, Italian and German).

Nicola Mendelsohn

Nicola Mendelsohn is VP for EMEA, Facebook, a role she has held since 2013. In addition, she is the co-chair of the Creative Industries Council alongside Secretaries of State for DCMS and BEIS – a joint forum between the UK creative industries and government. In 2014, she became a non-executive director of Diageo. She is also a Director of the Women's Prize for Fiction and serves on The Mayor of London's Business Advisory Board. Nicola and her husband are co-presidents of the charity Norwood. In 2015, she was awarded a Commander of the British Empire (CBE) for services to the creative industries in the UK. Prior to joining Facebook, Nicola worked in advertising for 20 years notably at Bartle Bogle Hegarty, Grey London and Karmarama. Her greatest joy in life comes from her husband Jon and her four children Gabi, Danny, Sam and Zac.

Bart Michels

Bart Michels is Global CEO of Brand and Marketing Consultancy Kantar Added Value, and has been with WPP since 2003. An experienced brand marketing practitioner, Bart started his career client side, as a senior marketer at Kellogg's, Coca-Cola, GSK and Virgin Media where he held a number of roles including UK & ROI Media Controller,

GB Head of Marketing Innovation, and Group Brand and Communications Director. Bart is an Economics graduate of UCL, and an alumnus of London Business School.

Jonathan Mildenhall

Jonathan Mildenhall spent the first 15 years of his career in the London Advertising industry. In 2006 he joined The Coca-Cola Company as VP, Global Advertising Strategy and Creative. Jonathan joined Airbnb as CMO in June 2014. He has never worked harder, never worked smarter, and never felt more creative.

Kevin Murray

Kevin Murray has been advising leaders and leadership teams for three decades. He specializes in leadership coaching and strategic communication, and gives talks on leadership around the world. He has worked as Director of Communications of British Airways and Chairman of the Public Relations Division of Chime group. His previous books includes 'Language of Leaders' and 'Communicate to Inspire', both shortlisted for the CMI Management Book of the Year Awards, and published in multiple languages around the world.

Stephen Odell

Stephen Odell is Executive Vice President, Global Marketing, Sales and Service, leading the company's continued efforts to improve the Ford Motor Company image globally by connecting more closely with customers. As Ford expands to be both an auto and mobility company, Odell is leading the team reinventing the customer experience with offerings like FordPass, while also introducing consumers to new alternative mobility solutions. All of this will ultimately change the way consumers travel and allow Ford to continue to distinguish its steadfast commitment of providing affordable transportation solutions and improving the lives for all. Previously, Odell led Ford of Europe and over the course of his 37 years at Ford Motor Company, he has managed a variety of Product Development, Purchasing, and Marketing, Sales and Service operations.

Izzy Pugh

Izzy Pugh leads the global Cultural Practice at Kantar Added Value. She has spent the last 15 years helping clients understand how they can connect their brands more powerfully into culture.

Dr Mukund Rajan

Dr Mukund Rajan serves as Chief Ethics Officer of the Tata group, and chairs the Tata Global Sustainability Council. Dr Rajan has held a number of senior executive positions through his 22 year career with the Tata group, including CEO of one of the group's telecom businesses, head of private equity, and member of the Group Executive Council at Tata Sons. In 2007, the World Economic Forum honoured Dr Rajan as a Young Global Leader. Dr Rajan graduated from the Bachelor of Technology program at the Indian Institute of Technology, Delhi in 1989, and received a Rhodes Scholarship to study at Oxford University, where he completed a Masters and Doctorate in International Relations.

John Rice

John G. Rice is Vice Chairman of GE and President & CEO of GE Global Growth Organization based in Hong Kong. He joined GE in 1978, and has held several leadership roles, including CEO of GE Transportation Systems and GE Energy. From 2005 – 2010, he served as Vice Chairman of GE and CEO of GE Industrial and then as Vice Chairman of GE and CEO of GE Infrastructure.

Dr Ian Robertson

Dr Ian Robertson (HonDSc) has been a member of the BMW AG Board, responsible for Global Sales and Marketing, since March 2008. After achieving a BSc in Maritime Studies, Ian joined the Rover Group in 1979 and has worked in the car industry ever since. From 1988 he held various senior management roles at the Rover Group and was Managing Director of Land Rover Vehicles from 1994. In 1999, he was appointed Managing Director at BMW South Africa before becoming Chairman and Chief Executive of Rolls-Royce Motor Cars Ltd in 2005, remaining Chairman until 2012.

Syl Saller

Syl Saller is the Chief Marketing Officer for Diageo and a member of Diageo's Executive Committee. Diageo is the world's leading premium drinks business operating in 180 countries with a collection of over 400 brands including Johnnie Walker, Smirnoff, Tanqueray and Guinness. Syl oversees all Global Marketing, Design, Innovation, the Futures Group, and Reserve, Diageo's luxury division, worldwide. Before this, Syl was Diageo's Global Innovation Director, responsible for Diageo's innovation strategy, including all new product development, launch programmes and R&D. Prior to that, she was Marketing Director for Diageo Great Britain.

Professor Klaus Schwab

Professor Klaus Schwab is Founder and Executive Chairman of the World Economic Forum, the International Organization for Public-Private Cooperation. In 1998, he created the Schwab Foundation for Social Entrepreneurship. He has received numerous international and national honours.

John Seifert

John Seifert is Worldwide Chairman and CEO of Ogilvy & Mather, one of the largest marketing communications companies in the world. Throughout his 38 year career with Ogilvy, John has worked in a wide range of client leadership and general management positions and led multi-discipline global brand teams for some of the world's most famous brands including American Express, BP, DuPont, Siemens, among many others. John is a frequent lecturer at universities and business forums on the subject of "Enterprise Branding." He is a National Board member of buildOn, a non-profit group targeting at risk high school students in the most dangerous urban communities across the U.S.

Sir Martin Sorrell

Sir Martin Sorrell is the founder and CEO of WPP, the world's largest advertising and marketing services group. WPP employs approximately 200,000 people (including associates and investments) in more than 3,000 offices in 112 countries. In October 2016, Harvard Business Review named Sir Martin as Britain's best-performing CEO, and the second best-performing in the world. He received his knighthood in January 2000 for services to the communications industry.

Tim Stevenson
Tim Stevenson is Chairman of Johnson Matthey PLC and Lord Lieutenant of Oxfordshire. Previously, he was Chairman of Morgan Advanced Materials PLC and Travis Perkins PLC. Tim Stevenson's executive career included multiple senior roles, among which serving as Chief Executive of Burmah Castrol PLC and Castrol International.

Michel Taride
Michel Taride started his career with Hertz in 1980 as Station Manager at Cannes airport in the south of France. He is now the Group President of Hertz International, responsible for Hertz car rental operations in Europe, Middle East, Africa, Asia Pacific, Latin and Central America. He plays a leading role in determining the mobility strategy and is passionate about the shared economy.

Michel is the Chair of the Advisory Board for the GTTP (Global Travel and Tourism Partnership) that supports education in 12 countries and has also joined the WTTC (World Travel and Tourism Council) Membership Committee. Michel developed an early passion for travel. He currently resides in London with his wife and children and enjoys sailing, music and mountaineering.

Adrian Tripp
Adrian Tripp began his entrepreneurial journey straight out of university, building Quest Media into the premier global publisher of Customer Management information. Following the sale of that business, Adrian focussed his attention on the European Business Awards, the social enterprise focussed on fostering and creating a stronger business community for the benefit of all of Europe's citizens. Whilst on this mission he has turned the Awards into one of the biggest business competitions in the world. In addition to the Awards he has also built a successful film and video production business called Tracc Films.

Takeshi Uchiyamada
Takeshi Uchiyamada was appointed Vice Chairman of the Toyota Motor Corporation (TMC) Board of Directors in June 2012 and Chairman in June 2013. After joining TMC in 1969, he held multiple roles, including chief engineer of Vehicle Development Center 2 - which developed the Prius, the world's first mass-produced gasoline-electric hybrid car. He was named to the Board of Directors in June 1998 and successively oversaw Vehicle Development Center 3 (from 1998), Development Center 2 (from 2000) and the Overseas Customer Service Operations Center (from 2001). Mr Uchiyamada was made a senior managing director and chief officer of the Vehicle Engineering Group in June 2003. In June 2004, he became chief officer of the Production Control & Logistics Group, and in June 2005, an Executive Vice President.

Dr Nick Udall

Dr Nick Udall is the CEO of Nowhere, and was a co-founder and the former Chair of the World Economic Forum's Global Agenda Council on New Models of Leadership. Nick has a degree in Product Design and a doctorate in Consciousness and Creativity, and since the age of 23 has been working with executive leaders of global corporations, choreographing transformation journeys, designing and catalysing breakthroughs and working with key leadership teams.

Keith Weed

As Chief Marketing and Communications Officer, Keith Weed is a member of the Unilever Executive Committee and responsible for the Marketing, Communications and Sustainable Business functions. His responsibilities are aligned to support Unilever's vision: to grow the business while reducing its environmental footprint and increasing positive social impact. Keith sees sustainability as a driver of consumer-led profitable growth. He led the creation of the Unilever Sustainable Living Plan and has also pioneered new ways of integrating sustainability into the business.

Greg Welch

Greg Welch is a senior partner in Spencer Stuart's Consumer Practice and served as its global practice leader for five years. Now in his 20th year of search, he has placed over 500 CMO's for many of the world's best brands and today he is widely viewed as the world's top CMO recruiter. Greg launched the firms marketing officer practice, is the co-founder of the Marketing 50 and he created the annual Spencer Stuart CMO Summit which is the industry's premier event. Greg is a frequent contributor to leading industry publications including Forbes, the Wall Street Journal and Ad Age. Greg is based in the firm's Chicago, Illinois office.

David Wheldon

David Wheldon is the Chief Marketing Officer of RBS and the President of the World Federation of Advertisers. He started his career as a graduate at Saatchi & Saatchi and progressed through the agency world to become the MD of Lowe Howard-Spink in London. Throughout his career he's been both agency-side and in-house, working for some of world's largest brands including Coca-Cola, Vodafone and Barclays.

Huib Wursten

Huib Wursten is co-founder of itim International and specialized in advising organizations on how to translate global strategies into country specific implementation. Since 1989 he has been working with Fortune top 100 companies, including long-term assignments with IBM, the IMF and The World Bank.

NOTES & REFERENCES

All illustrations have been credited directly in the text.
The notes below relate to additional usages.

Chapter 1

1. A study with Millward Brown Optimor:

    http://www.jimstengel.com/grow/research-validation/ -

    http://www.businesswire.com/news/home/20120117005066/en/Millward-Brown-Partnership-Jim-Stengel-Reveals-50

2. Campaign – Unilever http://www.campaignlive.co.uk/article/1345772/unilever-says-brands-purpose-growing-twice-speed-others-portfolio

3. Havas Group - http://www.meaningful-brands.com/

Chapter 2

1. The Authentic Enterprise
    An Arthur W. Page Society Report – 2007

2. What is Organization Culture? And why should we care?
    Michael D. Watkins, *Harvard Business Review* – May 15 2013

3. Good to great
    Jim C. Collins - October 2001

4. Leading with Culture – Point of View 2015
    Spencer Stuart - January 2015

5. An introduction to organizational behavior – v 1.0
    Dr. Talya Bauer and Dr. Berrin Erdogan

6. Where does organizational culture come from?
    James Thomas, Leadership & Management – May 14, 2014

7. International marketing and culture
    Huib Wursten and Tom Fadronhc
    https://www.academia.edu/22416733/International_marketing_and_Culture

8. Heineken https://www.youtube.com/watch?v=dKVn5z8U3ZU

9. Nike USA https://www.youtube.com/watch?v=WBXiuGBeJC0

10. VW https://www.youtube.com/watch?v=aCbQoqtMjL8

11. Audi https://www.youtube.com/watch?v=xb4W9Yu3Kc4

12. Pedigree https://www.youtube.com/watch?v=EcvG548aMJA

13. Jaguar https://www.youtube.com/watch?v=CyZL0xdKj0E

14. Alpha Romeo https://www.youtube.com/watch?v=qmJLwLEce5c

15. Nike Japan https://www.youtube.com/watch?v=WvvpKGVOf0Q

Chapter 3

1. Unconscious Branding: How Neuroscience can empower (and inspire) Marketing
    Douglas Van Praet - March 2014

2. The Science of Emotion in Marketing: How our brains decide what to share and
    whom to trust
    Courtney Seiter - August 18, 2014

3. Neuromarketing – Emotional Ads work best
    Roger Doolcy - 2009

4. Brain influence: 100 ways to persuade and convince consumers with
    neuromarketing
    Robert Dooley - 2015

5. Rational versus emotional appeal in advertising: which is the right approach
    Nathan King - June 17, 2016

6. Lovemarks – The future beyond brands
    Kevin Roberts, Stanford Management Institute Business Book Summaries - 2004

7. Emotional Branding: The new paradigm for connecting brands to people
    Marc Gobe, Allworth Press - 2001

8. The Hidden Persuaders
    Vance Packard, Ig Publishing Reissue Ed edition - 2007

9. Lovemarks – The future beyond brands
    Kevin Roberts, Powerhouse Books - 2004

Chapter 4

1. iCrossing - https://www.slideshare.net/icrossing/icrossing-connected-brands-primer

2. Entrepreneur 2012 - https://www.entrepreneur.com/article/223125

3. The Tipping Point - Malcolm Gladwell
    Little Brown & Company - 2000.

4. Truth - www.truth.ms/blog/culturally-connected-brands

5. The Economist July 9th, 2016 - http://www.economist.com/news/business/21701798-smaller-rivals-are-assaulting-worlds-biggest-brands-invasion-bottle-snatchers

6. http://www.theatlantic.com/business/archive/2013/08/airbnb-ceo-brian-chesky-on-building-a-company-and-starting-a-sharing-revolution/278635/"

Chapter 5

1. Fortune Magazine, October 2016
    fortune.com/2016/10/26/best-global-companies-to-work-for/

2. The Insider, January 2016 - http://uk.businessinsider.com/tony-hsieh-explains-how-zappos-rebounded-from-employee-exodus-2016-1?r=US&IR=T

3. Spencer Stuart, 2014 - https://www.spencerstuart.com/research-and-insight/tomorrows-cmo-chief-magic-or-logic-officer-survey-results

4. Egon Zehnder, 2017 - http://www.egonzehnder.com/leadership-insights/c-suite-perspectives-the-cmo.html

5. McKinsey Quaterly, February 2015 - http://www.mckinsey.com/business-functions/marketing-and-sales/our-insights/the-dawn-of-marketings-new-golden-age

6. Marc de Swaan Arons, Frank van den Driest, Keith Weed, "The Ultimate Marketing Machine", *Harvard Business Review*, July-August 2014

Chapter 6

1. Strategic Partnering: Remove Chance and Deliver Consistent Success
    Luc, Raphael and Guillaume Bardin – Kogan Page, November 2013
2. Intangible business, 2005 - http://www.intangiblebusiness.com/news/
    marketing/2005/11/ingredient-branding-case-study-intel

3. PwC 18th Annual Global CEO Survey - http://www.pwc.com/gx/en/ceo-
    survey/2015/assets/pwc-18th-annual-global-ceo-survey-jan-2015.pdf

4. The Fourth Industrial Revolution, Klaus Schwab - https://www.weforum.org/
    about/the-fourth-industrial-revolution-by-klaus-schwab

5. The Harvard Business Review, 9 May 2016 - https://hbr.org/2016/05/build-your-
    brand-as-a-relationship

6. Josh Feldmeth, Interbrand - US 2016
    http://interbrand.com/best-brands/best-global-brands/2016/articles/the-alpha-of-
    cohesiveness/

Chapter 7

1. Marketing 2020 - Marc de Swaan Arons, Frank van den Driest, Keith Weed, "The
    Ultimate Marketing Machine", *Harvard Business Review*, July-August 2014

    http://www.mbvermeer.com/portfolio-item/insights2020/

2. The Foresight Factory - https://www.foresightfactory.co

3. Siegel + Gale Global Brand Simplicity Index 2017
    http://www.siegelgale.com

4. PwC Research 2014 - https://declara.com/content/kaZnB43a

Chapter 8

1. The Fourth Industrial Revolution, Klaus Schwab - https://www.weforum.org/
    about/the-fourth-industrial-revolution-by-klaus-schwab

2. Super Intelligence: Paths, Dangers, Strategies,
    Professor Nick Bostrom, OUP Oxford, July 2014

3. Connectography: Mapping the Future of Global Civilization
    Parag Khanna, Random House Inc, 2016

4.   Ford Motor Company - http://corporate.ford.com/microsites/sustainability-report-2014-15/index.html

5.   In the future of retail, we're never not shopping – Werner Reinatz
     https://hbr.org/2016/03/in-the-future-of-retail-were-never-not-shopping

6.   Haier - http://www.haier.net/en/

7.   China's Philosopher-CEO Zhan Ruimin – Strategy+Business November 2014
     http://www.strategy-business.com/article/00296?gko=8155b

8.   The Haier Road to Growth – Strategy+Business April 2015
     http://www.strategy-business.com/article/00323?gko=c8c2a

Chapter 9

1.   The European Business Awards - http://www.businessawardseurope.com

2.   EffWeek - http://effworks.co.uk

3.   CNN, July 25 2012 - http://edition.cnn.com/2012/07/25/sport/olympics-london-2012-google-apple/

4.   Olympic News –December 2016
     https://www.olympic.org/news/how-do-we-know-that-rio-2016-was-a-success

5.   The Olympic Charter - https://stillmed.olympic.org/Documents/olympic_charter_en.pdf

Chapter 10

1.   Unilever Full Value Chain Approach - https://www.unilever.com/sustainable-living/the-sustainable-living-plan/reducing-environmental-impact/greenhouse-gases/Our-greenhouse-gas-footprin

Chapter 11

1.   Readers Digest Survey, 2016 - http://tmbi.com/readers-digest-announces-2016s-trusted-brands/

2.   Edelman 2016 Trust Barometer - http://www.edelman.com/insights/intellectual-property/2016-edelman-trust-barometer/

3.   Kevin Murray - People with Purpose, February 2017
     The Language of Leaders, April 2013

4. The Reputation Institute 2016 Global Rep Track ® 100 -
    https://www.reputationinstitute.com/research/Global-RepTrak-100.aspx

5. Lord John Browne - Connect: How companies succeed by engaging radically with
    society
    Virgin Digital, September 2015

6. BlaBlacar - Strategy+Business
    http://www.strategy-business.com/blog/To-Foster-Online-Trust-Build-a-
    Community?gko=7433c

7. Tata, The Evolution of a Corporate Brand
    Morgen Witzel, Portfolio Penguin - 31 May 2012

Chapter 12

1. Marketing Week, November 2015 – Diageo, Syl Saller
    https://www.marketingweek.com/2015/11/05/diageos-syl-saller-to-drive-growth-
    brands-must-embrace-change-but-respect-marketing-fundamentals/

2. Campaign June 2015 – Diageo, Syl Saller
    http://www.campaignlive.co.uk/article/1350489/diageos-syl-saller-ego-free-
    leadership-creativity-connects-growth

3. Brandfather
    John Murphy, Book Guild Publishing - January 2017

4. Brand Finance - http://brandfinance.com

5. Management Today - http://www.managementtoday.co.uk/chinese-takeovers-
    western-companies-arent-bad-thing/article/1382100#rbYQG8rpwakWF9V7.99

6. Fortune, March 2016 - http://fortune.com/2016/03/18/the-biggest-american-
    companies-now-owned-by-the-chinese/

7. 2016 Fortune 100 best companies to work for - http://reviews.greatplacetowork.
    com/google-inc?utm_source=fortune&utm_medium=list-page&utm_
    content=reviews-link&utm_campaign=2016-100-best

8. Siegel + Gale Global Brand Simplicity Index 2017
    http://www.siegelgale.com

9. The Reputation Institute 2016 Global Rep Track ® 100
    https://www.reputationinstitute.com/research/Global-RepTrak-100.aspx

Chapter 13

1. US Department of Defense – Crisis Communication Strategies
    https://www.ou.edu/deptcomm/dodjcc/groups/02C2/Johnson%20&%20Johnson.htm

2. 100 Days of Gushing Oil – Media Analysis and Quiz, Pew Research Center, 2010
    http://www.journalism.org/2010/08/25/coverage-bp-fared-worse-obama-white-house-and-gop-may-be-part-reason/

Conclusion

1. Allison Rimm, The Joy of Strategy
    Routledge, October 2015

2. The Happiest Brands in the World, Forbes
    https://www.forbes.com/sites/meghancasserly/2011/10/06/the-happiest-brands-in-the-world/#2a8582ef6c06

3. Kevin Murray - People with Purpose, February 2017
    The Language of leaders, April 2013

AUTHORS

Luc Bardin

Luc advises blue chip companies, governments and academic institutions on their brand, marketing and partnership strategies. Prior to this, he was group vice president for 12 years in BP and notably group chief sales and marketing officer, CEO of multiple global branded businesses and a member of the BP Downstream ExCo. Luc is an adjunct professor and member of the advisory board of the strategic marketing MSc at Imperial College Business School. His previous book '*Strategic Partnering - Remove chance and deliver consistent success*' was published in 2013.

Clara Bardin

Clara is studying medicine at the University of Reims and at Ecole de l'INSERM (France). With a global approach, she is interested in the relationship between industry, brands and patients in a highly connected world.

Elsa Bardin

Elsa is studying business management at the Lycée Sainte Genevieve in Versailles (France). A child of the world and competitive swimmer, one of her interests lies in sport brands and marketing.

ACKNOWLEDGMENT

Without you, this book of a heartfelt conviction would never have existed.

Thank you wholeheartedly to the extraordinary leaders who have contributed to '*THE Enduring Strategic Brand*'. You are life guides and role models, deep friends or dear colleagues, inspiring leaders and brand epitomisers – and to me, all of the above. Over the last 35 years, you have influenced my life more than you will ever realize and are the entirety of '*THE Enduring Strategic Brand*'.

Thank you to 'my' brand team over the years, whatever their position - Ian Conn, Duncan Blake, Kathy Leech, Shelly Lazarus, John Seifert and David Fowler. They deserve superlatives and have taught me the world of brands.

Thank you to the Castrol and BP brands for colouring my blood in red, green and yellow; to Matthew Smith and Urbane Publications for the considerable endeavour of publishing this book; to Deborah Parkes for her friendly and skilful support; to Philip Smith for his design excellence; to Evgenia Lunina for her thoughtful and patient assistance.

Thank you to Geraldine Prieur and her Rouge Absolu team for their striking cover design and stating that their *"graphic and aesthetic vision emanated from Luc Bardin's strategic knowledge on brands which he disseminates across businesses"*

Thank you to my cherished co-authors, Clara and Elsa, and to Francoise, Raphael and Guillaume for their infinite love and patience.

Thank you, thank you…thank you!

Luc